ISRAEL

ISRAEL

ITS LIFE AND CULTURE

III—IV

BY

JOHS. PEDERSEN

PROFESSOR OF SEMITIC PHILOLOGY IN THE UNIVERSITY
OF COPENHAGEN

GEOFFREY CUMBERLEGE   BRANNER OG KORCH
OXFORD UNIVERSITY PRESS   29, ST. KONGENSGADE
LONDON   COPENHAGEN

FIRST PUBLISHED 1940
REPRINTED (FOTOPRINT) 1947
REPRINTED (FOTOPRINT) 1953

PRINTED IN DENMARK
BY
DYVA & JEPPESEN

THIS volume, which brings to an end my account of the culture of Israel, is to be viewed in connection with the preceding volume, I—II, published in English in 1926. The present volume appeared in Danish in 1934. A few alterations and additions have been made, chiefly as a result of the Ras Shamra finds, the first published texts of which became available only just before I completed the Danish edition. The notes have been revised in accord with this and other new material. The translation has been done by Miss Annie I. Fausbøll M. A. I have myself gone through it in manuscript and discussed all doubtful points with her. I wish to thank Miss Fausbøll for the perseverance with which she has carried through her difficult task. While the translation was being prepared I received a welcome offer of help from Professor V. Burch. He has read the entire manuscript and made a great many suggestions which have all been adopted. Miss Fausbøll and I tender our best thanks for his valuable help.

I owe special thanks to the Trustees of the Rask-Ørsted Foundation for financial aid which has rendered possible the publication of this as well as of the preceding volume.

Copenhagen, March, 1940.

Johs. Pedersen.

CONTENTS

III.

HOLINESS AND ITS UPHOLDERS

IV.
THE RENEWAL AND THE SOURCE OF HOLINESS

V

III

HOLINESS AND ITS UPHOLDERS

WAR

ALL life in Israel depends on the interaction of the psychic forces of the people. Hence normal life can only prosper where the blessing is active and where peace prevails. This applies to daily life in the human community and to all its activities with the cattle and in the fields. But it applies even more to the great crucial situations when much is at stake. Then supreme effort is made, and the feeling of fellowship is quickened in all who share in it. A renewal of strength beyond the normal is needed, and the men who are to wield it create a renewed organism. In time of war the Israelites form such a regenerated community with increased strength.

In early Israel war was a natural condition, because life, honour, and peace had to be constantly created and recaptured. Just as the individual and his kin must maintain their ground by unwearying fighting and reprisal, so also the larger family communities and the whole people had to make a place for themselves among other nations by struggle and strife. The fighting of a people, too, might be an act of "vengeance" to uphold the honour of the nation (Judg. 11,36; 1 Sam. 14,24), and the Israelites entertained no doubt that the right won by the strong man measuring his strength against other men in war was a true right (Judg. 11,21 ff.; 18,9).

The leading part played by warfare in the life of the people is shown by the fact that the wanderings in the desert are described as a military expedition. The men are organised according to tribes in the camp around the sanctuary. Each unit gathers round its pennon or banner (*'ōth, deghel, nēs*) as its rallying point, an arrangement no doubt reflecting the organisation of the monarchical period. The sanctuary is carried in front

of the people on the march, certain trumpet blasts are the signal
for breaking camp, and it is expressly stated that the same
trumpets are used both in war and in the cult assembly (Num.
1,52; 2; 10; 26). The whole people is one great host of warriors.

This impression of the importance of war is confirmed by the
old historical narratives, and we have a single poem which,
more than any other, gives direct expression to the psychic condition engendered by war in the earliest times. This is the Song
of Deborah, which may be rendered thus:

 2. For vehement action in Israel, for the noble deeds of war-
    riors, [1] bless ye Yahweh.
 3. Hearken ye kings, give ear ye princes. Sing, sing will I
    unto Yahweh, I will chant unto Yahweh, the God of Israel.
 4. Yahweh, when thou wentest out of Seir, when thou advancedst
    from the steppe of Edom, the earth quaked, yea, the heavens
    o'erflowed, [2] yea, the clouds o'erflowed with water.
 5. Mountains crumbled before Yahweh, [3] before Yahweh, the
    God of Israel.
 6. In the days of Samgar ben Anath, in the days of Jael, the
    high roads lay deserted, wayfarers stole along tortuous paths.
 7. Hamlets (?) [4] decayed, they decayed in Israel, until thou
    arosest Deborah, thou arosest, thou mother in Israel.
 8. New gods are chosen, then is there fighting about the gates; [5]
    but no shield or spear is seen among the forty thousand of
    Israel.
 9. My heart is with the chiefs of Israel, those who proved noble
    among the people. Bless ye Yahweh.
10. Riding tawny she-asses, sitting on rugs, or wandering on
    the road. Chant!
11. ... [6] among the water troughs they sing the righteous acts
    of Yahweh, the righteous works of his ... [7] in Israel. Then
    the people of Yahweh went down to the gates.
12. Forward, forward, Deborah. Forward, forward, chant a lay.
    Rise up Barak, seize thy captives, Abinoam's son.
13. Then ... descend unto the mighty, Yahweh's people descend
    for me among heroes. [8]

14. From Ephraim is their root; "after thee, Benjamin, among thy kinsmen". [1]
Chiefs came down from Machir, from Zebulon those who wielded the sceptre. [2]

15. Thy chieftains, Issachar, [3] were with Deborah; ... and Issachar are loyal to Barak; into the valley were they sent in his train.
Great were the heart-searchings in Reuben's divisions. [4]

16. Why didst thou sit among the cattle-pens listening to the piping of the shepherds? For Reuben's divisions the heart-searchings were great.

17. Gilead lives beyond Jordan; why does Dan dwell like a sojourner near ships?
Asher sat by the seashore, remained by his creeks.

18. Zebulon is a people that endangers its life unto death, and Naphtali dwells on the high expanses.

19. Kings came and fought, then fought the kings of Canaan; at Taanach on the waters of Megiddo they gained no spoil of silver.

20. The stars fought from the heavens, from their courses they fought against Sisera.

21. The river of Kishon swept them away, the primeval river, the river of Kishon. My soul, go forth with strength.

22. Then thundered the horses' hoofs, in his stallions' fiery chase.

23. Cast off Meroz, says Yahweh's mal'ākh, cast off its citizens forever. For they did not come to Yahweh's assistance, to Yahweh's assistance among the heroes.

24. Blessed among women is Jael, the wife of Heber the Kenite, blessed among women in tents.

25. He asked water, she gave him milk, in a lordly bowl she gave him sour milk.

26. She put out her hand to the tent-peg, put out her right hand to the workmen's hammer; she smote Sisera, shattered his head, split and fractured his temple.

27. He swayed, sank, lay at her feet; he swayed, sank at her feet; where he swayed, he sank, slain.

28. Out of the window she peered, behind the lattice she wailed, Sisera's mother. Why is his chariot so long in coming, why delay the hoof-beats of his team?
29. The wise among her ladies made answer, [1] nay, thus she made answer to herself:
30. No doubt they are taking and dividing the spoil: a woman, two women to each man. Spoil of dyed stuffs for Sisera, spoil of dyed embroidered stuff, doubly embroidered and dyed stuff for my neck. [2]
31. Thus, o Yahweh, let all thine enemies perish; but those who love Him are like the sunrise in its might.

The vigorous stanzas of the poem present a series of pictures, the import and profundity of which partly elude us. Expressions are used which have since become obsolete in the language, allusions so slight that we do not understand them and in some cases the text is probably corrupt.

The opening lines indicate the theme, the magnificent feat performed by the people, but the glory for it is given to Yahweh. The poem begins and ends with the God of the people; it is His might which has been active throughout the great achievement. Hence His power is first described, and to begin with the narrative takes us back to the earliest history of the people. While Heaven and earth quake, Yahweh advances from the southward plains where the fathers of Israel wandered. In a few lines (vv. 6-8) the poet then draws a picture of the state of things before the battle. Uncertainty prevails everywhere, communications are being interrupted, men have to steal warily from place to place, Israel was decaying, for as yet no real leader had arisen. A change of culture is setting in. New gods are adopted and the people is faced by the struggle for the strongholds (if this reading of the second half of the first line in verse 8 is correct); and yet the Israelites, few in number though they are, are unprepared and unarmed.

But out of this confusion of disintegration, all at once there appears a people led by mighty chieftains, willing to abandon themselves to the passion of war, some riding their asses, others afoot, all with a single aim. Their objective is the "gates", the fortified cities; the confidence of the chiefs is due to the fact that the God is with them, it is by His strength and righteousness that they have hitherto maintained their position as a people (vv. 9-11).

The poet has now arrived at the point when the battle is about to begin. Without any transition a call is addressed to the leaders. Deborah, the woman who urged the people to fight, is requested to let her rousing war song be heard; Barak, the hero, is to open the battle. But just as it is about to begin, the poet reviews the tribes. Ephraim, Benjamin, Machir, Zebulon, Issachar form the core. The more distant tribes hesitate, or they have settled down and disregard the summons (vv. 12-18).

Suddenly there is a change in the spirit of the poem. The battle is described in short stanzas. The poet does not enlarge on what is happening, the exploits of the Israelite army are not even mentioned. Only the enemy is referred to, but the few and hastily sketched pictures convey a powerful impression of the defeat of the hostile army, and thus of the victory of Israel. The battlefield is at Taanach and Megiddo. Here came the Canaanite kings, sure of their prey, but they took no gain. They had no luck, even the stars fought against them. Two pictures suffice to call up all their misery. We see their corpses being whirled away by the river Kishon, and their horses dashing riderless across the plain (vv. 19-22).

Thus victory and defeat are completed. Now Israel is left victorious in all her power. But the poet has still a few words to add. An Israelite community, Meroz, has failed Yahweh, and yet — it must be taken for granted — it was near the battlefield. This conduct has placed it outside Israel, it cannot belong to the people any more (v. 23). Possibly its betrayal became apparent during the flight of the Canaanite chief, whose ignominious death is the next incident to be described in the poem.

The narrative centres round a eulogy of the woman Jael, only half Israelite, who caused his death. We merely learn his name, Sisera, in passing. Three stanzas describe the scene with his murder. He is standing in her tent asking for water; not content to comply with his request, she pours out milk for him in a lordly bowl, thus making him feel as safe as an honoured guest. But while he is drinking, and his face is hidden behind the bowl, she seizes the hammer and tent-peg and fractures his temple. All this is narrated in few and brief words, but the poet lingers over the description of how the smitten foe sways, sinks to the ground and lies at the feet of the woman.

This important incident does not, however, exhaust the sweetness of victory to the poet. The defeat of the foe is to be followed up to the last detail. He takes his hearers into the enemy's camp, and measures the greatness of his people's victory by the disappointed expectations of the women left at home. He does not mar his joy by words of mockery. With a clear and restrained objectivity he describes the expectation of the hostile chief's mother as she is sitting in her bower with her women. Their talk, as repeated here seems sober enough. Why does he not come? The wisest of the women agree with her; the spoil is so enormous that the distribution takes time. No comment is made on the conversation, and no superfluous remark describes the mother's reception of the message of defeat when it comes at last. The picture of the expectation of the women is left clear and unobscured; therefore it reflects the victory of Israel in its whole extent. Immediately after this, the poet breaks into a song of triumph: Thus shall the enemies of Yahweh perish, but His people shall continually renew its power, like the rising sun.

The clearness and objectivity characterising the pictures of the poem cover a strong passion which sometimes breaks out in ejaculations, in praises of Yahweh, and in cries to the leaders. The most impetuous manifestation is when the poet sees the Kishon sweep away the bodies of the enemy. At this sight he feels his soul overflow with an overwhelming power which urges it onward.

The poet's mood is not due to a purely individual inspiration; it is the outcome of the state in which the people finds itself.

The Israel revealed to us in the Song of Deborah consisted of a number of tribes which had settled among the Canaanites, chiefly in the highlands of Canaan. The mixing with the Canaanites had not yet gathered headway, but it had begun. The people was becoming acquainted with new gods, and at the same time it lived in fear of the strong Canaanites ensconced in their cities and ruling by such means as civilisation gave them. Thus the nation was threatened by weakening and disintegration both from within and from without.

The poem shows that the tribes did not form an organised unity. Some stayed away, others were half-hearted, those who came, gathered to the assistance of Yahweh upon the summons of the leaders. In the monarchical period the ruler tried to establish a regular army to be mustered and to fight at his pleasure. In early times the Israelites could only be induced to concerted action by their feeling of fellowship, and it exerted its influence as far as it went. No external framework kept the tribes together, those who hung back were threatened by the curse, by repudiation from the psychic fellowship. The upbearer of this fellowship was the ancient God of the people. This means that the unity was a unity of soul. It was due to a community of kind and a common history, which manifested itself in a uniform cult. But whether this inherited cult had found common forms after the immigration into Canaan is a question not easily answered.

The psychic unity which characterised early Israel was preserved more or less, and became especially conspicuous during war, because all the forces of the people were concentrated in it.

In the Song of Deborah we see how everything is intensified, how events loom larger than usual and attain cosmic dimensions. The first stanza, we may resume, sets forth the elation filling the souls of the warriors. A woman, herself carried away by her enthusiasm, urges them onward and sets the forces in motion. All depends on the chieftains, but most of all on the leader, in whom the will of all is bound up. The river that witnesses the fight is no ordinary stream, it is a primeval river. All space takes part in the battle, in the heavens the stars in their courses fight against the enemies of Israel.

The intense effort made by the people to gather all its strength is seen from the fact that it is Yahweh, the fountain-head and source of all Israelitish life, who directs the battle and brings it to an end. It is his strength and will which animate the chieftains and the people. He advances in all His might from His old home where the real history of the people began. The poem reaches its climax as it proclaims the death of His enemies and the eternal growth of His friends.

We hear nothing of the gods of the Canaanites; but it is a matter of course that they participate in the battle on the other side. [1] The hostile armies meet in battle, each bringing its entire world with it. Each people appears in all its strength, with its history, and its God.

The picture of warfare in early Israel shown to us in the Song of Deborah corresponds entirely to what we learn from other traditions. All efforts are directed towards creating and maintaining that state of increased psychic strength which is requisite in war.

For the army to preserve its concentrated strength it is necessary that every man in it should possess absolute purity. We know that purity is consistent with the integrity of the soul; impurity destroys its integrity and therefore impairs the strength of the soul.

Some of the Israelite military laws exemplify the strictness with which purity had to be maintained. Among the things which cause impurity are the issues of the body, especially such as belong to sexual life. Hence one law lays down that a warrior who has had an issue of the body in the night shall keep outside the camp all day and only be admitted to the camp again at sunset after washing. Similarly the waste products voided from the body are to be kept outside the camp and carefully buried in the ground (Deut. 23,10-15).

The rules mentioned in the narratives of the wanderings in the wilderness, that all who were suffering from an impurity caused by leprosy, an issue, or contact with a dead body, should leave the camp (Num. 5,1-4), applied in the first place to the army, even though they were only a more stringent enforcement of rules that applied, also, to the daily life of the community in general.

Altogether, the special demands made on the army rendered it necessary to carry caution to extremities. The least breach in the tense integrity meant a danger which might be fatal to the army and thus to the whole people. In the small collection of Deuteronomic military laws for instance, the Israelites are instructed to say expressly to the army going into action: If any man be timid or fearful (literally thin of heart), he shall return to his house that he may not weaken [1] the heart of his brethren like his own (Deut. 20,8). Similarly, in the story of one of Gideon's fights, he is directed to proclaim in the army that all who are timid and apprehensive shall return home (Judg. 7,3). A subsequent narrator interpreted this, according to his lights, as a command to reduce the forces lest the Israelites should believe that their numbers made them victorious and so forget to give glory to Yahweh (7,2). Fear spreads like wild fire; once it is admitted to the army, the defeat is inevitable; it is like an impurity attacking the firmness of the force, only that it acts directly and violently, while uncleanness accomplishes its disintegrating work in secret and by devious ways.

There are other rules showing the same solicitude that the army should only admit to its ranks men who can be entirely merged in the whole and act as part of it. In the military laws of Deuteronomy we find the following passage: If any man has built a new house but not dedicated it, he shall return to his house lest he die in the war and another man dedicate it. And if a man has planted a vineyard, but not taken the fruit of it, he shall return to his house, lest he die in the war and another man shall begin to take the fruits of it. — And if a man has betrothed a woman and not taken her, he shall return home lest he die in the war and another man take her (Deut. 20,5-7).

In these three laws we find the same considerate spirit which prevails in many of the laws of Deuteronomy and which is generally characterised by the honourable name "humane". A close inspection will show, however, that the laws are not considering casual instances, but something greater and more profound. In all three cases a man has started a new, important undertaking without having finished it yet. In such a case something has been created, which is greater than the man himself, a new totality has come into existence. To make a breach in this prematurely, that is to say, before it has attained maturity or has been finished, involves a serious risk of sin. This risk must be avoided for the sake of the cause itself, and the man who came to the army after committing such a breach might mean a danger much more than a help in the psychic whole constituted by the army.

It is a matter of course that a warrior must scrupulously abstain from intercourse with women, since such intercourse always involves a risk of contamination. When David came to Nob and wished to eat of the holy bread with his men, he expressly informed the priest that he and his soldiers had not touched women for several days (1 Sam. 21,6).

The story of Uriah and David is based on this feature of the warrior's life. When Bathsheba told David that she was expecting a child of which he was the father, David tried to conceal this fact by recalling her husband, Uriah, from the war. When David was informed that, in spite of his invitation Uriah had not gone to his house and his wife, but had spent the night with the guard at the entrance to the royal palace, he summoned him and asked him: Why didst thou not go to thine house? Uriah answered David: The Ark and Israel and Judah live in huts, and my master Joab and my master's servingmen are encamped on the plain. Why then should I go to my house to eat and drink and lie with my wife? By thy life, and thy soul's life, by no means I will do this! (2 Sam. 11,11).

Here Uriah describes the life of the warrior as a life under abnormal conditions and a life of renunciation. That the separation from his wife is a very important feature in this connection will appear from the sequel. For David invited him to a feast and made him drunk; but even then he would not go to his house but preferred to spend the night with the king's men. Only then did David give up his plan and sent Uriah back to the field, where David's faithful servant Joab saw to it that he was killed.

In other ways, too, the warrior had to avoid a normal life.

We do not know whether abstention from food belonged to the general preparation for war since we have only quite secondary testimonies to this (Judg. 20,26; 1 Sam 7,6). But there is a narrative which shows that it might be imposed on warriors during a campaign, when some great feat making unusual demands on them was the object.

When Jonathan, by an audacious act, had won a victory over the Philistines, it was urgently necessary to follow up his success and inflict a complete defeat on the enemy. Then Saul said: Cursed be the man who eats any food before evening, that I may take vengeance on mine enemies! (1 Sam. 14,24). The further course of events shows the seriousness of the duty imposed. The story goes on to say that the warriors eat nothing that day; even when they found some honey in the wood, they did not touch it. But Jonathan had heard nothing of his father's command, and when he discovered the honey he took a little on the point of his rod and refreshed himself with it. When a man informed him of the duty imposed on the army by his father, he answered: My father paralyses the land. See how clear my eyes have become because I have tasted this morsel of honey. Had but the warriors eaten today of the spoil they have taken from the enemy! Now no great defeat has been inflicted on the Philistines (1 Sam. 14,29-30). When Saul, later on, could get no answer from the oracle, he understood that a sin had been committed. Upon the drawing of lots Jonathan was designated as the guilty person, and when Saul asked him what he had done, he answered: On the end of this rod in my hand I have tasted a little honey. Lo, I must die. Then Saul said: "God do so, and may he so continue, thou shalt surely die, Jonathan" (vv. 43-44). The people, however, redeemed Jonathan and so saved his life.

Jonathan's spontaneous ejaculation, when he heard of his father's command, clearly implies a criticism of it; indeed, it seems as if he rejects fasting altogether, as a means to fortify the warriors. He says that it weakens the people to abstain from food, they had much better fall upon the booty and strengthen themselves by eating. The force of his words seems obvious; the early Israelites, too, knew that food is necessary for keeping up one's strength. And yet Jonathan's words must merely be taken as a momentary impulsive outburst, not as a more acute criticism of abstemiousness as a warlike measure. As will appear from the sequel, Jonathan fully recognises that he has committed a sin and is ready to take the consequences.

Food is necessary for the normal maintenance of life; but the warrior is in an abnormal state, because he acts with an intensified strength of soul, which has its own law. In everyday life a man draws strength from his food and accepts the risk of contamination involved therein, but in the warrior's state all contamination must be avoided; when at his highest level, therefore, he must also dispense with food. Abstemiousness means purification, it inclines the soul to pliability, the effort may be further increased, ecstasy becomes the natural form of action of the soul. [1]

_____

The Israelites call the warrior's state *ḳōdesh*, the term which we render by the word "holiness". Holiness has its root in the soul, it is a common force impregnating all the warriors. Not merely they themselves, but everything that belongs to them is pervaded by the same force. The warriors are "the sanctified of Yahweh" (Isa. 13,3; cf. Jer. 22,7; 51,27 f.), but their weapons, too, are sacred as long as they themselves are in the war-like state (1 Sam. 21,6; cf. Jer. 22,7). This property can be transferred to the weapons by anointing them (2 Sam. 1,21; Isa. 21,5). [2] The entire camp constitutes a sacred sphere, from which all that is unclean must be kept away, as well as from the persons of the warriors (Deut. 23,15). Thus the camp with the army forms a firm coherent organism. The unity is given through the common spirit of the people, but it is intensified in the same degree as the common strength is increased and all disrupting impurity kept away.

The army is the people in a condensed and intensified form. As the army assembles and prepares for war, the holiness is created which is the prerequisite of its power to act. To be carried through successfully a war must be "sanctified" (Jer. 6,4;

Joel 4,9; Mic. 3,5, cf. Jer. 22,7; 51,27 f.). In the first place the relation to the source of power, the God of the people, must be in good order, that he may constantly take part in the battle. Therefore the war is ushered in by a sacrifice. We hear about it in the old days, when the chief acted for the people (1 Sam. 7,9; 13,9 f.), and from the monarchical time we have a psalm which shows us in a brief glimpse part of the ceremony by which war was sanctified in the temple at Jerusalem.

The psalm runs as follows: May Yahweh answer thee in the day of trouble, may the name of the God of Jacob defend thee. May He send out thy help from the sanctuary, may He support thee from Zion. May He remember all thy sacrifices, accept as valid thy burnt offering. [1] May He grant thee according to thy heart, may He fulfil all thy counsel. Let us rejoice at the victory, raise the banner in the name of our God. May Yahweh fulfil all thy petitions. — Now I know that Yahweh will grant victory to His anointed, will answer him from His sacred Heaven with His right hand's victorious deeds of strength. Those put their trust in chariots and those in horses, but we glorify the name of Yahweh, our God. They stagger and sink, but we stand erect and hold our own. Yahweh, grant victory to the king! May He answer us when we call! (Ps. 20).

In this psalm we see that a war is imminent, and that it rests entirely on the king. The war is his war, and he petitions for victory. We do not see who is speaking, but he speaks on behalf of the people. The king has offered his sacrifices, and now the people add their petitions to his. The object is to create victory in the soul of the king. And in the last stanzas certainty has come. The God of Israel is the strongest, he has given victory to his anointed, all the rest waver and flee, only the army of Israel stands firm. The victory begins in the sanctuary, there it is achieved, for the decisive thing in war is to have "counsel and strength", so as not to appear with vain "lip-words" (2 Kings 18,20), which involve defeat, because they are nothingness.

Strengthened by their sanctification and the surety of victory thus acquired the warriors can now go to war. They must preserve what they have acquired by avoiding an infringement of their holiness. If they succeed, God's strength and thus God Himself is with them throughout. "Yahweh, thy God, walks with thee in the midst of thy camp to save thee and deliver up thine enemies to thee; therefore thy camp shall be sacred, that He may not see anything abominable in thee and turn away from thee" (Deut. 23,15, cf. Num. 5,3).

By carrying sacred objects with them in the camp, the army further sought to secure this divine presence. Taking into account the Israelite views in general it is a matter of course that their ensigns and banners were to them not merely practical signs, under which they assembled. They were "symbols" and thus an external expression of a special psychic power. But when much was at stake, the most sacred treasures of the people were exposed to the danger of war in the hope that they would secure victory. A narrative describing a battle with the Midianites in the wilderness time records how the priest Phinehas took his place in the army with the sacred objects (Num. 31,6).

We know this best from the old stories about the Ark. When the Israelites were unsuccessful in the war against the Philistines, they fetched the Ark, and the Philistines at once felt ill at ease to see the strong gods of the enemy enter into the contest (1 Sam. 4,3-8). But it was just as natural as their own practice af carrying some of their idols with them when they were at war (2 Sam. 5,21). Therefore it is not to be wondered at either, that in the narratives describing the journey of the Israelite hosts through the wilderness, it is the Ark that leads the people. When it started Moses pronounced the characteristic words: Rise up Yahweh, let thine enemies be scattered. Let thy foes flee before you. And when it halted he said: Return, Yahweh! The myriads of Israel's tribes. (Num. 10,35 f.). Surely we have here the cries with which the Ark was greeted when it was at war. That it also took part in David's campaigns appears from the story of Uriah (2 Sam. 11,11).

Thus we obtain full corroboration of what we learned from the Song of Deborah. Yahweh was with the Israelites in the battle. They fought "before the face of Yahweh" (Num. 32,20 ff.), they were "Yahweh's hosts" (Ex. 7,4; 12,41), the war was His war, the enemy His enemy.

_____

Everything that the Israelites did on preparing for war meant a strengthening of the soul, and this strengthening showed itself in the perfect certainty of victory. They sought to confirm it in many ways. A chieftain might fortify himself and the compact with God by making a promise. The promise might be of an offering, preferably of special significance, as we know it from the story of Jephthah (Judg. 11,30). Or such renunciations as we have heard about might be made still more binding by a special promise, as was precisely the case when Saul made the vow which Jonathan unwittingly happened to break (1 Sam. 14,24 ff.). Or the promise may be to surrender completely what is captured (Num. 21,2 f.). In all these cases the holy state of the warriors is intensified.

The Israelites seek by every means to secure the participation of the might of Yahweh in their undertaking. When Gideon had been called by Yahweh himself to fight against the Midianites, he wished to have the blessing giving victory confirmed by a sign. He decided himself what the sign was to be. The fleece of a sheep was to be wetted by the dew, while the earth around it was dry. And when this had been done, the opposite was to take place (Judg. 6,36-40). The fulfilment of these petitions assured Gideon that a real force with the right will was behind him. But this was not all. With his servant he stole across to the outposts of the enemy in the night and listened to their talk. He then heard a man tell another man of a dream in which he had seen a barley loaf roll down and overthrow the camp of the Midianites; and his hearer at once exclaimed that this meant Gideon's victory over the Midianites (Judg. 7,9-14). Now Gideon knew that defeat was in the soul of the enemy, and victory in his own soul, and so "his hands were strengthened" (v. 11); the issue was a matter of course.

It is the powers, the invisible powers at work behind, which decide the issue. But the warrior must assure himself that they are active in him, and act more vigorously than the forces filling his opponent. Herein he may secure potent aid from the *prophets*. The history of Ahab affords the best testimony to this. We know the scene preceding his and Jehoshaphat's fight against the Aramæans. Both kings were before the gates of Samaria, and many prophets filled with the spirit stood before them, creating victory in word and deed. But it was a lying spirit that spoke through the prophets. Only Micaiah, the son of Imlah, saw the discomfiture prepared for the kings, and Ahab sought in vain to crush the germ of defeat by keeping the prophet in subjection (1 Kings 22). [1] In this attempt we see what the co-operation of the prophets meant for the issue of the war.

We have another story about Ahab in which a prophet contributes to his victory. It deals with a war in which Ahab was encamped with his men opposite a hostile Aramæan army. It runs thus: And lo, a prophet came to Ahab, Israel's king, saying: Thus saith Yahweh: Hast thou seen all this great host? Lo, I deliver it into thine hand to day, and thou shalt know that I am Yahweh. And Ahab said: By whom? And he said: Thus saith Yahweh: By the young men of the chiefs of the provinces. And he asked: Who is to open the battle? And he said: Thou. (1 Kings 20,13 f.). The prophet remained continually with Ahab, and interfered in the course of events. When Ahab had conquered, the prophet again came to him, saying: Go, strengthen thyself and know and see what thou shalt do, for at the turning of the year Aram's king will come up against thee (v. 22). And later on, when the enemy had come, the man of God came back and promised Ahab victory, because the Aramæans had offended Yahweh by calling him a mountain god (v. 28).

Thus the prophet takes part in the war throughout, and in his own way he helps to create events; for there is a continual desire for his strong counsel. When the united kings of Israel, Judah, and Edom had gone on an expedition against Moab and were roaming the wilderness unable to find water, the king of Judah said: Is there no prophet of Yahweh here, that we may seek Yahweh by him? (2 Kings 3,11). Then Elisha was sent for, and he showed them water. Numerous stories have recorded such achievements of the prophets. During a battle with the Aramæans Elisha could see where the enemy had laid his ambush — as Samuel could see what had become of some asses that had strayed —, and the king of Israel acted accordingly (2 Kings 6,8-12), just as he constantly sought his advice (v. 21).

The prophet could help to bring about victory, not only by his words but also by special actions.[1] Elisha put victory into King Joash by making him shoot shafts of victory against Aram, and strike the ground with arrows (2 Kings 13,14-19), just as the King of Babylon procured signs by shaking arrows, looking at liver, and consulting Teraphim at the cross-roads (Ez. 21,26).

Whatever the procedure of the army-leader, his object is always the same: to increase his strength, and this can only be done by constantly keeping up the connection with the source of strength. During the war the Israelite commander turns continually to Yahweh. He does so when he solicits the advice of the prophet, and he can obtain the same result when by the aid of the priest he consults the *oracle,* the appurtenances of which in the early times were generally carried along in war time.

We know this from the history of Saul. When he had defeated the Philistines, and the people had taken the spoil, he did not know whether to pursue the enemy further. He then asked the oracle: Shall I go down after the Philistines? Wilt thou deliver them into the hands of Israel? (1 Sam. 14,37). But the oracle failed to answer, and Saul at once understood that something must have happened to separate the army from Yahweh. A fresh casting of lots revealed the sin of Jonathan, the holiness of the army was no longer complete; it was clear now that it had not what was requisite to proceed with the fight. Then the Israelites and the Philistines went each to his own land (v. 46). When Saul had reached the end of his resources, he was to learn what it meant to be abandoned by Yahweh. He sought hither and thither to find a remedy for the perplexity that beset his exhausted soul, "but Yahweh did not answer him, neither by dreams nor by Urim, nor by prophets" (1 Sam. 28,6).

When David went out to fight the Philistines this, too, was

on the strength of the oracle which said that Yahweh would deliver the Philistines into the hand of David (2 Sam. 5,19); and in the course of the campaign, when he was in doubt as to what further policy to pursue, the oracle gave him Yahweh's decision (v. 23). It is, therefore, perfectly in accord with the usage of earlier times that the narratives make the oracle constantly active during Israel's conquest of Canaan and during the wars in the age of the judges (Judg. 1,1; 20,18).

Thus weapons are very far from deciding alone the issue in war. All of them, sword, spear, and lance were of great importance. But it was of infinitely greater importance that those who were to use them possessed the proper psychic force, and we have seen that the efficiency of the weapons themselves in the battle depended on their consecration and consequent pervasion by holiness.

Hence weapons were not the only means by which the Israelites fought their enemies. Both armies, the Israelite and the hostile host, were under the same law. When Israel increased its psychic strength through its god, the enemy fortified himself through his own god. The object of the contest was to weaken and paralyse the enemy, and the best thing was to hit in the centre of his soul. This could be done by means of the curse.

Among the Arabs the curse constituted a very essential part of the battle. In the Old Testament, curiously enough, we only hear of it once, and then it is not employed by Israelites. But when we are told that Balak, the king of Moab, summoned Balaam, the man of God, to curse the Israelite tribes (Num. 22-24), we may take it for granted that the custom here mentioned was well known in Israel. And actually the Israelites made that psychic attack on the enemy which was inherent in the curse by the prayers for his defeat offered up in the temple.

The result aimed at by means of the curse might, however, be attained in other ways also. If the Israelites could strike terror directly to the soul of the enemy, it would become paralysed and divided, and the victory would be won. We hear several times of the contest taking this course, chiefly after unexpected assaults. When Jonathan with his armour-bearer had secretly made his way into the camp of the Philistines at Michmash, the sudden appearance of the two men caused a wild panic. It began with the surprised outpost, but terror spread swiftly throughout the camp. Disorganisation followed, the earth shook, the confusion increased, the whole army behaved like a troop beset by a curse, a crowd of people running among, and fighting each other. As the narrator expresses it, they had been stricken by a terror of God, *ḥerdath 'ᵉlōhīm*, and he says: thus Yahweh gave Israel the victory on that day (1 Sam. 14,6-23). In the same way Yahweh confused *(way-yāhom)* Sisera and his Canaanite warriors in the Deborah battle, according to the description of the battle contained in the prose narrative accompanying the poem (Judg. 4,15). And in the days of Samuel Yahweh struck terror to the hearts of the Philistine host by a loud thunderclap (1 Sam. 7,10).

There is much evidence to show that noise played a great part in war, and also that it had its effect. *Tᵉrū'ā*, the term for loud, uncontrolled clamour, which is also used about the shrill blast produced by the ram's horn bugle *(shōphār)* is unseparably bound up with warfare (1 Sam. 17,20.52; Jer. 4,5; 49,2; Ez. 21,27; Am. 1,14; 2,2; Zeph. 1,16; Job 39,25). The blare of the ram's horn bugle is the signal to make ready for battle and to break camp (Num. 10,1 ff.; Judg. 3,27; 6,34; 7,8.16.20; 2 Sam. 2,28; 18,16), but it also mingles with the shouting throughout the battle itself.

The noisy clamour of the fighters calls for no further explanation; it is a spontaneous expression of the spirit of the battling warriors. And as intensely as it rises out of the ecstatic certainty of victory, in the same degree will it be able to influence the enemy and weaken the firmness of his soul. When the Ark was brought into the Israelite army during the war with the Philistines, it raised their drooping strength, and they broke into a loud shout, making the earth shake. And the Philistines were terrified to hear it, for they knew what it meant; a mighty God had entered the Israelite army, and gave it new strength (1 Sam. 4,5 f.).

What such a noise meant we learn best from Gideon's battle with the Midianites. Gideon had 300 men. Each of them was provided with a horn, a jar, and a torch; the latter was hidden in the jar. They surrounded the enemy, and at a given signal they broke the jars, swung the torches, and blew the horns. A hopeless confusion ensued. Yahweh directed one man's weapon against the other, the rout was complete (Judg. 7,19 ff.). Thus Yahweh confused His own and Israel's enemies.

These old narratives show us how largely war was a psychic contest. Yahweh worked in harmony with men, because he worked in their souls. But we also have war stories in which the shouting, the old manifestation of the ecstasy of the people, and the sacred objects, do the work by themselves, so that events seem like miracles, produced by a divine arbitrariness. We have a typical example of this in the story of the conquest of Jericho.

According to this story the Israelite army went in procession round the city for six consecutive days. First came a division in special armour *(ḥālūṣ)*, then seven priests with ram's horn bugles, then the Ark, and finally the rest of the army. For six consecutive days the army went once round the city. On the seventh day they marched round the city seven times, and the seventh time the warriors broke into loud shouting while shrill blasts were blown on the ram's horn bugles. Then the walls fell, and the city was in the power of the Israelites (Josh. 6). [1]

In this story we find elements which we know from the warfare of early times. The presence of the Ark, the shrill noise of the bugles, the clamour of the warriors, are familiar to us from a time when weapons were not the only important thing in war. The march round the city in solemn procession, also, we understand, is a means of appropriating the city, og procuring psychic ascendancy over it. But in our narrative these things are not in harmony with the action of the people. They are not organic but independent, they act quite by themselves, as miraculous agencies. The hostile armies are of no importance as active participants. In marvellous wise the walls fall down, and the

Israelites have merely to put out their hands to take the gift bestowed on them.

By a very slight change the narrator has created quite a new picture of war out of the old elements. It corresponds to a change in the whole conception of divine action, which was to become of such significance for Israel's view of God and man. We meet with this conception of Yahweh's activity in war in the whole history of Israel's campaigns from the exodus from Egypt to the conquest of Canaan (Ex. 14,24; 17,8 ff.; 23,27; Deut. 2,15; Josh. 10,10 f.; 24,12 etc.).

At the end of the war the warriors returned to their normal condition. If they returned with defeat, they stole shamefacedly home along byways, as the story runs about David's men on one occasion (2 Sam. 19,4), but if they brought home victory, they were received by the women with timbrels and dancing, as we hear about Jephthah (Judg. 11,34). And when the Israelites had vanquished the Philistines, the women from all the towns came out singing and dancing, rejoicing with tabrets and triangles, ¹ greeting the victors with songs (1 Sam. 18,6).

No doubt the warriors observed certain rules when they were to pass from the holy into the normal condition, but we have no positive information of this. The psalter of the Old Testament contains psalms which have evidently been recited in the temple after a war had been successfully concluded (e. g. Ps. 9; 68; 76; 118); on that occasion, too, the offerings were made on the altar which the chieftain or king had promised before the war. Only when the sacred vows had been fulfilled was the holy period of war at an end.

A story of the wilderness time records the admission to camp of the warriors after they have carried through a successful war against the Midianites (Num. 31). They return with a rich spoil of women, children, and goods. Moses then commands the men to put to death the women who are not virgins. Next, everyone who has killed anybody, or touched a corpse, is to keep outside the

camp for seven days; on the third and seventh days they are to
purify themselves and the rest of the captives, as well as all
clothes and objects (v. 19 f.). It may be doubted whether the
command applies merely to those who kill the captives, but the
sequel, which forms a supplement to this, shows that it applies
to the warriors in general. For here Eleazar gives them further
instructions as to how they are to purify the different objects,
partly with water, partly with fire (vv. 21—23), and then goes
on to say: Then you shall wash your clothes on the seventh day,
and you shall be clean, and thereafter you shall enter the camp
(v. 24).

According to this account the warriors would be excluded
from the camp for a week after their return. If we consider the
narratives of the books of Samuel, they do not convey the impression that such an exclusion from the community was a general
rule, and it is probable that we have here a certain theorising on
old customs, as we know it from the Pentateuch. This would
also seem to be indicated by the fear of contamination by killing
or by corpses which runs through the story, in accordance with
the later development in Israel. But that there is something real
at the root of this theorising is certain enough, and not least
when the texts deal with the captured spoil.

When the hostile armies stand facing each other, cleansed
from all impurity, at the highest level of holiness, they constitute
two spheres sharply marked off from one another. In the battle,
however, these two spheres intermix, and when the battle is over,
the victor is left the possessor of goods and property which have
belonged to the hostile sphere. It is readily understood that it
must be a question of grave import how the victor may gain
ascendancy over the spoil he has acquired and appropriate it to
himself without doing injury to his soul.

The Israelite's desire for spoil was no less than that of his
neighbours, and was not diminished through the ages. In the
old days, apart from the human captives, they took in the first
place the enemy's cattle (1 Sam. 14,32; 15; 30,20 et al.), but
also clothes, as shown by the Song of Deborah (Judg. 5,30),
and treasure of a costlier kind; special mention is made of half-

moons, known nowadays from the excavations, and gold rings, chains etc. (Judg. 8,21.24-26). And gradually they appropriated all that they were able to carry with them of the goods found in the towns (Deut. 2,35; 3,7; 20,14 et al., cf. Gen. 14,11.16). It was part of the nature of the great king to be the winner of booty, (*'abhi 'adh)*, (Isa. 9,5), and the joy of participating in the distribution of the spoil is mentioned as an example of the highest form of pleasure (Isa. 9,2).

As among the Arabs, certain rules were evolved for the division of the spoil. The chieftain no doubt had his special portion assigned to him, but he could ask the warriors to give up part of their portions for a common purpose, as when Gideon made an ephod of the gold objects distributed among his men (Judg. 8,27). We learn that those who stayed by the baggage were to have a share in the booty together with those who fought, and this rule is referred to David (1 Sam. 30,24 f.). Under a law ascribed to Moses the spoil was to be divided into two equal parts, of which one fell to the warriors, the other to the rest of Israel (Num. 31, 25 ff.).

The law required the enemy's trees to be spared to some extent. It says: When thou besiegest a city for many days, in thy fight against it to capture it thou shalt not damage its trees by cutting them with an axe; thou mayest eat of them, but thou shalt not cut down the trees themselves. Are the trees of the field human beings[1] that they should be laid siege to by thee? But trees of which thou knowest that they are not trees with edible fruit, such thou mayest destroy and cut down and build of them a siege-wall against the town waging war against thee, until it surrenders (Deut. 20,19-20).

Here there is a demand for the moderation characteristic of the old time. Life is to be respected, it must not be entirely destroyed. But this law was not generally valid. When Jehoram and Jehoshaphat were waging war against Mesha, king of Moab, Elisha, stating the commands of Yahweh, said: You shall reduce every fortified town and every prominent city, and you shall cut down every good tree and stop all fountains, and every good plot of land you shall damage with stones (2 Kings 3,19); this command was carefully carried out (v. 25).

The severe measures demanded by the prophet were common in the case of human beings. But here, again, there are shades of difference. In one of the stories from the age of the Judges we learn that two noble prisoners are merely killed because the law of revenge exacts precisely their lives, while otherwise they would have been spared (Judg. 8,19). In the war against the Amalekites David put to death all who fell into his hands, only 400 succeeded in saving their lives by flight (1 Sam. 30,17). When a city or a land had been taken, so many were killed that the enemy suffered a grave reduction of his forces. The victor rejoiced when he could seriously humiliate the vanquished chief, who could not expect any gentle treatment. We hear of Adonibezek having his thumbs and great toes cut off (Judg. 1,6); he himself had had the happiness of treating 70 kings in the same way. The vanquished foe had to grovel in the dust and let the victor tread upon his neck (Jos. 10,24), a violent expression of the fact that he had no longer any will of his own. But under normal conditions there is no question of a general extermination. When David had captured the Jebusite town of Jerusalem, no massacre took place; even the owner of the rock sanctuary remained in undisturbed possession of his property until David later bought it of him at its full value. After the successful war against Moab, David had the men measured and caused the tall, well-grown ones to be put to death, whereas the short ones were allowed to remain alive (2 Sam. 8,2).

Here we find the same principle as that which the law enforces for the trees. Reduction is allowed, but not extermination. Contrasted with this, however, we have the tendency with which we have also become acquainted, that of having as many as possible put to death. That tendency has been clearly expressed in one of the martial laws of Deuteronomy. It says here: When thou approachest a city to make war on it, thou shalt offer it peace. If then it answer thee with peace and open unto thee, all the people to be found in it shall do forced labour for thee and shall serve thee. But if it do not make peace with thee, but wage war against thee, then thou shalt besiege it. And if Yahweh, thy God, then deliver it into thine hand, thou shalt kill all males in it with the sword. But the women and the little children and the cattle and all that is in the town, all the plunder in it thou shalt seize for thyself, and thou shalt consume the spoil of thine enemies which Yahweh, thy God, giveth thee (Deut. 20,10-14).

Under the provisions of this law enemies who give up all resistance shall be allowed to live, but as slaves. If they rise like men against the Israelites setting upon them, all the males are to be exterminated, while women, young children, and all property fall to the Israelites as spoil, provided they are victorious. In either case this law means that the hostile community is wiped out. For the community is based entirely on the male, and whether the men cease to be free, or are exterminated, their community will be dissolved, for their will is no more. Women merely act as helpmeets in the maintenance of the community and, when surrendered to the enemy, must contribute towards the prosperity of his community. Therefore the difference in the treatment of men and women is so great. A woman captured in war may even be taken as a wife, and when this has happened, she cannot be sold as a slave to another man (Deut. 21,10-14).

The law of the extermination of all men, despite its absolute terms, hardly indicates a fixed rule always acted upon, but is the consistent expression of a certain tendency. We have not a few stories, however, according to which the rule laid down by the law is carried into effect. In the narrative of the Midianite war in the wilderness period it is stated that, after the victory, the Israelites killed all males, while women, children, cattle, and property were carried off as spoil; but Moses and Eleazar also demanded that all boys and all women not virgins should be put to death, while the plunder was to be subjected to a purification (Num. 31,7-9.17-18.20 ff.). We have evidence of a similar procedure, the killing of all except the young virgins, in another story of late origin (Judg. 21,11).

A clause has been added to the aforementioned Deuteronomic provision as to the treatment of the vanquished foes. It is to the effect that the decree merely applies to "cities very far from thee, which are not of the cities of the nations here" (Deut. 20,15). And the text goes on to say: But in the cities of these peoples, which Yahweh thy God delivereth into thy possession, thou shalt let no breath live (16). Thou shalt completely banish them, the Hittites and the Amorites, the Canaanites and the Perizzites, the Hivites and the Jebusites, as Yahweh thy God hath commanded thee (17), lest they teach ye to act according to all their abominations which they exercise before their gods, and ye sin before Yahweh, your God (18).

The conquest of Canaan and the neighbouring tracts is described in accordance with this precept; all breath is destroyed, sometimes all the spoil also (Num. 21,1-3, cf. Judg. 1,17; Deut. 2,34 f.; Josh. 6-7; 8,2.27 f.; 10,28.35.37.39 f.; 11,10 ff.).

We have thus two laws in Deuteronomy concerning the treatment of the enemy and his property, the one more rigorous than the other. There can be no doubt that the first is meant to be a law of general application. That the second, which requires all breathing things to be exterminated, has been added later, appears from the fact that it begins with a restriction of the first law (in verse 15) which one would otherwise have expected to have been stated in the first law itself. The question is whether all are to be exterminated, or whether women and children are excepted.

In reality it applies to both laws that they have generalised and made absolute statements, where life itself must have presented many variations, as a consideration of the early history will show us. In so far both laws, whether they exact the extermination of all Canaanites or they merely spare women and children, are to be regarded as the outcome of a theoretical construction. They take for granted the claim of the monarchy to the whole of the country, but further they imply that this claim means that the whole population must be uniformly Israelite. In this form the claim would agree but poorly with conditions in the monarchical period. But it is in perfect agreement with conditions in post-exilic times, when the Israelites had to regain for themselves a position in the land, and as a background to their war against the other peoples settled there had the consciousness of a historical right which had grown to be absolute to them by the fact of its detachment from reality during the exile.

The same applies, however, to the martial laws of Deuteronomy as to the other theoretical laws; they are by no means utterly baseless. There was, a foundation in the early history of Israel for the demand for the complete extermination of enemies, and this is connected with the whole character of war.

Deuteronomy states that the Canaanites must be exterminated lest they should teach the Israelites their rites (Deut. 20,18). We see here the dread prevalent in exilic or post-exilic times that regenerated Israel should suffer the same fate as early Israel which acquired foreign customs and thus obliterated the boundary-line between Israelite and alien. Therefore the law, in fact, exacts the same treatment for an Israelitish city which proceeds to introduce the worship of alien gods, as for the strangers, i. e. extermination (Deut. 13,13-19). According to this rule hardly any Israelite city of the monarchic time would have survived. The rule, however, is merely a one-sided consequence of the old Israelite view of the relation between the Israelite and the hostile army. We have already seen in what this consists. The enemy and all his property was pervaded by a soul foreign to Israel. In order to preserve themselves the Israelites had to exercise the utmost caution towards what was alien, and in all instances only appropriate what they could actually assimilate.

We have seen that he who took foreign land sometimes appropriated it by setting up a sign bearing his name on it (1 Sam. 15,12; 2 Sam. 8,13 et al.) [1], but in the very first place Yahweh's name was mentioned over land appropriated by Israel (Am. 9,12, cf. Isa. 63,19). The upholder of Israel's strength must make it his own for it to become truly Israelite. The same fundamental view marks the relation to the spoil.

For the appropriation by the Israelites of the foreign spoil normally takes place by surrendering part of it to Yahweh. When it is consecrated to Yahweh he causes his might to pervade it, thus making it possible for the Israelites to appropriate the rest. The whole of it is made Israelitish, and the Israelites avoid

the terrible discord which would arise if they were to take over
something which was incompatible with their God. In the old days
there were hardly fixed rules as to how much was to be dedicated
to Yahweh, it was left to the judgment of the leaders; but naturally it must not be the poorest part. Thus we hear of Gideon
that he made all his men give up all gold things and treasures to
make a sacred object, an ephod (Judg. 8,24-27). A valuable
treasure such as Goliath's sword was kept in Nob's temple (1
Sam. 21,10), just as, on the other hand, Saul's weapon was
placed by the victorious Philistines in a temple to Ashtoreth (1
Sam. 31,10). And we are told that David dedicated to Yahweh at
Jerusalem all objects of precious metal which he took in his
wars (2 Sam. 8,7 f., 11 f.).

It is possible that gradually certain rules were formed as to
how large a portion of the spoil was thus to be dedicated to
Yahweh. At any rate a rule is given in the oft-mentioned story
of the Israelite war with Midian in the wilderness period. It
says that the warriors are to give a five hundredth part of their
share, while the rest of the community are to give a fiftieth part
of their share to Yahweh; in addition the warriors sanctified the
gold they had taken and the jewels (Num. 31,25-54). The consecrated spoil constituted a considerable part of the sacred gifts
of the temple and was under the supervision of a special functionary (1 Chron. 26,26-28). When part of the spoil is consecrated,
the consecration takes effect on that part also which is taken
over by men. No one could safely enjoy his booty if he was not
sure that a suitable portion had been dedicated and surrendered
to Yahweh.

It is a matter of course that there were certain things which
it was especially natural to dedicate to Yahweh. He had a claim,
not only to treasures in the common sense, but there were things
which were so pervaded with the soul of the alien people and so
sacred that it was beyond the power of humans to appropriate
them. Often the Israelites entirely refrained from taking sacred
objects, but if such were carried off, they were given to a temple.
It then became a question whether the god of the victorious people
was strong enough to take possession of them, or whether the

result would be the same as when the Ark was taken by the Philistines, and wrought mischief both to gods and men wherever it went (1 Sam. 5).

How long Israel continued to consecrate spoil of war we do not know; but we have evidence to show that at a certain time there was a change in this procedure. A prophecy against Tyre dating from post- exilic times utters this warning: And its income and profit shall be dedicated to Yahweh; it shall not be stored nor put away, but those that dwell before Yahweh shall of its income have food to satisfy them and choice raiment (Isa. 23,18). Here we find the old term for the treatment of the spoil, when it says that it is to be consecrated to Yahweh; but quite a different construction has been put upon it. Nothing is said of setting apart some of the booty for Yahweh. The whole of it is given up to him, but it is done by the people who dwell before his countenance taking possession of it. It is not difficult to see that this form of consecration of the spoil is due to a change in the conception of holiness.

The taking over of the spoil always implies that a psychic appropriation is possible. But there are enemies whose whole soul is so incompatible with that of the Israelite that appropriation is difficult or quite impossible. Then the relentless law of extermination comes into force for the enemy and all that is his. What is thus given over to destruction is designated by the word ḥērem, the absolute contrast to holiness. The Israelites must carry through the extermination in order to assert themselves.

Hence the extermination of the hostile ḥērem is pleasing to the Lord, and the narratives have examples of a war beginning with defeat, but when the Israelites took a vow to make the hostile city ḥērem, Yahweh blessed the war, and it was successful. Thus it is related of a Canaanite city in the south of Judah that by virtue of such a vow it was exterminated and the name of the site, ḥormā, recalls the event (Num. 21,1-3, cf. Judg. 1,17).

The most detailed description of how a city was made ḥērem is given in the narrative of the capture of Jericho. When the town was at the point of surrendering, Joshua said: The city and all that is in it shall be a ban (ḥērem) before Yahweh — a doom

from which, however, Rahab is excepted. "But beware of the ban,
lest you ban and then take of what is banned and thus place the
camp of Israel under a ban and so paralyse it. And all
silver and gold and implements of copper and iron shall
be consecrated unto Yahweh and shall go into Yahweh's treasury"
(Josh. 6,18 f.). The text goes on to say: They then banned by the
sword all that was in the city, both men and women, young and
old, oxen, sheep and asses (v. 21). And the city and all that was
in it they burned with fire, but the silver and gold, and the
implements of copper and iron they gave up to the treasury of
Yahweh's house (v. 24). And Joshua then adjured them at that
time, saying: Cursed before Yahweh be the man who takes upon
himself to rebuild this town, Jericho. He shall found it at the
cost of his first-born, and at the cost of his youngest shall he
erect its gates (v. 26).

   We see that certain things are excepted from extermination.
The costly treasures are not to be destroyed, but are given to the
temple and sanctified in the usual way. That the existence of the
temple, by which, of course, is meant the sanctuary at Jerusalem,
is taken for granted is not to be wondered at, since all the narratives of the book of Joshua bear the mark of a later time. Yahweh
is mighty enough to appropriate the treasures that are his due,
and he does not waive his right to them. We may conjecture,
however, that in earlier times there have been cases also in which
everything without exception came under the doom of destruction; for this seems to be implied in the nature of the ban itself. ¹

   The grim seriousness of the ban appears from the sequel to
the story. One of the Israelites, Achan, the son of Carmi, took
some of the spoil under the ban, a Babylonian mantle and some
gold and silver. Immediately the blessing left the army of Israel
and it suffered an unexpected defeat. Then Joshua learnt from
Yahweh what had happened: the Israelites had taken some of
the spoil under the ban and had therefore come under the doom of
the ban; Yahweh's wrath was on them. By the drawing of lots
Achan was found to be the delinquent, and he at once confessed
his sin. Then Joshua took him, his sons and daughters, his oxen,
asses, sheep, and tents, besides what he had stolen. And Joshua

said: As thou hast paralysed us, Yahweh shall paralyse thee on this day. And the Israelites stoned him and all his and burnt them up with all that belonged to him (Josh. 7).

When the ban is placed on a family this means that it is rooted out. Every trace of it must be removed, because everything connected with it is a danger. A hostile city placed under *ḥērem* was to be exterminated so as to leave no living thing in it. Its name was to disappear and must never be revived, lest Israel be contaminated by contact with it.

In earlier times it was sometimes demanded that single individuals should be placed under the ban, especially the responsible leader of the hostile army (1 Kings 20,42). Even in narratives showing evidence of the mode of thought of a later age, the enemy's king occupies a special position when the ban is placed upon a people, as in Saul's war with the Amalekites (1 Sam. 15,3.8 ff.). How frequently a radical extermination was carried out in the old days we cannot decide. But it is certain that there was an increasing demand for it.

This increased demand for the extermination of the enemy is, as previously mentioned, most readily to be understood in the post-exilic time, but the way for it had been prepared by the passionate assertion by the prophets of the peculiar character of Israel, and the complete dissimilarity of its God to the gods of other peoples. We see these contentions culminate in the demand of post-exilic prophets that whole nations should be made *ḥērem* (Isa. 34,2 ff.; Mic. 4,13). In this period Israel took the full consequences of the old view of the holiness of war and the absolute gulf between Israel and the enemy, and this could be done all the more easily because the consequences were merely of theoretical importance. The law of *ḥērem* became a general demand for the extermination of enemies, and the old stories of the early Israelite wars with Canaan were shaped accordingly, as may be seen in the book of Joshua and occasionally in other narratives.

Israel's demand for self-assertion had become a demand for the subjugation of all other peoples through the mighty intervention of her God. This involved a change in the conception of war and the holiness connected with it.

Our consideration of war gives us a picture of the people as it was when all its strength was concentrated. It shows us that the blessing could only act in harmony with still stronger and deeper forces, which extend through men and things and are rooted in the divine powers. But it was not only in war that holiness was necessary for the renewal and maintenance of the blessing. All life needed the addition of strength gained through holiness. The responsibility for this constant renewal rested with the leaders of the community, and the renewed strength was acquired in places where there was a special concentration of holiness.

CHIEFTAIN AND KING.

IN the book of Judges the following statement is twice met with: In those days there was no king in Israel, every man did what was right in his own eyes (Judg. 17,6; 21,25). According to this statement the monarchy was not only the upholder, but also the creator of law and order in Israel; it was preceded by chaos and lawlessness.

Our examination of the social organisation, the law of psychic life and the law of values has shown us that early Israel, even without the monarchy, was law-regulated; for the law was created from within and pervaded the social organism in a vital manner. It is true that the monarchy aimed to be the absolute centre point in the life of the people, but this aim was never wholly attained. Prior to, but also under the monarchy, Israel consisted of a number of small communities, essentially self-contained.

Men and chieftains from such communities won the victory on the plain of Jizreel. The Song of Deborah calls the chiefs princes, *śārīm* (Judg. 5,15), or leaders, *ḥōḳeḳīm* and *meḥōḳeḳīm* (5,9.14, cf. Isa. 10,1; 33,22), words cognate with *ḥōḳ*, the term for the law. They are also called "the noble", *nedhībhīm* (Num. 21,18; 1 Sam. 2,8; Job 12,21; 34,18; Cant. 7,2), those who possess nobility, *nedhībhā* (Job 30,15), "men af valour", *gibbōr* or *gibbōr ḥayil;* sometimes they are also called the "head", *rō'sh* (Judg. 11,8; 1 Sam. 15,17; Job 29,25 et al.). [1] They constitute the "elders", the upholders of the community.

From the book of Job we learn how a single man, through the blessing bestowed on him, may rise amongst the noble men, and become the cornerstone of the community. In the Song of Deborah there is such a leader of the Israelites; he is mentioned by his name, Barak ben Abinoam. No name is given to the position he occupied, and we are not told how he had obtained it or in what it consisted.

We have no knowledge whatever as to whether the Israelites in the earliest times had established forms denoting their common life together. But we have narratives which show how a man in the old days could become the elected chief of a larger community of Israelites. Job was the leader of his community by virtue of his strong counsel, his wealth, and his happiness. War might, however, reveal such extraordinary strength in a man that he was raised to be the leading chief merely on account of this strength, though he was neither by descent nor by wealth what the Israelites understood by a "man of valour".

The term *gibbōr ḥayil* is used about the Gileadite Jephthah (Judg. 11,1). Legend raises him to the sphere of the progenitor of the race by making him a son of Gilead himself, but he did not possess the privilege and honour of a family. His mother was a harlot, therefore his brothers turned him out without any inheritance, and he became the leader of a band of outlaws; they were called *rēḳīm,* "empty", the opposite of *nikhbādh,* "the man rich in substance, full of honour" (Judg. 11,3). Even so he had the strength, and his tribe made him chief, that he might lead them in the war against the Ammonites. "And the spirit of Yahweh descended upon Jephthah" (Judg. 11,29), he led his tribe in the war and triumphed.

To be blest a man must have Yahweh with him, no one can act without this. But in ancient Israel the chief, when he was to perform great exploits, must have the spirit of Yahweh in him. This is the expression by which the Israelites denote that increase of psychic strength without which no war could be carried through; it manifested itself in the ecstatic state.

If we consider the process taking place in the chieftain's soul, the essential element in it is intense concentration. It affects the centre of gravity, intensifying all psychic sensations, bursting all bounds. The totality prevails, self-consciousness is obliterated or renewed, the man's heart is regenerated, and a new strength pours into him. What is this strength, and whence does it come? The Israelite is in no doubt about the answer. It comes from the great source of strength underlying all psychic life and whose workings are in the depths of the soul. In the supreme power of this strength he recognises its divinity, therefore he calls it Yahweh's spirit or soul. The great exploits, and the curious and violent gestures of which we hear (1 Sam. 10,10; 19,24), are equally manifestations of the divine psychic strength.

The divine soul is active in the chief on definite occasions and within limited periods. But not everybody is capable of rising above the common measure and participating with the God in his strength. A special election is necessary. This is sometimes expressed in the stories about the rise of a chief.

Gideon was chosen directly by Yahweh, who came to him in the shape of his *mal'ākh* when he was threshing wheat inside a wine press, and greeted him with the words that Yahweh was with him (Judg. 6,12). Gideon dared not accept this greeting, for the people had no luck, but Yahweh said: Go in this thy might and thou shalt deliver Israel out of the hand of Midian, verily I send thee! (6,14). And when Gideon referred to the inferiority of himself and his kin, Yahweh said: Surely, I will be with thee, and thou shalt smite Midian as one man (6,16).

Yahweh's promise to be with Gideon means that he needs the blessing for his deed, but it is further added that he is to act with a special force. The relation between Yahweh and Gideon is indispensable for his whole activity. This is confirmed by the strange sacrifice which follows, and when Gideon calls the altar "Yahweh is peace" (6,24), he gives expression to the security of the pact. But how close was the union between Yahweh and Gideon only becomes clear when the story of his achievements begins. It opens with the statement that "Yahweh's spirit clothed itself in Gideon" (6,34). It was Yahweh's soul which filled him and was active in him. This gave to his activity the character and importance which the story expresses by letting it arise out of a personal meeting with Yahweh.

Other stories make the election of the hero take place already before his birth, by which his nature and character are seen to bear the impress of Yahweh from the very beginning. This was the case with Samson.

3*

It is related that Yahweh's *mal'ākh* came to Manoah's wife, saying to her: Thou art barren and hast not borne children, but thou shalt conceive and give birth to a son. And now, beware and drink not wine and strong drink and eat nothing at all which is unclean. For thou shalt conceive and give birth to a son, and no razor shall touch his head, for the boy shall be a *nāzir* unto God from his mother's womb, and he shall begin to deliver Israel out of the hand of the Philistines (Judg. 13,3-5). Later on the same messenger returned and repeated his story in the presence of Manoah, and the whole was confirmed by a sacrifice of a similar kind to that mentioned in the story of Gideon.

The narrative shows that it was no mere chance that Samson was brought into the world. Yahweh's will was behind the event from the beginning; by virtue of it he was born to a life shaped by the fact that Yahweh's spirit worked in him. There was a close connection between the accession of strength which meant to be possessed by the spirit of Yahweh, and Samson's whole conduct in life. He was a *nāzir*, which means that his soul was cleansed and sanctified. He was to be constantly in a similar state to that in which warriors found themselves while under the law of war. He was to be kept away from impurity to such an extent that even his mother must abstain from unclean food, and from wine, which was foreign to prę-Canaanite Israel. He himself must not have his hair cut, the vital force which displayed itself in the growth of the hair must not be diminished. And gradually as he grew up, it became apparent that Yahweh bestowed his blessing on him, and soon Yahweh's spirit began to urge him.[1] The divine soul moved in him and took command (Judg. 13,24 f.).

Samson was to use his excess of strength for saving Israel from the Philistines. It was, indeed, they who came to feel his strength. He killed 30 of their men at one stroke (Judg. 14,19). When Yahweh's spirit was not in him he could be very gentle. He willingly suffered himself to be bound when his timid countrymen proposed to give him up to the Philistines, but only to rage with all the more violence when he came into the camp of the enemy. Yahweh's spirit entered into him, he burst his bonds as if they were flax, and the foe went down before his blows on all sides (Judg. 15,9 ff.).

The possession of Samson by the spirit of Yahweh depended entirely on his conduct as a *nāzīr*. When his hair was cut by the aid of a designing woman, Yahweh forsook him and he had to surrender himself to a life in captivity and humiliation (Judg. 16,19 ff.). Only when his hair grew out again did his strength return, and he performed his last and greatest feat when he pulled down a whole temple on to the assembled Philistines.

Samson has this in common with Gideon and Jephthah that his greatness is due to the absorption of divine soul which urges him to perform great exploits among hostile peoples. All three of them are ecstatic heroes. But their relation to their peoples differs widely.

Samson goes his own way entirely. He commands no one, he has no followers, and his countrymen are against him rather than with him. Quite otherwise with Jephthah. His authority extended to the whole of his tribe and lasted as long as he lived. It was based on a fixed compact, but it took its origin from his power to lead the people in war, driven by the spirit of Yahweh. When the elders of his tribe saw that they could not do without him as a leader, they went to him, saying "Come and be a leader unto us *(ḳāṣīn)*, that we may fight against the sons of Ammon". Jephthah then complained that they had driven him away, and only approached him when they were in distress, and he exacted a promise from them that they should keep him as their chief *(rō'sh)* if he was victorious. "And the elders of Gilead said to Jephthah: Yahweh heareth what is passing between us. Surely as thou hast spoken, so will we do. And Jephthah went with the elders of Gilead, and the people made him a chief and leader *(lᵉrō'sh ūlᵉḳāṣīn)*. And Jephthah uttered all his words before Yahweh at Mizpeh" (Judg. 11,10-11).

The chief must have the blessing of the leader, and the people readily submit to his will as long as they need his strength and good fortune. The stability of the relation between the chief and the people is due to the fact that it is a compact sanctified before

Yahweh and thus rendered fixed and inviolable. By such a compact a people may leave all its fate to the care of its chieftain, its blessing is the same as his.

We have a clear example of how this may work in the story of Goliath. The huge Philistine shouted to the Israelite army: Why do you go out and prepare for battle? Am not I the Philistine, and you slaves to Saul? Make a pact with [1] a man and let him come down to me. If he is able to fight with me and beats me, we will be slaves to you. And if I prevail against him and beat him, you shall be slaves to us and serve us (1 Sam. 17,8-9). The people is so closely identified with the man that comes forward on their behalf that its victory or defeat is entirely decided by him. That this was seriously meant may be gathered from the fact that the whole of the Philistine army fled, defeated, the moment Goliath was slain (v. 51).

From the story of Jephthah we see that the luck of the chief in war need by no means result in a lasting recognition of his authority, even though this is a natural consequence. This is confirmed by an incident related in the history of Gideon. After the description of Gideon's victory over the Midianites, it says: And Israel's men said to Gideon: Rule thou over us, both thou, thy son, and thy grandson, for thou hast delivered us out of the hand of Midian. And Gideon said to them: I will not rule over you, neither shall my son rule over you, Yahweh shall rule over you (Judg. 8,22-23). Immediately after this it is then related that he let them give up part of the spoil and made an ephod of it which he set up in Ophrah.

According to this story Gideon, immediately after his victory, was offered that which had been demanded by Jephthah, a continued chieftainship even in time of peace. There was nothing remarkable about this, nor perhaps about his refusal. And yet the story contains strange features. The authority is offered to Gideon by "the men of Israel". This is most naturally interpreted to mean the men representing the whole of Israel (as in Josh. 9). But Gideon can only have been the leader of his nearest kinsmen, who were joined by some few of the northern tribes. It is quite possible that "the men of Israel" may denote these, but the expression is most naturally viewed against the background of the later Israelite unity. That the dominion of a man means the dominion of his family and is normally continued by his son is a natural thing from an Israelite point of view. But each new generation must assert its inherited right through action for it to be recognised. Therefore it is strange that the rule is at once offered to Gideon and his descendants. This, too, would seem to indicate that the incident has been described with the established hereditary monarchy as a background.

But the most remarkable thing is the reason Gideon gives for his refusal. He and his family must not rule, Yahweh must rule. Here a contrast is implied between the divine and the human ruler, which can hardly be said to be in the spirit of the early times. For when the chieftain acted, he was driven by the spirit of Yahweh; when he pronounced judgment, it was Yahweh's law that he enforced, and when he was victorious, it was Yahweh's victory. Yahweh made his influence felt among the people precisely through the rulers; this applies to the earliest time as well as to the monarchical period. The statement is made by a man for whom this does not hold good; the ruler does not act in harmony with Yahweh but against him. We meet with a similar consideration in the history of Saul. It has a natural background in the priesthood, who far down into the ages arrogated to themselves the prerogative as Yahweh's elect, and therefore regarded the old king-ruler as a rebel against the true rule of Yahweh. This does not mean that criticism of the ruler was foreign to earlier times, as we may learn from the history of Abimelech.

Abimelech was the son of Gideon and a slave woman from Schechem. Gideon who, in the aforementioned narrative, is said to have refused to be the ruler of Israel, was still recognised as chief in his town of Ophrah and probably in its immediate vicinity, for we see his sons, 70 in all, settled as an aristocracy in Ophrah with an authority recognised in Schechem also. Like Jephthah, Abimelech was not a full son, on account of his mother, and therefore he became a dangerous man. He ingratiated himself with the men of Schechem, his mother's native place, and made them see that it was better that the power be given to him, one man, who was at least their relation, than that the 70 sons of Jerubbaal, his half-brothers, should sit in Ophrah and rule over them. They gave him money, and like Jephthah he gathered "empty" men, that is to say, men devoid of honour about him and killed his 70 half-brothers, except Jotham who escaped. The men of Schechem then made Abimelech king under a sacred tree in that town (Judg. 9,1-6).

By a pact Abimelech had thus been made chief of the citizens of Schechem. This event Jotham, who had escaped, illustrated for the men of Schechem by a story which he related to them from the top of Mount Garizim. It was a fable about the trees who desired to choose a king for themselves. It turned out that the valuable trees such as the olive, the fig and the vine which produced fine fruit themselves, refused to be rulers, because this meant that they would have to give up the production of their good fruit merely to sway above the other tree-tops. Only the small prickly bramble was willing, but the result was that the good trees had to bend under it and thus be arrested in growth if they would not draw down upon themselves all kinds of disaster (Judg. 9,8-15).

The picture here drawn of the monarchy is a caricature. The ruler is not a man leading the people because he is capable of being the upholder of the community, he is not a man who bestows things but a man who demands things, he does not uphold the others, but checks them. Such rulers the Israelites might learn to know in the Canaanite city communities, but the story does not give the common view of the leader in early Israel. The Israelite view appears precisely in the sequel to the story which shows that Abimelech perished because his rule was based on violence. 1

In early Israel the chieftainship had the peculiar free character which corresponded to the psychic quality of the people and the social organisation. A totality is formed under the leadership of an individual in whom the totality rests and is concentrated. What totalities come into question depends on how large a unity the joint life embraces at the given moment. It may be a tribe as in the story of Jephthah, or several tribes, as in the story of Gideon, or it may be a town, as shown by Abimelech's abortive attempt.

When a Greater Monarchy arose in Israel it endeavoured to set fixed limits to authority and establish a firm and lasting rule. The transition seems abrupt, because this rule brought something quite new into the history of Israel. And yet the Greater Monarchy was introduced into Israel in close association with the old chieftainship by the eminent political ability of one man, David. But once introduced, it rapidly strove to adapt itself to conditions in the rest of the oriental kingdoms.

The rise of the Israelite monarchy is described in the narratives contained in the books of Samuel, whose principal characters are Saul, Jonathan and David, who are joined by Samuel. They are marked by the view that there was a sharp distinction between the monarchical period and the earlier, kingless time. The monarchy was introduced through a special act, determined by Yahweh. The first king was Saul, who, however, merely prepared the way for David, Yahweh's favourite. In the description of how Saul acquired his power, the stories are meant to show how the monarchy was introduced into Israel.

A short series of narratives concerning Saul's election show evidence of the dislike of the monarchy with which we have met in Gideon's history also. But side by side with these we have a group of stories that allow us to see the events develop in a clear psychological coherence and in full agreement with conditions in the early times.

The contents of these stories (1 Sam. 9,1-10,16; 11; 14) are as follows: A man of the tribe of Benjamin, a *gibbōr ḥayil* by name Kish, had a son, Saul, a fine youth, a head taller than any of the people, in every respect what the Israelites called a good man. When some of Kish's asses had strayed, Saul was sent out with one of the servants to look for them. They then came to the seer Samuel, intending to ask him to divine where the asses were. Only the day before Samuel had learnt from Yahweh that Saul was coming, and Yahweh had commanded Samuel to anoint him to be chief *(nāghīdh)* in order that he might free the Israelites from the yoke of the Philistines. Now when Samuel met Saul, he invited him to a sacrificial meal just about to begin and told him that the asses had been found. To this he added these words: To whom belongs the glory of all Israel? Is it not for thee and all thy father's house? (9,20). To this Saul answered that he belonged to the smallest family in the smallest tribe.

At the sacrificial meal Samuel showed great honour to Saul, and the next morning, when he went part of the way with him, he anointed him, saying that Yahweh anointed him to be chief *(nāghīdh)* of his people Israel. And Samuel mentioned some signs to him which were to confirm this, namely, that he should meet various persons, last of all a band of prophets in ecstacy. "Then the spirit of Yahweh shall descend upon thee, and thou shalt be ecstatic with them, and thou shalt be changed into another man" (10,6).

When Saul left Samuel, "God gave him another heart", and when he met the prophets, it happened as Samuel had foretold. When his ecstasy had ceased, he went home, but he disclosed nothing of what Samuel had said (1 Sam. 9,1-10,16).

Soon afterwards Saul had an opportunity of showing his new strength. When the city of Jabesh in Gilead was threatened with ignominy by Nahash, king of the Ammonites, its inhabitants sent word to the other Israelites to solicit their help. When their men reached Gibeah with their message, Saul was just coming home from the field with his oxen. The moment he heard what had happened, the soul of God entered into him (11,6). He cut to pieces a yoke of oxen and sent out men "into the whole territory of Israel", with the message that he who would not follow him should have his oxen treated in the same way. The Israelites were stirred by the power emanating from the son of Kish, a dread of Yahweh came upon them, and they rallied round Saul. The Ammonites were defeated, and now the Israelites went to Gilgal, in the sanctuary of which they made Saul king before Yahweh, sacrificing to Yahweh (1 Sam. 11). At this event in Gilgal Samuel again appears in the story (vv. 12-14). Later came the war with the Philistines, in which Saul established his authority supported by his son Jonathan, who behaved like a son worthy of a chief (1 Sam. 13-14).

Through these stories we are introduced into the very same community that we know from the book of Judges. Historically the main point is the description of how Saul won the position of a leader through action. He lived on his father's farm, engrossed in the management of it, as the son of a farmer in a large way, just as Gideon had done. Then there came a cry of distress from Jabesh, a city east of Jordan. The Israelites had no instrument in common that could act in such cases, but that the fellowship was felt is apparent from the very appeal to the Israelitish towns. Saul became leader because he was filled with the divine soul. It gave him strength and a claim to leadership, and it was this which directly influenced the Israelites. It affected them with an irresistible dread and bent their wills under his. Saul was a leader of the same kind as Gideon and Jephthah.

It says that Saul's summons was sent to the "whole territory of Israel". There is nothing to indicate, however, that the summons was of the same comprehensive character as that of Deborah and Barak, when the fortune of all Israel was at stake. The respite was brief, and the danger imminent. As in the story of Gideon and Jephthah, it was probably the leader's own tribe and perhaps its nearest neighbours that came.

The victory confirmed the fact that Yahweh's spirit was in Saul, hence it was only natural that the people should want to establish his position as a chief, as we know it, too, from the histories of the other heroes. It is stated that the whole people made him king *(melekh)* in Gilgal, before Yahweh. The relation between the chief and the people rested on a pact, sanctified and confirmed before Yahweh in the sacred place, as in the story of Jephthah.

In these narratives we have an account of how a man of unusual strength of soul is aroused, displays his strength in great exploits, and thus acquires the leading position which corresponds to his greatness of soul. And the story of the wars with the Philistines shows how this greatness increased and the authority of the chieftain grew. It is in the light of this that we must see the story of Saul's election. Just as the greatness of Gideon and Samson is expressed in stories which show Yahweh himself going forth to consecrate them, so also the story of Saul shows us Yahweh consecrating Saul for his task, in this case with a holy man as his instrument. The narrative is intended to exhibit how the greatness later displayed by Saul is implanted in him at the outset by Yahweh, with the aim towards which his exploits tended, that of asserting the independence of the Israelites of the Philistines. In such stories the reality is intensified and idealised, and it would be hopeless to attempt to find out how much may be regarded as "historical" in the beautiful tale of the consecration of the future great leader.

But on one point there seem to be distinct traces of this idealisation. In the narrative Yahweh says that Saul is to be anointed to be a chief "over my people Israel" (9,16), over Yahweh's "property" (10,1); he is to inherit all the glory of Israel (9,20). The narrator doubtless meant this in the full sense of the word.

The dominion of Saul was hardly in any respect of a strictly limited character. Nearest to him gathered his kin. His right hand, Abner, was his near relative. His authority depended in the first place on the recognition of his kinsmen. When seated under the tamarisk in his town among his men, he was surrounded by Benjaminites (1 Sam. 22,6 f.). But his success in war attracted other Israelites. In the campaign against the Philistines the Israelites of the whole of the central highland must have gathered round him, and Abner's conduct after his fall shows that considerable portions of these tribes both east and west of Jordan must have regarded him as their chief, so that he could be called chief of Israel. His power was greater than that of Gideon and Jephthah, but how far it actually extended is unknown. Since Israelites and Canaanites lived intermixed among each other, a common Israelite rule would only be possible if Canaan as a whole was subject to one man's will. We hear that Saul fought against the Amalekites settled south of Judah and set him up "an Hand" in the Judæan Carmel (1 Sam. 15,12). [1] This does not warrant the conclusion that he ruled over all Judah. More probably scattered Israelite communities were settled down there which appealed to the great chief for help.

The chief was the natural leader in war, which he conducted filled with the spirit of Yahweh. With him rested the responsibility of preserving the holiness of the army intact, as will appear from the narrative of Saul's vow during the war with the Philistines (1 Sam. 14,24). Naturally he must have taken care that holiness was created at the outset, and have conducted the sacrifices necessary in connection with the war, even though the reminiscences hereof in the history of Saul have only come down to us in a completely garbled version (1 Sam. 13).

In time of peace the chief was recognised through his judgments. This recognition was manifested in the fact that the appropriate present was brought to him (cf. 1 Sam. 10,27). As the bearer of all responsibility in the community the chief must, in time of peace also, be the natural centre at the festivals, when the holiness of the people is renewed. But it is precisely on this point that we clearly see the difference between the monarchy of Saul and that which developed in Jerusalem.

Saul had no sanctuary which ranked above the ordinary local sacred places. The sacred Ark, the ancient rallying point of the people, was not even connected with his town. He lived on his farm, no doubt the ancestral property, and here, like any other large farmer, he directed the feast, surrounded by his men (1 Sam. 20,24 f.). There is no indication whatever that he conducted feasts which assembled the Israelite tribes or had any direct significance outside his intimate circle.

Altogether, there is nothing in Saul's position which raises him above the nation and gives to him a special position in relation to the tribes. He is precisely a typical early Israelite chieftain of consideration. On his farm he has about him men of his family and tribe, but he also surrounds himself with other vigorous and able men (1 Sam. 14,52), among them the Bethlehemite David. He may even take a stranger, such as the Edomite Doeg, into his service as his trusted man (1 Sam. 21,8; 22,9). He is entirely determined by his kin, and he raises his family to be the first in Benjamin; and the others join him because he is the greatest Israelite chief, a combination of Gideon and Job, but greater than either of them.

Saul is entirely in the old style. The fact that he is called *melekh*, the common designation for "king", means nothing, for this word has had highly varying connotations. It is employed indiscriminately about the mighty rulers of the great empires and about the small chiefs of the Canaanite communities (Judg. 5,19; 9,6; cf. Gen. 20,2; Josh. 10,1; 11,1). And the distinction made in the tradition between the "judge", *shōphēṭ* of the earliest times and *melekh*, the king of later times, dates from the systematisers of a later age. The term *shōphēṭ* does not happen to occur in any of the old narratives of the book of Judges. Gideon, who is called a "man of valour" (*gibbōr ḥayil*), is mostly characterised as *mōshīᵃ*, "saviour" (Judg. 6,14; 8,22). Abimelech is called *melekh*, Jephthah *ḳāṣin* and *rō'sh* (Judg. 11,6.9.11), and no special epithet is given to Samson.

The reason why Saul has come to be regarded as the person who introduced the monarchy and thus marked an epoch in the history of Israel is that his chieftainship, greater than any other in early Israel, happened to prepare the way for the monarchy proper, which was founded by David. Saul's meeting with David determined his fate, and it also came to determine his place in the tradition.

The narratives dealing with Saul and David give us a picture with a far-reaching perspective. We see how Saul perishes in his struggle to uphold the blessing, and how he draws Jonathan with him in his fall. And out of their ruin rises David, filled with their blessing, ready to give an entirely new foundation to Israelitic life by instituting a monarchy which had not previously been seen in Israel.

Hence the narratives purpose to give us more than an interaction of the fates of persons chosen at random. The subject is the kingdom of Israel. And the issue is between the old chieftain-

ship which had grown up directly out of the soil of popular life
on the one hand, and a kingship on the other hand, which required
the adaptation of the people. The difference between the two com-
batants is so great that they almost seem to fight each other,
backed up by a different god. But to the narrator it was a matter
of course that it was the same Yahweh who was behind them
both, pulling the strings in the great drama.

This puts Saul and David on a line; they succeed each other
as holders of the kingship, Saul first chosen by Yahweh but since
rejected to give place to Yahweh's new elect. Saul is viewed in
the light of the later kingdom, and yet the narrator has been able
to give a strictly objective presentation of the entire growth of
the psychic interplay between Saul and David; he has thus drawn
two characters of incomparable clarity. In these he has described
two widely different types of rulers, both Israelites, but almost
like the representatives of two peoples. The main stress in the
presentation is laid on the psychic aspect. Sometimes the same
event is related in two different ways and in different contexts,
just as there are some few passages that have no connection with
the context (e. g. 1 Sam. 19,18 ff.). This is what must be expected in popular narratives of the kind. But it is not probable that
our narratives should have been made up of several continuous
stories. [1]

Just as the future greatness of Saul was expressed in a story
of his dedication which shows the powers that developed later
implanted in his soul at the outset through a special consecration, so also there are stories showing us how his abasement lies
concentrated in the germs of disaster laid down in his soul from
the very beginning. And since the blessing, which the chief was
to uphold for himself and his people, had its origin in the sphere
of holiness, it is natural for the root of Saul's disaster to be
found in a ritual sin. Two stories deal with this subject, but
none of them is entirely in the old spirit.

The way is prepared for one of them by a remark added to
the story of the dedication. Samuel bade Saul go to Gilgal and
wait there for seven days, until Samuel came to offer sacrifice
(1 Sam. 10,8). The story itself is inserted in that of the prepara-

tion for the great fight with the Philistines (13,8-14). The host is assembled at Gilgal and all are waiting for Samuel. When he delays and people begin to scatter, Saul himself offers up the burnt offering. At that very moment Samuel arrives, and he now says: Thou hast done foolishly. Hadst thou but [1] obeyed the commandment of Yahweh, thy God, which he commanded thee, Yahweh would now have established thy kingdom over Israel forever. But now thy kingdom shall not continue; Yahweh hath chosen a man after his own heart, and Yahweh hath destined him to be a chief (nāghīdh) over his people, because thou hast not kept Yahweh's commandment (v. 13-14). Thus Saul is rejected seven days after he has been elected.

The second story is connected with Saul's war with the Amalekites. Samuel carries the message to him that Yahweh will punish the Amalekites for their conduct towards Israel during the journeying in the wilderness: therefore Saul as Yahweh's anointed is to put the ban on them and kill all, men as well as cattle. Saul carried out the command, but spared Agag, the king, and the best of the cattle, killing only the bad cattle. Then Yahweh said to Samuel: It repenteth me that I have made Saul king, for he hath turned away from me and he hath not obeyed my word (15,10 f.).

When Samuel met Saul and reproached him with his conduct, Saul humbly excused himself: Agag he had taken with him, but it was the people who had kept back the best of the cattle so as to sacrifice it to Yahweh. Upon Samuel's stern answer that Yahweh preferred obedience to sacrifice, Saul replied that he acknowledged his sin, and he asked Samuel to go with him to entreat Yahweh. But Samuel's answer was: Since thou hast rejected the word of Yahweh, Yahweh will reject thee from being king over Israel (v. 26). And upon the continued entreaties of Saul, he answered: Yahweh hath today rent the kingdom of Israel from thy hand and given it to thy fellow who is better than thou. Verily, the Glory [2] of Israel doth not lie nor repent, for he is not a man that he should repent (v. 28 f.) Saul again besought Samuel and finally they went together to Gilgal. Here Samuel cut down Agag before Yahweh, whereafter he and Saul parted for good.

These narratives exhibit a definite tendency, that of glorifying Samuel at the expense of Saul. Ecclesiastical circles who saw Samuel as their representative, rejoiced at humiliating the fallen king through him. The proud, god-inspired chief has become a trembling sinner who is entreating the mercy of the great priestly prophet, and his sin against Yahweh consists in disobedience to the command of Samuel. The author or authors who have drawn this curious picture of the greatest chief of early Israel, are so far removed from that time that it even becomes a sin for the chief to offer sacrifice, a typical manifestation of the claims of the post-exilic priesthood. And the second story implies a conception of ḥērem and its possibility of being changed into sacrifice, which shows that the old meaning of the ban had been forgotten.

Both narratives, we may suppose, have been made up of older elements. Behind one of them we catch a glimpse of a description of the chief who is offering the common sacrifice for the holiness of the army before it goes into action against the Philistines. And it had surely nothing to do with Saul's disaster, for it inaugurated a successful war that confirmed the blessing of Saul. But in the second story the account of a sacrilege was in place, for it terminates Saul's period of success with its victories and progress, just at the point of David's appearance among his men. It is therefore highly probable that we have here an adaptation to the spirit of a later time of an old narrative relating how Saul, after the war with the Amalekites, transgressed the laws of the ban, and thus received the curse in him which was to destroy him.

The stories of the rejection of Saul are intended to prepare the way for the rise of David; hence they are followed by a tale of how David was chosen and anointed by Samuel as Saul had once been anointed. Yahweh commanded Samuel to go and anoint the successor of Saul, one of the sons of Isai at Bethlehem; he was to take with him a heifer and summon the people to a sacri-

ficial feast, then Yahweh would provide the rest. Thus Samuel
came to Bethlehem. The men of the city came out to meet him
full of fear of what he had now to bring them, but he merely
bade them sanctify themselves and come to his sacrificial feast.
He also invited Isai and his sons. Although they were fine well-
grown youths, Yahweh informed Samuel that he had not chosen
any of them, for Yahweh looked upon the heart, not upon the
outward appearance. Then the youngest, who had not even come
to the feast, had to be fetched home from the flocks. This was
David, and he was anointed by Samuel. "And from that day
forward, the spirit of Yahweh came upon David" (1 Sam. 16,
1-13).

This story is on a line with those that tell of Saul's rejection. The underlying idea is Yahweh's arbitrary election. He had
tried Saul first, but Saul was disobedient, so then he chooses
David. Samuel is the representative of Yahweh, the doer of his
will, by whom kings are deposed and made, a stereotyped figure
without any living relation to those about him. His mere appearance in a city strikes terror to the hearts of the people, and
though Bethlehem is quite outside Samuel's sphere of activity,
he acts as a person conducting a sacrificial feast for the inhabitants, who immediately obey his summons. But here again we
must assume that the story has been formed out of an earlier story
of how David was consecrated beforehand for his mighty task.

In the narrative of David's anointment we feel there is some
of the pleasure of the fairy-tale recounting how the most neglected
and the least of all is drawn into the forefront at the expense
of all the others. But this feature is utilised for emphasising the
pure arbitrariness of Yahweh's choice. It is this which gives a
peculiar character to the stories about Saul's rejection and David's
election.

The dedication legends of Gideon and Samson are typical
expressions of the old Israelite view of the great achievement.
Action is a direct expression of the wholeness of the soul, and
when a man performs great feats, it is a manifestation of what
has been in his soul from the very beginning, implanted there
by Yahweh. In the stories here discussed, everything is put down

to Yahweh. Everything turns upon his decision. This corresponds to the view of Yahweh which became prevalent in later times.

Of the first meeting of Saul and David we have two accounts. One of them is closely related to the account of the anointment. We are told that David's three brothers fought against the Philistines under Saul, and he himself, a shepherd, was sent to see them. Here he saw the Philistine giant Goliath, who had challenged the Israelites to single combat, and he learnt that the king had promised the man who could vanquish him riches, his daughter, and a higher rank for his kin. David took up the challenge despite the scorn of his elder brothers, and felled the Philistine with his sling, whereupon he cut off his head with the giant's own sword. By this act he had inflicted a defeat on the whole army of the enemy, and Saul admitted him on his farm (1 Sam. 17).

Here again David is the young, unknown shepherd and his feat suddenly raises him above the multitude. In this story we also perceive something of the view of Yahweh which dominates the story of his anointment. The little David behaves like a preacher to Goliath, says that he comes in the name of Yahweh, and Yahweh alone gives victory without considering sword or spear. But this means that Yahweh gives his blessing to the poor weapon of the shepherd in the fight against the mighty equipment of the stranger. The story must have been one of the many popular stories current about the war with the Philistines. Another account makes the Benjaminite Elhanan the slayer of Goliath (2 Sam. 21,19). Of these other narratives only some few insignificant fragments remain (vv. 15-22).

The question should not be raised as to whether a story like this is historical in the sense that this was actually the beginning of David's career. Such a question cannot be answered. But the story shows that David could be regarded as the man who rose through the quite unexpected luck sent him by Yahweh.

Whether the second story gives us the external events which led David to Saul is just as doubtful, but it takes us directly to the heart of their mutual relationship. In immediate continuation of the story of the anointment it is here recounted: And the

4*

spirit of Yahweh departed from Saul and an evil spirit from Yahweh came upon him. And Saul's servants said to him: Behold, an evil spirit from God cometh upon thee. Let our Lord but command, thy servants are before thee, let them seek out a man who understands how to play the harp. Then, when an evil spirit from God cometh upon thee, he shall pluck the strings with his hand, and thou shalt feel well (1 Sam. 16,14-16). Then, it is related, they fetched David, a fine warrior and *gibbōr ḥayil*, with whom Yahweh was, a man who understood how to speak, and how to play. In this way David came to Saul and became his squire so that, when the spirit of God came upon Saul, he might play the harp, and soothe him, the evil spirit then departing from Saul (v. 23) [1].

In the shape in which this story has come down it is meant to be viewed in connection with the one immediately preceding it, concerning the anointing of David. This ended with the statement that from that day on the spirit of Yahweh came upon David (16,13). The same expression is used here as about the possession of the old heroes by the spirit of God. But on this very point more than on any other David differs widely from the old chiefs. His whole character excludes that state of soul which finds expression in ecstacy, and nothing was farther from him than that his soul should be filled with the divine soul. When he appeared before King Akish in a prophetic frenzy, this was dissimulation, a means to escape from a difficult situation (1 Sam. 21,11-16).

The narrator uses a well-known expression when he says that the spirit of Yahweh came upon David; but he hardly used it in the old sense. No doubt he meant that the anointment imparted to David a special grace and a special privilege, which made him the sole rightful king. To possess this right is to possess the spirit of Yahweh. Only one can possess it, hence it left Saul when it was given to David.

But the stories of the evil spirit that entered into Saul have a profound psychic reality; to understand them we must start from the old conception of divine possession. If we ask how the evil spirit worked, we have the answer in one of the stories. When the women had sung that David had slain ten thousand while

Saul had only slain a thousand, Saul waxed exceedingly wroth, saying: Now he will surely also have the kingdom, and from that day onwards he cast evil looks at him. Then the story goes on to say: And the next day an evil spirit from God came upon Saul and he raved (behaved like a prophet) in the house, while David plucked the strings with his hand as he usually did every day. And Saul had his spear in his hand. And Saul flung the spear, thinking: I will pin David to the wall. But David evaded him twice. Then Saul was afraid of David, for Yahweh was with him, but had left Saul (1 Sam. 18,10-12).

A similar scene is described once more. Saul tried to get rid of David by giving him difficult tasks in the war with the Philistines, but Yahweh was with David, and he succeeded in everything. Jonathan tried to make peace between them, and David came back to Saul. But when David had won new victories, the evil spirit came upon Saul again, while David was playing to him, and again Saul flung his spear at him in vain. Then David fled (1 Sam. 19,8-10).

The curious thing is that Saul's acts under the influence of the evil spirit are psychically quite well founded. We have followed Saul in his conduct towards David and seen that everything he does is a struggle for the blessing, a continuous chain of desperate attempts to assert himself. Thus his possession by the evil spirit does not mean insanity in the ordinary sense.

From the story of Samson we know what it means when the spirit of Yahweh departs from the chief. It means that strength leaves his soul. It means the same thing to Saul. His soul can still expand so that he behaves ecstatically, but his ecstacy is not identical with his possession by God. The question is, what it is that fills the soul. Is it the divine positive strength or is it a caricature of it? If blessedness is in the soul, it is Yahweh's spirit that fills it. But if, like Saul, a man has lost the blessing, he can, indeed, be carried away by ecstacy but the ecstacy is false. It is not an accession of power, but on the contrary a manifestation of the disintegration of the soul, an affection of the mind which does not urge him to healthy action, but to abortive attempts, to misdeeds.

Possession by the soul of God carried Saul to the greatest heights. Impelled by it he became the greatest chief of Israel, leading the people from victory to victory. But when he had met his superior who took the blessing from him, the spirit of Yahweh in him was transformed into an evil spirit, his ecstasy became empty and powerless. What had been a divine power had become a delusion. Thus the history of Saul shows us that when a great chief loses the blessing, he loses more than an ordinary man. For he loses that soul of Yahweh with which his soul has been filled, and thus he loses his own soul.

No great importance need be attached to the fact that the story of David's arrival at Saul's farm describes Saul as losing Yahweh's blessing before David came to him. For the spirit of Yahweh is lost with the blessing, and the narrator sees this perish in Saul before his intercourse with David begins, because events, according to the Israelite way of thinking, are always an expansion of something that is present in the soul at the outset. Thus from the very beginning Saul's ecstasy becomes a manifestation of a disease which David is to alleviate by his music.

The difference between Saul's and David's gaining of the power is not that David acquired easily what Saul had to fight for. David, too, obtained the power by virtue of his conquests. While Saul, however, made conquest in psychic ecstasy, filled with the spirit of Yahweh, and then acted consistently with his victories, David's acts are continually those of the calculating politician. Saul was driven to action by the instinct which was the living core of the early Israelite psychic values, those which are denoted by the blessing, honour, the covenant. David acted with definite plans in view, and he used the laws which bound the men among whom he acted as a means to gain these ends.

The pact is the means by which he gains access to the powerful house of the chief, partly by his marriage with Saul's daughter, partly by his friendship with Jonathan. Outwardly he does not seek to obtrude himself. He who has gained great victories and rightfully won the king's daughter, declares that he is too insignificant for this honour (1 Sam. 18,18.23). He does not identify himself with the pact, but he would not do without it, whatever the cost; for this only can give him a share of the blessing of the chieftain which is necessary for his purposes. When Saul has cursed him and sought his life, he does not fight for his right and honour, accepting victory or defeat; he merely thinks of regaining his position in the house of the chief, with the man who hates and curses him. At his meeting with Jonathan he asks the latter to kill him if he has done wrong, and so compels Jonathan to strengthen the pact to the utmost (1 Sam. 20,8).

The figures of Saul and David are most clearly contrasted in the scene in the desert, when Saul's life chanced to be in David's power. We have two accounts of the event, but the same reason is given for David's conduct in both. In one account Abishai says to David: God hath today delivered thine enemy into thine hand. And now let me pin him to the ground with my spear with one stroke which I shall not repeat. But David said to Abishai: Do him no harm. For who can stretch out his hand against Yahweh's anointed with impunity? And David said: No, by the life of Yahweh! Yahweh will smite him, or his day will come and he will die, or he will go to the wars and be cut off. Yahweh forbid that I should lay hands on Yahweh's anointed (1 Sam. 26,8-11).

By these words, which are not very different from those of the other story (24,7), David has revealed his innermost motives. Abishai speaks as any one in early Israel would think, but David thinks otherwise. His sparing of Saul is not the result of the generosity of the great chief who would rather give than take, because it is in harmony with the greatness of his soul. Nor is it from an inward need to keep the pact which in spite of all he had with Saul, and which was still such a strong bond between him and Jonathan.

David refuses to kill Saul because he does not want to risk Yahweh's revenge if he kills his anointed; but also because he is convinced that it is unnecessary. Saul will soon be on the highroad to destruction, why should David take the responsibility of hastening his doom?

Even to Saul himself David explains his position, saying: Yahweh maketh return to every man for his righteousness and his faithfulness, as Yahweh hath today delivered thee into my [1] hand, but I will not stretch out my hand against Yahweh's anointed. And behold, as thy soul was great in mine eyes today, so shall my soul be great in Yahweh's eyes, and He shall deliver me out of all tribulation (1 Sam. 26,23 f.).

It is more than doubtful how much Saul understood of David's calculation here with regard to Yahweh, but in his own way he understood what had happened. He was humiliated by generosity and so he was doomed. Now he could only acknowledge David with the words: Blessed art thou, my son David. Thou shalt surely act, and surely thou *canst* (v. 25). This decides Saul's destiny.

The essential point in David's words is his reference to Yahweh's anointed. We have seen that when the chief in early Israel acted, he was filled with the spirit of Yahweh, and normally he was consecrated to his position among the people by a pact in the sacred place, at which a ceremony of anointment probably as a rule took place (cf. Judg. 9,8). This, however, did not mean that his position was assured forever. If the blessing left him, it meant that Yahweh had abandoned him, and he would have to cede his place to the man who had a greater blessedness.

David's words imply that by his consecration the king is placed under the charge of Yahweh, thus becoming inviolable. This view differs from the old one by a mere shade. The independence of the divine power seen behind the chief is more strongly accentuated and extends the range of his inviolability beyond that which is displayed in the personal ability of the king. If Yahweh has deprived the king of the blessing, it is for Yahweh to destroy him. But a man who stretches out his hand against the person once for all elected by Yahweh exposes himself to the divine wrath. It is the idea of the kingship which is expressed in David's words. It has grown up out of the old idea of the chieftainship by the special accentuation of a single aspect.

David's conception of the kingship explains why he constantly shrinks from Saul, yet without ever deserting him. David never ventures to raise his hand against Saul, and he desires to keep close to him so as to get a share in the blessing which Yahweh's anointed only possesses. This is the double foundation on which

David's whole policy towards Saul is based. By this policy he created his monarchy.

David's conviction that Saul would perish one day was soon fulfilled on Mount Gilboa. David did not move a finger to harm him, though he had joined Achish, the king of the Philistines, who thought he had secured an ally against Saul in David. And David let him remain in that belief. He made incursions into Judah, and while Achish thought he was making war on his countrymen, he actually merely attacked the foreign tribes, and even prepared the way for himself among the Judaeans settled around Hebron by goodly gifts (1 Sam. 27; 30,26-31). When Achish went out against Saul, things very nearly went wrong, but the suspicious Philistines saved David by demanding his dismissal from the army (1 Sam. 29).

When Saul had died, David was ready to reap the fruits of his policy. He might now have come forward with a claim to the power, but he kept on along the lines he had once laid down. There was no need for him to fight, he took possession of what Yahweh's anointed had acquired as his heritage. This was done by a series of acts, the leading idea of which was that Saul was Yahweh's anointed, and David his avenger.

An Amalekite, who at the request of Saul had administered the death blow to him, carried word of it to David and even brought Saul's diadem and ring. He hoped for a reward, but received a very different treatment. David rent his clothes and lamented over the fallen, over Saul and Jonathan, but then he had the messenger put to death, saying: How wast thou not afraid to stretch forth thine hand to bring down destruction on Yahweh's anointed? And he added: Thy blood shall be upon thine own head, for thy mouth hath testified against thee, saying: I have slain Yahweh's anointed (2 Sam. 1,14.16). In this way David got rid of Saul without any infringement of his inviolability; and by making himself his avenger, he claimed his heritage.

The following stories show how David contrived to create the monarchy by carrying through his policy step by step. It began by his being made king of Hebron, an important centre near his native place, where he had prepared the way for himself (2 Sam. 2,1-4). Starting from this he sought to arrogate to himself Saul's inheritance. His first attempt was made on Jabesh in Gilead, the inhabitants of which had attended to Saul's body and buried it. He sent men to them with the following message: And now may Yahweh show love and fidelity unto you, and I also will show the same goodness to you since you have done this. And now let your hands be strengthened and become men of valour, now that your lord Saul is dead. And further I have been anointed by the house of Judah to be king over them (2 Sam. 2,6-7).

No plainer hint could presumably be given, but the hint was not taken, for the inhabitants of Gilead thought that Saul's son, Ishbaal, must be Saul's heir, not David. It was Abner who carried through this idea, but it was only for a time. Ishbaal could not assert himself against Abner, who even took the liberty of taking one of his concubines. When Ishbaal protested, Abner turned to David. He wished to serve a real lord, and offered to secure Israel for David by a pact. We have seen how David conquered the difficulties involved in this pact. [1] First he demanded that his wife Michal, Saul's daughter, should be restored to him, and then made the pact with Abner and the Israelites as Saul's son-in-law. And when all seemed lost, because Joab, David's most trusted man, killed Abner, in whom he could only see a rival and against whom he even had a claim for revenge, David got out of the difficult situation by concentrating the guilt on Joab alone through a curse, and at the same time giving passionate expression to his grief for Abner. "And all the people and all Israel understood that day that it was not of the king to slay Abner, the son of Ner" (2 Sam. 3,37). David had secured for himself the pact with Israel as the heir of Saul, and the difficult problem which the relation between Abner and Joab must present, had been disposed of without responsibility for David.

Now there was only Ishbaal between David and the power; but this difficulty, too, was easily overcome. A couple of Benjaminites understood what David's wishes must be and were eager to gain credit in the eyes of the new ruler. So they killed their lord, carrying his head to David with the words, so natural to them:

Here is the head of thine enemy Ishbaal, Saul's son, who sought thy life. Yahweh has this day avenged my lord the king on Saul and his seed (2 Sam. 4,8).

But the two obliging men did not know David; they had done him a greater service than they knew or would have cared to do. Not only had they rid David of his rival but also of the responsibility of doing away with him, and David accepted both these benefits without hesitation .He said: By the life of Yahweh who hath delivered my soul from all tribulation. The man who announced to me: Saul is dead, who in his own view [1] was a messenger of joyful tidings, him I ordered to be seized and killed at Ziklag, though he came in order that I might give him a messenger's reward. And now that wicked men have killed a righteous man in his house on his couch, should I not demand his blood at your hands and exterminate you from the earth? (2 Sam. 4,9b-11). He immediately had them put to death and the bodies desecrated, but he caused Ishbaal's head to be buried.

Shortly afterwards David captured Jerusalem and thus secured to himself a strong capital in the border-land between his own kinsmen, the Judaeans, and Saul's kinsmen, the Benjaminites. But in central Canaan the Philistines held sway; after the death of Saul the Israelites had even been forced to abandon the towns on the plain of Jizreel and on Jordan (1 Sam. 31,7). [2] They could not but regard David as a rebellious vassal and advanced against Jerusalem. David would not submit to a siege in the town, but like the Bedawin, retreated to the desert where he was in his own element, and in the end he twice completely routed the Philistines (2 Sam. 5,17-25). By these victories David became master of Canaan, and later on he extended his dominion to the neighbouring peoples.

Thus David had made good his policy and replaced the chieftainship of Saul by a real kingship. Jerusalem had again obtained a ruler, but now a far mightier one than before. For the first time we have a realm comprising Canaan "from Dan to Beersheba", and this realm is Israelitish. David's power, however, extended farther, from the Euphrates in the north to the Egyptian frontier and the bays of the Red Sea on the south. "And David realised that Yahweh had set him up as king over Israel and had exalted his kingdom for the sake of His people Israel" (2 Sam. 5,12).

David's mighty work was carried out so rapidly that his kingdom could not have any great coherence. When Joab had put an end to Absalom's revolt, it appeared that David had established a realm, the nucleus of which was composed of people who still held the old view of their relation to the chief. Judaeans and Israelites fell to quarrelling about who had the greatest share in the king, and the Benjaminites, under the leadership of Sheba, the son of Bikri, set on foot a movement to break away from the kingdom of David. This shows that it was not a jealous affection for the person of David that was at the heart of the conflict. The Benjaminites wanted a chieftain with whom they felt at one, and they demanded that the chief should procure honour for them as the first of the tribes, the honour that they had under Saul. It is the same feature with which we are acquainted in the behaviour of the Ephraimites towards Gideon. The tribal communities consider themselves the decisive units, and fight each other for the sake of honour only. It is the spirit of the old chieftainship turning against the monarchical spirit.

The movement was subdued by Joab, the man to whom David owed most after Jonathan, and whose strength he exploited to the utmost, whereupon he abandoned him to destruction (2 Sam. 19,10-16.42-44; 20). It was to arise again later and destroy David's work. But his most important achievement, the establishment of the monarchy, was then so firmly consolidated that no one thought of attacking it any longer.

David founded the monarchy for himself and his house. To the very last he dominated the remnants of Saul's kin. His interest in it manifested itself in the question so characteristic of his whole policy, whether there were still any members of Saul's house left to whom he could show affection for Jonathan's sake (2 Sam. 9,1). It turned out that there was a son of Jonathan, Meribbaal, who was a cripple, and David showed his love for him in his own peculiar way. He presented him with Saul's house and land, but one of his own men, Siba, was to manage it; Meribbaal himself was to have the honour of living with David and eating at his table

This disposed of surprises in that quarter. And the other survivors of Saul's house were given over by David to the blood revenge of the Gibeonites (2 Sam. 21). Now there was no one left who could encroach upon David's kingdom by virtue of his descent.

The establishment of the Davidic monarchy gives an entirely new foundation to the history of Israel. No cultural domain remained unaffected by the revolution it meant in the life of the people. It created a new rallying point for the people, raised above the small communities and necessitating the creation of a new unit. The conflict of Saul and David became no mere personal matter; it was the old and the new type of ruler confronting each other. But therein lay the art of David that he preserved continuity between the old and the new, for he saw to it that his work should inherit the whole of the blessing from the greatest chieftainship that had ever arisen in Israel.

David could carry through this work because he was entirely at home in the old culture, and yet was not bound by it. He knew thoroughly the laws that bound the others, but he himself was only partly bound by them. He could operate with the men around him and use them as pawns in his game; he was always superior to them because he knew them, while they could not see through him. Many years later, Mohammed occupied a similar position among his countrymen.

Apparently there is no difference between David and his surroundings. He knows the necessity of having the blessing and the strict demands of the covenant. He knows what blood-guilt is, and is terrified to the depths of his soul at the thought of its contagion, and his fear of assaulting Yahweh's anointed is greater than any of his supporters understand. But precisely this inordinate anxiety points to a profound difference between David and the men of the old type. It is as if the forms created by the psychic values have acquired an independent and so an intensified importance, while the psychic life from which they have sprung has become stereotyped or dry. The spontaneous instinct characteristic of the men of the old time, which vitalises their actions, has given place to calculation in David. And his calculation concerns itself with the form, because this has become the actual reality. Hence he can live in a compact with Jonathan and yet take his blessing; he can keep close to Saul though the latter has cursed him and attacked him; and he can carefully spare Yahweh's anointed out of respect for his consecration and yet work for his destruction; he can shrink from Joab's blood-guilt and yet attach him to himself and exploit all his power. Even emotional outbursts David can utilise so as to make them serve his purpose, as he showed at the death of Saul and Abner. In all respects David is a contrast to the old chief possessed by the divine soul, who went forth without any definite purpose, urged by an inner power, filled with the vitality of the tribe and with its thirst for exploits and honour. Many of the features with which we become acquainted in later Israel's transformation of values are present already in the person of David.

How does a type like David suddenly appear among Saul's men? It is as difficult to answer this question as it is to explain how any new type arises. But just as, in the case of Mohammed, we can point to Jewish and Christian circles which brought foreign elements into the Arabian communities, so also we must consider that the Israelites in Canaan lived in an environment where there was a great mingling of cultures. Judah, to which David belonged, was on the periphery of Israel. It is not even mentioned as an Israelite tribe in the Song of Deborah. The reason why David could appear in the land of the Philistines is, however, that there were Israelite communities in the territory of Judah (1 Sam. 27,12), and this is also the natural explanation of the fact that Saul leads military expeditions to this place. As a matter of fact, Judah appears in the history of David, and later on, as the brother of Israel proper, and there is no doubt that both peoples call their God Yahweh. The probability is, therefore, that, intermixed with other tribes, there have been scattered Israelite colonies in Judah, which allied themselves more or less with the Israelites. Kaleb was such a semi-Israelite tribe, the Kenites were another.

David was descended from such border peoples. It is characteristic of him that as king he draws much support from foreigners, just as he makes a non-Israelitish town his capital. But he appropriated Israel through his covenant with Saul's kin, and he crowned his achievement when he carried up the Ark, Israel's ancient and most sacred treasure, to his capital.

By the new monarchy the Israelite communities were drawn out of their isolation. Saul lived on his land as any large farmer might do, rooted among his kin, and his rule was a form of the greatness of his kin. David created a monarchy which isolated itself from the small communities. It soared above all the tribes and so could command dominance over them all. As founded by David, it was further developed by his son Solomon. For three quarters of a century it survived in its full extent, and when the disintegration of the realm followed, the institution of the monarchy had become so firmly established that it persisted till the nation perished.

Passing from Saul's home to the new residence of the king, we come to a new world. Gibeah was an Israelitish town; here Saul was settled, surrounded by his kin. He could admit strangers, as the Bethlehemite David, and even the Edomite Doeg; they were his servants, but they could not make up for his kin, who formed the absolute centre round which all gravitated. David had won his capital by fighting. And the inhabitants of the city, the Canaanite Jebusites, continued to form an essential part of its population (Josh. 15,63; Judg. 1,21). It was the seat of the new ruler of Israel, and his power rested in great part on a body of warriors, *gibbōrīm* (2 Sam. 10,7), the nucleus of which was formed by foreigners. First of all are mentioned the Cherethites and the Pelethites (2 Sam. 8,18; 20,7; 1 Kings 1,38.44), together with the Gattites (2 Sam. 15,18) two of whom are known by name, viz. Obed Edom (2 Sam. 6,10) and Ittai (2 Sam. 15,19). It was the population of the Mediterranean coasts thus serving as mercenaries. They were faithful to David during his flight from Absalom, and Ittai was ready to join him with 600 men. Other foreigners, too, joined him, as for instance the Hittite Uriah.

The monarchy was not based on a feeling of kinship among the Israelites, but on the support of foreign warriors. And the king did not live on the ancestral land but in princely style in a palace built by a foreign architect with the art and the aids of civilisation. Here a new kind of court life developed with choice meat and drink, and singing-men and women, as we hear from Barzillai when David invites him to his court (2 Sam. 19,36). David already had no small number of wives and concubines (2 Sam. 5,13-16; 15,16), but under Solomon they grew into a whole host, and he displayed a splendour which was to raise him to the level of the kings of the great empires.

Through the monarchy Israel entered into the international political game. David, who ruled over the neighbouring eastern countries, formed a covenant with another Canaanite prince, Hiram of Tyre. The covenant was inherited by Solomon, who further, by a marriage, entered into a compact with Egypt and other countries. He utilised the situation of Canaan as a corridor country and carried on a far-reaching international trade, for which he even built a fleet. [1] All this was bound to lead to an entirely new military system, extending beyond the old popular customs. Already when David captured it, Jerusalem was a strongly fortified city. Solomon enlarged the fortifications and moreover built a series of new forts for the security of the trade routes. [2] He also organised an army with cavalry and war chariots on a large scale.

The peculiarities so far mentioned in the new monarchy were sufficient to bring about a great revolution among the people. The kingdom was Israelite, but it comprised the entire population of Canaan and a great part of this was not Israelite. The position of the king in regard to the Canaanite population recalls that of the Khalifah in regard to his non-Moslem subjects several centuries later, and in both cases things developed in the same way. The old population of the country merged into the ruling people and was called by its name. But it communicated its own culture to the ruling people, and thus transformed the latter after its own likeness. The Canaanites became Israelites, but at the same time the Israelites became Canaanite. This process cannot be traced in detail, but its cultural effects appear in all domains.

The levelling of differences between the Israelites and the Canaanites forms the basis of that view of Israel's relation to the country which came to prevail later on. The population is regarded as uniformly Israelite; this uniformity is maintained for the country in its entire extent under David and Solomon, and is referred back to the time of the immigration itself, when the country was divided (Josh. 13 ff.; cf. Deut. 11,24; Josh. 1,4 et al.). The result of the transformation of the people, even in an idealised form, is regarded as the starting-point of its history in Canaan. That the actual course of events was as described above may be inferred from numerous testimonies, and we have a list of cities which the Israelites did not conquer in the earliest times (Judg. 1), just as we have information of cities that formed a covenant with the Israelites, for instance Shechem (Gen. 34), Gibeon, Chephirah, Beeroth, Kirjath Jearim (Josh. 9, 17). Of a couple of the tribes, Naphthali and Asher, it is even said that they lived among the Canaanites (Judg. 1,32 f.), whereas the opposite expression is otherwise generally used. What is of interest to us here, however, is the significance of the monarchy for this great fusion of nations.

It is said about the Canaanite cities of the plain of Jizreel that "when Israel grew strong, she put the Canaanite to labour, but she did not drive him out" (Judg. 1,28), and a similar statement is made about the Canaanites in other cities (vv. 30.33. 35 and 29, cf. Josh. 16,10; 17,12 f.). In all probability these statements refer precisely to the monarchical period. At the beginning of that period the Canaanites inhabited some cities, others they had lost, and in others again, for instance Jerusalem, they lived in company with the Israelites.

Neither David nor Solomon carried on any direct warfare with the Canaanites. Both were surrounded by foreigners and had no reason to wage war against their Canaanite subjects. We also see David respecting a demand for blood revenge on the part of the Gibeonites (2 Sam. 21). The question then arises whether the king treated the two elements of the population quite alike, and this leads us on to the question of the nature of the royal administration.

Under the monarchy the smaller communities continued to exist as independent units. The king only created something new where his purposes required it, therefore he did not introduce a new administration which immediately overthrew the old order. The officials needed by David to carry out his plans were a commander of the army, a captain of the body-guard, priests, and two leaders of the administration, *mazkīr* and *sōphēr* (2 Sam. 8,16-18). To this must be added the leader of the labour gangs (*mas*, 20,23-26). We see what new features the king introduced. His power depended on the army and the body-guard, and these were organised. Further he required new buildings for himself and for the military, and his subjects had to furnish the working power. His administration merely serves his own special purposes, for which the population is exploited. Of an organisation of the entire life of the people there is no question.

Solomon had the same kind of administration as David, only his needs were much greater. Further, he made the people provide for his expensive court establishment by dividing the country into 12 districts, each with an officer *(niṣṣābh)* who was to procure what was necessary for the king's household for one month (1 Kings 4,7 ff.). Only geographical considerations seem to have been taken into account, so all classes of the populace, Canaanite and Israelite, had to pay their tribute. They had all become subjects, "slaves" of a common master. With respect to the bond service somewhat similar conditions obtained.

It was by the recruitment of labour gangs that the kings of nearer Asia usually carried through the construction of roads and especially the erection of buildings which were necessary to them. They used partly captives of war, hence the subjugated foreigners, partly the lowest orders of the native population. [1] It was not any different in Israel. That a beaten foe becomes a bondman *(lāmas)* is attested as a familiar fact in monarchical Israel (Isa. 31,8; Lam. 1,1). In accordance herewith it is said about Solomon: All the people that were left of the Amorites, Hittites, Perizzites, Hivites, and Jebusites which were not of the children of Israel, their sons that were left after them in the land and whom the Israelites were not able to banish, upon those

Solomon levied a tribute of bond-service unto this day. But of the Israelites Solomon made no bondmen, they were men of war and his servants, and his chiefs and his chariot fighters, and rulers of his chariots and his horsemen. These were the chiefs of the officers that were set over the work by Solomon: 550 which had the command of the people that took part in the work (1 Kings 9,20-23).

It is probable that Solomon, like the Egyptians, organised his bondmen as military troops. Or how else could he have sent his legions of workmen in orderly fashion up to Hiram? (1 Kings 5,27-32). And the principle of letting the ruling people serve in the army, and the subjugated people as bondmen, is so common that it would seem reasonable to apply it. But it does not agree with other information about Solomon, according to which he especially levied tribute of bond-service on the Israelites (1 Kings 5,27). And this is probably correct, for it was that which gave rise to the discontent, amongst others of the Ephraimite Jeroboam, a *gibbōr ḥayil* who was himself a bondman and later on the leader of "all the charge of the house of Joseph" (1 Kings 11,28), and it led to the disintegration of the kingdom.

For it meant a disruption of the old fellowship which bound the people of Israel together and set them apart from the Canaanites. A large number of the Israelites were put on an equal footing with the Canaanites as bondmen. And all, Israelites and others, had to pay tribute to the king's household. This would tend to level the difference between Israelites and Canaanites and to do away with the common responsibility in the old Israelite communities. A quite similar mixing of peoples and cultures took place later on in the provinces of the Moslem khaliphate.

The influence of the monarchy depended on the power it actually acquired in the community. It was not due to the sudden overthrow of the old order. The new institution, in spite of the revolution inherent in it, developed on a line with the old customs.

The power of the chief normally depended not only on the victories to which the spirit of Yahweh helped him. As the first in time of peace he must also be great by his possessions. If he had not inherited property from his kin, he might acquire it in other ways, by what he captured in war. We know that he obtained his special share of the spoil (1 Sam. 30,20). And when he conquered new territory, as when David captured Jerusalem, the leader was no doubt given his share of land, just as his helpers obtained their share. Saul takes it for granted that David will give those that join him fields and vineyards and make them captains of thousands and hundreds (1 Sam. 22,7). There is no doubt that the Israelite kings had great possessions. In fact, in the Chronicles we hear about Uzziah that he had big herds and flocks and was a farmer on a large scale (2 Chron. 26,10), and something similar is said of Hezekiah (32,28 f.). The history of Ahab shows that he owned landed property in Jizreel, that is to say, outside the city in which he lived.

Both the chief and the king were, however, bound to respect the laws relating to family property. David bought the threshing-ground of the Jebusite Arauna at its full value in order to make it into a sanctuary (2 Sam. 24,24), and much later Omri bought Mount Samaria of its owner because he wished to build his capital there (1 Kings 16,24). We have the best illustration of this in the story of Ahab and Naboth, which shows, however, that the king's respect for the old property laws was not absolute.

Ahab had his palace *(hēkhāl)* in Jizreel and hard by lay Naboth's vineyard which the king wished to add to his grounds. When Naboth would not commit the crime of giving up his ancestral property, Ahab fell ill with mortification, and was mocked by his wife, Jezebel. Dost thou govern the kingdom of Israel? she asked. What Ahab dared not enforce, she easily carried through. By means of false witnesses she caused Naboth to be condemned for the blaspheming of God and the king and thereupon had him done to death by stoning. Then she said to the king: Arise, take possession of the vineyard of Naboth the Jizreelite, which he refused to give thee for money, for Naboth is not alive; he is dead. — The king went down and took possession of the vineyard, but shortly afterwards Elijah proclaimed to him the doom of Yahweh for what had happened (1 Kings 21,1 ff.).

The story teaches us that the king is bound to respect the proprietary right of the family. This is implied not only in Elijah's denunciatory words, but also in the king's own conduct. The Phoenician Jezebel, however, knows another law which does away with the right of the family: as a king, Ahab may act according to his fancy, as one of the Amarna letters has it.[1] It is the arbitrariness of the despot which Ahab, though with some hesitation, agrees to assert in Israel in spite of the old proprietary right. It appears from the story, however, that it became law in Israel for the property of a delinquent to fall to the king. He obtained a means of acquiring property beyond what was warranted by the old family law.

The tendency of the king to appropriate property in this arbitrary fashion is traceable not only in the northern kingdom. David already, on no better ground than sheer libel, took Meribbaal's patrimony from him without ceremony and gave it to his treacherous servant Siba (2 Sam. 16,4); and just as arbitrarily he returned only half of it when the groundlessness of the accusation was discovered (19,30). We know the complaints of the prophets of the liberties taken with property by the royal chiefs,[2] and Ezekiel emphasises how important it is that the king's land around Jerusalem should have fixed boundaries, "and my princes shall no more oppress my people" (Ez. 45,7-8, cf. 48,21).

Thus the basis for the king's self-assertion by means of property was the property law of the family, but his special position gave him the opportunity to appropriate the possessions of citizens who were outlawed, and his power even led him to go beyond the limits of the law. It was not easy to decide where right ceased and might alone settled the matter; for might established a new right, even though it was not able to penetrate to those minds which were entirely dominated by the old conditions.

The bond-service already mentioned was established in this way. Under David it was organised by Adoniram (2 Sam. 20,24), and it was considerably extended under Solomon. Rehabeam promised his subjects that it would be even worse under him.

"And now, my father laid a heavy yoke upon you, and I will make your yoke heavier; my father chastised you with scourges, and I will chastise you with scorpions" (1 Kings 12,11.14). We know the consequences of these arrogant words, but not the weight of the yoke Rehabeam laid on those who remained under his rule.

That the people must give a gift to the ruler was implied in the whole nature of their relationship, and is expressly stated in the case of Saul (1 Sam. 10,27). And there are indications that the kings took a tithe which they used for their servants, though it was perhaps actually intended for the maintenance of the cult (1 Sam. 8,15.17). The facts relating to this tithe are, however, obscure. In Ezekiel we find that the prince is to have $1/6$ efa of each chomer of wheat and barley, i. e. in all $1/60$; and further probably $1/10$ bat of every chor of oil, [1] $1/100$ in all; and, again, a lamb out of each 200 (Ez. 45,13-16). It is expressly stated that the prince is to use these imposts for the cult.

The scattered information as to imposts which we gain from various periods is not sufficient to give us a true picture of this important side of the king's administration. But we know that Solomon's energetic collection by bailiffs of taxes in kind throughout his realm was continued down through the ages. A chance allusion in Amos shows us that the first mowings of the grass were reserved for the king, of course for his horses and his mules, which were indispensable, especially for the army (Am. 7,1; cf. 1 Kings 18,5). The excavations in Samaria, however, have shown that in Ahab's time taxes in kind were still collected in the northern kingdom according to the system of Solomon. In the store rooms of the palace were found remains of vessels, with inscriptions showing that they must have contained wine and oil collected from the various districts by the royal tax-collectors. A great many handles of jars found in Judah, bearing the legend "belonging to the king", indicate the same thing, and show that here, too, Solomon's system was retained until the last days of the kingdom. [2] The king could well use these taxes in kind, not only for his household, but also for the troops quartered in the fortresses (2 Chron. 11,11).

As to what part of the king's income was derived from his own land and what was his revenue from taxation, we are unable to say. Hezekiah built new store-houses in Jerusalem for corn, oil, and wine (2 Chron. 32,28), but we cannot see whether it was for the crops from his own fields or from those of his subjects.

It must, however, be kept in view that the monarchy did not create a state which at any point formed an institution independent of the king. The king of Israel had taken over the rôle of the chief, that of identifying himself with the whole, only now it was a more comprehensive whole. It was his endeavour to assert this to the farthest possible extent, and the organisation he set on foot was entirely connected with his personal greatness. We have heard how Omri possessed his capital through purchase, while David took possession of his by conquest. Solomon acquired great treasures by his own trade and by taking duties from the merchants (1 Kings 9,28; 10,14 f.). Later kings, too, accumulated considerable riches in their treasuries, and would exhibit them to strangers to convey an impression of the greatness of their honour (2 Kings 20,13). The wealth of the king was identical with the greatness of the kingdom.

The growth and authority of the monarchy depended largely on the power the king acquired through his immediate surroundings. The court raised him above his subjects.

His numerous wives and concubines were an expression of his self-glorification; and in this he imitated the rulers of the great empires. Though the wives of course, under these circumstances, obtained a position very different from that in the simpler household of the chief, their influence on the king might, none the less, be very considerable. Jezebel induced Ahab to act in ways that were foreign to Israelitish customs and sense of justice. The accounts of the last days of David show how his wives plotted against each other and formed parties among the men attached to the king. Thus Bathsheba managed to get her son Solomon accepted as David's successor against her rival Haggith's son Adonijah (1 Kings 1).

The queen mother, *gᵉbhīrā*, occupied a special position among
the ladies of the court. Special honour was due to her, as was
the case in Egypt and among the great kings of the East. ¹ When
Bathsheba went in to her husband David she prostrated herself
before him like any other subject (1 Kings 1,16.31). But when
she became queen mother, the case was reversed, her royal son
rose, prostrated himself before her, ² and seated her on his right
hand (2,19). The position of the queen mother is so important
that "the king and *hag-gᵉbhīrā*" are often mentioned together
(Jer. 13,18; 29,2), and the books of the Kings, under each Judaean
king, give the name of the queen mother as well. That she
occupied a similar position in the northern kingdom would seem
evident from the fact that the Judaean princes went up to pay
their respects to "the king's sons, and the sons of the queen
mother" (2 Kings 10,13). From this it would appear that the
brothers of the king obtained their authority through her. She
held a dignity involving definite rights. Asa deprived his mother
of her dignity as *gᵉbhīrā*, because she supported the Canaanite
cult (1 Kings 15,13). We even have an example of how a queen
mother, when her son had been killed, caused the rest of the
family to be put to death and seized the power herself, keeping
it for seven years (2 Kings 11). The foreign conception of the
position of this woman readily gained ground in Israel because
it was related to the early Israelite conception of the mother.

The king's sons, as we see from the history of David, were
attached to the palace but had a certain degree of independence,
and might sometimes cause their father trouble enough. There
does not seem to be any question of a participation in the government in conjunction with the king.

If we enquire who were the men that, gathered about the king,
constituted the staff and stay of the community, Isaiah mentions
the following, using that very term: the man of valour *(gibbōr)*
and the warrior; the judge *(shōphēṭ)* and the prophet; the seer
(ḳōsēm) and the elder *(zāḳēn)*; the captain of fifty and the
honourable man *(neśū' phānīm)*; the counsellor *(yōᶜēṣ)*, the skilled
magician *(ḥᵃkham ḥᵃrāshīm)*, and the expert in exorcism *(laḥash,*
Isa. 3,2-3). All these, says Isaiah, shall fail, and the whole com-

munity shall crumble. Boys shall rule, the dishonourable occupy the posts of the honourable, all shall resolve itself into mutual strife. The fact that the king is not mentioned no doubt means that he occupies a special position, above the others.

Among the aforementioned pillars of society we know several from the old community. The elders are the leading men in the communities; *gibbōr* is the responsible strong man; the judge, the man of authority whose decision is sought; *nᵉśū' phānīm* probably means "he who raises his face" and is one of the terms for the proud and honourable [1] (cf. 2 Kings 5,1; Isa. 9,14; Job 22,8). The elders, the "honourable", and the prophets were the leaders of the people, "guiding its steps" *(mᵉ'ashshᵉrīm* Isa. 3,12; 9,15), and the counsellor denotes a man of Job's kind.

These pillars, in the time of Isaiah, had no doubt adapted themselves to the new conditions under a king. "The man of valour", who is mentioned with the warrior, constitutes the nucleus in the king's army, in which the captains of fifty are the most numerous class of officers. And the prophet, seer, counsellor, and the two kinds of exorcists surely did not practise their calling among the people alone, but gathered round the king, so as to help him to form the right decisions. The many classes mentioned show how eager was the endeavour to create the highest psychic strength.

We know from the history of David that the king had a special "counsellor" *(yō'ēṣ)* attached to him; the counsel of Ahitophel was as though a word from God had been solicited (2 Sam. 16,23). It was Rehabeam's fault that he consulted the young and his own inclinations instead of the older counsellors (1 Kings 12,6 ff.). To obtain counsel which contained psychic strength because it was rooted in the divine power itself was the great and difficult task of the king. Therefore he continually sought the counsel of prophets, and had a priest at his side who supported him by consecrating the cult and obtaining oracles for him which were a direct expression of the divine will.

It was a sign of the exalted isolation of the king that those who came to the royal palace and belonged to his entourage were called "those who saw the face of the king" (2 Kings 25,19). It

was a special distinction to be called "the king's friend" *(rēᵃ'*
1 Chron. 27,33, *rē'e* 2 Sam. 15,37; 16,16; 1 Kings 4,5), a term
which was common in Egypt, but the meaning of which is not
clear in Israel. [1]

Gradually as the court grew, its administration required a
special class of officials. Solomon already had a special keeper
of the palace (1 Kings 4,6), but subordinate court officials were
added. Thus we know that there was a special keeper of the wardrobe (2 Kings 22,14). Isaiah once uttered some severe threats
against Shebna, the keeper of the palace, and announced that
Eliakim should have his office: And it shall come to pass on that
day, then I will call my servant Eliakim, the son of Hilkiah, and
I will clothe him with thy robe, and gird him with thy girdle,
and I will commit thy authority into his hand, and he shall be a
father to the inhabitants of Jerusalem and to the house of Judah.
And I will lay the key of the house of David upon his shoulder,
and when he openeth, none shall shut, and when he shutteth,
none shall open. And I will fasten him as a nail in a sure place,
and he shall be a seat of honour to his father's house (Isa. 22,
20-23).

This shows us how important the position of the keeper of the
palace had become; his authority is felt in the capital and in the
whole of the country, because he watches over the exalted king.
A certain robe with a girdle belonged to his position, and we may
perhaps read out of the words of the prophet that his installation
into office took place by investing him with this robe and placing
on his shoulder the large master key of the palace. His family of
course rise with him to high rank, and a subsequent addition to
the words of the prophet show that in course of time they became
such a burden to him that they brought about his fall.

There can hardly have been any fixed rule for the relation of
the royal officials to the heads of the local communities. As a
rule the king was no doubt satisfied if his purposes were carried
out without any severe encroachments on the rights of the old
local authorities who sustained the order of society. But the royal
power was a central power whose operation was of incalculable

range. Therefore the relation was probably always marked by a certain vagueness.

When Ahab encroached upon the rights of Naboth, neither he nor Jezebel ever dreamed that he would be able to do so by his own direct action. Jezebel wrote to the elders in Jizreel where Naboth lived and they, that is to say, the leading men of his family town, to please the king, convicted Naboth in an outrageous trial (1 Kings 21,8 ff.). The elders of the capital could influence the political decisions of the king when they specially affected the citizens. When Ahab was besieged in Samaria by Benhadad and received his invitation to surrender on severe conditions, he submitted the matter to the elders, and took the advice given by them and the people (1 Kings 20,7 f.).

It is not clear what conditions were in Jerusalem in this respect, but we obtain a certain insight into them through the history of Jeremiah. When he foretold the destruction of the sanctuary in the court of the temple, a large throng gathered around him, and he was detained by some priests and prophets. They took him towards the entrance of the temple, surrounded by all the crowd. Here they met the officers (haś-śārīm) coming from the royal palace, and they took charge of the affair. The priests and the prophets brought forward their accusation, but Jeremiah insisted that he had only spoken the words of Yahweh. The officers declared him to be innocent, and the whole people supported them. And they were seconded by some elders who came forward and mentioned examples of prophets who had spoken in a similar way in earlier times (Jer. 26).

Here we see the elders come forward and give evidence, but the decision lies with the officers, who represent the king. Still, far-reaching conclusions should not be drawn from this incident, since it takes place within the precincts of the temple. It might have been different perhaps if the matter had concerned the town.

That śārīm denotes the king's men in this story appears clearly from the context, but we have not always such clearness. Before the monarchical period the word denoted the prominent men, identical with the elders (Judg. 8,6 ff.; Job 29,9) just like *ḳāṣin* (Isa. 1,10; 3,6.7; Mic. 3,1, who also has: *rō'sh,* "head"). Later on it came to designate the royal officers and others who as officials were entrusted with high royal charges (Jer. 36-38). Therefore they are often mentioned in conjunction with the king (Jer. 4,9; 49,38; Hos. 3,4; 13,10; Am. 1,15), and they constitute a special class, distinct from the population (Jer. 26,11. 12.16; 34,10). But at the same time the term still, in the monarchical period, denotes the leading, distinguished men of the community (2 Kings 10,1).

This is precisely because there were no definite, sharp limits to the power of the king. In the large towns he had his *śar* who was to watch over his interests (1 Kings 22,26; 2 Kings 23,8), but the class of officials thus formed must have mixed with the old aristocracy, to which no doubt they often belonged. The new aristocracy withdrew the old aristocracy from that relation to the people which was one of the fundamental features of the earlier communities. The obscurity of the relation to the old local authorities is a sign that the monarchy never embraced the whole people. A radical centralisation of the administration was never achieved.

———

The history of David shows that the kingship did not arise out of nothing. He created it in direct continuation of the old chieftainship. Even though the figure of the king was looked upon in a different way to that of the chief, his relation to the people had, nevertheless, grown out of the leading position of the chieftain.

Like the early leaders, the king had a covenant with the people. This expresses the psychic bond between them, but here it had the special character, for which the Arabs had a peculiar term, that one party became subordinate to the other. When David founded his monarchy, it took place by his entering into a covenant, at Hebron, with the Israelites, which had been prepared by Abner beforehand. The pact was made between him and the elders before Yahweh, and they anointed him to be king

(2 Sam. 3,12.21; 5,1-3). Here much the same kind of thing takes place as we heard of in the histories of Saul and Jephthah.

We do not happen to hear anything of the making of such a covenant when the later kings take over the rule. But we hear of instances where the people undertook an important obligation, giving a new colouring to the relation between king and people, and confirmed by a renewed covenant between them. This was the case when the law book had been found under King Josiah. Then the king and the people met in the temple, the king took up his stand by the "pillar" and made the covenant before Yahweh, binding them to follow Yahweh and his law (2 Kings 23,3; cf. Josh. 24,25). And when Zedekiah wanted to enact a law relating to the liberation of the Hebrew slaves and slave women, it was done by the making of a pact with the people at Jerusalem (Jer. 34,8 ff.). The pillar at which the king stood was presumably one of the pillars of the entrance from which he was visible to the crowd in the court.

The enthronisation of the king was identical with the making of the covenant with the people. What visible expression this was given in the customs associated with the ceremony we can only partly say. In two cases we have information of the enthronisation of a king. When Solomon was enthroned, David himself prescribed the ceremonial. He was mounted on the king's mule and taken to the spring of Gihon, surrounded by the prominent men and the body-guard. Here the priest anointed him king with the holy oil, and all cried "May the king live", to the blowing of trumpets. Surrounded by the cheering people he was conducted through the town to the royal palace, where he took his seat on the throne (1 Kings 1,32 ff.).

The anointment, homage, procession in royal wise, and taking possession of the throne are the most important features of this solemn rite. It is the holy anointment by the priest to which weight is attached, and since it was carried out at the spring of Gihon this must have been a holy spring. Adonijah's attempt to obtain consecration as a king took place at the spring of Rogel and was connected with the slaughtering of cattle, which probably means that a sacrificial meal was eaten (1 Kings 1,9). The

most important features were the consecration and the actual
following of the royal customs by conducting a procession and
taking possession of the royal throne.

The account of the enthronisation of Joash agrees with this.
Solomon's temple was adjacent to the royal palace, and the first
part took place here. The priest, Jehojada, led young Joash
forward in the temple, put the diadem on his head, and anointed
him. The people broke into loud acclaim, clapped their hands
and shouted "May the king live" to the blowing of trumpets.
Meanwhile the king stood in his place "by the pillar", and the
priest made the covenant between Yahweh, the people, and the
king, that they were to be Yahweh's people. Then the king was
conducted by the body-guard to the royal palace, where "he took
his seat on the throne of the kings" (2 Kings 11). The holy
consecration and the ascending of the throne are always the
two prominent features of the enthronisation of the king. His
consecration by anointment endows him with secret power which
at once changes his character and gives him authority, as shown
by the history of Jehu (2 Kings 9,1-13).

The whole equipment of the king is included in his honour.
It was probably part of the consecration ceremony that he should
show himself in it for the first time. The king wore magnificent
robes (Ps. 45,9), but his royal honour was especially associated
with the diadem that ornamented his brow. We have seen that
Joash was crowned with it upon his enthronisation, and Saul
wore both a diadem and bracelets (2 Sam. 1,10). The diadem
was the typical sign of dignity, which, characteristically enough,
was worn by the post-exilic high priest who in part inherited the
position of the king. It is called *nēzer*, a word derived from the
same root as that which denotes the exalted state of the old
heroes and others who have been consecrated. It was not a
specially Israelitish attribute of the king. If a king took another
king's crown, it meant that he usurped his royal honour, as
David did with the king of the Ammonites (2 Sam. 12,30). [1]

Another attribute of the king is the sceptre *(shēbhet, matte,
mᵉḥōḳēḳ)*. It stands between the feet of the ruler (Gen. 49,10),
and it is often mentioned as the special symbol of the royal

dignity (Num. 24,17; Isa. 14,5; Am. 1,5.8; Ps. 45,7 et al.). But this was an attribute which the monarchy had taken over from the old chieftainship (Judg. 5,14), [1] probably an ancient sign of the dignity of a man. A prophet designates the ruler's sceptre as a shepherd's crook: "Guard thy people with thy rod, the flock of thine heritage" (Mic. 7,14), a comparison which is natural, for among the Israelites, as among the Babylonians, the kings are often called shepherds.

The rites of enthronisation show us how great was the importance of the throne for the royal dignity. It, too, had its history, which points back to the origin of the kingship from simpler conditions. In the earliest times, the customs in this respect were probably in Israel as among the Arabs. As a rule the men sat on the ground, or perhaps on a mat or a rug, while the chief or the judge sat on a higher seat, a chair. We hear that a man like Eli sat on a chair *(kissē')*, just like Eglon the king of Moab (Judg. 3,20; 1 Sam. 1,9; 4,13.18). In the monarchic period chairs had probably become common, for a *kissē'* belonged to every house of any standing (2 Kings 4,10), and at the same time the more refined townspeople used elegant couches (Am. 6,4). When, nevertheless, the chair, *kissē'*, far down into the ages remained the symbol of judges and regents (Prov. 20,8; Neh. 3,7) and quite particularly of the king, such rulers' seats were no doubt distinguished from others by their splendour and size. In fact, under the later khaliphas, the old Arabian chieftain's seat developed partly into a regular throne, partly into the raised pulpit in the mosque.

In narratives from David's time the king and his throne *(kissē')* are mentioned as if the latter stood for the monarchy itself (2 Sam. 14,9; cf. 1 Kings 1,13 etc.; 2,12.24; 7,7; 8,20). Like the sceptre and the diadem, the throne was pervaded by the royal soul; this was what gave it a peculiar significance. Hence it was natural for kings to carry their thrones with them to foreign territories which they had conquered and set them up there (Jer. 1,15; 43,10), just as we know that the earlier khaliphas carried their small thrones with them on journeys in their empire.

When Solomon was to display the glory of the kingdom which David had created, he procured a new throne in the style of the great empires, as well as a new palace and temple. The throne stood in a special throne room in the palace where the people to be judged by the king were summoned before him (1 Kings 7,7). It is described as a large throne of ivory overlaid with pure gold; it had six steps and a round upper part and on both sides of the seat there were arms, beside which stood two lions. On either side of the steps stood six lions. "There was not the like made in any kingdom" (1 Kings 10,18-20; cf. 2 Chron. 9,17-19).

Normally every throne had a footstool (Ps. 110,1), but a royal throne with six steps seems to have been something quite unique in the ancient east, nothing quite like it having actually been made before. It is doubtful, however, whether we have here a realistic description before us. [1] Be this as it may, it vividly illustrates the difference between the exalted king and the chief sitting on a simple seat among his men.

The outward symbols of the kingship show how it grew out of the old conditions, and the external forms express the inner relationship between them. The covenant exacts the same fundamental qualities of the chief and of the king, above all what the Israelites understand by righteousness. When the Israelites got a king, it seemed natural to them to turn to him for judicial decisions, because they were accustomed to go to the mightiest for judgments. In David's time people would come to his palace in the morning to solicit his help if they thought they had been wronged. It was on such occasions that Absalom stood at the gate and promised them all help and support if he were made king (2 Sam. 15,1-6). Solomon, whose wealth surpassed that of all others, and who imposed such heavy burdens on the people, had the reputation of being a great judge who saw that righteousness prevailed. According to one story, Yahweh at his request gave him the power to distinguish good from evil and to judge the people (1 Kings 3,9), and this is illustrated by the well-known example of how he pronounced judgment between two women.

There is no question of the king pronouncing a sentence on

behalf of the state which the state authorities then proceed to execute. The king's authority is personal like that of the chief. He must have a greater righteousness because he has more power, his will must be identical with the covenant, and he must bring his authority to bear and aid those who have been wronged. When Elisha wished to make return to his hostess at Sunem for her hospitality, he knew of nothing better than to put in a word for her with the king or the commander of the army, but she refused his help on the plea that she lived amidst her people and hence did not need any aid (2 Kings 4,13).

The king is a helper, $m\bar{o}sh\bar{\imath}^{a\varsigma}$, as was Gideon. Homage is paid to him by hailing him with a $h\bar{o}sh\bar{\imath}'\bar{a}$ $ham\text{-}melekh$, "save, king" (2 Sam. 14,4; 2 Kings 6,26), for this very hail means that you acknowledge his kingship. And his help is a result of his righteousness. A king upholds a country by righteousness $(mishp\bar{a}\underline{t})$, but a man who merely demands taxes, overthrows it (Prov. 29,4). By "judging" the lowly with truth, the king establishes his throne (v. 14).

When the Israelites speak of the king, they may strongly stress the arbitrariness which comes of his power. They record as a matter of course how Pharaoh wilfully raises and overthrows his baker and his butler, and how his vizier, Joseph, without whom no one could raise hand or foot in the land of Egypt, plays with his own brothers as a cat with a mouse (Gen. 41,44). But here we are concerned with conditions among a foreign people. It was the duty of the Israelite king as of the Israelite chief to maintain law and order. We have seen that this had become so much a part of their nature that the people could regard the time without a king as a time without law and order, and Habakkuk compares a disintegrated community with the fishes of the sea and the creeping things of the earth, "among which there is no ruler" (Hab. 1,14).

All this shows that the king may be regarded as a chief on a large scale, a man who has grown up to occupy the same position in relation to the people as a whole as the chief occupied in the smaller community. The fellowship produced by the covenant manifested itself in the great responsibility of the king.

Saul, the great chief, brought famine upon the Israelites because
he incurred blood guilt among the Gibeonites. When David had
sinned by counting the people, he was given the choice between
three disasters, three years of famine, three months' flight from
the enemy, or three days' pestilence, all plagues that came upon
the people, and when he chose the pestilence, it only befell the
people. It ravaged the country, but when the angel of death
approached Jerusalem, David said: Behold, I have sinned and
I have acted wickedly, but what have these, the herd, done? Let
thy hand be against me and against my father's house (2 Sam.
24,17). Then Yahweh caused the pestilence to cease, and thus
David and his house entirely escaped it.

David's words imply a recognition of the fact that he and
his house are chiefly responsible. But the whole story shows that
the people share in the responsibility of the king and must take
the consequences of his action, even if they have not taken part
in it. This is a result of the psychic fellowship instituted by the
covenant. The blood guilt of Manasseh in Judah elicited a threat
from Yahweh that he would make Judah an abomination among
the nations (Jer. 15,4).

And in Genesis we see this relation between the king and the
people mentioned as something self-evident. When Abimelech had
taken Sarah from Abraham without knowing that she was
another man's wife and afterwards learned the truth, he said:
How have I sinned against thee that thou hast brought so great
a sin on me and my kingdom? (Gen. 20,9). The king's sin
against a strange husband is the sin of his realm.

This of course is only the reverse side of what constitutes
the chief factor in the whole position of the king. Like the chief,
he is the man from whom the people obtains its blessing. Hence
rejoicing over a king expresses the greatest joy, the glory of
the king is the greatness of the people. He brings the elation
of victory and keeps all enemies in subjection (Num. 23,21;
24,7.17 f.). What the king meant to the community is expressed
in vigorous and plain terms in the lament for the destruction of
the monarchy: The breath of our nostrils, Yahweh's anointed,
was caught in their pit, he under whose shadow we thought to

live among the peoples (Lam. 4,20). Just as the great king in the vision of Daniel is described as an immense tree reaching to the heavens and spreading all over the earth, so that all can obtain shelter and food under it, so also the Israelite king is here called the tree under whose shelter the people could live. He is the breath of their nostrils, whence all their life streams.

We are here confronted with the quality characteristic of the king in distinction from the chief. It is not the decisive factor that one position is hereditary, while the other is not. It is natural to both that the family upholds the blessing, though the chief's son must, indeed, acquire his heritage and uphold his blessing in another way than the son of the king. Nor is the decisive factor the different extent of the field of action. There are great kings and small kings. But the wider range of the king's power contributed to establish a special position for him, and this, too, was so in Israel. The king who resided in Jerusalem and ruled over the whole country obtained an isolated position as a potentate. But his power did not consist in mere external display.

The significance of the chief of the old community lay in the fact has he was in the midst of his people. The forces inherent in the community were released through him, he realised the will of the totality when he went forth, filled with the spirit of Yahweh. The king was self-glorified, was elevated above the community. David created this position through his policy and the use of power. When it had once been gained, however, the whole view of the king which prevailed in the empires of the time followed naturally. The king possessed the entire blessing. He was a superman of inconceivable strength of soul. The community must do all it could to uphold him, for it was through him that strength flowed into it. From the Psalms we see how the people associates its victories, its fertility, all its future with him.

The chief led the field in battle and won the victory for his people, whereas under David we already meet with the idea that the king should keep outside the battle, so as not to "extinguish the lamp of Israel"; for the king is worth ten thousand other men (2 Sam. 18,3; 21,17). There is nothing absolutely new in

6*

this, for the fall of the chief, too, was decisive; but a shade of difference. is expressed which is significant because it accords well with the increased importance attached to the king's person. Like the Pharaoh the king can say "I and my people" (Ex. 9,27). Like the other peoples the Israelites learned to say that "the heart of kings is unsearchable" (Prov. 25,3), i. e. incomprehensible in depth and range; the king speaks words of superhuman force; "there is *kesem* in the king's lips, his mouth faileth not in judgment" (16,10); life radiates from the light of his countenance; with his eyes he scatters all that is evil (16,15; 20,8.26; cf. Isa. 33,17). Even a deposed and slain king was so full of this force that people washed themselves in his blood to obtain the blessing (1 Kings 22,38).

All this was due to the fact that the king stood in quite a different relation from other people to the source of the blessing. He is "the shoot of Yahweh" (Isa. 4,2), and even more: he is Yahweh's son (Ps. 2,7). This means that he has a divine soul, for which reason he is also called a god (Ps. 45,7). The close relationship between the god and the king is felt in many ways. God and the king should be feared (Prov. 24,21). He who curses them must undoubtedly die, for he is attempting to corrupt the very springs of life (Ex. 22, 27; 1 Kings 21,10.13). In the regeneration of Israel it is a matter of course that Yahweh and the king take the lead (Mic. 2,13).

It is this ideal background of the kingship which gives it significance and strength. The Israelite king created a new totality and placed himself above it. It was by the ingenuity of David that the new totality was linked up firmly with the past history of the community. He did it by constituting himself the heir of the most powerful of the Israelite chiefs, but also in other ways.

We do not know how the Israelite fellowship manifested itself in earlier times. The small separate communities had each their chief; there was no political unity, and yet there was a fellowship. It centred round the ancient sacred treasure common to them all, the Ark of the Covenant, and it is hardly conceivable that the people, after the dispersal throughout Canaan, should have been without common ritual assemblies, all the more so since the ancient and chief festival, the Passover, meant a re-living of the old common history. Attention has justly been drawn to the information we have about assemblies of the people. [1] When Rehabeam became king, the people assembled at Shechem to consult together and take a decision (1 Kings 12,1). To this very place where Jacob founded a sanctuary (Gen. 33,20; 35,4) the narratives localise an assembly of the people, and Joshua made a covenant (Jos. 24). The contents of these narratives, it is true, show evidence of a much later time. And to Shechem also the stories refer the setting up of stones for a united Israel and the pronouncing of solemn blessings and curses (Deut. 27; Josh. 8,30-35). In this we may venture to see hints that common assemblies have been held, with a renewal of the covenant, in continuation of the feasts held before the immigration of the people. On this point, however, we have no light, for the documents are incomplete, and transmitted from an age that no longer knew anything of the circumstances. And the Ark of the Covenant was at Shiloh, not at Shechem. It is possible that the prominence given to Shechem is due to conditions which developed in the monarchical period.

Whatever the forms that expressed the unity in earlier times, it is a fact that they were transformed under the monarchy and given a new centre. And on this point, too, David created a continuity by taking the Ark up to his capital; thus the new centre drew to itself the whole of the old Israelite fellowship. When the temple was built, the idea of the kingship was realised, the idea of creating a fixed spiritual centre for Israel.

The royal temple must be the place that gathered all around it. Here the assemblies of the people were now held which were required by custom if a new law involved a new covenant (2 Kings 23,3; Jer. 34,8.15). Here the people's feasts were to be celebrated. But above all the temple must uphold the greatness of the monarchy by its cultus.

In the cult, too, the chief was the person through whom the community acted. He was the leader at the feasts, just as he was the man through whom Yahweh's spirit worked, when great deeds were to be performed. In the same way the king was, as a matter course, the leader of the cult which was adopted for the whole country. But he was more than that. Yahweh's spirit did not work in him with ecstatic violence on special occasions. The power was present in him as a constant possession, because he was Yahweh's anointed and Yahweh's son, and this power of the king's could only be upheld by constant renewal in the cult. Hence we can say with certainty that the whole position of the king demands a cult which serves especially to strengthen him.

How much the king actually did himself was not of great importance; he had army leaders and ministers to carry out his purposes. But the maintenance of the royal blessing was incumbent on him, and it was renewed in the temple, where a priesthood became his assistants. By means of the temple the king created a new centre, so important that it retained its importance as the rallying point of the totality, even after the destruction of the kingdom. And it grew in importance, till at last it strangled all other rallying points. When the monarchy disappeared, the institution had become so powerful that not only could it assert itself without the king, but it could even regard the king's activities in connection with it as an usurpation.

———

The monarchy which grew up in Israel beside the Judaean, could never become the representative of all Israel like that of Jerusalem. Here was the monarchy founded by David as the common Israelite monarchy, and here was the great temple with the Ark of the Covenant.

It is against this background that we must view the criticism Hosea directs against the Ephraimite kingdom. "They have set up kings, but not by me, chiefs without my knowledge" (Hos. 8,4). "Oh where is thy king that he may save thee ... thou saidst: Give me a king and chiefs. I will give thee a king in mine anger and take him away in my wrath" (13,10 f.). Hence the Israelites waver. "Now they say: We have no king ... what can the king do for us?" (10,3). And Hosea announces his destruction (10,15). This does not mean that Hosea is against the monarchy as such, on the contrary, it is a punishment to be without a king. "For many days shall the Israelites abide without a king, and without a chief, and without a sacrifice and without a *maṣṣēbhā*, and without an ephod and without teraphim. Afterwards shall the Israelites return and seek Yahweh their God, and David their king, and come timidly to Yahweh and to his happiness at the end of the days" (3,4-5).

It cannot of course be proved that these words were spoken by Hosea in that very form. But everything would seem to indicate that they express his conception of the monarchy, just as Amos doubtless believed in the inward power of the falling hut of David (Am. 9,11). The Davidic monarchy had acquired a place in the life of Israel, precisely because it absorbed the old tradition and undertook to sustain it.

The stability of the Judaean kingdom was evidenced by the fact that the house of the founder retained its position till the destruction of the realm. Even though the greatness of the king depended on his consecration, the view of his house as the upholder of the blessing asserted itself none the less, and David's posterity lived by his blessing. A slave who rises to be king makes the earth totter (Prov. 30,22). It was only the descent from the father which was decisive; the mother need not be of royal birth (e. g. Jer. 52,1). When the people shouted, "May the king live", or "May the king live forever" (2 Sam. 16,16; 1 Kings 1,31.34.39), this meant that he himself should be filled with life, but the perpetuation of his soul in the family was implied in this. Hence the fortune of the Davidic house is dependent on the fact that it shares in David's covenant with Yahweh. His covenant is the pact of his house. The experience of the monarchical period in this respect is referred to David. In some obscure utterances purporting to be David's last words, we see him look down through the ages.

The beginning runs thus: Sayings of David, the son of Jesse, sayings of the man who was raised up on high, the anointed of the God of Jacob, the beloved of the songs of Israel. The spirit of Yahweh speaketh by me, his word is in my tongue; the God of Israel saith, the Rock of Israel speaketh to me: A just ruler

among men ruleth in the fear of God. As the light of morning
when the sun riseth, a morning without clouds ... But my house
is not so with God, for he hath made with me an everlasting
covenant, ordered in all things and preserved (2 Sam. 23,1-5).
In the sequel it is mentioned that evil-doers shall perish. So much
we can gather, that there is an allusion to the just king who
suppresses the wicked, and that he is found in the house of
David, which is secure in its royal power because of Yahweh's
covenant with David.

The same thing is said in plainer words in a promise which
the prophet Nathan is said to have given David at the beginning
of his career as a king. It runs as follows: Thus saith Yahweh
of the hosts: I took thee from the pastures, removed thee from
the flocks, to be a chief over my people, over Israel. And I was
with thee whithersoever thou wentest, and rooted out all thine
enemies for thee. And I will make thee a great name like unto
the name of the great men on earth, and I will appoint a place
for my people, for Israel, and I will plant it, and it shall dwell
in its place, and suffer no more anxiety, and evil-doers shall
humiliate it no longer as in the beginning, and since the day
when I commanded judges over my people Israel, and I will give
thee rest from all thine enemies; and Yahweh telleth thee that
Yahweh will make thee a house. When thy days are full and
thou sleepest with thy fathers, I will let thy seed survive thee
which issues from thy body, and I will establish its kingdom.
It shall build an house to my name, and I will establish the throne
of its kingdom forever. I will be a father to it, and it shall be a
son to me, so that if it sin, I will chastise it with the rod of men
and with the stripes of the sons of men. And my love shall not
depart from it, as I let it depart from Saul whom I removed for
thee. And thine house and thy kingdom shall stand secure forever
for thee, thy throne shall be established forever (2 Sam. 7,8-16).
David confirms these words before Yahweh, concluding thus:
And now Lord Yahweh, thou art God and thy words are truth,
and thou hast spoken this goodness to thy servant. Then bless
thou now thy servant's house that it may live forever before thee;

for thou, Lord Yahweh, hast spoken, and with thy blessing the house of thy servant shall be blessed forever (7,28-29).

In this speech we meet with the ideal which arose in Israel when the great fusion of Israelites and Canaanites had taken place. Israel's foes shall be exterminated and the people shall live in security, but this shall be accomplished by the house of David, because its dominion rests on Yahweh's unshakable promise to David. His house shall build the temple, and Yahweh, the Davidic king, and the temple are inviolably bound together, therefore this royal house shall be stronger than time. Its happiness depends upon the fact that it possesses the blessing of Yahweh, and only with David's line does the true history of Israel begin. For true life means security, but its prerequisite is the monarchy; what preceded it was all unrest with constant hostile invasions. Here then we find one more aspect of the view that makes the monarchy the starting-point of law and order in Israel. Before it chaos prevailed. Without the house of David the people could not live.

The monarchy, owing to its nature as well as its effects, meant the most radical revolution in the history of Israel. There were features in the psychic life of Israel which must make it suited for the monarchy. It obtained a strong central power under which it could seek shelter. But it was in conflict with old Israelite custom for one man to become so much exalted over the rest as the king, and the disintegration of the old social order could not take place without complaints. These complaints were bound to meet with great sympathy in circles remote from life in the capital and the other large cities.

The prophets directed their criticism against the effects of the monarchical régime, against the decline of Israelite law and custom, against the encroachments of the new magnates, and against the oppression of the humbler class of Israelites. Violent attacks were made on the new magnates. They are called the friends of thieves; they love bribes and decree unrighteous decrees for widows and the fatherless, they are oppressors and lead the people astray (Isa. 1,23; 3,12.14 f.; 10,1 ff.). They live in luxury, while the people perish (Am. 6,1 ff.). Micah says that they eat the flesh of the people and flay off their skin (Mic. 3,1-4.9-11). We may also see prophets, as Isaiah and Jeremiah, turn upon the possessors of the kingdom, accusing and threatening them; but this does not involve a rejection of the Davidic monarchy. Its solidarity with Yahweh had sunk deep into the minds of the people.

We find here the same duality of judgment as we are able to observe later in Islam. When the Khaliphate had transformed itself after the model of the old great kingships, the conservative theorists created an ideal of a Khalipha which was a combination of the great king and the simple Arab sheikh of the early days of Islam; and this ideal was identified with the first khaliphas, while at the same time there was a constant expectation of its realisation in the future. [1] In the same way the Israelites formed a picture of David. In him the idea of kingship had been realised, as it was to arise again. He combined the power of the great monarch with early Israelite simplicity and solidarity with the lowly, he was Israelite justice personified. The power of the great monarch is for the good when it is employed to uphold the people of Israel and their ancient manners and customs, and not for his own glorification.

This royal ideal is described in the prophetic writings. We read in Isaiah about a time of rejoicing, when the yoke of the foreigner has been so thoroughly broken that the boots of the warrior and the garments rolled in blood can be burnt, and in this connection the prophet goes on to say: Unto us a child is born, unto us a son is given, and the government shall be upon his shoulder, and his name is called Wonder-Counsellor, Hero-God, Father of Booty, [2] Prince of Peace, for the increase of government and for peace without end, over the throne of David, and over his kingdom to establish it firmly and support it by righteousness and justice. From henceforth and forever the jealousy of Yahweh of the hosts will do this (Isa. 9,5 f.).

The same expectation marks another utterance of Isaiah: A

branch shall spring from the stem [1] of Isai and a shoot shall rise from his roots. In [2] him dwells the spirit of Yahweh, the spirit of wisdom and insight, the spirit of counsel and strength, the spirit of skill and the fear of Yahweh ..... And he shall not judge by the sight of his eyes, nor guide by the hearing of his ears, he shall judge the poor with justice, and guide with equity the humble in the land, and he shall strike down the violent [3] with the rod of his mouth, and with the breath of his lips shall he slay the wicked. Justice is the girdle of his loins and truth the belt of his hips (Isa. 11,1-5). The text goes on to say that all dissension in nature shall cease, the Israelites shall dwell in security, hostile peoples being put down.

It is impossible to decide whether these utterances can really be ascribed to Isaiah, but it is highly probable that they date from the monarchical period, for they vividly portray the Israelite ideal of a king, no doubt in close connection with the cult connected with the king.

In the two descriptions we find traits always associated with an Israelite chief. He is to be a counsellor, full of wisdom, of power, and ability to carry out his purpose. And above all he is to be just and sustain the humble. He has in him the spirit of Yahweh, not as the inspiration of a moment, but as a permanent possession and it is identical with his power and his ability. He, who is pervaded by the fear of Yahweh, is yet in the first utterance called a hero-god. His powers are enhanced to the grand proportions of the monarchy. His counsel is a marvel; he creates peace in acquiring spoil, because he puts down all opposition; and he raises the house of David to undisputed power. But he uses his great power to put down men of violence and uphold the humble. Thus the king is to realise the early Israelite *mishpāṭ* and *ṣᵉdhāḳā;* he is to restore the order of society which the monarchy itself had dissolved, and put down its spoilers who followed in his own footsteps. Then "the throne shall be stablished by love and upon it shall sit in truth in the tabernacle of David a judge and one who is bent upon justice and one who is practised in righteousness" (Isa. 16,5).

We see in these utterances how the ideal of a royal ruler has been adapted to suit the Israelite way of thinking. Sometimes the adaptation is carried to such extremes that the very foundation of this ideal of power is renounced. In the book of Micah mention is made in the usual way of the mighty Israelite king, whose dominion is universal, lifted high into concentrated time: And thou Beth-Ephrath, [1] tiny though thou be [2] among the houses of Judah, yet out of thee shall one come forth unto me that shall be ruler in Israel, and his origin shall be from of old, from the days of eternity... And he shall rise up and be a shepherd in the strength of Yahweh, in the glory of the name of his God Yahweh, and they shall abide, for now he grows unto the ends of the earth (Mic. 5,1.3).

There is no end to the greatness which the power of the king was to reach. But after the announcement of the great victories the text goes on to say: And on that day, saith Yahweh, I will cut off thy horses out of thy midst and I will destroy thy chariots. And I will cut off the cities of thy land, and throw down all thy strongholds (5,9 f.). That is to say, chariots and horses, strongholds and great cities, all those means, unknown to earliest Israel, by which the monarchy was upheld, all these were to disappear with other non-Israelitish things such as sorcerers and idols. The king is an ideal figure who by the miraculous help of Yahweh acquires world power in virtue of his inner qualities alone. He does not employ the usual royal instruments of power, because they are un-Israelitish, even superfluous.

So far could the Israelites be carried in their accentuation of the psychic as the one thing needful for the king. This incursion right into unreality was due to the incongruity, constantly obtruding itself, in the relation between the ideal of kingship and Israelite tradition, but it was also due to the firm belief that Yahweh was the power behind and could never break the covenant he had made with David.

And yet justice was essential if Yahweh were to uphold the covenant of David. Hence Jeremiah says to the king that it is not splendour, but justice to the lowly which makes the king (Jer. 22,15 f.). And he says to the king of Judah "that sittest upon the throne of David", and also to his servants, that they shall do justice and righteousness, deliver the spoiled out of the hand of the spoiler, not oppress widows, orphans, and *gērim,* do no wrong, nor shed innocent blood. If they do this, then kings shall continue to sit on the throne of David, but if not, the palace shall be destroyed (Jer. 22,1-5).

The curious combination of universal power with lowliness exhibited in the Israelite ideal of a king still persisted after the fall of the monarchy. In a post-exilic utterance relating to the still expected scion of David, this duality in the royal person is very marked. It says: Rejoice greatly, o daughter of Zion: shout for joy, daughter of Jerusalem, behold thy king cometh unto thee: he is just and having salvation: lowly and riding upon an ass, upon a colt, the foal of she-asses. And I will cut off the chariots of Ephraim, and the horses from Jerusalem, and the battle bow shall be cut off, and he shall speak peace unto the peoples. And his dominion shall be from sea even to sea, from the river even to the ends of the earth (Zech. 9,9 f.).

Here again the Israelite king is ruler of the world in the most absolute sense, and yet all instruments of war are discarded. He brings peace because all subordinate themselves to him, and he gains this great victory merely by virtue of his righteousness, as an instrument in the hand of Yahweh. He wins it as the representative of the lowly, those who constituted the true Israel, as opposed to the self-satisfied cultivated people of the towns. As *'ānī,* humble, meek, he belongs to the common people, he rides on his ass, the animal used of old for riding by the Israelites, and still reserved for the lower class. That such a humble man should appear as the ruler of the world is a manifestation of the miraculous activity of Yahweh.

This utterance shows that the people kept intact its ideal of a king and upheld the covenant of Yahweh with David as that which guaranteed to Israel the greatness, and especially the claim to greatness which the monarchy had created for it. At the same time, however, it rejected what was needed for this greatness, that is to say, the exalted position of the king in the organism of the people as a superman with a divine soul. The history of Israel, which made it a nation of people in humble circumstances, contributed to this, but also a new conception of humanity. The more divinity became a thing apart, exalted above mankind, the more impossible it became for individual man to raise himself within the human community to the divine sphere.

The belief in the covenant with David persisted, and it exacted righteousness in the king if the covenant were not to be dissolved and the monarchy fall. When the monarchy actually did fall, the explanation was not far to seek. The kings had not been just. The old expectations of a ruler who was to renew the royal house and carry out the covenant now assumed a new aspect, they were changed into a hope of the restoration of the monarchy. In Jeremiah we read a lament about the shepherds who have destroyed and scattered the herd of Yahweh. For this misdeed they are to suffer, but the herd shall again be assembled, and then Yahweh will raise up a scion of David who is to be king with wisdom, justice and righteousness. Israel shall again be delivered as out of Egypt, and shall live in security under the just king who shall be called "Yahweh is our righteousness" (Jer. 23,1-8).

It is probable that this utterance dates from the time of the exile, though Israelites had gone into exile even before that time, [1] and it shows how much the happiness of the people is made to depend on the king and his righteousness. The people's belief in the future must therefore be a belief that a man should come to occupy the throne of David. The important thing is the upholding of the covenant of David, and a prophetic voice calls it as safe as the covenant with day and night in their regular alternation (Jer. 33,15.17.20 f.). It is David himself who is perpetuated in his scion and keeps the covenant (30,9).

The same ideas recur in other post-exilic prophets. "I will make an everlasting covenant with you, the sure love of David", we read in Deutero-Isaiah, who predicts the regeneration of the people (Isa. 55,3). The covenant of David is to him a loving union of souls between David, the king, and the people. And in Ezekiel as in the book of Jeremiah we read accusations against the shepherds who have fed themselves and not the flocks; they took wool, milk, and animals to kill, but they did not help the weak. Now Yahweh himself will gather his flocks, and set up

David as their shepherd. Then there shall be peace and safety, and all that is hostile shall be paralysed (Ez. 22,6; 34; 37,24 f.; 45,9 f.). Yahweh will plant a cedar on the lofty mountain of Israel, in the shadow of which all birds shall dwell (17,22-24), and the last treacherous king was only removed to give place to him to whom the right belongs, and to him it shall be given (21,30-32). That is to say, the kings have been bad, but the ideal of a king lives, embodied in the covenant with David, and now only, after the kings have disappeared, shall this covenant be properly introduced and realised. And the peace he brings consists in Israel receiving everything from Yahweh, with him as the mediator. This determines his mission.

The monarchy in Israel created the conception of an ideal king which was more lasting than the monarchy itself, and forever retained its power in the life of Israel. But the ideal comprised such heterogeneous elements that it must necessarily be subject to a strong inner tension. Hence it was most vital as an idea, without coming too closely into contact with reality. Confronted with concrete conditions it was transformed into a vigorous source of criticism.

We shall see later on how the priesthood created by the king grew gradually more and more powerful and drove the king out of the sanctuary. This, too, was a war of ideas, for it was only waged when the king was no more. We find here an inclination to consider the king as an invader in the Israelite community, and these ecclesiastical circles thought they had a right to an opinion on the matter, for the king was to be righteous, and they alone knew what righteousness was.

Such presuppositions led to the forming of the Deuteronomic law relating to the king, no doubt during or after the exile. It runs as follows: When thou shalt come to the land which Yahweh thy God giveth thee, and shalt take possession of it and dwell in it and shalt say: I will set me up a king like all the peoples around me, then thou shalt set up a king over thee which Yahweh thy God shall choose. Out of the midst of thy brethren thou shalt set up a king over thee, thou canst not set up a stranger over thee who is not thy brother. But he must not procure many horses for himself, nor lead the people back to Egypt to procure many horses, for Yahweh hath said to you: You shall return no more this way. And he must not take many wives unto himself that his heart may not be turned away, nor must he accumulate abundant silver and gold. And when he sitteth on the throne of his kingdom, he shall write in a book a copy of this law which he receiveth from the Levitic priests, and it shall remain with him, and he shall read it all the days of his life, that he may learn to fear Yahweh, his God, and keep all the commandments of this law and these statutes, and carry them out, that his heart may not be exalted above his brethren and that it may not swerve from the commandment right or left, that he and his sons may prolong his days over his kingdom in the midst of Israel (Deut. 17,14-20).

It is here indicated that the kingship is un-Israelitish, introduced after the custom of other peoples, by the will of the people, not really by that of Yahweh. If it is to be, however, then the people must abide by Yahweh's choice which here coincides entirely with that of the priests. The King is to be Israelite, a demand which could not possibly be made as long as the Davidic dynasty existed, for then the idea of a foreign ruler would be absurd. He must not make a grand display like Solomon to whom the writer clearly alludes in the passage about the horses, Egypt, the numerous wives, and the wealth. He must not be a despot. He must not exalt himself above other Israelites, but must conform to the humble conditions which were the lot of the true Israelite. And notably he is to submit to the priests from whom he is to receive the Deuteronomic law, of which he is to make a copy that he is to read daily.

We find features here which we have seen elsewhere; the king is a humble man because he is a true Israelite; the upholder of the life of the nation has become a meek disciple of the priests. After the fall of the kingdom, the king existed as an ideal only, and a subject of theorising. But this very theorising shows that the work of reconciling the real kingship with the Israelite ideals was constantly going on.

The monarchy cast back its shadow over the earlier history of Israel. Some few pronouncements show that the kingless period came to be regarded as a time of chaotic confusion. But a new point of view brought a certain order into this chaos. It made out Israel to be a unity governed by a succession of provisional kings. This view was only consistently adopted when by means of notes on the book of Judges, the heroes and chieftains of the past were transformed into a series of "judges", successive leaders of Israel. In this way, however, a succession of rulers was obtained which, starting from Moses and Joshua, passed on through the time of the judges to Samuel, Saul, and the whole list of kings. Saul who, as we know, was closely connected with David, had already become the first king in the earliest narratives about him. And Samuel was raised to the line of rulers as the last representative of the old time, the link between the judges and the kings.

The critical view of the monarchy now intervened, and asserted itself in a new presentation of the rise of the monarchy interwoven with the old narratives of how Saul became king (1 Sam. 8; 10, 17-27; 12). Here we are told that when Samuel grew old, he let his sons judge, but they did not follow in his footsteps. Then the elders of Israel went to Samuel, saying: Behold, thou art grown old, and thy sons walk not in thy ways; so now make us a king to judge us according to the custom of all the nations (1 Sam. 8,5). Samuel grew angry with them, but when he laid the matter before Yahweh, he was commanded to give in to them. "Not thee do they reject, but they reject me as king over them", says Yahweh (v. 7), and he adds that it is in accordance with their behaviour since he brought them up out of Egypt, for they have constantly forsaken him to serve other gods; and now they are treating Samuel in the same way. But Samuel was once more to warn them of what they were letting themselves in for.

Samuel did so by giving them the following description of the kingship: This shall be the behaviour (mishpāṭ, right and custom) of the king, he who is to be king over you. Your sons he shall take and put them to his chariot and his horses, and they shall run before his chariot, and he shall make them captains of thousands and captains of fifties, and let them plough his ploughing, and reap his harvest, and make his weapons and the appointments of his chariots. And your daughters he shall take for mixers of ointments and for cooks and bakers. And he shall take your fields and your vineyards and your goodly olive trees and give them to his servants. And he will take the tenth of your seed and your vines and give it to his eunuchs and to his servants. And he shall take your slaves and your slave women and your fine young men and your asses and use for his work. He will take tithes of your flocks, and you yourselves shall be his bondmen. And you shall cry out on that day to be rid of your king whom you have chosen for yourselves, but Yahweh shall not answer you on that day (1 Sam. 8,11-18). The people however, insisted, and Yahweh commanded Samuel to procure a king.

Once more Samuel collected the people at Mizpeh. He reminded them in the name of Yahweh of how Yahweh had brought them out of Egypt and rid them of all their oppressors, yet now they rejected their God who had rescued them from all evil, and demanded a king. Then the drawing of lots began. First Benjamin was selected, then the family of Matri, and then Saul. He had to be fetched out of hiding, and received homage as the king chosen by Yahweh through the oracle. Then Samuel wrote down the "law (mishpāṭ) of the kingdom" and deposited it before Yahweh (10,17-27).

Samuel's parting speech (1 Sam. 12), which has been removed from its context, belongs to this narrative. Samuel had now fulfilled the wish of the people and procured a king for it, while he himself retired. He then called the people to witness that he had not taken any man's ox or ass, had not committed any transgression or wrong, and not taken any bribe. He then gave a general view of the history of the people of the same kind as the "framework" of the book of Judges. Yahweh had showered benefits on the people ever since they were brought up out of Egypt; still they had constantly fallen away from him, but when they cried out to Yahweh, he had sent them saviours. Now they had claimed a king, though Yahweh their God was their king (v. 12), and Yahweh had enthroned him. Their fate in the future would depend on whether they were obedient to Yahweh. As evidence of how great a sin they had committed, by demanding a king, Samuel called forth a thunderstorm, and the people acknowledged its sin. Then Samuel again warns them to obey Yahweh, and no other gods, and he will not cast off his people.

The description of the king which we find in the law of the kingdom as set forth by Samuel is related to the criticism of the monarchy met with already in as early a document as the fable of Jotham. But now other conditions form its background, it gives a picture of the powerful despotic king with whom Israel became acquainted from Solomon's day. It is no exaggerated criticism. It claims that the Israelites are to be subjects used by the king for his military purposes, for bond service, and for his extravagant household. The people is to contribute to the glory of the kingdom. This is a correct description which strictly speaking might date from the earlier monarchical period, when the exactions of the king had already led to revolts.

A characteristic feature of the description is its purely negative character. It says nothing about the blessing of the king constituting the happiness of the people, or about Yahweh giving victory to the people through the king. The charges made against unfaithful shepherds in the books of Jeremiah and Ezekiel have here been elevated to be the law of the kingdom. That such a document was to be deposited before Yahweh as an embodiment of the prerogatives of the king can only have been imagined by a narrator who was far removed from the actual monarchy.

To this one-sided view of the king corresponds the description of his enthronisation. But here there is a duality. The king has been set up by Yahweh, has been approved and elected by him. And some men who speak in depreciation of the choice of Saul are sharply reprobated (1 Sam. 10,27; 11,12 f.). On the other hand, the strongest disapproval of the whole monarchy is expressed. The people that, according to the description of the king, is made to suffer for everything, has itself, in its obstinacy, demanded a king, merely to imitate other peoples. In reality, however, this is a heinous sin, no less than when it began to worship alien gods in Canaan. For the introduction of the monarchy meant that

7*

the people no longer wanted Yahweh for a king — he who had brought them up out of Egypt and showered benefits on them. Samuel emphatically points out this sin to the people, and it humbles itself and asks forgiveness. But by then it already had the king.

In a narrative about Gideon we met with the view that the introduction of the monarchy meant the abolition of Yahweh's kingship, and on that occasion we saw how difficult it was to reconcile it with the earlier view of the relation between Yahweh and the king. In the narratives here concerned there can be no doubt as to what this idea means. In these the introduction of the monarchy is identical with the discontinuance of Samuel's rule. Samuel is the idealised priest-prophet. He has immediate access to the presence of Yahweh and is an obedient instrument of his will; so it can be said that the people reject not him, but Yahweh. He has ruled like the true Israelite ruler, has not done violence to the weak, nor appropriated their oxen or their asses. The criticism which must from the beginning be directed against the kingship by the common people and the conservative classes, and which is known from the prophets' censure of the social conditions arising under the monarchy, was adopted in ecclesiastical circles, and led to a complete condemnation of the monarchy. At the same time, however, a priestly ideal of a ruler was set up, which assimilated the well-known Israelite demand for righteousness in the king, and made the ruler a priestly executer of Yahweh's will in law and cultus, whose government, therefore, was equivalent to the rule of Yahweh. There can hardly be any doubt that this priestly ideal, represented by Samuel, took shape among the exilic or rather the post-exilic priesthood. It is an expression, in historical form, of the struggle of this priesthood against the king, its former head, who had disappeared but still lived on in history.

These stories of the rise of the monarchy are clearly the strongest expression we possess of Israelite criticism of its own monarchy, its introduction being designated as a regular revolt against Yahweh. Yet this point of view is not consistently carried through. Even the post-exilic priesthood dared not deny that

Yahweh had approved of the monarchy and chosen its founder himself. The author of the story is then led to maintain that the monarchy, which only existed to oppress the people, was introduced exclusively to satisfy the people; and they demanded it in sheer defiance of the rule of Yahweh which had been all righteousness and goodness. And Yahweh had agreed to this, merely to humour the people which rejected him. At last the people had to acknowledge it and confess its sin, the demanding of a despot who would oppress it; but it did not go to the length of deposing him.

Such was the mental attitude towards history of the ecclesiastical circles holding the power after the downfall of the monarchy. In reality the point of view is not very different from that met with in the "Law of the Kingdom" in Deuteronomy. Here, too, it is hinted that the monarchy is introduced because the people desires to imitate the other peoples. It is true that this desire is not directly called sinful, but to make up for it a picture is drawn of the true king which corresponds entirely to the priestly claims, the positive counterpart of the negative picture given in the aforementioned stories.

The new description of the rise of the monarchy is connected with the narratives which make Saul's disobedience to Samuel the cause of his fall (1 Sam. 13,8 ff.; 15,10 ff.). They give a fresh shading to the picture of Saul's fate. Already in the early stories he was placed beside David as the first king, and he perished because David obtained the blessing. In the narratives bearing the priestly impress he is condemned from other points of view, for disobedience to the priest-ruler. And even though he had been chosen by Yahweh, he still came to figure as the first representative of the kingship proper, the institution which the narrator detested. Thus he came to bear the burden of the hatred directed against the founder of a monarchy which his mortal enemy created by destroying him. So strangely can the judgment of history be formed.

The ideas and view points left in the minds of the people by the monarchy were bound to influence the conception of Moses, the leader of Israel at the time of its foundation. We have seen examples of how the old stories from the nomad period were filled with the problems and views of a later time; decrees and ideas obtained authority by being referred to the founder of the nation. It is not possible to show what part of the narratives about Moses is derived from the traditions of the nomad period, what part bears the impress of the monarchical period, and what part dates from the time that lived by the traditions of the monarchical period after the monarchy had disappeared. On the whole it may be said, however, that there is least of the first; but the artificial clothing given to the stories often obscures their contents.

In the conception of Moses as a leader traces of the monarchy are not directly apparent. No account of the authority of Moses immediately reflects the position of the king. But just as Samuel was changed into the ideal ruler of all Israel precisely as a contrast to the king, thus Moses was in still higher degree depicted as the genuine Israelite leader. He lived in the humble circumstances of the true Israelite; he united in himself all leadership as chief, priest, and prophet; and he only let himself be guided by Yahweh with whom he spoke face to face. Like the king he made the covenant for the people, by which it pledged itself to the law of Yahweh. The old legend of the great ruler found in a reed basket and drawn up out of the river was told about him. Narratives dealing with the authority of Moses cannot escape the stamp of that conception of authority which was created through the kingship.

The story of Dathan and Abiram records a revolt against Moses as the master. Moses leads the people about in misery, and then he even sets up to be their master. Moses' defence is that he has not taken as much as one ass from them, nor done evil to any one of them (Num. 16,15), and the ordeal settles the dispute, the rebels being swallowed up by the earth. Moses' defence is that of Samuel (1 Sam. 12,3); he has been a just ruler, and the judgment confirms his rule. Behind the account looms the ideal of the king and the dispute about the right of the kingship in Israel, and the judgment acknowledges the just ruler.

Another revolt was raised against Moses by Aaron and Miriam when he had married a Kushite woman. It is the priest and the prophet rising against the self-glorification of Moses. "Hath Yahweh spoken only by Moses and not by us?" There is a certain obscurity in the connection between the two things which caused the anger of the two: the marriage to a strange woman, and the claim for equal honour as the inspired of Yahweh. Yahweh intervenes, saying that Moses is a man apart, he speaks directly to Yahweh, while others merely have indirect revelations by means of visions and dreams (Num. 12, 1-8). Here we are exclusively concerned with the person of Moses. The story emphasises that he is quite isolated, above priests and prophets; its conception of prophecy points to a time when this was no longer living, and it is difficult to say whether the account has any definite background in the history of Israel.

A couple of narratives deal with Moses' relation to other authorities among the people. We hear how he organised the administration of justice (Ex. 18). All the people came to Moses, occupying all his day in pronouncing judgments. But on the advice of his father-in-law he set up rulers of tens, fifties, hundreds, and thousands, to pronounce sentence in lesser cases, while the more important and difficult ones were to be referred to Moses, who was to lay them before God and then instruct the people in the right laws (v. 19 ff.).

All that we hear of judicial proceedings in the history of Israel shows that there was no stable relation between the various judicial authorities. Only in Deuteronomy do we find an endeavour in that direction, and it corresponds pretty closely with the story of Moses, to which reference is made in the introduction to Deuteronomy (Deut. 1,12 ff.). It is to the effect that in the towns there are to be judges and officers to judge in lesser cases, but more difficult cases are to be referred to the priest at Jerusalem and "the judge that shall be in those days" (Deut. 16,18; 17,8-13). That the Israelites should have had an ordered administration

of justice before the immigration, and then have begun over again
with a simple and variable scheme of a lay judiciary, to arrive,
finally, at the same arrangement as they had had in the early
times of their history is hardly likely. The Mosaic narrative no
doubt deals with the same conditions as Deuteronomy. This does
not exclude the possibility that the story of Jethro may contain
relics of an old tradition. Moses stands for the central authority,
the priestly type of which is implied in the fact that the cases are
to be laid before God, i. e. the oracle. This central authority at
Jerusalem was closely associated with the kingship, united in
Moses with the priesthood and prophethood to an ideal unity.
But most probably the provisions of Deuteronomy date from the
time after the fall of the monarchy. The vague allusion to "the
judge that shall be in those days" would fit in with a time when
it was not known whether the king would return, or what was
to take his place. The lucid organisation described in Deuteronomy
did not exist during the monarchy but was an ideal inspired by it.
The central priestly authority of post-exilic times was derived
from the king, and Moses is the ideal representative of this
authority.

On another occasion we hear about Moses' relation to the
elders. In historical times these were the maintainers and
representatives of the people. We are told that 70 elders represented the people. Of such a general representation we have
no information from the monarchical period. The elders accompany
Moses when he goes up to Yahweh for the making of the
covenant, but not only Moses but also the priests rank above
them (Ex. 24,1 f. 9-11.14). Of the task of these elders we hear
in another narrative. When the Israelites wept because they
received no flesh, but merely manna, Yahweh's wrath was kindled.
Then Moses began to complain. He could not procure flesh, and
he could no longer be the sole upholder of the people, he would
rather be killed. Yahweh then bid Moses gather 70 of the elders
of Israel at the sanctuary; he would impart to them part of the
spirit of Moses, and they should be the maintainers of the
people with him. And the people should be prepared for flesh

in abundance, of quail which Yahweh would send. All this happened. The elders assembled at the sanctuary, Yahweh descended, took part of the spirit of Moses and gave it to the elders, and they raved prophetically. So did two of the elders chosen who had remained with the people in the camp. Moses. was at once informed of it, and Joshua requested him to stop them. But he said: "Art thou jealous for my sake? Would that all Yahweh's people were prophets, and that Yahweh would put his spirit into them" (Num. 11,1-30).

Thus the elders are to share the responsibility with Moses and help him to uphold the people. Their installation into office is associated with the complaints about the lack of flesh; there is no inner relation between the two things, but the complaint of the people is a good motive for Moses' outburst, and the whole story forms a well-connected whole. [1] What particularly interests us here is the way in which Yahweh's spirit is mentioned.

We know that the infusion of the spirit of Yahweh created the chief, and the consecrated king held it as a lasting possession. This knowledge of the spirit has, however, been employed in our story in a merely mechanical way, as if the fact of participating in authority were identical with the possession of the spirit. Nowhere in the early literature do we hear that the elders consulting with the chief were consecrated for this activity by an ecstatic inspiration. The identity of authority with the possession of spirit is so consistently adhered to in the story that the quantity of spirit taken from Moses corresponds to the amount of authority which he gives to each. And the independent possession of spirit, without the leadership of Moses, can be regarded as a kind of revolt, an attempt to secure authority for one's self.

The whole character of the story removes us to a time which was far from the old view of the action of the spirit of Yahweh. The position of Moses as the upholder of the whole people undoubtedly bears the mark of the kingship, but cannot be called a direct reflection of it. More probably the narrative received its form in the postexilic time which operated with the old ideas, now lifeless. In the monarchical period there is no background for the idea of 70 elders sharing in the authority and responsibility of the leader; but in the succeeding period the possibility at any rate is there.

Thus at various points of history we find direct and indirect traces of the effects of the monarchy in the conception of persons and events, in ideas and moods. The judgments passed on the monarchy range from the view of the king as a divine being to the sharpest condemnation of him. This diversity originates from the sudden introduction with the monarchy, under foreign influence, of new institutions which had not grown up organically from the soil of Israel itself. But the monarchy left behind it an ideal of a king and an expectation of its realisation which became of the greatest significance for the descendants of the early Israelites far down into future ages, and no less so for other peoples which inherited it.

THE PROPHET

THE chief was the principal maintainer of the community in early Israel, because the blessing and the will of the community were identical with his. When the king raised himself above the people, the old type of chieftain might still be found in the smaller communities. He had, however, lost his old character of leader in war, and little by little he probably lost his inspiration, being changed into an instrument of the will of the king. The prophet could not by his special faculty acquire importance of the same kind as the chief. But the motive power of both was the same, Yahweh's spirit filled their souls. Hence in early times their activities would sometimes be closely related. And the prophet lost none of his importance when the monarchy became the foundation of Israel. The judging magnates *(śārīm)*, the soothsaying prophets, and the torah-teaching priests were the authorities with which the people became acquainted and by whom they were constantly led till the fall of the monarchy (2 Kings 23,2; Jer. 2,8.26; 4,9; 8,1.10; 13,13; 14,18; 18,18; 26,7.11; 29,1; 32,32; Ez. 22,25-28; Mic. 3,11; Zeph. 3,3 f.; Neh. 9,32). The existence of the people depended on these authorities.

The difference between the chief and the prophet does not lie in the greater or less strength of their inspiration. Both experienced that expansion of psychic power which meant that they were filled with the divine soul. But in the chief this power is converted into violent outward action, into war against enemies, and it strengthens his will to act as a leader. In the prophet it especially produces visions and inward experiences. He can influence things by his power and induce others to act. He has not the chief's responsibility for the community, but he cultivates his inward experiences as something of independent value, hence they are more subtly varied than those of the chief. That the psychic states of the chief and of the prophet do not, however, differ in essence we may learn from the story of the youthful Saul, who meeting a band of prophets joined in their ecstatic ravings, being possessed by the same spirit (1 Sam. 10,10-13; 19,24). But in order to be one of the prophets one must normally become a member of their societies, and this Saul was not. Hence the proverbial saying: Is Saul also among the prophets?

It is true that we hear of prophets acting singly. It is possible that some few individuals might receive the spirit and see visions without associating themselves with others, as Amos says about himself, and as the chiefs experienced it. But everything, the account of Amos too (Am. 7,12 ff.), would seem to indicate that the prophet belonged to or had issued from a society in which he was taught the prophetic experience as an art, as has been the case in corresponding societies in the later history of the East.

The experience aimed at was the ecstacy, in which the divine soul passed in and the self disappeared. The prophets whom Saul joined came down from Gibeah's sanctuary, raving ecstatically, playing the harp, the tabret, the flute and the cither (1 Sam. 10,5). Elisha was transported into a prophetic ecstacy on listening to a man playing the harp (2 Kings 3,15). Each society no doubt had its own rules for it. In a story about Saul we are told that when David had fled to Samuel at Ramah, Saul sent some messengers for him, even three times, but each time they were transported on seeing the prophets surrounding Samuel; and the same thing happened to Saul himself when he came. He stripped off his clothes and fell down naked at the feet of Samuel and lay in this state for a whole day and night (1 Sam. 19, 18-24).

In any case it can hardly have been a common experience to be carried away into an ecstacy and achieve all that the prophets aimed at, merely by watching the ravings of a band of prophets. But the description of Saul's condition is based on sure knowledge of the effect of the ecstacy. Thus 400 prophets stood before King Ahab and King Jehoshaphat raving ecstatically (1 Kings 22,10).

The members of a prophets' society are called "the sons of prophets" *(benē han-nebhī'īm)*. They were to be met with in all the cities of the land, and probably they lived together in a kind of monastery. [1] The societies in the various cities must have had a certain connection with each other. When Elijah and Elisha came to Bethel, they met the "sons of the prophets" there (2 Kings 2,3), as also when they came to Jericho (2,5); and when Elijah was carried up to heaven, 50 prophets' sons stood at some distance and witnessed the event (v. 7).

Of their organisation we know nothing beyond the fact that they had a master. The above-mentioned story of Saul makes Samuel the leader of the prophets' society at Ramah (1 Sam. 19), which is no doubt right even though the story does not seem to bear the stamp of authenticity. On departing this life, the great master might bequeath his psychic power to a close friend and disciple. Elisha received a portion of Elijah's spirit when he passed away (2 Kings 2,9.15), which of course means that he became the leader of his society. The members of the society regarded the leader as their master whose will they obeyed absolutely, and before whom they prostrated themselves deeply (2 Kings 2,15; 6,3.5). Sometimes they would be sent out on a prophetic mission to act with his authority (9,1). They lived with him and had their meals in his company (2 Kings 4,38; 6,1). But neither the leader nor the members were tied to the society.

The sons of prophets from one society might set out to visit a great master (2 Kings 5,22), and they could, like members of Moslem monasteries, have a wife and children outside. Throughout the country one came across such wandering prophets, and people willingly offered them hospitality and gifts (2 Kings 4,8.42; 5,22), for no one doubted that they brought the blessing with them wherever they went. Perhaps they lived solely by gifts; it is possible, too, that, as in Islam, they followed a trade in addition to practising their ecstatic exercises. Of course the support given to their families was not lavish. The widow of the "son of a prophet" who had just died came to Elisha, complaining bitterly, because a ruthless creditor, immediately after her husband's death, had come to carry off her two boys as slaves (2 Kings 4,1).

Elisha himself with his society of prophets had a house at Gilgal (2 Kings 4,38), but it became too small, and they desired to build a new one near the Jordan (6,1). In addition he had his own house at Samaria (2 Kings 5,9; 6,32; 13,17), with a servant to wait on him (4,12.25 ff.; 5,22), no doubt a disciple; here he received the king and foreign statesmen, a great lord, like the leaders of the Sufi societies of Islam. Often he travelled far, thus he went regularly to Sunem, his fixed abode being with a family who built a special chamber for the holy man (4,8 ff.). It was considered a great honour and blessing to house a man of that kind. Elijah wandered still farther, going right down to Horeb.

The prophet wore a mantle of skin with a leather girdle (2 Kings 1,8; Zech. 13,4). Perhaps the skin, as has been conjectured, was that of a sacrificial animal. At any rate the mantle played a prominent part; it was entirely pervaded by the prophetic soul. When Elijah invited Elisha to follow him, he threw his mantle to him, and when Elijah was carried up to heaven, Elisha inherited it with a part of his soul. Both Elijah and Elisha could part the waters of the river with it (2 Kings 2,8.13 f.).

Whether the baldness of Elisha was natural or belonged to the character of the prophet — as opposed to the Nazir, who expressly let his hair grow — we cannot say. Elisha was jeered at for his bald pate by some boys, who had to pay dearly for their mockery (2,23 f.). Altogether the prophets were often ridiculed because they were mad (mˤshuggā', 2 Kings 9,11; Jer. 29,26; Hos. 9,7), which as we know belonged to their calling, but people's mockery did not express their true opinion of the prophets; they entertained the deepest respect for the spirit that stirred them. The same duality of the popular judgment is known from Islam.

What the prophets did in their societies has not been transmitted to us, but we have sufficient hints of it in the accounts of their behaviour and in their own words to enable us to form an idea of it. The ecstatic state played an important part, and continued to do so down through the ages. The designation "mad" is heard both in the time of Hosea and of Jeremiah, and no one has given stronger expression to the ecstatic transports of prophets than Jeremiah and Ezekiel. Altogether the old forms hardly altered much in the monarchical time. Almost by chance we hear that Isaiah was surrounded by a band of disciples and that he calls them his sons (Isa. 8,16.18), just as the prophets' sons of earlier times called their leader father (2 Kings 2,12). The whole institution belonged to Canaan and was closely connected with Canaanite culture. We hear of purely Canaanite prophets, and the Israelite prophets might join them entirely (1 Kings 18,19.40; 2 Kings 10,19; Jer. 2,8). In the course of time Israel brought forth a specially Israelitish type of prophet, produced by the friction between the two cultures. But their distinctive character did not at first influence the nature of prophetism itself, and it is doubtful whether the Israelites from the first had their own special kind of prophecies. The term *nābhi'* is perhaps derived from the ecstatic incoherent cries. The fact that we are told in the story of Saul's anointment that "seer", *rō'e*, was an earlier term for the later *nābhi'* (1 Sam. 9,9, cf. vv. 11.18 ff.) can hardly be interpreted as evidence of an earlier, more Israelitish type, but only as a sign of an altered usus loquendi. A "seer" the prophet had been all his days, and though in later times he was rarely called *rō'e* (as in Isa. 30,10 and in the Chronicles), another term for seer is often met with *(ḥōze,* Isa. 29,10; 30,10; Am. 7,12; Mic. 3,7 et al.).[1]

The ecstatic state was not an end in itself, it accompanied that possession by the divine soul which was the real nature of the prophet. By their exercises the prophets of the societies impelled the presence of the spirit, thus they contributed to uphold the spirit of God and spread holiness throughout the land. They were holy men because the divine spirit dwelt in them, and they carried this quality with them as an inherent character

(2 Kings 4,9). They were "spiritual men" (Hos. 9,7) or men of God, *'īsh hā-rūªḥ* and *'īsh 'ᵉlōhīm* (Judg. 13,8; 1 Sam. 2,27; 9,6 ff.; 1 Kings 13,1; 17,18 etc.), expressions which say the same thing, viz. that the divine soul was in them. This endowment with divine soul gave to the prophet as to the chief a new self-assertiveness, but it also brought him into a new relation to things, and through this he acquired his great importance for the world in general.

The prophets always distinguish between what their own heart says and what the divine spirit says through them. It would be difficult to show how they felt the distinction themselves, but the divine soul must entirely remould their own soul, so that it yielded to what was done with it. The "symbolic acts" of which we hear so often, mean that the prophets personally pass through the entire fate they behold in their vision. Hosea experienced Israel's relation to Yahweh in an unhappy marriage to an unfaithful wife, and their children had names that expressed the fate of the peoples. The names "Graceless" and "Not-my-people" include at the same time the children of the prophet and the children of Yahweh, they are not symbolical the one of the other (Hos. 1-3). We know the same method from names such a "Quick-spoil", "Sudden-prey" (Isa. 8,1-4), and we are acquainted with similar acts, as when prophets butt with horns to express victory (1 Kings 22,11), or go barefoot as "a token" of the abduction of the Æthiopians and the Egyptians (Isa. 20), or carry a yoke like Jeremiah; or when the prophet loses his wife but is forbidden to wear mourning (Ez. 24,15 ff.). [1] Often it must be assumed that these actions have not been carried out by the prophet, but are part of his vision; thus, for instance, the marriage of Hosea by which his experience of the greater fate becomes more intense.

The substance of the prophecy was so intimately a part of the prophet's soul that an influence working on his soul also affected the prophecy. Therefore Ahab could punish Micah, the prophet of evil, and seek to keep him under; and Elisha's servant who carried his rod imbued with power was forbidden to greet others lest he effect a spiritual exchange with them (2 Kings 4,29).

When a man of God had uttered his prophetic threat against the altar at Bethel, and Jeroboam had received proof that he really spoke words full of power, Jeroboam invited him to a meal and offered him a gift, but the man of God refused. For by receiving such gifts from the king he was drawn into his sphere, and this might affect his prophetic purpose. The sequel to the story is peculiar. An old prophet invites the man of God to his table, falsely pretending that it is by the command of Yahweh, and then pronounces Yahweh's judgment on him when the man of God obeys him, thus breaking the command he has himself received from Yahweh (1 Kings 13). This narrative gives us a peculiar insight into the way in which men might attempt to sway destiny through the prophet, but also into the curious manner in which prophets might try whether their fellow prophets were obedient to the spirit of Yahweh.

The feeling that he was filled with the spirit of Yahweh gave to the prophet a high-strung selfconsciousness. Through him Yahweh says "I". His speech is not his own, it comes from the depths where all power is concentrated. This makes the prophet highly sensitive to injuries, those who aim at him, hit Yahweh, for he is Yahweh's mouth (Jer. 15,19).

When Amos was driven away from the royal sanctuary at Bethel by the priest Amaziah, he pronounced violent curses against the priest in the name of Yahweh: Now listen to the word of Yahweh: Thou sayest: Prophesy not against Israel and utter not words against the house of Isaac. Therefore Yahweh saith thus: Thy wife shall be an harlot in the city, and thy sons and thy daughters shall fall by the sword, and thy land shall be divided by line: and thou thyself shalt die on polluted soil; for Israel shall be carried away from its land (Am. 7,16 f.).

Jeremiah is just as violent to those that oppose him. He says to the men of his native town: Thus saith Yahweh against the men of Anathoth that seek thy life saying: Thou shalt not prophesy in the name of Yahweh that thou die not by our hand! — then Yahweh of the hosts saith: Behold, I will punish them; the young men shall die by the sword, their sons and their daughters shall die by famine. And no remnant shall be left of them, for I will bring evil upon the men of Anathoth in the year of their visitation (Jer. 11,21-23). And when the superintendent of the temple in Jerusalem had put Jeremiah in the stocks for a whole day because of his seditious speeches, Jeremiah raised his voice, saying: Yahweh doth not call thy name Pashhur, but "terror-far-and-wide". For thus saith Yahweh: I will make thee a terror to thyself and to all that love thee. They shall fall by the sword of their enemies while thine eyes behold it. .... and thou Pashhur and all that dwell in thine house shall go into captivity, and thou shalt go to Babylon, and there thou shalt die, and be buried there with all thy friends to whom thou hast prophesied lies! (Jer. 20,1-4.6). King Jehoiakim, too, is cursed by Yahweh when he has burnt the roll with all his prophecies (36,29-31), and Jeremiah treats similarly an opponent who has requested the superintendent of the prophets to deal with the rebellious prophet (Jer. 29,25 ff.). Attacking his prophecy is sacrilege, because he knows that it is Yahweh who utters it through him.

Conversely, those who support Jeremiah in some way or other obtain his blessing as the helpers of Yahweh. Baruch is to be saved from the general disaster (Jer. 45,1-5). The Kushite Ebed Melech, who has pulled Jeremiah out of a cistern, in the mud of which he was about to perish, has shown his trust in Yahweh: I will deliver thee, and thou shalt not fall by the sword, but thy soul shall be given thee as thy spoil because thou hast put thy trust in me, saith Yahweh (Jer. 39,18). Thus the personal moods and feelings of the prophet grow with his consciousness of being filled with the spirit of God. His friends and his foes are raised into being for or against Yahweh.

Just as we have narratives recording how Yahweh called some of the early chiefs to their office, so also we have stories of the consecration of prophets. In these the sum and substance of the prophet's mission is concentrated in one, first, pregnant experience. This applies to Jeremiah and to Isaiah. Both saw visions and were told by Yahweh what their teaching was to be. The vision of Isaiah was the most sublime, for he saw Yahweh himself sitting on a throne, his huge train filling the temple, and beings from among his following, Seraphim, consecrated the prophet's lips with a live coal from the holy altar (Isa. 6,1 ff.). To Jeremiah Yahweh's words were: Before I formed thee in the belly I knew thee, and before thou camest forth out of the womb I sanctified thee, and I ordained thee a prophet unto the nations (Jer. 1,5).

The intimate connection of Isaiah's experience with the sanctuary is no chance feature, it is, on the contrary, characteristic of the activities of prophets. The holiness created by them was, as we saw, to be found precisely in the sanctuary. They could draw inspiration from it, just as they contributed to maintain the power of the holy place by performing their exercises there and making the spirit of Yahweh appear.

When the great decisive struggle took place between Yahweh and Baal, it was a ritual battle, centring round the sacrifice. But prophets alone officiated at the religious rites, Elijah on the one side and 450 prophets of Baal on the other. They moved round the altar in a circle with rhythmic motions and wounded themselves with sword and spear "according to their custom" (1 Kings 18,26.28). Here we get a hint of the important part played by the prophets in the Canaanite cult, and of course they became equally prominent when the Israelites adopted it. When Jehu gathered Baal's staff in his temple, it consisted both of prophets and priests (2 Kings 10,19).

We have already seen that the prophets are constantly mentioned in connection with the priests, but there are only slight indications of their special participation in the Canaanite cult of the Israelites. Such are perhaps to be found in Isaiah's mockery of the drunkenness of priests and prophets (Isa. 28,7, cf. Mic. 2,11), and Jeremiah's complaint of the adultery committed by the prophets with the daughters of Israel (Jer. 29,23). But we possess clear evidence of Canaanite prophetic custom being continued in Israel in an undatable utterance which says that Yahweh will entirely destroy the idols; "and the prophets also and the spirit of impurity I will expel from the land. And if a man will still behave like a prophet, his father and his mother who bore him shall say unto him: Thou shalt not live, for thou

8*

art speaking lies in the name of Yahweh. And his father and his mother who bore him shall stab him when he behaveth thus. And on that day the prophets shall be ashamed each of his vision when he is prophesying. Neither shall they put on a hairy mantle to deceive. And he shall say, I am no prophet, I am an husbandman, for a man made me an owner from my youth. And if they say to him: What are these wounds between thy arms, he shall answer: Wounds I have given myself in the house of my lovers". (Zech. 13,2-6).

The prophet shall be put to shame and denied by his nearest relatives and friends, if he does not give up his activity of his own accord. And we recognise the old features of this activity. He wears a hairy garment, speaks prophetic words, and he has taken part in the Canaanite rites and gashed his skin in the house of the lovers, i. e. in the sanctuaries of the Baals.

Altogether, we hear constantly of the connection of the Israelite prophets with the cult and the temples. The prophet Samuel officiated at the offerings, and his holiness was so great that on festival days he went the round of the towns and blessed the offerings of the inhabitants. The prophets which Saul met when he left Samuel, were just descending with music from the sanctuary of Gibeah, still in the ecstatic state to which they had been transported in the sanctuary. The prophet, like the priest, belonged to the sanctuary. Hosea mentions, as one of the numerous signs of lawlessness, that the prophet is pursued in the house of his God (9,8). When Amos desired to speak to the people of Ephraim, it was natural to him to do so in the royal temple of Bethel, but he was told that he had nothing to do there. Jeremiah always speaks in the temple at Jerusalem, and he complains that priest and prophet alike desecrate the house of Yahweh (Jer. 23,11); and the Lamentations express grief at the killing of priest and prophet in Yahweh's sanctuary (Lam. 2,20).

The prophets, when urged by their inspiration, might appear singly in the temple with their pronouncements, but they might also, as their whole character made it natural, appear in a body.

They constituted a stable part of the staff of the temple, and we learn that in the temple of Jerusalem they were organised under a leader who was responsible for them (Jer. 29,26). Priests and prophets belonged together in the temple. The priest Pashhur, who had a leading position in the administration of the temple, prophesied, too (Jer. 20,6), and prophets like Jeremiah and Ezekiel were priests (Jer. 1,1; Ez. 1,3). As late as the post-exilic period people could apply to the priests and prophets of Yahweh's temple with enquiries concerning the continued observance of the day of lamentation at Jerusalem; and the prophet Zechariah intervened in the matter by announcing Yahweh's decision as it had been revealed to him (Zech. 7,3 ff.). When vital prophecy disappeared, the prophetic activity in the temple ceased of itself. But it is probably a correct observation that the organisation of the temple prophets reappears in the Levite mentioned as the leader of the oracles (1 Chron. 15,22.27). [1] This answers the question as to what finally became of the prophets associated with the temple.

––––––––––

The prophet is known especially as the man of words. "Torah will not perish from the priest, nor counsel from the wise, nor the word from the prophet" (Jer. 18,18). The word is to the prophet what action is to the chief. Behind the word, however, lies the experience to which it gives expression, something seen or heard. Often the prophet's speech gave no clear presentation of his experience. It is described as cries from stuttering lips, and mockers imitate its babbling incoherence (Isa. 28,10 f.). In the ecstatic state it might consist of mere exclamations, a fact which shows that the tense feeling had gained the mastery; all control of the self had gone.

The words and actions of the prophets show that their experiences were closely related to those undergone and described by many mystics. When possessed by the divine soul the prophet acquired a new relation to things. He saw what was behind them, their totalities or their souls, not their single components, but that from which they sprung. Behind the surface he came near to things, their usual laws were suspended, everything was possible. The soul of the prophet could govern them and bend them to his will; what was distant approached: he saw events lie as in a bud not yet expanded. These were the experiences which he expressed in his words and acts.

In a heterogeneous collection of prophetic sayings we are given a picture of the type of prophet which was no doubt the commonest in the whole pre-exilic period. He is in the sanctuary, wearing his hairy garment, transported by his ecstasy, wounding himself with savage gashes, and during or after this he announces the visions he has had, in the name of Yahweh (Zech. 13,1-6). The stories of Balaam are a testimony to the connection between the rites of the temple and the inspiration of the prophet. Balak is ordered to build no less than seven altars and sacrifice a bullock and a ram on each. In this way a sphere of holiness is created, and the prophet may expect the divine presence. Balaam then goes alone to a bare hill. And God comes towards him and inspires him with the vision which he then puts into words (Num. 23,1 ff. 14 ff. 27 ff.). The inspiration is still active in the form of the utterance, which is rhythmical like the speech of poets.

A number of stories which must be derived from prophetic circles describe how things take on an altered shape when they come in contact with the psychic power of the prophet. When Elisha's friends at Sunem lost their son, the prophet came to their aid. First he sent his servant with his rod which he was to lay on the face of the boy, but he was to be careful not to disturb the psychic power of the staff by exchanging greetings with anyone. The rod turned out to be useless. Then Elisha came himself, shut himself up with the boy, and prayed to Yahweh. Thus strengthened and concentrated, he covered the boy's dead body with his own, and shortly after the boy came to life (2 Kings 4,18-37). During the famine the same man of God could make oil flow in the empty jars (4,1-7); he would feed a hundred people with some few barley loaves (4,42-44); he would bless a bath in the Jordan so that the Aramæan leader was healed

(2 Kings 5); he would make an axe dropped into the river float (6,1-7), and so forth. After his death even, he could call the dead to life, when they touched his bones (2 Kings 13,21). Remarkable events spring up around the figures of the prophets. Fiery hosts appear and defeat a hostile army surrounding the prophet's native town (2 Kings 6,17 f.), fire comes down and burns up messengers from the king who intends evil to Elijah (1,10.12), he himself, finally, is taken up to heaven in a chariot of fire — all this expresses that there was no limit to the power of the strong prophetic soul to recreate its environment. It is the prophet's own feeling of his relation to things which is transformed into these stories.

Very often people applied to the man of God, asking him to heal them. He was the physician who was to bring new strength to the sufferer, and if they found no help with one, they tried another, perhaps as in Naaman's case in a foreign country. We learn from Naaman's words that on such occasions the man of God sought to gather new strength by moving his hand towards "the place", i. e. the sacred place (2 Kings 5,11). Sometimes they did not directly apply for help but merely asked how things would fall out. Jeroboam's wife went in disguise to the prophet Ahijah at Shiloh to ask what would be the end of her son's illness, and received the stern answer that he was to die for the sins of his father (1 Kings 14). Ahaziah sent word to Ekron to learn, not from Yahweh but from Baal Zebub, what would be the outcome of his illness, but Elijah saw to it that the king received the message of Yahweh, though he would rather have done without it (2 Kings 1,1-8).

These appeals show that the people recognised the power of the prophet to see behind things, and they took advantage of it in all the events of life. If some asses had strayed, you could ask a man of God to divine where they were to be found. He could see people far away and understand distant talk (2 Kings 5,26; 6,12.32 f.); he could see rain coming and behold far-off events (1 Kings 18,41; 20,13 ff.; 2 Kings 8,10 ff.), not only could he heal, but he could strike with disease and disaster (1 Kings 13,4 ff.; 20,36; 21,19 etc.). It was necessary to bring a gift for the prophet as an acknowledgment that he had given something, and so must be honoured. Saul and his boy very carefully searched their sacks to see what they had before they could think of going to Samuel to ask him about the asses (1 Sam. 9,7 f.). Jeroboam's wife took with her ten loaves, a jar of honey and other food on her journey to Shiloh (1 Kings 14,3). And Naaman took a large amount of gold and silver and ten festival robes to Elisha, but this time the prophet would not risk depreciating his own gift, so he refused to receive that of the stranger (2 Kings 5,5.15).

There was strength in visiting a man of God and being near him. He was visited especially on the holy days which corresponded to his own character (2 Kings 4,23). And sometimes people brought him gifts from the first fruits of the land (4,42), for it was a good thing to share the harvest with him that it might obtain a share of his holiness.

There was, at any rate in the old times, no fixed limit to the spheres in which a man of God might exercise his activities; his deep insight and his strong words were always in request. Only, it was necessary to find one, of whom it could be said that Yahweh did not let his words fall to the ground, or that what he said was sure to come true (1 Sam. 3,19; 9,6). The word he spoke when moved by the spirit of God was a word from God, and any one who possessed such a word could always easily reach him whom it concerned (Judg. 3,20).

The prophet, whose whole nature associated him so closely with the activities of the priest in the sanctuary was thus, in a different way from the chief, a counsellor of the people. He could see a connection which was hidden from the chief, and could therefore give counsel by pointing out the way; but the chief was the leading will and power in action. A prophetic voice might be raised and rouse the wills of the whole community, even that of the chief, as when Deborah roused all Israel to action. But most frequently the prophetic, God-inspired counsel was sought by those who needed it in the grander or more humble circumstances of life. It would not be easy to find the way without the advice and guidance of the men of God. It paralysed the people's power of action if Yahweh's word did not come, if it was "precious" (1 Sam. 3,1), because they could not act without it. Amos describes the disintegration that this would mean: Behold, the day shall come, saith the Lord Yahweh, when I will send hunger in the land, not hunger for bread, and not thirst for water, but to hear the word of Yahweh. They shall wander from sea to sea, roaming from north to east in quest of the word of Yahweh, and shall not find it (Am. 8,11 f.). When Amos spoke these words, there was not always the old harmony between the prophet and those who desired prophetic guidance.

The activity of the prophet was so nearly related to that of the chief that sometimes they were bound to coincide. When people went to the prophet for a word which carried authority, it seemed natural to solicit his judgment in judicial cases too. We learn that Deborah, the prophetess *(nebhī'ā)*, sat under the Deborah palm, somewhere between Ramah and Bethel, and pronounced judgment in all cases the Israelites brought before her (Judg. 4,4 f.). A man of God like Samuel is described in the tradition as a chief, a priest, and a prophet.

The great importance of Samuel may be gathered from the story of how he was born after his mother Hannah had made a special vow in the sanctuary at Shiloh. In her desire for the honour of motherhood, she dedicated to Yahweh for the whole of his life the son for whom she was praying, and vowed that no razor should touch his head (1 Sam. 1,11); thus he was to have the character of a Nazir. And Eli, the priest of the temple, promised her that her prayer should be granted. When Samuel had been born and weaned, his mother did take him to the temple of Shiloh, and here he grew up as a servant of the temple before Yahweh, dressed in priestly robes (1,24; 2,18 f.). In the night too he remained in the sanctuary, where he slept, and here he was awakened by Yahweh's voice speaking to him. He did not yet know the voice of Yahweh, so he thought it was Eli call-

ing him. The third time, however, Eli understood that it was
Yahweh and bid the boy say: Speak Yahweh, thy servant
heareth. This happened, and now Yahweh announced to Samuel
the impending fall of Eli's house (3,1-18). Samuel grew up and
Yahweh continued to reveal himself to him at Shiloh. And he
let none of his words fall to the ground; all Israel realised that
he was a true prophet (3,19.21). Thus Samuel imperceptibly
advances from being the servant of a priest to being a prophet,
and was acknowledged as such by all Israel.

In the story of Saul's anointment (1 Sam. 9) we meet with
Samuel as an honoured man of God. Here he is a man visited
as a seer, not only by people from his own town. At the sacrificial
feast he blesses the victim, and at the meal he acts as the chief
officiating at the ceremony. But the nucleus of the narrative is
the description of how Samuel as prophet anoints Saul to be
king of Israel. This is the culmination of Samuel's prophetic
activity. In the account of the anointment of David Samuel's
figure is of the same kind, but has grown; he is a maker of
kings who travels from city to city, striking terror where he
goes; and he officiates as a matter of course at sacrificial meals
in other towns.

Samuel's character of chief appears more plainly in other
narratives. It is recorded that he acted as judge, and settled
cases at Bethel, Gilgal, and Mizpeh besides in his native place
Ramah, where he built an altar (1 Sam. 7,16-17). Thus he went
on circuit in an area with his home town for its centre, but this
is expanded to the statement that "he was judge of Israel all his
days" (7,15). In this capacity we have already become acquainted
with him in the narratives in which Saul's kingship is first introduced. Even after his death his authority is felt, when Saul
conjures him up to ask his advice (1 Sam. 28).

It is true that he never becomes a warrior. But he causes
the defeat of the Philistines in a way that accords with a later
view as to how a victory should be won. After Samuel had made
the Israelites abolish the alien gods, he gathered them for a
solemn repentance at Mizpeh, where he then held a court of
justice. Now the Philistines advanced against them. But Samuel

offered a burnt offering to Yahweh, and immediately Yahweh made a thunderstorm break over the enemy; they were confounded and Israel won an easy victory which was complete and final (1 Sam. 7). Here Samuel is the mighty priest-prophet and chief whom we know from the hostile description of the election of the king (8; 10,17-27; 12). He fills in the empty space before Saul as an ideal figure created by the later priesthood in their own image, but having traits of the king, since he carries out the work of a ruler, but without the means and equipment of the monarch.

The transformation of the figure of Samuel has probably brought to development elements already present in the old narratives. But the various sides of his activity have been extended without inward coherence, so that his figure lacks life. In a psalm he is mentioned beside Moses and Aaron as one of the great priests of the past (Ps. 99,6). It is in his capacity of priest that he acts as a superior to the unhappy king whom he continues to chastise and humiliate, though he has given up his office as a ruler to give place to Saul. The starting-point of this great power may be that Samuel, in the old narratives too, was honoured as a counsellor and judge in virtue of his authority as a "man possessed by the spirit". We may find a hint of such traits in the story of his activity as a judge (1 Sam. 7,16 f.), but a literary separation of them is not feasible.

But even of what should be the core of Samuel's personality, the priestly and the prophetic, and the mutual relation of these two aspects, we obtain no clear picture. The only really vivid stories of these things are those dealing with his growing up in the temple at Shiloh and the anointment of Saul, but they are without any mutual connection. And even in these perspicuous and vivid narratives we must sometimes ask ourselves whether they have really come down to us in a form giving us images in complete agreement with Samuel's own time. The story of Saul's anointment takes it for granted that Saul is chosen through the instrumentality of Samuel as the first king of the people of Israel. He has been elevated to the line of kings which otherwise began in Jerusalem. Here already Samuel is the instrument

by which Yahweh carries out his decisions concerning his people
Israel. And in the story of Samuel's first prophetic experience
it is to him that the fall of the house of Eli as a hieratical line
is announced. In spite of the sinister message, there is something
idyllic about the night scene in the temple which does not perhaps
quite agree with the passionate prophesying of the old time.
Samuel hears the voice of Yahweh but does not know it yet.
Yahweh's voice seems to be imagined as something quite external,
perceptible, and Samuel hears it as a human voice giving him
some message, without any inner stirrings. This was how in
later ages, remote from it, the intercourse of the old men of God
with Yahweh was conceived.

That does not exclude the presence in these narratives of old
subject matter, and we may divine in it a prophetic figure of
grand dimensions, a man whose abilities gave him an activity
extending from that of the prophet not only to the domain of
the priest but also to that of the chief. Later ages, in their
eagerness to make his figure more prominent have obliterated
its features and deprived it of its original life.

In the old days the men of God filled the country with their
holiness, and made it possible for the people to live its life by
their counsel and pregnant word, and altogether imparted to it
their strength in the way required by circumstances. When the
monarchy strove to gather all authority to itself, it also had to
subordinate to itself the mighty force of prophecy and turn it
to account. We have seen that Isaiah mentions among the pillars
on which the kingdom is based the prophet and the soothsayer
(nābhi' and kōsēm) besides two kinds of exorcists (Isa. 3,2 f.).

Between the prophet and the soothsayer there cannot
originally have been much difference. For kesem must have meant
a strong word (Prov. 16,10); a typical man of God like Balaam
is called a soothsayer (kōsēm, Josh. 13,22), and the term is used
several times in connection with the word "seer" (hōze). Whether
the fact that it is as a rule false seers that are discussed in that

connection, [1] is characteristic, is not easy to say, but we sometimes hear that soothsaying is the task of prophets (Mic. 3,11).
Still it is curious that *kesem* is occasionally regarded as an
abominable practice as opposed to prophecy. Deuteronomy puts
it on a level with various magic arts and the act of passing one's
children through fire. It is said that the Canaanites listen to
people who practise such arts (Deut. 18,10.14, cf. 2 Kings 17,17).
In historical accounts, too, we find it designated as a sin.

The difference between prophecy and soothsaying lies in the
fact that in the latter the decision is the important thing, and
it can be gained by various strange practices; behind prophecy
lies the psychic experience of the prophet and it is made Israelitish by happening in the name of Yahweh. This does not apply to
the methods of the soothsayers and the exorcists when they try
to get behind the surface of events. Although both prophecy and
the other practices were originally Canaanite, the former could
therefore separate itself from the Canaanite element, whereas
exorcism could not. *Kesem,* which at first included both forms,
then incurred reproach together with exorcism. We see it used
about the procuring of oracles by calling up the souls of the
dead (1 Sam. 28,8), and we even have a complete account of
how a Babylonian king secured a *kesem* for himself by strange
practices (Ez. 21,26). It is not only Deuteronomy which mentions
that Israel's nearest neighbours had people who could give
them *kesem,* besides prophets, interpreters of dreams, sorcerers
(kashshāphim) and other diviners (1 Sam. 6,2; Jer. 27,9) just
like the Israelites (Jer. 29,8).

Saul is said to have forbidden the calling up of the dead, but
had recourse to it himself, when his perplexity had reached the
point of desperation. As the normal means of getting behind
the surface of things and finding an expedient, three things are
mentioned, viz. dreams, prophets, and the oracle. Any one could
receive a message through a dream from the events which had
not unfolded themselves, but in this respect, too, the special
power of the prophet appeared, [2] so it was all the more important
to have good prophets.

It was especially when great events were impending that the

king needed prophets, mostly before and during a war. Therefore he had a whole order of prophets attached to his court. Jezebel, Ahab's wife, had 450 prophets of Baal, and 400 prophets of Ashera who had their meals at her table (1 Kings 18,19), but in addition a large number of Yahweh prophets were in the service of Ahab. We become acquainted with them in the scene describing how Ahab and Jehoshaphat tried to ensure victory over the Aramæans at Gilead. Jehoshaphat wished to hear the word of Yahweh. He summoned 400 prophets. Transported into the ecstatic state, they saw the victory which they expressed in words and triumphant gestures, all except Micah, the son of Imlah. The king sought to suppress him, but his vision was the profoundest (1 Kings 22).

During a previous war with the Aramæans a prophet had promised Ahab the victory in the name of Yahweh and shown him who was to open the battle. Afterwards he could let the King know that the Aramæans would take up arms again at the new year. We know that in such cases deliberation and calculation must play a prominent part, but it is nevertheless in the last instance instinct which determines the able leader's decision. In the depths of the prophet's soul instinct created a vision of spontaneous certainty which he felt to be infused by God. It was of the greatest importance for the king to have such a man at his side, and we learn, in fact, that the above-mentioned man of God accompanied him in the various events of the war (1 Kings 20,13.22.28).

We have similar stories of other kings. When Jehoram and Jehoshaphat with the king of Edom went on an expedition against Mesha of Moab, they ran short of water on the plains. They then agreed to question Yahweh through Elisha, for "with him is the word of Yahweh". Elisha sent for a minstrel, and when he had played for some time, "the hand of Yahweh came upon him" (2 Kings 3,15). He commanded them to dig a hole in the chasm. Here he saw water in abundance, and he saw Moab's defeat. And what he had seen was confirmed (2 Kings 3). We have other stories of how Elisha perceived the King's plans so that he could always communicate them to the king of Israel, and it became possible to prevent them. And when the enemy sent out people to capture this strong prophet, they were stricken blind, and Elisha led them about as he liked (2 Kings 6,13-23). No wonder that the king made so mighty a man responsible for the troubles that befell Israel (2 Kings 6,31), but now Elisha saw the victory which was to free them from distress. Yahweh let the enemy hear the noise of an advancing army, and they fled for their lives (2 Kings 7,1 ff.). As late as when Elisha was lying on his deathbed and was visited by King Joash, he let the king shoot a victorious arrow against Aram, laying his hand upon that of the king, so that his power passed into the victorious act (2 Kings 13,14 ff.). The victories of the great Jeroboam II were promised him by Jonah, the son of Amittai (2 Kings 14,25).

Some of the stories show a tendency to magnify the active power of the prophets to enormous dimensions. The stories of the prophets exhibit the idealisation in prophetic circles of their great men of the past, but the idealisation is merely a magnification of what was familiar from the activity of the prophet.

When entering upon important undertakings the king constantly applied to the prophets for a word from God. David had Gad and Nathan; Rehabeam, Shemaiah (1 Kings 12,22); Jeroboam, Ahijah (11,29 ff.); Jeroboam II, Jonah, and so forth. When the book of law had been found in the temple, Josiah sent a message to a prophetess, one Hulda by name, to hear Yahweh's decision about it (2 Kings 22,13 ff.). As late as the last days of the monarchy we hear prophets foretell the ruin of Babylon in the temple (Jer. 28). Since prophets, as we have seen, were appointed at the temple of Jerusalem, the king must no doubt have employed their power here in the cult as a psychic foundation for the monarchy. Like the king, however, the prophets have entirely disappeared from the ritual laws, a sign that these reflect conditions at the post-exilic temple, where prophecy had died out, just as the king had gone. But relics of the oracle-giving activity of the prophets may perhaps still be traced in some psalms. [1]

The relation between the king and the prophet is of a peculiar kind; the prophet is in the king's pay as his helper and servant.

But he is so by virtue of a power that gives him an importance of his own, and since it is rooted in the divine power itself, it endows him with an authority, which is by no means always minded to subordinate itself to that of the king, but may even claim to be greater than it.

Prophets may intervene in the course of events and make kings. Elisha sent one of the members of his prophets' guild to the army of Israel to anoint Jehu, a commander, to be king. When his fellow officers asked him what the "madman" wanted (v. 11), Jehu answered contemptuously that they must know how that kind of people usually behaved. And yet they all attributed the greatest authority to the anointment. Neither Jehu nor the others were in doubt that by the action of the prophet Jehu had become transformed, and they carried through his election (2 Kings 9). We even learn that Elijah was commanded by Yahweh to anoint a king outside Israel, viz. Hazael of Aram (1 Kings 19,15). This story stands apart, but another prophet story connects Hazael's election with Elisha. He was in Damascus when Benhadad was ill. The king, desiring to question Yahweh through the medium of the foreign man of God, sent him an enormous gift by Hazael. And now the latter was told that Benhadad was to die, that Hazael was to become king, and that the prophet's people would suffer for it. This utterance made Hazael a claimant to the throne. He thought it most convenient to hasten on events, so he smothered the sick king with a wet towel (2 Kings 8,7-15).

As a rule the authority of the king need not conflict with that of the prophet, however great this may be, because they are so different. The prophet did not want to be a king. Elisha was acknowledged at his death by Joash, king of Israel, who bent over him weeping, and crying out: My father, my father, Israel's chariots and horsemen! (2 Kings 13,14). He was the upholder of the people's strength, worth as much as all its military defences.

The mixture of independence and subordination which characterised the prophets' relation to the king might make them active members of the factions that grew up round the monarch. The prophet Nathan was one of the principal men among those who worked for the succession of Solomon at the court of David (1 Kings 1,8.10.11.22 ff.). The prophets whose discourses have come down to us were constantly intervening for or against political plans. As late as post-exilic times, when Nehemiah was at Jerusalem, and he was suspected of wanting to be king, it was asserted that he had ordered prophets to cry: King of Judah! (Neh. 6,7), just as his opponents used prophets to further their designs on him (6,12.14).

The prophet's independence of the king might make him censure the king's actions, and he might then be a source of danger to the king, for he was in no doubt as to the divine origin of his authority, and the people thought the same. We have seen how a prophet might abandon the ranks of the other prophets and see other visions than those desired by the king; but this was of the nature of prophetism, and it was the king's business to balance the various testimonies against each other. Even then, however, he could not be sure of having finished with the prophets.

When Ahab had won his second victory over Benhadad and taken his enemy prisoner, he agreed to come to terms and set Benhadad free in return for getting back some bazars which his father had owned in Damascus. A "son of a prophet" thought this a sin, and resolved to let the king know it in a forcible way. He made another son of a prophet wound him. Then he tied a bandage over his face and stood as a wounded warrior by the roadside where the king was to pass. When the king came, the wounded man complained that he had let go a prisoner for whom he must answer with his own life or a talent of silver. The king declared that he could not escape that responsibility. The prophet then removed the bandage, the king recognised him and understood what it all meant; he had pronounced his own doom. The prophet gave him the judgment, saying in the name of Yahweh: Because thou lettest my banished man escape out of thy hand, thy soul shall be responsible for his soul, and thy people for his people. — Indignant and despondent the king returned to his capital (1 Kings 20,35-43).

It was not the only time Ahab had to hear a prophet's censure of his actions. Elijah spoke sternly to him for the outrage done to Naboth, when he wanted his family property, and Elijah waged a constant war against him for his Canaanite cult. After the murder of Naboth Elijah foretold the ruin of his house (1 Kings 21,19 ff.). And when he had won his victory over the prophets of Baal, he had them cut down (18,40).

Here we meet with the prophet in another aspect of his relation to the king, an aspect which we are constantly coming across. Even David had to submit to the reproaches of Nathan after having sinned with Bathsheba. By his story of the unscrupulous wealthy man who took the poor man's only lamb, he led David — like Ahab — to pronounce judgment on himself. And Nathan added: Why hast thou despised Yahweh's word by doing what is evil in his sight? (2 Sam. 12,9). Gad, who had supported him when he was a fugitive (1 Sam. 22,5), announced Yahweh's condemnation of the census he took of the people (2 Sam, 24,11 ff.). Jehu, the son of Hanani, announced to Baasha his impending ruin (1 Kings 16,1-4.7). In the books of the Kings it is almost the rule that every king had his prophet who was to chasten him and announce Yahweh's doom to him.

This has been reduced to a mere form and exaggerated by the author of the books of the Kings; it harmonised with his whole character to represent the prophet as the man who chastened and humiliated the king, as a congenial spirit had described it in his stories about Samuel. But behind this lies the historical reality of which the whole of the prophetic literature gives evidence, viz. that a series of prophets very forcibly asserted their authority against the king, being conscious that Yahweh spoke through them.

It is, however, a characteristic of these prophets that their independence of the king does not consist merely in their differing from other prophets, against the wishes of the king, as was the case, for instance, with Micah ben Imlah. Their censure is based on more than a momentary difference of opinion.

It appears most plainly in the history of Ahab. Elijah, in the name of Yahweh, announces to him God's punishment, because he has broken the old laws of Israel, first by violating the law of ancestral property, later by sanctioning an open murder.

Further he fights Ahab because he keeps up the Canaanite cult, especially in its Phoenician form; and against the upholders of this form of cult Elijah first fights the intense ritual fight, and later he has them all killed. And if we ask what blame the above-mentioned prophet's son laid upon the King, the answer is that it was the same thing for which Samuel blamed Saul, when the latter allowed Agag to live. He had broken the stern law of war, under which Yahweh demanded the extinction of his enemies; for this sin the prophet made him responsible.

The sum of it all is that the aforementioned prophets adhered to the traditional Israelite customs. On this foundation they formed their utterances and their actions. All they aimed at was a reaction against any breach of the old Israelite law, whether it was a breach of family law, violence and bloodshed, the acquisition of an alien mentality by the practice of an alien cult, or showing mercy to the enemies of Israel.

The type of reactionary prophets with which we first meet in the time of Ahab persists down through the ages, and it is the type with which we are most familiar, because all the prophets whose utterances have come down to us belong to it more or less. It arose as a protest against the mixing with the Canaanite element, but only — as is usually the case with reactions — when the mixing was in the main completed, and had also set its stamp on the reactionaries.

The presupposed position of the prophet among the people in the earliest times was that he and they stood on the same level. The prophet only differed from the rest by his experience which created strength among the people and gave him faculties which it might turn to account. Among the reactionary prophets circumstances are entirely different. A rupture has occurred in the people, and the prophets occupy quite a different ground from the greater part of those around them. To fight for this ground, the special Israelite element as it developed in the revolt against the Canaanite culture which had pervaded it, became the chief mission of these prophets. To speak from this ground was to speak in Yahweh's name, to fight for traditional Israelite custom, was to uphold the word of Yahweh.

It is clear that this must bring about a considerable change in the nature of prophetism. The ecstatic state with its holy power, its experiences and visions, no longer became the only or the essential thing. The background acquires much more importance. It must be purely Israelite in the sense of the prophets of the reaction. To maintain it must come before everything else, for a word which does not accord with Israelite *mishpāṭ* cannot be a word from Yahweh. Hence we see from the behaviour of Elijah that the fight for what is Israelite ranks far above everything else. Towards the prophets of Baal, he behaves not only as a prophet, but also as a warrior. And the messages which both he and the wounded son of the prophet utter have nothing to do with ecstatic experiences. They are simply dooms pronounced on those who have committed a breach of Israelite law. Thus the prophet became the motive power in the fight against what was alien to Israel, a chastiser and a propagandist, the constituted guardian of Israelite psychic life.

The rise of this transformed type does not mean a complete rupture with the character of traditional prophetism. We know traits of the life of Elijah which tell us that he knew the ecstatic state like other prophets, as when he ran in front of the king's chariot at Jizreel, seized by the hand of Yahweh (1 Kings 18,46), or when he was suddenly carried from place to place by Yahweh's spirit (18,12), and he wandered for 40 days after having eaten one meal only (19,8). His visions he experiences while squatting with his face between his knees (18,42) or standing up, with his head covered (19,13). In that position he heard the voice of Yahweh as a soft and gentle sound.

The history of Elijah shows that already in his time the prophets were divided into two bodies. He says that the prophets of Yahweh were killed (19,10). He himself killed Baal's prophets. The story of the wounded "son of a prophet" shows that there were prophets' guilds of the traditional type which joined reactionary prophetism.

If we pass down the ages to the first prophet whose discourses have come down to us, viz. Amos, we see him standing apart from the prophets' guilds. The priest Amaziah expelled him from the royal temple at Bethel, saying that he could go to Judah and prophesy and gain his livelihood there. But Amos answered: I am no prophet *(nābhī')* and no son of a prophet, but I am a shepherd and dress the sycamore. And Yahweh took me from my flocks, and Yahweh said unto me: Go and prophesy to my people Israel (Am. 7,12-15).

The words of Amaziah show us that the prophets at that time played as important a part as in the old days. They prophesied to the people, and received gifts in return; and the sanctuary seemed to Amos the natural place to do it. But the remarkable thing is that Amos denies being a *nābhī'* or the son of a prophet. This means that he belongs to no prophets' guild, hence has not received that training in prophetic experiences which in the early days was the chief thing for the prophet. Hence he says, as a contrast to this, that Yahweh took him directly from his flocks, to tend which was his daily task.

And yet Amos does not feel isolated. Yahweh speaks in him and lets him see visions like other prophets. He feels at home in the ranks of the prophets. He says in the name of Yahweh: Among your sons I let some appear as prophets and among your young men some as nazirites, is it not thus, Israelites? saith Yahweh. But you gave the nazirites wine to drink, and you bid the prophets: Prophesy not (Am. 2,11 f.). He shows how necessary the prophet is to the people when he speaks of the hunger that shall come for the word of Yahweh, but which shall not be satisfied. And he has experienced the constraint to which the prophet is subject. Yahweh does nothing without revealing his secrets to his servants, the prophets. And when he has spoken the prophet must needs prophesy, as surely as the roar of a lion excites fear (3,7 f.).

Thus the prophets are as much needed as ever, and it is just as necessary for them to speak when impelled by Yahweh. Hosea, too, feels his kinship with the circle of prophets. No one escapes from his chastening words, king, priest, or layman, the prophet only is an exception, he who is Yahweh's mouthpiece, through whom He tries to guide the people (Hos. 6,5; 12,11). And he blames people for calling the prophets and the spiritual men mad *(mᵉshuggāʿ)* and fools (9,7). The prophet is the true leader of Israel. She was brought up out of Egypt by a prophet, and later on preserved by a prophet (12,14). And with these Hosea associates himself.

In Hosea and Amos we see the prophetic type first met with in the time of Ahab (9th century) continued. The contrast has become more marked. The discourses of the two prophets show how they resented the whole life of the Israelite community, not only the Canaanite cult of the Israelites and the rupture with the Israelite social organisation in its relationship to the lowly, but the whole refined way of living involved by city culture. Just as the Wahhabi coming from their poor desert villages were amazed at the sumptuousness of life in the cities of Islam that had entirely altered the old Islamic customs to which they themselves still adhered, thus also the Israelite prophets were shocked at the life of luxury they witnessed, which their fellow countrymen believed to be Israelite. Their objection was to the whole luxurious life of the towns, the magnificent houses of ashlar and cedar, the artistic architecture, with arches, panelling, and ivory in the halls (Isa. 9,9; Jer. 22,14; Am. 3,15; 5,11); the life of the citizens with its dainty food, wine, and oil, with singing and playing of harps, which they enjoyed while they lay stretched on couches of ivory, was all levity (Am. 6,4-6, cf. 8,3), wild grapes in the vineyard of Israel (Isa. 5,4). Antagonistic to all this, the prophets demanded the reintroduction of the old manner of life in Israel. The old social spirit with its truth and love, *ʾᵉmeth* and *ḥesedh* (Hos. 4,1), was to reign once more, Israelite *mishpāṭ*, Yahweh's old law, was to prevail, foreign customs obtruding themselves were to be abhorred. Thus the prophets came to form a party, a cultural type within the people. They claimed to represent Israel proper, and hence to be the conscience of the people, and their actions derived strength from the fact that they spoke with the authority of prophets, in the name of Yahweh and inspired by him.

The prophetic experience no longer derives its importance from the fact that it creates holiness for the prophets and the community, but from the circumstance that it affords security that Yahweh is behind the prophetic utterances. A definite limitation is given to the revelations, they are entirely determined by the fundamental view of the prophets and the relation of the people to it. This could not fail to influence the very nature of the inspiration.

When Amos says that he is not a prophet's son, this means that he takes no part in the common exercises which create a common holy spirit and therefore, so to speak, are an end in themselves. Nor indeed does he need them. The visions and the message, which were but the fruit of the ecstasy and the holy state to the early prophets, are all to Amos. He and his like were "sent" by Yahweh, they had been entrusted with a mission, a message to announce for a definite purpose. They are the speakers of words that slay (Jer. 23,29; Hos. 6,5).

The speeches of the reactionary prophets pronounce a doom on the cultural life of Israel. Their teaching is that it will lead to destruction, because it is against the law of Yahweh and hence sinful. In this respect there is a striking uniformity in the speeches transmitted to us, and as a rule we do not find much in them which shows evidence of ecstatic prophecy. But to the ancients both the poet and the speaker were divinely inspired, as we know it for instance from the Arabs; for all spiritual exaltation and concentration is regarded as an inspiration. Therefore the Israelite prophets could become speakers fighting for a certain manner of life, and yet feel no change from the prophetism of the old days. The visions in which they saw the ruin of the depraved people, and the passion with which they denounced the existing conditions, arose from an agitation of the soul identical to them with the early prophets' possession by the spirit. And they could not doubt that it was the spirit of Yahweh by which they were possessed, for they were urged onward in the service of Yahweh. The connection with early prophetism was constantly felt, too, in the conduct of the prophets. The lives of Isaiah, Jeremiah, and Ezekiel all show features of an ecstatic character. But like Amos they hardly worked up the ecstasy in company with others for the sake of gaining the holy power. Inspiration was a vocation, an election by Yahweh; hence it turned to the individual. Not only was it to fill his soul, it was also to give him a mission to carry out, a struggle with those about him which, as we know from Jeremiah, might fill him with unspeakable pain.

Isaiah calls the prophet a watchman (Isa. 21,11 f.). Expressions such as scout and lookout are also used (Isa. 21,6; Jer. 6,17; Ez. 3,17). This means that they are to watch over the people and its fate. They are its admonishers, who see the danger threatening from within, and hearken when it draws nigh from without, with the armies of the Assyrians and of other foreign powers. Unlike the early prophets their attention is always directed outward towards the political combinations, for they feel assured that it is from there the inevitable punishment will come.

Their activity consists entirely in correction and chastisement. When Jeremiah is called to be a prophet, Yahweh says that he will make him a fortified city, a pillar of iron, and walls of bronze against Judah and all its authorities (Jer. 1,18 f., cf. 15,20 f.). Therefore he is to lead a solitary life, remote from his countrymen (Chap. 16). Again and again we hear him complain of his loneliness and the persecution and mockery of his foes. And yet he has not taken this burden upon himself; Yahweh has laid it upon him and must, therefore, take vengeance for him on his enemies (15,10 ff.; 17,14 ff.; 20,7 ff.).

In Isaiah the contrast with the people is even more sharply emphasised. The people is so far removed from the prophet that his speeches have the opposite effect to that intended. Yahweh has poured out upon the people a spirit of slumber, so that the prophet's speeches have become to it as the words of a sealed book (29,10 ff.). This makes the prophet so indignant that he sees this detestable issue as the very result Yahweh wanted his speeches to bring about — Isaiah is to appear merely in order to stupefy this people hardened in sin. "Go and tell this people: Go on hearing, yet understand not; and go on seeing, yet perceive not. — Make the heart of this people dull, and make their ears heavy, and shut their eyes, lest they see with their eyes, and hear with their ears, and their heart understand, and convert, and be healed" (6,9 f.). The admonitions of the prophet become a regular act of vengeance for their perversity. No longer uttered to guide the people, they are a doom. The prophets are judges, even of the entire world, says Jeremiah (1,10), because they represent the only true type of man.

The new type of prophet must have arisen in circles of the people to whom the prevailing culture was foreign. Though the continuity with the old type was preserved, the new type was nevertheless so far removed from it that the dissimilarity was greater than the similarity. As the old type did not, of course, disappear because a new one arose, there were now two kinds of prophets. We know the reactionary type best, because their speeches have come down to us. The others we know only from the point of view of the latter. Hence they are called false prophets.

It is especially Micah and Jeremiah who are concerned with them. Micah says: Thus saith the Lord concerning the prophets who lead my people astray, who announce peace when they have something to bite with their teeth, and consecrate a war against him who putteth nothing into their mouths: Therefore a night shall come unto you, that you shall not have a vision, and it shall be dark unto you, that you shall not divine. The sun shall set upon the prophets, and the day shall darken over them. The seers shall be put to shame and the soothsayers confounded, and they shall all cover their lips for God gives no answer. But I am full of power, of the spirit of Yahweh, of judgment and of strength to declare unto Jacob his transgression and to Israel his sin. Hear this, you heads of the house of Jacob, and you judges of the house of Israel, who abhor justice and make the straight crooked, who build up Zion with blood-guilt and Jerusalem with iniquity. Its chiefs judge for bribes, and its priests give oracles for gifts, and its prophets divine for silver. They lean upon

Yahweh and say: Is not Yahweh in our midst? No evil shall befall us. Therefore shall Zion for your sake be ploughed up as a field, and Jerusalem shall become a heap of ruins, and the temple-hill as wooded heights (Mic. 3,5-12).

The first thing we notice in this attack is that the prophets are classed with chiefs and priests, that is to say, with the maintainers of the people. We are not concerned with a few insignificant prophets who have been led astray, but with the whole normal prophetic type, they who, with the other authorities, form the foundation of the people's life and, as we gather from Isaiah (Chap. 3), are among the pillars of the kingdom.

What Micah blames the prophets for is not that they have no right to call themselves prophets. On the contrary, the implication is that they do have prophetic visions; but they lead the people astray by declaring peace, i. e. happiness, where there is no peace. Micah accuses them of doing this when they receive gifts, while they exhibit the most violent hostility, when these are not forthcoming. The charge against them is that they treat God's word with levity, and Micah blames them for taking any money at all for their prophecies. This probably refers to their conduct when people applied to them personally. But when it comes to the question of the great peace, of the fate of the people, then they rely on Yahweh dwelling in their temple, and trust that he is sure to keep away disaster. As a punishment for the levity with which they treat the visions, they shall be entirely deprived of them, and their blind reliance on the temple shall come to an end with its destruction.

From this utterance it will appear that a prophet of Micah's type did not give prophecies for gifts. Nor would his utterances have been suitable for it, for they do not deal with the kind of questions in which the people asked the prophets' advice. The prophet speaks of the conduct of life, Yahweh's law, and Israelite *mishpāṭ*. He has the prophetic power, which he does not deny to the others, but which they are to lose; he is full of strength and the spirit of Yahweh. And unlike the others, he is to use this inspiration to judge the people for their sins, declaring that their whole conduct of life is a failure, is non-Israelitish. Therefore it is impossible that Yahweh should ensure their continued happiness. To announce this is true prophetism. The curious thing is, however, that he regards his own and the others' prophetic inspiration as being in the same class.

The prophet complains that people listen willingly to the other prophets, and in a passage whose interpretation is doubtful, he accuses them of giving ear to a prophet who is given to wine and strong drink (Mic. 2,11). Isaiah, too, speaks of prophets and priests who reel with wine and totter with cider, and stumble in their trances (28,7), a testimony that these prophets, like the priests, were closely connected with the Canaanite cult. It is the normal prophet whom Micah is describing and combating, because he is an important maintainer of the Israel which Micah wishes to reform. And the features here described by an antagonist agree very well with what we know of the prevailing type of prophet in Israel.

In Jeremiah's struggle with the prophets we again find the same traits as in Micah. He says: Both prophet and priest, they are all false dealers. They heal the wounds of my people lightly, saying, Peace, peace, and there is no peace (Jer. 6,13 f.; 8,10 f.). Therefore the punishment will not fail to come. And it shall come to pass in that day, saith Yahweh, that the heart of the king shall perish, and the hearts of the princes; and the priests shall be appalled and the prophets confused. And then said I, Alas Lord Yahweh, surely thou hast deceived this people and Jerusalem, saying, Ye shall have peace, whereas the sword hath cut unto the heart! (Jer. 4,9 f.). The prophets are in the main responsible for the people besides the king, śārīm, and the priests, (13,12 f.; 32,32), for they have always promised the king and the people victory (14,13 ff.; 27,9.14 ff.; 37,19). We are here given a picture of the Israelite community in decay: king, magnates, priests, and prophets are paralysed in their souls, and there is a general collapse. It will happen because they are living an unrighteous life, and yet the prophets try to hide the impending ruin by announcing peace. Jeremiah does not, any more than Micah, deny that the prophets have visions from Yahweh. He may even go a step further and say that it is Yahweh that has inspired them with the deceitful promises of peace, just as he once caused a lying spirit to enter into Ahab's prophets (4,10, cf. 1 Kings 22,22). It may be because the prophecies are presented as part of the cultus of the temple, or because they are uttered in ecstasy, in the proper form, that Jeremiah dare not deny that they are inspired by Yahweh.

In any case, we have other instances that Jeremiah is not afraid of accusing the prophets of speaking out of their own hearts. He once had an encounter in the royal temple of Jerusalem with a prophet Hananiah, in the presence of priests and others, in the period between Nebuchadrezzar's two descents upon the city. Jeremiah went about carrying a yoke of wood as a sign that the subjugated people must submit to the yoke of the Babylonians. Then Hananiah came forward, saying in the name of Yahweh that the yoke of the king of Babylon was broken and the exiles would return with the holy vessels of the temple. Jeremiah expressed a doubt, but Hananiah broke the poles of his yoke; thus would Yahweh break the yoke of Babylon. Later Jeremiah received a message from God that Yahweh would make a yoke of iron, and lay it upon the people like a yoke of Babylon. Now he said to Hananiah: Listen Hananiah! Yahweh hath not sent thee, but thou hast made this people trust in a lie. Therefore thus saith the Lord: I will cast thee from off the face of the earth; this year thou shalt die, because thou hast taught rebellion against Yahweh (Jer. 28).

We see how Jeremiah is carried from doubt to certainty the moment God inspires him with his word, and from that hour he is certain that Yahweh has not sent the other prophet, hence he has sinned against Yahweh. The same thing is said directly as a message from Yahweh against those who proclaim peace: The prophets are prophesying lies in my name, I have not sent them, neither have I commanded them, neither spake I unto them. They prophesy (mithnabbe'im) unto you lying visions and soothsaying (ḳesem), and phantasms and the deceit of their own hearts (14, 14). The old expression for being in a prophetic ecstasy is here, characteristically enough, used about the utterance of a prophecy, and the old term for the powerful word has here become a caricature of prophetism. For such are the utterances of the prophets of fortune: "they speak a vision of their own heart, and not out of the mouth of Yahweh" (Jer. 23,16). "I sent not the prophets, and yet they ran, I have not spoken to them, and yet they prophesied" (23,21). It is even hinted that they steal the word of Yahweh from each other (23,30), and so speak at second hand. Competition had entered into prophetism, it became necessary to impose one's self and utter prophecies that would enhance the authority of their author.

Jeremiah fought against prophets all his life. Even among the exiles there arose prophets whom he combated (29,8). Thus he realised his vocation as a man of strife. He speaks of plots against his life and meets his opponents with violent curses (18, 18-23; 28,16). Zephaniah, too, says that the prophets of the country speak boastful and insincere word (3,4) and Ezekiel compares the prophets to people who paint a wall with whitewash which is quickly washed away by the rain; they speak out of their own spirit, having had no vision (Ez. 13,3.10 f.; 22,28).

With these warring prophets the people was in a very difficult position. This was nothing new, we know it from the days of Ahab, when Micah ben Imlah alone held out against all the other prophets. In the case of men whose whole conduct gave evidence of emptiness and imitation, it was important to distinguish a genuine inspiration from a fictitious one; but neither Jeremiah nor Micah deny that the others may have visions, it may be Yahweh who sends a lying spirit into them. What, then, was the people to believe?

Jeremiah says to Hananiah: The prophet who prophesies peace, when the word of the prophet shall come to pass then shall it be known that Yahweh hath sent the prophet with truth (28,9), i. e. it is neither his own invention nor a deception sent from Yahweh. And Deuteronomy says: If the prophet speaketh in the name of Yahweh, and the word doth not happen and doth not come to pass, then it is a word which Yahweh hath not spoken; it hath been spoken by the prophet in his presumption, thou shalt not fear him (Deut. 18,22). Here there is no reference to a deception from Yahweh. But the facts are to show who spoke Yahweh's truth.

This is quite in accord with the nature of prophetism. The visions are to contain the reality which unfolds itself later; but this is no good to people at the time they hear the prophecy. In reality of course there was no possibility of security. The prophets tried to get behind the events and penetrate to their root; but they had to compete about who could go deepest; he only whose power was entirely divine could penetrate to the bottom. The prophet saw the truth in the same measure as he received strength from Yahweh, but the presupposition was that he did receive it from Yahweh. Here we have come to what was the characteristic feature of the reactionary prophets in Israel. It was not as in the old days enough to have a purely psychic power to let one's self be filled with the spirit. The prophet had to be Yahweh's man in the sense that he knew and acknowledged His demand for a genuinely Israelite behaviour. To maintain this was the first duty of the prophet, and he must know that any deviation from it was a sin which would lead to disaster. A prophecy not in accord herewith could not be derived from Yahweh (Jer. 23,26 ff.), hence it was a false prophecy. In that case it was no matter whether one acted like the prophets of Samaria who prophesied in the name of Baal (Jer. 23,13), or uttered prophecies in the name of Yahweh, a name which they tried designedly to make people forget (v. 27).

The new type of prophet had a revolutionising effect on the authorities which formed the foundation of Israelite popular life. It caused dissension among the prophets and weakened the old prophetic type. The magnates were condemned with the prophets, as also the priests, whose activities in the Canaanite-Israelite cult were so closely akin to those of the prophets (Isa. 28,7; Jer. 2,8; 5,31; 8,10; 23,11; Hos. 4,5; Mic. 3,11; Zeph. 3,3 f.). To make up for it, the prophetic castigators proposed to lay a new foundation, or rather strengthen the old one, by inducing the people and their authorities to be guided by the old law of Yahweh, adopting its simple customs, Israelite solidarity against everything foreign, and faithfulness to Yahweh.

The relation to the king was determined by the whole character of the new prophetic type. The prophetic figures familiar to us did not reject the monarchy, especially the Davidic monarchy, any more than they rejected prophetism or priesthood, but their criticism was aimed at the actions of the king no less than at those of the others. Their interest in dangers threatening Israel from the great powers was bound to direct their attention to what the king was doing. They showed the same frankness to the king as the early reactionary prophets had done.

Hosea says that the Ephraimite kings were chosen without the consent of Yahweh, set up by the people themselves, who are already beginning to feel that the king is no good (7,3.7; 8,4; 10,3). Hosea seems to have had no direct relations with the king, but clearly he blames him as the protagonist in the whole of that conduct of life which offends him (see especially Hos. 7). And his condemnation of the appeal to Egypt and Ashur (7,11) shows him to be consistent in his demand that Israel should preserve her old manners and customs and have no dealings with strangers. Political relations with other countries are an evil; Israelites should trust to Yahweh alone. They should only come into contact with foreign powers when these descend upon them and destroy them for their sins.

It was impossible for the kings to feel safe with these troublesome men. The king was, or was to be, the centre of the blessing, gathering all powers to himself, and he had prophets at his disposal so as to be able to fulfil his task. But these prophets stood on another level than the king, and they did not bow to his authority, for they had the highest authority, that is, direct from Yahweh. And encounters could not be avoided, for the prophets were always occupied with that for which the kings were responsible, the relation of their people to foreign powers.

When the kings of Damascus and of Ephraim were going to attack Jerusalem, King Ahaz had to submit to being rebuked for his fear by Isaiah who declared that they should do nothing and was willing to offer any miracle as a proof. The king of Israel could safely remain inactive, merely trusting to Yahweh (Isa. 7). What would have happened if the king had accepted the prophet's

offer, we shall never know. But the king would not leave the
responsibility to the uncalled prophet; he rejected his offer.

Isaiah behaved in a similar way to Hezekiah, when he was
besieged by the Assyrian king Sennacherib. But according to the
narrative the king himself sent for Isaiah, who declared that the
city would not be taken (2 Kings 19; Isa. 37), and on another
occasion Isaiah is said to have reproached Hezekiah because he
showed his treasures to some Babylonian ambassadors (2 Kings
20,12 ff.; Isa. 39). There is another story of how Isaiah is sent
for by King Hezekiah in the way of the ancient men of God,
and heals him with a fig plaster (2 Kings 20; Isa. 38). Apart
from this narrative the information we have of Isaiah's relations
with the king conveys the same impression. The king is to keep
aloof from strangers and merely put his trust in Yahweh. And
on this point Isaiah speaks as one who has greater authority than
the king. With the same force he declared that the sins of the
country would lead to its destruction.

When the last days of the kingdom drew near, and misfortune
after misfortune befell the people, Jeremiah, like a watchman,
announced the coming of disaster. This is the last encounter between the prophet of evil and the authorities of the realm.
Jeremiah constantly saw calamity threatening Judah, and he
made Baruch write down his utterances and read them in the
outer court of the temple to any one who cared to listen. But
such messages of disaster were not appreciated within the precincts of the temple; other voices were usually heard there. The
king was informed, he had the speeches read to him, and as they
were read, he burned them on a brazier, by which act he sought
to check the danger; he tried also to secure the person of
Jeremiah, just as Ahab had previously seized Micah ben Imlah
(Jer. 36).

But misfortune made the king feel insecure. When Zedekiah
had ascended the throne, he tried to win over the dangerous
prophet, but he, too, heard only words of ill omen from Jeremiah (21,1 ff.; 37,1 ff.). After the prophet had been imprisoned,
the king's respect for the strong man of God was still so great
that he secretly asked him for a word from God (37,17). When

the Chaldaeans were approaching, Jeremiah stood in the midst of the general confusion, proclaiming loudly that the inhabitants could only save themselves by flight, and the officers would have had him put to death, because he "weakened the hands" of the warriors and the people (38,1 ff). Once more Zedekiah turned to Jeremiah, and he then received the answer that he could only save his life by flight .The prophet knew the risk he ran by his utterances, for he made the king swear first that he would not kill him because of the word from God (38,14 ff.).

It is characteristic that one of the prophets of the opposition was imprisoned, and was then on the eve of the general collapse asked for advice by the king in the last days of the monarchy. Even after the great disaster, the people with some of their officers entreated Jeremiah to ask Yahweh where they were to go, and what they were to do (Jer. 42,3). It was ten days before the message came from Yahweh, bidding them stay in Canaan and not go to Egypt. But they accused him of speaking lies, Yahweh could not have said that they were not to go. They thought that he wanted to entrap them (43,2 f.), so they went to Egypt after all, taking the prophet with them.

On comparing Hosea or Amos with Jeremiah in their relations with king and people, we see that Jeremiah is drawn more into the events of the day. His advice is even asked in special affairs, because his prophecies of evil have proved truer than the predictions of others. He was regarded not only as a judge of conditions in general, but as a man of God who, like the other prophets, could guide the people and tell them what was to be done in a certain situation. But they only did it reluctantly, and even without confidence.

In reality there was, indeed, a difference between Jeremiah and the other prophets. The officers complained of the rebellious prophet, saying: This man seeketh not peace for this people, but disaster (Jer. 38,4). They demanded of a prophet that he should stand by his people as one of its supporters. He was to use his psychic powers to see visions which could show them the way out of difficulties, onward to peace and happiness, as the prophets may be supposed to have done in the cultus at the temple. But

Jeremiah and his sympathisers stood on quite a different ground. They also desired happiness for Israel and believed in it. But the Israel in which they believed was quite different from that to which they spoke, it was an ideal only existing in their minds. They did not wish to abolish either the monarchy with its chiefs, or the priesthood, or prophetism, but they wanted them all to be transformed together with the people, and when this came to pass, the blessing would come of its own accord. All their talk about the future was determined by this fundamental view.

During and after the exile prophets continued to appear who sought to influence the political situation by their utterances. Between the two falls of Jerusalem Hananiah proclaimed in that city the exiles' deliverance from Babylon, as we know from Jeremiah's conflict with him (Jer. 28). In Babylonia Ahab and Zedekiah delivered the same message, but were stopped by the Babylonian government (29,21 f.). The importance attached to the conduct of the prophets may be gathered from the fact that Jews in Babylonia sent accusations to Jerusalem against Jeremiah while he, in a letter, denounced those who proclaimed deliverance in Babylonia (29,24 ff.). And Ezekiel continued the activity of the earlier prophets of doom, his words being addressed both to the exiles and to those at home. When Cyrus began his Persian campaign of conquest, Deuteroisaiah prophesied the return of the exiles and the regeneration of the people; and the restitution, especially of the temple cult, was largely due to the intervention of Haggai and Zechariah. When Nehemiah undertook to arrange affairs at Jerusalem, he too had to fight against prophets who supported his opponents. A whole series of nameless prophecies which have come down to us seem to date from the post-exilic centuries.

Thus the ancient institution of prophetism continued to exert its influence on the life of the people far down through the ages. As late as the Maccabaeans no one dared decide what was to be done with the desecrated altar stones in the court of the temple because there was no prophet to guide them, and the decision was postponed until the advent of a prophet who could help (1 Mac. 4,46, cf. 14,41).

Gradually prophetism lost its spontaneity. The visions did not arise intuitively in the soul of the prophet, but were determined by tradition. From the prophecies of the past, visions of the future were extracted which were arranged and systematised, and such visions of the future, detached from their origin, obtained an independent meaning. The prophecy was supplanted by the Danielic type of apocalypse.

Prophetism, however, acquired its greatest importance by the fundamental view which the prophets of doom fostered among the people. The chief significance of the early prophets was that they formed centres of holiness throughout the country, and by virtue of their holy power they could see behind things and become spiritual supporters of the people. The reactionary prophets laid the whole stress on their teaching. It required no ecstatic experience in itself, but it appeared in the form of prophetism, compelled by the tradition which governed psychic life. Hence the ecstatic character is more or less prominent. Such traits abound in Ezekiel, but in Deuteroisaiah there is no trace of them; he is a speaker, and a poet, yet he is fully entitled to a place in the series of prophets, a prophet devoid of prophetism in the original sense.

The responsibility of the prophet, therefore, becomes essentially that of the moralist. When he has warned the sinner he may wash his hands of him, whereas he is co-responsible for the sin if he refrains (Ez. 3,16-21). And if he gives helpful advice to an Israelite apostate, his guilt is so great that he, as well as the sinner, must suffer death (14,1-11).

The sharp line of distinction drawn in the population between true and untrue Israelites was the work of the prophets. In the monarchical period they formed, as it were, a cell of another kind in the organism of the people; their idea of the true Israel was so different from the prevailing state of affairs that they could not fail to become an element of discord. As late as just before the fall of the kingdom we see how the king tried to keep Jeremiah at arm's length.

After the fall of the kingdom, all this was altered. The monarchy and the priesthood of Jerusalem, the chief pillars of the common life of the people, had been shattered, but the prophet survived. That the predictions of the prophets of evil had been fulfilled must be a testimony that it really was Yahweh who had spoken through them. Their zeal for the purely Israelitish in contrast with what was foreign tended to preserve the Israelite community in its exile. And the above-quoted utterance of Ezekiel shows how sternly the solidarity was enforced. Thus it came to pass that the spirit of the prophets of doom set its mark on exiled Israel from which the new community of Judaea was built up.

This spirit makes itself felt in the historical view transmitted to us. It shaped the ideal of a king which we have seen grow up after the fall of the kingdom. And while history lets the king recede into the background, it exalts the prophet. He rebukes the king and shows him the way. Nathan is no longer a mere helper among those about David, he is an intermediary between Yahweh and David, a man who acts with Yahweh's authority towards the king. Samuel is the ideal prophet, who has the full authority and therefore chastens and disciplines Saul. Already in early times Moses was regarded as a prophet. "By a prophet Yahweh brought Israel out of Egypt" (Hos. 12,14). He became the prototype of all later prophets (Deut. 18,15); for he had the spirit. Yahweh appeared to him as to a prophet in the burning bush in the desert. But he was greater than all other prophets in his own age or in later times, for whereas Yahweh spoke to others in visions and dreams, he spoke to Moses mouth to mouth, and Moses beheld Yahweh himself (Num. 12,6-8; Deut. 34,10). The other prophets received revelations as to single questions only, but to Moses the whole of Yahweh's will was revealed in the law.

All this implies a changed conception of the prophet. He is no longer the living instrument of the divine soul filling him, but a man speaking with authority as the mediator between God and man. The prophets are men of God in the sense that they are especially dear to God. The patriarchs become prophets

(Ps. 105,15), Abraham is called a prophet and it is added that when he prays for Abimelech, he shall live (Gen. 20,7.17). Chronicles lets Isaiah write Uzziah's history (2 Chron. 26,22), because he was the spiritual man of the period. Every period has its authority, and this is a prophet.

THE PRIEST

OF the three leading authorities among the people the priest retained his importance the longest. While kingship disappeared abruptly upon the fall of the kingdom, and prophetism ebbed out in the course of time, the priesthood survived and acquired a steadily increasing power and influence. In the light of this development one might in post-exilic times speak of "our kings and our priests" as the men responsible for the fate of the people under the monarchy (Ezr. 9,7).

In the early times no one could be a leader of the people without being an instrument of the spirit of Yahweh. But whereas the chief and the prophet obtained their authority through the inner power which their spiritual inspiration gave them, the priest acted as the servant of the spirit at some sanctuary where it was present. About the priests at such sanctuaries we possess a few accounts from the earliest days. [1]

A man by name Micah, who lived in the mountainous district of Ephraim, procured an idol, and at the temple in which he placed it, he appointed one of his sons priest, he "filled his hand". [2] However, there was a young Levite *(lēwī)* of the house of Judah who was staying at Bethlehem as a sojourner *(gēr)*. He left the town to seek his fortune as a *gēr* in another place, and when he happened to come to Micah, he was asked to stay there. "And Micah said unto him: Stay with me and be a father and a priest unto me, and I will give thee 10 shekels of silver a year and a suit of apparel and thy victuals" (Judg. 17,10). The Levite then stayed with Micah, and the latter said: Now I know that Yahweh will do me good, seeing I have the Levite to my priest (v. 13). — At that time the Danites were seeking another dwelling-place. They sent out some scouts who on their way

put up for the night at Micah's house. Recognising the voice
of the Levite, they went to him and questioned him. And they
begged him to ask God whether they would prosper on their way.
The answer was that Yahweh would prosper their undertaking
and they went on hopefully until they found a suitable dwelling-
place. When later on the tribe passed the same way, they invaded
Micah's sanctuary, took the sacred objects with them and the
priest too, saying that he should be their father and priest and
thus become priest to a tribe and house in Israel instead of being
priest to a single man. They then continued on their road, seized
the town chosen for them, later called Dan, and there they set
up the captured idol. And Jonathan, the son of Gershom, the
son of Moses, officiated as priest at the sanctuary of Dan, and
his descendants after him, until the country was conquered and
the inhabitants carried into exile (Judg. 17-18).

The last remark shows that the narrative must have taken
shape after 734, and it cannot be supposed to have been preserved
unaltered through the succeeding centuries. The story purports
to describe the origin of the sanctuary at *Dan,* the most important
sanctuary next to Bethel in the northern kingdom, and likewise
to give the history of its priesthood; thus it affords an insight
into the conditions of the priesthood in earlier times. A man
might have a private priest, and might give this post to his son,
but it was preferable that he should be a Levite. He has the
requirements necessary for acquiring the authority of a "father".
His activity was entirely confined to the temple, its idol, and
its oracles. He was a Levite and as such he would settle wherever
his services were in request, and he traced his descent from Moses,
the first chief of the people. The story shows us how easy of
access the calling of a priest was, but also that a priest who
was attached to a certain sanctuary would found a line of priests
at the sanctuary, a natural result of the Israelite conception of
the family.

We know such priestly dynasties from other temples. At
Shiloh Eli was priest with his two sons, Hophni and Phinehas.
We hear of the death of all three; the sons were slain in the war
with the Philistines, when they took part in it as the guardians

of the Ark, and Eli fell from his chair and was killed in his terror at the evil tidings (1 Sam. 4,11.18). However, his house was not extinct. Phinehas' widow gave birth to a son, Ichabod, immediately after the death of her husband (4,19 ff.). But another son of Phinehas, Ahitub, carried on the dynasty, for his son Ahijah accompanied Saul as his priest in the war against the Philistines (14,3.18).

At the same time there lived at *Nob* a priest, Ahimelech, the son of Ahitub, as leader of a community of priests (1 Sam. 21,2; 22,9). He is often regarded as identical with Ahijah who is then supposed to have left Shiloh and gone to Nob. This, however, is hardly likely. Ahimelech was the head of a very large family of priests at Nob (22,11.18) which must therefore have had a long history. Hence it is inconceivable that the head of the house should have been transferred to the place from another temple one generation earlier only. It is, in fact, probable that Ahijah was still priest at the sanctuary of his forefathers in Shiloh (1 Sam. 14,3). The priestly house of Nob, which was so predominant in the town that it was actually called "the priests' town" (22,19) came by a terrible end. Ahimelech aided David in his flight from Saul unaware that he was helping an enemy of the great chief. An Edomite informer brought the news to Saul, and this sealed the doom of the priesthood. The informer himself was ordered to cut down all its members; they were jointly responsible for the help given by their head to Saul's enemy (1 Sam. 22,18 f.). After the fall of the kingdom, when there was an endeavour to interconnect the various priesthoods, the priests of Nob also were brought into relationship with those of Shiloh (1 Kings 2,27).

Only one of the priests of Nob escaped disaster. This was Abiathar. For him there was only one thing to do, to fly to David, who at once owned himself guilty of the destruction of his house. He therefore entered into a covenant of faith with him, saying: Stay with me. Fear not, for he who seeks my life seeks thine also [1]; surely thou art in safe keeping with me (1 Sam. 22,23). David kept the covenant. During his wanderings he had always Abiathar with him, and received oracles from him (23,6.9; 30,7 f.).

We hear of no priesthood in Gibeah where Saul lived. It may be taken for granted that there were priests at the sanctuary of the city, but it is characteristic of the position of the chief in early times that there is no mention of such a priesthood having played any prominent part among those immediately about the chief. In crucial situations the priests at Shiloh, where the Ark was, came into the forefront. And Ahimelech's defence before Saul (22,15) shows that there was often communication between Nob and the chief's place when an oracle was required, for its priesthood possessed the authority.

David who founded a new monarchy, also laid the foundation of a new priesthood at *Jerusalem,* which was to become of overwhelming importance for Israel. As David's priests are mentioned his own sons, about whose priesthood, however, we learn nothing further (2 Sam. 8,18), and besides them, Ira, of the family of Jair, which belonged to the district east of Jordan (2 Sam. 20,26), and in the first place Abiathar ben Ahimelech from Nob, who had faithfully followed him, and Zadok, the son of Ahitub (2 Sam. 8,17; [1] 20,25); these were both with him when he fled from Absalom (2 Sam. 15,24 ff.). On that occasion we learn that they had sons; Abiathar, the son Jonathan; Zadok, the son Ahimaas (v. 27.36), so they could both found a dynasty of priests.

The various priests may have served at different sanctuaries in Jerusalem, and of course there must have been many more priests in that city than the above-mentioned. There is a conjecture that Zadok was connected with a sanctuary at Jerusalem before David captured it. [2] The story of the conquest of Jerusalem cannot easily be reconciled with the destruction of sanctuaries and priesthoods, hence it is probable that under David there were priests from earlier times in the town. Whether Zadok was among them cannot, however, be proved. Together with Abiathar he was connected with the Ark, the Israelite shrine in the strictest sense (2 Sam. 15,24-29), and the two priests seem to be equals. When David's death was drawing near, they became opponents, Abiathar supporting his son Adonijah, while Zadok backed Solomon (1 Kings 1,7 f. etc.; 2,22). This settled their further destiny. When Solomon became king, he banished Abiathar to his property in Anathoth with the remark that in reality he was a man marked for death (2,26) and only his faithfulness to David in his evil days had saved him. Thus Zadok became head priest without opposition at the very time when the new royal temple was built, and the cultus assumed forms requiring a priesthood quite different from the former; and this foremost place he had acquired for his family for good.

The new priesthood was bound to become rapidly the most important one, and one day it was to rise to be the only one in Israel. Just as the kingship could be traced back to earlier ages through a series of precursors, thus also the priesthood of Jerusalem was regarded as the perpetuator of an earlier priesthood, which had served the previous main sanctuary. This would then be the house of Eli, which had guarded the Ark. Just as the shifting of the power from Saul to David has been expressed in prophetic utterances that took shape in much later times, this is also the case with the transference of the priesthood from the house of Eli to that of Zadok. The projection into the past of the governing ecclesiastical dynasty appears plainly from the narrative. A man of God came to Eli, announcing the doom over his house. Already during the bondage in Egypt Yahweh had chosen it to serve as priests, ascend the altar and wear the ephod before Yahweh. But the members of the house have sinned by taking what was best among the sacrificial gifts, Eli has honoured his depraved sons above Yahweh. Therefore his house is to be reduced, Yahweh takes back his promise to it. In somewhat obscure terms it is mentioned that a man shall be preserved for the family at the altar, but the rest of the house is to die, [1] and the sign Eli shall receive thereof is that his two sons shall die on the same day. "And I will raise me up a faithful priest that shall do according to that which is in mine heart and in my mind, and I will build him a sure house, and he shall walk before mine anointed forever. And everyone that

is left in thine house shall come and crouch to him for a piece
of silver and a loaf, and he shall say: Let me enter, I pray
thee, into one of the priesthoods, that I may eat a morsel of
bread" (1 Sam. 2,27-36).

This prophecy is connected with an earlier story about the
two sons of Eli who sinned against good priestly custom. They
were men of b*eliya'al* (2,12) who forcibly appropriated the
sacrificial meat. But Eli's admonitions were of no use, "for
Yahweh wished to kill them" (v. 25). Here we learn that the
sons of Eli perished on account of a breach of the cult and
priestly law, and Samuel is set up as their counterpart. It might
then be expected that the story would go on to describe how
Samuel took their place; but this is not the case, nor do we know
whether Samuel continued to be associated with Shiloh.

This old narrative, which merely mentions the destruction of
the two sons of Eli, is now continued in the aforementioned
prophecy of the replacement of the Elides by the Zadokides.
For Zadok is the reliable priest who walks before the king,
and he is promised security to his house, just as Nathan promised
security to the house of David. It is evident that the house of
Eli must have survived far down in time, and this agrees with
the fact that the line was continued in spite of the death of
Hophni and Phinehas. We may take it for granted that it
survived until the destruction of Shiloh, an event that took place
in the monarchical period, and made a deep impression though
it cannot be dated (Jer. 7,12.14; 26,6.9) [1]. The priesthood must
then have sought refuge at the great royal sanctuary, and done
what it could to secure a place in the mighty order of priests
there. In spite of the factitious idea underlying the utterance,
there is no reason why the gravitation of the unattached priesthoods to the central sanctuary should be regarded as unhistorical.

A peculiar member of the priesthood of Shiloh is Samuel.
From his history we may learn how a man might become a priest
in Israel. The childless Hannah, Elkanah's wife, accompanied
her husband on a pilgrimage to Shiloh, and there prayed to
Yahweh for a son, making this promise: "Yahweh of the hosts!
If thou wilt look on the affliction of thine handmaid, and re-

member me and not forget thine handmaid, but wilt give unto thine handmaid a man-child, then I will give him unto Yahweh all the days of his life, and there shall no razor come upon his head" (1 Sam. 1,11). The next year Samuel was born, and when he was weaned, his mother took him with her to Yahweh's house at Shiloh and gave him to Eli, for he was to belong to Yahweh (v. 24).

Samuel was not descended from any family of priests, his father was of the Ephraimite house of Suph. But when he was given to the sanctuary it meant that he was to be entirely incorporated in the priesthood and serve "before the face of Yahweh" (1 Sam. 2,18; 3,1). Therefore he wore the usual priest's dress, a linen ephod (2,18), and he even slept at night in the sanctuary where the Ark was placed (3,3). What became of Samuel's priesthood in later times we do not know. As already mentioned, it might have been expected that his priestly functions would have been displayed at Shiloh, when the house of Eli declined, but we hear nothing of this. We see him acting as a highly respected seer in various towns, and as a mighty sacrificial priest. But those who have thus glorified his figure have deprived it of the features which would have allowed us to see him act as a prophet of great authority, and at the same time as a priest at some sanctuary.

The narrative shows us that just as an animal from the herd or part of the crops of the field might be given to the sanctuary, so also a human being might be offered as a gift, and in both instances sanctification was achieved, an increase of psychic power. We are told about Samuel that his head was not to be shaved. We have already met with this way of concentrating the psychic power among the warriors and the ancient heroes, and it attests the close relationship in early times between the different types of maintainers of the community. The chieftain, the priest, and the prophet were all to be pervaded by that holiness which was communicated by the enhancement of the psychic power. Normally the divine spirit flowed in these three separate streams, but they might approach each other, or merge in one, and the source was the same.

What characterises the priest in distinction from the others is that he is the servant of a sanctuary. But his activities are not far removed from those of the prophet, and they often coincide. The fact that there were upwards of a hundred priests in a town such as Nob does not mean that so many were necessary to perform the external functions of priests. It was their duty to maintain the holiness of the place, and this maintenance of holiness was also the mission of the early prophets. Since prophets, as we have seen, continued to officiate at the sanctuaries, we may take it for granted that the priests took part in the ecstatic exercises with them; we have also seen examples of priests who prophesied, and the terms used for priests would likewise seem to indicate a kinship with the prophet. [1] But the priest was a servant of the temple, entirely identified with it and its sacred objects.

The holiness possessed by the priest invested him with authority, and gave him the possibility of fortifying and guiding the people, as did the chief and the prophet. When Saul commanded his men to kill the priests of Nob, they shrank from laying hands on Yahweh's priests who possessed his holiness (1 Sam. 22,17). This did not mean that they were invulnerable, any more than the god-inspired chief. Saul did not fear to attack them, and later on Solomon regarded Abiathar as a man assigned to death because he had opposed his succession to the throne, and he removed him without ceremony from his priestly office. Priests could be appointed and dismissed; Micah appointed his son, and again dismissed him. Any one might be sanctified and again lose their sanctity. Descent was no decisive factor, but as in all other relations it was of great importance. The family once attached to a sanctuary, did not relinquish it again unless great events had happened. And in the narrative about Micah we see that from olden times the Levites constituted a family possessing a special priestly blessing. If you could get a Levite, you were fortunate. And those who belonged to this special family could wander about alone like prophets, and settle down as gērīm wherever fate offered them a resort.

In the old days there was the same lack of fixed rules for

priests as for other authorities. They were attached to the sanctuaries, yet they had a certain freedom of movement. Any one could become a member of the priesthood, and yet it showed a tendency to arrange itself by families. It had its independent power and importance by the side of the chieftainship, and a chief would apply to the priesthood best suited to render assistance at any given moment. But of course the priests had no protection from his acts of violence if respect for their holiness did not restrain him.

The function of the priest as the guardian of the sanctuary brought him into contact with the offerings brought by the worshippers. But in early times he held no leading position at the sacrifices. Indeed, it is questionable whether his cooperation was necessary. It was the chief and the head of the family who sacrificed. Even when a family went up to the sanctuary to sacrifice and partake of a meal, it was the head of the family who served the sacrificial meal, as is evident from the story of Elkanah who took this meal at the sanctuary of Shiloh with his two wives and his children (1 Sam. 1,4 f.). But no doubt a custom early developed according to which the priest helped by giving Yahweh his share. For after this had been done it was customary for the priest to take a share for himself (1 Sam. 2,13 ff.). The priest may also be supposed to have blessed the offering (cf. Deut. 21,5). According to the accounts of Samuel, a prominent man of God might bless the offerings of the families of his town and conduct the sacrificial meal (1 Sam. 9,12 ff.); but this does not warrant any conclusion as to the general functions of the priest. In that respect a decisive change took place at the large temples in the course of time.

The power reserved for the priest as the guardian and servant of the temple was that of procuring guidance through oracles. The question had to be put in such a way that the answer could be in the affirmative or in the negative, and when the priest enquired by the sacred lots, the decision was holy, i. e. it was Yahweh's. The Danites coming to Micah's sanctuary begged the Levite to ask Yahweh about their journey, and they received the answer that it would be successful (Judg. 18,5 f.). Any one might ask questions of the priest. David often came to Nob to obtain an oracle (1 Sam. 22,15).

It was not necessary to go to the sanctuary for the oracle. The sacred objects could be taken out, and this was always the case in war. Then the priest accompanied the army and was at the disposal of the chief, when he wished for enlightenment in order to find ways and means. In the battle of Michmash Saul was accompanied by Ahijah. He decided by an oracle whence the defeat came; it was Jonathan who had broken his father's promise of fasting for the army (1 Sam. 14,18.41 ff.). And Abiathar accompanied David on his wanderings, always ready to question the oracle (1 Sam. 23,6). It guided him in difficult situations (23,9 ff.; 30,7 ff.).

This confirms the close kinship between the priest and the prophet; for the prophet, too, was able to procure utterances from the power that lay behind to elucidate what lay at the surface, and prophets, too, accompanied the armies in war as helpers of the commander. When both oracles and prophets were silent, all was lost (1 Sam. 28,6). The difference between the prophet and the priest was in the way in which they communicated with the powers behind. The prophet spoke out of the strength filling his own soul, the priest made the sacred objects speak by the force that pervaded them. It was his connection with the sacred objects which gave the priest his power. The prophet might anoint kings, but the use of the holy oil for this purpose was actually one of the tasks of the priest (1 Kings 1,34.39). Prophet and priest were always closely connected, for the priest, too, must have in him so much holiness that he was able to deal in the proper way with what was holy.

The introduction of the monarchy did not of course at once affect the priesthoods at the many sanctuaries of the country, but in general it tended to strengthen their authority. The importance of the priests at the royal sanctuaries was enhanced by the growth of the temples and their connection with the king.

And while the monarchy must endeavour to restrict the authority
of the local chiefs, it had no reason to interfere with the authority
of the priests which had nothing to do with the direct exercise of
power. As a matter of fact, the speeches of the prophets in the
monarchical period convey a strong impression of the overwhelming influence of the priesthood. Both in the north and
the south they are made responsible for the condition of the
people, and many of the speeches are addressed directly to them.
When the last remnant of the Israelite kingdom perished, the
general grief found expression in the complaint that Yahweh had
rejected "king and priest" (Lam. 2,6).

The priest still derived his importance from the fact that he
maintained the holiness of the sanctuary, and the practical use of
this to the people was peculiarly evident in the guidance he could
give them as to the will of Yahweh through the oracle. Like the
prophet he came to speak of their fate and their conduct, but in
the nature of the case mostly about the latter. People asked:
What am I to do? and he had to answer them. But there was
nothing accidental about Yahweh's will, it did not stray
capriciously hither and thither. It was determined by the totality
of Israelite customs, *mishpāṭ*, and was expressed in the laws. The
people pledged itself in the sanctuary by a covenant on the laws
(2 Kings 23,3), and we have reason to suppose that such a
covenant was regularly renewed at reunions in some holy place.
There is a close connection between the law and the sanctuary, as
between the law and the oracle. The oracle would merely come in
to supplement the law in individual instances or to apply it.
Therefore the priests, who administered the oracle, had to be quite
familiar with what was already established as Israelite custom
and expressed in the law.

The priests are teachers of Israelite law. This is expressed
in "the Blessing of Moses" which presumably dates from the
earlier monarchical period. The poet says to Yahweh about the
priests: Thy Thummin and thy Urim (i. e. the lots of the oracle)
belong to the people of thy faithful man (i e. the priests) . . . .
They teach Jacob thy customs *(mishpāṭēkhā)* and Israel thy law

(tōrā) ..... (Deut. 33,8.10). The oracle and the teaching are closely connected and constitute the domain of the priests. The priestly instruction is called *tōrā* (Deut. 17,11; 33,10), the common term for the law, the standard of Israelite conduct.[1] The prophets bear witness in their speeches that the responsibility of communicating it rests with the priests, and frequently we hear that they do not act up to it. Micah blames them for giving instruction for pay (3,11), the same thing of which he accuses the prophets. Hosea goes much further. He says that the country lacks truth, charity, and knowledge of God, all that on which peace depends, hence it must perish (Hos. 4,1-4). But the responsibility for this rests with the priests. Therefore the prophet goes on to say: My people perisheth for want of understanding. Because thou hast rejected the proper understanding, I will reject thee, that thou shalt be no priest to me. Thou hast forgotten the instruction of thy God *(tōrā)*, so I will also forget thy sons. The more they multiplied, the more they sinned against me, therefore will I change their honour into shame. They feed on the sins of my people, and the desire of their soul is for their guilt. Therefore shall the people and the priest fare alike. I will punish him for his ways, I will requite him for his doings. They shall eat and not be satisfied, they shall commit whoredom and not increase, for they have ceased to take heed of Yahweh (Hos. 4,6-10).

This speech gives us a clear picture of where the chief responsibility of the priest lay. We hear the same complaint during the last days of the kingdom. Zephaniah says that the priests "desecrated the sanctuary, violated the *tōrā*" (Zeph. 3,4), and Jeremiah sounds a similar note. All are agreed that it is the duty of the priest to take care of the *tōrā*. The opponents of the prophet hopefully say: The *tōrā* will never fail the priest, nor counsel the wise man, nor words the prophet (Jer. 18,18). But Jeremiah asserts that the priests do not teach the proper *tōrā*, any more than the prophets pronounce the proper words. Those who teach the *tōrā* do not enquire about the nature of Yahweh, they know him not (Jer. 2,8), priests and prophets lie (6,13; 8,10). We hear the echo of these complaints in Ezekiel (7,26; 22,26).

The priests and the prophets were both to teach Yahweh's

words. The utterance of the prophet was a *tōrā* too (Isa. 8,16.20), and priest and prophet were jointly responsible for what the prophets of doom called the desecration of the temple (Jer. 23,11). The condemnation of them both implies the same view of Israel, the dislike of the absorption of anything foreign in the social life and the cultus. As teachers of the *tōrā* the priest and the prophet were on a line. But the activity of the priest had not the same free character as that of the prophet. He had to watch over the continuity of the doctrines, a more scholastic knowledge of the laws was demanded of him.

The result of the development in the time of the monarchy is found in the laws formulated after its fall. It is said expressly that people apply to the priests for instruction in case of leprosy, and have to follow their precepts (Lev. 13 f.; Deut. 24,8), and the priests are to direct them in everything appertaining to purity, holiness and the like (Lev. 10,10 f.). But a more far-reaching provision is to the effect that difficult cases are to be laid before the priests for decision. It says: If there arise a case too hard for thee in judgment *(mishpāṭ)* between blood and blood, between right and right, and between stroke and stroke, cases of controversy within thy gates, thou shalt arise and go up to the place which Yahweh thy God shall choose. And thou shalt go to the Levitic priests and to the judge who shall be in those days, and thou shalt enquire and they will let thee know the legal decision. And thou shalt act in accordance with the decision they give thee from this place which Yahweh thy God shall choose. — The text goes on to say that any one who defies the instructions of the priests or the judge shall die (Deut. 17,8-13).

The priesthood here referred to is that of Jerusalem, and the "judge" is that judge who is to succeed the king. The utterance shows how great an influence the priesthood had obtained as teachers of the *tōrā*. Whatever the role of the judge, it is clear that it rests entirely with the priests to decide what is *mishpāṭ* in Israel. But this means that they lay claim to the entire domain of law, even the pronouncing of sentences. In this way they have subordinated to themselves a domain with which they had but little to do in the old days; for the settling of legal disputes was a matter for some powerful man, mostly a leader of the community. But gradually as tradition created more comprehensive and more complex laws, the expert knowledge of the priesthood was necessary for their administration, and this, again, gave them the power.

The influence of the priests as oracle-givers and in conjunction herewith as teachers of the *tōrā* may be traced throughout the history of Israel, which shows us how their first activity was gradually limited and finally vanished entirely, whereas the second acquired an ever-increasing significance. The importance of the king in connection with this activity was that he took the lead in the making of the covenants at the temple, by which the people pledged themselves on the law, and he was at all times the highest judge. But gradually as the expert knowledge of the priests came to play a greater and greater part, we must assume, though we know nothing about it, that he came to lean largely on the priests in his function as a judge. We do not know according to what rules it was exercised in the later years of the kingdom, but the vague statement of Deuteronomy shows that the priesthood could do without him. The story of Moses' distribution of the judgeships (Ex. 18) affords but little help, since we do not know whether Moses here represents the authority of the king or that of the priest, just as we do not know to what time the whole story must be assigned.

As servant of the sanctuary the priest had to give his aid at sacrifices. As oracle-giver he had a certain independent position in relation to the king, but as participator in the cult he was entirely the king's assistant. Just as the head of the house and the chief performed the sacrifices for their households, thus the king officiated at the holy rites in the state temple. David conducted the transference of the Ark to Zion. The story of this has no doubt been shaped in accordance with the customs prevalent for such processions in the monarchical period. The king himself danced before the procession clad in the special priestly garment (2 Sam. 6,14). Solomon not only built the temple, but he conducted its entire inauguration (1 Kings 8). We are told that he sacrificed three times a year on the altar (9,25), and he took the lead in the stupendous offerings at its consecration; he addressed himself to Yahweh, was the people's spokesman, and blessed the people. The temple belonged to the king. He had the necessary repairs made, and its treasures were at his disposal (2 Kings 12,5 ff. 19). Ahaz, who introduced a new altar, settled questions of cult himself, and gave orders to the priests about them (2 Kings 16,10 ff., cf. 21,4 ff.). Right down to the last days of the kingdom it was the king who decided questions of cult, on the advice of the prophets, and sternly carried through his intentions, thus Hezekiah and Josiah (2 Kings 18,4; 23). In the northern kingdom the same conditions prevailed. Jeroboam introduced a new cult into Bethel after the pattern of Jerusalem, and mounted the altar himself at the sacrifice (1 Kings 13,1). And the judgment pronounced on the kings in the book of Kings was dependent on the cult they practised at their temples.

The relation of the priest to the king was that of a servant. This is mentioned in the judgment on the Elides where it is said of Zadok: He shall walk before the face of my Anointed forever (1 Sam. 2,35). But the priest was a very valuable servant, for he helped the king with what was the most important thing of all, the maintenance by the cult of the holy strength on which the whole kingship depended. The king and "his priests" were inseparably bound together (2 Kings 10,11). Gradually as the cult developed at the large temples, the activity of the priest was extended more and more. The king could not manage the numerous offerings himself, and it must be for the priests to perform at any rate the bulk of them. In the Blessing of Moses it is mentioned as their chief duty besides the service at the oracle. "They send the smoke of the sacrifice into thy nostrils, and put whole burnt offerings upon thine altar" (Deut. 33,10). And when the fortifying of the king's strength became an important part of the cultus, the priesthood was bound to acquire a significance of their own by the actions which were to create this holy strength for the king, as was the case too in the great states to the south and to the east.

The only priesthood about the organisation of which we know anything is that of Jerusalem, a simple consequence of the fact that the temple of Jerusalem was the only one to survive through the ages. We know its organisation of the post-exilic time best, but this was based on pre-exilic conditions; some parts of the post-exilic organisation point to a certain connection between the priesthood of Jerusalem and that of the other sanctuaries.

The fall of the northern kingdom of course caused the royal priesthood of that kingdom to lose its importance, but this by no means meant that the priesthoods in the various towns were dissolved. To them the event was hardly of any great significance, except to those who were deported by the Assyrians. It is mentioned, for instance, that the sanctuaries at Bethel and other cities survived long after the fall of Samaria (2 Kings 23,15, cf. 19).

The priesthood at the royal temple of Jerusalem was organised under a leader even in the monarchical period. The first in Solomon's time was Zadok, from whom the whole of the ruling priesthood traced its descent. The leading priest is called the "great priest" (hak-kōhēn hag-gādhōl, 2 Kings 12,11) or the "head priest" (kōhēn hā-rō'sh, 2 Kings 25,18). He was closely connected with the royal house. The head priest Jehoiada was married to a sister of King Ahaziah, by name Jehosheba (2 Kings 11,2; 2 Chron. 22,11). He might interfere in political questions, and it was Jehoiada who was responsible for the overthrow of Athaliah. He had brought up her successor, Joash, in the temple and thus obtained an influence over him. The stories about him show that the priests managed the property of the temple and carried out the repairs in it according to the instructions of the king (2 Kings 12,5 ff.).

From the succeeding period but few names have come down to us. Under Ahaz the chief priest was Uriah, who set up a new altar by the order of the king (2 Kings 16,10 ff., cf. Isa. 8,2). Under Josiah Hilkiah is mentioned; he managed the funds of the temple and took charge of its maintenance for the king as Jehoiada had done (2 Kings 22,3 ff.). In Jeremiah's time Pashhur is mentioned as the leader, *nāghīdh* and *pāḳidh* in the temple, and he maintained order there by putting a rebellious prophet like Jeremiah in the stocks in one of its gates (Jer. 20,1.3). It is doubtful whether this enforcer of order is identical with the chief priest, more probably it was a special office to exercise surveillance. Several priests had such a leading position in the temple. Zephaniah, the son of Maaseiah, is mentioned by Jeremiah as the superintendent *(pāḳidh)* who is to keep in order all such as are mad or carried away in a prophetic frenzy in the temple, a post which had been held by the priest Jehoiada, and he was empowered to put prophets in the stocks or in an iron collar (Jer. 29,25 f.). Here we receive an impression of the great role prophets must have played among the staff of the temple, and likewise of how large and complex this had become. The prophets were lodged in the temple by guilds (Jer. 35,4).

Among the varied host of servants of the cultus many have quite disappeared from our sight. A remark about Josiah's reform opens up quite a new perspective (2 Kings 23,7). It reveals that there were "holy men", i. e. male priests of a sexual cult, at the temple of Jerusalem. They had special chambers, and their special organisation as well. We may infer from this information that there must have been priestesses of the same cult at the royal temple, the *ḳedhēshōth* known from the sanctuaries of Canaan. To this must be added the priests of the foreign cults who gradually gained access to the royal temple, especially in the Assyrian period, the same who were combated by Josiah, and still flourished in Ezekiel's time (Ez. 8). Of priestesses, who were so common among the Phoenicians, [1] we hear nothing beyond some doubtful allusions. In the story of the iniquity of Eli's sons it is mentioned that "they lay with the women who served at the entrance to the tent of the revelation" (1 Sam. 2,22), which is perhaps an allusion to the above-mentioned sexual cult, but it may be a quite arbitrary remark of late origin. Miriam's appearance by the side of Aaron (Num. 12) suggests that she represents a female element in the personnel of the cultus; she is then to be sought among the prophets of the temple, since she is called a prophetess (Ex. 15,20). At the Passover she conducts the dances performed by the women.

To the lower priesthood belonged the watchmen at the gates, who are expressly designated as priests (2 Kings 12,10). They played rather an important role in the external management of the temple; they received the gifts offered towards the repair of the temple and put them in a box (ib.; 22,4). A chamber is mentioned which is set apart for the keeper of the threshold, Maaseiah, the son of Shallum (Jer. 35,4); probably it belonged to a guild of keepers of the threshold. This section of the ecclesiastical class waited upon the chief and second priests, as e. g. when cult objects were to be removed at the reform (2 Kings 23,4). When the Babylonians sacked the temple, they carried off the two above-mentioned leading priests and three janitors with other important men (2 Kings 25,18 = Jer. 52,24). For chopping wood, carrying water etc. foreigners were partly used. We know, for instance, that Canaanite Gibeonites were employed (Josh. 9,26), and Ezekiel shows us that in the last years of the kingdom foreigners were employed to assist the priests at the sacrifices (Ez. 44,7).

As far back as the first conquest of Jerusalem (597 B. C.), Nebuchadrezzar deported a number of priests to Babylonia (Jer. 29,1) and this was repeated at the second conquest in 586 or thereabouts. Even if a good many priests were left behind, the priesthood of Jerusalem was, nevertheless, dissolved. But it proved strong enough to survive the dissolution. The organisation had created a strong order of priests, whose distinctive character was determined by their descent, and whose task it was to teach the people the *tōrā*. It is probable that the cult had not become quite extinct at the ruined temple. But in the exile the whole work of the priest must be to teach the *tōrā;* and here the priesthood, if it were to preserve its special Israelite character, had to model itself on the requirements of such prophets as Jeremiah and his brother spirits. The maintenance of the Canaanite cult ceased of itself in the priesthood of the exile. As the upholder of the purely Israelite tradition its strong order was prepared to take over the leadership of the people.

A factor of the greatest importance for the future of the priesthood was the disappearance of the king. He whose holy strength was a centre of the cult and of whom the priests were merely servants, he who had created the entire priesthood and from whom all its authority was derived, was no more, and the community organised itself entirely without him. But then the priesthood of the great temple had already attained such a degree of independence that it could exist without him, nay even claim to rise above him.

A peculiar manifestation of this tendency is seen in that outline of a new order of things which is to be found in the book of Ezekiel. The work is pervaded by the idea that the priests only possess that holiness which allows one to officiate in the inmost court of the temple. The view held of the king appears from the complaint that the temple has been polluted by the nearness of the palace and the royal tombs (Ez. 43,7 f.), — which in earlier times was the best warrant for the maintenance of the holiness of the temple! On the other hand, tradition required that the king should have a place in the cultus, hence Ezekiel tries to make a place for him. "The prince" *(han-nāsi̓)* is to receive certain taxes from the people, and out of these he is to defray all the sacrifices demanded by the prescribed cultus (Ez. 45,9-17). He is to make certain offerings both at the daily service and at the festivals (45,22-46,15); but the offerings are intended to be made by the priests (46,2), while the prince is to stand in the inner gate of the forecourt of the temple, and there he is to prostrate himself. The sacrifices of the priests, which used to be a task in which they assisted the king, have now become a privilege at which the royal person merely has the right to be present and at which he must prostrate himself. But he is allowed to stand in the inner gate of the temple, which may be approached by no one outside the circle of the priests, and there he is to partake of a meal (44,3).

Thus the prince acquires a prerogative, but without encroaching upon the self-glorifying privileges of the priests, and he is quite superfluous and might keep away without any harm. The actual good he does is only to procure the necessary material for the

cult of the priests. It is possible that we here find the effects of
the old criticism of the kingship, which achieved its greatest
triumphs after the fall of the king. It may also be that Ezekiel's
plan dates from the time shortly after the return, when Israel had
no king but merely a Judaean "prince". In both cases we have
here an attempt to make the king's traditional and privileged
position in the cult form part of the system which made the priests
sole masters at the temple.

After the first return, about the year 520 B.C., we find the
regent Zerubbabel, a descendant of David, fully occupied in
rebuilding the temple in cooperation with the high priest Joshua.
Zerubbabel may then be presumed to have occupied a position in
the cult somewhat similar to that of "the prince" in Ezekiel. The
very expression "prince of Judah" is employed about the leader
of the return journey (Ezr. 1,8). Various utterances show how
Israel dreamed that Zerubbabel might be the shoot from which
David's kingdom was to grow forth again. But he and the chief
priest are mentioned as equals; they are to occupy the throne
together in full harmony, but the chief priest is to reign in
Yahweh's house and guard the courts of the temple (Zech. 3;
4,6 ff.; 6,9-15, cf. Ezr. 3,1-6; Hag. 1-2). This harmony evidently
had not yet been confirmed by the facts.

Soon, however, there came foreign regents, and now the possibility vanished of letting the ruler of the country occupy the
traditional position of the king in the temple; we still have a
reminiscence of him in the law of sacrifice which demands a
special sin offering for the head of the tribe (Lev. 4,22). The
cultus was wholly the business of the priests. A man like
Nehemiah emphatically refused to enter the sanctuary (Neh. 6,11).
Only in history did the king now live as high priest, but there,
too, he was pushed into the background by posterity. This is
evidenced in the books of the Kings, where remnants only of this
royal activity remain, and even more in the Chronicles where the
kings are merely administrators, while they are severely punished
if they venture into the domain of the cult (2 Chron. 26,16-21).

In the laws the king has entirely disappeared as leader of the

cult, apart from the traces thereof which may still be found in the
conduct of Moses. But these are too vague to give us a clear
picture, for the figure of Moses has a distinctive character.

We know the priesthood best at the height of its prosperity,
in the post-exilic period, because our most important sources date
from that time. Since the temple of Jerusalem was the only
recognised one, our entire knowledge is limited to its priesthood.
We know that it traced its descent from Zadok, the guild here, as
under other circumstances, being regarded entirely as a family.
But we see that only the higher priesthood was in later times
regarded as belonging to this family, while the whole priesthood
of Jerusalem was referred to the house of Levi. In this way a connection is created between the priests of Jerusalem and the early
Israelite priesthood.

We have seen that in the old days there were priests of quite
different families, but that it was preferable for a priest to be a
Levite. Such a Levite was the founder of Dan's priesthood, who
traced their descent from Moses (Judg. 18,30). Of another Levite
we hear that he lived as a gēr in the highlands of Ephraim
(Judg. 19,1), and in the legend of the Passover Aaron as priest
is called "the Levite" (Ex. 4,14). From the sparse allusions it
appears that the Levites formed a special family with special
priestly blessedness. And just as prophets might leave their guilds
and wander about the country, so also the Levites. The Levite
then lived as a gēr in the family that admitted him to their midst
and profited by his blessing. In this way Levite communities might
arise within various tribes and families. The Levite who became
the progenitor of the Levite community in the house of Dan had
formerly belonged to Judah (Judg. 17,7). The Danites knew him
by his speech, and were surprised to find him in the highlands of
Ephraim. That the Levites belonged to the south may be inferred
from their connection with Reuben and Simeon. [1] We do not
know how numerously they were represented in the old sanctuaries
of Israel. [2]

That mixture of respect and antipathy with which holy men are often regarded in the East was experienced by the Levites too. It is expressed in the Blessing of Jacob in these words: Simeon and Levi are brethren. Instruments of violence are their weapons (?). My soul shall not enter into their counsel, mine honour shall not be united with their assembly. For in their wrath they slew men, in their wantonness they disabled oxen. Cursed be their anger for it is fierce, and their ire for it is hard. I will divide them in Jacob, and I will scatter them in Israel (Gen. 49,5-7). Just as the Arabic tribal legends are connected with the old poems and elucidate them, so also this utterance of a poet finds its commentary in a story, dealing with Simeon's and Levi's assault on Shechem with which Israel had just made a covenant (Gen. 34).

The Blessing of Jacob probably dates from the early monarchic period. It is a peculiar trait that the scattered life of the Levites is here regarded as a punishment from Yahweh, and the house of Levi is put on an equal footing with a vanishing and dissolved tribe like that of Simeon. The punishment befalls Levi for violence. A judgment is here pronounced on the priestly tribe reminiscent of Hosea's judgment of the conduct of Jehu (Hos. 1,4), which, however, was regarded by others as especially pleasing to Yahweh. The victims of the violence of Levi were the Canaanites, as is evidenced by the story about Shechem, and it may be assumed that cult controversies have been the cause. But precisely in the neighbourhood of Shechem disputes must have arisen in which the struggle of some priests to assert themselves must have gone so far that those who were the guardians of Israel's *mishpāṭ* renounced all connection with them. Of such struggles Hosea says: As robbers [1] lie in wait, a band of priests murder along the roads to Shechem, for they commit shameful deeds (6,9). They may be resident priesthoods that are being ousted, or priests who, like the prophets, roam about the country "without knowledge" (Jer. 14,18) seeking for a place to settle. Hosea may be thinking of Levites in these struggles; or perhaps of their opponents.

A poem, the Blessing of Moses, which must probably be assigned to a time not far from that of Hosea, gives us a picture of the importance of the house of Levi as an Israelite priestly house, and here also there is a reference to priestly disputes in which Levi was mixed up. These words are addressed to Yahweh: Thy Thummim and thy Urim belong to the people of thy faithful man whom thou didst prove at Massah and whom thou lettest strive at the waters of Meribah. He who said of his father: [1] I see him not, who did not acknowledge his brethren, nor knew his sons. For they observed thy word and kept thy covenant. They teach Jacob thy customs and Israel thy law. They send the smoke of the sacrifice into thy nostrils and put burnt offerings upon thine altar. Bless, Yahweh, his power. Accept the work of his hands. Crush the loins of his enemies, and let not his foes rise (Deut. 33,8-11).

In this utterance the work of Levi is that with which we have become acquainted as the task of the priest. He manages the oracles and teaches the people Israelite law, and he performs the offerings. Yahweh is entreated to bless this work and to crush his foes ruthlessly. Thus it is a life and death struggle, as in Jacob's blessing, but here Levi seems stronger and the poet identifies himself with his struggle.

If we ask what the struggle is about, it is evident that in the Blessing of Moses it is regarded as a fight for the word of Yahweh and his covenant. In this Levi has disregarded all consideration for family, for father, brothers and sons, and the struggle seems to have been concentrated in an event that was assigned to Massah and Meribah. The latter place was situated south of Canaan at Kadesh, and two different stories show how it obtained its name "strife", because the people there demanded water of Moses (Ex. 17,1-7; Num. 20,1-13). In reality there is every reason to suppose that Meribah means "legal dispute" [2] and that the two names indicate a place in which sentences were pronounced. Our poem suggests that Levi here had his priesthood confirmed; thus the history of Levi is associated with Kadesh and Moses' activity there. But we do not know the story referred to.

We may conjecture, however, that it has been related to

another story which has come down to us, and which is to show how the Levites obtained their priesthood through a ritual struggle no less violent than the struggles we heard of above. It is described in the story of the golden calf how the Levites rallied round Moses after he had destroyed the hateful image. While the people was in a religious ecstasy, Moses called upon all who would join him to take their swords and go forth and slay the people without consideration for son or brother. It was the Levites who gathered upon his call, and killed a large number of Israelites. Moses then declared that by their lack of mercy to son or brother they had acquired the blessing (Ex. 32,29), that which was to make them true priests. It is the ruthless fight against Israelites who practise the Canaanite cult which gives Levi the blessing. The same trait recurs in the legend of the dedication of the priestly house of Eleazar. This family acquired the blessing by slaying Israelites who had dealings with foreign women in connection with the cult of their gods (Num. 25,1-13); here doubtless is a reference to the Canaanite sexual cult.

According to these narratives, the blessing of Levi would, then, be connected with the struggle against the Canaanite cult, and its growth as a tribe of priests would depend on the intensity with which it carried on this struggle. The account of the introduction by Jeroboam of the cult of the bull in the northern kingdom, at Bethel and Dan, points in the same direction. He is said to have arranged high places for sacrifice, and appointed all kinds of people who were not Levites to be priests (1 Kings 12,31 f.; 13,33).

This takes us to the very heart of the question of the great struggle between the Israelite and Canaanite cult which fills the whole history of Israel. In reality there is nothing more natural than that the strife of the priests should in the first place be the result of the struggle between the cults. It is not possible, however, simply to regard the Levites as priests who adhered to old Israelite custom as opposed to those who adopted Canaanite practices. No such hard and fast line was drawn, as would appear when the struggle had finally come to an end.

We learn that the priesthood of Bethel was not Levitic, but

at Dan, where the cult was not different from that at Bethel, the family of the abducted Levite were the leading priesthood as long as the northern kingdom survived (Judg. 18,30). At Jerusalem the descendants of Zadok survived down through the ages as the leading priesthood, and yet the alternate introduction and abolition of foreign cults was constantly going on under the same priesthood according to the inclination of the kings. Ezekiel gives the name Levites to the priests who "are gone away from Yahweh" as well as to the others (Ez. 43,19; 44,10; 48,11).

A close study of the narrative of the golden calf would seem to warrant the conclusion that there was strife even among the Levites themselves in the matter of the Canaanite cult. The Levites were rewarded because they spared neither son nor brother, but these too were Levites. However, the story is hardly meant to be interpreted thus. In all probability it received its present shape in post-exilic times, and then it was natural for the recognised priesthood to base their authority and right on the fact that they had the only true cultus which excluded the Canaanite elements. In pre-exilic times the Canaanite cult found servants among the Levites too, but it seems only natural that the opposition to the Canaanite element to be found among the priesthood should have its principal stronghold in Levitic circles, which formed the nucleus of the old Israelite priesthood. This tendency might assert itself with varying strength in the different parts of the country and at different times. The fact that the Blessing of Jacob so sternly denounces the violence of this tribe of priests, quite agrees with the character of the narratives in Genesis. The relation to foreigners here bears the mark of peace, very unlike the wilderness stories and Deuteronomy.

Neither the prophets nor the old historical writings [1] mention the Levitic priestly house; but towards the close of the monarchical period, it had made such progress that it quite dominated the priesthood of Jerusalem, which was regarded as entirely Levitic, and in the main also the other priesthoods. This appears from Deuteronomy and Ezekiel; they must both be supposed to reflect the conditions that had developed before the exile. Deuteronomy constantly speaks of the "Levite *(hal-lēwī)* who is within your gates" (12,12.18.19; 14,27.29; 16,11,14 etc.) and for the towns mentions "the priests *(hak-kōhᵃnīm)*, the sons of Levi" (21,5, cf. 24,8), and similarly the priests of Jerusalem are referred to as "the Levites who stand there before Yahweh" (18,7) or "the Levitic priests" (17,9.18; 18,1; 24,8; 27,9). Ezekiel mentions "the priests.... namely Zadok's sons, who among the sons of Levi approach Yahweh..." (40,46), "the Levitic priests of the seed of Zadok" (43,19), "the Levitic priests, the sons of Zadok" (44,15), just as he speaks of the Levites who "are gone away from Yahweh" (44,10).

Two circumstances here are remarkable. One is that the old Israelite priestly house, which is not mentioned at all at the founding of the priesthood of Jerusalem, suddenly appears to be the one from which it traces its descent. The other is that the priests of the various sanctuaries are regarded as belonging to the same house as the priests at Jerusalem. How this has happened we do not know. The unity of the priesthood may be due to the fact that the small sanctuaries felt themselves dependent on the great sanctuary. This must induce their priests to seek connection with its priesthood, and all the more so because the priests' teaching of the *tōrā* would naturally lead to a connection between them gradually as the striving of the monarchy for unity made itself felt. The interest taken by the king in the priests of the smaller sanctuaries is evidenced by the statement that he dismissed them (2 Kings 23,5). And that the Zadokites became Levites may of course be due to the fact that they were so originally, though this is not recorded; or they may later have sought to associate themselves with Levi, the ancient Israelite family of priests, a proceeding which would seem natural to them since they were the highest priesthood of Israel. It would be in good keeping with David's policy, if he had at once secured priests for himself of this ancient line.

The general subordination of the priesthood to the house of Levi tended to emphasise the significance of the relationship for the priest. It was the same in the case of the chief. In the old days one might become a chief if he were impelled by the spirit, and the conditions required it, but the tendency was then for the blessing to remain with his house. This tendency later led to the blessing being entirely associated with the house. One was born to priesthood as well as to kingship. If a man was of priestly descent he also had the priestly blessing.

This development brought the Israelites into difficulties when the old state of affairs was to be revived. Only the temple of Jerusalem was recognised, the other sanctuaries were rejected. But their priesthoods were recognised in so far as they were regarded as belonging to the true priestly house of Levi. This question is taken up in Deuteronomy, which makes a vigorous demand for the sole right of the temple of Jerusalem.

The monopoly of the great temple results in its priesthood being made the highest court of appeal in questions of the *tōrā*, to which all Israelites are to refer difficult questions (Deut. 17,9.12). It is implied that the priests remain in their towns. We are told that questions of disputes and physical injuries are settled by them (21,5), and in that context certain cases are quoted in which they give assistance; in particular the question of leprosy comes up (24,8). This may then be understood to mean that the general instruction was left to them, while more difficult cases were submitted to Jerusalem; but there is some obscurity about the relation of the priests to other authorities who pronounce judgments (19,17 f.). Festivals cannot be held nor sacrifices performed in the towns. But when people go up to Jerusalem, they are to take their Levites with them, and they are to take part in the cult practices together (12,12.18; 16,11.14; 26,11). The Levites are put on an equal footing with widows, orphans, and *gērīm*, whom the Israelites must never fail, because they have no "part and inheritance" with the other Israelites (12,12.19; 14,27; 16,11.14; 26,11). Deuteronomy proposes to remedy the miserable state of all these by letting them have the tithe every third year (14,27-29).

Besides this charitable measure the inference is consistently drawn from the fact that all Levites have the rights of priests. We are told that the tribe of Levi have no part or lot with the Israelites but live on the offerings and property of Yahweh, and it is enumerated what they are to have. Of the sacrifice the shoulder, the jaws, and the maw, further the first fruits of corn, cider, oil, and wool (18,1-5). To this is added: And if a Levite come from any of thy gates out of all Israel, where he sojourned, and come with all the desire of his soul unto the place which the Lord shall choose, then he shall minister in the name of Yahweh his God, as all his Levitic brethren do, who stand there before Yahweh. They shall enjoy a share as a share..... (v. 6-8).

The most concrete element in all this passage is the rule about the sharing of the priests in the offering and the first fruits; it must indicate what it was customary for the priests to get at Jerusalem in the last days of the kingdom. As long as the tradition remained unbroken, any special motive was therefore superfluous; that given here is a mere abstraction. Levi was not to have any particular territory assigned to it, because its members were dispersed among the other tribes. The author regards the land as divided up among the tribes on purely abstract lines; this means that priests cannot possess landed property, and the offerings are their compensation. It was of course true that many priests subsisted on the sacred gifts. We are further told that they received money for sin- and guilt-offerings (2 Kings 12,17), and they may perhaps also have sold some part of their portion (Deut. 18,8). [1] But this has wrongly given rise to the principle that priests must dispense with landed property. David's priest, Abiathar, had landed property at Anathoth to which he was banished by Solomon (1 Kings 2,26). The priest Amasiah at Bethel owned land which according to the threat of Amos, was to be divided among others (Am. 7,17), and Jeremiah, who was a priest, after the enactment of the law of redemption, repurchased his uncle's land at Anathoth (Jer. 32,6 ff.). This shows that as owners of land priestly families followed no other rules than other Israelite families. And as late as post-exilic times we learn that priests and Levites lived each on their own land in the cities of Judah (Neh. 11,20).

We may therefore venture to assume that there have been both rich and poor priests; some had landed property, others

had none. The account we have from Nehemiah's time shows
us what priests would generally do if they lost connection with
a temple; they settled on their landed property. Among the
usurers who mortgage the property of poor Jews in Nehemiah's
time priests also are mentioned (Neh. 5,12). But the law, which
is of an entirely abstract character, regards them all as un-
propertied; they live as *gērīm* among the tribes (Deut. 18,6).
It is then a matter of course that charity should be extended
to them as to other distressed Israelites. But how are we to
understand the rule that they were to be taken to Jerusalem at
the festivals? We know that the Israelites went up to the festivals
by families. On whom, then, did the duty devolve of taking the
priests of the town with them? In the provisions of the law
we constantly meet with abstractions.

We can hardly think otherwise about the rule that any Levite
could go to Jerusalem and serve at the temple with the same
right to a share in the offerings as the priesthood there. This
provision which, incidentally, would render the above-mentioned
admonitions superfluous, is, as we have already said, the result
of all Levites holding the privileges of priests, but Jerusalem
only having a right to the temple. It is quite possible that in the
monarchical period, as this view of the temple and the priesthood
gradually ripened, there was a right for priests to come from
without and take part in the cult at Jerusalem. The priest
Jeremiah, it is true, did not participate in the cult, but he
appeared like other prophets in the temple, and was subject
to its rules, though he was a native of Anathoth. It seemed
natural for unemployed priests to go to the great temple and
seek admittance there, as the house of Eli are said to have done
when they could no longer stay at Shiloh (1 Sam. 2,36). In the
Talmud the provisions of Deuteronomy are interpreted to mean
that priests from the country could take part in the sacrifices
at the festivals and have a share in them, [1] while they could
not be admitted to the temple service for good. It is doubtful,
however, whether the provision can be understood thus. More
probably the law has here once more elevated a certain general
practice into a principle. But it is difficult to understand how

an existing, organised priesthood like that of Jerusalem could allow priests from other sanctuaries to pour into the temple as their full equals with no other limitation than their own wish, "all the desire of their soul".

The tentative measures of Deuteronomy show how difficult it was to set aside the numerous sanctuaries and at the same time acknowledge their priests. The law was founded in custom but to this basis it added more comprehensive views; it did not confine itself to making ordinances for Jerusalem and Judah, it would be valid for all Israel. All this is most readily understood if the law came into existence in the period when the nation was occupied with the regeneration of Israel after the fall of the kingdom, during the exile or immediately after it.

Among the kings bent on reform there was one who treated the priests in a way which reminds us of the demands of Deuteronomy. This was Josiah, whose reform is, as a matter of fact, generally connected with the law. But Josiah had not the abstract view of the law of a universal Israel. According to one account he slaughtered all the Bamah priests in Samaria (2 Kings 23,20), but this account does not perhaps originally belong to the context; at any rate we do not hear of his doing anything for the priests of northern Israel. In Judah he removed the idolatrous priests (kᵉmārīm) in the towns and the vicinity of Jerusalem (v. 5), and he brought thither the priests (kōhᵃnīm) from the towns (v. 8), "nevertheless the Bamah priests did not go up to Yahweh's altar at Jerusalem, but they eat unleavened bread among their brethren" (v. 9).

We are not told whether Josiah brought all the priests or only some of them from the towns of Judah to Jerusalem, nor whether they were Levitic priests he brought with him, or if not, what was his choice. He admitted them to the temple; however, they did not obtain the full rights of priests, but only a certain recognition. Here, then, we hear of the introduction into the temple of Jerusalem of priests from without, and the form of the communication would seem to indicate that they came to constitute part of the lower priesthood. The demands of Deuteronomy were not complied with; according to these they

should be able to come whenever they liked, and be given quite
the same standing.

Deuteronomy is concerned with the state of affairs which will
arise in the whole of Israel when she has only one temple but
many priesthoods. The laws of the book of Ezekiel enter more
fully into the internal organisation of the temple of Jerusalem
when the general restitution comes.

As in Deuteronomy, we find the statement in Ezekiel that
priests must have no landed property, for Yahweh is their inheritance; but they are to have a share in offerings and holy
gifts (Ez. 44,28-30), and their habitations are to be on a piece
of land laid out round the temple itself. Here it turns out that
Ezekiel distinguishes two orders of priests. A piece of ground
is to be laid out for "the priests *(hak-kōh^anīm)* who minister to
the sanctuary, those who come near in order to minister to
(shārēth) Yahweh" (v. 4), and another for "the Levites, the
ministers of the house" (v. 5). The same division occurs in the
arrangement of the cells. The northern cells are reserved for
"the priests who serve at the altar, namely Zadok's sons, those
of the sons of Levi who approach Yahweh to minister to Him"
the southern ones belong to "the priests *(kōh^anīm)* who serve
the house" (40,45 f., cf. 43,19). Connected with the cells there
are kitchens where the priests *(hak-kōh^anīm)* boil and bake the
offerings, and others in the outer court where "those who minister
to the house" boil the offerings of the people (46,20.24). One is
the higher order of priests who make the sacrifices and enter
into the inner sanctuary, the other one "ministers to the house".
A comparison of the different expressions shows that there is
no fixed designation. They are all called priests and Levites,
but the first order constitute the priests in the proper sense, they
are descended from Zadok within the family of Levi, therefore
the others are "Levites" in a special sense. This accords with
what we might have expected. Priests regarded as belonging
to the old Levitic priestly family have been admitted to the
temple, but of course they could not attain the same standing
as the ruling Zadokides, and so they form an order of priests

of the second rank; and in the course of time people were probably also admitted to it who were not originally regarded as Levites. The history of Josiah tells us of a special increase in the lower priesthood, but of course a lower priesthood existed at the royal temple even before that time. Ezekiel's classification of the priests forms the basis for the ordering of the temple service, and even, as we have seen, for the arrangement of the temple. It may therefore be taken for granted that his rules are based on traditions from the monarchical period. It accords with this that the division between priests and Levites was maintained among those who lived in Babylonia, as we can see from the accounts of their return. It was necessary for the service of the temple that both orders should return home. This must be because the temple tradition required it.

Ezekiel attaches much importance to the rule that all priests, even the lower ones, should be of Levitic descent. He states that previously people who were not Israelites *(beně někhār)* were allowed to come and serve in the temple, but this must not take place any more. "But the Levites who went away from me when Israel went astray, straying from me after their logs of gods, they shall bear their sin. They shall serve in my sanctuary, having charge of the gates of the temple and serving in the house; they shall slay the burnt-offering and the sacrifice for the people, they shall minister unto them (i. e. the people) and serve them. Because they served them before their logs of gods, and caused the house of Israel to fall into sin, therefore I lift my hand against them, saith the Lord Yahweh, and they shall bear their sin. And they must not come near unto me to do the office of a priest *(lekhahhēn)* unto me, nor come near to any of my sanctuaries, to the very holiest things, and they shall bear their shame and their abominations which they have committed. And I make them keepers of the temple with all its work and all that is to be done therein. But the Levitic priests, the sons of Zadok, that had charge of my sanctuary when the Israelites went astray from me, they shall come near to me to minister unto me, and they shall stand before me and bring me the fat and the blood, saith the Lord Yahweh. They shall enter my sanctuary, and they shall come near to my table to minister unto me, and they shall keep my charge" (44,10-16).

Ezekiel's statement shows that strangers have been used for the subordinate temple service. The allusion here is hardly to the priests of the foreign cults which Ezekiel testifies flourished within the temple (chap. 8), for he refers to some priests who take part in the normal sacrifices (44,7). It is nothing unusual for strangers to be employed in the temples for such services, it has even happened in Mohammedan mosques, and we know that Canaanite Gibeonites worked as woodcutters and water carriers in the temple of Jerusalem (Josh. 9,27). Ezekiel shows that this use of strangers was continued right down to the fall of the kingdom, but of course not that the lower priesthood consisted exclusively of strangers. Now, however, they are to be dismissed, Levitic descent is to be decisive; for the lower service those Levites can be used who, by taking part in foreign cults, have lost their right to priestly service proper.

Ezekiel's demand accords with the events in the reign of Josiah, but his utterances show that the matter was not settled with what happened then. The problem of the Judaean priests outside Jerusalem continued to exist all through the period of transition. As in Deuteronomy, Ezekiel's utterances consist of proposals and claims, but they are based on something already extant. At Jerusalem there were already two kinds of priests, the Zadokites, who, in Ezekiel's opinion, had kept to the true cult, and the Levites, who had gone astray (Ez. 48,11). It is this system Ezekiel wishes to be continued. What the relation is between Ezekiel and the various demands of Deuteronomy it is difficult to decide.

It is certain that gradually many new priests became attached to the temple of Jerusalem, and most frequently, it may be supposed, they had to join the ranks of the lower priests, though hardly them alone. A reminiscence of the origin of a number of Levites from Judaean cities may perhaps be found in the later genealogies. [1]

Of the significance of Ezekiel's diatribe against the strangers who had performed subordinate priestly services in the temple it is difficult to judge, since we do not know of whom he is speaking. If he is thinking of the temple slaves working from the time of Solomon, his words were without effect for they continued to work after the return home; and "the Levites" did not perform such inferior work as they did.

The unity of the priesthood aimed at by the gathering of them under the tribe of Levi, was accomplished at the restitution after the exile, when the sanctuaries still in existence outside Jerusalem fell entirely outside the framework of recognised Israel. The restoration of the priesthood was now one of the most important tasks, for it was essential to the establishment of the cultus. The priest was no longer a mere oracle-giver and assistant at sacrifices, he was an authority on the law, but also the only one who could perform sacrifices and other temple rites. He had become the mainstay of society.

Upon the return home it was necessary to bring back all classes of the temple staff. At the first return, which took place around the year 538 after a little more than 40 years' exile, mention is made of priests, Levites, and temple singers, viz, Asaph's sons, janitors, persons given to the temple (*nethinim*), descendants of the slaves of Solomon (Ezr. 2; Neh. 7, cf. 12). The same classes are mentioned at the return associated with the names of Ezra and Nehemiah (Ezr. 7,7; 8,15 ff.; Neh. 10,29; 11). The orders of the priests and the Levites are even mentioned separately in the royal decree which gave permission for the return (Ezr. 7,13, cf. 8,30; 9,1). Great weight was attached to the return of both orders of priests. When but few Levites joined, a special message was sent to them (Ezr. 8,15-20). The two groups of temple slaves mentioned last were not always kept distinct. In the return journey of Ezra 220 temple slaves (*nethinim*) are mentioned who had already been given by David and his men to serve the Levites (Ezr. 8,20). The classification of the staff is rooted in tradition. [1]

The lists of the returning Israelites on both occasions show an enormous number of priests, but very few Levites (Ezr. 2; 8). The recognition of the priests depended on their being able to make good their right by genealogical tables (Ezr. 2,61-63). If there really was such an overwhelming number of priests (in the first return journey alone a number of 4,289 are mentioned, Ezr. 2,36 ff.; Neh. 7,39 ff.), this may be because many have got in who ought really to have been among the Levites. The Levites who were not admitted to the highest order must then in part have preferred to remain in Babylonia. The whole matter is, however, obscure.

The great number of the temple staff is the clearest evidence of the new position of the priesthood. There was no need for so large a staff to maintain the temple cult, but the priest did not exist for the sake of his office. By belonging to the priestly family a man obtained his share of the priestly blessing with all that the covenant with Yahweh implied; he was born to the prerogative of being admitted to what was holy, a prerogative to be respected if holiness were to be maintained.

Only part of the large staff of the temple settled in Jerusalem. A list gives us the families who established themselves there in the time of Nehemiah; mention is made of priests, Levites, and janitors, likewise of temple slaves, who lived in Ophel (Neh. 11,10-19.21). In another context we learn that the high-priest had his dwelling along part of the city wall (Neh. 3,20 f.), and the priests likewise by the city wall near the horse gate (3,28). Other families settled on their property "in their cities", and this happened both after the first and the second return (Ezr. 2,70; Neh. 11,3.20). It was the case both with priests, Levites, and temple slaves. It is said about a number of Levites and singers that they had built themselves farms in the neighbourhood of Jerusalem, even down in the valley of the Jordan (Neh. 12,27-29). When the Levites did not receive their dues, the officiating Levites and singers moved out on to their land (Neh. 13,10). There were Levites in the area of Benjamin, too (11,36).

We are evidently here confronted with two categories: partly Levites who moved out of Jerusalem and built themselves new farmsteads in the neighbourhood of the city, often somewhat far away, partly representatives of all classes of the temple staff who settled on properties "in their cities". The expression would seem to denote that from olden times, that is to say, from before the exile, they had family property in these cities. They, or rather their fathers, may like Abiathar have been priests in Jerusalem before the exile, and at the same time have had family property in other cities. But it seems most natural to suppose that their family had been priests in these cities and that they had then, either before the exile or upon the return, become recognised as priests in Jerusalem. If this is right, it means that men from the other cities were admitted as members to all orders of the priesthood of Jerusalem, and not merely to the Levite class. A story in the book of Joshua tells us of temple slaves originating from Gibeon (Josh. 9,27).

Thus the organisation after the return cannot have been based exclusively on the demands of Ezekiel, and it is by no means these that first gave rise to the division into classes. The records of the return show that the division was already an accomplished fact among the families in exile, and since it cannot, of course, have been introduced at a time when there was no temple cult, and when they were moreover in a strange country, it must be based on an early tradition from the monarchical period. Priests as well as Levites were later divided into 24 groups, each serving a week in the temple. This arrangement was referred to David (1 Chron. 24 f., cf. 9,25 f.; Luke 1,8) [1]. The rest of the time the priests might then live wherever they liked. The hereditary priesthood, both of the highest and the next highest order, counted so many members that it by far exceeded the number necessary for the temple service. But it had become a holy aristocracy, effective by its mere existence no less than by its activities. The chronicler takes it for granted that this state of affairs had always been prevalent. Hence he can say that all priests and Levites in Israel came to Jerusalem in the reign of Jeroboam to serve there, because Jeroboam discharged them and appointed people who were not Levites as priests (2 Chron. 11,13-15).

In the priestly laws formulated at the temple of Jerusalem

in post-exilic times, the whole priesthood are united in one genealogy with Levi as their first ancestor, the priests proper being sons of Aaron. We have previously seen that the priests of Jerusalem were regarded as descendants of Zadok. Now we see the Zadokides coordinated with other families as descendants of Aaron. According to the genealogy, Aaron who was descended from Levi, had four sons: Nadab, Abihu, Eleazar, and Ithamar (Ex. 6,14 ff.; Num. 3,14 ff.; 26,57 ff. et al.). The family of Eleazar was identical with the Zadokides (1 Chron. 5,27 ff.; 24,1 ff.), but the genealogy shows that they were now no longer the only priestly family recognised in Jerusalem. About Nadab and Abihu, the fathers of the two first-mentioned families, we are told, however, that they committed a ritual offence and hence perished (Lev. 10,1-7; Num. 3,4; 26,61). [1] This means that these priestly families were recognised as belonging to the priesthood, but were afterwards excluded. Ithamar survived, but only with 8 of the 24 groups, so that 16 were assigned to Eleazar (1 Chron. 24,4); the Ithamarides traced their descent from Ithamar through Abiathar, Zadok's fellow priest under David (v. 6). All this shows that other priests besides the Zadokides were actually admitted to the priesthood of Jerusalem, but it did not happen without a struggle, some were admitted and again excluded. This must have occurred during the changes which took place when the country priests were trying to obtain recognition at Jerusalem.

The priestly genealogies and the legends associated with them give us in their own language a contribution to all this part of ecclesiastical history. They show us that the whole thing was not so systematically carried through as the proposals of Deuteronomy and Ezekiel would seem to imply. Both the higher and the lower orders of priests received members from without. Some families were admitted for a time and then expelled. In the meanwhile the Zadokides still retained their position as a leading family. Eleazar's line, which, as we saw, was identical with it, was the most important family of priests (1 Chron. 24,4) and the high priest belonged to it (5,34). Its superiority is established in a legend of the same kind as the one showing how the Levite priesthood originated through the fight against the cult of the calf. We are told that the Israelites, before the immigration into Canaan, committed fornication with foreign women and took part in their cult. Then Eleazar's son Phinehas killed an Israelite who was with a foreign woman, and this put an end to the plague, which had been sent by Yahweh as a punishment (Num. 25,7-9). In postexilic times the fight against the foreign cult was regarded as a duty by the true priesthood, it gave them the right to be priests.

The lower priests have the descent from Levi in common with the higher priests. Levi had three sons. Gershon or Gershom (thus in 1 Chron. 6,2 ff.; 15,7) had the sons Libni and Shimei, names reminiscent of the Judaean town Libna, and of Simeon, the families of which were neighbours of the Judaeans. Merari had the sons Mahli and Mushi. Kehat had four sons; Amram was the father of Moses and Aaron and thus of all priests; his brothers were Izhar, Hebron, and Uzziel. Among these names we recognise the well-known city. Thus some Levites are more closely connected with the priests than others.

The Levites are the subordinates of the priests. Only the priests can perform the actual rites and sacrifices, the Levites are their servants. It is even expressed in the terms that the Levites have been given to Aaron and his sons as "temple-given" (n^ethûnîm), being assigned to the priests as a compensation for the first-born (Num. 3,5-9.11-13.41.45 ff.; 8,16-19). The priests minister directly to Yahweh, the Levites to the sanctuary, taking charge of the vessels and preparing everything for the priests (Num. 4; 1 Chron. 23,28-32). In the course of time the temple treasure and the sacred gifts were given into their charge, and later on they were also given functions pertaining to the administration outside the temple (26,29 ff.). The history of the priesthood in the uncertain period of transition shows that many of those who became subordinate priests must have fought for a position as priests of the first class. We have a reminiscence of this struggle in the narrative of Korah's revolt. The house of Korah were closely related to the priests, their first ancestor being the son of Izhar, brother of Amram, the progenitor of the priests. They claimed the right to be priests, and the matter was to be decided by Korah and his 250 men trying to offer incense together with Aaron. Yahweh then pronounced his doom, letting Korah and his men be consumed by a rushing fire (Num. 16 f.). Thus unlike Nadab and Abihu, this family did not become recognised, but had to be content with a place among the Levitic subordinate priests.

Janitors and singers occupy a special position. They are not mentioned separately in the priestly laws. Ezra, Nehemiah, and the Chronicler sometimes refer to them side by side with the Levites (Ezr. 2,41 f.; Neh. 7,44 f. et al.; 1 Chron. 9,17 ff.; 25) and may even designate them as brothers of the Levites (1 Chron. 6,33; 15,16; 2 Chron. 35,15), but in other cases these classes are called Levites (Ezr. 3,10; Neh. 11,17.22; 12,8.25.27; 1 Chron. 9,33 f.; 15,17; 16,4; 23,30; 2 Chron. 7,6 et al.). The three families of singers Heman, Asaph, and Ethan (for whom we sometimes meet with Jeduthun) are then distributed among the Levite families Kehat, Gershom, and Merari (1 Chron. 6,18 ff.), while the janitors are assigned to Korah and Merari, and the guardians of the treasure to Gershom (1 Chron. 26). Either each Levitic family had originally its group of singers, or the association with the Levites is late and secondary, and they have been quite arbitrarily distributed among these families. Among the families of singers we find the last remnants of the temple prophets incorporated. [1] Just as Levite means partly priest in general, partly subordinate priest, so it came to denote partly subordinate priest in general, partly such subordinate priests as were not singers or janitors. It is this duality which we find in Ezra, Nehemiah and the Chronicler.

The right of the priesthood was not only a privilege which allowed them to perform the ritual acts, it also admitted them to a share in offerings and sacred gifts. During the growth of the order in post-exilic times, its claims in this respect grew too, as shown by the priestly laws. A comparison of Deuteronomy with Ezekiel will make this clear. Besides a share in the sacrifices the priests received the firstfruits of all growing things and first-born animals, to which was added a compensation for the first-born of human beings and unclean animals, and a large part of the tithes. All this was collected by the Levites and placed in cells in the temple (Neh. 10,38 ff.; 12,44 ff.; 2 Chron. 31,4 ff.).[1] In the Priestly Code we find the same reflections on priestly property as in Deuteronomy and in Ezekiel: Thou shalt have no inheritance in their land, neither shalt thou have any part among them. I am thy part and thine inheritance among the Israelites (Num. 18,20). But just as Ezekiel would, nevertheless, assign a share to the priests, thus also the Priestly Code. It takes it for granted that the whole of Canaan belongs to Israel, and quite in the abstract divides the country between the tribes which, be it said, no longer existed after the exile. In this division 48 cities are assigned to the Levites, each provided with common land for their cattle (Num. 35,1-8). They are found in every tribe, and to the priests proper are given 13 of the cities in the tract around Jerusalem (Josh. 21; 1 Chron. 6,39 ff.). Thus the idea has been realised that sanctuary and priests are not inseparably associated. There is one sanctuary, but the priesthood is distributed over the entire land, being held together by their kinship. It is an expression of the fact that the whole country is Israelite. The priesthood spreads a net of Israelite holiness over the land. It is of benefit merely by its existence, and hence its members receive their share of the sacred revenues, if only they figure in the genealogies (2 Chron. 31,19).

The power and significance of the priesthood among the people in post-exilic times found its supreme expression in the position of the high-priest. Already under the king the chief priest had a great and special importance as the representative of the priesthood. After the first return we see him placed by the side of the regent. The regent is mentioned first, but nevertheless the high priest is his equal (Hag. 1,1.12.14; 2,2.4); they are the two "anointed" (Zech. 4,14). It is true that there were still some who looked forward to the coming of "a shoot" that should wear the crown, that is to say, as king, but the high-priest was to rule in the temple (Zech. 3; 6,11 ff.). There was a certain doubt, but it ceased when it became clear that the king was not coming. While he lived on in the ideal realm of expectation, remote from reality, the high-priest acquired more and more importance as the person who was the upholder of the Israelite community. It is this state of affairs which is expressed in the priestly laws.

The high-priest is called "the great priest" (Num. 35,25.28), "the anointed priest" (Lev. 4,3.5.16), "the chief priest" (2 Chron. 19,11) or merely "the priest" (Ex. 31,10; 35,19 et al.). He is of Eleazar's family and is "Levi's prince of princes" (Num. 3,32). The law of holiness calls him "the priest who is greater than his brethren" (Lev. 21,10). The same thing is expressed in genealogical form by the statement that Aaron, the first high-priest, was the father of the priests. "Aaron and his sons" is the usual designation of the priesthood. As the representative of the priests he wears over his robe the instruments of the ancient oracle (Ex. 28,30) that with which the activity of the priest was especially associated in the old days. And as the mainstay of the community he had the Israelite tribal names inscribed on precious stones on the bag containing the oracular lots (Ex. 28,17-21.29). Now it was the high-priest who was to secure through the cultus that strength for the people which it had previously been the duty of the king to create. However, it is particularly the negative element which comes into the foreground. A sin committed by him reacts on the whole community, therefore special expiatory offerings are made for him (Lev. 4,3 ff.; 16). How largely the whole psychic life of the people with its responsibility was associated with him may be seen from the fact that murderers were exempted from their blood-guilt when the high priest under whom they had incurred it died (Num. 35,25.28.32).

The position of the high-priest and his relation to the priests at the post-exilic temple is directly reflected in the stories of Aaron and his sons from the time of the founding of the nation, in which Aaron figures as the brother of Moses. This has brought about a certain obscurity in the position of Moses, for previously Moses himself was the chief priest of the people, because he was its highest chieftain. Dan's priesthood traced its descent from him, Gershom being a son of

Moses (Judg. 18,30). It was Moses who founded law and justice for the Israelites (Ex. 15,25), he procured oracles in difficult judicial questions (Ex. 18,19); he received revelations from Yahweh in the sacred tent (Ex. 33,9). It is impossible to determine with accuracy where he acts as a priest and where he does not. We still find traces of the old time when the chief was the head of the cultus, as in the making of the covenant on Sinai (Ex. 24, 6-8); but precisely because tradition attributed a power to him which later came to be a priestly function, such power was continually attributed to him even after the function of the priest had become an office apart, and this had been assigned to Aaron. It was still Moses who was nearest to Yahweh and received his revelations, he was the intermediary between Yahweh and Israel. Even the story of Moses' distribution of the offices of the judges (Ex. 18) must no doubt have taken shape under post-exilic conditions. Aaron was merely a priest, but Moses continued to have traits of both the ruler and the priest, just as he had also the spirit of the prophet. In a psalm it is therefore possible to refer to both Moses and Aaron as priests of Yahweh (Ps. 99,6).

Tradition has thus exerted its influence on the stories, so that Aaron always appears as second to Moses. In so far they reflect the relation between the king and the chief priest, but they give no clear picture of this relation, because the picture of Moses also shows evidence of the post-exilic view of the great priest, and therefore he occupies a purely individual special position throughout. In the legend of the Passover Aaron is Moses' assistant, his "mouth" (Ex. 4,16), and the intermediary between him and the people; sometimes he also accompanies Moses to Pharaoh (5,1 ff.; 7,1 f.; 8,4 ff.; 9,27; 10,3.8). He helps Moses in war (17,10 ff.), and assists him when the covenant is made on Mount Sinai (19,24; 24,9 ff.). It is Moses who appoints Aaron and his sons to the priesthood (Ex. 28,1 ff.) and carries out their cultic consecration (29,1 ff.). Here it is the priest who appoints the priest. It is difficult to decide what is implied in the story of Aaron and Miriam, who opposed Moses when he had married a Kushite woman (Num. 12,1 ff.). It may be a priestly and prophetic opposition to the king which has left traces in this narrative, but more probably it is meant to show that Moses is a person quite apart, raised above the priests and prophets of Israel.

The most remarkable story we are told about Aaron is that of the calf of gold which he made, allowing the Israelites to celebrate a great religious festival before it while Moses was on the mountain with Yahweh (Ex. 32). The result was that the Levites were given the priesthood, because of their zeal in cutting down their apostate countrymen. But how is it possible that Aaron, the greatest of all Yahweh's priests, could be the leader in a cult regarded in later Israel as the greatest of all sins? This raises the question of who Aaron originally was. We only know the name as a designation for the high-priest of Jerusalem in post-exilic times. At the same time as new families were admitted to the priesthood of Jerusalem and the priests were collected under the genealogy of Levi, Aaron appears as the man from whom the Zadokite priesthood traced their descent, together with the other ecclesiastical families admitted to the temple at Jerusalem. Just as Levi was the old Israelite priestly family which can hardly originally have had anything to do with Jerusalem, thus Aaron may have become the recognised first ancestor, because he could be shown to be an early Israelite progenitor of priests. Probably he obtained recognition as a progenitor together with Eleazar and Phinehas. Now, it is said about the latter, whose conspicuously Egyptian name, which means negro, is the designation of one of Eli's sons (1 Sam. 4,11.19 f.), that his city was Gibeah, and that Eleazar was buried there (Josh. 24,33). It has been inferred from this that Aaron, too, originally belonged to Ephraim, [1] which may be right. It is then supposed that Aaron, in the narrative of the golden calf, represents the North Israelitish cultus to which, as we know, the calf belonged.

This conclusion seems correct, but is not entirely so. The narrative undoubtedly contains genuine features of the Canaanite-Israelite cult, but it is also marked by the conception of a later period. It cannot reasonably be affirmed that Aaron is here quite a different person from the Aaron of the other narratives, that is to say, the head of the priesthood. The story is only narrated to condemn the Canaanite cult, and to show that the true priesthood is associated with this condemnation. If there should really lie behind our story a cult tradition of a North Israelite priest, Aaron, who founded the worship of the calf, then the story has been changed to its contrary. As we know it, it gives a picture of the great struggle between the cults in which the priesthood played a prominent part. It shows how tainted the priesthood of Israel was as a whole, and how great the danger was, when even the highest members of it indulged the inclinations of the people. Both Moses and Aaron, we know, sometimes showed that they also could be recalcitrant and defy the will of Yahweh. What would most seem to show that the narrator is working with old refractory material is the curious lack of consistency in the behaviour of the Levites, who win their blessing by a sanguinary battle against that which their own leader has founded.

When Moses, the unique man of God, had died, the great office of the high-priest became more prominent. To Joshua was assigned part of the honour *(hōdh)* of Moses, he was to lead the people; but it is emphasised that he is to ask the high priest Eleazar for oracles and act in accordance with them (Num. 27, 20 f.). Here we find a similar obscurity in the relationship between the two authorities to what we know from the above-mentioned historical accounts of post-exilic times; but there is an attempt to insist upon the superior rank of the high priest, exhibited also in the fact that the reference now is to "Eleazar and Joshua" (Num. 34,17).

In the history of the monarchical period as presented in the Chronicles we find a certain analogy to this view of the authorities. The chronicler has preserved the tradition of David and Solomon as founders of the temple and the cultus. They appear as the leaders of the ritual ceremonies, the priest taking no prominent part in them. But under the later kings it is otherwise, now the high-priest takes the lead in the service at the altar and rebuffs the king's attempt to invade his domain. The otherwise highly esteemed Uzziah wished to enter the temple to offer incense, when he was met by the high-priest and 80 priests who turned him out of the sanctuary; and when he would not yield, he became leprous (2 Chron. 26,16-20). From the history of Hezekiah and Josiah we see how the Chronicler understands the matter (2 Chron. 29-31; 35). The king was to manage external affairs, and defray expenses, but the cult concerned the priests only. The principle is expressed by Jehoshaphat. There are two domains, that of Yahweh and that of the king, and he says: Behold, the high-priest Amariah shall be your superior in all that concerns Yahweh, and Zebadiah, the son of Ishmael, the head of the house of Judah, in all that concerns the king ... (2 Chron. 19,11).

This division had been aimed at as far back as the time of the laws of Ezekiel. It had begun by a claim on the part of the priests that they should be sole masters on the ground of the temple, and the fact that foreign regents ruled the country favoured their claim. But in reality it could not be carried through. The cultus was the basis of the whole life of the people, and all the laws were an expression of the will of Yahweh. The segregation of the priests turned the people into laymen, but for that very reason they could not do without the priests, neither their holiness nor their teaching. Ezekiel who attached so much importance to the maintenance of holiness, in accord with the tradition, accentuates the duty of the priest to teach the people, settle legal disputes, and watch over the torah (Ez. 44,23 f.). The priestly laws also bid the priests teach Israel (Lev. 10,11; 13 f.). And the Chronicler who attempts to draw a distinction between the domains of Yahweh and the government, will not of course give up the claim of the Levites and priests to take part in the administration of justice (2 Chron. 19,8.11). Both Levites and priests teach the people the law in post-exilic times (Neh. 8,7; 2 Chron. 17,7-9; 35,3).

The maintenance of holiness and the keeping of the law were essential to the survival of the community, hence the priests were necessary to the people. But often the priests felt merely like a privileged class who by virtue of their birth were entitled to service from the people. Nehemiah who himself kept carefully to the domain of the layman (Neh. 6,11) devoted all his energy to providing the service at the temple, and the maintenance of the rights and duties of the priesthood. Hence he had to fight both the lay population and the priests. When the Levites did not receive their dues, they left the temple and went to their landed property (Neh. 13,10). Nehemiah regarded the organisation of the priesthood as his greatest achievement (13,29 f.).

Severe words are pronounced against the priests by the nameless prophet usually called Malachi: And now, ye priests, this commandment is for you! If you do not hear, and do not lay it to heart to give glory unto my name, saith Yahweh of the hosts, I will send curses upon you and curse your blessings ... Behold, I threaten your seed and throw dung upon your faces ... And ye shall know that I send you this commandment that my covenant may be with Levi, saith Yahweh of the hosts. My covenant was with him for life and peace and I gave them to him, for fear, and he feared me and was afraid of my name. The torah of truth was in his mouth, and injustice was not found in his lips. He walked with me in peace and equity, and he turned many away from guilt. For the lips of the priest preserve knowledge, and they seek torah at his mounth, yea, he is the messenger *(mal'ākh)* of Yahweh of the hosts. But ye are departed from the way, have caused many to stumble against the torah, ye have corrupted the covenant of Levi, saith Yahweh of the hosts. Therefore I have caused the whole people to despise and slight you as you keep not my ways but are partial in the torah (Mal. 2,1-9). He also accuses the priests of neglecting the cult by offering unclean bread and imperfect animals, whereby the whole offering becomes useless. (1,6 ff.). But a messenger shall come who shall redress everything, a messenger from God to Israel. Possibly the prophet is here thinking of the expected king (Mal. 3,1). [1]

The stern accusations mean that the priests are not doing their duty as the maintainers of holiness and the law, but not that they are superfluous; on the contrary, the passionate utterances are due to the very fact that Israel cannot do without them. That the prerogatives of the priesthood could be opposed, however, is evidenced by the revolt in the desert (Num. 16), but this was merely a passing incident. The pre-eminence of the priesthood was impregnable. The ordeal of the laying of the rods in the temple showed it, for only Aaron's rod flowered (Num. 17,16-26). Just as prophecies of the appearance of a true scion of the house of

David are attributed to Jeremiah, thus also in connection herewith we find the assurance that Yahweh's covenant with the Levites shall never be broken; they shall always have descendants who shall serve before the face of Yahweh and present his offerings (Jer. 33,18.21). At what period this utterance was formulated, which adheres to the connection between the true kingship and the true priesthood, cannot be decided, but the post-exilic period is implied.

The interaction between the monarchy and the priesthood is one of the most important features in the history of Israel. It was the monarchy which created the possibility of a large and powerful priesthood. The priests were the servants of the king, who were to create and maintain the holiness that enabled him to be the upholder of the people. But the old independence of the priest as the teacher of Israelite law and the steward of holiness was not forgotten, and the more powerful the king made the priesthood the greater became its claims as an independent power. The monarchical attempt at centralisation collected the priesthood; the great temple of the king gathered to itself the priests; thus they became united as a caste, possessors of holiness by virtue of their birth. When the kingdom fell, this whole development of the power and function of the priesthood had been securely accomplished. Now they proceeded to rid themselves entirely of the fallen king, to live as an independent holy aristocracy with the high-priest as leader. This is what Josephus calls theocracy.

The high-priest could to a certain extent take the place of the king, but not entirely; his actions were determined by quite different traditions. He could not take charge of the cult associated with the king. This is evidenced by the fact that only reminiscences of it are preserved in the temple hymns, while it has entirely disappeared from the cult, with, perhaps, a single exception. [1] Hence the rule of the high-priest meant a new epoch in the cultural history of Israel. The chief was the person in whom the community gathering round him felt their own strength and will made active, hence there was a perfect fellowship between them. The king was an isolated person, who, aided by the priest, increased his psychic strength through the cult, that he might again impart of it to the people. The strength of the high-priest was due to the fact that he was the person round whom a holy aristocracy gathered, which found its nature and its strength expressed in him. The strength which he was able to impart to the people came to it by way of the holy priesthood.

Simon, one of these high-priest rulers, is praised by Jesus, Sirach's son as the greatest among his brethren, the priests, and the ornament of his people. In the description of his conduct during the rites, homage is paid to him which recalls that previously given to the king. He goes forth like the morning star, like the sun, like the rainbow, dressed in his magnificent robes (Sir. 50). When the Hasmonaean high-priests allowed themselves to be made kings, a natural cycle of development was closed.

Once the priestly aristocracy had been created, there was no getting round it. It formed the transition between the human and the divine world, but thus it blocked the way for the other Israelites to the highest thing life could offer. As Joel dreams of a time when all Israelites will be prophets, another prophet consistently sees Israel made perfect by all Israelites becoming priests (Isa. 61,6, cf. Ex. 19,6). Thus the people would by devious ways attain the same state as that in which it was living under the primitive conditions of the old times.

HOLY PLACES AND HOLY THINGS.

TO the Israelites, mankind and the land they inhabited formed an entity with a fixed harmony. The land of man was the land of the blessing, and the land pervaded by the blessing of Israel was Canaan. But just as there were people whose souls were filled with the strength of holiness, so also there were places which were marked by an immense concentration of sacred strength. Such places were holy places.

The Israelites never forgot that they had a history before they entered Canaan, and this fact has set its mark on their tradition of the holy places. Among all these the mountain in the desert, Sinai or Horeb, occupied a special position, because it was there the God of the people had revealed himself and made the covenant on which its life was based; it was there Moses built an altar in order to confirm the covenant by sacrifice (Ex. 24, 4-8), and it was there all laws were given which were of decisive importance for the life of Israel. Hence the holy mountain of the desert is to the Israelites their original sanctuary, the starting point of all Israelite life. In Israelite poetry we also sometimes meet with the statement that Yahweh comes from Sinai (Deut. 33,2; Judg. 5,5; Ps. 68,9.18), [1] which expresses that the God of Israel dwells there.

The strange thing is, however, that the Israelites did not keep up the connection with the primal holy mountain. We are told that Elijah, wearied by his struggle with the new gods, retired to Horeb (1 Kings 19,8), but apart from this we hear nothing of pilgrimages, far less of a regular Israelite worship at the place. This means that the mountain is no longer any real sanctuary to the Israelites. A close study of the records confirms this. The mountain is sometimes called Horeb, sometimes Sinai. Deuter-

onomy, except in the Blessing of Moses (33,2), has Horeb
(1,2.6.19; 4, 10.15 etc., cf. Ex. 3,1; 17,6; 33,6); otherwise Sinai
is the name usually employed. Certain features which are referred
to Sinai in the Pentateuch, are referred to Horeb in other writings
(1 Kings 8,9; Mal. 3,22; Ps. 106,19). Thus the two names have,
at any rate in later times, been used about the same place. We
cannot say whether two traditions have become merged here, or
whether there may have been two mountains, so close to each
other that both their names could be used for the holy place.

This obscurity is further increased if we attempt to determine
the position of the mountain or mountains on the basis of the
narratives of the wanderings. The great difficulties encountered
in these attempts are probably caused by the fact that the narrators no longer knew anything about it themselves. In the Song
of Deborah we read: Yahweh when thou wentest out of Seir, when
thou didst advance from the plain of Edom ... (Judg. 5,4) and
another poem runs thus: Yahweh cometh from Sinai, breaketh
forth out of Seir to them, radiates from the mountain of Paran
(Deut. 33,2). This conveys the impression that Yahweh's dwelling-
place is in Edom, which is not reconcilable with the legends of
the wanderings. Possibly these poetic utterances (as in Hab. 3,3)
are merely intended to express that Yahweh came from the south.

The only natural explanation of the fact that Sinai-Horeb
came to play such a prominent part in Israelite tradition is that
pre-Canaanite Israel really resorted to this mountain as a main
sanctuary. Through the cultus it has then constantly been
commemorated as the place of Yahweh's covenant with Israel. Thus
it came to be regarded as the original sanctuary, the point of
departure for all covenants with Yahweh and for Israelite law.
Its position became a matter of indifference, it was an imaginary
place of supreme importance. Hence the old traditions as to its
geographical situation were forgotten, and replaced by "learned"
reconstructions.

In addition to the holy mountain the Israelite nomad community had movable sanctuaries which they could carry with them
on their wanderings, partly a tent, partly a chest, "the Ark of the
Covenant". The people still preserved these sacred treasures after

they had settled in Canaan, an external testimony to the continuity
of their history; hence we must consider them more closely in
connection with the other sanctuaries which Israel possessed in
Canaan.

We have two different descriptions of the tent as a movable
sanctuary. According to one Moses erected it on the camping
ground outside the camp. When Yahweh was to be questioned,
Moses went into the tent, the Israelites remaining outside as
humble witnesses. Inside he spoke face to face with Yahweh; but
Joshua was always there as a servant (Ex. 33,7-11). Besides this
account we have the detailed description of the large sanctuary
placed in the middle of the camp, in which the entire cult of
Jerusalem was instituted (Ex. 25 ff.). The fact that the whole of
this large building, constructed of wood and provided with
hangings, was called a tent, shows how strong was the tradition
that a tent constituted the sanctuary of the wandering tribes.
Actually the entire description, as has been long since discovered,
is a mere reflection of the temple at Jerusalem. The post-exilic
priesthood could not imagine an Israelite existence without this
temple as the basis of the maintenance of life, least of all in the
period of the founding of the nation, when all the leading
institutions were created; therefore the old tent was transformed
in their eyes into a complete temple building. But the other description also cannot be taken as a simple historical document. Moses
is already here the unique intermediary between Yahweh and
Israel as the conveyer of the revelation.

In both presentations the tent is called *'ōhel mō'ēdh* (Ex. 27,21;
28,43; 33,7 et al.), a designation very difficult to translate, but
a characteristic expression of what the sanctuary was. *Mō'ēdh*
denotes place, time or condition, fixed and made prominent by a
definite agreement, a custom, or a special psychic content giving
it a particular significance. Therefore it may denote an arrangement, a place or time agreed upon, or an appointment; but it also
denotes time or place set off from their surroundings by a special
character. When the realm of death is called *bēth mō'ēdh* (Job
30,23), this term hardly indicates the house where people gather
as much as the house which in a quite peculiar sense becomes a

dwelling-place for all living beings. Hence *mō'ēdh* is used about time in a special sense, its climaxes, that is to say, festive occasions, and in the same way it denotes a place prominent among all places, because a special power attaches to it. The earlier translations of *'ōhel mō'ēdh* as "witnessing tent" or "tent of the covenant" render approximately what is implied in the expression. It denotes the tent where the divine power has revealed itself, where it is present to the Israelites. It is the place of the spiritual union between God and man. It may presumably be regarded as purely accidental that the word *mō'ēdh*, which is constantly used about hallowed times, is only on rare occasions used about the greatest Israelitish sanctuary, the temple of Jerusalem (Ps. 74,4, cf. 8; Lam. 2,6). On one occasion it is employed to denote the mythical, foreign, holy mountain where the gods dwell *(har mō'ēdh* Isa. 14,13), but otherwise we only find it employed about the sacred tent of the wilderness time, and then as a rule in the form mentioned. Besides this, there also occurs *'ōhel* or *mishkan hā'ēdūth*, "the witnessing tent or dwelling" (Ex. 38,21; Num. 1,50.53; 9,15; 10,11; 17,22 f. et al), and similar expressions are used about the Ark and other holy things, all in the sense described above. [1]

The inherent power of the holy places caused the ancient sanctuaries to be respected throughout the history of the people. For that very reason they were transformed and idealised in the spirit of a later time. Thus the mountain and the tent, in the tradition of Israel, became an expression of what later Israel sought at the holy place, as well as a reminiscence of the nomadic past of the people.

───────────

When the Israelite tribes entered Canaan they found a land filled with sanctuaries. The simplest form of sanctuary is known from the investigations in Israelite territory as well as in Phoenicia. It was an enclosed, uncovered space, with one or more holy stones, besides trees or wooden poles; further a reservoir for water, and occasionally a building with an altar in front of it. By the outer walls there might be closed cells for the use of the priests or for sacred treasure; frequently, also, subterranean caves might be found. [1] We know too that a holy place might be connected with a spring. The Canaanite sanctuary was a part of the Canaanite landscape itself.

From this simple starting-point there developed sanctuaries in which the building played a more prominent part. This is attested by the archaeological discoveries which are beginning to be made. They show how foreign influences, too, asserted themselves in this field. The four temples found at Bethshean were all built by Egyptian potentates to Canaanite gods, one in about the year 1400, three about 1300. In the earliest one the underlying Canaanite plan is still evident: an open space with stone pillars and an altar. Inside the temple building were found sacred objects, idols of Astarte etc., pointing to an Egyptian, Hittite, and Aegaean origin. The two youngest temples, dating from the time of Rameses II, contained a hall with pillars; one was dedicated to Astarte as queen of the heavens, the other contained objects of a Cyprian-Aegaean character. Perhaps they belonged to the Philistines who ruled here at the time of Saul. [2]

An open space with an altar and possibly stone pillars is also found at Shechem. From the open space a staircase leads towards the north to a hall which again opens into a hall divided into three aisles by rows of pillars; in the middle there is the pedestal of an idol or the like. [3] Here, too, details of an Egyptian or an Aegaean character can be demonstrated, and the temple may be presumed to be the one dedicated to Baal berith, mentioned in the book of Judges. The holy place is of the true Canaanite type, and the building, too, in so far as it shows that mixture of foreign elements which was typical of Canaan.

The foreign influence was especially evident in the temple buildings. As a rule they probably contained an idol and other sacred objects, but they were also a gathering-place for the participants in the festivals. The Old Testament tells us of Canaanite temple buildings, and we learn that they were filled with the worshippers at the festivals. The temple of Gaza contained an image of Dagon (1 Sam. 5,2 ff.); from the story of Samson we learn that it was filled with men and women diverting themselves with the sight of the eyeless hero (Judg. 16,23 ff.). We hear of the temple of Baal at Shechem that the citizens sat in it eating and drinking and cursing Abimelech (Judg. 9,27). The temple of Baal at Samaria, too, was filled with worshippers on occasion (2 Kings 10,21).

Like other conquerors the Israelites appropriated the sanctuaries of the country, but it did not happen suddenly, and as long as they had to content themselves with being shepherds and small farmers, they possessed no large temples like those to be seen at Bethshean. Their sanctuaries had the simple Canaanite forms. For some of them we have consecration legends associated with the heroes of the time when the Israelites settled in Canaan, the time of the judges.

In connection with the sanctuary at *Ophrah* which was regarded as belonging to the tribe of Manasseh, we have a consecration legend in two forms directly connected with each other. One runs as follows: Gideon, the son of Joash of the family of Abiezer, was at Ophrah threshing wheat in his wine press, when Yahweh appeared to him under the terebinth in the shape of his *mal'ākh;* he greeted Gideon and summoned him to fight against the Midianites. Now Gideon understood his guest to be a man of God speaking in the name of Yahweh, and he wished to confirm what had happened by a meal. When he came with the meat of a kid and with soup and bread, the stranger asked him to lay the meat and the bread on the rock and pour the soup over it. When he did this, Yahweh touched it with his wand, a flame leaped out and consumed the food, and Yahweh disappeared. Then Gideon was afraid and Yahweh promised him peace. And Gideon built an altar to Yahweh which he called "Yahweh is peace", and, says the narrator, "it stands to this day in Ophrah of the Abiezrites" (Judg. 6,11-24).

The second story is given as a sequel to the first and so has probably lost its original beginning. In this we are told that Gideon, upon the command of Yahweh, pulled down his father's altar to Baal, and cut down the asherah beside the altar. Then he built on the rock an altar consisting of various layers and sacrificed a bull, using the asherah as fuel. This happened at the dead of night. The next morning the townsmen raised objections, but yielded to threats on the part of Gideon's father (Judg. 6,25-32).

The two narratives agree in referring the altar of Yahweh at Ophrah to two of the heroes of the fighting period. They show us the struggle by which Israelite sanctuaries developed out of Canaanite ones, but only the last story has entirely this character. The first one is a purely Israelite consecration legend, intended especially to confirm and motive, in the shape of such a legend, the character of the sanctuary at Ophrah as a holy place. It is a holy place because Yahweh himself appeared there and consecrated the rock to be a place of sacrifice. The story is highly condensed and rich in details. We hear that a terebinth stood near the place, and that Yahweh sat in its shade; this elevates it to the sphere of holiness. Near by a press had been cut in the rock and served as a threshing ground for Gideon. The whole place belonged to him and his family, not to the city community. The most important part of it was a projecting rock, for the holy strength of the place was chiefly gathered there. Hence special mention is made of it in the legend. By his meal Gideon wished to make a covenant with the unknown man of God, and thus confirm the promise he had received of the blessing in his fight against the enemy. He obtained what he wanted, but not in the way he had imagined. It was Yahweh himself who consumed the meal by his flame, and thus he took upon himself his part of the covenant that Gideon desired. And the covenant was inseparably associated with the holiness of the rock, for it was confirmed by the sacrificial fire which Yahweh kindled on it. The altar is called "Yahweh is peace", because it was the agency by which the covenant that Yahweh made with the Israelite chief was maintained.

The legend explains the holiness of *the place*, and of the terebinth and the rock upon which the sacrifice was made. The statement that Gideon built an altar there and gave it the above-mentioned name (v. 24) need not conflict with this. The holiness of the place was the permanent feature, the altar might vary.

But it is quite possible that originally there was no mention of a place of sacrifice other than the rock, the altar having crept in from the sequel.

In that narrative the altar plays the leading part. It is more like an ordinary story than a consecration legend. The place was already a holy place with an altar to Baal, when Gideon pulled it down together with its asherah and built an altar to Yahweh, on which he offered the first sacrifice. The story merely acquires its peculiar character by this being done in obedience to the command of Yahweh. Thus a Canaanite was transformed into an Israelite holy place, by the chief of the period of the foundation giving it a new altar. The story is not so full as the first one, and it may be doubtful whether it gives a true picture of the fighting period. Gideon's name Jerubbaal, "Baal is fighting" would seem to indicate that he belonged to circles where no sharp distinction was drawn between Yahweh and Baal, and the attempt made to give the opposite meaning to the name (6,32) shows that it is remote from the time of the event. According to another narrative, Gideon secured to the sanctuary at Ophrah an Ephod made of 1700 shekels of gold (Judg. 8,22-27). So probably there also belonged a temple building to the old natural sanctuary, but we hear nothing of this. It was the rock itself which was the actual holy place.

About the holy place at *Zorah* there is a consecration legend associating it with Samson's birth. Yahweh's mal'ākh came to Manoah's wife promising her that she should give birth to a son who should be dedicated to God. Upon the prayers of Manoah Yahweh's revelation was repeated, and now Manoah wished to know the name of the man of God in order that he might honour him when his promise was fulfilled, but he was merely told that the name was wonderful. Like Gideon he then wanted to offer a meal to the stranger, but the man of God bid him offer it to Yahweh on the rock. When Manoah, acting upon his command, made an offering upon the rock, the stranger disappeared in the altar flame. Then the husband and wife understood who had been present (Judg. 13). The story purports to show how Samson acquired the blessing and was consecrated by the spirit of Yahweh.

But his sanctification was associated with the holiness of the rock, in the sacrificial fire of which Yahweh revealed himself.

The consecration legends associated with the time of the Judges show how the holiness of two sanctuaries was created or confirmed by Yahweh himself appearing on them and identifying himself with the sacrificial fire kindled in them. They take us directly into life, showing us that Yahweh himself was present in their holiness.

In the tract south of Judah proper there were some sanctuaries which were associated with the name of Moses, especially *Kadesh*. Here the people are said to have stayed for a long time, and scouts were sent northward from there (Num. 20,1; 32,8; Josh. 14,6.7). There was a well on the spot called the well of the ordeal, *ʿēn mishpāṭ* and *mē merībhā* (Gen. 14,7; Num. 20,13.24; Deut. 33,8; Ps. 81,8 et al.). There can be no doubt that it was a holy well, and this is expressed in a story of how it sprang forth when Moses smote the rock with his staff at the bidding of Yahweh (Num. 20,1-13; cf. Ex. 17,1-7). [1] Close by there was an altar to Yahweh at Rephidim (Ex. 17,14 f.), and Aaron's death is localised to the mountain of Hor (Num. 20,28; 33,38; Deut. 32,50), which must surely mean that pilgrimages were made to his grave there. This series of sanctuaries belonged to the region on the outskirts of the Israelite land; Kadesh was included in the territory of Judah (Num. 34,4; Josh. 10,41; 15,3). The reason why the holy places are associated with Moses and Aaron is perhaps that the traditions about Moses originally belonged to the people of these parts.

The tradition shows evidence of the Israelite lack of interest in the sanctuaries after the temple of Jerusalem had become their only holy place. The holy well at Kadesh became a remembrance of that defiance which even Moses and Aaron showed to Yahweh (Ex. 17,1 ff.). And yet the Israelites could not quite give up the ancient holy places, where their forefathers had confirmed their covenant with Yahweh; for they had been centres of the blessing which bound Israel and the country together. This is expressed in the narratives about the patriarchs.

It is probable that the patriarchs were originally associated with definite sanctuaries; each must then have been honoured separately as the hero who founded the sanctuary, and whose God the worshipper found at the shrine.[1] As we know them, the patriarchs are the fathers of the whole nation, and the blessing by which the whole people lives is derived from them. The narrators represent them as going about the country thus making it an inheritance of Israel. The institution of sanctuaries is made into episodes occurring during their wanderings, by which they appropriate the country and make it the foundation of the blessing of Israel. The stories may be based on ancient consecration legends, but they do not themselves describe a living cult as do the narratives associated with Ophrah and Zorah.

One of the chief Israelitish sanctuaries during the monarchical period was situated at *Bethel*. Jeroboam equipped it as a royal sanctuary, a rival of Jerusalem (1 Kings 12,29 ff.). Under Jeroboam II it retained this standing, as we know from Amos (7,13), whose words likewise show that it contained a temple with pillars (9,1). The sanctuary is said to have been desecrated by Josiah during his ritual campaign (2 Kings 23,15, cf. 1 Kings 13,1 ff.). But it was not Jeroboam who founded the sanctuary in the first place. We hear about it in earlier times, not only in the curious narrative at the end of the book of Judges (20,26; 21,2), but also in the stories of Samuel (1 Sam. 10,3). The general importance for Israel of this sanctuary is acknowledged by assigning its foundation to the time of the first ancestors of the people.

Of Abraham we are told in the usual brief way: And he went up from there to the mountain east of Bethel, and he pitched his tent with Bethel to the west and Ai to the east, and there he built an altar to Yahweh, and called upon the name of Yahweh (Gen. 12,8). It is impossible to say whether the sanctuary of Bethel was outside the town, or whether we may here be concerned with a holy place at Bethel other than the main sanctuary. The significant feature is that Abraham also sanctified Bethel. But the most important foundation legend referring to Bethel is that associated with the name of Jacob. It runs thus:

And Jacob left Beersheba and wandered to Haran. And he

came upon the place and stayed the night there for the sun had
set. And he took one of the stones of the place and laid it at his
head, and he lay down to rest in this place. And he dreamed, and
behold, a ladder was set upon the earth and the top of it reached
to heaven; and behold, God's *mal'ākhīm* ascended and descended
it. And behold, Yahweh stood before him, saying: I am Yahweh,
the God of thy father Abraham and of Isaac. The land on which
thou liest I will give to thee and to thy seed. And thy seed shall
be as the dust of the earth, and thou shalt spread abroad to the
west and to the east, to the north and to the south; and in thee
and in thy seed shall all the families of the earth be blessed. And
behold, I will be with thee and will keep thee wherever thou
goest, and I will bring thee back into this land; for I will not
leave thee until I have done all that I have spoken to thee of.
And Jacob awoke out of his sleep and said: Surely Yahweh is
in this place, and I knew it not. And he was afraid and said:
How dreadful is this place. This is none other but a house of
God, and this is the gate of heaven. And Jacob rose early in the
morning and took the stone that he had put for his pillow and
set it up for a *maṣṣēbhā,* and he poured oil over the top of it. And
he called the name of that place Bethel (i. e. house of god); but
the name of the city had from early times been Luz. And Jacob
vowed a vow, saying: If God is with me and keeps me on this
way that I am going, and he gives me bread to eat and raiment
to put on, and I come back again to my father's house in peace,
then shall Yahweh be my God, and this stone which I have set
up for a *maṣṣēbhā* shall be a house of God; and of all that thou
givest me, I will give a tenth part to thee (Gen. 28,10-22).

Here again, the foundation of the sanctuary is made a link in
the life and wanderings of the patriarch. It is even emphasised at
the beginning of the narrative that it was merely by chance
(way-yiphgaʿ v. 11) that Jacob happened to stay the night there.
But we soon discover that this chance is a feature of the narrator's art. It was not the first ancestor's own idea to found a
sanctuary there, he was guided by a stronger hand, in accordance
with the teaching which runs like a leading thread through all
the narratives in Genesis.

A close scrutiny of Jacob's experience in the place to which he was led will show that there is no event which, as in the story of Gideon and Manoah, consecrates the cult of the holy place. Jacob has a dream in which he sees the place directly connected with Heaven, and thus with the seat of God. And if he were to doubt that this was the meaning of the ladder, his doubts must be dissipated when he sees divine beings moving up and down it. Hence there is nothing strange in the fact that Yahweh suddenly appears to him and speaks to him. There is nothing in the words of Yahweh to recall the sanctuary; he confirms the blessing which Jacob has already received from Isaac: he shall possess the land and the blessing shall become active in his seed; it shall fill the entire earth. It is the covenant with his forefathers which is transferred to Jacob in this place; here the father of the people received the blessing by which the people lives, and a promise of the land it claims.

When Jacob awakes the next morning he confirms the covenant by which Yahweh's blessing is bestowed on him. He establishes that it is a new and unexpected gift which has been conferred on him. The place is dreadful to men as are all places frequented by divine beings, but little did he suspect that it was a place which belonged to Yahweh, and as such must be given to him. And he consecrated the stone to be a *maṣṣēbhā* by pouring oil over it. The consecration has a special meaning, it was a confirmation of the blessing and the covenant which the night had witnessed. Yahweh had promised him to take care of him and bring him safely back. If Yahweh kept his word, he should always be the God of Jacob, and the consecrated stone he had set up should be a house of God, at which he would give tithes. Thus the story ends in a conditional promise requiring a sequel. And as a matter of fact this comes upon the return of Jacob from the land of the Aramaeans.

When Jacob was at Shechem, he was commanded by God to go to Bethel and build an altar to the God that had revealed himself to him. "And Jacob said unto his household and to all that were with him: Remove the strange gods that are among you, and purify yourselves and change your garments. And let us arise and go up to Bethel and there I will build an altar to the

God that answered me in the hour of my distress and was with me in the way which I went" (Gen. 35,2-3). Now they gave Jacob all their strange gods and the rings they wore as amulets, and he buried them under the terebinth by Shechem. Then they left the place, and the family went unmolested to Bethel, for all the cities around were struck with terror. Here Jacob built an altar in the place of the divine revelation. And again God appeared to him and confirmed his blessing; where it happened Jacob set up a *maṣṣēbhā,* which he consecrated with oil, and he called the place Bethel (vv. 4-7).

In the first narrative Jacob was promised the land and Yahweh's protection; in the second he admits his Aramaean household to the Israelite community by making the members cast out all strange gods which they had brought with them. Then he fulfils his promise and founds the sanctuary by building an altar, and again the divine blessing is confirmed, his name being changed to Israel (v. 9 ff.). The story does not link up with the former one in the way we should expect. It might have been thought that there would be a hint that Jacob, by founding the sanctuary, had fulfilled the promise he had made, and likewise an indication that the *maṣṣēbhā* he set up was the one he had already consecrated. However this looseness of construction is to be explained, there is no doubt that the two stories are intimately associated, and taken together are meant to give the history of how the sanctuary at Bethel came into existence.

We have already said that the narrative has not the character of a consecration legend proper which has been formed by the living cult. What does it mean that Jacob promises his God to make the stone a house of God? The narrator is trying to reproduce the old way of thinking, though he does not quite know it any longer. In the old days it was the God himself who revealed his presence in the holy place, thus showing that it was "a house of God". The very point of the legends is that it was not man who chose the holy places at his own pleasure. Jacob could promise to honour the holy stone that Yahweh had chosen, and to build a temple in Yahweh's holy place. There are other features which are not derived from early times. In later Israel, after the exile, the abolition of the foreign idols and amulets became a natural condition for the admittance of strangers, but it is not in accord with the old time, least of all with the cult which was current at the main sanctuaries in northern Israel.

The narrator did not wish to give the background nor the divine confirmation of the cult which was prevalent at Bethel, for it was quite alien to him. What he wanted to show was that here Yahweh was present. At the old main sanctuary Yahweh made a covenant with the father of the race, bestowing on him the blessing and the land. The founding of the sanctuary at Bethel means that the country to which it belongs is Israelitish property. To the narrator this is the significance of the altar and the *maṣṣēbhā* in the ancient and famous sanctuary. [1]

Of a similar kind are the foundation legends relating to the sanctuary of *Shechem* situated a little to the north of Bethel. In one of the stories about Jacob we hear an echo of the fights of the Israelites and Canaanites for the possession of this city (Gen. 34). Here Gideon's son Abimelech was king for a short time, and we hear of a temple to Baal berith, but it was destroyed with the town by Abimelech during his struggle for the power (Judg. 9), which does not mean, of course, that the sanctuary was abolished for good. The city became the capital of Jeroboam I (1 Kings 12,25), and there seems to be a reminiscence of its importance for Israelite cultus in the account of how an altar was erected there at the immigration, blessings and curses being pronounced there (Deut. 27,1 ff.; Josh. 8,30 ff.). The legends we possess about Shechem carry us back to the time of the conquest as well as to patriarchal times.

The foundation of the altar is attributed both to Abraham and to Jacob. The story about Abraham is, as usual, quite short. On his wanderings he came to Shechem "when the Canaanite lived in the land", and found himself at the soothsayer's tree. Yahweh promised him the land for his property, and Abraham built an altar to Yahweh (Gen. 12,6-7). The story is a part of the plan according to which Abraham builds altars to confirm the blessing and his right to the possession of the land. And it is no different with Jacob. An isolated fragment of an old tradition

14*

makes Jacob promise Joseph "a shoulder *(shᵉkhem)* above thy brethren which I have taken from the Amorite with my sword and with my bow" (Gen. 48,22). But in Jacob's history we are told that when he came to Shechem on his journey from the land of the Aramaeans, he settled before the town, and he bought the site of Hamor's sons on which his tent had been pitched, and there he erected an altar which he called El, the god of Israel (Gen. 33, 18-20). Here again the legend says that the Israelites are fully entitled to the sanctuary; it has been lawfully founded by their first ancestor.

To this must be added a feature related a little later. Jacob buried all the strange gods and the other sacred objects which his family had brought with them from the land of the Aramaeans under the terebinth of the sanctuary (Gen. 35,4). And further, in another passage, we are given the supplementary information that Joseph's bones were buried in the place where Jacob founded the sanctuary (Josh. 24,32).

The feature that the foreign gods were abolished at Shechem is meant to emphasise further the Israelite character of the sanctuary in the most rigorous sense, but it shows clearly that we have not an old consecration legend before us, but a didactic story of later times. It is true that the foreign gods were combated in the pre-exilic struggles, but a story like the present implies that the struggle is ended. It is taken for granted that the eradication of the foreign gods is the chief condition for the founding of an Israelite sanctuary.

This trait appears even more distinctly in the stories about Joshua. We are told that after the war had come to an end, Joshua collected the tribes at Shechem. Addressing them he reviewed their history, and showed how they had been led by Yahweh and owed everything to him (Josh. 24). He exhorted them all to keep to Yahweh and abolish the foreign gods they had worshipped in their exile (vv. 14.23). Thereupon they made a covenant, and Joshua set up a stone under the oak standing in Yahweh's sanctuary, saying that the stone had heard the words and was to stand there as a witness that they would not deny their God (v. 26 f.).

Thus we learn that the grave of the progenitor of the tribe of Joseph belonged to Shechem, and that there was a holy tree and stones in the sanctuary. But what the legends communicate beyond these elements is marked by the conception of a later Israel.

Wandering southward through the country, Abraham came to southern Judah, he and Isaac founded sanctuaries in this part, and Jacob departed from here in the opposite direction to Abraham, going up through the country and eastward. A sanctuary near Kadesh, a well called *Be'er laḥai ro'i*, was associated with Yahweh's promise of greatness to Ishmael (Gen. 16,6 ff.; 21,13 ff.). Thus the area of the stories concerned with Abraham brings us close to the regions with which the legends of Moses were associated. The sanctuary at *Beersheba* was founded by Isaac, who built an altar there and called upon the name of Yahweh (Gen. 26,24 f.); here, again, there was a well. And the founding of the sanctuary has the same character as the other consecrations in the stories of the patriarchs; it is associated with Yahweh's promise of his blessing and of countless offspring.

The most important of the southern sanctuaries was *Hebron*. Here David had for a time been king, there he made the covenant with Israel before Yahweh (2 Sam. 5,3), and his family still went to this sanctuary (2 Sam. 15,7). That, too, had been founded by Abraham. When Yahweh promised him the whole land and numerous offspring, he settled among the terebinths of Mamre at Hebron and built an altar to Yahweh. The altar was to confirm the fact that Yahweh had given the land to Abraham (Gen. 13, 14-18). At Hebron the patriarch received visits from Yahweh (Gen. 18), here he purchased for his lawful possession a cave (Gen. 23) in which he buried Sarah, and later on he himself, Isaac, and Jacob were buried there. At Hebron were the tombs of the forefathers; it was the centre from which the blessing spread over Israel, a guarantee that the promises which the covenant with Yahweh covered would be fulfilled.

It is impossible to say why the stories of the patriarchs have to do particularly with these sanctuaries, the founding of which they describe. It is of special interest to note that the chief sanctuary of the people, the temple of Jerusalem, is not represented as founded by the patriarchs, and this is all the more remarkable since Jerusalem was not far from the route of Abraham, when he wandered from Bethel to the Dead Sea and thence to Hebron. It is possible that the allusion in the story of the sacrifice of Isaac is to the rock at Zion, so that the sacrifice showing the obedience to God of the first ancestor is after all associated with the great sanctuary, but there is no direct mention of the foundation. This need not imply any hostility towards the temple of Jerusalem. But the narrator of the stories, who has preserved so lively a picture of early Israelitish life, desired to show that this life was peculiarly the simple existence of the nomad and the agriculturist, and that the ancient sanctuaries scattered about the country were a token of Yahweh's covenant with his people and therefore a guarantee of its blessing and its right to the possession of the land. Thus the stories maintain the continuity of the people with the early institutions, in spite of the strong feeling against the scattered sanctuaries aroused by the conflict of the cults. They entirely disregard this conflict and maintain that, in spite of all, the sanctuaries were Israelitish sanctuaries.

In connection with the sanctuaries we continually hear of wells and trees, of tombs and stones. Wells and trees are living parts of nature in which holy energy is active. Through the tombs the strength and blessing of the ancestors are present, and often the power emanating from them is embodied in the stone.

The reason why stones are of such great importance in Israelite as well as other Canaanite and Semitic sanctuaries is that they have a power of absorbing and embodying a psychic content. This substantial, and almost unchangeable element, which plays a prominent part in the landscape of Palestine, like everything else in the world, has its own peculiar nature, its soul, and it is highly receptive of what is communicated to it. The vitality present in every stone is present in concentrated strength in the stone of the sanctuary. Hence man can draw power from the stone by approaching it, just as, conversely, the force of the stone is strengthened by the approach of man. Of what kind the energy is that is inherent in the stone depends on the tradition. The force which men have by experience found to be contained in the stone, will be found there over and over again.

In the simplest form of sanctuary there was no doubt only one stone, a piece of rock, as in the sanctuary of Ophrah. Here man encounters the divine power, and when his gifts are laid on the rock and consumed, it is the God himself who is in the stone and accepts the gift, as is clearly shown in the foundation legends for Ophrah and Zorah. But there may be also, as in most instances, a special altar and several holy stones. This was a Phoenician practice. The stone is then, as a rule, an upright pillar (*maṣṣēbhā*).

We know that it was usual in Israel to erect such a stone in order that it might bear a man's name or record some great event. [1] The maṣṣēbhā erected on Rachel's grave (Gen. 35,20) enabled the Israelites constantly to meet with the mother of their race. Samuel perpetuated a victory over the Philistines by a stone which he called "the stone of help" (*'ebhen hā'ēzer*, 1 Sam. 7,12). In Gilead, perhaps at the town of Mizpeh, there was a stone memorial which embodied and preserved the covenant between the Israelites and their neighbours and kinsmen, the Aramaeans. We do not know whether regular worship took place at the memorial, which included a maṣṣēbhā and a cairn; but the stones were witnesses of the covenant, and punishment from them would befall any one who broke it (Gen. 31,44-54). The forces embodied in the stone might act for the good, or for evil, as did, for instance, the cairn set up over the sinner Achan (Josh. 7,26).

Hence the stone could also retain and embody the forces in all their tremendous potentialities, so that, like the stone at Bethel, it might become the abode of a god. We cannot now tell what the Israelites saw in every single stone. Two stones of quite similar exterior might be quite different, and several stones in the same sanctuary might embody each its own content. Thus far the statement that Moses erected a maṣṣēbhā for each tribe beside the altar which he built at Sinai agrees with the early way of thinking (Ex. 24,4). One maṣṣēbhā might be the seat of forces emanating from Yahweh which were determined by the experiences of the patriarchs; while the fundamental strength of some Canaanite community might be inherent in another.

This is the reason why we find various conceptions of the maṣṣēbhās represented in the Old Testament. One prophet, Hosea, mentions these stone pillars as a fixed part of the sanctuaries; but since he denounces these as non-Israelitish in nature, his threats are also directed against the maṣṣēbhās (Hos. 3,4; 10,1 f.), and it is quite in accord with this campaign against foreign cults that a number of clauses in the Law demand the destruction of the Canaanite maṣṣēbhās (Ex. 23,24; 34,13; Deut. 7,5; 12,3); even though this demand, in the shape in which it has come down to us, has perhaps been formulated after the fall of the kingdom. It is otherwise when the Israelites are simply forbidden to erect maṣṣēbhās, as in Deuteronomy (16,22); and the reason alleged is that the maṣṣēbhās were identified with idols (Lev. 26,1; Mic. 5,12). This brings us to the way of thinking of post-exilic Judaism, which is also evinced in the retrospective remarks on the history of the monarchy found in the books of the Kings (1 Kings 14,23; 2 Kings 17,10). When we are told of the two reformers, Hezekiah and Josiah, that they did away with the maṣṣēbhās, the meaning of this information is not clear. Perhaps it is only part of the two kings' strife for unification; or perhaps the post-exilic author's hatred of the stones has found its way into the historical account.

On the other hand, as late as post-exilic times the significance of the stones had by no means been forgotten by everybody, and a narrator whose way of thinking is not far removed from that of the author of Deuteronomy can say about the circle of stones at Gilgal that it was a sign of Yahweh's wonderful guidance of the people across Jordan (Josh. 4,20 ff.). Similarly the maṣṣēbhā at Shechem was set up by Joshua as a witness to Israel's covenant with Yahweh (Josh. 24,26 f.), and a prophet in the time of the Diaspora speaks of an altar in Egypt and a maṣṣēbhā at its frontier as a token of the activity of the God of Israel in a foreign land (Isa. 19,19).

There is no actual difference between an altar and a maṣṣēbhā. But a maṣṣēbhā may express a limited content, while the altar is the place where man meets with the entire divine power, and where normal worship takes place. Just as a maṣṣēbhā may be erected at any time, thus also it is not all altars which are assigned to the earliest ancestors. After his victory over the Philistines Saul set up an altar of stone at Michmash that his men might sacrifice there; the account reads thus: And Saul built an altar unto Yahweh; it was the first time he built an altar unto Yahweh (1 Sam. 14,35). [1] And just as the holy altar stone was consecrated at Ophrah by Gideon, the heroic chief of the place, so also the altar at Ramah was ascribed to Samuel, whose native place it was, and whose grave was shown there (1 Sam. 28,3). We are here on the borderline between foundation legend and historical record. Altars were continually built and dedicated through all the history of Israel.

Most frequently Israelitish altars do not consist of a single stone but are built up of several. They may not even be made of stones but may be built of earth. An old law says about this: An altar of earth thou shalt make unto me, and shalt sacrifice thereon thy burnt offerings, and thy peace offerings, thy sheep, and thine oxen. In every place where I record my name I will come unto thee and bless thee. And if thou make me an altar of stones, thou shalt not build them as hewn stone, for thou hast lifted thy tool upon them and profaned them. And thou shalt not go up upon mine altar by steps, lest thy shame be uncovered thereon (Ex. 20,24-26).

This passage of the law has preserved to us a description of an altar in the old sanctuaries which we do not possess in any other place. It is only here that we learn that the altar might be of earth, and the excavations at Shechem have possibly brought to light an instance of this. [2] The difference between the altar consisting of one stone and that now described is that the latter presents a larger surface and is therefore better suited for larger offerings. It makes no difference in the character of the altar, just as we have seen that there might be memorial stone-heaps as well as memorial stones. It is a strongly emphasised requirement that the stones must be unhewn. It means that they are to be *living* stones, the life of which has not been injured by human interference, as is expressly said. This is the place where the name of God is recorded and that means that the divine soul is present there; hence the altar is the point from which the blessing emanates. [1] The interdiction against altar-steps expresses disapproval of the types leading beyond the simple form, the reason given must no doubt be regarded as rather accidental.

This type of altar however did not persist as the only one in Israel. Within the temple of Jerusalem there were magnificent altars of quite another type, and likewise outside it. The altar of Jerusalem was so high that it had to be mounted by means of steps (cf. Lev. 9,22; Ez. 43,17), as was the case at Bethel (1 Kings 12,33); a feature considered normal in later times, precisely because Jerusalem indicated the norm. And this great altar was provided with horns, by which are meant upstanding projections (Ex. 27,2; 30,2 f., Ez. 43,15.20 et passim). It is clear that we have here a type other than the ancient earth or stone altar. It must be hewn of stone or, as in Jerusalem, elaborately made of another material. We know that the main altar of Jerusalem in David's time had horns (1 Kings 1,50 f.; 2,28), and the same was the case with the main altar at Bethel in the time of Amos (Am. 3,14).

These horned altars were known by the Phoenicians, and one or two small specimens of them have been found at Shechem. [2] As a matter of course they were adopted by the Israelites as a type already familiar in Canaan. And the adoption of them is not without interest. The ancient requirement that the altar was to consist of living things unshaped by any human hand had been given up. The altar was an instrument so contrived as to be most serviceable for carrying the victims. But the tradition as to the character of the altar was so firmly rooted that it was transferred to the artificial altar, and the horns were even regarded as the holiest part, to which any one seeking protection clung, and on which the priest sprinkled the blood of the victim.

Whether the sanctuary contained the ancient sacred stone only and the kindred natural altar, or a more elaborate one, the altar remained its central feature. It was always the altars of the sanctuaries which were said to have been founded by the patriarchs. Where there is an altar there is a sanctuary too. The altar may record a name, and thus, like the *maṣṣēbhā*, have an individual content, though not very precisely defined. *Yahweh shālōm*, i. e. "Yahweh is peace" was the name of the altar at Ophrah (Judg. 6,24), a designation that would be suitable for any altar to Yahweh; and an altar on the frontier of Amalek was called *Yahweh nissī*, "Yahweh is my banner" (Ex. 17,15), a name fitted for a place where Yahweh was often the God of war. Any one who pulled down the altars of Yahweh warred against him, because he was present in them. Elijah, who built an altar to Yahweh on Mount Carmel in order to combat the god who was his enemy (1 Kings 18,32), breaks out in lamentations: They have thrown down thine altars, they have slain thy prophets (1 Kings 19,14), two forms of the same war, because the same spirit was active in the prophet and the altar. And when later prophets, from the time of Amos, entered on their campaign against the various places of worship, it was the altars they turned against: Ephraim hath built more and more altars, and they have all turned to sin, therefore it is first of all the altars that Yahweh will strike at and shatter (Hos. 8,11; 10,1; Am. 3,14). When the deported Judaeans returned home from the exile, their first task was to rebuild the altar at Jerusalem; the essential part of the cult could then be resumed, even though the temple was in ruins (Ezr. 3,3 ff.). Hence at Sinai, too, an altar was necessary, for here the fundamental covenant was made between Israel and Yahweh (Ex. 24,4-8), just as the founding of altars to Yahweh was evidence of the extension of Yahweh's territory and his power (Isa. 19,19 ff.).

Thus, when Deuteronomy condemned all sanctuaries other than that of Jerusalem, it condemned all other altars at the same time. Nevertheless Deuteronomy has, from its transmitted material, preserved a curious tradition of how Moses after the crossing of Jordan commanded Joshua to set up an altar on

Mount Ebal at Shechem and to sacrifice there, and a later story tells us that Joshua obeyed his command. But it is characteristic that this material in Deuteronomy has been amplified by explanations of how the stones were whitewashed at the bidding of Moses, and the whole Deuteronomic law inscribed on them. Hence the altar has preserved its value as a centre, but a different meaning has been assigned to it, it has been made a banner of the law (Deut. 27,1-8; Josh. 8,30-35). Another story in the book of Joshua is of a similar kind. When the tribes of Reuben and Gad, and the east-Jordanic group of Manasseh, left the other tribes, they built an altar near Jordan. The other tribes were immediately ready to avenge this breach of the Deuteronomic law. But the tribes assailed declared that they had by no means built the altar for sacrifice, but merely as a witness that they belonged to Yahweh's people (Josh. 22,9-34). Thus, in post-exilic times an attempt could be made to preserve the Deuteronomic interdiction against the numerous altars and yet not give up the history of the past. The altars were not altars, they were witnesses to the ownership of Yahweh. This is not very different from what the foundation legends of the patriarchal history purported to inculcate, and as we saw, Joshua, too, explained the maṣṣēbhā at Shechem in the same way. There is something of the ancient tradition in this, only what was once an actual fact has here become merely a symbol.

Thus in early times the simplest form of an Israelitish-Canaanite sanctuary was a stone or a plain altar, perhaps flanked by one or several stone pillars; probably it was surrounded by an enclosed space. At the same time there were sanctuaries of quite a different type, of which a single instance has been preserved in the book of Judges, viz. in the above-mentioned story of Micah (Judg. 17-18). The beginning runs thus: There was a man of the highlands of Ephraim, whose name was Micah. He said to his mother: The eleven hundred shekels of silver that were taken from thee, and for the sake of which thou utteredst a curse and said while I heard it [1]: ... I have that silver, I took it. And his mother said: Blessed be my son before Yahweh. And he returned the eleven hundred shekels of silver to his mother, and his mother said: I dedicate the silver unto Yahweh from myself for my son to make a carved and a molten image thereof, and here I give it to thee. [1] And he returned the silver to his mother, and his mother took 200 shekels of the silver and gave them to the silversmith; and he made thereof a carved and a molten image, and it was placed in Micah's house. And the man Micah had a house of gods, [2] and he procured an ephod and teraphim, and he filled the hand of one of his sons, and he became his priest (Judg. 17,1-5). Then follows the account of the arrival of the Levite who was installed as priest in his house, by which is probably meant his house of gods (v. 12), and of the Danites who first sent out five scouts, and came afterwards with 600 men, intending to go northward. When they arrived at the houses, one of which was Micah's, the five who had been there before said: Know you that in these houses there is an ephod and teraphim and a carved and molten image?Learn what ye have to do. They, i. e. the five, then proceeded "to the house of the young Levite, Micah's house (of gods)" (18,15), while the troops of warriors remained by the gates of the small town; [3] and the five took the carved image, the ephod, the teraphim, and the molten image. The priest raised objections, but realised that it was better to become the priest of a tribe than to remain in the house (i. e. the family v. 19) of a single man. So he took the sacred objects, went out to the band of warriors and left with them. After a while Micah and his neighbours pursued the Danites, and when they asked him what ailed him, he replied: Ye have taken my God which I have procured and likewise the priest and are gone away, and what have I more? How can you say to me: What aileth thee (v. 24). But the Danites drove him home and proceeded on their journey. When they had captured the town they had chosen, viz. Dan, they set up the carved image there. [4]

This is the story of how the later royal sanctuary at Dan and its priesthood first came into existence. Of that, however, we hear no more, but we become acquainted with a sanctuary of a different type from the open space with a natural altar and a stone pillar. Micah's sanctuary is a house, which acquires its character from the sacred objects of which it is the repository.

It is doubtful whether an altar belonged to the place, at any rate it is not mentioned. It is the images which make the house a sacred house. What the difference is between the four objects purchased with the sacred gift of the mother (17,4 f.) cannot be clearly shown. *Pesel* denotes an artistically formed image. As the one here mentioned, it may be made of silver, i. e. a molten image (cf. Jer. 10,14), or it may be of wood (Isa. 44,15.17; 45,20), but also of stone or other material; hence it is the most comprehensive term for idols (Ex. 20,4; Lev. 26,1; Isa. 40,19 etc.). The other term, *massēkhā,* is used in a more restricted sense, being applied to a molten image only, either of silver (Hos. 13,2) or of gold (Ex. 32,2 ff.). The two terms often occur together as a general designation of idols. [1] As a rule the precious metal probably formed merely a coating over a figure of some other material (Isa. 30,22; 41,7). That the images often represented a calf appears from the story of the golden calf, from the cult arrangements of Jeroboam at Bethel and Dan, and from prophetic utterances (Hos. 13,2); but there is no reason why this should be the only possibility. That Micah possessed a real image is evidenced by his own exclamation.

In addition to the two objects already referred to, designated after the way they are made, ephods and teraphim are mentioned, objects which we also find conjoined in other accounts (Judg. 17,5; 18,14.17 f.20; Hos. 3,4). We hear most frequently of ephods, and we are most familiar with them in the shape of a garment for the priest. In the laws relating to priests we have a description of the dress of the high-priest. Here the material of the ephod is described, but not its shape. It was made of gold, purple, and byssus twined in threads, and it was hung over the shoulders by straps fastened to each edge of it (Ex. 28,6-13; 39,2-7). A richly embroidered pouch *(hōshen)* containing the two oracular stones was fastened to the same straps (Ex. 28,15-30; 39,8-21), and over it all the high-priest wore a mantle called the mantle of the ephod (28,31; 39,22). The ephod, therefore,

constitutes an essential part of the priestly robe for great
occasions; under it was worn a short under-jacket *(kᵉthōneth);*
a girdle, linen trousers and a turban with a frontlet completed
the costume (Ex. 28,4.36 ff.; 39,27 ff.). The upper part of the
costume consists of the ephod, breast-pouch and mantle. The
shoulders and back must have been covered by the mantle, the
chest by the pouch. Since the latter is fastened to the shoulderstraps
of the ephod, the ephod itself must be lower down on the front
of the body, as an apron covering the less splendid trousers.
Behind, these are covered by the mantle, and that the ephod is
an apron, not a skirt, is shown by the fact that its two edges are
mentioned. This, then, was what the ephod was like in post-
exilic times. There is no reason to believe that it differed much
from the ephod of earlier days.

"He who wears a (linen) ephod" is the designation of a
priest in early times (1 Sam. 14,3; 22,18). As part of the
priestly outfit it is worn by the young Samuel in the temple of
Shiloh, and by David when he danced the cult dance before the
Ark. Of each of them it is said that he was *"girded* with a linen
ephod" (1 Sam. 2,18; 2 Sam. 6,14), which shows that it was
worn round the loins, and when we are told that the dance
uncovered David, this could take place much easier if the ephod
were an apron than if it were a skirt.

The case would thus be fairly clear if we did not possess
other information. We are told that when Abiathar fled to David
from the temple of Nob "the ephod went down in his hand"
(1 Sam. 23,6). The reference cannot be to a common ecclesiastical
garment, which every priest must have had at his disposal, but
to some noteworthy treasure from the temple. It is the sacred
thing itself which departs of its own accord, an idea with which
we are familiar from other peoples as well, when their idols are
transported from one place to another. That the reference is here
to a special treasure of the temple appears also from the way in
which its place in the temple of Nob is brought to notice. The
sword of Goliath "stood behind the ephod" (1 Sam. 21,10). It
was of great importance in the service of the oracle, which, as
we know, was the special business of the priest. When David

wished to consult the oracle, he said to Abiathar, "Bring me the ephod!" (1 Sam. 23,9; 30,7). In a similar situation in the history of Saul we hear the priest say: Let us go over here to the God! whereupon Saul questions the oracle (1 Sam. 14,36 f.). This reminds us that the ephod, in the story about Micah, is mentioned in connection with the idols, and a narrative about Gideon points in the same direction. When he had defeated the Midianites, and the people had in vain requested him to be their king, he made his countrymen give up their spoil of gold: nose-rings, crescents, the collars of the camels, 1700 shekels in all, besides purple robes. "And Gideon made an ephod thereof and set it up in his town of Ophrah, and all Israel went awhoring after it there, and it became a snare to Gideon and his house" (Judg. 8,26 f.).

In the last remark the ephod comes under the same denunciation as the idols; hence it betrays the later narrator; but the gist of the story is that a cult object was made of gold and perhaps of purple, and that it was an object that could be erected. "Ephod" never seems to denote an image in general in any other passage, but it is often mentioned in conjunction with the oracle, and this connection is confirmed by the fact that it also appears in the costume of the high-priest, which was made of gold with purple threads interwoven. It might then be supposed that the ephod was a sacred apron which the priest put on when he ministered to the oracle. Such an apron, in which there was much gold, might also be supposed to be able to stand, if supported against a pillar. But the various statements about the ephod would seem to indicate that it belonged to an idol, and the most natural assumption is then, presumably, that it was an apron of the same kind as that of the priest, and that a pouch containing the oracular stones was fastened to it, as to the robe of the high-priest. It was then placed on an idol, to which the designation "ephod" was transferred. If this surmise be correct, the idol must have had human likeness. The ephod had its fixed place in the sanctuary (1 Sam. 21,10), but the priest could carry it with him when called upon to accompany the chief and to assist him, especially in war.

Teraphim *(terāphīm)*, which are mentioned in connection with the ephod, also belong to the oracle. We are told that the king of Babylon consults the teraphim and interrogates the liver (Ez. 21,26), and in a prophetic utterance the teraphim are compared with the false soothsayers, and are said to speak lying words *('āwen,* Zech. 10,2, cf. 1 Sam. 15,23). And, as a matter of fact, they are mentioned among the cult objects which Josiah removed (2 Kings 23,24). A peculiar feature of the teraphim is that they belong to private houses. Rachel stole her father Laban's teraphim, and when Laban overtook Jacob, he at once asked him why he had stolen his God (Gen. 31,30). It is no large object; Rachel was able to hide it in the camel's saddle and sit on the top of it (v. 34 f.). In David's house, too, there were teraphim. When he had fled, his wife Michal deceived his pursuers by putting it in his bed; at some distance, then, and by night, it might convey the impression of a man in this position (1 Sam. 19,13.16). The connection with the ephod might be that the teraphim denoted the idol on which the ephod could be placed; ephod would then denote the apron with the stones, teraphim the idol, and both words may mean the idol with the oracular garment, apron and pouch. [1]

Even though we can merely form conjectures concerning the ephod and the teraphim, the connection with the oracle is indubitable, and so we return to our point of departure, Micah's sanctuary. In this we find a sacred place of another kind than the Canaanite open-air sanctuary, where the actual holy thing is a rock or an altar of stone or earth, or perhaps a stream. In Micah's sanctuary holiness is concentrated in an elaborately made object kept in a house; and since this object is used for the oracle, it requires a priest to serve it.

Micah's sanctuary is closely connected with a private house. From the narrative of David's flight we may take it for granted that the houses generally contained holy objects, household gods, with which the blessing of the house was associated. Excavations have shown that there might also be small altars in the houses, intended for household worship. [2] Whether Micah had such an altar we do not know. What gave Micah's sanctuary its special character was evidently the oracular objects, which had to be served by a priest.

The open-air sanctuary and the closed house containing the holy objects are the two types of sanctuaries found in early Israel. As a rule they were probably combined. At Shechem the excavations show an open space as well as a temple building, and what we know about Bethel agrees with this.

In a vision at *Bethel* Amos saw Yahweh standing by the altar, commanding that the temple should be destroyed (Am. 9,1). This would seem to indicate that the altar stood outside the building. From the legend of Jacob (Gen. 28,18.22) we know that there was a maṣṣēbhā in the holy place. But the altar was an artificial altar provided with horns (Am. 3,14). Amos threatens "the altars of Bethel" with the visitation of Yahweh. The allusion may be to several sanctuaries, but more probably he is referring to the fact that, as at Shechem, there were several altars in the main sanctuary. [1]

The temple buildings were not only used as a repository for sacred objects, but there was no doubt a difference according to the size and importance of the temple. At any rate we know that a temple hall *(lishkā)* was sometimes used for a sacrificial meal, and it must then be able to hold the leading men of the town, as we know from Shechem and Ramah (Judg. 9,27; 1 Sam. 9,22); probably it was the main hall, in which there may also have been sacred objects. At Shiloh the pilgrims took the sacrificial meal by families, but we do not know whether it was eaten in the temple. In it stood the Ark in a cell guarded by a man consecrated to be priest, and a lamp was burning in it, but it was put out at night (1 Sam. 3,3). At Nob we only know the temple as a house with an ephod, behind which the sword of Goliath was standing; we hear that holy bread was lying in it (1 Sam. 21,1-10; 22,13), but whether there was a hall for meals, and whether there was an open holy court in front of it we do not know.

Even when temples became common among the Israelites, the

open-air sanctuary still remained the predominant form, and the sanctuary proper was the altar. Hosea complains that Ephraim is continually adding to its altars, and they all turn to sin (Hos. 8,11; 10,1); Amos too as we saw, turned against the altars, even those founded by the patriarchs.

The holy place was most frequently situated on a hill. "They sacrifice on the tops of the mountains, and they send up smoke from the hills" *(hag-gᵉbhā'ōth)* (Hos. 4,13). Such utterances are met with over and over again in the prophets, not least in the later ones, as for instance Jeremiah. The hill is called bamah *(bāmā,* 1 Sam. 9,12; 10,13), and the temple, the house of bamah (1 Kings 12,31; 2 Kings 17,29 et al.), but the word bamah is also used about the sanctuary situated on the hill (1 Kings 3,4; 11,7; Hos. 10,8; Am. 7,9 et al.).

To a sanctuary belonged not only stones but also trees. The holy places are to be found "under every green tree" (1 King 14,23; 2 Kings 16,4, cf. Ez. 6,13; 20,28), "under oaks, poplars, and terebinths" (Hos. 4,13). Just as Shechem had its holy terebinth (Gen. 35,4), so also Beersheba had its tamarisk; and like many altars, it was traced back to Abraham, who planted it there, calling upon the name of Yahweh, the eternal God (Gen. 21,33). Some holy trees had their own special name, such as Deborah's weeping oak at Bethel (Gen. 35,8) and the terebinth at Mamre in Hebron. Like the stones, therefore, they might embody a certain historical content.

We often hear of an asherah belonging to the holy place, but mostly we merely learn that the prophets condemn them. That the asherah represents a tree is certain; we hear that it is to be burnt (Deut. 12,3; 2 Kings 23,6), cut down or uprooted (Judg. 6,2; Mic. 5,13). It is possible that sometimes, as the Talmud has it, it was a living tree; the asherah which Gideon cut down would then be identical with the tamarisk under which Yahweh's mal'ākh sat (Judg. 6,11.25 ff.). There is no certainty in the matter. We can infer nothing from the fact that the asherah could be "planted" (Deut. 16,21). Conversely, mention is made of an asherah being "formed" (1 Kings 16,33; 2 Kings 17,16 et al.). Here the narrator was probably thinking of an idol *(pesel hā-'ᵃshērā)* representing the goddess who constituted the life of the tree. But often the asherah was probably an unhewn pole, as is known from other Mediterranean regions. [1] It is mentioned in the large sanctuaries at Samaria and Jerusalem (2 Kings 13,6; 21,7).

That a spring was often holy has already been stated. Thus were the springs of Kadesh and of Rogel near Jerusalem (1 Kings 1,9). But a spring cannot normally be said to belong to every Israelitish open-air sanctuary. However, there was no doubt always water in reservoirs, if no spring was present.

The temple building must have contained holy objects, like those in Micah's sanctuary. At Bethel and Dan there were figures of bulls which represented Yahweh (1 Kings 12,28 f.); such were also to be found in Samaria (Hos. 8,5) and Gilgal (Hos. 12,12). [2] It was a common custom of the people to "make themselves images" everywhere (Hos. 13,2). We learn most about this from Deuteronomy and the exilic and post-exilic prophets through their attacks on the "abominations", "logs" and "idols", gods that are merely of stone and wood. We meet with the same things always in the Israelitish sanctuaries as among the Phoenicians and other Canaanites.

The scattered information which has come down to us of the ancient sanctuaries thus gives us a certain idea of them, and behind it we catch a glimpse of the two types represented by the holy place in the open and the temple building, the repository of holy objects. The sanctuaries were of highly varying importance. The private citizen had his smaller or larger household sanctuary, and the city community had its public sanctuary, accessible to all. Among the city sanctuaries some were in special repute, and were therefore visited by pilgrims. "Go not to Gilgal, go not to Beth-Awen, swear not by the life of Yahweh," says Hosea (4,15). "Seek not Bethel and go not to Gilgal, and pass not to Beersheba", says Amos (5,5). And we are told how every year Elkanah went up to Shiloh with his family to sacrifice to Yahweh (1 Sam. 1,3) .It is expressly stated that Jeroboam built his big sanctuaries at Bethel and Dan in order to attract pilgrims and keep them away from the great new temple at Jerusalem (1 Kings 12,26 f.), just as later on the Umayyad Khalifa built his grand mosque at Jerusalem to prevent pilgrimages to Mecca.[1] This shows the connection between the pilgrimage sanctuary and the ruling power, and the words of Jeroboam express a recognition of what the temple of Jerusalem already meant. Gradually it was to acquire signal importance for the life of the people as the sole sanctuary in which all holiness was centred.

When David had made a capital for his new dominion by capturing Jerusalem, he resided as a Judaean ruler with his people among strangers; for apart from those who had fallen in the struggle about the city the Jebusites remained in the country (Josh. 15,63; Judg. 1,21). David's aim would now be to make the place Judaean, but he did not do it by drawing a sharp distinction between the Judaeans and the strangers; on the contrary we know that he surrounded himself by many strangers from whom he drew support. But his policy towards Saul and his family shows throughout that his object was to obtain ascendancy as an Israelite king, without making any difference between Judah and Israel proper.

His actions in respect of the cult agree with this. For the chief of these was his transference of the Ark to Zion. By this act he appropriated the earlier history of Israel and made Jerusalem the centre of its further development. It was David's crowning act; it won for him more than Saul's blessing, for it made the monarchy of Jerusalem the maintainer of the earliest tradition, leading right back to the origin of the people. The Ark was the most sacred treasure of the nation, embodying its earliest history, a nomads' shrine carried down from the past into the land of the fixed sanctuaries.

Tradition records that in the earliest settlement period the Ark was kept at Shiloh, where it had a cell in the temple (1 Sam. 3,3), and was ministered to by the priesthood of Eli. Of its significance in the cult there we know nothing, but we hear what it meant in war.

When the Philistines were at war with the Israelites and victory inclined to the former, the elders of Israel said: Wherefore hath Yahweh smitten us today before the Philistines? Let us fetch unto us the Ark of the covenant of Yahweh out of Shiloh; and when it (or he) cometh among us, it (or he) shall save us out of the hand of our enemies! (1 Sam. 4,3). Then people sent to Shiloh, and the Ark was fetched, its two priests Hophni and Phinehas accompanying it. When the Israelites saw it, they sent up a mighty shout. The Philistines, hearing the shouting and learning that Yahweh's Ark had come into the camp, were afraid, "for they said, gods are come into the camp, and they said, Woe unto us, for such a thing hath not been heretofore. Woe unto us, who shall deliver us out of the hand of these mighty gods? These are the gods that smote the Egyptians with all manner of plagues in the wilderness. Take courage and be men, Philistines, that ye may not toil for the Hebrews, as they have toiled for you; be men and fight!" (1 Sam. 4,7-9). Then the Philistines fought and won, the Ark of God was captured, and Hophni and Phinehas, the two priests accompanying it, were both killed. We are now told how the news was brought to the aged Eli, who was sitting on a chair, waiting; when he heard about the loss of the Ark, he fell backwards and broke his neck. Phinehas' wife was so shaken that she gave birth to her child prematurely, and she called the boy "Ichabod" or "bereft of honour", for Israel had been deprived of its honour, its *kābhōdh,* by the loss of the Ark.

With great art the narrator has attempted to characterise the Philistines' conception of the God of Israel. He makes them speak in the plural on purpose, as if Israel had several gods. [1] Behind the narrative we catch a glimpse of the Israelite hearer, who is filled with pride at the thought of how thoroughly the Philistines are mistaken. But precisely in this instance, where the arrival of a single sacred object is concerned, the reference to several gods seems little appropriate. The rather pronounced irony, expressed in a wealth of words somewhat reminiscent of the story of Goliath, would, however, seem to indicate that the narrative acquired its present shape at a time when the contrast between monotheism and polytheism was the important thing to the Israelites, and when, as in the book of Joshua, they imagined the other peoples to be terrorstruck because of the wonders happening on the journey when the Israelites came up from Egypt. We must not, therefore, lay too much stress on the details of the narrative, but it gives us a clear idea of what the Ark was, a central sacred treasure of the Israelites, which could be carried into battle to secure victory to the nation.

The succeeding tales show us how the Ark displayed its power among the Philistines, so that they decided to send it back. In this way it came to Bethshemesh, but since it also caused disasters there, it was taken on to Kirjath Jearim. Here it was placed in Abinadab's house, and his son Eleazar was dedicated to watch the Ark. Thus like Micah, Abinadab had his own private sanctuary, but the sacred object he was guarding was of greater importance than a common ephod.

When David had established his power at Jerusalem and defeated the Philistines, he set out with his warriors to carry the Ark up to Jerusalem. This was to be the final reparation for the Philistine oppression of early Israel. The Ark was placed on a cart, and the procession started, but an accident happened; one of the two sons of Abinadab who were guarding the Ark was killed because he rashly touched the sacred object. Then David would not take the risk of carrying on the Ark to his royal city; he had it placed in a house to try whether it brought good or evil with it. It was a Gattite, Obed-Edom, on whom was conferred the honour of housing the Ark. Again this shows that David's entourage was not unmixed, which is all the more remarkable in the present instance where the guarding of a costly Israelitish treasure is concerned (2 Sam. 6).

When it turned out that the Ark brought blessedness to the house in which it had been placed, it was clear that it did not object to be brought up to the royal city, and the transference was now made with great festivity. It was placed in the city of David. "And they brought in the Ark of Yahweh and set it in its place in the midst of the tent that David had pitched for it, and David offered burnt offerings before Yahweh and peace offerings" (2 Sam. 6,17). The priests Zadok and Abiathar were charged with the office of guarding it (2 Sam. 15,24; 1 Kings 2,26).

Under David, too, the Ark was carried into battle. We have evidence to show that it was with the army on the expedition against the Ammonites, for Uriah, on being recalled from it and invited to dwell in his house, made the following answer: The Ark and Israel and Judah dwell in arbours, and my lord Joab and the slaves of my lord are encamped in the open fields, should I then go into mine house etc. (2 Sam. 11,11). When the Ark was moved it was sometimes driven (1 Sam. 6,7 ff.; 2 Sam. 6,3 ff.), but generally carried (2 Sam. 6,13), and in that case by two priests (2 Sam. 15,24.29).

Of the appearance of the Ark the early sources tell us nothing beyond what is implied in the name 'ārōn, which shows that it was a kind of chest or box, and the tradition that the tables of the law were kept in it agrees with this. When in its fixed place, it might, as we have seen, be in a temple, or some other building, or it might be in a tent, as was the case in Jerusalem in the time of David (2 Sam. 6,17; 7,2). This seems also to agree with the fact that it was carried out on warlike expeditions, for on such excursions it had to have a portable shelter. But according to the statement of Uriah it dwelt in an arbour, sukkā, under those circumstances, and it seems as if this was in contrast with the normal, everyday conditions. Thus we are given no perfectly clear picture of the dwelling-place of the Ark, but its character implies that it must have had a movable abode at its disposal.

The impression we gather from the sources, that the Ark was an Israelitish sanctuary of central significance, which took the lead on the expeditions of the people, is fully confirmed by David's conduct. The fact that he attached such weight to the transference to Zion, affords strong evidence of the importance of the Ark in the earliest times.

The question now arises how much farther back we may trace the tradition. The narratives dealing with the wanderings assign signal importance to the Ark all through the wilderness period.

It is a matter of course that this should be so in "the priestly code", for here the sanctuary in the wilderness, around which the people are encamped, is a prototype of the temple of Jerusalem where the Ark stood in the inmost room (Ex. 25,10-22; 37,1-9). But the Ark also occupies an important position in stories of another kind. Yahweh's Ark and Moses form the rallying point of the camp (Num. 14,44). During the wanderings in the wilderness the Ark would sometimes go on in front to find a new camping place for the Israelites, who followed it (Num. 10,33). The place which the narratives assign to the Ark in the campaign in the wilderness no doubt corresponds to its importance on the warlike expeditions of historical times. And, in fact, the shouts with which it was greeted in the wilderness stories, when the people started or rested, originate from that usage. The story runs: When the Ark started, Moses said: Arise Yahweh! Thy foes shall be scattered and thine enemies flee before thee! (Num. 10,35). And when it rested, he said: Return Yahweh! Thousands of ten thousands of Israel (v. 36). [1] Throughout the story of the immigration the Ark is described as the rallying point of the people or their leader, and from the character of these narratives we see that it is the incarnation of Yahweh's sovereign power and will. Before it the waters of Jordan divide, and the enemy's towns fall into ruins when it has circled them.

It has already been indicated that in the wilderness narratives we have traditions of a portable tent sanctuary of another kind than that described in the laws. It says about this: And Moses took the tent and pitched it [2] outside the camp, at some distance from the camp, and called it The Tent of the Revelation (*'ōhel mo'ēdh*), and every one who sought Yahweh went out to the tent of the revelation, which was outside the camp. And when Moses went out to the tent, all the people rose up, and each stood at the opening of his tent; they looked after Moses until he entered the tent (Ex. 33,7 f.). Here Moses came face to face with Yahweh, afterwards returning to the camp, while his servant, the young Joshua, son of Nun, remained in the tent.

We have here a regular tent sanctuary, and it is possible that there are other references to a holy tent in the wilderness period. [1] It is remarkable that nothing is said as to the Ark being in this tent. It is true that the remark about Joshua, who reminds one of Samuel in the temple of Shiloh, would seem to indicate that there was something to guard in the tent; but there is no certain connection between the tent and the Ark in this tradition. This has led to the surmise that the two things have no connection with each other. The tent is then supposed to be the nomadic sanctuary proper, as known from the tent-like camel saddle of the Syrians and Arabs in which their gods were conveyed; whereas the Ark is supposed to be a Canaanite shrine, little suited to be carried about on wanderings in the wilderness.

However, peoples settled in the Mediterranean countries also had holy tents; so far both might be Canaanite. But the early history of Israel and the whole policy of David show that the Ark was the ancient common treasure of the people with which the covenant and victories of Yahweh were associated. This is decisive evidence that the Ark belongs to the pre-Canaanite history of the people and hence must date from that period of its existence. It was doubtless for traditional reasons that David placed it in a tent, but this does not prevent the tent from having its own independent importance as a holy place. Hence it is doubtful whether the Israelites, in addition to the tent of the Ark, had a separate holy tent.

Since the Ark was a box, it doubtless contained something, but what this was, we do not know. It is an idea of post-exilic Judaism that it held two tables inscribed with the sum and substance of the law, which to them was the holiest of all. It is possible that it contained a holy stone, but it may have been any other holy object. The chief thing was that the Ark embodied the early history of Israel, and that the whole interaction of the people and its God was associated with it. Hence it is called the Ark of God or the Ark of Yahweh (1 Sam. 3,3; 4,6 et al.); or the Ark of the covenant and the Ark of the covenant of Yahweh (Num. 10,33; Josh. 3,3.6.8; 4,9; 1 Sam. 4,3; 1 Kings 6,19 etc.), but also the Ark of the testimony, the holy Ark, or "the Ark of thy strength" (Ps. 132,8), all expressing that the holy strength of Yahweh and his covenant with the people were embodied in it. [1]

_____

According to the books of Samuel David had intended to build Yahweh a temple at Jerusalem, but gave up the idea after Yahweh had spoken to him by the prophet Nathan. The part of the narrative, already mentioned, which is of interest here, runs as follows: And it came to pass when the king sat in his house, and Yahweh had given him rest round about from all his enemies, that the king said unto Nathan, the prophet: See now, I dwell in an house of cedar, but the Ark of God dwelleth within tent-curtains. And Nathan said to the king, Go, do all that is in thine heart, for Yahweh is with thee! And it came to pass that night that the word of Yahweh came unto Nathan, saying, Go and tell my servant David: Thus saith Yahweh, Shalt thou build me an house for me to dwell in? Whereas I have not dwelt in an house since the time that I brought up the children of Israel out of Egypt even to this day, but have walked in a tent and in a tabernacle. As long as I have walked with all the children of Israel, spake I a word with any of the tribes (1 Chron. 17,6: judges) of Israel, whom I commanded to guard my people Israel, saying, Why build ye not me an house of cedar? Now therefore so shalt thou say unto my servant, to David: Thus saith Yahweh of the hosts, I took thee from the pasture-land, directly from the flocks, to be ruler over my people, over Israel. And I was with thee whithersoever thou wentest, and have cut off all thine enemies out of thy sight; and will make thee a great name, like unto the name of the great men that are in the earth. Moreover I will appoint a place for my people Israel, and will plant them, and they shall dwell in their place, and forever they shall fear no more; neither shall the children of wickedness distress them any more as in the beginning, and since the time that I commanded judges to be over my people Israel; and I will cause thee to rest from all thine enemies; and Yahweh telleth thee that Yahweh will make thee an house. And when thy days be fulfilled, and thou shalt sleep with thy fathers, I will raise up thy seed after thee, which shall proceed out of thy bowels, and I will establish its kingdom. It shall build an house for my name; and I will establish the throne of its kingdom forever. I will be a father to it, and it shall be a son to me etc. (2 Sam. 7,1-14).

This story contains a piece of philosophising on the history of Israel viewed from post-exilic times, when the Davidic dynasty and the temple of Jerusalem had long since come to occupy the chief place in it. The contrasts are sharply set up against each other. With David began the time when all Israel had rest, all enemies were crushed; it attained its fullness when Yahweh, too, was given rest, obtained a fixed place in which to dwell, David's seed building a fixed temple to his name. The preceding time is exclusively a period of unrest and wandering; Yahweh, having no house, passed from place to place in a tent. Thus the whole period before David actually becomes a mere continuation of the wilderness period, a time of preparation. And even if David did not build the temple, it is associated with his name; his seed built it, so to speak, on his behalf. The utterance, perhaps based on a temple hymn (Ps. 132,11 ff.), is mentioned in Solomon's temple speech (1 Kings 8,15-19) and as far back as his address to Hiram (1 Kings 5,17-19).

The question why David did not build Yahweh a house comes up several times. According to the accounts we have of Solomon, this son and successor of David wrote to Hiram that David had not been able to build a temple because he was always at war, Solomon only, having entirely peace from his enemies, was able to do it (1 Kings 5,17 f.). The same point of view appears here; peace, rest, is required for the temple to be built. Two viewpoints meet here. Rest means that the king need not go to war; but in the story about Nathan and David there is also another more essential point of view, the contrast between Yahweh's wanderings and his fixed habitation. The utterance does not give any reason why David is not to build the house, which his son was to erect. But it establishes the fact that hitherto Yahweh had not desired a house. It was in harmony with his nature to wander from place to place in a tent.

Thus the ancient nomad sanctuaries are raised to essential importance. They give expression to Yahweh's character. But these considerations depend on a transformation of the history of the earliest occupation period. Yahweh has been in one place only, viz. his tent, whereas the numerous sanctuaries throughout the country which the Israelites took over entirely disappear. So tremendous an event did David's transference of the Ark to Zion become; it spread, and filled the period, to the exclusion of everything else. It created a continuity between the past and the temple, but at the same time happened to create that contrast to the temple which came to characterise the whole preceding period. We see here where the line runs that led to "the priestly code" assigning the whole of the temple with its appurtenances to the wilderness, transformed into a portable tent-house.

The strong contrast set up between the past when there was merely a tent, and the succeeding period, when there was only the temple at Jerusalem, is due to a one-sided emphasising of individual parts of the cult history both of the early times and of the monarchical period. But what was the state of affairs in David's own time?

We are told that David had the Ark brought to the city of David, "And they brought it in and set it in the tent which David had pitched for it" (2 Sam. 6,17). We learn nothing about the place of this tent beyond the fact that it was in the city of David, hence on Zion, the south-eastern hill of Jerusalem, where the ancient city stood, and where David had built his new palace, his "house of cedar". It was from there, also, that Solomon later on had the Ark brought up to his temple (1 Kings 8,1).

When we are told that David sought the countenance of Yahweh or "the God" (2 Sam. 7,18; 12,16; 21,1), the obvious assumption is that it was in the tent with the Ark. Here, too, the holy oil was kept with which the king was anointed (1 Kings 1,39). But as we know, the Ark was merely a sacred object previously kept in a temple at Shiloh, and it seems likely that David set up the Ark with its tent in a holy place already in his possession. It is inconceivable that, when he captured the city of Zion, he should not have taken possession of the sanctuary of the town. This may have been an open-air sanctuary like those described above, but according to the state of affairs then prevalent in the cities of Canaan, it seems most natural to suppose that there was a temple building in the place.

There are, in fact, circumstances which would seem to indicate that in the days of David the city had a temple, "Yahweh's abode" *(nāwe)*, the place where the Ark was housed, and where David after being put to flight by his son longed to see Yahweh again (2 Sam. 15,25). On his numerous campaigns David had acquired much spoil which he dedicated to Yahweh, and to this must be added the gifts of foreign princes which he likewise consecrated (2 Sam. 8,7 f. 10 f., cf. 1 Kings 7,51). Even if we must suppose that in the open-air sanctuaries such goods were placed in caves or separate buildings within the holy precincts specially devised for the purpose, it seems much more natural to assume that such treasures, here as in Nob and other places, were lodged in a temple building; and it would be very strange if David, who desired to establish a kingdom resembling the great empires, should have neglected to provide the most important thing, a temple to secure the holiness of the kingdom. Hence there is no reason to try to get round the text when we meet with the direct statement in one of the narratives that David entered "Yahweh's house" (2 Sam. 12,20). But the temple of Solomon came to overshadow everything else by it greatness.

It is not, of course, possible to say whether the tent with the Ark stood within the temple building itself or in the holy court outside it. It is mentioned in connection with the altar, which was not here the ancient type of stone or earth but an artificial altar with horns (1 Kings 1,50; 2,28 f.). When we are told that Joab fled to Yahweh's tent and clung to the horns of the altar, this does not necessarily imply that the two were standing close to each other. "The tent" was the essential thing in the sanctuary, after which, therefore, it was named, and perhaps Uriah's words about the Ark having to dwell in a tent during the war (2 Sam. 11,11) are more easily understood, if it dwelt in a house under ordinary circumstances; but we can say nothing certain about this.

David's sanctuary, of which we hear nothing later on, and which has probably vanished without leaving any trace, was not the only holy place near Jerusalem in the time of David. By the Rogel south of the city, now the well of Job, lay a stone, the Zoheleth stone, which was probably a holy stone (1 Kings 1,9) at which sacrifices were made. And the temple court which, through Solomon, was to become of such great importance to Israel, was, according to tradition, instituted as a sanctuary by David.

The foundation legend for this sanctuary runs thus: When the pestilence ravaged the land because David had sinned by numbering his subjects, David entreated Yahweh to stay his hand against the innocent people. The angel of the pestilence then stopped at the threshing-place of Araunah [1] the Jebusite. In the book of Samuel we are told that after this the prophet Gad came to David bidding him erect an altar on the threshing-floor. But Chronicles gives us a much clearer picture of how David saw the ravaging angel of Yahweh standing by the threshing-floor, towering between heaven and earth; terror-struck David fell on his face beseeching Yahweh for mercy, and at this moment Gad came and commanded David to erect an altar where he had seen the angel. The story now goes on to say that David went up to the threshing place where Araunah was threshing wheat; the latter prostrated himself before the king, asking what he desired, and David stated his intention of buying the threshing place for the purpose of raising an altar there that the people might be freed from the pestilence. Araunah offered the king the place with his oxen, and the threshing implements for fuel, all without payment. But David would not accept what was to be dedicated to Yahweh as a gift, and paid Araunah a sum of money, according to the book of Samuel 50 shekels of silver, according to Chronicles 600 shekels of gold. And David built an altar to Yahweh and offered a sacrifice thereon, after which the pestilence ceased (2 Sam. 24; 1 Chron. 21).

Just as the sanctuary at Ophrah was referred to the great

hero of the settlement period, thus also this legend connects the chief holy place of Jerusalem with the great Israelite founder of the city. The holy place, a rock at the top of the hill, is of the usual Canaanite type. It seems most natural then to suppose that it was really an ancient Canaanite sanctuary. This does not exclude the possibility that there may have been a threshing-floor close to the place, nor that the whole area may have belonged to one man and his family. ¹ It would seem natural to go one step further and assume that David's sanctuary, where the Ark stood, was in reality within the later temple precincts. But this would conflict directly with what our sources tell us. According to these David's chief sanctuary was within the ancient city that he captured, the city of Zion, which is also called "the city of David".

In the introduction to the account of Solomon found in the book of Kings it says that the people sacrificed at the various sanctuaries because the temple was not yet built. The book of Kings, in the form in which it has come down to us, is entirely dominated by the post-exilic idea of unity, and views the past from this angle. In this context we are told that Solomon sacrificed at Gibeon, for the great sanctuary was there (1 Kings 3,4), but later he sacrificed in Jerusalem before the Ark (1 Kings 3,15). These remarks about Solomon prove how little we know about the conditions of worship in early times; for we have no other information to show that Gibeon was specially important among the sanctuaries of early Israel. On the contrary, other accounts give us the impression that Gibeon preserved its non-Israelite character (Josh. 9). Perhaps the detached account of Solomon's sacrifice conceals a story of how Solomon captured the town and made it Israelitish. There is nothing remarkable in the fact that an Israelite king offered sacrifices at various native sanctuaries. To the author of the Chronicles the problem arose how Solomon, himself the founder of the only true temple, could sacrifice outside

Jerusalem; but he saves his idea of unity by placing the tabernacle, the sanctuary uniting the people in the past, at Gibeon (2 Chron. 1,3). He shows, however, that he felt some scruple at having the Ark with its tent in Jerusalem at the same time (v. 4), since he would then have two sanctuaries; but he has no means of getting over this difficulty.

In antiquity it was a natural task for kings to build temples. For the most important task of the king was to keep alive holy energy. David had begun from the bottom, but Solomon began with the great kingdom that David had created, as an Asiatic potentate, connected by marriage with the Egyptian empire. This glory required a new palace and a more dignified sanctuary, which was erected outside the narrow city of David, on the top of the hill near the old rock sanctuary. How new all this was in Israel may be seen from the fact that Solomon had to go to the Phoenicians to find builders. In "the priestly" description of how the sanctuary in the wilderness came into existence, Israelite artisans are selected for the work (Ex. 31,1 ff.). The new feature was not that Israel only now obtained a temple, for earlier she already possessed enclosed sanctuaries, but it was, that a temple was built which was worthy in size and splendour of the kingdom of David.

Temple and palace were closely connected, enclosed by a common wall. The court of the temple was again an enclosed part of the common court. We have seen instances of holy places which were owned by private individuals. The new temple was owned by the king, its significance to the people was associated with the importance of the king.

The Canaanite character of the holy place was preserved. The holy rock, in the open air, was still the actual place of worship, separate from the closed building. Here in the open air Solomon built a new altar (1 Kings 9,25). At other sanctuaries, too, we have seen that altars were erected on or by the holy rock. [1] But the altar of Solomon was of bronze (1 Kings 8,64; 2 Kings 16,14 f.), a pronounced artificial altar instead of the ancient altars of earth or stone. When the temple was consecrated, Solomon consecrated the whole of the court around the altar as a place of sacrifice (1 Kings 8,64), which shows how things were managed when there were many sacrifices to be offered.

The altar, which is said to have been renewed under Asa (2 Chron. 15,8), was replaced once more under Ahaz. After his meeting with Tiglat Pilesar at Damascus he sent a model of an altar there to the priest Uriah, who built a new one from this model, and the old altar was moved to the north of the new one (2 Kings 16,10-16). [1] Ahaz' altar is probably the one which was Yahweh's altar-hearth all through the monarchical period (Isa. 29,1; 31,9), the holiest thing in Jerusalem, and this was made after a foreign model. Since it is kept distinct from "the bronze altar", it must no doubt have been of stone or bricks. [2] In the description of Ezekiel, which is based on recollections of conditions in the monarchical period, the altar consists of four parts built up by steps, the upper one of which was the altar-hearth ('*ari'ēl*), running into horns at the corners (Ez. 43,13 ff.). [3] The altar of the "priestly code", also, has horns, besides being surrounded by a grille, but it is so formed as to be light and portable (Ex. 27,1-8; 38,1-7). The altar was so high that it had to have a flight of stairs (Ez. 43,17); this was also the case in other large sanctuaries (1 Kings 12,32 f.; 13,1). Here the law of the ancient open-air altar was broken; it prohibited such steps which introduced an artificial element, and uncovered the worshipper in the presence of what was holy (Ex. 20,26).

At the destruction of the temple the altar, too, was destroyed. It preserved its importance as a centre to such a degree that the rebuilding of it was the first task of the returned exiles, after which the interrupted cultus could be resumed little by little (Ezr. 3,1-6). The new altar was built according to the ancient altar-law, of unhewn stones, and according to the measurements given in Chronicles for Solomon's altar. [4]

The accounts mention various sacred objects which Solomon placed in the open court of the temple: a large basin, the sea, supported by twelve oxen, and ten bronze carts decorated with lions, oxen, and cherubim on panels set in a framework ornamented with palmettos and garlands, all of them bearing lavers (1 Kings 7,23 ff.; 2 Chron. 4,2 ff.). Some of them were removed by Ahaz, and the rest also vanished, so that Ezekiel has nothing to say about them; and when 2 Chronicles says that the priests purified themselves in the sea, while all that belonged to the burnt offerings was cleansed in the lavers (2 Chron. 4,6), this is hardly based on a sure tradition. These were international cult objects. The carts are known from Cyprus, a "sea" was found in Babylonian temples, and undoubtedly it is what the name says, a reproduction of the sea, the primeval water, contained in the temple. [1] This does not exclude the possibility that the priests may have washed themselves in its water to sanctify themselves.

Thus the site of the ancient open-air sanctuary had been transformed into a temple court with artificial cult objects, foreign to the Israelite tradition. In this court stood the temple with its entrance facing east, opposite the altar. It was an overwhelming testimony to the greatness which the new Israelite dynasty attributed to itself and its kingdom.

The description in 1 Kings is not easy to make out in all its details, and Ezekiel's ideal picture is inspired by the appearance of the temple in the last days of the kingdom (1 Kings 6, cf. 2 Chron. 3; Ez. 40-42); but in a broad way there is no doubt as to the arrangement of the building. Its thick walls were of accurately hewn freestone, covered by a roof borne by beams of cedar. Its interior breadth was 20 cubits i. e. about 10 metres, but along the outer walls there were side buildings which only left the upper part of the walls free. A flight of steps led to the entrance hall which must have conveyed the impression of a tremendous height since it was 10 cubits deep and 30 cubits high. The wide entrance was flanked by strong pillars which each had a bronze column in front of it named Jachin and Boaz (1 Kings 7,15 ff. 41 f., cf. 2 Kings 25,13; Jer. 52,17.20). These had capitals shaped like lilies at the top, and afford fresh evidence of the transformation of the ancient open-air sanctuary, for these refined works of art were doubtless the successors of the old maṣṣēbhā. [2]

Apart from the entrance hall the temple consisted of two chambers, the long temple hall, which bore the same name as the whole temple *(hēkhāl)*, and the inner cell *(dᵉbhīr)*, the holy of holies, where Yahweh himself was present. This room was cubic; each side of the cube being 20 cubits, which is best explained by the fact that it was at a higher level than the hall.¹ This division of the temple, with its holiest chamber at the back, suggests the foreign models followed by the Phoenician builder.² The two principal rooms had the walls covered with panels on which were carved cherubim and palmettos (1 Kings 6,15; Ez. 41,15-20).

The descriptions mention various things which were kept in the temple hall. Ten lamps are referred to (1 Kings 7,49), later one lamp with seven arms (Ex. 25,31 ff.). In the background in front of the inner hall there was an altar of wood overlaid with gold, doubtless identical with the incense altar (Ex. 30,1 ff.; 1 Kings 6,22; 7,48; Ez. 41,21 f.);³ further, a table on which to lay the shew bread (1 Kings 6,20, cf. Ex. 25,23 ff.) besides various vessels and small cult objects (1 Kings 7,50). This is what we learn from the descriptions of the temple; the book of Kings lavishes gold both on the building itself and on the objects. It is not likely that the large hall, 20 metres long, should have been built merely to hold the holy objects. No doubt it was meant for processions; and as in other Israelitish temples for the gathering of worshippers. Perhaps also for the sacrificial meals of the king. No trace however, is preserved of this. In post-exilic times the priests had long since appropriated all the temple to themselves.

The holiest part of the temple was the cella at the back which was closed with a door consisting of two leaves (1 Kings 6,34; Ez. 41,24). It contained the holiest object, the ancient Ark, which David had brought up to Zion and Solomon had now conveyed to its temple cella. Thus the holy tent disappeared from Israelitish cultus, even though it may for a time have been kept in the temple (1 Kings 8,4).

By carrying the Ark into the new temple, Solomon remained faithful to David's idea and linked up the monarchy and its holiness with the ancient history of the people. Thus the Ark lost the last remnant of its early character as a wandering sanctuary. This transformation is strongly emphasised in the considerations accompanying the description of the consecration of the temple. The God of Israel now acquired a fixed habitation, while previously he had wandered. But of course the Ark did not from this time onward become a fixture in its temple cella. It was provided with carrying poles for processions; but of its participation in war we hear no more.

The writers who have described the inner room of the temple have been so preoccupied with the association with the early history of the people that their thoughts continually hover round the Ark. But the holy chest was not the only object found in the inner sanctuary. This appears both from the description in 1 Kings and from the factitious description of the temple we have in the narratives about the sanctuary in the wilderness.

The book of Kings tells us that Solomon placed two cherubim of olive wood overlaid with gold in the inner room. They were of large dimensions, 5 metres high; their wings measured 5 metres from tip to tip, and they were spread so as to touch each other on the inner side while each of the outer wings touched the wall. The Ark was now put in so as to be covered by the wings on the inner side; the poles, however, projected so that they could be seen from the temple hall, but not farther away. Second Chronicles repeats this description and adds that the faces of the cherubim were inward, which must mean that they were turned inward (1 Kings 6,23-28; 8,1-9; 2 Chron. 3,10-13; 5,2-10).

According to this description the inner room was entirely dominated by cherubim. They reached half-way to the ceiling, barred the whole room and covered the Ark. These figures were characteristic of Solomon's temple, whose walls were everywhere ornamented with their images. This shows Solomon's strenuous endeavour to give his temple an international character, for such winged creatures, made up of different animal figures or sometimes partly human were known from the whole of the near East.

In the description of the sanctuary in the wilderness there is an idealised picture of the Ark as a shrine entirely overlaid with gold and provided with gilded poles to carry it by. The Ark is covered with a *kappōreth* of gold, with a cherub, likewise of gold, at each end, the faces turned inward, and the wings stretched upward so as to cover the *kappōreth* (Ex. 25,10-22; 37,1-9).

Hence we must reckon with three things in the holy of holies, the Ark, the cherubim, and the *kappōreth*. The questions then arise: What is their relation to each other, and what is the *kappōreth?*

The book of Kings has an item which seems to be an actual observation, viz. that the bearing poles of the Ark could be seen from without, a statement which implies that the doors to the inner room were kept open. If the room was raised, it is understandable that the wings of the cherubim would make the Ark look insignificant. Their gigantic figures dominate the place, and we hear only about them and the holy Ark.

It is quite otherwise in the wilderness narrative. Here, too, the Ark is described, but the *kappōreth* placed over it plays a much more prominent part. And the cherubim are no longer the immense figures which entirely hide the Ark; whereas they are closely connected with the new holy object. Of what did this consist? The description gives its length and breadth which are identical with those of the Ark. It seems natural, then, to suppose that it was a slab laid over the Ark and supporting the cherubim, which covered it with their lifted wings (Ex. 25,18 ff.). It would then be nothing but a support for the cherubim. This, however, corresponds ill with its importance. For several hints would seem to show that it had become the actual sacred object.

When in post-exilic times the high-priest entered the cella, it was with this object only, not with the Ark, that he was concerned. It is prescribed that he shall at once place a pan with incense in the room in order that the *kappōreth* may be covered with a cloud of smoke, that he may not die at the sight of the holiest of all the holy objects. He is to sprinkle the blood of the victim on the side of it turning to the east, and then sprinkle it before it seven times (Lev. 16,13-15). It is clear that all this is concerned with the *kappōreth,* and it cannot be a flat slab, but must be some upright object.

Its holiness was due to the fact that Yahweh himself was

present upon it. "I appear in the cloud over *hak-kappōreth*" (Lev. 16,2). The cloud is the cloud of incense which the high-priest caused to ascend. Here we have the reality underlying the descriptions of how Yahweh always spoke enveloped in a cloud in Mount Sinai. When Moses in the tent "heard the voice speak to him from above *hak-kappōreth* which is over the Ark of testimony between the two cherubim" (Num. 7,89, cf. Ex. 25,22; 30,6), this is a reflection of what took place in the temple of Jerusalem. It is not without reason that 1 Chronicles calls the inner sanctuary the *kappōreth*-room (1 Chron. 28,11).

This evidence from the post-exilic period must be supposed to link up with the traditions of the monarchical period. The name *kappōreth* gives no indication of the appearance, but it is doubtless connected with the term for atonement, and merely denotes something by which this is accomplished. It must then be regarded as an indirect expression, resulting from the Jewish shrinking from direct mention of the holiest things. [1] But there are expressions which confirm the close connection which we have seen between this object upon which Yahweh reveals himself and the cherubim; for Yahweh is often called he "who is enthroned upon the cherubim" (1 Sam. 4,4; 2 Sam. 6,2; 2 Kings 19,15; Ps. 80,2; 99,1). This, as has often been maintained, can only mean that the cherubim carry a throne. It is this that has inspired the poet when he sees Yahweh swooping through space, riding on cherubim (Ps. 18,11). It suggests that *kappōreth* must be some kind of a throne.

We have, in fact, a clear statement that Yahweh dwelt on a throne in the temple of Jerusalem, and even a description of the throne, viz. in Ezekiel. He saw Yahweh return to the restored temple, and he heard him say from its interior that it was the place of his throne and his foot-stool (Ez. 43,6 f.), and the throne is described in the vision that the prophet had at Chebar (Ez. 1, cf. 9,3; 10,19 f.; 43,3).

The throne was carried by four winged beings partly human and partly composed of various animals, i. e. a kind of cherubim. While the cherubim on the temple wall had two faces in Ezekiel's description, that of a man and that of a lion (41,19), these had each of them four, of a man, a lion, an ox, and an eagle. They had the trunk of a man and calves' feet, with wheels on the outer side. A couple of wings covered the trunk, another pair were spread sideways, and the one pair of wings of the four beings together supported over their heads a slab or a board called *rāḳīaʿ*, the term   for the firmament. Above it there was, as it were, a throne, and on it something resembling a human form. From it there emanated an overwhelming radiance. It was the glory of Yahweh in visible shape (Ez. 1).

The description presents great difficulties, but it is excluded that it can be pure invention. It must be based on realities, and these can only be derived from the temple of Jerusalem as it appeared at the close of the monarchical period. The obscurity is in part due to the fear of a direct description. Mention is made of something that had "the semblance of" creatures, "the semblance of" a throne or of a human form. It is intended to inculcate that no common things are here described. The throne of Yahweh is borne by "the firmament", an expression of the fact that the throne is of cosmic importance and that the being seated on it is the same Yahweh that is enthroned above the firmament.

From Ezekiel's description we may, then, infer that in the monarchical period, before the destruction of the temple, there was in its inner sanctuary a throne, the base of which was supported by cherubic beings. These again rested on wheels, but it is not clear whether the wheels were fastened to the feet of the cherubim or whether they were part of a chariot on which the whole rested. The wheels seem to indicate that the throne was wheeled out in processions, perhaps within the precincts of the sanctuary. In all probability the throne was empty, Yahweh's honour might dwell there without any visible image. Ezekiel saw a human shape on it, but this need not mean that there actually was a human figure there. Empty thrones of gods were not uncommon in the Mediterranean countries, and they were well suited to be adopted by Israel. [1]

If we may rely on the description in the book of Kings, such a throne was hardly introduced into the temple under Solomon. Mention is merely made of the Ark and of cherubim, and the latter play quite a different role. If we are here really given a picture of conditions in the time of Solomon, the two great cherubim must have been removed by some later king and replaced by the new throne. The fact that Yahweh is often mentioned as he who sits enthroned on cherubim when the Ark also is referred to, would find its natural explanation if the Ark, the ancient sacred treasure, were lodged below the throne, just as a saint's shrine is placed below an altar. Thus Yahweh would be able to sit enthroned both above the Ark and on cherubim (Jer. 3,16 f.). The term for Yahweh as he who sits enthroned above cherubim was then transferred to the narratives of the Ark in the early days, before the royal temple came into existence (1 Sam. 4,4; 2 Sam. 6,2).

The description of the contents of the holy of holies in the wilderness sanctuary cannot be made to fit entirely that of Ezekiel. It only mentions two cherubim, but in the *kappōreth* we may see a hint of the throne, all the more so since the ritual of the day of expiation describes it as an upright object. However, the description (Ex. 25,17 ff.) is so incomplete that it is impossible to form any definite picture of it. The question then arises whether we have in this description a direct expression of conditions in post-exilic times, or whether the whole thing is a reminiscence of the past.

It is quite possible that after the exile the Israelites made good the loss of their sacred treasures by making a chest like the Ark and placing it under a *kappōreth* as described in Exodus; this need not have had exactly the same appearance as the former throne. In that case it would be possible that there was a basis of fact in the constant statements that the Ark contained two stone tables inscribed with the decalogue (Ex. 25,16; Deut. 10, 2 ff.; 1 Kings 8,9). A chest containing an abstract of the law would be quite conceivable in the holiest sanctuary of post-exilic Judaism. But the information we have about it may, indeed, merely be the outcome of imaginings about the past of Judaism.

That the ancient chief sacred object of the people continued to play a prominent part in their thoughts is evidenced not only by the description of the sanctuary in the wilderness, but also by

an utterance ascribed to Jeremiah: And it shall come to pass
when ye be multiplied and increased in the land in those days,
saith Yahweh, they shall say no more: the Ark of the covenant
of Yahweh; it shall not enter their minds, they shall not
remember it, and shall have nothing to do with it, and it shall
be made no more. At that time they shall call Jerusalem the
throne of Yahweh, and all the nations shall be gathered unto it ...
(Jer. 3,16 f.). This passage, which probably dates from the post-
exilic period, is the outcome of the passionate adherence, in the
later period of decline, to the early history and its sacred treasure,
a tendency which marks the whole conception of the wilderness
period. The utterance confirms that the Ark was understood to
be the throne of Yahweh. It shows that the idea of replacing
it when it disappeared seemed natural, [1] but it would be superfluous, because the whole of Jerusalem had taken over its
holiness. It does not appear from the utterance whether it
actually had disappeared or not.

If the holy objects of the inner sanctuary were replaced by
others after the exile, these, also, disappeared later on. Towards
the time of Christ the holy of holies was empty; only a stone was
found in the dark place. [2] But imagination occupied itself with
the Ark far down through the ages, and a tradition arose that
Jeremiah had rescued "the tent and the Ark" together with the
incense altar at the destruction of Jerusalem and concealed these
holy things in the mountain from which Moses looked into the
promised land; here they were to be found again when the people
were again gathered together (2 Mac. 2,4-7).

Solomon's temple was a typical expression of the new
monarchy. In its entire character it was foreign to early
Israel, composed as it was of elements from the great west
Asiatic cultures. But it preserved the continuity with the simple
Canaanite open-air sanctuary previously appropriated, the an-
cient holy place being retained. And through the Ark the con-

nection with the early history of Israel was secured. The altar in the open air and the Ark in the dark inmost room continued to be the two centres of the sanctuary.

The temple survived during the whole monarchical period until destroyed by Nebuchadrezzar in 586 or thereabouts. A large priesthood gradually grew up around it, who later gained the ascendancy among the people. A fixed, magnificent cult developed here on weekdays and at festivals, the whole of that temple ritual which was resumed in an altered form after the exile at the temple of Zerubbabel, as we know from the priestly code. It is a matter of course that throughout the monarchical period many changes were made in the temple, but we have no direct information of them.

From information in the books of the Kings it appears that there was a continual alternation between kings who favoured the foreign cult and others who persecuted it. Therefore there was a continual change in the cult utensils of the temple.

We are told about Asa that he removed "the logs" (gillūlim) which his fathers had made (1 Kings 15,12). Since Asa was the son of Rehabeam, it is the latter and Solomon who are his forefathers. The general character of this information, and the contemptuous term used for the idols, reveal the post-exilic author. But no doubt he based his account on an ancient tradition, and this means that the temple had from the beginning a more Canaanite character than the account of the building would lead us to suppose. Jeroboam set up images of calves to compete with Jerusalem; this would seem to show that Solomon had done something similar there. Asa destroyed a holy object [1] which his mother had made for the asherah (v. 13). Thus, in the reign of Rehabeam, or more probably even before he came to the throne, there was an asherah in the temple.

From early times the temple held an image of a serpent, called neḥushtān, until Hezekiah removed it (2 Kings 18,4). No doubt this, too, belonged to it from the beginning. The excavations have shown that the serpent, partly alone, partly with a goddess, was common in Canaanite temples. [2]

Under Manasseh the temple became a home for fresh foreign

cults. He set up an asherah in the temple (2 Kings 21,7), [1] but in addition "he built altars for all the host of heaven in the two courts of the house of Yahweh" (v. 5). We are here concerned with the introduction of Assyrian cults, but there was a restoration also, after Hezekiah's reform of the temple, and it was maintained by his son Amon. The account of Josiah's reform shows how full the temple was of cult objects. There were utensils for Baal and Asherah and all the host of heaven (2 Kings 23,4), more especially an image of an asherah (v. 6). There were cells for the male priests of the sexual cult where the women wove for Asherah (v. 7), and there were horses dedicated to the sun and sun chariots, an entire Assyrian Shamash sanctuary, [2] and on the roof of "Ahaz' upper chamber" there were altars (v. 11 f.).

The reform of Josiah did not prove permanent. Between the first and second conquests of Jerusalem both Tammuz and Shamash were worshipped in the temple, and the temple court harboured "the image of jealousy which provoketh jealousy" (Ez. 8,3.5), i. e. an image of an alien god. At one of the gates there were secret cells with animal pictures on the walls where Shaphan's son Jaazaniah conducted the cult (Ez. 8,7 ff.). Foreign priests, too, were drawn to the temple by these cults (Ez. 44,7 f.). These are the practices which the prophets designate as abominable and offensive *(shikkūṣ, tōʿēbhā,* Jer. 7,30; 32,34; Ez. 5,11 et al.). Altogether this shows that the royal temple must in the course of time have obtained quite a different appearance to that suggested by the description.

The close connection between the whole establishment and the monarchy appears from the fact that the buildings of the royal palace and the temple were surrounded by a common freestone wall. The common court was called "the great court" (1 Kings 7,9.12), but the temple had a special wall (v. 12). Several gates led from the site of the palace to the temple precincts and there was continual traffic here. Part of the king's body-guard was always stationed in the temple, which it entered on the sabbath (2 Kings 11,5 ff.), and the officials of the king passed in and out between the temple and the palace (Jer. 26,10; 36,11 ff.). The solemn entry of the king was made by the main entrance on the east, looking towards the altar and the front of the temple. Thus it is described in Ezekiel (46,1 f., cf. 44,3), and the eastern gate was "the royal gate" (1 Chron. 9,18). The gates were closed buildings. In one of them Jeremiah sat in the stocks (Jer. 20,2). The magnates would sit there and take counsel together (Jer. 26,10).

The temple hall corresponded to the hall of the old temples, the *lishkā,* and as indicated above, we may probably take it for granted that in the beginning it was used for the same purposes. But in the long run it was not sufficient. For the use of the priests, for stores etc. there were the side buildings along the temple, [1] but these, also, were insufficient. We have seen that new buildings were added for foreign cults on the site of the temple, but in the latter part of the monarchical period there were also a number of chambers, each termed *lishkā,* doubtless along the outer wall of the court. An ecclesiastical official, the janitor Maaseiah ben Shallum, had his own *lishkā,* above which "the chiefs" had theirs, and next to these the sons of Hanan ben Jigdaliah, the man of God, had their *lishkā* (Jer. 35,4). By "the new gate" a son of the king's official Shaphan had his chamber (Jer. 36,10).

Very different people had chambers in the temple. A guild of men of God had one chamber, either to live in or for their ecstatic exercises, as in the mosques of today. And the other chambers, which either belonged to a single person or to a particular circle, were probably used especially for sacrificial meals. This is confirmed by Ezekiel's plan of the temple, a simplified and systematised sketch based on conditions at the close of the regal period. Here an outer court surrounds the temple except on the western side, and there are entrance gates in each of the three outer walls. Along these there are buildings with chambers, and kitchens at the corners (Ez. 40,17 ff.; 46,21-24), where the temple servants were to boil the sacrifices of the lay population, from which it may be inferred that the adjoining chambers were intended for the consumption of the sacrificial meat. The court immediately surrounding the temple is again shut off as an inner court only accessible to priests. This court, too, is surrounded by a wall with three entrance gates; in and by these there are shambles for the slaughtering of the victims (Ez. 40,39 ff.), and in the court there are partly chambers for the functioning priests (40,44-46), partly kitchens and chambers where the priests were to eat the meat of their offerings (42,1 ff.; 46,19 f.).

All that is new in Ezekiel is probably merely his re-organisation of an older plan. The division into two courts is strictly adhered to, corresponding with the distinction between priest and layman. But the division into an outer and an inner court already existed at the early temple, though not from the beginning. At that time "the inner court of Yahweh's temple" or "the court that is before Yahweh's house" (1 Kings 6,36; 7,12; 8,64) was the same thing as the temple court, as opposed to the great court covering the whole site of the palace and temple (7,9.12). However, we find the division into an outer and an inner temple court in Ezekiel before the final destruction of the early temple (Ez. 8,16; 10,3.5; perhaps 8,3). In the time of Jeremiah mention is made of the "higher temple court", i. e. the inner one (Jer. 36,10, cf. Ez. 40,19), and already in Isaiah Yahweh calls the site of the temple "my courts" (Isa. 1,12, cf. 2 Kings 21,5; 23,12). Perhaps the division was made under Jehoshaphat or shortly before, for we are told that he stood "in Yahweh's house in front of the new court", an expression that must be due to the tradition (2 Chron. 20,5). In the temple of Zerubbabel the division had been carried out (Isa. 62,9; Zech. 3,7; Neh. 8,16; 13,7).

The question is of interest because, as we gather from Ezekiel, the division came to form the basis of the separation of the priests from the people. At first, however, it hardly brought about such a distinction, but it was connected with the trend of the development in the temple.

It had been founded as a royal temple, but it soon became a rallying-point for the varied multitude of the people. Not only at festivals did the Israelites crowd to the temple and "trample down" the court. On ordinary days, too, it was filled by the throngs listening to the speeches of the prophets, as when Baruch stood in the hall of Gemariah ben Shaphan and read Jeremiah's discourses to the people (Jer. 36,10). Prophetic guilds sat there practising their exercises; and the leaders of the people carried on their debates there. The priesthood grew and filled the side buildings. Many frequented the temple day and night. Thus it became a world of its own with a varied life, quite like the mosques in later ages. The king was the head of the temple, but it acquired importance independently of him. A royal child like Joash could live with his nurse in a bedroom in the temple for years without the ruling queen even suspecting it (2 Kings 11,2 f.).

The division into the two courts probably took place in connection with extensions required by the increasing activity at the temple. A certain shutting off of the sanctuary proper for the sake of order may also have been intended, but at any rate it did not mean that it was only the priesthood who were holy enough to enter the inner court. [1] As we saw, the nurse of Joash could live with the king's son in a chamber of the temple. The royal body-guard stood in a circle around the temple quite close to the altar (2 Kings 11,11), and it is implied that everybody can go up to the altar, perhaps even into the temple (2 Kings 12,10). This was in the 9th century. Shortly before 700 we hear Isaiah mention that the people filled the courts, and even shortly before the destruction Baruch read Jeremiah's speeches to the people in a chamber in the "higher court", i. e. the inner one.

After the exile we see Nehemiah engaged in removing strangers from the temple and its precincts, and he himself regarded it as sacrilege to enter the temple hall, whereas he does not seem to have made any distinction between the two courts (Neh. 6,10 f.; 13,4-9, cf. Ezr. 10,9). As late as the time of the Hasmonæans we have evidence that the lay population entered the inner court. Only after Alexander Jannæos had once been attacked there did he shut out the people. [2] Now the inner court was merely "the court of the priests". This was the case, too, in the temple of Herod which was even further divided, non-Israelites having access to the outermost part of the outer court only.

We see what a struggle there must have been about the temple. Nehemiah acknowledged that only priests should be allowed to enter the temple building, while he probably moved without fear about both the courts of the temple, but the leading priests did not see eye to eye with him in this matter. It was no doubt an early claim within the priesthood that only priestly holiness should be recognised as suited for the inner court, and this is strongly emphasised in Ezekiel's plan. Perhaps the inner court was also in post-exilic times called "the court of the priests" (2 Chron. 4,9) for it was here especially that they displayed their activity. But it required the fortuitous concurrence of a political event for their claim to be accepted that it should be entirely reserved for them.

The royal temple was completely under the control of the king. This was also the case at Bethel, where the chief priest did not interfere with Amos until he had consulted the king (Am. 7,10 ff.). The royal temple of Jerusalem was built and consecrated by the king, and he had sovereign power over its cultus. It was the king who introduced or abolished foreign cults. He caused the temple to be guarded, and when he entered it, he was surrounded by a bodyguard, "runners", who carried bronze shields which had replaced the gold shields of Solomon (1 Kings 14,26 ff.).

The importance of the temple might be measured by the treasure stored in it. This was in the main supplied by the king (1 Kings 15,15; 2 Kings 12,19), but a good deal came in, too, in the shape of cult gifts or dues (cf. 2 Kings 12). Not only royal temples had a temple treasure. At Shechem the men of the town took silver from Baal berith's temple to support Abimelech (Judg. 9,4). Enemies always knew how to obtain spoil from the treasuries of the temples. Already under Solomon's successor the king of Egypt secured his temple treasure (1 Kings 14,26), and the kings of Judah had continually to resort to the silver and gold of the temple to keep off an enemy or gain over a dangerous ruler; or the enemy might take it himself (1 Kings 15,18; 2 Kings 12,19; 14,14; 16,8; 18,15 f.; 23,33; 24,13). Hezekiah even had to peel the gold off the doors and pillars; thus it is difficult to understand how he could have a large amount of treasure to show to the Chaldæan envoys (18,15 f. and 20,13). When Nebuchadrezzar first captured Jerusalem he merely took the temple treasure and the gold vessels which he carried off to Babylon, but the second time he entirely despoiled the temple (2 Kings 24,13; 25,13; cf. Jer. 27,18 ff.; Ezr. 1,7 ff.).

The temple was managed by the priests, who were royal officials. We learn that Joash enjoined them to receive the gold dues or gifts [1] coming in and defray the expenses for the repairs of the temple out of them. When it turned out that the priests accepted the silver but let the temple decay, the king summoned them before him, with the chief priest Jehoiada, reprimanded them, and deprived them of the management of the silver gifts. The chief priest then caused a chest to be made which was placed by the altar on the right side of any one facing the temple, i. e. to the north. Here the priests who were on guard put the silver, and after a suitable space of time it was fetched by the king's minister *(sōphēr)* in company with the chief priest. They weighed the silver and gave it to the contractors who had undertaken the repairs, and these paid the artisans and purchased the materials without rendering any account, having pledged their faith. The money was not used for new utensils or an increase of the treasure, and the priests, as was evidently the custom, received the silver given for sin and guilt offerings (2 Kings 12,5-17). Thus the king's attempt to leave the entire administration of the temple to the priests was not a success, and this was no doubt because by tradition part of the temple revenues belonged to them, and they had not character enough to distinguish between what they were allowed to take for themselves and what was to be reserved for the temple. Under Josiah we hear of the same procedure as was introduced by Joash. The king sent his *sōphēr,* Shaphan, to the temple and in company with Hilkiah he arranged for the payment of the workmen exactly as had been done under Joash (2 Kings 22,3-9).

Within the priesthood it was the chief priest who was mainly responsible for the administration of the temple; along with him are mentioned the second priest and the janitors; these, according to the command of the king, were to arrange for the details of the cultus (2 Kings 23,4; cf. Jer. 52,24). The janitors had, indeed, a subordinate position; but in the administration itself they took an important part, dealing, as they did, with the temple gifts that were collected (2 Kings 12,10; 22,4). We have seen that there was also a special inspector at the temple, just as there was a supervisor of the prophets (Jer. 20,1 ff.; 29,26), and they were invested with authority to punish those who broke the rules of the temple. But the priests had no independent administrative authority, they were the king's men. Hence they were dependent on the king's other officials. When Jeremiah had prophesied the fall of the temple, the priests and prophets laid the matter before the royal officials, who then sat in the temple pronouncing judgment, and their judgment was final (Jer. 26). In another case the king's minister at the palace was informed of the rebellious conduct of Jeremiah in the temple, and he submitted the case to the king (Jer. 36,9 ff.).

Thus Ezekiel's claim that the temple should be entirely given over to the priesthood, whereas the king should only be allowed to come just inside the inner temple gate (Ez. 44,3; 46,2), goes far beyond conditions in the monarchical period; but, as we have seen, there was, in post-exilic times, a strong tendency to make the priests sole governors of the temple, because there was no ruler who could supply the place of the king. And yet it was a layman, Nehemiah, who restored conditions in the temple by virtue of his personal authority and the warrant he held from the Persian overlord. Thus he installed inspectors who were responsible for the temple chambers and for the payment of the holy dues, and these inspectors were priests (Neh. 10,38 ff.; 12,44 ff.; 13,4 ff.).

The claim that the holiness of the temple and of its priests should be maintained was not only an ecclesiastical claim intended to safeguard professional interests. It was the people who demanded that the centre from which the holy power emanated should be venerated, because their life was dependent on it.

The varied public activity displayed about the royal temple on Zion witnessed to the special importance of this temple as compared with others. Jeroboam's fear that people would continue their pilgrimages to the temple connected with David's house (1 Kings 12,26), was well founded. As late as the days after the capture of Jerusalem travellers came from Shechem, Shiloh, and Samaria, 80 in all, to offer sacrifice in Yahweh's temple (Jer. 41,4 f.).

The pilgrims coming to Jerusalem found other sanctuaries besides the rock temple there. Several of them had been built by Solomon. On the Mount of Olives, where there was also a sanctuary in the time of David (2 Sam. 15,32), he erected temples to the Moabite god Chemosh, to the Ammonite Milcom, and to the Sidonian Astarte (1 Kings 11,7 LXX.33). Altogether, he built temples to the gods of his foreign wives (v. 2); if this is truly historical, he must also have founded an Egyptian temple. These temples survived right down to the time of Josiah (2 Kings 23,13); but there were others also.

A temple to Baal, probably Phoenician, must have been built by Joram who married Athaliah, a daughter of Ahab, or she may have built it herself. When she had been overthrown and put to death, the population of the land pulled down the temple with its altars and images and killed Mattan, its priest (2 Kings 11,18, cf. 8,27 f.). Manasseh not only introduced Assyrian cults in the temple, he also rebuilt all the sanctuaries in the town which Hezekiah had demolished (2 Kings 21,3). By one of the city gates, at any rate, there were sanctuaries, "the gate bamahs", which were desecrated by Josiah (2 Kings 23,8). Toward the close of the monarchical period, there were altars to the queen of heaven in the streets of Jerusalem, (Jer. 44,17. 21), just as there were altars in the streets in Assyria.[1] To this must be added the numerous private cults, Adonis gardens (Isa. 17,10), and sanctuaries on the roofs, where the people offered sacrifice to "the host of heaven" (Jer. 19,13; 32,29). The most important were perhaps the sanctuaries to Baal in the valley of Hinnom to the south of the city; in one of these, *tōpheth,* children were sacrificed as a burnt-offering to Molech [1] (2 Kings 23,10; Jer. 7,31; 19,1-13; 32,35).

All this shows that we should obtain a quite incorrect picture of Jerusalem if we viewed it in the light of post-exilic times as a city with a single temple only. Jerusalem like the other large cities of antiquity was a town full of shrines to different gods, even though our sources have reduced them to a quite insignificant feature.

The numerous sanctuaries found in Jerusalem and elsewhere all had the important mission of being the centres from which the holy energy emanated which was a vital necessity for the people. This is clearly expressed in the older altar law in which Yahweh says: In every place where I record my name, I will come unto thee, and I will bless thee (Ex. 20,24). Here the divine power is present, and the blessing emanates from here. And the blessing has the same effect as any other blessing. In the dedication address ascribed to Solomon (1 Kings 8) it is victory and fertility he hopes to win from the new temple. And when the temple lay in ruins, it had to be rebuilt at any cost, that the people might regain happiness and fertility.

The prophet Haggai says on this subject:

Now therefore thus saith Yahweh of the hosts: Let your hearts consider your fates: Ye sow much and bring home little; ye eat, but are not satisfied; drink, but are not filled; clothe yourselves, but not to be warmed; and the wage-earner procures wages for a purse full of holes. Ye look for much, and it comes to little; and when ye bring it home, I blow upon it. Why? saith Yahweh of the hosts. Because of mine house which is left desolate, while ye run every man to his own house. Therefore the heavens withhold their dew from you, and the earth withholds its produce. And I call for a drought upon the land, upon the mountains and upon the corn, upon the wine and upon the oil, upon that which the ground bringeth forth, upon men and upon cattle, and upon all the labour of their hands (Hag. 1,5-6.9-11). And the same prophet describes how, in the time when the temple was desolate, people only had 10 measures of corn when they expected 20, only 20 measures of wine when they expected 50;

for hail and mildew destroyed the produce. But after the foundation of the temple no one need be afraid to sow the seed; vines, figs, pomegranates and olives will grow luxuriantly, "from this day will I bless you" (Hag. 2,19). It cannot be said more plainly how important the sanctuary is as the centre of the blessing.

Just as the strong men who are the upholders of the community create blessedness for it, because the spirit of Yahweh is in them or with them, thus also the creation of blessedness by the holy place is due to the divine spirit which dwells in it. This is what is expressed in the foundation legends, just as it has set its mark on the term for the holy tent of the wilderness which is called the tent of "the presence" or of "the testimony". In the old altar law it is expressed by the fact that Yahweh records his name in the place (Ex. 20,24), just as we are told in other passages that Yahweh's name is fixed there, the temple bears it (1 Kings 8,18 f. 43; 9,3); his name has been pronounced over the sanctuary (Jer. 34,15). This means that his *kābhōdh,* his honour, is in the temple (1 Kings 8,11, cf. Ex. 40,34 f.), his name, his eyes, and his heart are there (2 Chron. 7,16). We know that all these are the literal equivalents of the soul of Yahweh. He is present in the sanctuary himself and has his dwelling there (Ex. 15,17; 25,8; 1 Kings 8,13). As the stone in the ancient sanctuary is the abode of a god, thus also the temple with the holy objects is his dwelling-place. In the royal temple of Jerusalem Yahweh sat enthroned like a king in his castle.

Any one who had the spirit of God in him felt at home in the holy place, because there he was in his own sphere. And any one who had not the spirit of God in him, or required to have it revived, could receive it in the holy place. Here leaders drew inspiration to carry out their work. Under holy trees and by holy springs the judge was given power to speak the proper words of judgment, hence a holy well could be called a "well of judgment" (Gen. 14,7; Judg. 4,5). The men of God went to the holy place to awaken the spirit of God; and the sanctuary with its offerings inspired their soothsayings, as we know from the story of Balaam (Num. 23,13.27). Hence there is nothing strange in the fact that a prophet sees in a vision the temple at Jerusalem as the centre from which all divine revelation spreads over the earth (Isa. 2,2 = Mic. 4,1).

As the centres from which the blessing emanated the holy places represented the Israelite world. In holy stones, in trees and water, the forces working in the land of Canaan were present, and a stone or some other holy thing might embody part of the history of Israel and ensure the continuity with the past. By its stone the sanctuary on Zion was allied to the old open-air sanctuaries, and at any rate for a time there was an asherah there as a representative of the tree. But otherwise nature was represented by foreign cult objects, the water by "the sea", and the heavenly forces by objects associated with the sun. Thus the sanctuary became a cosmos, but it was not these things that rendered it significant.

The temple had been founded as a royal temple, it was the God of David who dwelt in it. And thus it continued to be, even though the realm governed by Jerusalem comprised but a small part of the people of Israel. Jerusalem was the ideal seat of the royal power, which was the rallying-point of the people, and the maintainer of the earliest history of the nation. Hence it became in ever-increasing degree the centre of popular life, and it was a natural result of the whole history of the people that after the exile it came to be regarded as the only sanctuary of Israel.

In this way the royal temple at Jerusalem was gradually raised above time. It was not enough that the rock was that mountain of Moriah where the progenitor had offered sacrifice and given the greatest proof of his obedience (Gen. 22,2; 2 Chron. 3,1). The place was assigned with the world itself to primeval ages and was to last forever, independently of the vicissitudes of time (Ps. 78,69; 125,1). Not only did the plan of the temple exist quite complete in the wilderness period at the birth of the nation; but its archetype, the tabernacle, was formed after a model which Yahweh himself had shown to Moses (Ex. 25,9.40). And in another connection we are told that Solomon got the plan of the temple from David, who had it from a writing in Yahweh's own hand (1 Chron. 28,19). Thus the Israelites, exactly like other peoples, gave expression to the importance of their temple by affirming that it derived its origin from the very God who dwelt in it. [1]

This central importance of the temple is also expressed by the idea that its place is in the midst of the people, a conception which we know from other peoples also, to whom their sanctuary is "the navel of the earth". [2] Ezekiel sees the people regenerated, with the temple in their midst, raised above the united Israel and Judah (Ez. 37,26-28; 48,8.10.21). From this place rich in blessedness a spring flows forth which shall bring life to the desolate salt plains, so that trees grow up in abundance and bear fruit incessantly for food, and fresh leaves for healing, "for its waters issue from the sanctuary" (Ez. 47,1-12, cf. Joel 4,18; Zech. 14,8).

The temple makes Jerusalem not only the centre of Israel, but of the whole earth. Here the ruler of all the world sits enthroned (Zech. 14,9), the rock of the temple towers above all peaks and draws all men unto itself, because they desire to share in the revelation emanating from it (Isa. 2,1 ff.). Thus the whole earth is transformed and becomes subject to the sanctuary of Israel, for it possesses all holiness and therefore also all the blessing.

SACRED AND PROFANE

HOLINESS is a force which is felt in all spheres of life, it is, indeed, at the root of all other kinds of energy. In men it manifests itself in various ways according to their nature, and in sacred places it is felt with differing degrees of strength. All kinds of holiness, however, have something in common. The force felt by the Israelite in the sacred stone is not dissimilar in its essence from that which he feels in his own soul when it works in the full intensity of its strength.

In Hebrew as in all other Semitic languages the term for holiness is connected with the root *ḳdsh*. A consideration of this root, however, affords no insight into the nature of holiness, since nothing is known about it except the very fact that it is used about what we call holiness.

From our consideration of war we learned that not only the elect could obtain the intensified and increased strength of soul which constituted holiness. All Israelite warriors acquired it and maintained it as long as the war lasted, and the way to it passed through isolation from the ordinary workaday world. In early Israel we meet with examples of men living a whole lifetime in this condition. We know it best from Samson, one of the old chiefs already mentioned.

Samson's powers as a god-imbued chieftain were connected with the fact that he was a *nāzīr*. The account of his birth and destiny gives us the external marks. His mother is not allowed to drink wine or strong drink, and must not touch unclean food, his head must never be shaved (Judg. 13,4 f. 14). The prohibition of wine and unclean food must of course have applied to himself even more than to his mother. How important was the free growth of the hair is evidenced by the story of the false

Delilah who wheedled out of him the secret of his unexampled strength. He divulged the fact that all his strength would leave him if his hair were cut, and thus it came to pass (Judg. 16, 17.19).

Samson is an ideal figure, the great Nazirite. The law of his life was, that the restraining forces of normal civilised existence should be kept away from him. His hair, in the growth of which every one might observe the spontaneous vital force, must not be artificially trimmed, uncleanness must not waste away any part of his soul and destroy its integrity. Wine must not contribute to increase the strength of his soul, for wine was Canaanite and did not belong to the Israelitish psychic totality.

From Amos, too, (2,12) we know that the Nazirites were forbidden to drink wine; the prohibition to cut the hair recurs in the history of Samuel (1 Sam. 1,11). The great importance of the Nazirites is evidenced by Amos, who places them on a level with the prophets (Am. 2,11). The affinity of their condition to that of the warrior is clear. As a *nāzir* Samson accomplishes his mighty deeds. He rends lions, carries off city gates, and slays whole hosts of Philistines. It is readily understood that the term *nāzir* comes to denote the consecrated chieftain (Gen. 49,26; Deut. 33,16; Lam. 4,7), *nēzer* his diadem (2 Sam. 1,10; 2 Kings 11,12; Ps. 89,40 et al.), and that the corresponding verb may be used in the same sense as *ḳdsh* (Hos. 9,10), while a cognate word in Arabic is employed especially concerning the consecration of a warrior. [1]

How deeply ingrained in the mind of the people were these fundamental ideas may be seen from the importance they retained through the ages. Any one could become a Nazirite for a short period and thus acquire renewed strength of soul. The law on this point has been preserved. It says: If a man or a woman would make the vow of a Nazirite to live as a Nazirite before Yahweh, he must practise the abstemiousness of a Nazirite from wine and strong drink. He shall drink no vinegar of wine or vinegar of strong drink, he shall drink no liquor of grapes, and he shall eat no fresh or dried grapes. In all the days while he is a Nazirite he shall eat nothing of what is produced from

the vine, neither unripe grapes nor fresh shoots. ¹ All the days
of his vow as a Nazirite no razor shall come upon his head;
until the days be fulfilled, in which he lives as a Nazirite unto
Yahweh, he shall be holy *(kādhōsh)*, and shall let the hair of
his head grow freely. ² All the days that he lives as a Nazirite
unto Yahweh, he shall come near no dead body. He shall not
make himself unclean by his father, his mother, his brother or
his sister, when they die; because his consecration to his God
as a Nazirite is upon his head. All the days of his consecration
he is sacred unto Yahweh (Num. 6,2-8).

The text now goes on to say that if the Nazirite should inadvertently be defiled by a corpse, he must purify himself when the
period of his consecration is over, and then resume the state of a
Nazirite for the normal period. Finally directions are given as to
how the sacred condition is to be terminated. The Nazirite must
make an offering. Then at the entrance to the sanctuary he shall
shave off his hair and cast it on to the altar under the sacrifice.
When the consecrated state is at an end, the Nazirite may again
drink wine (Num. 6,9-20).

The same elements which were found among the old Nazirites
are established in this law. The prohibition of wine has, with the
Israelite desire for consistency, been extended to include
everything that has any contact with the vine, even the dried
raisins. Among unclean things to be shunned special stress is
laid on corpses, and it is still a point of vital importance that the
hair of the head should be left intact. The free, unchecked
development of any natural growth is so important a component
of the concept that the word *nāzīr* can be used also about the
uncut vines of the year of Sabbath and Yobhel (Lev. 25,5.11).

The law calls the Nazirite sacred (Num. 6,5.8), he is "holy
unto Yahweh", "a *nāzīr* of God" (Judg. 13,5.7; 16,17). This
places him on a level with the warrior, the chieftain, the
prophet, and the priest. It applies to them all that their holiness
is a condition they can acquire and lose again, and they may
possess it in greater or less degree. Holiness is not consistent with
the claims of everyday life; normal souls acquire it for a time
after which they again discard it. The priests occupy a special

position, their holiness is due to their daily association with sacred things. There is a decisive difference between blessedness and holiness. Blessedness is a power which must never be lost if life is to be lived, and it has always a good effect only. Holiness has its special law, because it is the extraordinary, the greatly increased strength of the soul. It may serve to increase blessedness and is necessary to renew it. But if man approaches it unprepared, the force of it may do more harm than good.

The accounts of the old sanctuaries constantly record the fear men may feel when face to face with them. When Gideon discovered that he was standing in a sacred place by the rock in Ophrah, and that it was Yahweh's *mal'ākh* that had appeared to him there, he broke into lamentation: Alas, Lord Yahweh! I have seen Yahweh's *mal'ākh* face to face! But Yahweh said to him: Peace be unto thee! fear not! thou shalt not die (Judg. 6,22 f.). The same thing happened to Manoah in Zorah when Yahweh consecrated the sanctuary there. Then he cried to his wife: "We shall surely die, for we have seen a deity" (Judg. 13,22). And when Jacob dreamed his dream at Bethel and understood that the place was a sacred place and the house of God, he was struck with terror, though Yahweh had promised him his help and his blessing. "And he was overwhelmed with fear and said, How dreadful is this place! This indeed is a house of God, and this is the gate of Heaven!" (Gen. 28,17).

This sense of fear is caused by the mighty power of holiness. It surpasses what is *known* to ordinary human beings, hence they cannot control its laws, and do not know whether it will serve to strengthen or to destroy them. This is illustrated by the stories of the Ark.

When Yahweh's Ark was brought into the war against the Philistines it was accompanied by the two sons of Eli and caused great rejoicing among the Israelites, and fear among the Philistines. Nevertheless it was taken by the enemy and its two priests were killed. The Philistines dealt with it as was their habit with sacred spoil. They placed it in a temple at Ashdod beside the god Dagon who had now become lord of the Ark. He was, then, to appropriate to himself the alien sacred shrine, but

this he was unable to do. The Philistines might defeat the Israelites, but Yahweh's Ark could not be conquered by the hostile god,
and next morning Dagon lay before the Ark, his head and his
hands broken off. This was not all. Disaster befell the town, the
inhabitants were smitten with a plague of emerods. The men of
Ashdod realised whence the misfortunes came. They decided to try
whether the temples of other towns could get the better of the
troublesome spoil, but neither Gath nor Ekron were more successful. Wherever the Ark went, the plague followed it, and death
spread throughout the cities of the Philistines (1 Sam. 5).

It was now plain that the Philistines could not appropriate
the Ark, so they had to restore it; this could not be done, however,
without at the same time making reparation to it. The priests and
the diviners advised that a propitiatory offering should be made
to the Ark of a mouse and an emerod of gold for each of the five
lords of the Philistines; thus they would "give glory unto the God
of Israel" (1 Sam. 6,5). These gold objects were to be laid in a
receptacle to be put with the Ark on a new cart, to which were
to be harnessed two cows that had just calved and had never
been under the yoke, and from which the calves had been taken.
"And watch, if it goeth up to Bethshemesh by the road to its
own land, then it is He who hath done us this great evil; but if
not, then we shall know that it is not His hand that smote us; but
it was a chance that happened to us" (1 Sam. 6,9).

This advice was followed. The cows went straight to Bethshemesh, lowing incessantly and hardly looking either to the
right or the left, accompanied to the border by the lords of the
Philistines. The people of Bethshemesh were reaping their wheat
harvest; they rejoiced to see the Ark again and sacrificed the
cows where they stopped, in Joshua's field, using the wood of
the cart. And, the text goes on to say, the Levites took down the
Ark and the gold objects, and put them on the great stone:
and the men of Bethshemesh made offerings to Yahweh. The
Ark, however, was not willing to remain here either, and it smote
seventy men because they rashly looked in its direction (6,19).
"Then the men of Bethshemesh said: Who is able to stand before
this holy God Yahweh? And to whom will He go up from us?"

(6,20). Now they sent messengers to Kirjath-jearim, whose inhabitants fetched it. And they placed it in the house of Abinadab, where his son Eleazar was consecrated to guard it (6,21-7,1). Here, then, the Ark remained until David removed it. Of this event it is recorded that it was placed on a new cart, and Uzza and Ahio, the sons of Abinadab, accompanied it, while David and the people of Israel followed in festive procession. When the draught-oxen suddenly failed, [1] Uzza put out his hand to the Ark, but then "the anger of Yahweh was kindled against Uzza" and he killed him on the spot in the place since called *pereṣ ʿuzzā*, "Uzza's breach". Under these circumstances David dared not proceed any further with the Ark but placed it in the house of Obed Edom, the Gittite. Here it remained for three months, and Yahweh blessed Obed Edom and all his household. When David learned this, he brought up the Ark to the city of Zion (2 Sam. 6).

The Israelites have recorded in their own way what happened to the Ark among the Philistines. How far this corresponds with the actual facts is of no interest in this connection. But it appears with all plainess from the narratives that the Israelites by no means regarded the Ark as what we understand by a thing. As a weapon or a garment is pervaded by its owner's soul, so also the Ark is the true counterpart of the soul of the deity. Men might have a divine soul, but no man could possess it in so high a degree as this sacred chest. It is referred to in the same way as Yahweh himself, what is done to the Ark is done to Yahweh. In several passages it is not even possible to decide whether the words apply to the Ark or to Yahweh (1 Sam. 6,3.5.8.20). Similarly, the starting and resting of the Ark on the journey was identical with that of Yahweh (Num. 10,35 f.).

The Ark has firm and decided will power and jealously guards its honour. The Philistines understand this and attempt to do penance and make reparation to it. As they have put it on a cart that is quite new, and thus directed by no other power, any more than are the cows harnessed to it, it is the Ark alone which decides whether it will go one way or the other (1 Sam. 6,9), just as it is the Ark which selects the camping places in campaigns

(Num. 10,33). It had a very unmistakable way of showing its will power. When it was received in Bethshemesh with the honour due to a sacred thing, all was well at first, but when it was dissatisfied, it at once killed people, and people asked themselves where it wanted to go next. Then it came to Kirjathjearim, whence David set out with it towards Zion. Why should it kill once more, this time even a man who wanted to help it? Uzza was no unhallowed person whom disaster befell because he lacked the qualities necessary for touching what was sacred; he and his brother were the guardians of the Ark; they must, then, have been prepared for their office, and had no doubt placed the Ark on the cart. Uzza's sin may have been that he did not act in the right way, but more probably it was just his good will that was his sin. It offended the Ark, which did not need his help; he was struck down by the jealousy of Yahweh whose honour was outraged. But where there was entire harmony, there blessedness grew up around the ancient shrine, even in the house of a stranger.

The holiness of the Ark signified a tremendous fund of energy and what we may call will-power, which was so great because it was entirely divine. Even Yahweh's divine honour and susceptibility to offence resided in it. Its force was so intense that its workings seem arbitrary. And yet its holiness, like everything else of the soul, showed a certain conformity to law. The more man was able to enter into spiritual relationship with holy things, the more did his dread of their holiness disappear.

Holiness shows itself in its most pronounced character in the sacred place and in everything belonging to it. Just as the blessing has its contrast in the curse and cleanness in uncleanness, so also what is sacred has its contrast in that which is denoted by the root *ḥll*, the profane. The sanctuary with everything that belongs to it is *ḳōdhesh*, everything lying outside the sanctuary is *ḥōl* (Ez. 42,20). It is the duty of the priests to know exactly where the line is to be drawn between the two worlds, a duty which, according to Ezekiel, they do not always discharge in the proper way (Lev. 10,10; Ez. 22,26; 44,23).

The contrast to blessedness and cleanness is always evil, but this is not the case with the contrast to what is holy. In holiness psychic strength is so intensified that it rises above the contrasts of good and evil prevalent among men. The profane is equivalent to what is normal, what belongs to daily life. The ordinary bread of daily nourishment is *ḥōl* (1 Sam. 21,5); the same term is applied to a site belonging to Jerusalem but not to the sanctuary (Ez. 48,15).

To profane *(ḥillēl)* means to draw into the sphere of normal life. It acquires a negative meaning by the fact that it is always used to denote a withdrawal from the sacred sphere into daily life, and the more sacred the sphere the more does the profanation acquire the character of a debasement, a violation. The sacred altar stones should be living, should not be encroached upon by man. To cut them with a tool would be to bring them into the normal sphere and profane them (Ex. 20,25). The fruit of the vine must be sanctified in the fourth year (Lev. 19,24 f.). Then, when men first appropriate it, they withdraw it from the sacred sphere into daily life; this, too, is naturally called a profanation (Deut. 20,6; 28,30; Jer. 31,5). But whereas the profanation of the altar is sacrilege, because it is against the nature of the altar, the profanation of the grape is consistent with the order of life. Usually the word is employed as a condemnatory term for the violation of what is sacred, of Yahweh, of the covenant, of the sanctuary, of the sabbath; and altogether of the precepts of Yahweh. The idea of violation may come to loom so large in the concept that no more thought is given to the question whether the offence is committed against something holy (Gen. 49,4; Isa. 23,9).

There are other expressions much more emphatically denoting antagonism to what is sacred. While *ḥll* designates that which is not sacred, *ḥnp* denotes that which resists what is sacred. Jeremiah speaks of priests and prophets doing evil in the house of Yahweh; he says that they commit sacrilege *(ḥānᵉphū,* Jer. 23,11). Through blood-guilt and other sin the whole country becomes pervaded by this unholiness (Num. 35,33; Isa. 24,5; Jer. 3,1 f.; Ps. 106,38). Therefore the curse will come, and harry the land, and its priests and prophets must grope their way in darkness and perish (Isa. 24,5; Jer. 23,11).

The Israelites have a specific term, *ḥērem*, for the sphere which is utterly incompatible with what is sacred, for that which is hostile and alien, and, because incapable of assimilation, must be destroyed. We have seen the part played by this concept in war. The enemy was *ḥērem*, but the Israelites, too, might become *ḥērem*. If they passed over to the alien in its most intensified form, as it operated in the cult, they were transformed from within and must be exterminated as *ḥērem* (Ex. 22,19; Deut. 7,26). A city which meddled with an alien cult was to be made *ḥērem*, according to the requirements of Deuteronomy, and burnt down to the ground with all that was in it (Deut. 13,13 ff.). To make *ḥērem*, or to place under a ban, means to root out of the community of Israel, to place entirely outside the Israelite psychic totality; and as a natural consequence this usually involves extermination, as we saw in the history of Achan. *Ḥērem* is identical with the curse in its most potent form. When Meroz did not obey the summons to come to the battle with Deborah, it was cursed (Judg. 5,23). When Jabesh did not take part in the general campaign against Benjamin, it was made *ḥērem* (Judg. 21,11). The two things are identical. Sometimes the idea of destruction, extermination, is predominant. The destruction of Jerusalem meant that Jacob was given to the ban, Israel to mockery (Isa. 43,28; Zech. 14,11). A shade of difference between exclusion from the community and destruction may also be found. The returned exiles were summoned to a meeting at Jerusalem, and if they did not appear, they were excluded from the community and their property placed under a ban (Ezr. 10,8). This means that it was destroyed.

The fact that the greatest contrast to what is holy is the utterly alien, that which is incapable of absorption in the whole, implies that holiness is, to a certain extent, determined by the relation of Israel to foreign peoples. In that respect there was a great difference between early and later Israel. In early times there was no difficulty about admitting aliens to the community, and thus making it possible for them even to enter the sacred sphere. Doeg, the Edomite, held a position of trust with Saul, and could dwell in the Israelite temple at Nob before the face of Yahweh (1 Sam. 21,8; 22,9). David could even leave the Ark in the house of a Gittite, whose name, "worshipper of Edom", shows the relation of his family to another god; and yet the Ark blessed his house (2 Sam. 6,10 f).

In Israel the state of affairs was as among other peoples. Aliens had generally the qualifications for associating themselves with, and being admitted to, the sphere of holiness. As a matter of fact, the Israelites had no hesitation in allowing strangers to serve in the royal temple, and as late as post-exilic times the priest Eliashib could place an Ammonite who had become a member of his family in a temple cell (Ez. 44,7; Neh. 13,4). But when the alien element was utterly hostile, and especially when it clothed itself in its own holiness as opposed to that of Israel, then a union was impossible, it was ḥērem. And of course it was always a gross defilement of the sanctuary of Israel, if hostile strangers invaded it; that was desecration in the most literal sense (Jer. 51,51; Ps. 79,1.; Lam. 1,10).

The fierce contest waged in the time of the monarchy between the Israelitish and the alien element in Canaan taught those Israelites, who wished to keep the soul of Israel intact, how difficult it was for them to assimilate the alien element and yet keep it under control and preserve their own selves. This created a tendency in them to withdraw into themselves and surround their own inner life with a shell so as to defend themselves against the alien element. All that was alien now became hostile, it was impossible to absorb any part of it in the sacred sphere. This tendency prevailed during and after the exile, when events had established the weakness of Israel in relation to strangers. This view is predominant in Ezekiel, it is a gross infringement of holiness that strangers have entered the sanctuary (Ez. 44,7). The law forbids not only alien cults as a violation and a profanation of what is sacred (Lev. 20,2 f., cf. Ez. 20,39; Am. 2,7 et al.). A stranger must not consume anything that is sacred, not even if he is in the service of the priest (Lev. 22,10), and a stranger who approaches the domain of the Levites or the priests is invariably to be killed (Num. 1,51; 3,10). Post-exilic prophets look forward to a time when the temple will be truly holy, when the Canaanites are kept out of it (Zech. 14,21), and preferably out of the whole of Jerusalem, which is one great sanctuary (Joel 4,17; Ob. 17). It was in this spirit that Nehemiah acted when he drove the Ammonite Tobiah out of the temple.

If holiness had previously been a psychic strain, it now became an overstrain. This marks its place in the culture of the people. Isolation from uncleanness was always the indispensable condition for being sanctified, for uncleanness is the alien element which militates against the psychic totality. This applies to the warrior as to the Nazirite, and Isaiah was sanctified to be a prophet when the altar fire wiped out his uncleanness (Isa. 6,7). The laws contain several precepts which agree with this. No one must enter the sanctuary or touch the sacred objects in an unclean condition (Lev. 22,3.6.7; Num. 19,20). It applies to the priest also, when leprosy or an issue makes him unclean, and to any one who has been branded as abnormal by a physical defect (Lev. 21,23; 22,4). It applies to the woman in childbed, who must remain unclean for 33 days (Lev. 12,4). He who is to meet what is sacred must be sanctified himself, and this takes place by a purification which also comprises the washing of the robes (Ex. 19,10.14; Lev. 6,20; Num. 11,18; Josh. 3,5; 7,13). If the uncleanness is disappearing, the person in question must sanctify himself, thus acquiring a surplus of renewed strength of soul, which affords a possibility of resuming an entirely normal life. Hence it says that the woman "sanctifies herself" from her impurity (2 Sam. 11,4), and the law prescribes how this sanctification is to take place through an offering in the sanctuary (Lev. 12,6 ff.). If a camp has been defiled by the presence of ḥērem in it, the people must sanctify itself so as to obtain strength to cast out the dangerous element (Josh. 7,13).

All this accords with the old conception of purity and impurity and their relation to holiness. But the growing terror of the alien element was a fear of uncleanness. Post-exilic Israel's convulsive

struggle to exclude the foreign element involved an increase of
the impurity of what was alien and of the holiness of what was
native.

In the monarchical period Canaan was the pure land, because
it bore the impress of the Israelite soul, while foreign countries
were impure (Hos. 9,3; Am. 7,17). In post-exilic times this
contrast was not strong enough, now it consisted in holiness and
unholiness. The land of Israel was holy land (Zech. 2,16; Ps.
78,54), its cities sacred cities (Isa. 64,9). The presupposition is
that Israel as such is a holy people. This idea of course is not
absolutely new. "Israel is a sanctuary to Yahweh, the first growth
of his crop", says Jeremiah (2,3), and this signifies nothing but
what Hosea means when he calls Israel Yahweh's son (Hos.
11,1); it denotes the close connection between Israel and her God.
But the new feature is that it is holiness which is made the
foundation in the consideration of the people, holiness expresses
its nature in contrast with that of other peoples. The Israelites
are to be "a kingdom of priests, an holy nation" (Ex. 19,6). "Ye
shall be holy, for I am holy", says Yahweh (Lev. 19,2; 20,26).
The Israelites are "the holy seed" (Ezr. 9,2, cf. Dan. 8,24). Hence
marriages with strangers are an infringement of holiness (Mal.
2,11), and both Ezra and Nehemiah fought against them with
all their might. There is nothing strange in the fact that the laws
forbid the people to make themselves unclean by reptiles or by
consuming the flesh of cattle that have been killed by beasts of
prey and therefore are unclean, and it may date from any period
of the history of Israel; but the reason given, that it militates
against the holiness of Israel (Ex. 22,30; Lev. 11,44, cf. 20,7)
more probably belongs to the later history of Israel.

The extravagant demand for the holiness of the people as such
must of necessity mean a change in the character of holiness. In
early times the people was normally in a state of purity, though
in continual contact with impurity which must be removed. And
it had always the possibility of sanctifying itself in war and in
the cult; thus it attained a level of gathered psychic energy
which it might abandon, when taking again to normal life. Only
those who possessed great strength of soul remained, in higher

18*

or lower degree, in the exalted condition, and the priests were in this state in so far as they were in continual contact with sacred things. Now, when it is said that the nation shall be as priests, that they are a holy seed, this would mean that they would continually be in this exalted condition. In reality it means that the conception of holiness has been weakened, the old gold has no longer its full value. Holiness is no longer an exceptional condition, a strain on the soul for those Israelites that assume it. It becomes a characteristic of the Israelite, which he maintains by following Israelitish customs.

––––––––––

The extravagance of the demand for holiness had the peculiar but very natural effect of attenuating holiness, so that it came to include within its domain what had previously been called purity. But this did not mean that everything Israelitish was equally holy. On the contrary, the increasing craving for holiness caused a growing isolation of the temple at Jerusalem, with all that belonged to it, as the centre of all holiness. Spontaneous holiness, directly connected with the life of the people, was thrown into the background. All the more stress was laid on the holiness radiating from the temple where Yahweh himself had his dwelling.

The history of the royal temple shows a continuous tendency towards a limitation of its area. First the altar in the open court as well as the inner temple cell, with the ark and what else there was there, were the two special dwelling-places of holiness. The hall of the temple was probably a cult hall where at any rate the king's men could gather with him. But if this was the case, all trace of it has disappeared. Holiness spread from the inner cell and kept ordinary people away from the hall, even after the most assiduous sanctification. In Ezekiel and the "priestly" Code this is a matter of course. Yahweh sanctified the house when Solomon built it (1 Kings 9,3.7; cf. Num. 7,1). In early times this meant that the people could come here and draw strength from it; now it began to mean that the people must not approach it because its holy power was too great. The holiness of the temple is accentuated and is expressed in the name. The hall is called "the sanctuary", the inner cell "the holy of holies". Only the high priest possesses holiness enough to enter the holy of holies, and this only once a year. Previously, at any rate, other priests had to be admitted too, when the Ark was to be carried out in solemn procession. Ezekiel tried to exclude the people from the inner court of the temple, thus indicating a characteristic tendency which, however, was only carried through much later.

Like everything else which is of the soul, holiness has a power of spreading and operating through its surroundings; hence it is natural that in the monarchical period Mount Zion had its share of the holiness of the temple. "Zion, my holy mountain," says Yahweh (Ps. 2,6; 3,5; 24,3; cf. Isa. 11,9 et al.). But in Ezekiel this is even more pointedly expressed in the fact that the whole domain around the temple is sacrosanct (*ḳōdhesh ḳodhāshīm*, Ez. 43,12), and Jerusalem becomes, in a special sense, the holy city in the holy land (Isa. 48,2; 52,1; Joel 4,17; Ob. 17; Dan. 9,20; Neh. 11,1.18).

At the same time that holiness is diffused in a new way throughout Israel, it is segregated as a world apart within Israel, not only differing from daily life, but on the way to lose its connection with the life of the people. The laws of holiness are developed as a separate system. To deal with what is sacred requires a whole technique by itself, which can only be mastered by priests.

The previous activity of the priest as guardian of the temple, giver of oracles, and instructor in the commands of the law had become transformed at the temple of Jerusalem as its sphere of action gradually widened. The priesthood had developed into a large organisation maintaining the holiness of the temple by their work, but also by their holiness. As his birthright the priest had a certain character which gave him the priestly blessing, and thus the qualification for being consecrated to the vocation of a priest. In post-exilic times the *Qedēshōth* had disappeared from the temple; and in so far as the prophets still played any part in the cult, they had become merged in the ecclesiastical order. It was the latter which maintained the holiness of the temple.

It was never forgotten that the peculiar character of the priest was associated with the sanctuary. The priests are called "Aaron and his sons who guard the sanctuary" (Num. 3,38), and Ezekiel speaks of them partly as those who perform the service of Yahweh in the sanctuary, partly as those who, as subordinate priests, serve in the house. They give not only outward service, "they bear the sin of the sanctuary" (Num. 18,1); this implies that they have the full responsibility of maintaining the holiness of the temple. They receive holiness from the temple, and they themselves strengthen its holiness.

It is a matter of course that the priest was sanctified for his vocation; it was always the essential condition for his ability to officiate in the temple. In early times any one could be sanctified as, for instance, Micah's son and Abinadab's son (Judg. 17,5; 1 Sam. 7,1); holiness acted freely and spontaneously. In post-exilic times it was confined to a single family consecrated by Yahweh together with the sanctuary (Ex. 29,44); the holiness of the sanctuary and that of the priest were intimately connected.

The consecration of the priest is described by a peculiar term, adopted from the Assyrians, "to fill the hand" (Ex. 28,41; 29,9; Lev. 8,33; 21,10; Judg. 17,5.12 et al.); perhaps it is merely a term for giving authority to a person. Like the king and the sacred objects the priest was anointed with sacred oil (Ex. 29,7; 30,30; Lev. 8,12). We know the mode of procedure for the consecration, at which the investment with the ecclesiastical robes, the anointment, and certain sacrifices in which the novice takes part, constitute the main point (Ex. 29; Lev. 8). His robes are "sacred robes" pervaded by his spiritual dignity (Ex. 29,29; 31,10; 35,19.21 et al.), most of all the sacred diadem, *nēzer haḳ-ḳōdhesh* (Ex. 29,6; 39,30; Lev. 8,9).

The priest has to comply with special requirements in order to be able to maintain his holiness and approach the sacred things. He must not marry a woman who has broken her marriage vows or been repudiated by her husband, nor a woman who has otherwise lost the full honour of an Israelite woman (Lev. 21,7). [1] And if his own daughter breaks the marriage laws of Israel, his holiness is so seriously imperilled that she must be exterminated and burnt (V. 9). Ezekiel demands that a priest should never marry a woman who has belonged to another man, unless the latter was a priest (Ez. 44,22), that she may not have received the impress of a character incompatible with that of priesthood.

A man of priestly descent must not perform ecclesiastical duties if he has a physical defect, whereas he may eat of the sacred meat (Lev. 21,16 ff.); hence he still possesses a certain holiness. A priest must keep his body in a normal state. According to Ezekiel he must neither shave off all his hair nor allow it to grow freely, but he must trim it (Ez. 44,20), a custom which was of course based on a definite tradition. One law forbids priests to cut off all the hair of the head, to trim the edge of the beard or gash their flesh; "they shall be sacred to their God and must not offend against the name of their God" (Lev. 21,5 f.). These were the same customs which all Israelites were forbidden to follow when in a state of mourning (Lev. 19,27 f.; Deut. 14,1). [1] They were alien customs, hence they were not reconcilable with the soul of Israel, and least of all among those who were the maintainers of holiness.

Altogether, the priest must, even more scrupulously than other Israelites, avoid uncleanness. Thus he must not touch any corpse except of his next-of-kin, (which he could only with difficulty avoid), his father, mother, brother, unmarried sister, son or daughter (Lev. 21,1 ff.; Ez. 44,25 ff.). The high priest was subject to all these rules in a still more rigorous form, for his holiness was much greater. He was only allowed to marry a virgin, of course of Israelite origin, and he must not defile himself by touching any corpse whatever (Lev. 10,6 f.; 21,10 ff.).

When the priest entered the sanctuary he had to free himself from what was profane. He must not drink wine or strong drink (Lev. 10,9; Ez. 44,21), a precept showing the continued relationship between the holiness of the priest and that of the Nazirites. Before the service he was to wash his hands and feet (Ex. 30,17 ff.; 40,31 f.). Ezekiel wants the priests to change their clothes and put on the linen ecclesiastical robes at the entrance to the inner court of the temple, taking them off again when they leave, and putting them away in the sacred cells (Ez.

44,17 ff.). Similar demands are found in the laws commanding that the robe employed in the sanctuary should be kept strictly apart from the profane garment (Ex. 28,40 ff.; Lev. 6,3 f.). Stress is laid on its not being of wool, and the reason given (a typical and secondary one) is that the priest must not perspire. The use of linen was based on tradition, and had possibly its root in Egypt.

All that was present in the sanctuary was sacrosanct, the altar, the implements, and the water used there (Ex. 29,37; 30,10.29.36 et al.). And because of their holiness the priests have the power to maintain the character of the temple by anointing and sanctifying what is in it. The temple and the ecclesiastical order had come to be two institutions which upheld each other.

The hierarchical degrees were dependent on the differing strength of the holiness of the priests. In post-exilic times the holiness of the subordinate priests depended also on their descent and on a consecration which is described in great detail (Num. 8,5 ff.). Their inferior degree of holiness only enabled them to be the helpers of the priests. If they were to approach the altar itself, their holiness would not suffice, and they would die (Num. 18,2 ff.). Most remote were the people; they had now become laymen and could only receive. We have noted the efforts of the priests to get them further and further removed from the temple, out into the outer court. Ezekiel insists on it, and a priestly law says: The Israelites shall no longer approach the tent of revelation, whereby they would incur sin and die (Num. 18,22). The expression "no longer" which strictly speaking makes no sense in this context, shows that the person who formulated the law was aware that he was putting forward a new demand.

———————

Thus the Israelites gradually made holiness subject to certain well-marked limitations. It had its centre in the temple of Jerusalem in the holy of holies and it operated in a less and less intensified form as one withdrew further and further from the temple. And to this corresponded a division of the people into classes according to their holiness, from the high priest by way of priests and subordinate priests to laymen. Israel and the area inhabited by it indicated the limits of holiness.

A terrible thing always, was holiness in Israel, at least for any one who was not sure of being prepared for it. A person standing on sacred ground showed his reverence by taking off his shoes, the part of his clothing which came into the closest contact with the earth (Ex. 3,5; Josh. 5,15).

The laws for the workings of holiness became, as it were, more fixed and definite in post-exilic times. Most conspicuous is its power to act on the surroundings through contact or in other ways. In this it is no different from other forces of the soul. But disaster invariably befalls any person who comes into contact with what is holy without being prepared for it.

It is expressly pointed out that he who touches the altar or other sacred objects, becomes sacred (Ex. 29,37; 30,29). When an implement has once been approached to anything sacred it becomes sacred and must be handled accordingly (Num. 17,2 ff.). The sacred ointment is so important because, when poured over kings and priests or over the objects in the temple, it transfers the force of holiness to them (Ex. 30,22 ff.). The offering, too, sanctifies any one who touches it, therefore it is often the priests alone who may consume it (Lev. 6,10 f. 20.22). The highly sacred sin-offerings must not be brought into the court where they would sanctify the people, just as the people would be sanctified if the priests went out to them in their consecrated robes (Ez. 44,19; 46,20), and such holiness they could not receive without injury.

People who secretly practised private cults sometimes said to one another: Keep to yourself, do not touch me, for I shall hallow you [1] (Isa. 65,5). The prophet blames people for seeking holiness by devious ways, but he does not censure the view that holiness acts through contact and may be dangerous to the unprepared. Holiness occupied men's thoughts, and the priests had to expound its laws. How far did its action through contact extend? This question is answered in a pronouncement in Haggai: Thus says Yahweh, the Lord of hosts: Ask the priests for a *tōrā*, saying: If a man is carrying sacred meat in the skirt of his robe and touches with his skirt any bread or pottage or wine or oil or any food whatever, shall it become sacred? And the priests answered and said, "No". And Haggai said: If any one unclean through a corpse touches any of all these things, will it become unclean? And the priests answered and said: "It will become unclean". (Hag. 2,11 f.).

The answer implies that uncleanness spreads faster than holiness, an expression of the fear of the Israelite of everything associated with the curse. But the most significant feature of the whole pronouncement is the way in which psychic conditions such as holiness and uncleanness are now regarded, they are assumed to act entirely of themselves, almost according to automatic laws, regardless of spiritual presuppositions.

Through sacred acts and the contact with the sacred things holiness acts on people's souls. Those who are capable of receiving it by virtue of their own consecration are filled with and strengthened by its power; but he who is touched by holiness unprepared is in no better way than the man on whom the curse falls, and the same applies to the person who touches what is profane when in a holy state. These and all other infringements of holiness create guilt in the perpetrator, and the outcome must be disaster and death. This is what happened to Uzza when he offended the Ark; and the priest entering the sanctuary in profane garments will "incur guilt and die" (Ex. 28,43). The Levites who were to carry the holy objects during the wanderings of the Israelites must only convey them wrapped up; if they came into direct contact with them or saw them, they would die (Num. 4,15.19 f.).

All depended on holiness, therefore an infringement of it was always so dangerous a transgression that the sinner must be exterminated. This applied not only to the person who desecrated Yahweh's name and made his holiness unclean by a non-Israelitish cult (Lev. 20,1 ff.); but also to any one who entered the sanctuary or touched the sacred things in an unclean state (Lev. 22,3.9; Num. 19,20), or any one who treated the sacrificial meat wrongly or in other ways violated what was sacred in Israel (Lev. 19,8;

Num. 18,32). Yet there was a possibility that the sin might be expiated if it had happened inadvertently (Lev. 5,15 ff.; 22,14.16).

For their own sake the Israelites had to exterminate any person who committed sacrilege. But if they did not do so, the guilt remained with the sinner, and would invariably, sooner or later, carry him and his kin to destruction. This is said expressly about those who sacrifice to Molech (Lev. 20,1 ff.), and it is in perfect agreement with the whole view of life of the Israelites.

The development which led to the powerful concentration of holiness at the temple in Jerusalem, and among the priesthood belonging to it, did not pass off quite uneventfully. This is not remarkable, for it coincided with the movement which made the people of Israel as such feel with increasing strength that they were a sacred nation. Evidence of the opposition to which it gave rise is afforded by the story of the revolt led by Dathan, Abiram, and Korah (Num. 16-17). It has previously been mentioned that it embodies both a protest against a single man's leadership of the people and against the pre-eminence of the priesthood, but both protests unite on the question of holiness.

The account given is that there are two parties which rebel. One is led by Korah, progenitor of a family of the lower priesthood, the other by two Reubenites, Dathan and Abiram. Korah represents the lower priesthood, the two Reubenites the lay population; two hundred and fifty prominent Israelites join them. They unite against Moses and Aaron, saying: Is it not enough for you that the whole congregation are, all of them, sacred and that Yahweh is in their midst? Why then would you raise yourselves above the community of Yahweh? (Num. 16,3). Here it is clearly expressed that it is holiness which is at issue. All Israelites are sacred, hence a caste with special claims should not be set apart.

The difference between the lower priests, who have some holiness, and the lay population appears from the following.

Moses answered Korah and his adherents that they should come
the next day each with his incense-pan and burn incense before
Yahweh, Yahweh himself would then show them who was sacred.
Aaron, Korah, and the two hundred and fifty were each of them
to offer incense (16,4-7.16-17). This speech is interrupted by a
special address partly to Korah and partly to Dathan and
Abiram. To Korah Moses said that the sons of Levi must be
content to be set apart from the community to do service in the
temple, but if they aspired to perform the ecclesiastical service
proper, it would be rebellion against Aaron and Yahweh (16,8-11).
He then sent word to Dathan and Abiram, begging them to come,
but they refused. Moses had failed to fulfil his promise of leading
them to a good land, and now he even wished to set himself up
as a ruler above them. Then Moses turned to Yahweh, assuring
him that he had not taken one ass from them or done them any
harm (16,12-15). It will appear from this that Korah's desire
is not, as a matter of course, to deprive the priests of their
privilege, but to obtain a share in it himself, whereas the lay
population are altogether dissatisfied with the leadership of
Moses.

The story now goes on to say that Korah and his adherents
came with their pans, and the entire congregation assembled
outside the sacred tent, where Moses and Aaron were present.
Yahweh would have destroyed all the congregation, but Moses
and Aaron begged him not to destroy them all for the sake of
one instigator of rebellion. It is now related that the people withdrew from the dwellings of the rebels, and these were swallowed
up by the earth (16,18-34). But the story then records that fire
issued from Yahweh, and consumed the two hundred and fifty
men who had brought the incense. And Aaron's son Eleazar was
commanded to take the pans from the burnt bodies and have
them beaten into a coating for the altar to commemorate the event,
which showed that only Aaron's sons were allowed to offer
incense.

This is not the end of the incident. Now the congregation are
indeed stirred up against Moses and Aaron and say that they
have killed Yahweh's people. But when they force their way into

the sacred tent, the honour of Yahweh descends as a cloud on it, and he begins to strike them down. Aaron, at the request of Moses, comes with his incense pan, which contained incense and coals from the altar. Where he stood, the ravages of death were stopped; the wrath of Yahweh subsided and the people was saved; but 14700 Israelites had perished. Then a rod for each tribe was laid in the sanctuary, Aaron's name being inscribed on Levi's rod. This alone blossomed and sprouted; thus it was proved that Aaron's sons alone, and none of the other tribes, possessed holiness.

The narrative contains two obscure points of importance. One is the alliance between the two different groups, the lower priests and the laymen, the other is the two different modes of death, swallowing up by the earth and burning by fire from the sanctuary. The first obscure point, however, results largely from the very contents of the tale. Lower priests and laymen ally themselves; there is nothing strange in this, but it necessarily makes the character of the opposition somewhat complicated. One party merely desires extended ecclesiastical privileges, the other party goes against the hierarchical aristocracy altogether. But the two things cannot be separated, as if one party were rebelling against the ruling power, while the other was merely fighting for special ecclesiastical rights. For both parties the object is a share in holiness. This appears from the beginning of the narrative, but also from its conclusion. The whole affair terminates in the placing of a rod for each tribe in the sanctuary to settle where the holiness is, and Levi's rod wins. But here again we have the same obscurity as in the rest of the narrative. It is true that it is Levi's rod which is chosen by Yahweh, but Aaron's name is inscribed on it, Levi's holiness being thus conferred upon the sons of Aaron.

From the point of view of the leaders the claims of the two parties are identical, their aim being in both cases an attack on the special holiness of the priesthood proper. Hence the test both of Korah and of the two hundred and fifty Israelites consists in a divine ordeal with the object of showing whether they are really able to discharge the special ecclesiastical duties, or whether their holiness will fail when confronted with them. It is a typical

ecclesiastical legend. The narrator entertains no doubt that
disaster will befall the person who would perform sacred acts
without being sacred. The moral is that the people, when in
danger, can only be rescued by the intercession of the ecclesiastical leaders and by the sacred incense of the superior priest.

Whatever the circumstances connected with the obscure points
in the form of the narrative, there is no doubt that it came into
existence entirely in the post-exilic period. [1] It is dominated by
the problems of that time, by its conception of holiness and the
way in which this is associated with the composite cult at the
temple of Jerusalem. And the picture of Moses as the ruler which
has been inserted in the episode with Dathan and Abiram is of
quite the same kind as that which the post-exilic priests have
drawn of Samuel (16,15, cf. 1 Sam. 12,3).

The representatives of the lay population are said to belong
to Reuben, the tribe which had long since disappeared, because
Reuben was the eldest of the sons of Jacob. This is undoubtedly
a fictitious feature, but the contents of the legend are real enough.
They reflect struggles of which otherwise we hear little, rebellion
against the course of development taken by holiness. But it was
a struggle against the tendency of the time. In the legend the
ecclesiastical view-points gain the day, and this is in accordance
with the facts.

_____

The spiritual history of Israel shows clearly a movement from
spontaneity and multiplicity towards conformity to law, limitation,
and uniformity; but no generation in Israel was in doubt about
the necessity of holiness for the maintenance of life, and the
essential characteristic of holiness was always the same. It was
invariably the intensified strength of the soul.

In the old days there was always a possibility of holiness
where there was soul life: in the life of the spring, the stone,
the tree, in the life of animals and human beings. All forms of
life drew their growth from holiness, because their vital force
emanated from it. The question was merely where it was especially
to be found. It was important for man to realise this, for it

was the essential condition enabling him to get into the right relationship to it, to derive a blessing from it and not a curse. There were men who possessed as a special gift the capability of being filled with the divine soul and acting or seeing with intense strength; but anybody had the possibility of sanctifying himself, and thus of being filled with a strength of soul beyond the ordinary. And the same strength revealed itself in sacred places, in the stone, the spring, or the tree.

Thus holiness becomes a regulating principle in life, because it constitutes the central points of life. Holy men are centres of force in the community, as are the sacred places on the earth. The monarchy of Israel endeavoured to concentrate the holy strength at one point, in the monarchy itself, and this holiness was established and strengthened in the temple which was intimately associated with the monarchy. Here we have the predisposition for the development of holiness in Israel.

The temple of the monarchy required a priesthood, its numbers constantly increased and its task was to create holiness. Holiness was drawn from nature into the artificial temple. Far down into the ages holiness might act spontaneously in men in the manifold ways of early times; but the holiness of the priests became more and more predominant, because it was associated with the rallying point of all holiness, and because it was safeguarded by the acts and rites handed down by them. This tendency finally prevailed in post-exilic times. Nature and spontaneity were thrown into the background, holiness was subjected to definite laws. In these the direct experience of the early times had to make way for ecclesiastical custom, and on this foundation the work was carried on, the aid of logic and scientific argument being called in.

Holiness dominated the whole of life, and in the early days permeated it. Holiness exerted its influence not only on places, on things, and on human beings, but also on time. There were days and periods set apart from all the rest by their holiness, this made them a source of strength to the other periods, just as holy men were a source of strength in the community. These days were the festival days.

A day may become so full that it is consecrated to Yahweh as a holy day. This happened when Ezra read the law to Israel and laid the foundation for their regeneration. The leaders declared: The day is hallowed to Yahweh, your God, mourn not and weep not. And further: Go and eat fat things and drink sweet drink, and send portions as gifts to him who has nothing certain, for the day is holy unto our Lord. And do not mourn, for the joy of Yahweh is your strength. And the people obeyed (Neh. 8,9-12).

Usually, however, the festival days are fixed by tradition. Each festival has its peculiar character and thus its special justification. And not all of them are of a pleasant character, like the festival day just mentioned. But they have this feature in common as holy days that they are outside the nature of ordinary days, just as man can only sanctify himself by discarding the habits of everyday life. This means that the festival day is no working day.

In a calendar of festivals (Lev. 23) this is expressly pointed out for the Sabbath, the New Moon, the Day of Atonement, the Pentecost, and the first and last days of the Passover, as well as the Feast of the Tabernacles. The law even fixes a whole year, every fiftieth, as a holy year, the year of yōbhēl, in which the ordinary laws do not hold good. Fields must not be tilled, and ownership brought about by purchase is to be dissolved (Lev. 25,10-12). [1]

The rule as to the cessation of work obtained the greatest importance in the case of the sabbath. This day was a weekly experience, so it made itself especially felt, particularly when the Israelites were living among aliens. The temptation to break it was often strong, hence it is all the more rigorously enforced. It is mentioned not only in the aforesaid calendar of festivals, (Lev. 23,2-3), but also in other law codes. "Remember the sabbath to keep it holy; six days shalt thou labour and do all thy work, but the seventh day is sabbath to Yahweh, your God. Thou shalt do no work whatever, thou, nor thy son, nor thy daughter, nor thy man-servant, nor thy maid-servant, nor thy cattle, nor thy gēr that is within thy gates" (Ex. 20,8-10, cf. 23,12; 34,21; Deut. 5,12).

In earlier times it was a matter of course that the New Moon and the Sabbath were excepted from the days of business. Incidentally we learn that on those days especially people visited holy men (2 Kings 4,23), a most natural way of spending holy days. In Amos we hear how the shameless oppressors long for these holy days to come to an end that they may resume their trade and secure wealth by fraud (Am. 8,4-6), but there is no indication that it was conceivable to break the rule of the holy days themselves. In later times when Israel came more into contact with strangers, there was a change, and now we hear the prophets enforce the command to rest on the sabbath. Jeremiah says: Watch over your souls and carry no load on the sabbath, nor bring it within the gates of Jerusalem, and carry no load out of your houses on the sabbath, and do no work whatever; and you shall hallow the sabbath day as I have decreed for your fathers (Jer. 17,21 f.).

Breaking the sabbath is a breach of what is holy. Therefore the whole life of Israel depends on its maintenance. Jeremiah says that if the people will refrain from carrying loads on that day, the monarchy shall endure and Jerusalem shall not fall eternally, but if the sabbath be broken all shall perish (Jer. 17,24-27). Ezekiel teaches the same lesson (Ez. 20,20; 44,24), and another prophet from about the same period says: If you keep your foot from the sabbath, from carrying out your tasks on my holy day, and call the sabbath a delight, Yahweh's holy day, honoured; and you honour it, not carrying out your projects, nor seeking your business and holding converse, you shall feel delight in Yahweh, and you shall ride on the hills of the country and enjoy the heritage of Jacob, your father. Yea, Yahweh's mouth hath spoken (Isa. 58,13 f.; cf. 56,2). Here again, the hallowing of the sabbath by refraining from work is a condition of the life and happiness of Israel.

When Nehemiah worked for the re-establishment of the Israelitish community at Jerusalem, he made the people pledge themselves to abstain from trade on the sabbath and other holy days (Neh. 10,32). But he had to take vigorous steps to prevent them from working in the fields and vineyards or doing business on

the sabbath, and he ordered the gates to be closed so as to hinder
Phoenicians and others from bringing in provisions and trading
on the holy day (Neh. 13,15-22).

In some few passages the reason given for the command to
keep the sabbath holy is, that those who serve must rest. The day
is to be one of rest "in order that your ox and your ass may rest,
and that your woman-servant's son and the alien citizen may
renew their souls" (Ex. 23,12). Deuteronomy says: . . . so that
your man-servant and your woman-servant may rest; and you
shall keep in mind that you were a bondman in the land of Egypt
and Yahweh your God brought you out with a strong hand and
stretched-out arm. Therefore Yahweh your God commanded you
to observe the sabbath day (Deut. 5,14 f.).

The idea here is that the sabbath exists for men and their
domestic animals to gather strength. In Deuteronomy this is
connected with the characteristic idea, which we know from the
prophets also, that the Israelites must not oppress their subordinates, because it is against their nature as Israelites to exalt
themselves above others: they have themselves been a people in
bondage.

This idea cannot be said to conflict with the character of the
sabbath: for it is a matter of course that men and animals are
to draw strength from it. But there is a deeper and wider motive
for the rest on the sabbath day than that pointed out here. It is
not the welfare of this worker or the other which is the decisive
factor. On the sabbath and other feast days work ceases because
these days are holy. From the force gathered around them the rest
of the time derives its strength, therefore all life is dependent on
the maintenance of their holiness. But a primary part of this is
that they are set apart in character from ordinary days and all
that fills them.

So great is the holiness of the sabbath that it has its root in
remote antiquity. Just as the sacred temple dates from the time
of the foundation and is formed on a model shaped by the God
of the people himself, so also the law of the sabbath is not only,
like all other laws, imposed on Moses by Yahweh, but He himself
has introduced it in a special sense. In six days He created the

world, and on the seventh day He rested, and He blessed and sanctified this day (Gen. 2,2-3). No other law thus finds its justification in a myth, and as a matter of fact, it is repeated in the law codes (Ex. 20,11; 31,17). In the wilderness time, when Yahweh sent his people manna, it did not fall on the seventh day, and the people was to learn from this that no work whatever must be done on that day (Ex. 16,26-30).

To break the sabbath is a breach of holiness and hence exposes all life to unsuspected dangers. He who has been guilty of such a sin must therefore suffer the fate of the great offenders and be completely exterminated. "You shall keep the sabbath for it is holy to you. Whoever desecrates it shall surely be put to death, for whoever does any work on it, that soul shall be rooted out from the midst of his people" (Ex. 31,14, cf. V. 15; 35,2). This provision, as is sometimes the case in the books of Moses, is referred to a decision in a definite case. Some Israelites discovered a man gathering firewood on the sabbath and took him to "Moses, Aaron, and the whole congregation". They took him into custody since there was not as yet any clear decision in such a matter. Then Yahweh's revelation came to Moses, and after that they led the man outside the camp and stoned him to death (Num. 15,32-36).

Nehemiah's endeavours testify that transgressors were by no means always treated so summarily; but the law gives expression to the ideal, completely consistent view.

As in the other domains of holiness, abstention, here expressed in the giving up of work, is merely the negative aspect. The sabbath and other festival days derive their positive force and holiness from what fills them. This makes them days of pleasure, not in a superficial sense, but because the people draws strength of soul from them. Therefore it is a serious threat which is uttered by Hosea: I will cause all her (i. e. Israel's) joy to cease, her festival, her new moon, her sabbath, and all her solemn feasts (Hos. 2,13).

But here as in other fields, the negative aspect came more and more into the forefront. The very danger of an infringement caused people to ask themselves with growing anxiety how far

abstention from daily life was to be carried. This is evidenced in
the narratives of the wanderings. In the story of the manna it
says that "every one shall stay where he is, no one shall leave
his place on the seventh day" (Ex. 16,29). Another passage has:
You shall light no fire in any of the places where you stay on the
sabbath day (Ex. 35,3); and in one of the stories cited above we
have seen that the gathering of firewood was not allowed (Num.
15,32-36). We have here the beginning of those discussions which
were continued later on in the history of Judaism, and which are
quite analogous to the treatment of the other problems of holiness.

Holiness was still something serious, but it was no longer
spontaneous, rooted directly in the experience of the soul. The
motive given in Deuteronomy for the observance of the sabbath
shows that the strong and simple feeling of what it really meant
no longer existed, and this is indicated, too, by the difficulty
Nehemiah had in enforcing it. For that very reason the demand
for its observance grew all the more urgent in another quarter,
and logic set to work where intuitive feeling failed.

―――――――

Just as blessedness spreads and creates life and progress of
various kinds according to its nature and force, so we see holiness,
also, unfold itself in many ways, and the sanctuary is a centre of
all. How intimately holiness is associated with the life of the
people is seen in war; and we shall see it once more if we consider
more closely the sacred acts that take place in the sanctuary. The
contrast to holiness is the utterly alien; hence it is an indispensable
condition of holiness that the soul should be moulded after the
pattern of Israelite custom. Corresponding to the sharp demarcation from what was alien, which became so prominent a feature
of the later history of Israel, there is the importance attached to
the preservation of the Israelitish type. This also was to leave its
mark on the conception of holiness.

From olden times the disposition of the Israelite was determined by the custom, *mishpāṭ*, which innate characteristics and
external conditions involved. When custom did not suffice, the
Israelite sought *tōrā*, instruction, and this was obtained in the

sanctuary, for it was the priest who was the guide to what was right. He would perhaps consult the holy oracle, and the *tōrā* was the will of Yahweh. It is probable, too, that the people confirmed the pledge on the law in the sanctuary. Thus the *tōrā* sprung directly from holiness, it was a source of strength because it gave the Israelite the possibility of asserting his nature. There is, then, an intimate connection between the holiness of Israel as a people and the holiness of the *tōrā*.

This, however, does not imply that an Israelite becomes holy because he lives according to the *tōrā*. In the earliest times holiness was a psychic concentration, an increase of the strength of the soul; in order to achieve it the soul must be healthy; this meant that it was what the Israelite understood by "righteous". Part of this was that it absorbed the proper instruction, but this did not yet mean a conduct shaped in all its details. In order to become holy the soul must have this normal character, but it did not become holy simply because it was normal.

Circumstances were to bring about a change in this. The war waged by a series of prophets against the alien element which had invaded Israel, was in great part a fight for traditional Israelite custom against the sanctuaries and their practices. The sacred character of the *tōrā* thus became more accentuated; and real holiness, that which was created at the sanctuaries and by the festivals, was denied. We learn from Zephaniah that the priests have desecrated what was holy by making light of the *tōrā* (Zeph. 3,4), and Ezekiel says exactly the same thing (22,26).

The presuppositions for this view of the *tōrā* were given at the outset, for the *tōrā* was derived from Yahweh. But by becoming identified with holiness itself it acquires a new significance. And this trend in the conception ran parallel with that by which holiness in the old-fashioned sense was severed from the organic connection with natural life. The whole apparatus of the temple and the priesthood persisted, even in an intensified form, but as the sphere of holiness became a special domain for priests, the temple cult lost its root, which had drawn nourishment from the life of the people. It then itself sought for justification in tradition, in the law.

This was of the greatest significance in the psychic history of Israel. Just as holiness came to include and cover purity, so also a readjustment took place between holiness and righteousness. Holiness was no longer as before exclusively an increase of the strength of the soul, the highest level of psychic life; it was becoming a constant common characteristic which was acquired by quite ordinary acts, by carefully observing the law. The whole of this development is identical with that which led to the Israelites being regarded as holy by the mere fact of being Israelites.

In the laws of later times and in other writings we several times meet with the idea that the Israelites become holy by observing the law. The Israelites are commanded to carry certain tassels "that you may remember and carry out all my commandments, and be holy unto your God" (Num. 15,40). It is Yahweh who makes the people holy, but it is achieved through fulfilment of the law. "Yahweh will make you into a people holy unto himself, as he has sworn to you, in that you keep the commandments of Yahweh, your God, and walk in his ways" (Deut. 28,9).

We know that this did not prevent the assertion of the special holiness of the priests, but the two points of view are united in the expectation that the whole people shall achieve priestly holiness, and this happens if it carefully observes the covenant, i. e. the law. This is expressed in Yahweh's saying: And now, if you listen to my voice and keep my covenant, you shall be a possession unto me above all the peoples, for all the earth belongs to me. And you shall be unto me a kingdom of priests and a holy people (Ex. 19,5 f.).

The increasing sanctification of the law, and the tendency to change holiness into an observance of the law, made holiness a requirement by adhesion to which the Israelites fulfilled their destination. The old demand for purity and other provisions of the law are accompanied by general commands that the Israelites should sanctify themselves, because Yahweh is holy, by keeping his commandments (Lev. 11,44 f.; 19,2; 20,7,26). "The holy ones" may therefore simply come to denote those who "fear Yahweh" (Ps. 34,10).[1]

From this later period of the history of Israel we have several visions, in which the prophet looks into the future, seeking a new world in which Israel forms the ideal centre. Everything then centres round the ancient sanctuary of Jerusalem, the temple on Mount Zion, as it did also under the monarchy. But to the later prophets the temple is not only the central point from which holy strength overflows the people and the land. All the world is to come to the temple, because it is the home of the *tōrā*, the point from which the proper instruction comes (Isa. 2,2 f. = Mic. 4,1 f.).

The history of holiness in Israel gives a picture of the psychic history of the people. The spontaneous power with which it manifested itself in the old days in men and in nature did not remain unaffected in the artificial community of city life. It was subordinated to restricting rules, and it was adjusted to other aspects of soul life; to a certain extent we may say that it became stereotyped. But holiness never lost its true nature as the force on which life depended and from which it was renewed.

Therefore holiness went right down to the roots of existence. It was the element which connected men and other living things with the powerful beings who sustained life, all divine beings, above all Yahweh, the God of the people. If holiness in men was more or less perfect, it was found in its pure form in the divine beings, who were entirely holy. The maintenance of life depended on the interaction between them and man. Just as the great sustained the small through the blessing, and received the blessing in return, so also men sanctified their God and were sanctified by him. In this way holiness was maintained, and with it life.

IV

THE RENEWAL AND THE SOURCE
OF HOLINESS

THE SACRIFICE AND ITS EFFECTS

WHAT is holy has its value in itself by virtue of its sovereign power. But it is not immutable; holiness can be acquired and lost, just as it can deteriorate and be renewed. If all holiness vanished, life would perish because the blessing draws its nourishment from holiness. But it is in man's power to contribute to the renewal of holiness; by so doing he will secure the maintenance of his world and his own life. This life-sustaining activity is exercised through the cult in the holy places.

The multifarious places of worship, from the simple stone to the magnificent temples, were bound to become the background of a heterogeneous cultus. At the large temples there developed an ever-increasing ritual activity which must needs give rise to new shades in the whole character of the cult. We may to a certain extent follow this development at the only temple which held its own far down in time, viz. the main temple at Jerusalem. Some few indications show that other temples, too, had a rich ritual apparatus, but the history of these temples has been lost. The old narratives and laws, however, allow us to observe certain general features, and we see that the cult at the sanctuaries of Israel, also, is made up of common elements. The chief of these is the sacrifice.

The Israelite sacrifice does not differ much from that in common use among other Canaanite peoples, but to a certain extent it has acquired a special Israelitish character. The significance of the sacrifice has many aspects, and in the course of time a few of these gained the ascendancy and spread, while others receded into the background.

In order to understand this it is natural to start from Israel's treatment of the new life produced by the increase among the cattle and in the fields, because it shows plainly the connection between the sacrifice and the Israelite people's view of nature. We know that fruit-trees — and among these were included the olive and the vine — were to live their own life, untrimmed for three years after they were planted. [1] But man cannot immediately after this begin to appropriate their fruits. "And in the fourth year all the fruit thereof shall be a holiness of festive rejoicing before Yahweh, and in the fifth year you may partake of its fruit that you may increase its produce for yourself. I am Yahweh, your God!" (Lev. 19,24-25).

Behind this ordinance lies an idea which we know from the treatment of the spoil. When something alien is to be absorbed, it must be sanctified, Yahweh being given his share; in this way it is prepared for appropriation by the special Israelite psyche. An assimilation takes place, and at the same time the fruit is filled with a holy strength; the blessing accruing therefrom maintains the growth and fruitfulness of the tree. This is what is stated in the law. [2]

A special law applies to the trees with their perennial life, but the same fundamental rule holds good for all the produce of the fields which the Israelites wish to appropriate. The appropriation can only take place by a sanctification which at the same time approaches the alien life to the soul of Israel and supplies a renewed strength for its maintenance. The provisions relating to the *first-fruits* are concerned with this. All the law codes contain ordinances about it; they do not form a continuous chain, even though a comparison of them clearly shows the trend of the development. [3]

The ordinance is found in its most general and comprehensive form in the book of the Covenant and the law of the Two Tables, in which it reads: The first of the first-fruits (*rē'shīth bikkūrīm*) of thy land thou shalt bring into the house of Yahweh thy God! (Ex. 23,19; 34,26). The first *(bikkūrīm)* of the first-fruits is that part of the crops which ripens first and is reaped first. First-fruit, *rē'shīth*, denotes partly the first, the beginning, partly the best, the main part. The term first-fruits does not render the concept in its full extension; for it is used not only about growth and crops, but also, for instance, about the beginning of a period of time. It is no mere accident that the two meanings: the first and the best, the most important, are combined in the word, it is closely connected with the whole Israelitish way of thinking and handling of ideas. The first ancestor of the Israelites, for instance, the first Israelite, is the archetype, in whom the whole Israelitish nature is inherent; the same applies to the progenitor of an animal species, the archetypal animal, and the first day of a period embodies in itself the whole character of the period, so that the following days unfold from it. Every totality is concentrated in its first origin.

This is what gives the first-fruits their importance. They are not the best in the sense that the best developed part of the fruits has been selected; but as the first of the produce they represent the whole; the entire power and blessedness of the harvest are concentrated in them. Hence the first-fruits have a special possibility of being holy and acting by their holiness on the growth of the rest of the produce. "The first of the first-fruits", then, means the representative part of the harvest that first grows ripe. It is to be brought to Yahweh's house so as to be sanctified by being given to the holy place. "First-fruits" and "holy" become synonymous ideas (Jer. 2,3; Ez. 48,14).

The book of the Covenant has another ordinance of a similar kind: Thou shalt not withhold thy increase *(melē'āthekhā)* and thy first drops *(dim'akhā)* (Ex. 22,28). The increase must denote the same thing as the first-fruits (cf. Num. 18,27), that in which the power and value of the crops is concentrated, and "the drops" must be "the first" of the expressed grape juice and oil. Thus the book of the Covenant contains an ordinance relating to the sanctification both of the crop just harvested and of the produce of the fruit harvest in its next stage, as the expressed juice.

The Israelites having three harvest seasons, the season of the barley harvest, the wheat harvest, and the fruit harvest, they had the produce of three periods to sanctify. This sanctification was done jointly and formed the basis of the three great agricultural feasts. That the first-fruits are concerned is only stated expressly about the second feast in the book of the Covenant. Here mention is made of "the first-fruits of thy labours, that which thou hast sown in thy field" (Ex. 23,16) or, as it is also put, "the first-fruits of the wheat harvest" (Ex. 34,22). It does not say in what form the harvest is sanctified, nor how the sanctification is to be carried out.

In the law of holiness more definite rules are given for the sanctification of the crops at the two grain-harvest feasts. Yahweh makes Moses say to the Israelites: When ye come into the land which I give unto you, and reap the harvest thereof, then ye shall bring the sheaf of the first-fruits of your harvest unto the priest, and he shall wave the sheaf before Yahweh to your advantage; the day after the sabbath the priest shall wave it (Lev. 23,10-11). Some ordinary offerings are to be added to this, and now the text goes on to say: And bread, roasted ears, or fresh dough of corn you shall not eat before this selfsame day, before you have brought the offering *(korbān)* for your God, as an eternal decree for your generations in all your dwellings (23,14).

On the fiftieth day after the above-mentioned sabbath the first-fruit offering of the wheat harvest is brought: Ye shall bring out of your habitations two wave loaves; they shall be made of two tenths of fine flour (i. e. of wheat), and baked with leaven, as first-fruits unto Yahweh (Lev. 23,17). To this must be added several other offerings. It is this day which the Priestly Code calls "the day of the first-fruits" in the festival under consideration (Num. 28,26). As regards the fruit harvest the law of holiness speaks of fruits and the boughs of trees (Lev. 23,40), but a sanctification of the fruit by offering the first-fruits in not expressly mentioned.

The sanctification of the barley sheaf is of most interest in this connection, because we have here a typical first-fruit offering. Doubtless it is an ancient custom here fixed in the form of a law. The first sheaf, i. e. the raw first produce, is brought to the priest. He waves it before Yahweh, by which act it is sanctified and absorbed in the sphere of Yahweh. Not until this sanctification has taken place can men venture to appropriate the crops to their own uses, whether to consume them as ordinary bread or as cakes of fresh corn or to eat the fresh ears roasted. We may take it for granted that such a sheaf was originally brought to the sanctuary from each farm, and perhaps this is implied, too, in the words of the text.

The sanctification of the sheaf is assigned to a certain day of the week, "the day after the sabbath". The first Sunday of the harvest might be meant, but more probably a definite day is meant, and then it can only have been the Sunday of the Passover week. [1] This dating is hardly old, the most natural assumption is that each farmer sanctified his sheaf as soon as it was reaped. On the other hand, it would be absurd to suppose that the law of holiness should not have known the feast of unleavened bread. None of the law collections available to us are complete. But the custom is an interesting testimony to the fact that the desire for sanctification of the crops was not satisfied by the ritual of Passover week and the part played there by the unleavened bread, even though it was probably also originally used to sanctify the new crops. The sanctification of the sheaf brought a living element into the treatment of the barley harvest. By becoming part of the Passover ritual, however, this act, too, gradually became merely a formal one, performed by the priest on behalf of the congregation with a single sheaf.

The first-fruit offering of the wheat harvest differs from that of the barley harvest in that it is not the fresh sheaf but two fully baked wheat loaves which are offered to Yahweh as the first-fruits, and sanctified by waving like the sheaf. They signify the termination of the grain-harvest. It is a question whether the reference made in the book of the Covenant to the first-fruits of what has been sown in the fields does not allude to the sanctification of the raw corn (Ex. 23,16, cf. 34,22). This would be nothing strange. We have seen that the book of the Covenant reckons with the sanctification of fruit in its different stages. The circles which the law of holiness has in view may also have sanctified a wheat sheaf, even though the law only mentions the finished loaf.

A sanctification of the corn in its different stages of preparation is evidenced in scattered precepts in the various laws. Reference is made to an offering of first-fruits to be brought in the shape of a cake baked of a fresh dough of crushed grain; it is to be mixed with oil and incense and its 'azkārā is to be burnt on the altar (Lev. 2,14-16). The first of the cakes baked of coarse flour are also consecrated: And it shall be that when ye eat of the bread of the land, ye shall select an oblation for Yahweh. The first of your coarse flour ye shall take out in cakes as a portion; as the oblation from the threshing floor, so shall ye take it out. Of the first of your coarse flour ye shall give unto Yahweh an oblation in all your generations (Num. 15,19-21). Here it is clearly stated that both the raw grain from the threshing floor and the newly baked bread is to be consecrated through its first batch, and this is confirmed by other evidence (Ez. 44,30; Neh. 10,38). At each stage man must sanctify the crops to be able to appropriate them. And the demand for the sanctification of the first-fruits was extended to other substances associated with the consumption of bread, such as honey and leaven; but that this demand was something secondary appears from the fact that this first produce was not allowed on the altar (Lev. 2,2, cf. 2 Chron. 31,5).

The book of the Covenant only states in quite general terms that the first-fruits are brought to the sanctuary. In the law of holiness we hear about a "waving" of the first-fruits by the priest in the temple, and in other laws we hear of a partial burning on the altar of what has been sanctified. In Deuteronomy we meet with the command that the Israelites are to put the first of all the fruits of the earth in a basket and give it to the priest who is to place it in front of the altar. The worshipper shall then say before Yahweh: My father was a miserable Aramaean, who went down into Egypt and sojourned there with a few, and there became a nation, great, mighty and numerous. And the Egyptians harassed and humiliated us and laid upon us hard bondage. Then we cried unto Yahweh, the God of our fathers, and Yahweh heard our voice and saw our misery, our toil, and our trouble. And Yahweh brought us out of Egypt with a mighty hand and with an out-stretched arm and with great terror and with signs and with wonders. An he brought us to this place and gave us this land, a land that floweth with milk and honey. And now, behold, I bring the first-fruits of the land which thou, Yahweh, hast given me. — And the text goes on to say: And thou shalt set it before

Yahweh thy God, and thou shalt prostrate thyself before Yahweh thy God. And thou shalt rejoice over every good thing which Yahweh thy God hath given unto thee and thine house, thou and the Levite and the *gēr* that is in thy midst (Deut. 26,1-11).

The import of the worshipper's prayer is that he gives Yahweh the first-fruits of the harvest of Canaan, because Israel has received Canaan as a sheer gift from her God. There is in this a change in the old idea of the first-fruits, which was that man sanctifies the gift of Nature for the purpose of strengthening it and so as to be able to appropriate it. The old relation of man to Nature has receded into the background, giving place to Israel's relation to her God through history. Apart from the prayer, we hear of a procedure consisting in the first-fruits being brought in a basket and sanctified by being set before the altar. We are told that the priest puts the basket there, but towards the close of the story only the worshipper himself would seem to be active. Probably, then, the narrative has been altered, and in that way perhaps both the cooperation of the priest and the text of the prayer have been introduced. This as well as other Deuteronomic laws probably gives expression to customs prevalent in Judaean cities, and employed by the author as a basis for cult requirements in Jerusalem. On the other hand, the command as to "the waving" mentioned in the law of holiness agrees with a sacrificial practice fixed in the Priestly Code and thus in common use at the temple of Jerusalem after the Exile.

Deuteronomy concludes with a command to the worshipper to rejoice in every good thing given him by Yahweh, and this means that he acquires the full right to use the crops when he has given Yahweh his share. It is the same idea as is expressed by Ezekiel; when the first-fruits have been sanctified there is a blessing in the crops (Ez. 44,30), but there is an accentuation of the note to which the prayer gives expression.

As indicated above, the offering of the first-fruits originally formed the nucleus of the agricultural feasts, but the idea itself was so deeply rooted in the relation of the Israelites to Nature that it continued to give rise to new forms. Gradually as the festivals were restricted to the large temples, especially to that of Jerusalem, the feast-offerings became public functions having no direct connection with the farming of the individual peasant. But then the first-fruit offerings of the individual came into use again, the land-owners bringing their first-fruits to the temple without these becoming part of the feast-offerings. We have seen evidence of this in the ritual described in Deuteronomy.

The peasant was driven to do this by his own desire to have his crops sanctified, but there was a class of men who were interested in keeping alive this desire, viz. the priests. What became of the holy crop when the first-fruits had been sanctified, either by being waved or by being set before the altar? Only in a single unimportant case in the late laws do we hear of it being burnt on the altar (Lev. 2,14-16); as a rule what is holy falls to the priests. The law of holiness says about the sheaf which is waved and its accompaniments that these are consecrated to Yahweh on behalf of the priest (Lev. 23,20).

This is a very natural procedure. The priest possessed the same holiness as the sanctuary and could therefore take what was holy without causing any breach in its holiness or bringing any ill-fortune upon himself. In the narratives about Elisha we hear that a man brought the man of God "bread of the first-fruits, twenty loaves of barley and coarse flour, in his bag (?)". The holy man had it distributed among the people and there was plenty for a hundred persons (2 Kings 4,42-44). We see the vitality of the idea inherent in the sanctification of the first-fruits. Where there was holiness the first-fruits could be used without following the fixed rules of a law. Possibly the loaves mentioned here had not been in the sanctuary, but acquired their sanctity by being given to the holy man.

The regular procedure, however, was to deliver the first-fruits in the sanctuary, where they fell to the priest, and this came to be exacted by the law. Deuteronomy has: The first-fruit also of thy corn, of thy wine, and of thine oil, and the first of the fleece of thy sheep shalt thou give him (i. e. the priest) (Deut. 18,4) Here the wool growing on the animals is co-ordinated with the produce of the soil. Ezekiel says: The first of all the first-fruits of all things, and every oblation of each sort of your oblations shall fall to the priests; and ye shall give unto the priest the first of your coarse flour that the blessing may dwell in thine house (Ez. 44,30), and Ezekiel emphasises that it is in the temple of Jerusalem that it is to be given (20,40). And finally it says in the post-exilic sacrificial laws: All the fat of the oil, and all the fat of the wine and corn, their first-fruits which they offer unto Yahweh, I give to thee. The first crops of all that is in their land which they bring unto Yahweh shall belong to thee. Every one that is clean in thine house may eat of it (Num. 18,12-13). The person addressed is the priest. He receives the first-fruits, but he may also let his family partake of them. It is true that they are holy, but not in any high degree. The designation of the first-fruits as the "fat" shows that the old view of this part of the produce as the essential part filled with power still survived, and from Ezekiel's words we learn that, as previously, the sanctification of the first-fruits had the object of creating blessedness in the houses of the Israelites. But a new factor has been added, the delivery of the first-fruits to the priests in the sanctuary being represented in the laws as a right belonging to the priests, an income to which they can lay claim.

The development of the first-fruit offering reveals certain lines determined by the fact that the official cultus became divorced from the life of the individual peasant or even entirely divorced from Nature, while the relation to Nature from which the offering sprang still survived among the peasants themselves. To this must be added the claims of the increasing priesthood, which were hardly at bottom related to the conception of the peasant, though the priests understood how to profit by it.

Considering the tendency of the first-fruits to become a tax, it is peculiar that the laws give no rules as to its amount. In that respect it has retained its spontaneous character; if any quantity is mentioned at all, it is a basket-full or a sheaf. But in addition to the law of the first-fruits we have a law relating to a similar sanctification of produce in which the quantity is brought into the foreground, viz. the law of *tithes*.

20*

Tithes are never mentioned in the book of the Covenant, but often in Deuteronomy. One passage runs thus: Thou shalt take a tithe of all the increase of the seed that the field bringeth forth year by year. And before Yahweh thy God, in the place where he chooseth to let his name dwell, thou shalt eat of thy corn, thy wine, and thine oil, and the firstlings of thy herds and of thy flocks, that thou mayest learn to fear Yahweh, thy God, always (Deut. 14,22 f.). The text goes on to say that if the way to the temple, i. e. to Jerusalem, is too long, the produce that would have been offered is to be turned into money and for this money the farmer may buy anything he likes of oxen and sheep, wine or other strong drink, or what else his soul desires, and eat and rejoice with his household before Yahweh. He is further enjoined not to forget the Levites in the cities throughout the land.

As is reasonable, other utterances in Deuteronomy command that the tithes must not be brought to other sanctuaries than that of Jerusalem, and we hear again that the tithe of corn, wine, and oil "is to be eaten before the face of Yahweh" in company with sons, daughters, slaves, slave women, and Levites (Deut. 12,16 f. 11 f. 17 f.). If we disregard the attacks on the sanctuaries outside Jerusalem characteristic of Deuteronomy, the text shows how people come by families with their tithes to the sanctuaries throughout the land and make their meal off them before Yahweh in company with the priests.

It is clear that these ordinances would result in the Levites throughout the country practically obtaining but a small share of the tithes. Hence we find another precept intended to secure compensation for them. The tithes of every third year are to be collected "within your gates", i. e. in the various towns, and there the Levite, the gēr, the orphan and the widow are to consume them (Deut. 14,28 f.). This provision has emerged from a fear of the social consequences when the tithe was abolished in the cities.

The result of this ordinance is a change in the character of the tithe, for in that year it is not sanctified. But that the true character of the tithe was not forgotten in that year either, appears from a declaration which, according to another statement, was to accompany its delivery: When thou hast finished taking all the tithe of thy increase in the third year, the year of tithing, thou shalt give it unto the Levite, the *gēr*, the orphan, and the widow; and they shall eat within thy gates and be satisfied. And thou shalt say before Yahweh, thy God: I have brought away the hallowed things from out of mine house, I have also given them unto the Levite, and to the *gēr*, and the orphan, and the widow, according to all thy commandment which thou hast commanded me. I have not transgressed or forgotten any of thy commandments; I have not eaten thereof in my mourning, and I have taken away nought thereof in an unclean state, nor given ought thereof to a dead person. I have obeyed the voice of Yahweh, my God; I have acted in accordance with all that thou hast commanded me. Incline thyself from thy holy habitation, from heaven, and bless thy people Israel and the land which thou hast given us, as thou swarest unto our fathers, a land that floweth with milk and honey (Deut. 26,12-15).

In this ordinance it is evidently implied that the giver of tithes is to go up to the recognised sanctuary to make this declaration, undeniably a peculiar compromise between the old custom and the new claims. But the remarkable thing is that the tithe has retained its old character as holy, though it is by no means brought to the sanctuary to be sanctified. And it is treated as holy, since it must not come into contact with any impurity caused by death or anything else, and yet it is to be consumed in a profane place by the indigent. Evidently these are old provisions relating to the tithe, which have been incorporated in this peculiar law.

Behind the artificial provisions of Deuteronomy we catch a glimpse of a practice which consisted in bringing tithes of the produce of the soil to the temple; we are not told what was done with them there to sanctify them, but they were consumed in the holy place.

This custom is adhered to consistently, abstractly, in the laws of the Priestly Code. Here it is not the produce of the fields only, but also animals; a tenth part of all is holy. It is quite clear, however, that "holy" here merely means "devolving to the sanctuary", i. e. to those who govern it. It is a mere tax. This appears with sufficient clarity from the provisions: All the tithe of the land, whether of the seed of the land or of the fruit of the trees, belongs to Yahweh, it is holy unto Yahweh. And if a man redeem ought of his tithe he shall add thereto a fifth part thereof. And all tithes of the herd or of the flock, whatsoever passeth under the rod, the tenth part shall be holy unto Yahweh. He shall not search whether it be good or bad, nor change it. And if he change it, both it and the change thereof shall be holy, and shall not be redeemable (Lev 27,30-33). The interest of the priests in the tax is plainly implied in the text.

Another statement in the Priestly Code establishes that the sons of Levi receive the tithe as a compensation because they have been given no tribal share of the country (Num. 18,21-24); from this it appears that the sons of Levi here denote the whole priesthood. But another provision is added, according to which the Levites, the lower priests of Jerusalem, are to receive the tithes as a wage for their work, and out of this they are to pay tithes to the priests (Num. 18,25-32).

We have now come to the stage that the tithe is a tax given to defray the wages of the temple servants. But we have been able to make out from various texts that it was, originally, something else, a sanctification of the produce. The question then arises as to what relation it bore to the first-fruits. For these, too, were part of the crops given to the holy place as a holy gift. The difference consists in two things only, partly in the fact that the tithe constitutes a definite quantity, one tenth, partly in the express statement that it was eaten in the holy place. In character both sacrificial gifts are the same.

That the tithe is not an invention of later legislators is shown by Amos' words: Come to Bethel and transgress, at Gilgal multiply transgression! Bring your sacrifices next morning, your tithes on the third day! (Am. 4,4). That it was the custom to give tithes precisely at the sanctuary of Bethel may also be gathered from its foundation legend, in which Jacob declares: And of all that thou shalt give me, I will surely give the tenth unto thee (Gen. 28,22).

Amos' words show that the giving of tithes was part of the ritual. But then they must have been in the main of the same importance as the first-fruits. In the nature of the case the fixing of the holy gift at a certain part of the harvest makes it impossible to set apart for the temple a portion until the harvest is finished. A measure, originally less precisely defined, for instance a basketfull for each tree, may later have been fixed as one tenth, and this measure may then have been transferred to all other produce of the soil; "tithes of all the increase of thy seed growing in thy field", and "tithe of thy corn, thy wine, and thine oil," says Deuteronomy (12,17; 14,22). It may have had some influence in the fixing of this quantity that in other countries of Nearer Asia, also, there were sometimes regular dues of a tenth part to be paid to the sanctuary or to the kings. ¹ In the warning speech against the monarchy ascribed to Samuel, he says that the king will take a tenth part of the people's flocks (1 Sam. 8,17). We do not know, however, whether this was actually done in Israel.

It is quite possible that the tithe was first introduced at certain temples, perhaps after a foreign prototype, and spread from these to others. As shown above, it seems originally to have been a first-fruit offering, the amount of which has become fixed; this gave it its own peculiar character, amongst other reasons because it could not be given until the harvest was over, and it then underwent a special development as a tax. Hence the sanctification of the first-fruits became a necessity in addition to the giving of the tithe; it was not even enough to sanctify the first-fruits once for all, the produce must constantly be sanctified in its various stages. Deuteronomy and the Priestly Code have commands exacting both tithes and first-fruits without any intermixture, and it is emphatically stated in Deuteronomy that the first-fruit offering brought at the feast of Weeks could be given in any quantity the giver chose (Deut. 16,10).

How largely the tithe developed into a mere tax may be gathered from the Priestly Code, where it is regarded as a right belonging to the priesthood. And this right became an abstract principle extended to include animals, too (Lev. 27,30 ff.), with the result that there is a complete rupture of the connection with the first-fruits. The principle cannot be arrested in its development until it has come to comprise everything. Jacob promises Yahweh "a tenth of all that thou shalt give me" (Gen. 28,22), and Abraham gave the priestly king Melchisedek a tenth of everything (Gen. 14,20). Both these statements, it would seem, took their shape from ideas dating from rather a late period in the history of Israel.

When the old customs were to be restored at Jerusalem after the exile, the background of the first-fruit offering did not exist in its original vigour, and it was necessary to bring home to the population its duty of giving both first-fruits and tithes as dues (Neh. 10,36-40; 12,44; 13,5). Somewhat later we hear a prophet complaining that the people is defrauding Yahweh of the tithe that belongs to him, and assurances are given that the blessing will come when the tithe is paid in full (Mal. 3,8.10). This does not mean the blessing in the old sense which permeates the whole crop from the sanctified first-fruits; here the blessing is a reward to the people for fulfilling the law.

The time when these prophetic complaints were heard is probably not far from the period when the priests were engaged in the final formulation of the old provisions, and amongst other things carried through a rigid demand for tithes. The priests would now indeed relate how zealously the people in the days of King Hezekiah had paid a tithe of everything, and how great was the blessing they obtained in that way (2 Chron. 31,5 ff.).

The sanctification of the produce of the soil was so important to the Israelites that it constantly generated new forms as long as their culture possessed vitality. These were not exhausted by the periodical sacrificial gifts previously mentioned. Thus in certain temples bread was constantly placed for sanctification. We happen to know this from Nob where it was regularly changed, and only sanctified persons were allowed to eat it (1 Sam. 21,5.7). In the great hall in Solomon's temple there was a special table or altar for the "shew-bread" (1 Kings 7,48; Ez. 41,22) [1], and we have a detailed description of it in the wilderness legends of the wanderings (Ex. 25,23 ff.; 35,13; 37,10 ff.; 39,36; 40,23). The law prescribes that it should be wheaten bread, twelve loaves in all, which are laid out with incense every sabbath; and the discarded loaves may be eaten only by the priests (Lev. 24,5-9).

According to one of the wilderness narratives a jar with manna was kept in the temple "before the testimony", that is, in front of the Ark, probably at the back of the temple hall (Ex. 16,32-34). Beyond this statement we hear nothing about it, but since manna is mentioned as part of the nourishment of prehistoric Israel (Ex. 16; Num. 11,6 ff.), we may here have an element from pre-Canaanite times which has been preserved in the cultus. To later Israel manna was merely holy bread, a heavenly food for "the mighty" (Ps. 78,24 f.; 105,40).

The whole of the sacrifice centring round the idea of the first-fruits is the offering of the agriculturists, and among the Israelites it is indissolubly bound up with the land of Canaan. This cannot be said about the cattle-breeder's offering, since the prehistoric Israelites, too, were a pastoral people, and in certain parts of Canaan these keepers of flocks adhered to their old customs without mixing with the world of the agriculturists. The ruling part of the population, however, combined both occupations, and as agriculturists they introduced the ox, necessary as a draught animal in the tilling of the soil. As a matter of fact, the laws relating to the first increase of the animals deal both with oxen and sheep, but they do not stop at animals; human beings, too, are included under them.

A passage runs thus: The first-born of thy sons thou shalt give to me. Thus shalt thou do with thine oxen and thy sheep; seven days it shall be with its dam: on the eighth day thou shalt give it to me (Ex. 22,28-29). From the context it appears that the reference is to the *first-born* of the oxen and sheep. They are to remain for a week with the dam, for the order of nature must not be broken, and they are to attain a certain development. What is to be done in the sanctuary with the first-born is not stated.

Further: All that openeth the matrix is mine; and all thy cattle [1] ... the firstlings of oxen and sheep. And the firstling of an ass thou shalt redeem with a lamb, and if thou dost not redeem it, thou shalt break its neck. All the first-born of thy sons thou shalt redeem, and none shall appear empty-handed before me (Ex. 34,19-20; almost as in 13,12 f.). Here the idea has been extended. All first-born creatures belong to Yahweh, and it is a duty to bring them as an offering in the sanctuary. But now there appears an obstacle. Some animals have not been so entirely appropriated by the Israelites that they can be sanctified. Among the animals used by them this applies especially to the ass. The difficulty is surmounted by letting a lamb or a kid represent the ass's foal. The sacrifice of one's own offspring is avoided in a similar way.

Both in Deuteronomy and elsewhere we meet with the principle that everything which opens the matrix is to be consecrated to Yahweh. "Sanctify unto me all the first-born, whatever openeth the womb among the Israelites, both of man and of beast; it is mine" (Ex. 13,2). We are told a little more about what is to be done with it: All the firstlings that come of thy herd and of thy flock, all the males, thou shalt sanctify unto Yahweh, thy God. Thou shalt do no work with the firstlings of thy bullocks, nor shear the firstlings of thy sheep. Thou shalt eat it year by year before Yahweh, thy God, in the place which Yahweh shall choose, thou and thy household. But if there be any blemish in it, as if it be lame or blind, or have any evil flaw whatsoever, thou shalt not sacrifice it unto Yahweh, thy God. Thou canst eat it within thy gates, the unclean and the clean together, as the gazelle and as the hart. Only thou shalt not eat the blood thereof; thou shalt pour it upon the ground as water (Deut. 15,19-23).

Through this law we get an idea of how the first-born were treated in the sanctuaries throughout the land. The first-born are the animals who prepare the way for the new generation which is to perpetuate and renew the life of the race to which they belong. This life is active in them in a special way, but only in the males, the fully valid representatives of the species of the animal, in so far, that is, as they are normal, without any blemish. Therefore man must not appropriate them, must do no work with them and must not shear their wool. Like the first-fruits of the plants they are to be sanctified in the holy place. How this is done appears from our text.

The sanctified animal is slaughtered, the blood is given to the altar, the holy stone, or whatever it is, and thus the holy soul of the animal is restored to the forces from which it sprang. For in the blood the soul is present in a special degree. The animal has become entirely absorbed into the sphere of holiness. In this way it sanctifies primarily the offspring later falling from the same dam; but in a wider sense it acts on all the rest of the species. The whole animal soul is strengthened by the sanctification, and the blessing will appear in renewed strength and fruitfulness. In sanctifying the animal, man, who sacrifices it, receives his share of holiness; and this is further strengthened by the fact that the worshipper with his fellows eat of the remains of the holy animal, making a meal off it in the holy place before Yahweh. All this is implied in the words of Deuteronomy.

All the laws agree that the giving up of the first-born to the sanctuary is a thing which Yahweh can claim. Thus there are two aspects of the case, but that does not imply a departure from the fundamental point of view, the sanctification of the sacrifice and through it of all that it represents. But when the temple priests become interested in the offering of what Yahweh can claim, more emphasis will easily be laid on this aspect of the matter, and the sacrifice of the first-born becomes a tax.

Thus it is in the Priestly Code. Where Yahweh enumerates the dues of the priests, he says: Everything that openeth the matrix in all flesh which they bring unto Yahweh, whether it be of men or of beasts, shall be thine. But thou shalt redeem the first-born of man, and the firstling of unclean beasts thou shalt redeem. And as for that which is to be redeemed, thou shalt redeem it when it is a month old, according to thy (usual) estimation, 5 shekels of silver of the shekel of the sanctuary, which is 20 gerahs. But the firstling of oxen, or the firstling of sheep, or the firstling of goats thou shalt not redeem; they are holy. Thou shalt sprinkle their blood upon the altar, and thou shalt change their fat into smoke for an offering for a pleasant savour unto Yahweh. And the flesh of them shall be thine. As the wave breast and as the right shoulder, it shall be thine (Num. 18,15-18).

It quite agrees with the character of these laws that the old point of view, that the animal is to be sanctified, is not only preserved but even strongly stressed. But in addition, the surrendering of the first-born had become a tribute which the priests could claim. The actual sanctification by means of offerings could still take place with such animals as belonged from early times to the Israelite world, i. e. oxen, sheep, and goats; and their sanctity had then become so great that the worshippers themselves were no longer allowed to touch their flesh; only the priests were so holy that they could take possession of it. But the offering of the first-born had developed into an independent principle consistently and abstractly applied, so that it held good for everything born in the possession of man, for clean as well as unclean animals. And since unclean animals could not be sacrificed, they must be redeemed; that is to say, their value was to be paid, a tax was simply levied on them.

It is immediately evident that this development is a parallel to what we found in the case of the first-fruits. But here perhaps we see more clearly how the exaction of a tax developed into a principle wholly independent of the principle of sanctification. On the other hand, we have seen how the principle of the tithe, evolved from the first-fruits, was extended to apply to animals, at any rate in theory, and brought them within its scheme. And just as the first-fruit offering in the spring must be regarded as a renewal of the old first-fruit offering which still survived in the use of the unleavened bread, thus also the sacrifice of the first-born is a renewal of the old offering of the firstlings surviving in the paschal sacrifice.

The priests put up a vigorous fight against a curtailment of any of the dues acquired as the right of Yahweh. "The firstling of the cattle which should be Yahweh's firstling, no man shall sanctify; whether it be ox or sheep, it is Yahweh's. And if it be of an unclean beast, then he can redeem it according to thy (usual) estimation, and shall add a fifth part of it thereto. If it be not redeemed, it shall be sold according to thy (usual) estimation" (Lev. 27,26 f.). This means that no gift is presented by the offering of the firstlings, for these already belong to the sanctuary. If anything is to be gained by sanctifying an animal of one's own accord, another animal must be given. At the same time the worshipper is admonished to pay a tax for the unclean firstlings, and this has even been augmented by a fifth part.

If we wish to form an opinion of the sacrificial customs of the Israelites, we must remember that in Canaan they met with a fully developed cult. Our knowledge of the Phoenician-Canaanite cult is now quite sufficient to warrant the conclusion that the greater part of the Israelitish sacrificial practices had been learnt from the Canaanites. We shall see later that the paschal sacrifice is probably pre-Canaanite, but it is indeed difficult to draw the line between what is Canaanite and what is strictly Israelite. The Israelites did not adopt the Canaanite custom as a dead system. The sacrifices, also, entered as a natural element into the organism of Israelite culture, not as a thing merely acquired in an outward sense. Behind the sacrificial practices adopted by Israel there lay deeply rooted elemental ideas, which lived in the Israelite people. Hence they could independently appropriate the entire sacrificial cult, but also create new forms and new viewpoints from it.

The sacrifice of the first-born, like the offering of the first-fruits, takes us to the nucleus of the Israelite idea of sacrifice, which sprang from the necessity for a sanctification of the produce of the soil throughout the world of Israel, in order that the species might be maintained through the sanctification, and the essential condition be created for man's appropriation of them. Therefore the objects of sacrifice were primarily the animals belonging to that world in the narrowest sense, i. e. oxen, sheep, and goats. But we have seen that the law was also confronted with two kinds of first-born of which it spoke with less certainty, viz. asses, and male children.

We know about the ass that very soon after the immigration into Canaan of the Israelites, it was used by them for riding. This is evidenced already by the Song of Deborah. But it was not admitted to their world in the same way as the ox. The fact that the law requires the firstling asses to be redeemed by a sheep or a kid, or to be killed (Ex. 13,13; 34,20), means that the ass has become so well established in the Israelitish world that it cannot avoid contact with the law of sanctification, but it has come too late to be sanctified by sacrifice itself; hence sanctification must take place by means of a substitute, a lamb or a kid. The firstling ass is given to holiness, but cannot be absorbed by it. If the claim to it is not satisfied, it becomes an animal of evil; man may not appropriate it, but must break its neck. Thus Israel combines the requirements of the time with an impregnable tradition.

The ass marks the outward limit where problems and doubts arise. Somewhat beyond this we find the camel, which also became an Israelitish animal, but never became so well established in the Israelite world as to give rise to any problem. The inner limit was as difficult to draw as the outer one. With respect to the human species doubts arose as in the case of the asses, but the difficulties were here of another kind.

It was the human world of animals and plants which was sanctified by the sacrifices, but it was man himself who was active in the sanctification, hence he obtained a share in it. And men could of their own accord sanctify themselves in many ways. Their activity made their relation to the cult different from that of the animals. And yet their life was analogous to that of the animals, they multiplied in the same way. If it were necessary for the maintenance of life to sacrifice the first-born animals, was it, then, less necessary for men to give their first-born to sanctification in the same way as the animals so closely related to man?

We know both from information about the Phoenicians and the Punic peoples, and from archæological discoveries in Palestine, that people within the Canaanite sphere of culture drew this conclusion. We have also evidence thereof in the Old Testament.[1] The Israelites largely acquired the Canaanite point of view. This is shown by the commandment in the book of the Covenant: The firstborn of thy sons shalt thou give unto me (Ex. 22,28). This makes the custom Israelite, it expresses Yahweh's demand for holiness. But there is another ordinance opposed to it: All the

first-born of thy sons thou shalt redeem (Ex. 34,20, cf. 13,13).
The claim then has been acknowledged, but as in the case of the
asses, there is a shrinking from fully accepting it. This may have
been the common solution in earlier times, but the narrative of
Jephthah and his daughter shows that it did not seem unnatural
to the Israelites when the occcasion called for it to sacrifice their
own children.

The redemption consists in substituting an animal for the
person to be sacrificed. We know an instance of redemption from
the story of Jonathan. When he was marked for death because
he had broken his father's promise, the people redeemed *(pādhā)* [1]
him (1 Sam. 14,45), and the same principle is known from blood-
revenge. Compensation might be made for the person to be
sacrificed. But from blood-revenge and from the above-mentioned
story we know that redemption is never the same as the actual
fulfilling of the claim.

The view that Yahweh demanded the sacrifice of male children
but was satisfied with a substitute, could not therefore be the
final solution of the question. Those who felt the demand strongly
must always be asking themselves whether they had done enough
by making compensation, and in times fraught with disaster this
question might become especially urgent. We hear in fact in the
second book of the Kings that King Ahaz, as also later on
Manasseh, sacrificed his sons (2 Kings 16,3; 21,6, cf. 17,17). It
is noted as something remarkable in their case.

Around the year 600, however, there came a revival of child
sacrifices, and at the same time there arose a violent reaction
against it. We learn this from Jeremiah and Ezekiel. These
sacrifices especially took place at a certain sanctuary, *tōpheth,* in
the valley of Hinnom near Jerusalem. The most natural assumption is that it was a sacrifice of first-born children, but this is not
certain; and both boys and girls are mentioned (Jer. 7,31; 32,35;
Ez. 16,20). [2] It is a strange fact, however, that according to the
prophets these sacrifices were not made to Yahweh but to alien
gods, and Molech is mentioned (Jer. 32,35; Ez. 16,20; 23,37 ff.).
But the worshippers themselves do not regard the cult as non-
Israelite. Ezekiel says that people enter Yahweh's temple on the

same day that they sacrifice their children in the valley of Hinnom (Ez. 23,39). Both visits then form part of a pilgrimage and belong together. Evidently it was a certain Canaanite cult which was here suddenly revived, and seemed natural to the worshippers, a realisation of an old command which had formerly been recognised at any rate in prominent Israelite circles. The whole phenomenon shows how closely the Canaanite and Israelite elements had become fused in large parts of the populace.

The two prophets condemn child sacrifice in severe terms and maintain that it is totally in conflict with the will of Yahweh. Jeremiah says: And they (i. e. the Judæans) have built the bamahs of Tophet in the valley of the sons of Hinnom, to burn their sons and their daughters in the fire, which I commanded them not, neither came it into my heart (Jer. 7,31), words which are repeated elsewhere, the bamahs being called "the bamahs of the Baal", and the victims are said to be sacrificed as burnt-offerings to the Baal or to Molech (Jer. 19,5; 32,35). The burning of children was hardly an old Israelite custom, [1] but of course it is the sacrifice as such, and not a certain rite, which Jeremiah condemns.

Thus Jeremiah entirely denies that Yahweh has demanded child sacrifice. Ezekiel, however, takes another view of the matter. He says: Because they did not observe my rules, but rejected my laws, and polluted my sabbaths and their eyes were after their fathers' logs of gods, I have also given them laws that were not good and rules whereby they cannot live. And I polluted them in their own gifts, in that they gave all that openeth the womb, that I might paralyse them, that they may know that I am Yahweh (Ez. 20,24-26).

Even though the old law was generally regarded as a compromise, there is a great gulf between it and the two prophets, whether we consider Jeremiah's pure denial of Yahweh's demand for child sacrifice or we keep to the demonic explanation of Ezekiel. These prophets represent a new Israel which had a different view of man, far removed from nature. Any mixing with animals was excluded. Man occupied an absolutely special position, nature was only an instrument to him, and the life of Israelite man was precious in Yahweh's eyes. Therefore the sacrifice of children became both foolish and revolting.

There are, indeed, laws which express this reaction against infant sacrifice and denounces it as a Canaanite custom incompatible with Israelite usage. Deuteronomy never mentions the old law relating to the sacrifice of the first-born, but expressly prohibits the practice of giving children to the fire, which is assigned to the same class as sorcery and similar obscure practices (Deut. 18,10). The law of holiness, also, which militates so much against the Canaanite element in Israel, prohibits the offering of children to Molech, by which the name of Yahweh is profaned (Lev. 18,21; 20,2-5).

According to the second book of the Kings, Josiah put an end to the cults in the valley of Hinnom (2 Kings 23,10), but Ezekiel bears witness that in his time children were still dedicated to the fire (Ez. 20,31). The sacrifice of the first-born continued to occupy people's thoughts. They could not rid themselves of the idea that it was an old command. The story of the sacrifice of Isaac inculcates didactically that the command merely applies to the worshipper's disposition, to man's readiness to obey to the utmost the will of God; when this disposition is present, God merely demands an animal sacrifice instead of the sacrifice of a son.

The old compromise of redeeming the first-born was retained in the Priestly Code. But here it is said that all that opens the womb is to go to the priest, a fixed payment being made for infants and unclean animals (Num. 18,15 f.). The demand for the sacrifice of the first-born has been extended to the utmost limit, but at the same time it has lost its character, the sacrifice being replaced by a tribute.

An idea which has no connection with this practical transformation of the old demand for sanctification of the first-born is what we find elsewhere in the Priestly Code, the idea that the Levites are given to Yahweh as compensation for the first-born. We read: Behold, I take the Levites from among the Israelites instead of all the first-born, all that openeth the matrix, among the Israelites, and the Levites shall be mine (Num. 3,12); and reference is made to the fact that Yahweh's demand for the first-born derives its origin from the events in Egypt. The idea is consistently adhered to, the Levites replacing the male first-born among men, and their cattle the firstlings of the herds and flocks (Num. 3,41.45). And when a count shows that there are fewer Levites than first-born, a redemption sum is paid for the surplus (v. 46 ff.). Indeed the idea of the Levites as a sacrifice is carried so far that the priest is commanded to swing them before the altar as prescribed in the ritual for the sacrificial meat (Num. 8,11 ff.).

The remarkable thing about these considerations is that they render superfluous all ordinances for the offering of the first-born or their redemption, for if the Levites supply the place of the firstborn, all claims must fall away upon their consecration. The idea is not utterly gratuitous, since the fundamental purpose in offering the first-born is sanctification, and precisely those who serve in the sanctuary are sanctified, or given to Yahweh. However, the wholly abstract character of the consideration would seem to indicate that it has merely a purely theoretical significance; nevertheless it is of great interest, for it shows that there was no getting rid of the idea that it was a duty the Israelites owed to Yahweh to sanctify all the first-born to him.

———————

The offering of the first-fruits and the first-born carries us to the very principle of the sacrifice, because this offering is an immediate necessity for the maintenance of the life of Israel. We have seen that great things are set in motion by it. The life that constitutes the world of the Israelites is sanctified and acquires renewed blessedness, it is appropriated and absorbed by the Israelites, and at the same time the Israelites themselves are fortified by obtaining a share in the holiness created by the sacrifice. And simultaneously with all this the Israelite strengthens the covenant with his God, nay he strengthens the God himself. All increase of holiness is a strengthening of the God, because holiness is the essence of his soul. By offering the sacrifice to the holy sphere the worshipper gives a gift to the

God, and here as among men the gift acts according to its nature; the receiver is honoured, and the covenant between the two parties is strengthened.

In the sacrifice all the threads of life are gathered together; renewed life springs from it, because the blessing is recreated in it, and its effects are felt in all the forces of life, in the world of God, the world of man, and the world of nature.

The multiplicity of significant psychic elements embodied in the sacrifice renders it understandable that it could not be limited to the first-fruits or the first-born. In their instance the sacrifice was a necessity, because the whole soul of their species was in them, and it would be a danger to life if they were quite simply allowed to enter everyday existence. But other representatives of animal and plant life might also be sanctified, and man might thus strengthen holiness and renew his covenant with the God.

While the offering of first-fruits and first-born was chiefly confined to certain periods, free-will offerings might be made at any time when the worshipper felt a desire for that which was acquired through the offering. The various aspects of the character of the offering may then come more or less into the forefront. As a rule the all-engrossing point of view is that the God is honoured and the covenant with him strengthened by the gift. The sanctification of the animal or plant species is then quite overshadowed by the special purpose of the worshipper.

The free-will offering is called $n^e dh\bar{a}bh\bar{a}$, a term meaning what is done or given of the worshipper's own inner impulse. The free-will offering attained great importance as an independent category of sacrifices. In a single instance it may denote the amount of the offering to be made at the feast of Weeks, because the amount is optional (nidhbhath yādh^{e}khā, Deut. 16,10); but otherwise it signifies the sacrifice which is offered quite freely. Most frequently it was probably offered by a person who had received a special blessing and desired to present his gift as a simple consequence of having received a gift himself. His sacrifice is in honour or praise of God. "I will freely sacrifice unto thee, I will praise thy name, Yahweh" (Ps. 54,8). The special praise-offering *(tōdhā)* is in the main identical with the free-will offering, even though the latter may probably also comprise other offerings; *tōdhā* belongs to the hour of joy (Jer. 33,11). It is offered of the worshipper's own free motion *(nᵉdhābhā* Ps. 54,8) and may also be compared to the votive offering (Ps. 56,13). When Amos says: Burn sacrificial smoke as a praise offering of leavened bread, ¹ proclaim loudly free offerings (Amos 4,5), his two utterances probably in the main express the same thing, and he gives us a hint particularly of the immense importance of this sacrifice. We hear how the offering of it is loudly proclaimed in the temples, and we understand that, just because it was voluntary, it was the outcome of special experiences on the part of the worshipper. The Psalmist calls his praises "the free-will offerings of my mouth" (Ps. 119,108).

Ezekiel takes it for granted that "the prince" also will offer *nᵉdhābhā* (Ez. 46,12), and immediately after the altar had been restored in the post-exilic time, "free-will offerings" were made besides the prescribed ones (Ezr. 3,5). The book of Chronicles even takes for granted that there must be a special priestly functionary to take charge of these offerings which were clearly not reduced in number in the course of time (2 Chron. 31,14). In the sacrificial laws *nᵉdhābhā* is mentioned as a special category of sacrifices, always simultaneously with the votive offering (Lev. 7,16; 22,18.21.23; 23,38; Num. 15,3; Deut. 12,6.17); these two kinds constituted the voluntary offerings made in addition to the prescribed ones (Num. 29,39).

The votive offering, as indicated by the name, is an offering performed in fulfilment of a vow. The *nedher* is used both about the vow and the offering. *Nedher* as well as *nᵉdhābhā* is a gift which strengthens the peaceful relation to the God, in that the worshipper honours him; and in both cases as a rule it confirms a relationship created through a blessing received by the worshipper. Both are offered of the worshipper's own accord, hence a votive offering may also be called *nᵉdhābhā* (Deut. 23,24). The only difference is that the worshipper making a votive offering has made a conditional promise to the God before the blessing was bestowed on him. This, however, gives an important shade of variation to the votive offering; for by his vow the worshipper tries to influence the course of events and call forth the object of his wish. However, the vow may also be made without any such condition.

The votive offering has a wider effect than the free-will offering. Whoever makes a vow at once enters into the sphere of the offering; he has laid a restraint on himself which will not be abolished until he has made his offering. By offering his sacrifice he makes his vow "complete" (*shillēm*, Isa. 19,21; Nah. 2,1; Ps. 22,26 et al.); his word is no mere lip-service, but attains its natural development. Hence it can also be said that he performs his vow (*'āśā*, Jer. 44,25), through the offering his vow is made to stand (ibd), it is accomplished. ¹

Many expressions show us how common votive offerings were. Votive offerings are constantly made to Yahweh in addition to the prescribed sacrifices which expressed the normal state of things (Ps. 22,26; 50,14; 61,9; 65,2; 66,13; 116,14.18), just as those who worshipped the queen of heaven also made votive offerings to her (Jer. 44,25). When Eliphaz has to say that Job will be happy, he puts it thus: he will be able to make his votive offerings (Job 22,27). So natural does it seem to be that a blessing gained is connected with a vow that has been made. And Nahum describes the happiness to come by saying that Judah shall keep her feasts and perform her promises of sacrifice (Nah. 2,1). The rise of an Israelite colony in Egypt is described in the words: the people there shall make sacrifices, and vow, and perform vows to Yahweh (Isa. 19,21).

We have also historical examples of the making of such vows. When Absalom planned his rebellion against David, he had to think of a pretext for going to Hebron without exciting suspicion. And the pretext was easy to find. He told David that during his exile at Geshur in Aram he had taken a vow that he would serve Yahweh at Hebron if he let him come back to Jerusalem. Though it was long since this wish had been fulfilled, David found nothing strange in the matter and bid him go in peace to Hebron (2 Sam. 15,7-9). This story shows how common such promises were, and it likewise tells us that the vow was made to a stated sanctuary.

The binding power of such a vow is shown by the history of Jephthah. When he went into battle against the Ammonites, he sought to secure his God's participation by a vow. "And Jephthah vowed a vow unto Yahweh and said: If thou wilt deliver the Ammonites into mine hand, then whosoever cometh forth out of the doors of mine house to meet me when I return with peace from the Ammonites, shall be Yahweh's, and I will offer him up for a burnt-offering" (Judg. 11,30 f.). It is clear that Jephthah has here promised Yahweh a human sacrifice, and it is doubtful whether he did not in the first place think of his daughter as the person most likely to greet him first upon his return, even if, by giving his vow a more vague form, he might hope that Yahweh would choose another.

The idea is that if a man wants to bind the God to do great things, he must give him something great in return. Thus we hear of King Mesha of Moab that he sacrificed his first-born son, when the Israelites seemed about to inflict a defeat on him. "And there was great indignation against Israel, and they departed from there, and returned to their own land" (2 Kings 3,27). The will of the God is influenced by the sacrifice, he stirs up the souls and induces them to put forth every effort, thus making them unconquerable.

Nor will Yahweh take less than Jephthah's daughter, his only child. This becomes apparent when she comes out to meet him in her usual way with timbrels and with dances. "And when he saw her he rent his clothes and said: Alas, my daughter, thou hast brought me very low, and thou art become the one that hast caused me woe. I have opened my mouth unto Yahweh, and I cannot alter it. And she said unto him: My father, if thou hast opened thy mouth unto Yahweh, do to me according to that which hath proceeded out of thy mouth, after Yahweh hath taken vengeance for thee over thine enemies, over the Ammonites (Judg. 11,35 f.). Like Jonathan in the case of Saul, his daughter knew that a child could not break her father's holy vow, and she willingly let the vow be fulfilled on her (v. 39). But that it was no everyday occurrence is manifested by the fact that it gave rise to a four-days' lamentation feast, at which Israelite women bewailed the girl who had to yield up her life in her virgin state to secure victory for her people.

It follows from the nature of the case that the vow need not concern an ordinary sacrifice. A gift to Yahweh is primarily a sanctification and may take place in several forms. A vow such as Jacob made at Bethel was of an unusual kind, a vow of the first ancestor to the God of the people. It was no less than that Jacob would make Bethel into a sanctuary and take Yahweh for his God, if he gave him a prosperous journey (Gen. 28,20 ff.). A vow of a more ordinary kind was that which Hannah made to Yahweh at Shiloh.

Hannah was childless, the glory of being a mother was denied her. One day when she was at Shiloh on the annual pilgrimage with her husband and his other wife, who had brought her children, Hannah went before the face of Yahweh, weeping and praying. "And she vowed a vow, saying: Yahweh of the hosts! If thou wilt look upon the affliction of thine handmaid and remember me, and not forget thine handmaid and give thine handmaid male issue, I will give him to Yahweh all the days of his life, and no razor shall come upon his head" (1 Sam. 1,11). Thus Hannah will achieve the honour of motherhood, and the boy will be given to Yahweh.

In the story of Hannah there is no indication that the law demands the sacrifice of the first-born boy, which shows that this requirement cannot at any rate have been generally accepted in early Israel. And yet the idea of the law is felt in the story. It is right that the first-born boy should be given up to a special sanctification. And it is worth noticing that Hannah prefers this to having a girl-child that she may keep, because the honour is greater.

Countless were the vows vowed by Israelite women to obtain the fulfilment of their desire for a male child. And gradually as the old times and their customs receded, when the sacrifice of the first-born had long since been replaced by fixed taxes and the idea of the sanctification of the first-born was vanishing, it was probably as a rule regular sacrifices that were promised. However, the desire for sons was so great that the vows made in order to obtain them did not cease. "The son of my vows" (Prov. 31,2) is a mother's name for a long-desired, and therefore beloved, son.

By her vow Hannah consecrated her son to be a Nazirite. But any person making a vow becomes to a certain extent consecrated. By his vow he has approached what is holy and is subject to its power until the vow has been fulfilled.

There are vows in which this state is the essential thing, and thus we see the close relationship between the votive offering and the condition of a Nazirite. In that condition the person sanctifies himself for a shorter or longer period after making a vow to that effect (Num. 6,2.5), and when the period has expired, it is terminated by a sacrifice (v. 10 ff.). The close relationship between the words *nedher* and *nāzīr* is no mere chance.

The precepts concerning such vows do not state that they are confined to the fulfilment of a certain wish, nor was this probably the common rule in earlier times. The sanctification was undertaken in order to gain strength. But if strength was desired for some definite purpose, this was a step on the way to the ordinary conditional promise. And gradually as the abstention itself, which was an adjunct of the sanctification, came to be regarded as an offering, a gift to God, this point of view also contributed to make people vow holy vows so as to compel the fulfilment of a wish. How common a feature this came to be in later Judaism may be seen from the Mishnah. [1]

But as early as before the completion of the Biblical laws a desire arose to limit the vows of abstention. If a woman made such a vow (*'issār*), she thereby abandoned married life, and her vow might thus conflict with her duties to her father or her husband. The law, then, lays down that a woman cannot by her vow limit her father's authority over her if she is unmarried, or the rights of her husband, if she is married. Her father can give her away in marriage, and her husband demand that she fulfil her matrimonial duty despite her vow, that is, if they raise objections as soon as they hear of her vow. If her husband first hears her vow and holds his peace, and later demands that she break it, he is responsibile for its fulfilment (Num. 30). In this law it is a jurist who is trying to limit and divide the responsibility, and it is clear that the old idea of sanctification with its absolute demands has here given place to the logic of the interpreter of the law.

As already mentioned, the votive offerings are made an important class of offerings in the sacrificial laws. Deuteronomy lays down the express command that votive offerings should be made at Jerusalem (Deut. 12,26). But it is pointed out in Deuteronomy that no one need make vows; if, however, such have once been made, they must be kept, or it will be a sin. "When thou vowest a vow to Yahweh, thy God, thou shalt not be slack to pay it, for Yahweh, thy God, will surely require it of thee, and there will (in that case) be sin in thee. But if thou forbear to vow, there will be no sin in thee. That which goeth out of thy lips thou shalt keep and perform according as thou hast vowed unto Yahweh, thy God, as a freewill offering *(nᵉdhābhā)*, that which thou hast spoken with thy mouth" (Deut 23,22-24).

The vow was to be performed exactly as it had been pronounced, for instance if a particular animal was concerned. Malachi curses the deceiver who with a male animal in his herd makes a vow concerning it and then offers a gelded animal in its place (Mal. 1,14). "The deceiver" probably regretted his promise and then excused himself on the principle that a substitute was allowed.

How common the votive offering was in later times may be gathered from Proverbs where we hear how harlots go about saying to men that they have just made a votive offering as a pretext for inviting them home (Prov. 7,14). And it is quite in the spirit of the pedantically prudent Proverbs when it is said that "it is a snare to man if one rashly says Holy and afterwards reconsiders vows" (Prov. 20,25), just as Ecclesiastes earnestly points out that the vows made to God must be fulfilled. "Pay that which thou hast vowed. Better is it that thou shouldest not vow than that thou shouldest vow and not pay" (Eccl. 5,3 f.).

Thus sacrifices filled the life of the Israelite, and not merely on the occasions provided by Nature herself. It shows how largely he was swayed by the world of holiness. By offering sacrifices he entered into communion with the holy sphere, either in order to influence the events emanating from it, or merely to place himself in the right relationship to the power from which he had received the blessing.

In every offering there is something of all the effects produced by the offering; but one or another element may become more or less prominent. In the Old Testament great stress is laid on the point of view that the offering is a *gift* to Yahweh. This is expressed by the word *minḥā*, ¹ a comprehensive term for the offering (Gen. 4,3-5; Judg. 6,18; 1 Sam. 2,17; 26,19 et al.) as also a word connoting the gift in all its forms.

This point of view is natural to the Israelite because nothing strengthens the bond of union between souls so much as the gift, it confirms the covenant and creates honour. And the Israelite knows that the Mighty One of whom he solicits a favour must be honoured by a gift; this applies both to the king and to the God. No one, as the laws have it, must appear before Yahweh empty-handed (Ex. 23,15; 34,20; Deut. 16,16). Even the Philistines realised that they could not send back the Ark to Yahweh without gifts (1 Sam. 6,3). The gift aspect does not conflict with the sanctification aspect, quite the contrary. In being sanctified the offering is given to Yahweh, because sanctity is identical with his nature. The relation is mutual. Of his holy power Yahweh gives corn, wine, and oil to the Israelites; and when they sanctify the first-fruits thereof, they return the gift to Yahweh.

In the sacrificial laws, but also in other texts (Judg. 13,19.23; 1 Sam. 2,29; 3,14; 2 Kings 16,13; Ps. 20,4; 40,7 et al.) *minḥā* became a special term for an offering of agricultural produce, while at the same time it retained its more comprehensive connotation. This was connected with the fact that specific terms were used for the animal sacrifices. But in addition to *minḥā* other terms appeared which expressed the gift aspect, particularly *ḳorbān;* [1] in the sacrificial laws all sacrifices offered to the sanctuary are called *t^erūmā,* which may best be rendered by the word "tribute".

The holy things, *ḳodhāshīm,* found in the temples, did not consist solely of animals or the produce of the fields. We have seen that after the wars part of the spoil was sanctified and handed over to the temples. We hear it about the weapons of Saul and Goliath (1 Sam. 21,10; 31,10) and of the treasures mentioned in the stories of Gideon and David. This sanctification provided a possibility of appropriating what was alien. But in the first place Yahweh was honoured and his holiness strengthened by it.

The Chronicler tells us that King David and his predecessors dedicated the captured spoil in order to maintain the strength of Yahweh's house (1 Chron. 26,27 f., cf. 1 Kings 7,51). We come across the same idea in Haggai, who says that the newly built temple is glorified by the gold which all the peoples of the world shall bring to it. "And I will shake all the nations and the treasures [2] of all the nations shall come, and I will fill this house with glory, saith Yahweh of the hosts. The silver is mine and the gold is mine, saith Yahweh of the hosts" (Hag. 2,7-8). Thus the glory of the new temple shall surpass even that of the first temple, though the latter was surrounded by the glamour of the great associations of the past.

That the precious metals in particular were given to Yahweh accords well with the story recording the capture of Jericho. As we know, this city was placed under a ban, *ḥērem,* and totally destroyed. But the order was given that "all silver and gold, and all objects of copper and iron were to be consecrated to Yahweh and taken to Yahweh's treasury", which was done (Josh. 6,19, cf. 24). This is called *ḳōdhesh.* But in the sequel we are told that Israel was defeated because Achan had appropriated some of the objects that were *ḥērem.* These were a magnificent garment and a large treasure of gold and silver, that is, things which were to be holy (Josh. 7,21).

Ḳōdhesh and *ḥērem,* the greatest contrasts conceivable, are here brought close together, and that indeed is consistent with the very nature of the concepts. What is banned is destroyed for the sake of Yahweh, because it is incompatible with the Israelite soul, but the treasures are given to Yahweh because by his power they can be absorbed in his holiness. If we consider that many of the offerings are consecrated to Yahweh by being destroyed in the fire, we shall understand that two concepts so directly opposed to each other may yet be approached to each other, and indeed become merged.

Though, as late narratives show, the idea of *ḥērem* as the hostile element, that in which the curse resided, was by no means abandoned, it was nevertheless to a certain extent blended with the idea of what was holy, and we find the rule that all that was banned was to fall to the priests (Num. 18,14; Ez. 44,29). The banned thing actually becomes a special kind of holy gift. "All banned things that a man shall ban before Yahweh of all that he hath, both of man and of beast and of the field in his possession must not be sold or redeemed. All that is banned is most sacred to Yahweh" (Lev. 27,28). It is here emphatically stated that the banned things are holy, but it does not appear from the text how, then, they are distinguished from ordinary holy gifts. That banned things have preserved a special character appears from the sequel. "All under a ban, which is banned, of human kind, shall not be redeemed, but shall surely be put to death" (v. 29). Here the old view of *ḥērem* seems quite unaltered. Theorising on old instinctive concepts might lead to curious contrasts.

Of course gifts of other kinds than enemy spoil might be presented to the temple and thus to Yahweh. Costly things were given to the temple which, being sanctified, strengthened its holiness and, together with other gifts, constituted its treasure. Every large temple had its treasure *('ōṣār)*, thus the temple at Shechem (Judg. 9,4); and at Jerusalem Solomon's temple was filled with treasures presented by the kings but removed again when they had to pay tribute to an enemy. [1] When the temple at Jerusalem became the only one, the old-time sanctification of private temples or cult objects belonging to them was discontinued, all holy gifts being given to the great temple. We hear of such an addition to the treasure of the temple in Zechariah's parable, in which the shepherd gives to the temple the 30 shekels of silver he has earned (Zech. 11,13).

The holy gifts were not reduced in course of time, and the temple became an important factor in economic estimates, as may be seen amongst other things from an expression such as a "sanctuary shekel" in use at the post-exilic temple (Ex. 30,13; 5,15 etc.). Landed property, too, might be sanctified, and the temples of Canaan were doubtless, as in other countries, large landed proprietors. The Old Testament has only a few reminiscences hereof where Jerusalem is concerned; partly in the temple plan of Ezekiel, according to which the temple was to own the surrounding land, partly in a law providing for the redemption of holy gifts in which houses and fields also come under consideration (Lev. 27).

The law shows how common it had become to present holy gifts to the temple. But as usual in the Priestly Code, it is not possible to tell with certainty where we are concerned with realities and where with theories only. When the law estimates the exact redemption sum to be paid for male or female persons given to the sanctuary all according to their age (Lev. 27,1-8), it may be concerned with persons actually given to the temple as in the old days; but the estimates may also be merely theoretical, intended to show how this kind of temple gift might be avoided if it were conceivable that it could be given. It is remarkable that the sanctification of unclean animals is taken for granted, for which a certain sum is then to be paid, as for unclean firstlings (vv. 11-13.27). If a man sanctifies a house, the priest is to estimate its value; if then the man wishes to redeem it, he must pay in addition one-fifth part of the sum at which it has been valued (v. 14 f.). Similar considerations apply to the fields, but here a more complicated estimation comes into play, since both the evaluation and the right of disposal are to be in accordance with the law of the year of yōbhel (Lev. 27,16-25).

Through the law relating to the redemption of holy gifts by payment of a sum of money the Israelites have carried the gift aspect of the sacrifice so far that there is not much left of the original idea of sanctification. The view according to which the giver sanctifies some possession of his and by it himself, has almost entirely disappeared, and the holy gift has become a mere tribute. This is the same development which we found for the first-fruits and the first-born, and it is a matter of course that it must be even more prominent where the holy gifts proper are concerned. But the law implies that it was a common custom to dedicate property of all kinds to the temple, as was the case among many other peoples, and as was still customary in the East when the sanctuaries had become mosques.

The central point in the sacrifice is the sanctification of the offering, the surrendering of it to the god. But it is not a matter of indifference what is next done with it, it may even be of prime importance for the effect of the sacrifice.

In early Israel the most important offering was probably that in which an animal was sacrificed and a *meal* was then made of its flesh in the holy place. We know the great significance of the meal among the early Israelites. Nothing was so well suited to unite souls and strengthen the covenant as a meal which gathered relatives and friends around the common food in a communal spirit. The meal of such a fellowship confirmed and strengthened the peace, the harmony on which all joint life was dependent.

How much deeper then must the effects go when the common meal was taken in the holy place. Everything was holy. The participants had sanctified themselves to be able to set foot in the holy place and take part in the holy rites. The slaughtered animal had been sanctified through the sacrifice, and naturally the God was present in all this holiness; for where holiness was, God was. The participants in the meal were his guests, his holy invited guests (Zeph. 1,7); for they were in his house. And since part of the animal was wholly given up to him and withdrawn from the approach of man, God and man were partakers of the meal in common; they formed a firm association where peace was recreated and strengthened.

It is not to be wondered at, therefore, that such offerings became peculiarly covenant offerings. The covenant with the God became their chief characteristic. This is doubtless implied in the designation *zēbhaḥ sheelāmīm*, which connotes the animal sacrifice with which a meal is associated; we note the relationship with *shālōm*, [1] the term for peace.

We do not possess such detailed information of the earlier time that we can form any reliable idea of these sacrificial meals. We hear of the Canaanites of Shechem that they "entered the temple of their God and eat and drank" (Judg. 9,27). And the Philistines gathered in the temple of their god for a great slaughtering in his honour and "to rejoice" (Judg. 16,23), and part of their rejoicing was that their prisoner Samson was brought in to entertain them.

We may imagine that the Israelites, too, gave themselves up to rejoicing and fully enjoyed what the meal offered. They were not content with the flesh of the animal; bread and wine were also included (cf. 1 Sam. 1,24; 10,3). We have noted that tithes of corn, wine, and oil, might likewise afford an opportunity for a meal in the holy place (Deut. 12). We gather from the story of Hannah that the priest did not regard it as anything unusual for the worshippers to become intoxicated with the wine served at the sacrificial meal (1 Sam. 1,13 f.).

Those who were to partake of the sacrificial meal sanctified themselves (1 Sam. 16,5). The blood of the animal was given to the stone or the altar; the soul was present in the blood in a special degree, hence the soul of the animal was given to the holiest part of the holy place itself. Not only was this a means by which the animal was sanctified, but it was also returned to the forces from which it had emanated. That the animal was treated thus may be gathered from the later laws for the shelamim sacrifice (Lev. 3; 7,11 ff.) and from a few other allusions (Ex. 24,6; 1 Sam. 14,34). According to the sacrificial laws other parts too were given to the God, such as the fat of the entrails and the kidneys, and this also was due to old custom (1 Sam. 2,15 f.). The fat was put on the altar and burnt (ibd.).

It depended on the character of the offering what kind of

people partook of the meal. At the old Israelite sacrificial meal at the Passover it was the family, and the entire ceremony was conducted by the head of the house. This also was the case on other occasions. Elkanah sacrificed at Shiloh every year and then took a meal with his family, evidently in some part of the sanctuary (1 Sam. 1,4 ff.). Even in the temple of Solomon meals must probably have been taken by families in the monarchical period, or at least by small groups, in the special chambers designed for that purpose. From Deuteronomy we learn that the sacrifice of the first-born might be connected with a meal (Deut. 12,17; 15,20), and consequently it must have been consumed by families.

Sacrificial meals were also celebrated at which the men of the town gathered in the temple. David excused his absence from Saul's new-moon-meal by the fact that his whole kin on that day offered their regular sacrifice in his native town of Bethlehem (1 Sam. 20,6). "The whole kin" here perhaps means the family ruling in Bethlehem *(mishpāḥā)*.

We hear also of the leading townsmen at Ramah partaking of a sacrificial meal. Saul came here when looking for the asses just as the meal was going to begin, and Samuel invited him and his servant to partake of it. There were about thirty people; they gathered in the hall *(lishkā)* of the sanctuary under the leadership of the seer, who blessed the sacrifice before the meal began (1 Sam. 9). It is a peculiar feature that Samuel, the great seer, should act as the leader of the sacrificial meal in other cities than his own. [1]

In the old days it was the father of the family or, at the city offering, the head of the ruling house, who officiated at the whole of the sacrificial ceremony. It is uncertain what part the priest played when the animal victim was offered at the old minor sanctuaries. Doubtless he assisted the sacrificer in some way, especially at the burning on the altar, and he received his share of the sacrificial meal. The latter fact we gather from the story of Eli's sons, the priests at the temple of Shiloh, who were not content to take their lawful share, but took what they wanted for themselves of their own accord.

For we are told about the sons of Eli that they did not acknowledge Yahweh, nor the customary relation of the priests to the people. When a man offered sacrifice, the priest's slave came while the meat was being boiled, put a three-pronged fork into the pot or pan or whatever vessel was used, and whatever he got hold of in this way was appropriated by Eli's sons. It might also happen that the priests' slave came before the fat had been burnt, that is, before the sanctification had taken place, demanding the raw meat for roasting instead of waiting for the boiled meat to be allotted to them. But he was answered that first the fat must be consumed by the fire and turn to smoke, then they could have whatever they liked. This obliging offer, however, was refused with threats (1 Sam. 2,12 ff.).

From this story we may learn that the prist had a customary right to a share of the sacrificial meat as soon as it had been prepared. The inference is that the original right of the priest is that of being a participator in the meal of the worshippers, as is only natural if he gives his assistance in some way at the sacrificial rites. That this was in fact the case may be gathered from Deuteronomy (Deut. 12,12.18 f.).

The charge brought against Eli's sons in the first case is that they appropriate their share of the meat as something separate; this has the character of robbery, for they simply take the law into their own hands. But they go still further in the second case. Here they demand the meat in the raw state, that is, before it has undergone any kind of preparation. This is not far from being sacrilege, for Yahweh had not yet received his share of the offering; though on the other hand the priests did not go so far as to take anything that belonged to the God. It appears from the story that the meat was generally boiled at the sacrifices, which agrees with other information we possess from early times (Judg. 6,19). Eli's sons, however, wanted to have their share roasted and this further removed them from the fellowship with the worshippers, their participation being confined to receiving a tribute consisting of a share of the sacrificial meat.

The indignation expressed in our story is of great interest. Eli's sons showed contempt for the sacrificial gift to Yahweh and incurred great guilt, and indeed these sinners came to an evil end. This shows that the story really dates from the old time. For the demands of Eli's sons point in the very direction which the development gradually took at the temple of Jerusalem. In the laws of the Priestly Code relating to sacrifices at the post-exilic temple the common meal of the worshipping family has receded far into the background, even though there were still chambers along the walls of the outer court where the lay population, as the worshipping people gradually came to be, could take their sacrificial meal. But large parts of the sacrifices could only be consumed by the priests, because they alone possessed holiness enough to do so, and of the animal bodies in the ordinary sacrifices great shares had to be given to them as a tribute which was their due. This is indeed mentioned in the Deuteronomic laws (Deut. 18,3, cf. Lev. 6 f.).

The sacrifice of an animal victim with the meal appertaining thereto is often merely called *zēbhaḥ* (Lev. 23,37; 1 Sam. 1,21; 6,15; 20,6; 1 Kings 12,27; Hos. 3,4; 6,6; Am. 4,4; 5,25 etc.), a term in which the main stress is laid on the killing of the animal. In reality it may indeed be said that the two concepts "killing" and "sacrifice" were very closely connected in the old days. If the Israelites wanted to celebrate a festival with a great meal of oxen or sheep, it often took the form of a sacrificial feast as when Adonijah invited his brothers and the Judaean courtiers to such a meal at the Rogel spring by the *zōḥeleth* stone, which must undoubtedly be regarded as a holy stone (1 Kings 1,9). This is quite natural. If cattle were to be killed, the Israelite shrank from taking the animal's whole soul, but took care that it was returned to its origin as far as possible; the blood at any rate must be handled with caution and must not be consumed by man.

Hence we find in the Old Testament a plainly expressed fear of making unlimited inroads on the herds and flocks. We have the most vivid illustration of this fear in the story describing the conduct of the Israelitish army after the battle of Michmash. It runs as follows: And the people flew upon the spoil and took sheep, oxen, and calves and slew them on the ground, and the people eat over the blood. Then they told Saul: Behold, the people sin against Yahweh by eating over the blood. And he said: Ye do wrong, roll a great stone up to me at once. And Saul said: Disperse among the people and say to them: Bring hither to me every man his ox and his lamb and slaughter it here, and then eat. But sin not against Yahweh by eating over [1] the blood. And all the people brought every one his ox [2] thither by his hand that night and slaughtered it there. And Saul built an altar unto Yahweh; it was the first altar he built unto Yahweh (1 Sam. 14,32-35).

The sin of the people consists in letting the blood run out on to the ground where they will eat their meal. Food and blood are not kept apart, the blood is treated like water. This must not happen, and Saul takes care that the blood shall run over a stone and be absorbed. This entirely removes it from the body of the animal which can then be consumed elsewhere. But afterwards Saul consecrates the place where such a great slaughtering has taken place, and builds an altar there.

The story has been interpreted to mean that the large stone rolled up to Saul was a holy stone, and on this assumption it has been asserted that in early Israel every slaughtering was a sacrifice. If this contention means that the early Israelites were only allowed to slaughter an animal at a sanctuary, it cannot be maintained. When Abraham received guests, he went out and fetched a calf and bid his slave hastily prepare it (Gen. 18,7), and it is not said that he had been at the sanctuary with it, any more than in the narrative of Jacob and Rebecca who prepare two kids for Isaac (Gen. 27,9). It might be conjectured that these were traits dating from a later time, but the books of Samuel, too, show that animals might be slaughtered at home, and that it was not necessary to take them to the sanctuary. When a guest arrived the fatted calf was hastily killed or perhaps a lamb or a kid (1 Sam. 28,24; 2 Sam. 12,4). When Elisha left his work in the field to follow Elijah, he caused the oxen before his plough to be killed on the spot and had the flesh boiled and distributed among the people (1 Kings 19,21).

Nor is there in the story about Saul and his warriors any indication that the stone on which the cattle was killed was holy.

22*

The altar was built afterwards. But the story plainly shows that the killing of cattle in early Israel had to preserve something of the character of the sacrifice. Even if the blood were not shed over the stone or the altar of the sanctuary, it was necessary to treat it with caution, it could not merely be poured out on the ground.

When the Israelites were limited to one recognised sanctuary, the old common meals at the holy places were bound to be discontinued. Deuteronomy prohibits them, they may only take place on the spot chosen by Yahweh at Jerusalem. To make up for it, it is emphasised that the Israelites may slaughter as many animals as they like in the cities, taking care only to drain off the blood entirely, so that they do not partake of it. Deuteronomy is so preoccupied with the purely negative aspect of forbidding sacrifices outside Jerusalem that it expressly enjoins the pouring of the blood upon the ground like water (Deut. 12,16.24). There is in this expression a profanation of the slaughtering which is not in the old spirit, and a sharp line is drawn between sacrifice and slaughter. The difference between the two things is of old standing, the new feature is the sharp distinction made between them. And the command meant that the sanctification of animals by sacrifice was growing rarer, it was then bound to lose its immediate connection with life.

The negative feature that men must not consume the blood was preserved, if anything with increasing care. Yahweh's share of the sacrifices must nót under any circumstances be appropriated by men; hence the command also applies to the fat. In the sacrificial laws of the Priestly Code this very motive is given for the interdiction. "Whoso eateth the fat of the beast of which an offering is made to Yahweh — the soul that eateth it shall be cut off from his people" (Lev. 7,25) and whoever consumes any blood of beast or bird shall suffer the same fate (v. 26 f.). As will be seen, the rule relating to the blood is somewhat stricter than that relating to the fat. This was because the blood had gradually acquired an independent significance in sacrifice. The whole matter concerns human beings only. The fat of animals that have died from disease or have been torn to pieces — which cannot be sacrificed — must not be eaten by human beings, though it may be used for other purposes (Lev. 7,24).

So important was the law forbidding the consumption of blood by men that in conjunction with the interdiction against the shedding of human blood it was referred back to the time when order was restored after the chaos of the deluge, the time when God made his covenant with Noah (Gen. 9,3 f.), whereas Israelite law in general is assigned to the wilderness period and Moses. Blood had become a thing apart, the law concerning it came before all other laws.

In the law of holiness, the remarkable collection of statutes in which purely abstract commands are found side by side with early Israelite rules, we find again the stern law that whoever consumes blood shall be cut off; and the blood of game is to be carefully covered up with earth (Lev. 17,13), that is to say, it is not to be treated like water. But as far as the animals are concerned, this law does not recognise that they can be killed anywhere outside the one true sanctuary. Whoever does anything of the kind shall be cut off from his people (Lev. 17,1 ff.). This law is evidently derived from circles who did not acknowledge the profanation of slaughtering. They wished to restore the old conditions and thought they could best do so by applying the principle, purely in the abstract, that slaughtering must only take place at the sanctuary. This might perhaps be possible if one imagined the whole people to be gathered in one camp, round one sanctuary, as was the case in the ideal Mosaic time with which the theorists occupied themselves. It meant little to them that the law could not be enforced when the people was scattered all over the country and at the same time had only one sanctuary. The law shows how much the contact with early times, which were concerned with realities, had weakened, a parallel to what we have seen in the social laws.

In early times there can hardly have been any rule prescribing when a meal was to be combined with the sacrifice. It was the remains of the offerings which were consumed. Just as the animal was sanctified by pouring out the blood, so also the wine was sanctified by part of it being poured on the altar. This libation is called *nesekh*. The wine libation constitutes an essential part of the normal offerings side by side with the blood and the bread. When Hosea prophesies that the Israelitish order of the world shall perish when the people is transported to Assur, he expresses it in the words that the Israelites shall no longer offer wine before Yahweh, nor sacrifices; their bread shall be unclean as the bread of mourners, so that it cannot be brought into the house of Yahweh (Hos. 9,4). And Amos complains that people sit at the altars, that is, in the holy places, on clothes laid to pledge, and drink wine, unlawfully acquired, in the house of the God (Am. 2,8).

It is no doubt by chance that we do not hear of a separate wine libation, unconnected with a meal. On the other hand, we hear on some few occasions about libations of water. It is not to be wondered at that water must also be included within the holy sphere of the temple. The fertility of the country depended on this element, it was the means by which the blessing worked. We have seen, as well, that water was still present in Solomon's temple where the sea was represented by a huge cauldron. Like the Egyptian and the Babylonian, the Israelite, too, could sanctify water by pouring it out in the holy place, and thus produce the effects of an offering. We hear in a narrative which bears the mark of a late date that Samuel gathered the Israelites at Mizpeh where they drew water and poured it out before Yahweh, doing penance for their previous worship of idols (1 Sam. 7,6). And we are told about David that three of his warriors, upon a wish lightly expressed by him, brought him water from the well of his native town Bethlehem, which was in the possession of the Philistines. But David shrank from taking water which had been obtained at such great peril. It could only have been procured by Yahweh's special blessing, and so it must belong to him, hence David offered it as a libation to Yahweh (2 Sam. 23,16).

We have no information as to a regular offering of water any more than a regular, separate, offering of wine, but undoubtedly such a libation must have taken place; and from post-exilic times we have evidence of the importance of libations *(nesekh)* besides offerings of the produce of the field *(minḥā,* Joel 1,13; 2,14). As in the offering of the first-fruits here also the basic idea of the sacrifice had so much vitality that it constantly put forth fresh shoots. At the feast of the tabernacles, in post-exilic times, a libation of water from the spring of Siloa was offered every day; it was mixed with wine and poured out before the altar. [1] This sanctification of water just before the rainy season is doubtless old, even though it is only attested in the older part of the Talmud.

Olive oil belonged to those gifts of nature of which the first-fruits were offered, but the oil was also offered as a libation by itself *(nesekh).* "Is Yahweh pleased with thousands of rams, with ten thousands of rivers of oil?" says one of the prophets (Mic. 6,7) and thus attests the importance of the oil libation. Like the other fluid sacrificial gifts the oil was poured over the holy stone, as shown by the story of Jacob at Bethel (Gen. 28,18; 35,14); and it must be supposed to have been poured out in the same way at the altar. Oil, like blood, acquired independent importance as a holy element, and it was used to consecrate persons, such as kings (Judg. 9,8; 1 Sam. 16,3.12 f.; 1 Kings 1,34.39 et al.), prophets (1 Kings 19,16; Isa. 61,1), or priests (Ex. 28,41; 29,7.29.36; 30,30 et al.), and likewise to sanctify implements of various kinds. The custom of anointment *(māshaḥ),* however, did not arise on Israelitish soil. The Israelites adopted it independently of their oil libations as a common eastern custom current among the Egyptians as well as the Babylonians, and also recognised in early Canaan (Judg. 9,8). Anointment as an initiation rite probably originates from the fact that inunction was part of the general care of the body, and it acquired a sanctifying character by being done with consecrated oil. Therefore the olive-tree in the fable of Jotham could speak about itself as that "with which one honours men and gods", just as the wine from the vine is that "wich pleases gods and men", who, as we know, all have their share of it (Judg. 9,9.13).

In all these sacrifices the offering to the God caused no difficulty. The stone or the altar absorbed the fluid sacrificial gift which, indeed, left traces, but which no man could take back again. This also was the case with the animal victim, but when it came to the kidneys and the fat, the withdrawal from the ordinary world must be effected in another way, and this occurred through burning, as when the spoil of the enemy was given to be ḥērem. It is mentioned not only in the sacrificial law for the shᵉlāmīm offering (Lev. 3,5.11.16), but also in the story of Eli's sons (1 Sam. 2,16).

The sacrificial laws speak of a special kind of offering, the sin-offering, in which the flesh of the animal is to be burnt outside the camp (Lev. 4,12). It has been conjectured that we have here a reminiscence of an earlier form of fire-offering. [1] In reality it would be quite conceivable that it was an ancient procedure to sanctify the animal by offering the blood and then destroying the rest of the carcase by fire, instead of eating the flesh. But the conjecture does not hold good for this sacrifice, since the usual parts of the entrails, the fat and the kidneys, are to be burnt on the altar (Lev. 4,8-10), the ritual of the sacrifice thus presupposing burning on the altar in any case. Altogether it is impossible to put the question whether the fire-offering developed from or after the meal-offering as one concerning the Hebrews only; for here both offerings are found side by side from the earliest times, just as they were among the Phoenicians. [2]

When the offering was burnt, it was normally done in the sanctuary on the altar itself. This largely affects the entire character of the sacrificial ritual. The altar cannot be a single stone, but must be built with a large surface or must be a large rock. When the whole animal is burnt on the altar, the burning becomes part of the ritual and will easily become the most important factor, because it forms the greater part of the ceremony.

A couple of the old cult legends of the book of Judges mention such offerings as are generally called *burnt-offerings*. When Yahweh visited Gideon in the shape of a man, perhaps a man of God, the latter set before him a meal of goat's meat, broth, and unleavened bread. The stranger bade him lay the meat and the bread on the rock and pour the broth over it. When this was done, Yahweh touched it with his staff, fire came out of the rock and consumed it, and Yahweh disappeared. Then Gideon understood what had happened (Judg. 6,11-24). He built another altar and burnt a bull on it for a burnt-offering.

In the narrative where Gideon meets with Yahweh at the sacrifice everything centres round the fire. Nothing is said about the blood of the kid being poured out in the holy place, but this is due to the nature of the story. Gideon does not know that he is preparing a sacrifice, he thinks that he is preparing an ordinary meal. But this interplay between an offering and a meal is only possible because the offering is regarded as a meal which is given to the God, and which he consumes by the sacrificial fire.

We encounter the same point of view in the narrative of Manoah and his wife. They, too, received a visit, from the angel of Yahweh, who promised them a son, and they set about preparing a kid for him. He asked them to offer a burnt-offering instead, and so Manoah brought the kid and the flour with it and offered it on the rock. "And it came to pass that when the flame went up from the altar towards heaven, Yahweh's *mal'ākh* ascended in the flame of the altar" (Judg. 13,20). The man and his wife fell to the ground in terror, when they discovered that it was the God they had seen. But the woman was reassured by the fact that Yahweh had accepted their offering and thus shown that he was well pleased with it.

When, later, part of the animal is also burnt on the altar at the meal-offering, the difference between the two ceremonies at the altar will merely be whether more or less is to be burnt, that is to say, whether Yahweh is to have all. But in both ceremonies the fire is of great importance. The ritual has begun to be complicated. The shedding of the blood cannot fail, but the fire may waver or burn clearly, it is a divine flame and according as it rises towards heaven or not, it is seen whether or not the sacrifice is a success, whether Yahweh accepts it.

The smoke of the sacrifice is noticed even more than the fire. "To turn into smoke" (*kiṭṭēr* and *hiḳṭir*) becomes the actual designation for sacrificing (1 Sam. 2,16; 2 Kings 18,4; 22,17;

23,5; Jer. 1,16; 7,9; Hos. 11,2; Am. 4,5, etc. and Lev. 2,2.9.11.16; 6,8; 2 Kings 16,13.15 etc.), just as *ḳᵉṭōreth* "smoke" becomes the term for the essential aspect of the sacrifice (1 Sam. 2,28; Isa. 1,13; Ps. 66,15). The smoke is the God's share, the form in which he receives his sacrifice, he smells it as a "sweet savour" *(rēᵃḥ nīḥōᵃḥ,* Gen. 8,21; Ex. 29,18; Lev. 6,8; 23,13.18 etc.).

The priestly laws of sacrifice have a special term for offerings that are burnt, viz. *ishshe.* [1] For the burnt-offerings there are two terms, *'ōlā* and *kālil* (1 Sam. 7,9: *'ōlā kālil).* The latter term, "holocaust", denoted that the offering was entirely given up to the altar; the former, "what ascends", has been explained either as that which is put on to the altar, or as that which ascends in the smoke. Both interpretations are possible, though the last-mentioned is perhaps the more probable (cf. 1 Kings 18,29.36; 2 Kings 3,20).

As previously indicated, meal-offerings and holocausts occur simultaneously already in the earlier days of Israel, [2] as is only natural since both kinds of sacrifices were doubtless in use among the Canaanites. It has been suggested that the holocaust developed from the human sacrifice, in which a meal was excluded; [3] but it is not necessary to seek such a specific origin. The consumption of the offering by fire was natural when elements were offered which were not like the blood and the fluid matter quite simply absorbed, and thus disappeared in the holy place; and it was necessary when offerings became so abundant that it was out of the power of the worshippers to consume the meat of the victims on the spot.

Hence the increase in the use of burnt-offerings is connected with a growing desire to augment the number of sacrifices. In this way special aspects of the sacrifice are accentuated, and new elements come into the forefront. A gift being given to the God by the sacrifice, an attempt is made to assure and enhance the effect of the sacrifice by increasing the gift. The more insecure life became owing to the political conditions of the 8th century, the more important it became to make every effort to retain the divine goodwill which was a prerequisite of peace and blessedness. With the external insecurity the internal uncertainty grew. No man could ever be sure that his gifts had been large enough; as the prophet says: Wherewith shall I come before Yahweh, bow myself before the God on high? Shall I come before him with burnt-offerings, with calves of a year old? Will Yahweh be pleased with thousands of rams, with ten thousands of rivers of oil? Shall I give my first-born for my transgression, the fruit of my body for the sin of my soul? (Mic. 6,6-7). The prophet has his own reply to this question, but what is of interest to us here is the question itself, for no doubt it expresses a general feeling among the people.

It is this feeling that explains the immense increase in the infant sacrifices. The importance of the gift is measured not only by its quantity but also by its quality. From olden times it was a matter of course that the animal victims were to be without blemish, for only a normal animal was a completely valid representative of its species; but to this was added the consideration that the normal animal was more valuable. And even though an animal victim might represent the first-born son, it was self-evident that the human child was more valuable. And if a valuable gift were to be offered to the God, what then could compare with one's children? This is the line of thought that is expressed in the above-quoted utterance of the prophet. And it was not a specifically Israelite idea, in virtue of it King Mesha of Moab sacrificed his first-born son for a burnt-offering when the Israelites were besieging his city and pressed him hard; and the result was at once manifested in the flight of the Israelites (2 Kings 3,27).

We have seen that there were three parties to whom the sacrifice was of great and positive importance: the God, the worshipper, and the element furnishing the offering. In the view-points here described the last-mentioned factor recedes into the background except as a means to an end. The sanctification of the world of Nature, as represented in the offering, vanishes from memory, the offering becomes merely an instrument by which the relation between the two other parties, the God and man, is strengthened.

The power of the sacrifice to create harmony between God and man made it natural and necessary to offer sacrifices on many occasions important to the worshipper. If he entered into some new relationship or was confronted with great events, the covenant with God required to be strengthened, and this might be done through sacrifice.

As we have seen from the free-will offerings and the votive offerings, affairs of a private nature might be involved. When Hannah gave her son Samuel to the temple at Shiloh in accordance with her vow, she consecrated him to his new position by offering a bull, [1], some flour, and some wine (1 Sam. 1,24). When unclean persons were purified, they had to sacrifice in order to prepare for their new lives in the normal state.

But sacrifices were especially necessary when the community was faced by new events and conditions. The choice of a king was confirmed in the sanctuary by sacrifices (1 Sam. 11,15), and sacrifice was one of the most urgent necessities in the preparation for war. This was the case both under the rule of chiefs and kings (Judg. 20,26; 21,4; 1 Sam. 7,9; 10,8; 13,8 ff.; Ps. 20). In the hymn to the king who is preparing for war one passage runs thus: May he (Yahweh) remember all thy offerings! (Ps. 20,4). Then comes the sudden cry: Now know I that Yahweh will save his anointed. — Victory is created by the sacrifice. When it has been normally offered, and Yahweh has accepted it, the covenant is assured and Yahweh's power is with the king.

A city was founded by sacrifice, even by human sacrifice. When Hiel rebuilt Jericho in the days of Ahab, he laid its foundation in Abiram, his first-born, and set up its gates in Segib, his youngest son (1 Kings 16,34). Thus he had to consecrate his work both at the beginning and at the end, by offering one of his sons. Excavations have shown that human foundation sacrifices were a Canaanite custom. [2] When Nehemiah had rebuilt the wall of Jerusalem, its future was secured by great offerings (Neh. 12,43).

It follows that a temple must be consecrated by offerings, as we are told of Solomon's temple (1 Kings 8,62 ff.). But the reception of a treasure such as the Ark must also take place with great offerings in order that it might be received in harmony and produce blessedness. When the Ark came from the Philistines to Bethshemesh, it was received with burnt-offerings and sacrifice, and when it was taken to Zion, sacrifices were offered after six steps (1 Sam. 6,15; 2 Sam 6,13.17).

Everything which brought the people into some new condition required sacrifices, because the covenant with the God must always be secured if the blessing were to be retained. Sacrifices were necessary to strengthen every covenant, both between men (Gen. 31,54) and between the people and its God (Gen. 8,20; Ex. 24,4 ff.); for God always had to be included in the covenant.

As soon as the offering had been detached from its immediate connection with the world of nature and acquired its own independent importance as confirmer of the covenant between God and man, there was no end to the ways in which it could be used. If it was necessary for the normal maintenance of existence, it must also be offered constantly. For that very reason a certain daily regularity of sacrifice might arise at the larger sanctuaries.

We do not know when regular daily sacrifices were introduced. In the story about Elijah's contest with the prophets on Mount Carmel, the time is given as "the hour when the offering *(hamminḥā)* ascends" (1 Kings 18,29.36), which means some time after noon. In a story about Elisha we read "in the morning, when the *minḥā* ascends" (2 Kings 3,20). According to these statements there should in the 9th century have been a fixed offering in the morning and one in the afternoon. But whether it was the custom at several sanctuaries and if so at which, we are not told.

The regular daily offerings quite naturally took their rise at the royal sanctuaries. The king was able to furnish the numerous sacrifices, and it was only reasonable that he should use his power to establish a regular and grand sacrificial cult, since everything depended on his constant perpetuation of the covenant with God. The increase of the offerings meant that they were more and more given over to the charge of the priesthood.

At the old sanctuaries the offering of the sacrifices was chiefly the duty of the heads of the families and the chiefs. When David had become king, he offered his sacrifices himself, both in the sanctuary where the Ark was placed (2 Sam. 6,17) and on the holy stone with which Solomon's temple was later associated (24,25). Solomon sacrificed at Gibeon himself (1 Kings 3,4), and officiated at the numerous sacrifices offered at the inauguration of the temple at which he, indeed, took the lead entirely, though he must have had assistants (1 Kings 8,62). But he sacrificed in company with "all Israel". This must mean that countless families must have offered their sacrifices in the temple court at the same time, so that the scene has somewhat resembled that of Arabs gathering under their chief in a place of sacrifice.

We are told that three times a year Solomon offered burnt-offerings and peace-offerings on the altar (1 Kings 9,25). This must indicate that he himself conducted the three feast-offerings associated with the seasons of harvest; but we possess no information as to what other kinds of sacrifices were offered in the days of Solomon. Jeroboam sacrificed at Bethel and conducted the autumn feast, just as he took charge of the cult at the sanctuaries in the Northern Kingdom (1 Kings 12,25 ff.). Jehu even summoned men to a sacrificial feast for Baal, and when the priests and prophets had gathered with the rest of the congregation, he offered a burnt-offering, as people were evidently accustomed to see the king do (2 Kings 10,18 ff.).

Thus we see the king as the person officiating at the sacrifices in the temples of his kingdom, but of the introduction of a regular daily sacrifice we have no other information from the earlier time than that found in the two above-mentioned stories of the prophets. We possess fresh, positive information about Ahaz in the last half of the 8th century.

Ahaz sent his priest Uriah a model of an Assyrian altar from Damascus. When Ahaz returned, the altar had been built; he ascended it and offered a burnt-offering and a flour-offering with a libation, and he sprinkled the blood of the victims on the altar (2 Kings 16,12 f.). The sacrifices seem to have been inauguration sacrifices; the altar could not be used until the king came home. The story goes on to say: And King Ahaz commanded him (i. e. Uriah, the priest) saying: On the large altar thou shalt let the

morning burnt-offering, and the evening *minḥā*, and the king's
burnt-offering, and his *minḥā*, and the burnt-offering of all the
people of the land, and their *minḥā*, and their libations, ascend
in smoke; and all the blood of the burnt-offering and of the
sacrifice shalt thou sprinkle on it! (2 Kings 16,15).

These records show us another stage in the development of the
sacrificial cult in Jerusalem, the stage which it had reached
shortly before the year 700. On special and important occasions
the king offers sacrifice himself, but the ordinary sacrificial
service is performed by his assistant, the officiating priest. An
extensive regular, daily, sacrificial system has been established.
We hear once more about the two daily sacrifices, a burnt-offering
in the morning, and in the evening a *minḥā*, which must presumably mean an offering of agricultural produce. But to this is added
a special burnt-offering and *minḥā* for the king and the same
for the people, with accompanying libations.

We see that the morning and afternoon sacrifices were so
firmly established by tradition that they entered into the regular
sacrificial service without argument. Hence it was necessary to
offer special sacrifices for the king. The most natural explanation
is that the reference is to daily offerings partly for the king,
partly for the people. It is indeed strange that the two things are
kept apart, for the king's peace was the people's peace. It would
mean that the two parties had not, after all, become entirely
merged; that would accord with tradition, for we have seen that
Solomon sacrificed *in company with* the people. But the people's
offering more probably means the many private sacrifices offered
by people throughout the year; and as regards the sacrifices for
the king it must be left open whether they were daily offerings or
special feast-offerings. That daily offerings were made for the
king may, however, be inferred with certainty from Ezekiel. Thus
we hear from Ahaz about a daily morning and evening sacrifice,
and probably about a daily double sacrifice for the king, besides
what is sacrificed by the people.

The system of which Ahaz' words inform us formed the
nucleus in the great sacrificial cult which developed at the temple
of Jerusalem in the monarchical period, under the leadership of an

increasingly strong priesthood. It forms the background of the plans sketched by Ezekiel. Here it is expressly stated that the people is to give a certain part of its income to the prince, $\frac{1}{60}$ part of wheat and barley, $\frac{1}{100}$ part of oil, and $\frac{1}{200}$ part of the lambs of the flock, out of which tribute the king is to discharge the regular offerings (Ez. 45, 13-17). It is probably merely on account of the incompleteness of the plan that wine and cattle are not mentioned. This must also be the reason why no daily offering is referred to other than that of the prince: a lamb for a burnt-offering every morning with an offering of agricultural produce and oil (Ez. 46,13-15). On the sabbath and at the new moon it is considerably increased, and in addition the prince offers various feast offerings and free-will offerings (v. 1 ff.). We possess plenty of evidence that the daily afternoon sacrifice was, indeed, preserved in post-exilic times.

The sacrifice of the prince was, according to Ezekiel, to be offered by the priest, in harmony with the prophet's entire conception of holiness. But the prince was to participate in the great special offerings which he made, by standing in the gate of the inner court and prostrating himself over the threshold towards the altar, while the people stood outside (vv. 2 f. 12).

The grand regular system of sacrifice gradually created by the Judaean kings at Jerusalem developed into an institution which had its own independent value. It was effective by its regularity and the close observance of the traditional procedure. In the interplay between the three parties to the sacrifice: the God, the worshipper, and the offering, the second party too receded into the background; for as to the result of the ordinary sacrifices, it mattered not who offered them, as long as the prescribed number of animals and amount of produce were sacrificed in the proper way and by the proper cult staff.

This view of the sacrifice lies behind the claims put forward by Ezekiel, but it comes out with the greatest clearness in the descriptions of the return of the Jews from the exile. According to these, the Jews held written promises, both from Cyrus and Artaxerxes, of support from the royal exchequer to procure the wherewithal for the sacrifices (Ezr. 6,9; 7,15 ff.; 8,25).

Of course this help did not suffice, the sacrifices had to be kept up by the Jews themselves. Instead of giving the taxes to the king who then took charge of the sacrifices, they were paid directly to the temple itself. Nehemiah succeeded in making the regenerated community of Jerusalem pledge themselves to pay each $\frac{1}{3}$ of a shekel for the maintenance of the temple service (Neh. 10,33); it was the institution and its whole apparatus which it was desired to keep up. In the Priestly Code the tribute is augmented to $\frac{1}{2}$ of a shekel, which every Israelite must give "to redeem his life" (Ex. 30,11-16), i. e. to acquire the right to live as an Israelite. This shows that the sacrificial service formed the background of all Israelite life.

Gradually the temple acquired means for the maintenance of the sacrifices from the numerous foundations by which holy gifts were presented to the temple (Lev. 27), and during the first period especially the establishment of the sacrificial service was rendered possible by voluntary gifts from the people. These conditions are reflected in the stories of the Pentateuch relating how the service at the Tabernacle was made possible by free gifts from the Israelites, presented either by private individuals or by tribes (Num. 7, cf. Ex. 35,29; 36,3 and 2 Chron. 31,6 ff.).

The fact that the king has entirely disappeared from the priestly sacrificial laws collected in Leviticus and Numbers affords the strongest evidence that these laws reproduce the practice at the temple of Jerusalem in post-exilic times. In the laws of Ezekiel it was still necessary to consider the king, and there was a careful attempt to place him outside the holy hierarchy of the temple. In the Priestly Code he had been entirely forgotten. And yet it was he who had created the whole tradition on which the post-exilic practice was based, and which it further developed.

The regular daily sacrifices were continued. We have seen that Ezekiel mentions the offering of a burnt-offering, a flour offering, and an oil offering every morning on behalf of the prince (Ez. 46,13-15), but that tradition further prescribed a burnt-offering in the morning and a *minḥā* in the afternoon. Immediately after the return, *'ōlath tāmīdh*, "the continual burnt-offering", was reintroduced (Ezr. 3,5), and in the agreement about the restitution of the cult to which Nehemiah made the returned exiles consent "the continual flour-offering, and the continual burnt-offering" *(minḥath hat-tāmīdh, 'ōlath hat-tāmīdh*, Neh. 10,34) are mentioned. In the Priestly Code the daily sacrifice, the *tāmīdh*-sacrifice, is performed twice, viz. in the morning and "between the two evenings", that is, at sunset; and on both occasions it consists partly of a lamb sacrificed as a burnt-offering, partly of a certain measure of wheaten flour, oil, and wine (Ex. 29,38 ff.; Num. 28,3 ff.).

In the time of Ahaz, as we have seen, a burnt-offering in the morning and a *minḥā* in the evening were a daily feature, and to these were added the burnt-offering and *minḥā* of the king, which may also have been daily events. This, then, is in reality the same number of daily sacrifices as were prescribed in the Priestly Code. Even though the earlier writings speak of a separate *minḥā* not mentioned in the post-exilic laws, the tradition of the monarchical period may nevertheless in the main be said to be continued after the exile, only that one set of offerings were no longer royal offerings, since the king had disappeared. But at the same time the post-exilic practice introduced a new daily sacrifice, viz. a flour-offering to be offered every morning and evening on behalf of the high priest (Lev. 6,12-16). [1] In the ritual of the Day of Atonement the latter likewise succeeds the king in his relationship to the people.

The various kinds of sacrifices mentioned in the post-exilic laws are the same which we know from the monarchical period, and the conception of them developed along the lines laid down at the royal temple. The bond with Nature had been severed, sacrifice had become a self-contained artificial institution. The offerings could no longer be regarded as living representatives of the world of nature with which the Israelites had made a covenant, they had become "sacrificial material".

The prevalent view of the relation between the worshipper and the offering must under these circumstances be that, depriving himself of some thing, he presented it as a tribute to the God. This as we have seen, does in fact accord with the essential features of the development of the idea of sacrifice. It was natural then that the offering of animals should come into the forefront. In animal sacrifice a life most nearly allied to man was offered, thus it was the costliest thing that could be presented to God. The person performing the sacrificial rite was always a priest.

The animals offered in sacrifice were the same as throughout the history of Israel, viz. oxen, sheep, and goats. To these were added birds, pigeons and turtle doves (Lev. 1,14; 5,7.11; 12,6.8; 14,22.30; 15,14.29; Num. 6,10), which are also mentioned as victims in the story of Abraham's covenant with Yahweh (Gen. 15,9), though otherwise only known as such from the laws. It is quite unknown when the pigeon, Astarte's holy bird in Canaan, was adopted as a victim by the Israelites. [1] The practice of offering both males and females for peace-offerings had developed (Lev. 3,1.6), while males only were sacrificed for burnt-offerings (Lev. 1,3.10). This was perhaps connected with the fact that the burnt-offering was the great offering, in which all was given to the God, and in which the best must be offered. Of course only animals without blemishes could be sacrificed (Lev. 22,17 ff.; Num. 29,2; Deut. 17,1 et al.).

The material for the offerings of the produce of the soil was stored in the store-rooms of the temple, under the charge of one of the priests (Num. 4,16). It consisted of the ancient harvest offerings, such as wine, olive oil, and grain of barley and wheat. The corn was offered in various forms, either in the ancient form of roasted ears of corn (Lev. 2,14) or as fine flour *(sōleth)* or baked as cakes without leaven, either in the oven or in a pan (Lev. 2). This offering could be made separately, as might be the case with private offerings (Lev. 2), and as was the case with the offering of the high priest (Lev. 6,12 ff.) and some other special offerings (Lev. 5,11; Num. 5,15), as well as with the shewbread which occupied a special position (Lev. 24,5 ff.). But in the sacrificial laws the offering of the produce of the soil is chiefly of importance as an adjunct to the animal sacrifices, both peace-offerings and burnt-offerings (Lev. 7,11 ff.; 8,26 f.; 9,4; Num.

6,14 f.; 15,1 ff.; 28,3 ff.). In the peace-offering it may take the shape of leavened bread (Lev. 7,13).

A wine offering was only made in connection with other offerings, not separately (Ex. 29,40; Lev. 23,13; Num. 15,5 et al.), and oil was used for pouring over corn or bread offerings (Lev. 2,1.4.5; 8,26; Num. 15,4.6.9 et al.).

To all these offerings must be added yet another, which occupies a special position, viz. the *incense offering*. In connection with the law of the incense altar it is said that Aaron is to produce a smoke *(hiḳṭir ḳeṭōreth)* of aromatic herbs *(sammīm)* on it every day in the morning and "between the two evenings" (Ex. 30,7 f.). Moreover, incense *(lebhōnā)* is sometimes used as an adjunct to the flour offering (Lev. 2,1.15.16), where, further, salt is employed (Lev. 2,13). It was likewise laid by the shewbread (Lev. 24,7), and on the Day of Atonement the high priest burnt incense in the holy hall at the back before he entered (Lev. 16,12 f.). On the other hand, two instances are expressly mentioned in which neither incense nor oil must be used, viz. if a special sin-offering is made (Lev. 5,11) or an offering by which the fidelity of a suspected wife is tried (Num. 5,15). Nor is incense used in connection with animal sacrifices.

What distinguishes incense from all other "sacrificial material" is that it is no product of the soil of Canaan. It was introduced by the trading caravans which kept up Israel's communication with the outside world, in this instance South Arabia (Isa. 60,6; Jer. 6,20). Incense does not belong to the natural Israelitish offerings; it was a means of beautifying the offering. It was only when the smoke had acquired an independent value as a "sweet savour" that there was any meaning in making it still more precious by filling it with what men regard as fragrance. The regular burning of incense within the temple hall was doubtless a transference to the temple of a custom prevalent in wealthy households.

Thus there is no doubt that the use of incense meant a refinement, but this does not tell us when it was introduced. The sacrificial cult of Israel did not develop gradually from the inside; the people, entering a new environment, found themselves in the midst of old cult traditions, and as soon as they had obtained larger and richer temples there was a possibility of adopting the refinements of the cultures around them. According to the latest excavations it is quite certain that incense, which was much used in the Egyptian cultus, was also employed in Canaanite temples; and it is indeed likely that it was already used by a ruler such as Solomon. We have conclusive evidence that it was employed in pre-exilic times, for it is mentioned along with other offerings in texts from the exile and the time immediately preceding it (Isa. 43,23; Jer. 6,20; 17,26; 41,5). But we possess no certain evidence from earlier periods, for the term for incense is the same as that for the ordinary smoke of the sacrifice. [1]

The temple had its own recipe for mixing the incense which was used by itself (Ex. 30,34-38). This acquired a special character as holy incense, the use of which for ordinary purposes was sacrilegious and entailed destruction (v. 38).

Oil, likewise used in everyday life for beautification by anointment, underwent a similar refinement. As in the Egyptian and Babylonian cult, anointment became a holy rite for the consecration of kings and priests and others to be sanctified, as well as for the sanctification of objects in the sanctuary. The holy oil for anointment likewise came to be made from a certain recipe, with various fragrant components, and it was a deadly sin to use it for anything else (Ex. 30,22 ff.).

Censers and shovels of fine metal were used for the incense (*maḥtā* Ex. 27,3; 38,3; Num. 16,6.17.18 et al.; *miḳṭereth* Ez. 8,11; 2 Chron. 26,19), they were probably placed on the incense altar filled with incense. Of course there were definite rules for the procedure. What happened when these were not observed may be gathered from the story of Nadab and Abihu, who offered "strange fire" before Yahweh and were therefore killed on the spot by Yahweh's fire. Their sacrilege was so great that the people were not allowed to observe the usual mourning customs for them (Lev. 10,1-7). The strange fire may be supposed to be fire not originating from Yahweh's altar. In the international cults connected with the temple, incense was also used, as may be gathered from Ezekiel, who, in one of the cult chambers of the temple, saw 70 elders standing before some images, each carrying his censer from which a fragrant smoke arose (Ez. 8,11).

In the Israelitish cultus the privilege of offering incense became the distinguishing mark of the priesthood proper. This was because these priests reserved for themselves permission to enter the temple hall where the incense altar was. The lower priests' fight for equal rights became a fight for the privilege of offering incense, as shown by the story of Korah's revolt. The priests asserted their privileges even against the king in the war they waged against him through the laws and the historical records. The Chronicler says about Uzziah that his power made him arrogant and caused him to revolt against God, so he took a censer and tried to carry it to the incense altar. But the priests barred the way to him and spoke severely and peremptorily to him, for they alone were holy enough to offer incense. Uzziah's anger did not help him, he was smitten by leprosy and had to be led away as a man stricken by Yahweh (2 Chron. 26,16 ff.).

When the returned exiles decided to take upon themselves the restoration of the temple cult, they agreed to pay a third part of a shekel "for the shewbread, the continual *minḥā*, and the continual burnt offering, the sabbaths, the new moons, the set feasts, the sacred ceremonies, and the sin-offerings; to make an atonement for Israel; and for all the work of the house of our God" (Neh. 10,34).

Here the whole temple cult centres round the view of atonement. This aspect must gradually have come much into prominence in the monarchical period. In Ezekiel, too, we read that *minḥā*, burnt-offerings, and peace-offerings are to be offered to effect atonement for Israel (Ez. 45,15.17), and in the priestly laws of sacrifice it is the predominant point of view. The law exacts half a shekel to meet the cost of the sacrifices. This requirement is met by the Israelites to "make atonement for their souls", and the money is "atonement money" (Ex. 30,15 f.). Spoil of war given to the sanctuary was likewise given to effect atonement for their souls (Num. 31,48 ff.).

We have encountered the concept of *kōpher* "an atonement fine". It denotes a gift by which some person who has been wronged is induced to give up a reasonable claim. [1] This introduces us to the ideas which find expression in the atonement *(kippūrīm)* and the acts intended to effect atonement *(kippēr)*.

Whatever the view taken of sacrifice, it always contained germs of what developed into the idea of atonement. The worshipper purified himself and was sanctified by the sacrifice, he presented a gift to the God, he partook of a meal with the God; in all cases a new peace was created for him through the sacrifice, a renewal of harmony. But man could only be in harmony with God when he was "whole". The sacrifice removed whatever was wasting away his integrity, what was called sin. This was brought about by man being sanctified while at the same time God was induced to be lenient towards him.

The essential condition for the sanctification of a man who wished to offer sacrifice was that he should first purify himself. This meant that he freed himself from the tarnish of everyday life which sullied his soul. Of course this was only possible if his soul was not poisoned by greater sins; he who approached what was holy with a corrupt soul merely hastened on its complete destruction. "The sacrifice of the wicked is an abomination to Yahweh" (Prov. 15,8; 21,27). But if the soul were normal and clean, it was renewed through the sanctification achieved by the sacrificial act; by an access of strength all that inhibited the soul was swallowed up or swept away, and the power of resisting it was augmented.

This, however, is only one aspect of the matter. Sanctification brings about a close communion between the worshipper and the source of sanctity and power, the source from which strength flows, viz. God. Sins not only stunt the soul and make it abnormal, they exert an inhibitory influence on its relation to the divine powers and cause disturbance in the covenant, because they evoke Yahweh's resentment. The sanctification, while rendering perfect the soul, does away with the divine anger. Yahweh's wrath subsides.

The purification of the soul and the propitiation of the God by sacrifice are thus two aspects of the same matter. The psychological law operates throughout, but the relation to the divine will brings in a certain element of arbitrariness. Yahweh loves pure souls, but if he smells the sweet savour of sacrifice, and if he receives large gifts, his will may be influenced; he is propitiated and extends forgiveness with all his power.

A couple of stories about David show clearly how these different points of view are linked together. Meeting Saul during his conflict with him, David said: And let my lord, the king, hear the words of his servant: If Yahweh have stirred thee up against me, let him smell a sacrifice, but if they be men, they are cursed before Yahweh ... (1 Sam. 26,19).

If men have not stirred up the hatred of Saul, then it has arisen from the bottom of his soul, and this means that it is Yahweh who has awakened it. In both instances healing is possible by cutting off the source of hatred. If they are men, they can be rendered harmless by that paralysis of the soul which is the result of the curse; but if Yahweh is the origin of the hatred, he can be propitiated by a sacrificial gift and its sweet savour. Then the hatred will die of itself, Saul's soul will be healed and made whole. This is the effect of the sacrifice on man and God.

The interaction here described may manifest itself in curious ways. Once David got the unusual idea of numbering his people, an action which ought not to have taken place. When it had been done, David was smitten with remorse and acknowledged that he had sinned. The narrator says quite plainly that God was angry with Israel, hence he stirred up David to the sinful act which was bound to draw down disaster upon the people. Through the message of a prophet Yahweh allowed David himself to choose between three evils, and the result was a three days' pestilence, preferred by David because it freed him from the humiliating cooperation of men. After three days Yahweh stopped the plague, and full harmony was restored when David consecrated the altar on the threshing-ground of Araunah and offered burnt-offerings and peace-offerings (2 Sam. 24).

Yahweh was angry with Israel, hence he made David sin, and for this David and the people had to take the full responsibility.

The covenant was restored by the sacrifice, it meant the final obliteration of the sin which Yahweh himself had evoked.

At the close of the book of Job we hear that Yahweh is angry with Job's friends. Hence they are to offer burnt-offerings for themselves, and ask Job to intercede for them, then Yahweh will not harm them (Job 42,7 f.). We meet with the same idea in the words of the Israelites to Pharaoh: Let us go three days' journey into the desert, and sacrifice unto Yahweh, our God, lest he fall upon us with pestilence or with the sword (Ex. 5,3). Sacrifice may both avert and put an end to disaster, because it is an act of sanctification and a strengthening of the covenant with God.

Atonement especially expresses the change that takes place in the soul when it is freed from all that inhibits it. It is difficult to say what was the primary sense of the verb *kippēr*, which we render by "appease" and "atone". It has been conjectured to be cognate with verbs meaning "muffle" and with others meaning "wipe away", and the word has implications which point in both directions.¹ Just as *kōpher* is used about a gift which makes an injured person give up his claim, thus *kippēr* can be used about inducing a person who has been wronged to forget his grievance and allow it to be wiped from his soul; he is appeased and harmony is restored. "Let me appease his face with the gift" (Gen. 32,21), says Jacob about Esau, from whom he has taken the blessing; and to the Gibeonites who have been offended by Saul, David says: What shall I do to you, and wherewith shall I effect atonement, that ye may bless the inheritance of Yahweh? (2 Sam. 21,3).

It would correspond to this if we could speak in the same way of "appeasing" God. Such, however, is not the *usus loquendi*. One may "appease the face of Yahweh", but "to atone" *(kippēr)* means to obliterate a psychic content which is of a negative, inhibitory kind. "The wrath of the king is the messenger of death, a wise man atoneth for it", says the proverb (Prov. 16, 14); this word can be used even about the dissolution of a covenant with death (Isa. 28,18), or about averting a menacing doom (Isa. 47,11). The term appears in its proper context when it denotes the obliteration of sin. When Isaiah in his ecstatic condition felt that his lips were touched by a live coal from the altar, a voice was heard to say: Thine iniquity is taken away, thy sin obliterated *(tᵉkhuppar* Isa. 6,7). And normally this takes place precisely through sacrifice, as expressed in an utterance about the house of Eli: The sin of the house of Eli shall not be obliterated *(yithkappēr)* by sacrifice nor *minḥā* forever (1 Sam. 3,14, cf. Isa. 27,9), even though this obliteration or atonement may also occur without sacrifice (Prov. 16,6).

What happens is that the evil poison in the soul, which threatens to spread and corrupt it, is taken away. The object of the offering is to "take away the sins of the congregation by making atonement for them" (Lev. 10,17). It may also be expressed by saying that atonement is effected "for" the sin (*ʿal* Lev. 5,13.18.26; Jer. 18,23; Ps. 79,9; *bᵉʿadh* Ex. 32,30, *lᵉ* Num. 35,33; Ez. 16,63) or obliteration "of" it *(min* Lev. 4,26; 5,6.10; 14,19; 15,30; 16,16, Num. 6,11). And what is from a psychological point of view an obliteration of sin, is forgiveness from a divine point of view; the sin which has been is no longer considered to exist. These are two aspects of the same matter (Lev. 4,20.26.31.35; 5,10; Num. 15,25). Hence it can be said that it is God who effects the atonement (Ez. 16,63), or that it is the priest, as is mostly the case in the sacrificial laws; or it may be another person who occupies the position of an intermediary (Ex. 32,30).

The sacrifice, therefore, is the culmination of the whole process of purification undergone by the worshipper. He purifies himself in order to approach what is holy, and with the sacrifice his purification is completed by an act of sanctification. The priest effects atonement "for" the Israelite (*ʿal* Lev. 1,4; 8,34; 16,10; 17,11; Num. 8,12.19; 28,22.30 etc. or *bᵉʿadh* Lev. 16,11. 17) obliteration "of" his sin (Lev. 4,26; Num. 6,11) or "of" his unclean condition (Lev. 14,19; 15,15.30), making him clean (Lev. 14,20.53).

Atonement being a thorough purification, it affects everything connected with the sanctuary. When the sanctuary is freed from the unclean condition, atonement is effected "for" it as for man (*ʿal* Ex. 29,36; 30,10; Lev. 8,15; 16,16.18 et al.); but it can also be said to be "expiated" (object Lev. 16,20; Ez. 43,20.26; 45,20) a usage not found about men. In this term "expiate" has become the equivalent of "purify".

The taking away of sin and the evils connected with sin need not take place by sacrifice. When an Israelite committed fornication with a Midianite woman and thus caused a pestilence to befall the people, Phinehas put to death the sinful couple, and the pestilence immediately ceased (Num. 25,6 ff.). Phinehas was rewarded for his act, and it is said that he "effected atonement for the Israelites" (v. 13). Atonement is here effected by extirpating the root of the evil in the same way as a murder is expiated by putting to death the perpetrator. Atonement by fine, which we know from the sphere of blood revenge, may also be employed when an offence against Yahweh is to be expiated. Sacrifice is here regarded from another point of view, which finds its characteristic expression in the trespass offering of the Priestly Code *('āshām)*. The Philistines sent a trespass-offering *('āshām)* to Yahweh, when they had offended him by appropriating the Ark (1 Sam. 6,3 ff.).

Altogether the idea of expiation by sacrifice had many shades of meaning. When a person was found slain and the murderer was unknown, the distance to the nearest town was measured; from this town the elders were enjoined to take a heifer that had never been under the yoke and lead it to an ever-flowing stream in an uncultivated valley. Here they broke its neck and washed their hands over it, saying: Our hands have not shed this blood, and our eyes have not seen it. Make atonement for thy people Israel whom thou hast redeemed, Yahweh. And lay not innocent blood unto the charge of thy people Israel, but let the blood be expiated for them. And the text goes on to say: Thou shalt take away innocent blood from among you, doing what is right in the sight of Yahweh (Deut. 21,1-9).

"Blood" here, as so often, means the guilt involved in the shedding of blood, and the "innocent blood" is probably that which would have been shed if vengeance had been taken on an innocent town. The expiation, then, consists in the dissolution and disappearance of the menacing guilt, and this is brought about by the above-mentioned solemn declaration over the slain heifer.

It is a peculiar fact that this act, which must doubtless have been a common custom in the cities of the monarchical period, is not performed in a sanctuary. But the place where it is performed is not under cultivation, the life of nature unfolds itself freely; there is no human intervention. And even though the killing of the heifer is not a sacrifice of the ordinary kind, the custom doubtless contains elements of the sacrifice; since the animal, which has not yet been under human control, must return its life to its origin. When life is thus given back, a communion with the God is brought about as in the sacrifices proper, and the words spoken acquire a special significance.

The story testifies to the importance of the idea of expiation in Israelitish popular life. This idea attained its full development in the evolution of the cult in the temple at Jerusalem. Everything in any way connected with sacrifice acquired an expiatory power, as seen from the story of Korah's revolt. The incense carried to the altar by the wrong hands involved disaster, and the people who joined the rebels perished in great numbers. But when Aaron came with his censer on which he had laid a live coal from the altar with some incense, he at once effected atonement, and the punitive pestilence ceased (Num. 17,11-13).

The desire for purification pervaded the people, and the priests had to provide means of purification, not only in the temple. They were ordered to kill a red heifer without blemish, which had not been under the yoke; the priest was to kill it outside the camp and sprinkle its blood in the direction of the sanctuary. Then it was to be burnt, body and bones, with cedar wood, hyssop, and scarlet. Then the priest and his assistants were to purify themselves, but the ashes were to be gathered together in a clean place outside the camp. There people could fetch it and put it into water, and this water could be used to take away sin (Num. 19,1 ff.).

There is nothing remarkable in the idea of the expiatory effect of sacrifice arising in Israel, for it developed quite organically from the nature of the sacrifice. But the remarkable thing is that it grew to be the most important aspect of sacrifice. This was because it satisfied an ever-increasing desire. Political uncertainty and social disintegration allowed little peace among the people. The more the blessing failed the community and the individual, the greater were the efforts to acquire it. But is was only obtained by righteousness, and in order to gain righteousness it was in the first place necessary to keep free from sin. As their fear grew, the negative aspect became more and more prominent, and the Israelite was constantly harassed by the thought of how to avoid the fatal effect of sin and of the curse on his soul.

This desire was satisfied through the temple. And simultaneously with the growth of the craving for expiation, the temple tended more and more to become a closed domain of holiness, a place apart, which possessed special powers capable of consuming sin and all the essence of the curse. The temple developed into a powerful institution for the healing of the soul, a place from which all healing emanated, and to which the individual could turn for purification and renewal of his soul.

Through the centuries sacrifice occupied the most important place in the temple cult. It is a matter of course that there were already at the early temples fixed rules for the preparation of a sacrifice. This is illustrated by the story of Eli's sons, which also shows, however, that the rules might give rise to conflicts. The event marks the boundary between a time when it was the family who performed the sacrificial rites themselves in a sanctuary like that of Shiloh, while the priest rendered assistance and received a share in return, and a time when the priesthood took the lead in the ceremonies, while the worshipper was a guest. At the great temple of Jerusalem this development ran its full course. The ritual for the treatment of each kind of sacrifice became fixed in the process of time and the more the sacrifice was cut off from nature and acquired a value of its own, the greater was the weight attached to the correct performance of the rites, though in this respect there was only a shade of difference between earlier and later times. Even when a person offered a sacrifice of his own accord, the duty of performing the ceremony devolved exclusively on the priest, but the rites establish that the worshipper will nevertheless gain blessedness from his offering.

The priestly laws of sacrifice codify the post-exilic practice at the temple. This was based on the custom of the monarchical period, but it is impossible to separate the later from the earlier elements. The sacrificial laws give no exhaustive account; thus there is no description of the rites for the daily burnt-offering. In the sacrificial laws we meet with the same kinds of offerings as in early times, and to these must be added the sin- and trespass-offerings. For all animal sacrifice it is still the rule that the animal is to be without blemish (Lev. 1,3.10; 3,1.6; 4,3 etc.); [1] only a normal animal can be sanctified and offered as a gift to God. The worshipper who wishes to sacrifice an animal must be the lawful owner of it, or he could not give it away. It is a sign of decay when Malachi complains that in his time people offered stolen or lame and sick animals (Mal. 1,13).

The laws for burnt-offerings and *shelāmīm* offerings show how the priest and the worshipper cooperate.

If a man wishes to offer a *burnt-offering,* the law demands a male animal, whether it be an ox, a goat, or a sheep. The worshipper must lead the animal to the entrance and lay his hand upon its head. By this act he establishes the fact that the animal is his property. It belongs to his sphere, and when it is sanctified, the sanctification primarily affects him. It is also the worshipper who kills the animal, near the altar, "before the face of Yahweh". [2] The actual sanctification, on the other hand, was performed by the priests. They received the blood and sprinkled it round the altar. While the animal was skinned and cut up, they attended to the altar fire, they put the pieces on the altar after the entrails and bones had been washed, and the whole of it was then burnt (Lev. 1,1-13). The skin, however, was kept apart and given to the officiating priest (Lev. 7,8). The procedure is less elaborate in the case of birds (Lev. 1,14-17).

The rites prescribed by the laws for *peace-offerings* (*shelāmīm*) are not essentially different from those relating to burnt-offerings. The animal may be male or female; the implication is, presumably, that this offering was not so important as the burnt-offering. The worshipper lays his hand on the victim and kills it as in the burnt-offering, and the priests sprinkle the blood on the altar. But here it is only the fat from the entrails, the kidneys with the fat on them, and the lobe of the liver which are put into the altar fire by the priests, and in the instance of the sheep, the fat tail as well (Lev. 3). These are the parts which from the earliest times were withheld from man and committed entirely to sanctification.[1]

As always in the early days, a meal, regulated by fixed rules, was associated with the *sh*e*lāmīm* offering. The temple contained special chambers designed for sacrificial meals. The rules for them varied somewhat according as the sacrifice was a thanksgiving-, a votive-, or a voluntary offering. Any one who was clean could partake of the meal; the participation of an unclean person was a breach of sanctity and entailed death (Lev. 7,20 f.). At the thanksgiving-offering the meal was to be finished on the day of sacrifice, at the other two the leavings could be eaten the next day. What was left after this was to be burnt, as well as what came into contact with the unclean. If nevertheless the worshippers partook of it, they would reap sin instead of happiness from the sacrifice (v. 15 ff.). At the thanksgiving-offering some cakes also were sanctified. They were the priest's share (vv. 12.14). The text runs: Besides the leavened cakes he shall make his offering together with his thanksgiving-*sh*e*lāmīm* offering (v. 13). The leavened cakes mentioned here must be something not belonging to the sacrifice; it shows that the worshippers brought leavened bread with them for the meal.[2] From the history of Hannah we know that in earlier times wine belonged to the sacrificial meal. The fact that it is not mentioned in the sacrificial laws may be due to their incompleteness.

The participation of the priests in the sacrificial meal in no way resembled the eating of a meal by the worshippers. If it had been customary in early times for the priest to join in the meal as a guest, this custom, which already the sons of Eli repudiated, had long been discontinued. According to the law the priests received their fixed shares, but these were not only given to them as their due. The holiness of the priests had become so great that their taking over of the sacrificial meat became part of its sanctification.

At the *sheᵉlāmīm* offering two portions of the animal fell to the priest. The breast was given to "Aaron and his sons", i. e. the priesthood, and the right haunch was the share of the officiating priest (Lev. 7,30-33). It could be consumed by priests and their families in a clean place (Lev. 10,14 f.). The law mentions that one portion, viz. the breast, and sometimes also the haunch, is waved (*teᵉnūphā*). This waving is also carried out according to certain precepts with the fat and the other parts brought to the altar (Ex. 29,24, cf. v. 26 f.; Lev. 8,27.29; 10,15 et al.). We have no account of how it was done; we merely know that the piece of meat in question was carried on the hands and "waved" before Yahweh. This must doubtless be understood to mean that it was moved towards the altar. The movement may then be supposed to signify that the victim was "symbolically" given to the holy centre; it is said, indeed, that the sacrificial meats are sanctified by this waving (Ex. 29,27). To "wave" (*hēnīph*) actually becomes a term denoting "to sanctify". It is employed of holy gifts given as a permanent institution to the temple (Ex. 35,22; Num. 18,11), and probably their sanctification was accompanied by a solemn ceremony like that just described. All this shows that the giving of certain portions of the sacrifice to the priests was regarded as related in nature to the giving of them to Yahweh.[1]

As to the offering of the crops of the field, we have seen that corn was offered in different forms; in the shape of sheaves, roasted grain, flour, or bread. The bread must never be leavened. This was not because leaven in itself was unholy; like honey it was to be brought to the temple as first-fruits, though it must not be laid on the altar (Lev. 2,12). But perhaps the prohibition against leavened bread was due to a tradition dating from a period before the introduction of leaven. Some salt was added to the offering (Lev. 2,13).

The law for the worshipper who proposed to make an offering of the produce of the soil, *minḥā*, laid down rules for the various forms of produce offered (Lev. 2). The offering may consist of fine wheaten flour (*sōleth*) with oil, to which is added some incense. It is taken to the priest, who removes a handful of it, its *'azkārā*,[2] to be burnt on the altar, while the rest falls to the priesthood. The offering is treated similarly if presented in the baked form, whether baked in an oven or otherwise (vv. 4.5.7), and likewise if given in the shape of newly roasted ripe ears of corn (v. 14 f.). Of baked things the priestly share goes to the officiating priest, while the unbaked things fall to the priesthood (Lev. 7,9 f.). They are to be consumed within the precincts of the temple, and only male members of the priests' family may have a share. It is most holy, like the holiest offering, and makes the person who touches it holy (Lev. 6,7-11).

Since all offerings of the post-exilic system had for their principal object expiation, i. e. the obliteration of sin and disaster, a special interest attaches to the sin- and trespass- offerings.

The *sin-offerings,* which are designated by the same term as sin *(ḥaṭṭā'th)* are offered to expiate some sin inadvertently committed. The question for whom they are offered to some extent determines the ritual. It may be the high priest, the Israelitish community, a prince, or an ordinary Israelite. The offering always consists of an animal which must of course be without blemish.

If the sacrifice is on behalf of the high priest, he must offer a bull. He takes it to the entrance, lays his hand upon its head, and kills it before Yahweh. Then he takes some of its blood into the sanctuary, and dipping his fingers, seven times sprinkles some of it before Yahweh in the direction of the hanging before the holy of holies, afterwards smearing some on the horns of the incense altar. The rest of the blood he pours out at the foot of the altar for burnt-offerings. The fat of the entrails, the kidneys with the fat on them, and the lobe of the liver are then, as with the peace-offering, to be given to the fire of the altar, while the rest of the animal is taken to a clean place where it is burned up (Lev. 4,3-12).

If it is the Israelite community which has inadvertently incurred sin, the procedure is the same, only that here the elders lay their hands on the victim and kill it (Lev. 4,13-21). In this instance another law demands that a bull be offered together with a flour offering and a libation, and a he-goat as a sin-offering (Num. 15,22-26). Since both these laws must represent the practice at the temple of Jerusalem, they show that the temple customs underwent a change, but it can hardly be shown what relation they bore to each other.

A prince offers a he-goat. He lays his hand on it and kills it, the priest smears some of the blood on the horns of the altar for burnt-offerings and pours out the rest at the foot of the altar, whereafter the same parts of the entrails as in the peace-offering are burnt on the altar (Lev. 4,22-26). In the same way ordinary Israelites among whom gērīm too are included (Num. 15,29), offer a goat or a sheep (Lev. 4,27-35; Num. 15,27-31 where a goat only is mentioned). The meat left over is in these instances to be eaten by the priests in a holy place in the court. It is most holy and strongly affects everything with which it has contact. If blood from it happens to be smeared on a garment, it must be washed off in the holy place; if the meat is boiled in an earthen vessel, this must be broken, while a bronze vessel is to be carefully scoured (Lev. 6,17-23).

For the trespass-offering ('āshām) the procedure is largely the same as for the sin-offering. Here the blood is sprinkled around the altar, the usual parts of the entrails are burnt, and the meat is to be eaten by the priests. "As the sin-offering is, so is the trespass-offering, there is one law for them" (Lev. 7,1-7).

The sin- and trespass-offerings resemble the burnt-offerings in that the worshipper commits them wholly to the sanctuary without receiving any share of the sacrificial meat. It is also prescribed that the killing is to take place in the same spot as for the burnt-offerings (Lev. 4,24; 6,18; 7,2). But they resemble the peace-offerings in that the same parts of the entrails are burnt on the altar, and except at the sin-offering of the high priest and of the community, the meat is eaten, but by the priests only. In spite of this latter fact, they are regarded as most nearly allied to the burnt-offerings, and sometimes are actually included among them (Ezr. 8,35), because the giving of them to the priests is an act of sanctification not very different from the giving of them to the altar. But the way in which the blood is used shows that the sanctification of the victim comes very much into prominence in these offerings.

Here the sanctity of the offering is intensified and renders the sin- and guilt-offerings in a special degree suitable for expiation. The law of sin-offerings opens as follows: If a soul sin inadvertently *(bish^eghāghā)* against any of Yahweh's interdictions, and acts against one of them: Thus if the anointed priest sin, burdening the people with sin, he shall for the sin *(ḥaṭṭā'th)* which he hath sinned bring Yahweh a bull from the herd without blemish for a sin-offering *(ḥaṭṭā'th,* Lev. 4,2-3). Similarly it is said about the other parties that if inadvertently they incur guilt by transgressing a command and then discover it, they are to make a sin-offering, and "the priest shall effect atonement for his sin which he hath sinned, and he shall be forgiven" (vv. 26. 35). Hence the sin-offering is made for the express purpose of effecting expiation for the sins committed. The same thing is emphasised in the other law mentioned above (Num. 15,22-29); it is merely a formal difference that the trepasses are here called failure through inadvertence to fulfil the commands of Yahweh. It is added that deliberate sins, such as are committed "with raised hand" *(b^eyādh rāmā),* are sacrilegious and entail death (Num. 15,30 f.).

As we have seen, the rites are chiefly the same for sin- and trespass-offerings, and it is difficult to determine the difference between them. The precepts for trespass-offerings contain ordinances which indicate that they are exacted in cases involving compensation. "If a soul commit a trespass and inadvertently sin against the holy things of Yahweh, he shall bring unto Yahweh as his trespass-offering *('āshām)* a ram without blemish out of the flock, which thou shalt estimate at several shekels of silver after the shekel of the sanctuary, for a trespass-offering *('āshām).* And he shall make good what he hath sinned against the holy things, and add thereto one-fifth part and give it to the priest. And the priest shall effect atonement for him by the ram of the trespass-offering, and he shall be forgiven" (Lev. 5,14-16). The reference is here to a man who, for instance, has omitted to make an offering

24*

to the sanctuary which it was his duty to present, or who has taken some of the sacrificial meat which was to go to the sanctuary and its priests, or the like. He is then partly to make ample reparation, partly to purify his soul of the sin adhering to it. This is done by means of the "trespass-offering". It must not be an insignificant offering, but is to consist of a ram of full value. Thus in the purification-offering also, the value is of some importance.

Exactly the same procedure is adopted when an Israelite has unlawfully appropriated something at the expense of his neighbour, either by not acknowledging property committed to his charge, pledged or found, or by other trespasses, or by swearing falsely. Though this is not stated, the reference must presumably be to mistakes. At any rate, when the sinner bethinks himself and perceives his sin, he is to restore the property unlawfully appropriated by him, adding one-fifth part, and presenting a ram as a trespass-offering by way of expiation (Lev. 5,20-26).

If we possessed these ordinances alone, we might say that the trespass-offering was employed to effect expiation in those instances when an offence required compensation. And the concept of compensation seems also to influence the ordinance concerning the offering itself, in so far as the value of the latter is to be estimated. But actually the trespass-offering is used for the same purpose as the sin-offering, and since their rituals are also almost identical, there is nothing strange in the fact that they are not kept rigorously apart. Just as in the case of the sin-offering, it is said that, if a man inadvertently incurs guilt by doing some of the things prohibited by Yahweh, he is to effect atonement by offering a ram as a trespass-offering (Lev. 5,17-19). The only difference is that here as in the other instances of trespass-offerings we hear of a ram, while the sin-offering for an ordinary Israelite consists of a female animal of the flock, a goat or a sheep. In a single instance the sin-offering is even called a trespass-offering (Lev. 5,6) in a context where we hear nothing of offences against others, but of guilt incurred in a wider sense.

We know how near to each other are sin and the curse. Both always cause disaster, because they waste away the health and strength of the soul, its righteousness and blessedness. It is the effect of the offering to strengthen the blessing through sanctification, but the negative side corresponding to this, i. e. purging the soul of evil, of sin and the curse, is the essential element in the action of the sin-offering. And the latter offering has always this effect, in so far as the evil is not deeply rooted. Hence it not only obliterates the light sins but also the evil entering the soul through curses or uncleanness. With such cases, too, the law is concerned:

And if a soul sin and hear the sound of a curse and hath been a witness or hath seen or known (of the matter), if he do not utter it and so bears his sin *('āwōn);* if a soul touch any unclean thing, whether it be a carcase of an unclean beast, or a carcase of unclean cattle, or the carcase of unclean creeping things, and if it be hidden from him, he being yet unclean and guilty *('āshēm);* or if he touch the uncleanness of man, whatsoever uncleanness it be that a man shall be defiled withal, and it be hid from him, when he knoweth of it and feels guilty; or if a soul swear rashly pronouncing with his lips to do evil or good, whatsoever it be that a man shall pronounce rashly with an oath, and if it be hid from him, and he then perceiveth it and feels guilty of one of these things, then he shall when he feels guilty of one of these things, confess what he hath sinned in that thing; and he shall bring his trespass-offering *('āshām)* unto Yahweh for his sin which he hath sinned, a female of the flock, a lamb or a kid of the goats for a sin-offering *(ḥaṭṭā'th)* and the priest shall make atonement for him concerning his sin (Lev. 5,1-6).

Here we are told of different kinds of evil which enter the soul from within or from without through a curse directed against an unknown sinner, by which the person concerned is affected because of complicity, or through contact with uncleanness of every kind, or through rash vows which are broken. The sin-offering — also called a trespass-offering — is effective as a healing remedy which destroys all the germs of this evil in the soul.

So important is it that people should have access to this healing of the soul that the law also provides for the indigent persons who cannot procure a lamb or a goat. For them two pigeons or turtle doves will suffice, the one being offered as a burnt-offering, the other as a sin-offering, the priest sprinkling some of the blood on the side of the altar and pouring out the rest at its foot. If this also is unattainable, the poor man may bring one-tenth of an ephah of wheaten flour without oil or incense, and the priest will present it as a sin-offering, pouring out a handful on the altar as *'azkārā* and taking the rest himself. It cannot be less (Lev. 5,7-13).

The law relating to sin- and trespass-offerings has been formulated in post-exilic times like the other sacrificial laws. Only at that time could so important a position among the people be attributed to the high priest in Jerusalem that the whole people incurred guilt because of a sin committed by him, and the importance ascribed to a *nāśi'* seems to indicate the same thing. But it is plain that the position given to the high priest in the law is a heritage from the king. This would seem to show that the sin-offering, too, like most other post-exilic cult practices, was inherited from the temple customs of the monarchical period.

It is true that from that time we have only a single instance of the use of sin- and trespass-offerings (2 Kings 12,17), and its meaning is not clear. But in Ezekiel's attempt at a reconstruction these offerings are mentioned several times, and even in a prominent place. We are told that in these offerings the animals are killed on the same slab as in the burnt-offerings (Ez. 40,39), and the sacrificial meat is stored together with other things of great holiness in special chambers for the priests (42,13, cf. 44, 29; 46,20). The nature of the sin-offering is indicated by the fact that it is used to consecrate and purify the altar and the sanctuary (43,19 ff.; 45,19 ff.).

At the dedication of the temple after the first return from the exile, twelve rams were offered for a sin-offering (Ezr. 6,17), and similar sacrifices were presented together with some burnt-offerings by those who returned with Ezra (8,35). The sin-offering is also mentioned among the institutions which the congregation pledged themselves to maintain at the initiative of Nehemiah (Neh. 10,34). All this may be taken as evidence that the sin-offering belonged to the stable traditions of the royal temple. [1]

In reality it was quite natural that sin-offerings should appear at the close of the monarchical period. It was the time when the idea of expiation obtruded itself; the desire for holiness as a protection from evil grew stronger. Influences from the East may have played a part, but the decisive circumstance was the fear generated in people's souls by the general disintegration. Everywhere evil was seen to burgeon, and there was no inner power to suppress it. Thus the fight against the negative came into the foreground. The dread of disgrace and the curse loomed greater than the confidence in the blessing and the glorious fight for honour. In the meantime the temple at Jerusalem was looked upon as the stable point. Here all holiness was stored up, by means of which evil must be combated. The chief means of maintaining this holiness were the sacrifices. Just as the people in early times gained fresh strength, blessedness, and peace through them, thus also they became to the people of a later age the most important and strongest weapon in the fight against evil.

FEASTS AND SACRED CUSTOMS.

SACRIFICE was only a single, though important, item in the acts by which the Israelite sanctified himself, thus renewing himself and his world. In its essence it was connected with the constant regeneration of Nature herself, when the crops ripened and the animals multiplied. Through it sanctification became associated with definite seasons of the year. But not only the harvest and the renewal of the herds and flocks were occasions for sanctification. There were other times to which nature and history gave signal importance and which must be remembered and sanctified. Thus, in the course of the year, there arose a series of special occasions which were sanctified by the Israelites partly by sacrifice, partly by other acts. Such occasions were called *mō'ᵃdhīm*, festive occasions.

The information we can gather from the various narratives dealing with the popular festivals by no means gives us any comprehensive picture of conditions in earlier times, though it contains features of importance.

In the book of Job we are told that once a year Job, the wealthy farmer and stockbreeder, gathered his sons and daughters for a feast. When the annual festival came, Job made them sanctify themselves and offered burnt-offerings for them in the morning; this was to obliterate the sins they might have committed (Job. 1,5). The book of Job describes conditions in the small towns, but we are not told what feast is concerned, nor do we know at what time it takes place. But this much we learn: the festival and its sanctification concerns the family, it is conducted by the head of the family, and we receive the impression that it is, at any rate in great part, celebrated on his farm. This was doubtless the case with several of the peasant festivals of early Israel.

The family was the established unit of life; by sanctification at the festival its common foundation was strengthened and its blessing renewed.

When we are told that Job offered burnt offerings, it seems most natural to suppose that it was at the sanctuary of the town. We do not know to what extent sacrificial rites could be performed in houses and on farms. But since sacred objects such as teraphim belonged to the houses, and the excavations have shown that there were sometimes household altars, it must have been possible to perform a certain part of the cult in the home, even though tradition does not seem to indicate that domestic worship was so important in character here as, for instance, among the Romans.

We possess historical evidence from earlier times of feasts which were, at any rate in great part, celebrated by each peasant on his own land. This applies to a typical cattlebreeders' feast such as the *Feast of Sheep-shearing*. This feast never attained the importance of the Passover, at which other elements than the sanctification of the flocks came into prominence; on the other hand it retained its character of a feast, whereas the sanctification of the first-born which came to form an additional part of the Passover, had merely the character of an offering without further rites.

The shearing of the animals of the flock meant the same to the stock-breeder as the reaping of the harvest to the farmer. Through it he appropriated part of the life around him, therefore it must be sanctified by sacrifice. We have seen that Deuteronomy demanded that "the first" of the sheared wool should be given to the sanctuary (Deut. 18,4).

From the stories in Genesis and the books of Samuel we see how important a part the sheep-shearing played in the life of the people. Even when the flocks were far away, the owner went out to them to conduct the work; this forms an integral part of the narratives. When Judah was on the way to Timnath, and had his fateful meeting with Tamar, he was to conduct the sheep-shearing there (Gen. 38,12 f.). And when Jacob wanted to flee secretly from Laban with his two wives, he arranged that he should be three days' journey from his father-in-law, who was occupied with the shearing of part of the flocks (Gen. 30,36; 31,19 ff.). The master of the house might always be expected to be where the shearing was going on.

Laban had "his brethren" with him (Gen. 31,23). The shearing was a family affair, and the relatives took part in the feast. We do not know what was the relation to the sanctuary. We may suppose that the master of the house brought "the first" of the wool to the nearest sanctuary, but after that, as the shearing proceeded, the feast was celebrated at his home under his auspices. It consisted in a meal with a social drinking *(mishte)*. It may be taken for granted that it was opened with a blessing and a word of sanctification by the head of the family. We hear of Nabal that he sat like a king in his house at Carmel among those who had assisted at the shearing; an abundance of bread, water, and slaughtered cattle was consumed, to which were added dainties such as cakes made of figs and grapes. Wine was indispensable for the revels, and Nabal became very intoxicated (1 Sam. 25,11. 18.36). David, we gather from the story, took it for granted that roaming bands might demand a share of the delicacies at such a feast.

A story about Absalom conveys a similar impression of the same feast. He was conducting the sheep-shearing at Baal Hasor, a good way from the capital, where he must probably have had a farm, and here he held a feast. He invited the king's sons and the king, i. e. his nearest kin. David declined, but allowed his sons to accept, though with some hesitation. The feast consisted of an abundant meal and much wine. We see that it was a family feast. The participants were in the first place "the household", but their circle was not clearly defined. The above-mentioned feast ended disastrously, for Absalom caused his half-brother Amnon to be killed in his intoxication (2 Sam. 13,23 ff.).

We hear of other feasts in early times which were celebrated by the master of the house on his farm. One narrative tells us of a new-moon feast on Saul's farm which fatally affected the relation between Saul and David. It took place at a time when the secret struggle between the two had begun, though David alone realised its character. "To-morrow is the new moon, and I shall sit

with the king to eat", said David to Jonathan (1 Sam. 20,5); but he
wished to avoid this meeting, and asked Jonathan to apologise
for his absence. The text goes on to say: And the day of the new
moon came, and the king sat down to eat. And the king sat upon
his seat as he had again and again sat upon the seat by the wall,
and Jonathan went up ... [1] and Abner sat by Saul's side, and
David's place was empty. And Saul spake not anything that day
for he thought: Something hath befallen him, he is not clean,
surely he is not clean! And it came to pass the day after the new
moon, the second ... [2] that David's place was empty and Saul
said to Jonathan, his son: Why hath not the son of Jesse come to
the meal, either yesterday or to-day? (1 Sam. 20,24-27).

On the day of the feast Saul gathers his men around him for
a meal; only the few men who are of special importance are mentioned, each has his fixed place. On the day itself the circle is
sanctified, as we gather from the fact that perfect cleanness is
required. An accidental uncleanness, brought on by no fault of
one's own, excuses a man's absence from the feast which is to
sanctify Saul's "father's house"; all others must be present and
take part in the sanctification. It goes without saying that here,
too, a blessing and holy words must have been pronounced. The
narrative would seem to indicate that it is merely on the day of
the new moon that cleanness is required. That day only is a holy
day. David's absence from the daily meal excites Saul's surprise
because he stays away two days in succession, [3] and the presumed
excuse on the holy day was not valid for a weekday. We hear
nothing of how the sanctification took place, nor of any visit to
the holy place.

The excuse which David invented for Jonathan to tell his
father ran thus: If thy father miss me, thou shalt say: David
begged leave of me to run to Bethlehem, his native city, for there
is an annual sacrifice there for the whole family *(kol ham-
mishpāḥā)* (1 Sam. 20,6). And Jonathan did, in fact, offer this
explanation to Saul in the situation in question. David had asked
to be allowed to go to Bethlehem: Let me go, for we have a family
sacrifice *(zebhaḥ mishpāḥā)* in the city ... and now if I have

found favour in thine eyes, let me get away and see my brethren (v. 29).

David had been admitted to Saul's house as a member of his household, and the narrative shows that as such he belonged to its cult assembly. But he still belonged to his own family, hence it was reasonable that he should be present at its feast. But the matter is not so simple. The moment his participation in the family feast acquires the character of independence of the master in whose service he is, a conflict will arise, and this is just what happened when the matter was submitted to Saul.

It is not quite clear what is meant by "family" in the present instance. It may be David's "father's house", i. e. the family in a narrower sense. But since the annual sacrifice is mentioned, that is to say, a regular annual feast, we are more probably concerned with the city community whose ruling men constituted a *mishpāḥā*. We then arrive at another basis for the festival, the community which next to the family played the most important part in early Israel, viz. the city. This, as far as the small towns were concerned, probably meant the family in an extended sense. We learn from the story that the public feasts of the city communities had their special character for each city. Saul could not possibly know that the great feast of Bethlehem was on that day of the new moon.

The father's house and the city community were the two social units with which the festivals of early times were associated. We do not possess any detailed account of these ancient feasts, but traits of some city festivals have come down to us.

When Saul and his servant came to Samuel's town, a feast was in progress, with sacrifices and a meal in the temple. The participants, the citizens, are "those called thither"; they partake of a meal in the temple hall *(hal-lishkā)*, but not until the sacrifice has been blessed by Samuel, the seer. The two strangers are invited and take part in the meal as honoured guests (1 Sam. 9). The reason why Samuel conducts the sacrificial meal must be because as a man of God he has the authority of a chief and leader in this city community, being the man whose blessing is at all times worth most. [1] Eating and drinking in the temple seem to have been prominent features of the common cult of the city communities, as well as the blessing spoken over the holy sacrifice. Blessings and curses might be pronounced during the feast, as in the Canaanite communities. The inhabitants of Shechem gathered the harvest of their vine-yards and pressed the grapes; then they went to the temple of their God, where they ate and drank and cursed Abimelech (Judg. 9,27). We can see from the narrative that here, again, it was the men who formed the festive gathering. The feasts were marked by joy and animal spirits. This also was the case among the Philistines. We are told that their chiefs gathered for a sacrificial feast to Dagon "and for rejoicing" (śimḥā), and they added to their delight in the good fortune their god had bestowed on them by leading the blinded Samson into the temple, where they enjoyed the sight of his humiliation (Judg. 16,23 ff.).

Of the special sacred customs of some few city communities we merely possess hints. At Shiloh the young women took part in the wine harvest festival by dancing in circles (Judg. 21,21.). It appears from the story that no man joined in this part of the festival, hence it gave the Benjaminites a favourable opportunity for carrying away the young women. We hear of another feast in which only the young women took part, in the neighbourhood of Mizpeh in Gilead. Here they celebrated annually a mourning feast of four days for Jephthah's daughter, who typefied the unhappy woman that died suddenly in her youth before she had known a husband or motherhood (Judg. 11,39 f.). [1]

The city communities demanded the presence at all their public feasts of all proper citizens; but the individual families were not strictly bound to the sanctuary of their own city. Just because each sanctuary had its special character, some sanctuaries might become more prominent than others and therefore become pilgrims' shrines. They could be visited at any time by families or individuals from other cities, especially at their annual festivals.

This is shown in the narrative about Samuel's kin. Elkanah of Ramathaim came annually with his two wives, Hannah and Peninah, and the children of the latter to sacrifice to Yahweh at Shiloh. We are not told on what occasion it happened. But the regular sacrifices were presented, besides the offerings which were to redeem special vows. A common meal was eaten by the family before Yahweh, prayers were offered to him and these were strengthened by vows, and on leaving, the family prostrated themselves before him (1 Sam. 1). The prophets of the monarchical period mention such pilgrimages to the sanctuaries of Bethel, Gilgal, and Beersheba (Am. 4,4 f.; 5,5), but of the rites performed there we merely hear that various kinds of sacrifices were offered, and there was singing and playing of harps (Am. 5,21 ff.), while the sacred images of calves were kissed where such were present (Hos. 13,2, cf. 1 Kings 19,18).

The scattered information we possess of the ancient feasts gives us no comprehensive picture of them, but it shows that they originated partly in the individual families, partly in the city communities, the two social units which were the mainstay of early Israelitish life. The feasts were celebrated in part in the homes, and in part in the sanctuaries. Hence they had a certain heterogeneous character, even though some of them were bound to the same seasons. Doubtless many local cults developed at the various sanctuaries in Canaan which were only practised at a single temple.

It is difficult to say whether special festivals for the people as a whole were celebrated in earlier times. Stories about covenant assemblies in the wilderness and immigration periods (Ex. 24; Deut. 27; Josh. 8,30-35; 24) perhaps contain traces of such common festivals celebrated in the central part of the country in earlier times. [1] It is clear that the Passover was such a popular festival before the immigration, and it is probable that in Canaan, too, Israelites from the various tribes gathered to it. In the Blessing of Moses we are told that Zebulon and Issachar assembled some of the tribes (*'ammīm*) on a mountain for "sacrifices of righteousness" (Deut. 33,18 f.). This shows that there must have been a great centre for Israelite festivals somewhere near the plain of Jizreel, perhaps on Mount Carmel — but the details are concealed from us. It was natural that the monarchy should strive to raise the festivals above the limitations of the small communities. This applies not only to the special royal festivals but also to the feasts which were rooted in the life of the people from ancient times.

The laws lay particular emphasis on three feasts, viz. the Passover and the Feast of Unleavened Bread in the spring; the Feast of Weeks in the summer; and the Feast of Ingathering in the autumn. Evolved from the life of the stock-breeder and farmer, they were intimately bound up with existence in Canaan as harvest feasts. The earliest laws lay down that each of these three festivals is to be celebrated in the sanctuary as a pilgrimage feast *(ḥāgh)* 1 They cannot, as for instance the feast of Sheepshearing, be celebrated on the farms. It is improbable that the customs connected with the feasts were quite identical at the different temples.

Gradually the royal temple at Jerusalem acquired an ever-increasing importance. The feasts celebrated there were influenced by the fact that they were conducted by the king; they were not for a small circle, but for the whole people and the kingdom. Therefore the feasts at Jerusalem became more important than in other places, though the local cults still survived. This tendency in the development is evident to us already in the first period after the division of the realm, when Jeroboam sought to counteract it by making Bethel the rival of Jerusalem (1 Kings 12,26 ff.). After the exile, when only the temple of Jerusalem enjoyed recognition, all other cults were branded as un-Israelitish; this is the situation established by the Deuteronomic law. Thus the ancient multiplicity disappeared; only the feasts at Jerusalem were known and recognised.

The centralisation of the festivals at Jerusalem gradually changed their nature. During the growth of that city in the monarchical period a new town life developed; for its inhabitants, like those of Samaria, lived chiefly as artisans and tradespeople. For them the ancient agricultural and pastoral feasts could not retain their original character. They were observed, as required by the tradition, but it was necessary to give them another meaning, a development which we have been able to follow in the instance of the sacrifice. We can also see, though it can hardly be shown in detail, that the participation and leadership of the king sometimes imparted a special quality to the cult festivals.

The movement towards Jerusalem meant a striving for uniformity, but at the same time a withdrawal from Nature. The festivals no longer signified the direct sanctification of Nature. The people were sanctified by them in virtue of the tradition and the ceremonial of the priesthood. This development was accomplished by the rupture in the life of the people caused by the exile. Complete uniformity was now introduced because what was outside was not regarded as belonging to Israel. The king had disappeared from the ritual of the cult, but his work survived. The temple of Jerusalem and its priesthood was the centre of the festivals. And yet the history of the Passover shows that it was not possible to connect all festivals with the temple.

These are the chief features of the development of the festivals, but they convey no impression of uniformity. Our sources testify to a change as far as the individual feasts are concerned, but it is difficult, often impossible, to elucidate the history of the festivals of Israel.

The laws relating to *the spring festival* illustrate the movement which we have just mentioned. In the book of the Covenant we read: Three times a year shalt thou keep a pilgrimage feast *(tāḥōgh)* unto me. Thou shalt keep the pilgrimage feast of unleavened bread *(ḥagh ham-maṣṣōth)*, thou shalt eat unleavened bread seven days as I commanded thee for the feast *(mōʿēdh)* of the month Abib, for in it thou camest out from Egypt; and none shall see my face empty-handed. — Three times a year all thy males shall appear before the face of Yahweh [1] (Ex. 23,14.15.17).

In the corresponding law it says: The pilgrimage feast of unleavened bread *(ḥagh ham-maṣṣōth)* thou shalt keep. Seven days thou shalt eat unleavened bread as I commanded thee for the feast *(mōʿēdh)* of the month Abib, for in the month Abib thou camest out from Egypt. — Thrice in the year shall all your men-children appear [1] before the face of Yahweh, the God of Israel. For I will cast out foreign nations from thy midst and make spacious thy domain, and no man shall desire thy land when thou goest up to appear before the face of Yahweh, thy God, thrice in the year. Thou shalt not shed the blood of my sacrifice over leaven, and the sacrifice of the pilgrimage feast of Passover shall not be left overnight till the morning (Ex. 34,18.23-25).

The two laws tell us that, like the other two main festivals, the spring festival is to be celebrated as a pilgrimage feast, with visits to the shrine. The obligation devolves on men only. This agrees with what we know about the cult assemblies of the towns, but not with the story in the book of Samuel about the annual visit of Elkanah and his family to Shiloh.

The laws give no information as to the sanctuary for which they were valid, or whether they applied to several. Altogether we learn very little about the character of the festivals. It is stated in the two laws that the feast lasts for seven days. It is called the *maṣṣōth* feast, because unleavened bread only may be eaten while it lasts; and it is celebrated in the month of Abib, for in that month Israel came out of Egypt. These ordinances have been assumed to warrant the conclusion that the two law-codes did not know of the Passover, but only of the *maṣṣōth* feast, which is then supposed to be a purely agricultural feast, a celebration of the barley harvest. This, however, is quite incorrect. For among the brief and incomplete ordinances we find the command that the blood of the Paschal sacrifice is to be kept apart from the leaven, and it must not be left overnight (Ex. 34,25, cf. 23,18). As will appear from this, the Passover and the *maṣṣōth* feast constituted one feast in these laws, named after the unleavened bread, while the term Passover *(pesaḥ)* is only used to denote the special sacrifice offered at the beginning of the feast.

From the above it will already be clear that it was no mere harvest festival, and this it further confirmed by the fact that the reason given for assigning the feast to the month of Abib is that the exodus from Egypt took place in that month. We have here the entire conception of the feast which we know from later times. Only the wheat harvest is called a harvest festival; whether this was once otherwise is a question apart. These circumstances do not warrant the conclusion that the absence of a definite date was due to the regulation of the festival by the barley harvest. The vague character of the dating may be due to the incompleteness of the brief laws. But if the laws were valid for several sanctuaries, there may also have been a certain margin for individual differences.

Incidentally a single feature shows that the said laws do not, in their present form, simply reflect earlier conditions. For the remark that Yahweh will drive all non-Israelites out of Canaan and take care that the land is not attacked by foreigners while the people go on their pilgrimages (Ex. 34,24) is typical of the exilic and post-exilic way of thinking. Thus did a later time imagine Israel's relation to other nations to have been. It may be taken for granted that the pilgrimages referred to in this passage are supposed to be to Jerusalem.

The ordinances of Deuteronomy run thus: Thou shalt observe the month of Abib and keep the Passover *(pesaḥ)* unto Yahweh, thy God: for in the month of Abib, Yahweh, thy God, brought thee forth out of Egypt by night. And thou shalt sacrifice the Passover unto Yahweh, thy God, of the flock and the herd in the place which Yahweh shall choose to let his name dwell in. Thou shalt eat nothing leavened with it; for seven days shalt thou eat unleavened bread *(maṣṣōth)* therewith, the bread of affliction; for thou camest forth out of the land of Egypt in haste; that thou mayest remember the day when thou camest forth out of the land of Egypt all the days of thy life. And there shall be no leaven seen with thee in all thy coasts for seven days. And none of the flesh which thou sacrificest on the evening of the first day shall be left overnight until the morning. Thou mayest not sacrifice the Passover *(hap-pesaḥ)* within any of thy gates which Yahweh thy God giveth thee, but at the place which Yahweh thy God chooseth to let his name dwell in, there thou shalt sacrifice the Passover at even, at the going down of the sun, the time *(mō'ēdn)* when thou camest forth out of Egypt. And thou shalt cook and eat in the place which Yahweh, thy God, chooseth, and thou shalt turn in the morning and go unto thy tents. Six days thou shalt eat unleavened bread, and on the seventh day shall be a solemn assembly *(ᶜaṣereth)* to Yahweh, thy God; thou shalt do no work. — Three times in a year shall all thy males appear [1] before the face of Yahweh, thy God, in the place which he chooseth: in the pilgrimage feast of unleavened bread, and in the feast of weeks, and in the feast of tabernacles; and they shall not appear before the face of Yahweh empty-handed, but every man according to the gift of his hand (i. e. what he has at his disposal) according to the blessing of Yahweh, thy God, which he hath given thee (Deut. 16,1-8.16-17).

The feast is here of the same character as in the two first-mentioned laws. Only one feast is referred to, and it is called sometimes the Passover (v. 1, as in Ez. 45,21), sometimes the Feast of Unleavened Bread (v. 16). On the day of the sacrifice and on six successive days *maṣṣōth* only may be eaten, and leaven must not be found in Israel. It is eaten as "the bread of affliction", in commemoration of the hasty departure from Egypt. The festival is throughout a feast of commemoration for Israel's deliverance from the yoke of Egypt, and this is the reason why it is celebrated in Abib — this is all as in the two smaller law codes. The slaughtering of the animals takes place on the first day at sundown, again with a view to the departure from the land of bondage; and the offering must not be left till the next day, that is to say, it must be eaten in the course of the night. This is another trait which was found in the other laws (Ex. 23,18; 34, 25).

The new feature in Deuteronomy is the provision that the feast must only be celebrated at Jerusalem. Thus it has become, like the other feasts, a feast expressing unity of the people. Here we trace the influence of the monarchy which we have already mentioned. It is strange that there is no reference to a special Paschal sacrifice, but only to the usual festival offerings of oxen and sheep. [2] It says that the sacrifice is to be *boiled* and eaten on the spot. Evidently the night passes in doing so. The next morning the participators in the feast are to turn "to their tents", but on the last of the feast days there is again a gathering with a festive assembly in the sanctuary, and this terminates the festival.

25*

Thus Deuteronomy lays down that the Passover is to be a temple feast, but it is uncertain what the participants do in the interval between the first and the last day of the festival. The question is what is meant by the return to their tents after the night of the Passover. Usually this expression means to go home (1 Sam. 4,10; 13,2; 2 Sam. 18,17; 19,9; 1 Kings 12,16; 2 Kings 8,21; 14,12 et al.). If the background of the Deuteronomic law is the state of affairs prevalent immediately after the exile, when Jerusalem and its nearest vicinity only are concerned, the expression may without difficulty be interpreted in its usual sense. But if it really refers to pilgrims from distant parts, a return home in the interval is not easily conceivable. We must then — if the command is not remote from all reality — consider the possibility that the allusion is to real tents.

In that case Deuteronomy might have preserved a good old tradition according to which it was customary to live in tents during the ancient nomadic feast. Such a tradition seems to be hinted at by the prophet when he says: I am Yahweh, thy God, from the land of Egypt, I will yet make thee dwell in tents, as in the feast days (Hos. 12,10). This, then, would mean that what was now only kept up in the days of the commemorative feast would again become full reality. At the Paschal feast the people must then, as in the wilderness period, have assembled round the holy place in tents, and Deuteronomy demands that this should take place at Jerusalem. If that is the case, however, the custom did not survive, for we find no trace of it later. [1]

As soon as the festival was entered in the calendar of feasts at the great temple, a date had to be fixed for it. According to Ezekiel and the Priestly Code, it began on the 14th of the first month, Nisan, and lasted for seven days. Like other holy feasts it was "proclaimed" (Lev. 23,4). Only in Ezekiel do we catch a glimpse of the participation of the king, by which it became a feast intended to secure the welfare of him and his realm. On the first day "the prince" sacrifices on behalf of himself and all the inhabitants of the kingdom a bull as a sin-offering; on each of the seven days of the feast he sacrifices as a burnt-offering seven bulls and seven rams, and as a sin-offering a he-goat, all with *minḥā* and oil (Ez. 45,21-25). Here the feast has become incorporated in the great atonement system of the temple.

The festival retained this character in the laws from the post-exilic temple. In one of these codes we read: In the first month on the fourteenth day of the month between the two evenings is the Passover *(pesaḥ)* to Yahweh. And on the fifteenth day of that month is the feast of unleavened bread *(ḥagh ham-maṣṣōth)* unto Yahweh; for seven days ye shall eat unleavened bread. On the first day there shall be a holy convocation *(miḳrā' ḳōdhesh)* for you. Ye shall do no work. And ye shall offer an offering made by fire unto Yahweh for seven days. On the seventh day there is a holy convocation. Ye shall do no work (Lev. 23,5-8).

A similar law states what offerings are to be made. In addition to the daily normal *tāmīdh* sacrifice, two bulls, one ram, and seven yearling lambs are to be sacrificed as a burnt-offering on each of the seven feast days, besides a *minḥā* with oil and libations, and one ram as a sin-offering (Num. 28,16-25).

We have here the post-exilic continuation of the order established under the monarchy. The feast is one, but the Passover stands out on account of its special character. It is a temple feast with an assembly on the first and last days. Each day has its own sacrifices, but these are merely of interest to the priesthood and the temple institution. The prominence given to the special Passover offering, however, draws, as it were, a line between the Passover and the *maṣṣōth* feast. This acquires a certain actual significance, because the latter feast must be celebrated for seven days subsequent to the Passover offering, while in Deuteronomy the gathering for the Passover offering takes place on the first of the seven days of the festival. It is clear that this principle of division at the time of the post-exilic temple does not help to elucidate the original relation between the Passover and the *maṣṣōth* feast.

The historical books give us very few particulars of the history of the Passover. The second book of the Kings informs us that Josiah reformed the feast. It says: The king commanded all the people; saying: Keep the Passover unto Yahweh, your God, as it is written in the book of this covenant. Nor has such a Passover been kept since the days of the judges, when they judged Israel, nor in all the days of the kings of Israel and Judah, but not until the eighteenth year of King Josiah was this Passover kept unto Yahweh in Jerusalem (2 Kings 23,21-23). This means that Josiah reintroduced the feast instituted by Moses; that again merely means that it was the true and proper feast, but we are not told in what it consisted. If the account is to be read in the light of Deuteronomy, it must mean that Josiah made the Passover more of a common Israelite temple feast at the temple of Jerusalem.

From the later post-exilic period we have two accounts of royal Paschal festivals at Jerusalem, viz. those of Hezekiah and Josiah described in the Chronicles. Here we are told (2 Chron. 30) that Hezekiah, his chieftains, and the whole congregation at Jerusalem decided to keep the Passover in the second month, because the priests had not sanctified themselves in the first month, and the people had not gathered at Jerusalem after the temple reform had been introduced. Runners were then sent out through the whole of Canaan with letters to invite the tribes, and great throngs assembled at Jerusalem to celebrate the festival which is now called the "Feast of unleavened Bread" (v. 13). Here, then, there is the same alternation of names as we have in the laws. — They slaughtered the Paschal offering (hap-pesah) on the 14th day of the month. The priests and Levites sanctified themselves and offered burnt-offerings. They stood in the usual place, and the priests sprinkled the blood which they received from the Levites, for there were many, we are told, who had not sanctified themselves, and so the Levites had to kill the victims for them. And yet, against the precepts, they took part in the meal. Then peace-offerings were offered every day, the priests and Levites giving thanks daily, and at the close of the feast they agreed to celebrate it for another seven days. The king gave towards the feast altogether 1000 bulls and 7000 animals of the flocks. Finally the priests blessed the people, who then returned home.

Of the feast of Josiah, the same that is mentioned in the book of the Kings, we are told (2 Chron. 35) that it began on the 14th of the first month. The king made the priests and Levites take up their station in the temple according to their families, and make ready to slaughter and prepare the Paschal offering according to the law of Moses. An obscure remark seems to hint at a procession with the Ark. The king gave as victims for the Paschal offering 30 000 lambs and kids and, in addition, 3000 oxen; to which various chiefs added their contributions (2600 and 5000 small cattle, 300 and 500 oxen). We are then told that the Levites slaughtered the victims for the Paschal offering, and the priests sprinkled the blood on the altar. The Levites roasted the victims over the fire and boiled "the holy parts" (v. 13); perhaps the reference is to other parts of the Paschal meal. They divided all this among the families of the lay population. After this they prepared a meal for themselves and for the priests, who were occupied with sacrifices till nightfall. While all this was going on, the singers remained in their places, presumably occupied with the temple music, and the janitors did not leave their gates. They, too, were helped by the Levites. Thus, we are told, Paschal offerings and burnt-offerings were presented on that day, and the Israelites there celebrated the Passover and the Feast of unleavened Bread for seven days. Finally the whole account is summed up in the statement that no Israelite king had ever celebrated such a feast before, its equal had not been known since the days of Samuel. The narrator evidently did not remember Hezekiah's Passover (2 Chron. 35,1-19).

It is impossible to establish how much in these narratives is tradition and how much the outcome of priestly ideals of a later age, but at any rate we see how the temple servants of a subsequent period pictured to themselves a Passover feast in the time of the monarchy. In both narratives the feast is a royal undertaking; it is carried out according to the directions of the king by the priesthood of his temple. It is the king and partly his chiefs who give the countless numbers of sacrificial animals. This withdraws the offerings from their direct relation to the families, and makes them a royal institution. Other sacrificial animals are brought to the feast besides the Paschal animals and the sheep and goats. This agrees with the later laws. [1] As in Deuteronomy, the whole feast lasts for seven days (35,17; cf. 30,22). Here then there is a deviation from the later sacrificial laws, presumably derived from an earlier tradition. Each feast day has its own offerings with thankgivings, but none of the later days equals the first evening and night.

We receive the impression of immense activity in the temple. The priests and Levites are occupied with the enormous numbers of sacrificial animals which are partly burnt on the altar, partly roasted, the blood only being sprinkled on the altar. The singers sing in their places, the people revel in the sacrificial meal, which is served to them according to their families by the Levites. The eating of this meal is the people's sole contribution to the festival, the killing of the animals and the preparation of the meal being the work of the Levites. This accords with the whole character of the narrative. For the lambs are given en bloc by the king, no family has any sacrificial animal it can call its own. It is all the more remarkable that precisely on this point there is some vacillation in the narratives. The story about Hezekiah tells us that the Levites had to kill the sacrificial animals because many of the assembly had not sanctified themselves (30, 16 f.); this implies that it was the normal thing for the people themselves to kill the victims. That was of course the case in earlier times when each family brought its own sacrificial animal, and it is still implied in Deuteronomy (16,2.6) and in certain priestly laws relating to private sacrifices (Lev. 1,5 f. 11 f.). But the tendency to withdraw offerings and festivals from ordinary family life, and transform them into institutions under the temple was bound to lead to the performance of all such undertakings by the personnel of the temple; that indeed is demanded as a generally valid rule by Ezekiel (44,11). And the same procedure is described by the Chronicler at the first Passover following the return of the exiles (Ezr. 6,19-22). Under these circumstances the only faint trace we have of the ancient custom is that the sacrificial meal is handed out to the lay population by families by the functionaries of the temple. That there is a certain vacillation in our narrative on that point proves that the change did not occur quite regularly.

The material which we have hitherto examined shows that all the laws only know of the spring festival as a temple festival celebrated in commemoration of the exodus from Egypt. We can follow the tendency to centralise the festival at the principal temple at Jerusalem, and see how it is thus in process of being withdrawn from the families and turned wholly into a temple rite. It is doubtful whether a withdrawal from Nature is to be found in the laws, for none of them shows evidence of any connection with the world of Nature. This does not exclude the possibility that such a connection may have existed in earlier times; but as a whole the laws tell us very little about the actual mode of procedure at the festivals. Our knowledge is considerably enlarged, however, by the circumstance that the Passover legend itself is preserved among the narratives of Exodus.

The most important part of the legend runs thus (Ex. 12): [1] And Yahweh spoke unto Moses and Aaron in the land of Egypt, saying: [2] This month is unto you the head of months, it is the first month of the year to you. [3] Speak ye unto all the congregation of Israel, saying: On the tenth day of this month they shall take unto them each a lamb, according to their father's houses, a lamb for the house. [4] And if the household be too little for a lamb, he and his neighbour next unto his house shall take (lambs) according to the number of souls; you shall make your count for the lamb according to the part eaten by each man. [1] [5] It shall be unto you a male lamb without blemish, a yearling; ye can take it out from the sheep and from the goats. [6] Then ye shall keep it up to the fourteenth day of the same month, and the whole assembly of the congregation of Israel shall kill it between the two evenings. [7] And they shall take of the blood and smear it on the two door posts, and on the lintel of the houses in which they eat it. [8] Then they shall eat the flesh in that night, roasted over fire, and with unleavened bread with bitter herbs they shall eat it. [9] Ye shall not eat of it raw nor boiled in water but only roasted over fire, with its head over its legs and over its belly. [2] [10] Ye shall let nothing of it remain until the morning, and what remaineth of it until the morning, ye shall burn with fire. [11] And thus shall ye eat it: your loins shall be girded, your sandals on your feet, and your staff in your hand. And ye shall eat it in haste, it is a Passover *(pesaḥ)* unto Yahweh. [12] And I will pass through the land of Egypt this night, and I will smite all the firstborn in

the land of Egypt, both man and beast, and on all the gods of
Egypt I will execute judgment, I am Yahweh. ¹³ Then the blood
shall be unto you for a token upon the houses wherein ye dwell;
and when I see the blood I will pass over you *(pāsaḥti)*, and
among you the destroyer shall not strike any blow, when I smite
the land of Egypt. ¹⁴ And this day shall be unto you for a
memorial, and ye shall keep it as a feast *(ḥagh)* to Yahweh,
throughout your generations ye shall keep it as an ordinance
forever. ¹⁵ Seven days shall ye eat unleavened bread, even the
first day ye shall remove leaven from your houses: for whosoever
eateth anything with leaven from the first day until the seventh
day, that soul shall be cut off from Israel. ¹⁶ On the first day
there shall be an holy convocation, and on the seventh day there
shall be an holy convocation to you. No manner of work shall be
done in them, save that which every soul eats, that only may be
prepared by you. ¹⁷ And ye shall observe this rule of the unleavened bread, for in this self-same day have I brought your
armies out of the land of Egypt, and ye shall observe this day in
your generations as an ordinance forever. ¹⁸ In the first month,
on the fourteenth day of the month, at even, ye shall eat unleavened bread, until the one and twentieth day of the month at
even. ¹⁹ Seven days shall there be no leaven found in your
houses. Nay, whosoever eateth that which is leavened, that soul
shall be cut off from the congregation of Israel, both the sojourner
and the children of the land. ²⁰ Ye shall eat nothing leavened, in
all your habitations ye shall eat unleavened bread.

²¹ And Moses summoned all the elders of Israel and said unto
them: Go out and take you a lamb according to your families and
kill the Passover *(hap-pesaḥ)*. ²² And ye shall take a bunch of
hyssop and dip it in the blood that is in the basin and ye shall
put some of the blood which is in the basin on the lintel and on
the two door posts, and none of you shall go out at the door of
his house until the morning. ²³ And when Yahweh passeth
through to smite the Egyptians and he seeth the blood on the lintel
and on the two door posts, Yahweh will pass over *(pāsaḥ)* the
door, and will not suffer the destroyer to come into your houses
and smite you. ²⁴ And ye shall observe this thing for an ordinance

to thee and to thy sons forever. 25 And when ye come to the land which Yahweh will give you according as he hath promised, ye shall keep this service. 26 And when your children shall say unto you: What means this service ye execute? 27 Ye shall say: it is a Passover offering *(zebhah-pesah)* unto Yahweh who passed over *(pāsah)* the houses of the children of Israel in Egypt, when he smote the Egyptians, but delivered our houses. And the people bowed down and prostrated themselves. 28 And the Israelites went away and did as Yahweh had commanded Moses and Aaron; so did they.

29 And it came to pass that at midnight Yahweh smote all the first-born in the land of Egypt, from the first-born of Pharaoh that sat on his throne to the first-born of the captive that was in the dungeon, and all the first-born of the cattle. 30 And Pharaoh rose up in that night, and all his servants and all the Egyptians, and there was a great cry in Egypt, for there was not a house where there was not one dead. 31 And he summoned Moses and Aaron by night, and he said: Rise up and get you forth from among my people, both ye and the Israelites, go and serve Yahweh as ye have said. 32 Both your flocks and your herds shall ye take, as ye have said, and be gone, and ye shall bless me also. 33 And the Egyptians were urgent upon the people that they might make them leave the land in haste, for they thought: We shall all die. 34 And the people took their dough before it was leavened, their kneading troughs being bound up in their clothes upon their shoulders (Ex. 12,1-34).

A brief account is then given of the departure, and the text goes on to say: 39 And they baked unleavened cakes of the dough which they brought forth out of Egypt, for it was not leavened, for they were thrust out of Egypt and could not get any peace, and they did not even procure victuals for the journey... 42 It was a night of watching for Yahweh for bringing them out of the land of Egypt. That same night was a watching for Yahweh for all the Israelites in their generations (Ex. 12,39.42).

Finally a series of regular ordinances follow: 43 And Yahweh said unto Moses and Aaron: This is the ordinance of the Passover, no stranger shall eat thereof. 44 And every servant that is bought for silver, if thou circumcise him, he may eat thereof. [45] A client *(tōshābh)* and an hired servant shall not eat thereof. [46] In one house shall it be eaten, thou shalt not carry forth ought of the flesh out of the house, and ye shall not break a bone thereof. [47] All the congregation of Israel shall prepare it. [48] And when a *gēr* shall sojurn with thee and he will keep the Passover to Yahweh, all his males shall be circumcised, and then he shall draw near and prepare it, and he shall be as the natives, but no uncircumcised person shall eat thereof. [49] One law shall be to the native and to the *gēr* that sojourneth among you. [50] And all the Israelites did as Yahweh had commanded Moses and Aaron, so did they. [51] And the selfsame day Yahweh brought the children of Israel out of the land of Egypt after their armies. [13,1] And Yahweh spake unto Moses, saying: [2] Thou shalt sanctify unto me all the first-born, whatsoever openeth the womb among the Israelites, both of man and of beast, it is mine (Ex. 12,43-13,2).

There follows a speech of Moses which is highly reminiscent of the style and diction of Deuteronomy. It sums up the main events of the festival. The day of the departure is to be commemorated by the absence of all that is leavened among the Israelites for seven days, and on the seventh day there is to be a feast to Yahweh. At the festival the Israelite is to tell his son what happened at the exodus, and when the Israelites come into Canaan, they are to give all the first-born to Yahweh, but redeem asses and their sons. This they are to do because Yahweh killed all the first-born of man and beast among the Egyptians. "And it shall be for a token upon thine hand, and for the frontlets between thine eyes, for by strength of hand Yahweh brought us forth out of Egypt" (Ex. 13,16). We have here an admonition which sums up and states with precision what the feast is about, and which has been added to the actual description of it.

That we have before us, in the passages quoted above, the legend of the Passover appears from the fact that the feast, with its essential elements, is described as something originating in the remote antiquity of the people, something connected with its own origins. Such a legend does not come into existence all at once, it is amplified and transformed in the course of years. It is hardly possible to assign it to various "sources"; at any rate it is difficult to find any clues to the history of the legend by this procedure.

The legend, as we have it, takes us into the land of Canaan. There, we are told, the customs of the feast are to be observed (12,25), and there the legend is to be perpetually transmitted, and brought home to the next generation (12,26 f.). The rules for participation in the feast are based on the social order in Israelitish Canaan. Strangers must not take part, nor *tōshābh*, nor hired men, though a slave may participate if circumcised. If *gērim* wish to celebrate the Passover as pure Israelites, they are free to do so if they submit to circumcision, not otherwise (Ex. 12, 43-49).

The main events pointed out in the legend are as follows: Every father's house among the Israelites shall, on the tenth day of the first month, select a male animal without blemish among the lambs or the kids. If a family is too small or too poor to provide a lamb, it may join with its neighbour in providing one. On the fourteenth day the feast begins, the lamb being killed in the evening. ¹ With a bunch of hyssop the blood is to be sprinkled on the posts and lintels of the doors in the houses where the lamb is eaten. It is a custom of essential importance, since it represents a principal motive for the feast; that is, the protection of the Israelites from the disaster about to befall the enemies of the people. The same night the meat is to be roasted and eaten up; should any part be left, it is to be burnt the next morning. With the meat they are to eat unleavened bread and bitter herbs. The meal is eaten hastily, and the participants are to be ready as for a journey, with staff in hand. On the following days unleavened bread only may be eaten; all leaven is to be kept far from Israelitish houses.

In this ordering of the feast it is very conspicuous that the family is the central point. The lamb is killed by and for the family, the meal is eaten in the houses of the families. These even play a special part, one of the objects of the feast being to protect them against evil by smearing blood on their doors, a

custom still well known in the East. [1] The precepts concerning
the unleavened bread imply that people normally spend the
Passover week in their homes. A certain connection with the
sanctuary is hinted at, especially in the command about a "holy
assembly" *(miḳrā' ḳōdhesh,* Ex. 12,16) on the first and seventh
days. But the main stress seems to be laid on what happens in
each family and in its house. The Israelites celebrate the festival
by families, and yet it is not exclusively a family feast. It is a
general Israelite festival which concerns the whole people and
its history.

The Passover expresses throughout the idea, which we also
found in the laws, that the feast is to commemorate the departure
from Egypt. Before considering this essential aspect, we must,
however, notice some other sides of it. According to the legend
itself, the connection with the exodus results from the fact that
the Israelites asked Pharaoh for permission to go into the desert
and celebrate a festival with sacrifices to their God, Yahweh.
The whole legend deals with the fight to obtain this permission
and the victory of the Israelites. It is impossible to elucidate the
underlying historical events. But the legend implies that the
feast was an ancient and customary one with the tribes, which
now acquired a fresh significance because of these events. It
seems quite natural, indeed, that the Israelites should have had
such a feast from the earliest times, and that it should be
associated with a sanctuary in the desert.

For the sacrifice which is the central incident of the feast
is in good accord with conditions in pre-Canaanite Israel. It
consisted of a lamb or a kid, that is to say, a Bedawin offering,
and typically Israelitish, because the tribes were keepers of
flocks. As in the case of the Arabian *'atīra* festival, the feast is
celebrated in the spring about the time when the young of the
flocks have been born. Hence we may safely assume that the
original nucleus of the festival was the sanctification of the
flocks on whose increase the life of the wandering tribes depended.

It is then natural to suppose that it was the first-born which
were sacrificed. Nothing is said about this in the main part of
the legend (Ex. 12) any more than in the laws. But a large part

of the legend centres round events connected with the first-born, viz. the saving of Israel's first-born and the killing of the first-born of the Egyptians. This would seem to indicate that we have here an element once predominant in the character of the festival. [1]

In the special way in which the lamb or kid is to be prepared an ancient Bedawin custom is doubtless preserved. It must not be boiled, a feature left out in one of the laws (Deut. 16,7), nor must it be raw; it is to be roasted whole without being cut up (as would be necessary if it were boiled), and if our reading of this passage is correct (Ex. 12,9), it is to hang with its head upwards. No bone must be broken in the animal (Ex. 12,46). All this is to preserve the body of the sanctified animal as intact and as near to the live animal as possible. The well-being of the flock in the year to come depended on the holy animal being protected from injury. The Israelites acquired an increased share in the holiness of the feast by eating the animal. But this must be done only on the holy evening of the festival. Leavings not eaten at once were to be destroyed that they might not be exposed to desecration, and thus perhaps become a source of incalculable harm.

With the meat, according to the legend, the people partook of bitter herbs and unleavened bread. How the former came to be used at festivals we do not know. They may have been herbs belonging to the meal in the nomadic period and so have been preserved as a ritual food at the Passover.

It is just as difficult to determine the significance of the eating of unleavened bread *(maṣṣōth)*. This, too, might be supposed to be due to a Bedawin custom transmitted through the ages. We know that the Arabs used unleavened bread *(faṭīr)*, and recent explorers tell us of the use made of it by the Bedawin. [2] It is not only Bedawin, however, who eat unleavened bread; it was also in use among the peasant population of Canaan (Gen. 19,3; 1 Sam. 28,24). Hence it may equally well be a Canaanitish custom which has become associated with the Passover.

The laws give no answer to the problem thus raised. We have seen that in some of the post-exilic laws a certain difference is made between the Passover and the *maṣṣōth* feast (Lev. 23,5 f.; Num. 28,16 f.), but this is a purely secondary distinction between the two main elements of the feast. The consumption of unleavened bread is peculiarly associated with the Passover. It is to be eaten in commemoration of the exodus from Egypt (Ex. 23,15; 34,18). For it is the bread of affliction, which recalls the hasty departure (Deut. 16,3). On the other hand, in the account of the immigration, we find the remark that at the first Passover after the crossing of Jordan the Israelites eat *maṣṣōth* and roasted corn of the crops of the land, at the same time ceasing to eat manna (Josh. 5,10-12). Here *maṣṣōth* is expressly associated with Canaan in contrast with the desert food. This information can hardly have any bearing on the early history of the festival, but it shows that there was a feeling that unleavened bread belonged to life in Canaan.

If the use of *maṣṣōth* dates from the time in Canaan it can not originally have been associated with the Passover. It is not unlikely that this was the position. The eating of unleavened bread for a whole week is such a significant feature that it seems more probably to indicate an independent feast than an amplification of some particular part of the customs associated with the Passover meal. In such circumstances this feast can only have been connected with the barley harvest, as has long been conjectured; and its combination with the Passover is simply due to the fact that the two feasts coincided. It must have symbolised the sanctification of the first produce of the soil, and the command to eat unleavened bread must be derived from ancient customs according to which the bread-corn was to be sanctified without any connection with foreign elements, the same principle we find at the sanctification of the roasted corn. [1] The omission of leaven, then, as is often the case with ritual duties, acquired an independent importance of unlimited range. No leaven at all was permitted to be found in the houses during the holy week, and any one who eat anything leavened was to be killed without mercy for his sacrilegious act (Ex. 12,19).

Thus the events of the spring festival warrant the presumption that it is a combination of two originally independent festivals, a pre-Canaanite pastoral feast which sanctified the first-born, and a Canaanite peasant feast which sanctified the barley crops. Both the laws and the legend, however, show us how closely the two festivals became knit together, so as to form one feast, called now by one, now by the other name. At the same time each of them lost what we may suppose was its original significance. The Passover did not exact the first-born only, but any sacrificial lamb could be used. And *maṣṣōth* has nothing to do with the first crops; not even the connection with the barley harvest is indicated in the laws, the entire interest centres round the removal of all leaven. The post-Biblical ordinances expressly allow the cakes to be baked of other than barley flour. [1]

The ancient double feast which sanctified the world of the Israelite farmer and stock-breeder suffered this transformation by being connected with the exodus from Egypt. The most natural supposition is that this connection, as recounted in the legend, was due to some historical coincidence, but as to this we can form no independent conjecture. The new character given to the feast made it a commemoration feast, that is to say, a feast through which the people re-experienced the events on which their existence as an independent nation was based. In all the laws it is with this that the festival is concerned, and the Passover legend is based on it. It is the history of the people which is sanctified.

The re-living of this experience, and that is what is meant by "commemoration", is carried through by simple and forceful means characteristic of primitive folk, or those unaffected by modern European culture. The participants in the feast repeat the exodus by eating the meal in the greatest haste, with staff in hand, with sandals on their feet, and with girded loins (Ex. 12,11). This is the essential feature which has been preserved, but doubtless there were others. We may conjecture that running and jumping movements were performed, for the name *pesaḥ* is related to words which denote such jumping movements. These movements, known also in Canaanitish cults (1 Kings 18,21.26), may have been thought to symbolise the hasty flight from the enemy's country. [2]

All the actions of the feast acquire a fresh character, adapted to its purpose, the commemoration of the exodus. The unleavened bread is eaten during the feast, because the people had to take hurriedly the unfinished dough with them in troughs carried on their shoulders, having no time to procure proper food for their journey (Ex. 12,34.39), a feature probably repeated in the ritual of the feast. Doubtless the bitter herbs are regarded as a reminder of Israel's bitter humiliation in the land of bondage.[1] The lamb was not offered as a sacrifice to win sanctification for the flocks; the offering was concerned with Israel's fight against Egypt. The blood was to be sprinkled on the doors of the Israelites; when Yahweh went forth to smite all the first-born of Egypt, he would pass over *(pāsaḥ)* the houses thus marked. Thus the Passover *(pesaḥ)* becomes a feast by which the Israelites are rescued and the offering saves their first-born.

The interest centres entirely around the first-born who are slain, that is, among the Egyptians; and the first-born who are saved, that is, among the Israelites. They hold the interest to such a degree that, as we have already noted, the ordinance concerning the Paschal lamb entirely disregards the command that it is to be a first-born animal which is sacrificed, though this must necessarily be the starting-point of the whole idea. It is not mentioned in the main legend, and has disappeared entirely from the laws, and quite similarly the unleavened bread has been separated from the harvest.

The actions mentioned here do not appear as isolated actions in the legend, but as the climax of a series of events concerned with Israel, in which, however, she is not active. It is a drama enacted on a higher level, for Yahweh is the motive power. Helped by Moses and Aaron, the leader and the high priest at the dawn of the nation, he carries through his campaign against his and Israel's foes, until he has attained his object, the deliverance of the people and his own glorification.

A firm and compact plan holds together the legend, in spite of irregularities in the details. It begins at the very beginning with the immigration of the forefathers of the Israelites into Egypt, the rapid growth of the people, and the Egyptian fear of their power. In order to check it Pharaoh imposed hard forced labour on them under taskmasters, and further sought to kill their men-children; first by commanding the midwives to do so, next by the general order that they were to be cast into the Nile (Ex. 1). This gave rise to the struggle which ended by the children of the Egyptians being killed.

After the situation has thus been outlined in the introduction, the legend proceeds, recording how Yahweh's instrument, the saviour and creative ruler of the people, was born. The story is connected with the command that all the male children were to be cast into the Nile. First the child is concealed, then it is put in a chest by the river, a feature recalling the legend of the birth of Sargon, the ruler of the early Babylonian empire. The child was found by Pharaoh's daughter, who took charge of it, and had it taught all the wisdom of Egypt. Thus the very daughter of the enemy came to foster the rescuer, and the Israelite does not deny himself a certain pleasure at the thought that she was cheated into paying the mother for nursing the child while it was small (Ex. 2,1-10).

The story proceeds apace and brings Moses very near to his task. He visits his people and is indignant at seeing a fellow tribesman struck by an Egyptian, whom, therefore, he kills. But the next day, when he wants to reconcile two quarrelsome Hebrews, they refuse to listen to him and even tell him that he is a murderer. He flies, and the legend connects him with Midian where he takes a wife and begets a child, a significant feature, because the future leader of the nation is thus connected with the plains in the regions frequented by the pre-Canaanite Israelitish tribes. And here, indeed, he received his consecration, the God of his fathers resolving to take charge of the people (Ex. 2,11-25).

The account of the consecration forms a central point in the progress of the story. For here Yahweh, as in a programme, sets forth all the events which are to develop in the rest of the legend. It happens in a holy place, Horeb, the mountain of God, where Yahweh appears to Moses. He reveals himself as the God of his fathers, of Abraham, Isaac, and Jacob, and then all that is included in the commemoration of the Paschal feast is unfolded. Yahweh has heard the cry of his people. He will bring them up out of the affliction of Egypt and lead them into Canaan, a land "flowing with milk and honey". Moses is to take this message to the elders of Israel, and they are to ask Pharaoh to let them go into the desert to sacrifice to Yahweh. But Pharaoh will not listen to them, and Yahweh will then smite Egypt with all His wonders and thus force him to do so (Ex. 3). To win authority, Moses is given power to perform miracles, especially with his rod, which turns into a serpent; and when he tries to excuse himself by his slowness of speech, he is commanded to take Aaron with him. "He shall be thy spokesman unto the people, he shall be to thee instead of a mouth, and thou shalt be to him instead of God" (4,16, cf. 7,1). After some time Moses is commanded to leave Midian and go to Egypt, and again it is intimated what is to happen: Moses is to work wonders, but Yahweh will harden the heart of Pharaoh so that he will not let Israel go. And the main theme of the Passover is strongly emphasised. The first-born of Pharaoh shall die, because he refuses to let Israel, the first-born of Yahweh go into the desert and celebrate a feast to him (4,22 f.). Then Moses goes to Egypt and meets Aaron, but in passing an episode is inserted into the legend which establishes the vital necessity of circumcision for the Israelites (Ex. 4).

Moses and Aaron interpret as a command not as an appeal Yahweh's demand that the Israelites shall be allowed to go into the desert and keep a feast to him (Ex. 5,1). This only leads to greater oppression, for Pharaoh does not know Yahweh (Ex. 5,2). The events that follow make Pharaoh acquainted with the might of the God of Israel. His hardness is but a factor in Israel's conflict with him. It is Yahweh himself who hardens his heart so as to be able to show his power over him with all the more violence (Ex. 7,3 ff.). In rapid succession follow Yahweh's judgments, executed by Moses or Aaron by means of the powerful rod. The Egyptians can imitate some of them, hence Pharaoh gets no idea of the power behind Moses, and his heart remains hard. But even when the power of the magicians fails them, Pharaoh's heart is hardened and he will not listen (Ex. 8,15.28; 9,7).

All this, however, is only part of Yahweh's plan. It is he who blinds the eyes of Pharaoh, that he may triumph over the mighty ruler and let the Israelites experience events which they can commemorate and transmit from generation to generation. Moses and Aaron actually invite Pharaoh to humble himself before Yahweh, and let the people go away to keep a feast to him. His own men entreat him to give way. During one of the previous plagues Pharaoh has allowed the Israelites to celebrate the feast in Egypt, but they have refused on the plea that the Egyptians would stone them if they sacrificed animals which it was an abomination to the Egyptians to kill (Ex. 8,22). Now he goes a step further and allows the men alone to go away and celebrate the feast; if they want to take their wives and children, and their herds and flocks as well, it shows that they have other intentions than that of celebrating a feast (Ex. 10,10 f.). The plague of the grasshoppers makes Pharaoh ask forgiveness, but when it has stopped, he is as he has been. A great darkness all over Egypt, except in the place where the Israelites live, makes Pharaoh offer to give up the men but not the animals. When this is refused, the struggle is at its height, the climax towards which the whole drama has been tending. At midnight all the first-born of men and animals in Egypt are slain, at the same time the Israelites are saved through their Passover. Thus Pharaoh is conquered. He who has been so hard now begs them to leave the country, and even asks for their blessing (Ex. 12,31 f.), and the Egyptians, their oppressors, press on them their deliverance.

Thus the Passover is the feast of the deliverance of the people. But the legend has a sequel. The humiliation of Pharaoh has not yet been completed. This only happens when Yahweh again hardens his heart, so that he pursues the delivered Israelites with horses and chariots, horsemen and warriors. Then comes the hour when Yahweh can finally triumph over him, when he lets him and all his host perish ignominiously in the sea. This terminates the war between Yahweh and Pharaoh about Israel.

The victory is celebrated in a hymn which fits well into the rest of the legend, establishing as it does the glory won by Yahweh in the fight (Ex. 15). It opens thus:

1 I will sing to Yahweh, for he is most mighty, the horse with its rider hath he hurled into the sea.

2 Yah is my strength and song, he is become my salvation. He

is my God, I praise him, my father's God, I exalt him.

3 Yahweh is a warrior, Yahweh is his name.

Then there is a description of how Yahweh destroys Pharaoh. He is lured into the sea, which Yahweh has dammed up by the breath of his nostrils. But Yahweh's breath went forth again, and the waves closed over the enemy's host. The song goes on to say:

11 Who is like thee among the gods, O Yahweh! Who is like thee, exalted in holiness!

Awful in glorious deeds, creator of wonders! 12 Thou didst stretch forth thy right hand, the earth swallowed them.

13 In thy mercy thou didst lead forth the people which thou didst avenge, thou didst guide them in thy strength unto thy holy habitation.

14 The peoples heard it and shook, a trembling seized the inhabitants of Philistaea.

15 Then the chiefs of Edom were dismayed, the leaders of Moab were seized with fear; all the inhabitants of Canaan were paralysed.

16 Fear and dread fell upon them, by the violence of thine arm they became still as a stone;

That thy people might go forth, Yahweh, that the people thou didst purchase might go forth.

17 Thou didst bring them in and plant them in the mountain of thine inheritance, a place thou didst prepare for thy dwelling, o Yahweh, the sanctuary which thy hands prepared.

18 Yahweh is king forever and ever.

A very valuable note is added to the hymn. In the introduction (Ex. 15,1) we are told that it was sung by Moses and the Israelites, but at the end it says: And the prophetess Miriam, Aaron's sister, took the timbrel in her hand, and all the women went out after her with timbrels and with dances, and Miriam sang to them: Sing ye to Yahweh, for he is most mighty etc. (15,20 f.). This means that the hymn has become part of the festival together with the women's dances, like the dances they performed when the victorious warriors returned (1 Sam. 18,6).

If we consider the Passover legend as a whole, it is not possible to regard it as a purely literary product. It contains facts, viz. actions which form the nucleus of the feast. These cannot be due to arbitrary invention, but must be based on a firm tradition, evolved from the historical events, the participants in the feast repeating and giving renewed life to them through the ages. It is not, however, the object of the legend to preserve the external happenings which once caused prehistoric Israel to leave Egypt. On the contrary, the individual events have no independent significance, they merely serve to paint a vivid picture of how Yahweh, in connection with the primeval festival, humiliates Pharaoh and exhibits his power over him in favour of Israel. Hence the legend does not present a historical development, where one event grows out of another. The result is a foregone conclusion.

The fight is so unequal that not only does Yahweh easily defeat the enemy, but he must even make his soul rigid, hard, and heavy, in order that it may offer resistance, and Yahweh may thus exalt himself at his expense. This play of Yahweh with Pharaoh gives coherence to the story; there is no logical coherence between the events, nor is Pharaoh's attitude psychologically consistent. Though the plagues are mostly cataclysms with which Egypt was familiar, they lose their natural character in the legend. They begin and cease quite arbitrarily; they assume monstrous dimensions; and though they befall all Egypt, the Israelites living in Egypt can escape them; so much does the story rise above the order of ordinary historical events. Hence the feast comprises great things: The foundation of the nation by its earliest leaders; the inauguration of its God's work for it; the transporting of the people from conditions of bondage in a hostile country to its own historic land surrounding the temple which was the seat of its God. [1]

It is impossible to cut out definite details from this drama and thus form a picture of how the exodus from Egypt took place; just as it is impossible on the basis of these documents to arrive at a more precise idea of the God of prehistoric Israel. As the Israel of this legend is the people which came into existence in Canaan, not the prehistoric earliest Israel, so also is it the

God of Canaanitish Israel, enthroned on Zion, whose fight with the enemy this legend glorifies.

It is remarkable that, though the two parties to the fight are so unequal, circumvention plays such a great part in the legend. It is thus in the commerce of the Israelites with their Egyptian neighbours. According to Yahweh's directions the Israelites asked the Egyptians to lend them their gold and silver things, and the eyes of the Egyptians were blinded by Yahweh, so they were cunningly cheated out of their valuable property (Ex. 3,22; 11,2 f.; 12,35 f.). But elements of craft are mixed even in the main story. Moses and Aaron only ask for permission to keep a feast, but in reality they want to take this opportunity of leaving Egypt for good. Pharaoh has seen through them, so he wants first the women and children and the cattle to remain behind, later the cattle only, and Moses cunningly answers that they are obliged to take the cattle with them as they do not know how many victims they will need (Ex. 10,10 f. 24-26). We may wonder that those who have so powerful a God on their side employ the weapon of the weak, nay, that their own God gives it to them; we may even say that it fits badly into the whole legend, which centres round the fact that Pharaoh is made to give in by force. But it is here as in the narratives about Jacob. Cunning also expresses the ability to attain an end, and the Israelites rejoice to see that Pharaoh, though he knows what is at stake, must yet succumb, because he is powerless.

Thus the whole Passover legend centres round one thing, the Israelitish God's display of all his cunning and power to make Israel the nation it became. The exodus from Egypt was celebrated in the feast as a fundamental event by which the people was uplifted; it means the decisive victory which its God won in the fight against his enemies, and by which he exalted himself above all other gods as the greatest in power and holiness. In this fight he used cunning and force and made servants of the elements. The order of nature had to be overthrown when he desired to call down plagues upon the Egyptians; wind and sea combined to destroy the enemy. And the emigration was part of a definite plan with the temple of Zion as its object. While the neighbouring peoples were seized with dread Yahweh led his people directly to the habitation which he had selected, and where he lived as a king. The dances performed and songs sung at the festival were a glorification of the Judaean royal temple and the God ruling there; and the Paschal feast was a re-living and commemoration of Yahweh's deliverance of the people by which the nation was actually founded. The fact that the feast is a spring feast acquires fresh importance: it is to be celebrated in the first month, which is the head and source of all the months (Ex. 12,2), and the event itself becomes the starting point of a new era.

Re-living the Paschal legend, the Israelites sanctified their history and thus strengthened the foundation of their life and the relation to their God. Through the Passover the great events were made more prominent, the exodus from Egypt acquired a unique importance as the beginning of all Israelitish history. Israel's God was called the God who brought them out of Egypt, and it is the participation in this historical event which decides whether or not one belongs to Israel (Isa. 11,16; Hos. 2,17; 8,13; 11,1.5; 12,10; 13,4; Am. 2,10; 3,1; Mic. 6,4; 7,15; Ps. 81,11; 135,8.9; 136,10 et al.). The repeated commemoration of this story of the founding of the nation laid a firm hold on their souls, and created the sure basis from which the Israelites drew self-confidence as a nation.

Yahweh's fight for his people at the deliverance from Egypt was not an ordinary historical event which had taken place within the normal bounds of time. It had happened in primeval times, hence it was of cosmic dimensions. The fight with Egypt was identified with the primordial fight when Yahweh created the world and its order out of Chaos, slaying its primeval monsters. In the prophets and in some hymns we meet with detached fragments of these ideas in the glorification of Yahweh. "Awake, awake! Put on strength, O arm of Yahweh! Awake as in ancient days, the generations of eternities. Didst thou not cleave Rahab, pierce the dragon? Didst thou not dry the sea, the waters of the great deep? Thou who madest the depths of the sea a way for the ransomed to pass over?" (Isa. 51,9-10; cf. 30,7; Ez. 29,3; 32,2 f.). [1] Deutero-Isaiah expects that the great events will be re-lived upon the return from the exile. And there can be no doubt that the incidents to which he refers have belonged to the mythical glorification of the exploits of Yahweh in the deliverance from Egypt, and that it was part of the cult by which these exploits were re-created and commemorated.

As we have seen, the ancient basis for the Passover and the *maṣṣōth* feast was entirely transformed by the whole feast being changed into a commemoration festival. If the *maṣṣōth* feast is of Canaanitish origin, there must have been a time when the Passover alone was celebrated for the purpose of sanctifying the flocks and commemorating the history of Israel. Of the *maṣṣōth* festival as an independent festival we know nothing, we can merely conjecture its existence. In all the sources it has already become part of the commemoration of the deliverance from Egypt. But it is quite possible that once, before the historical element became predominant, it meant in equal degree the sanctification of the animals belonging to the world of the Israelite, of his crops, and of his early history.

It is remarkable that when the early connection between the world of Nature and the Paschal offering and *maṣṣōth* had been broken off, it was re-established in new forms. When the Paschal lamb was no longer an offering of the first-born, fresh offerings of first-born were required, as we have seen, and an attempt was made to link them up with the Passover. Thus we see a general demand for the offering of first-born loosely inserted in the Passover legend (Ex. 13,2, cf. 34,19); and in the peculiar summary introduced into the legend (Ex. 13,3-16) the demand for the first-born becomes a principal point, the motive being the killing of the first-born. But elsewhere we find this demand without any connection whatever with the Passover (Num. 18, 15 ff.; Deut 15,19 ff.). Owing to the season in which the festival was celebrated the first-born animals were often brought to the sanctuary at the time of the feast. For the same reason the association with the barley harvest was revived, and it became customary to sanctify the first sheaf in connection with the spring festival. Hence the Mishnah takes it for granted that the Passover has some relationship with the harvest. [1]

As mentioned above, there are features of the legend which show that the great events were re-experienced at the festival through mimetic acts. It is not possible to estimate the extent of these. But we have seen that the entire legend forms a unity, the coherence of which is due to the ritual purpose. It contains the events which were given renewed life in the cult, and thus were identical with what was created in primeval time and was revived by the cult. It is unlikely that the mimetic acts should have been restricted to the few things directly mentioned. The entire deliverance of the people is re-lived. It is a matter of course that the texts were recited, but we may suppose that it took place by parts of it being assigned to different people, who dramatised the stories not only by reciting the words.

The form of the legend which has come down to us is of course in some degree accidental. It has become transformed through the ages. By being inserted in a continuous historical narrative, it has lost something of its character, and we have no indication as to how it was used. It appears clearly, however, that it was a nocturnal festival, beginning towards the evening and ending in the morning. In connection with the times stated, mention is made now of festival rites such as offerings, then of the events of primeval time. The two things are in reality the same. The whole story of the exodus takes place in the course of one night, the night of the festival. On the 14th of the first month at the beginning of the evening the victim is slaughtered (Ex. 12,6), at midnight Yahweh smites the first-born of the Egyptians (12,29). In the course of the night the people fly and Pharaoh pursues them, but the result is certain, it is a "watch-night" *(lēl shimmūrim)* to Yahweh (12,42). First he allows the pursuit full play, but at the time of the morning watch he looks out over the Egyptian host (14,24); the pursuit is now at its height, and Israel near annihilation. Then he intervenes, and at the dawn of day the waters close over the Egyptians (14,27). The drama, and thus the primeval events, have come to an end; the people rejoice and strike in with the triumphal chant; the women seize the timbrels and celebrate the victory by dancing, singing, and playing.

The pæan of victory which terminates and sums up the whole legend points to a feast at the royal temple of Jerusalem. The same would seem to be indicated by the demand for a holy assembly on the first and seventh days of the feast (Ex. 12,16). It would then be natural to suppose that we were here concerned with a nocturnal feast celebrated in the temple, where the different parts of the legend were gone through at the times indicated. But important parts of the legend conflict with this view. The Paschal lamb is eaten in the houses, which are marked with its blood, and no part of the meat must be taken out of the house (12,46). It is even forbidden to leave the house in the course of the night (12, 22). It is a family festival though it is at the same time a public feast. We are here faced by the old question of the relation between home and sanctuary at the feasts.

We may take it for granted that the form of celebration of the feast underwent changes according to the period and the place. Before the immigration, when it was still a purely nomadic feast, we must suppose it to have been celebrated similarly as when the Arabs celebrated a sacrificial feast, for instance in the sanctuaries around Mecca. They must have been encamped in their tents near the holy place, must have sacrificed and eaten a meal by families, and then performed the rites together. We have found intimations that such an encampment in tents also belonged to the celebration of the feast in Canaan (Hos. 12,10). It is, in fact, natural to suppose that the assemblies at the sanctuaries were of this type.

We do not, indeed, know how the feast was celebrated there. The question, then, is merely what its relation was to the temple at Jerusalem, and at the time when the Paschal legend received its final form this temple only could be concerned.

We have learned from the laws that there was a strong tendency to refer the feast to the temple as a temple institution purely in which the people took a small part only. Deuteronomy, like the other sources, requires the Paschal sacrifice to be offered in the evening; and it has another feature which we recognise from the legend, viz. the haste of the proceedings. But here the sacrifice is an ordinary temple sacrifice, we hear both of large and small cattle (Deut. 16,2), and the meat is to be boiled, and thus also cut up like other sacrificial meat, which is in marked contrast with the Paschal legend (Ex. 12,9, cf. the Book of Jubilees 49,13). Ezekiel, the Priestly Code, and other later sources likewise speak only of acts taking place in the temple, and there is no hint of a meal in the houses (Ezr. 6,19 ff.; 2 Chron. 30; 35). If we pass farther down in time we see that the Book of Jubilees (49,16) even says expressly that it is not permitted to eat the Passover meal outside the sanctuary; but from the Gospels we know that Jesus took the Paschal meal with his disciples in a private house (Mat. 26,18; Mark 14,14; Luke 22,11 f.) in accordance with the legend.

We see from this the uncertainty caused by assigning the Passover to the temple of Jerusalem. It became difficult to retain that combination of a family festival and a public feast which was doubtless the rule in earlier times. The legend, we have seen, probably shows traces of referring to a feast in and near the temple of Jerusalem, but in the form in which we know it, the prevailing point of view is that it is held in the houses, which must not even be left in the night (Ex. 12,7.22). This excludes participation in nocturnal public rites. Such, then, had been abandoned at the time when the legend received its present form. It is even possible that this form came into existence outside Palestine, where visits to the temple of Jerusalem were excluded, the Passover being, none the less, celebrated; just as the Mohammedans in the various countries celebrate the same sacrificial feast as the pilgrims at Mecca.

The combination of the private feast and the temple feast was a fixed rule at the beginning of our era, when people went on pilgrimages to Jerusalem but celebrated the Paschal night in private houses. We know little about the role then played by the temple. According to the Mishnah the lamb was first sacrificed in the temple and then taken to the house where the meal was eaten. [1] This is a compromise, but it is obvious that the feast has thus lost its old character. The Passover legend clearly shows that the nature of the feast demanded community.

From several periods we have evidence that the Passover was actually celebrated by Jews outside Canaan. The earliest is found in the Elephantine letters. A letter dated in the 5th year of Darius, i. e. 419, tells us that the king had sent an order to the governor, Arsham, and the sender of the letter, a Jew by name Hananiah, referring to this order, requests the Jewish garrison at Elephantine to observe various rules which clearly enough concern the Passover and the Feast of Unleavened Bread. That the Jewish garrison must have the special permission of the great king to celebrate such a feast is easily understood, partly because it involved some days of rest, partly because the slaughtering of lambs might lead to conflicts with the Egyptian Chnum priests, such as we know from the quarrels of Hindus and Mohammedans over the sacrificing of the ox. [1]

The Passover being by its nature of central importance to the Israelites, its observance was regarded as an invariable duty for every Jew. The book of Jubilees (49,9) even demands the extermination of any Jew who neglects it. All who were admitted to the Israelite community were to celebrate it, thus a *gēr* or a purchased slave, in so far as they were circumcised (Ex. 12,44. 48 f.; Num. 9,14); whereas a *tōshābh* and a man hired for the day were not allowed to partake of the Passover meal (Ex. 12,45).

A prerequisite for participation was of course always complete cleanness. Any one who was prevented by uncleanness or absence on a journey could keep the feast at the corresponding time in the second month. A post-exilic law states this in the form of a casuistical ordinance of Moses (Num. 9,1 ff.). It shows that the observance of the Paschal law had now become a part of the obligatory system of Judaism.

As long as the temple of Jerusalem existed, it attracted large bands of pilgrims for the Passover feast, as we learn from the New Testament and Josephus. [2] Philo calls the Passover the most important Jewish feast, because it celebrates the fundamental event in the life of the people. [3] The feast retained this importance down through the ages. What had originally been the nucleus, the sacrifice of the lamb, gradually fell into disuse outside Jerusalem, and after the final destruction of the temple in the year 70, the offering also ceased to be made there. [4]

The history of the Passover feast shows that it developed out of the sacrifice by which the cattle and later also the corn were sanctified. We know it in this form only that both these sacrifices subserved the purpose of sanctifying the history of the people, and of commemorating their delivery from the bondage of Egypt which is a basic feature of that history. This aspect of the character of the feast carries us far back in the life of the people, and it renders the feast suitable for acquiring central significance for the kingdom as a chief festival at the royal temple. The demand that it should be entirely subordinated to the temple was never fully nor consistently carried through, but the feast retained its signal importance during the whole life of the people.

The mixed origin of the festival has left its traces in the Passover legend, which carries us back to its earliest forms as a sacrificial feast for the first-born. It allows us a glimpse of the ancient common festivals with the commemorative re-living of the fundamental events in the national history, and it contains features which point to the royal temple on Zion. But it likewise shows us the family as the basis of the feast; and this ancient feature was through the development of conditions after the exile one-sidedly emphasised as the predominant trait. For there can hardly be any doubt that it was only after the exile that the legend obtained the form in which it has been transmitted to us.

The harvest formed the climax in the life of the peasant. It gave him the reward for his labours and was the foundation of his own and his family's existence. "The joy in harvest" (Isa. 9,2) is that exalted joy which recalls the feeling that fills the victorious host when it divides the spoil. The harvest season, which opens with the barley harvest (2 Sam. 21,9) and is continued with the wheat harvest, therefore constitutes "the weeks" in a special sense. The Israelites say confidently of Yahweh: He reserveth unto us the appointed weeks of the harvest (Jer. 5,24).

Though the harvest thus forms a coherent period, the crops of each separate species of corn were of course sanctified, just as the produce was sanctified in each of the stages from the sheaf to the loaf. We have seen that the Feast of Unleavened Bread probably originally sanctified the barley crops, and that this purpose of the feast was lost sight of, but was again revived, in so far as a barley sheaf was sanctified during the feast.

The sanctification of the wheat doubtless in early times was conducted in the same way as for instance the sheep-shearing feast, with a visit to the nearest sanctuary and also a festival on each farm; but all the laws that have come down to us require it to be celebrated as a pilgrimage feast, and since the first pilgrimage feast became entirely merged in the Passover, it became the harvest feast proper. Hence we read in the two minor law codes: And (thou shalt celebrate) the pilgrimage feast of harvest, the first-fruits of thy labours, that which thou sowest in the field (Ex. 23,16); and again: And thou shalt observe the feast of weeks (i. e. the harvest weeks), of the first-fruits of the wheat harvest (Ex. 34,22).

In Deuteronomy we have the command: Seven weeks shalt thou number unto thee. Thou shalt begin to number the seven weeks when the sickle begins to be put to the standing crop. And thou shalt keep the feast of (harvest-) weeks unto Yahweh thy God, all according to the free-will offering of thine hand which thou wilt give, according as Yahweh thy God blesseth thee. And thou shalt rejoice before Yahweh, thy God, thou and thy son and daughter and thy man-servant and thy maid-servant, and the Levite that is within thy gates and the *gēr,* and the fatherless, and the widow that are among you, in the place which Yahweh, thy God, shall choose, to let His name dwell there. And thou shalt remember that thou wast a bondman in Egypt, and thou shalt observe and keep these laws (Deut. 16,9-12).

If we disregard the demand that the feast should be celebrated at Jerusalem, we here gain an impression of the harvest festival as it was observed at the Israelite sanctuaries. A certain quantity of the crops was sanctified according to the farmer's own judgment in proportion as the crops were plentiful or sparse, and a feast of rejoicing was then celebrated, of course with a meal, of which in the first place the family, but amongst others the priest also partook. The Levite is probably mentioned as the person who generally joined in the sacrificial meals at the sanctuaries. But besides this Deuteronomy in its effort to prevent any one belonging to the people from perishing mentions several persons who are to be included out of charity. The feast being at the same time located at Jerusalem, the whole proceeding acquires an unreal and impracticable character. Behind the law we catch a glimpse of ancient ordinances to which certain fresh requirements have been added, without any thought for their suitability or feasibility. The reference to the people's bondage in Egypt is not meant to give a historical character to the feast, as was the case with the Passover, but to excite gratitude and thus exhort the people to obedience.

Deuteronomy dates the feast, though merely in part. It is to be celebrated seven weeks after the beginning of the barley harvest. It is inconceivable that the barley harvest should have begun on the same date throughout the country. It would seem to follow that the feast was celebrated by families for each farm, or at any rate for each village, similarly as it is recorded of the sheep-shearing feast. But the matter is obscure, and we must therefore ask why the wheat-harvest feast was to be kept precisely at a fixed time after this. There is probably here a vague attempt to establish a more stable calendar of festivals; the vagueness is the result of an attempt to combine this effort with the retention of an early custom.

In the actual statutes for the temple of Jerusalem the feast has become definitely fixed as part of the festival calendar of the great temple. It says: And ye shall count from the day after the sabbath, from the day that ye bring the sheaf of the wave-offering, seven complete weeks there shall be. Unto the day after the seventh sabbath shall ye number fifty days, and ye shall offer a new *minḥā* unto Yahweh. From your habitations ye shall bring wave loaves, two ... two tenth parts (ephah) of fine flour it shall be, it shall be baked with leaven as the first-fruits unto Yahweh. And ye shall offer, besides the bread, seven lambs without blemish of the first year, and one bullock of the large cattle and two rams; they shall be for a burnt-offering unto Yahweh with their *minḥā* and their libations, an offering made by fire of sweet savour unto Yahweh. And ye shall offer one kid of the goats for a sin-offering and two lambs of the first year for a peace-offering. And the priest shall wave them over the bread of the first-fruits, waving them before Yahweh [1], it shall be holy for Yahweh, for the priest. And ye shall proclaim on the selfsame day, it shall be a holy convocation unto you, ye shall do no servile work therein, as an eternal law in all your dwellings, throughout your genera-tions (Lev. 23,15-21). Another law has somewhat different rules about the sacrifices on the "day of the first-fruits, when ye bring a new *minḥā* unto Yahweh in your weeks" (Num. 28,26-31).

Here, too, the feast is limited to one day, with a holy con-vocation and all sorts of ordinary sacrifices. The connection with the harvest has not been lost sight of, but now it is a loaf which is sanctified, an ordinary loaf with leaven, such as was used every day. The whole feast turns upon this, nothing else has been associated with it, but we gather the impression from the law that the main object is not so much to sanctify a portion of the wheat crops as to consecrate the new sacrificial material of the year. Ezekiel's failure to mention the feast of weeks in his little calendar of feasts (Ez. 45) may be due to chance, but it may also mean that the mere offering of the wheat crops had not yet at the temple of Jerusalem attained the standing of a festival proper.

The last of the three pilgrimage feasts which is mentioned in the laws was associated with the fruit- and grape-harvest. The story of Abimelech gives some traits from the ancient Canaanite festival. We are told about the Shechemites: And they went out into the fields and gathered grapes in their vineyards and trod the grapes and kept *hillūlīm*. And they went to the house of their god, and did eat, and drink and cursed Abimelech (Judg. 9,27). According to this the feast falls into two parts. The first part takes place in the vineyards in connection with the gathering and pressing of the grapes, the last part in the temple, where a meal is eaten. From the story of the Benjaminite rape of women we learn that the women of Shiloh took part in the feast by dancing outside the vineyards (Judg. 21,20 f.), a custom which was probably not merely local; and the rape itself must have been part of the cult. Only men shared in the meal in the temple. This division of the feast, as we have seen, accords with conditions ir early times; but we are not told what actually happened. The harvest must have been sanctified in the temple, the wine must have contributed to the general elation. Even though the feast had its fixed forms, there was nevertheless an opportunity of ex· pressing the feelings with which the people were filled at the moment, in this case the hatred of Abimelech. The character of the vineyard feast is summed up in the word *hillūlīm*, which denotes the ecstatic festival mood that manifests itself in singing and shouting [1]. Our law says about fruit-trees that "in the fourth year all their fruits shall be a *hillūlīm* treasure to Yahweh" (Lev. 19,24). It means that the entire produce was to be sanctified at the festival which had the aforesaid character.

The brief allusions in the book of Judges show that the festival differed from several of the other ancient feasts by not being a family festival, but a festival of the city community. This may be due to the fact that there was a special community of viticulture, but conditions may have varied in the different places.

Among the laws the two minor law codes merely require the feast to be celebrated as a pilgrimage feast at the sanctuary, of the same standing as the Passover and the Feast of Weeks. It is called the "feast of Ingathering *(ḥagh hā-'āsīph)* at the end of the year, when thou gatherest in thy labour from the field" (Ex. 23,16) or "the feast of Ingathering at the turn of the year" (Ex. 34,22). Deuteronomy has more details.

It says: Thou shalt observe the pilgrimage feast of tabernacles *(ḥagh has-sukkōth)* seven days, at the ingathering from thy threshing-place and thy wine-press. — And thou shalt rejoice in thy pilgrimage feast, thou, and thy son and thy daughter, and thy man-servant and thy maid-servant, and the Levite and the *gēr,* and the fatherless and the widow, that are within thy gates. — Seven days shalt thou keep thy pilgrimage feast to Yahweh, thy God, in the place which Yahweh shall choose. For Yahweh thy God blesseth thee in all thy produce and in all the works of thine hands. Thou shalt surely rejoice" (Deut. 16,13-15).

The Priestly Code and the Law of Holiness are even more detailed: And Yahweh spake unto Moses, saying: Speak unto the Israelites, saying: On the fifteenth day of this seventh month is the pilgrimage feast of the tabernacles *(ḥagh has-sukkōth)* for seven days unto Yahweh. On the first day there is a holy convocation, ye shall do no servile work therein. For seven days ye shall offer an offering made by fire unto Yahweh. On the eighth day there is an holy convocation for you, and ye shall offer an offering made by fire unto Yahweh, it is a festive assembly, ye shall do no servile work ... Surely, on the fifteenth day of the seventh month, when ye gather in the fruit of the land, ye shall keep Yahweh's pilgrimage feast for seven days. On the first day there is a rest, and on the eighth day there is a repose. And on the first day ye shall take you the goodly fruit of trees, branches of palm trees and boughs of leaf-trees and of Arabah trees from the river beds, and ye shall rejoice before Yahweh your God for seven days. And ye shall keep it as a pilgrimage feast to Yahweh seven days in the year, as an eternal rule in your generations; in the seventh month shall ye celebrate it. Ye shall dwell in booths seven days, all that are Israelites born shall dwell in booths, that your generations may know that I made the Israelites to dwell in booths when I brought them out of the land of Egypt. I am Yahweh, your God! (Lev. 23,33-36.39-43).

As at the Passover, each feast day demands separate offerings, carefully enumerated in a list of offerings (Num. 29,12-38). Ezekiel merely says about the feast that the prince is to offer the same daily festival offerings as at the Passover (Ez. 45,25).

Deuteronomy interprets the feast as a festival for the wine and the threshed corn, but does not mention the fruit-harvest. It is doubtful whether we have here anything but a mere inaccuracy. There cannot well be any corn-harvest festival in the autumn, nor is it possible quite simply to regard all the demands of Deuteronomy as realities. In addition, Deuteronomy has the requirement that, as at other feasts, there should be a general exodus to Jerusalem with relatives and slaves and the indigent. If the feast were previously a common feast for the city community, the

decrees of Deuteronomy turn it into a family feast like the
Passover, at the same time as it becomes an institution of the
temple of Jerusalem.

We become acquainted with it in the Priestly Code as a temple
institution with daily offerings and a holy convocation on the
first and last days. [1] But both the Priestly Code and Deuteronomy
contain a new feature which throws light on the main autumn
feast. During the whole of the festival week the participants are to
live in booths, and the command to take fruits and branches from
various kinds of trees must be understood to mean that the
branches and the foliage are to be used for the booths (cf. Neh.
8,15). All Israelites are to dwell in booths or tabernacles to
commemorate their living in booths when they were brought out
of Egypt. Hence the feast is also called the Feast of Tabernacles.

As we saw, there is a possibility that the early Israelites dwelt
in tents at the Passover. The association of the use of booths at
the autumn festival with the deliverance from Egypt cannot be an
original feature, for booths have nothing to do with life in the
desert. But it shows the overwhelming importance attached to
the deliverance from Egypt. It formed the main subject of one
feast and was even transferred to the other. The use of booths
doubtless belonged to the early Canaanite feast and to that part
of it which took place in the vineyards.

Many explanations of this custom have been put forward. An
essential feature of it is that men leave their customary habitations
and become at one with nature together with which they are to be
sanctified through the feast. The green foliage and the fruits with
which the booths are covered are manifestations of the blessing and
fertility of nature which the feast is to re-create. We must imagine
the dance of the young women to be a wild abandonment producing
an ecstasy and a *hillūlīm* mood in which erotic excitement is a
conspicuous element. This ecstatic festival dance combines with the
other acts of the feast to strengthen the blessing that gives fertility
to the crops and to man. The feast was Canaanite but was appropriated by the Israelites and adopted as a feast for Yahweh.
How deeply rooted it was in these regions may be gathered from

the fact that feasts with exactly the same features, in which booths are also used, occur in other Mediterranean countries having similar cultural conditions [1].

The historical sources provide us with no direct evidence as to how this or other feasts were celebrated at the main temple in the monarchical period. But its great importance may be gathered from some few remarks. We are told that the Israelites assembled in connection with the consecration of the temple in the autumn in the month of Ethanim, and celebrated the »pilgrimage feast" *(he-ḥāgh,* 1 Kings 8,2.65) under the leadership of the king. This need not mean that it was the only pilgrimage feast, but its importance appears from the fact that Jeroboam introduced an imitation of it at Bethel in the eighth month, to prevent people from becoming adherents of the king of Jerusalem by taking part in his festival (1 Kings 12,26-33). The great significance of the feast is doubtless rooted in conditions in Canaan, where the vine, as the story of the spies shows us, plays a very conspicuous part; where the first care of the first agriculturist was to plant a vineyard (Gen. 9,20); and where it was recognised that wine pleased not only men, but also the gods (Judg. 9,13). But it is quite clear from the allusions in the book of Kings that the feast acquired a special significance under the leadership of the king; it would then be natural to suppose that he also gave it a new content.

By being subordinated to the temple of Jerusalem and withdrawn from the local orchards and vineyards, the feast was at any rate bound to lose something of its early character. The association with the fruit harvest was, however, never lost sight of, as is shown by the laws. The booths, too, were retained, but we can see that they gradually acquire a purely symbolical significance. It is, indeed, probable that the feast may still in the monarchical period, and presumably later, have been celebrated here and there as a local feast, but all that has passed into oblivion. After the exile the few thousands who returned determined the future.

The chronicler tells us that those who returned first, under Darius, after rebuilding the altar, celebrated "the pilgrimage feast of the tabernacles as it is written, with daily burnt-offerings, a certain number, regularly, the daily portion" (Ezr. 3,4); that is to say, as an ordinary temple institution with daily offerings, as in the post-exilic laws.

Of greater interest is the story of the Feast of Tabernacles which was celebrated when Ezra had come, and had read aloud his law book. The account runs thus: And on the second day were gathered together the heads of the families of all the people, the priests, and the Levites, unto Ezra, the scribe, in order to [1] gain insight into the words of the law. And they found written in the law which Yahweh had commanded by Moses, that the Israelites are to dwell in booths in the feast of the seventh month, and that they are to publish and proclaim in all their cities and in Jerusalem: Go forth into the mountains and fetch olive leaves, oil tree leaves, myrtle leaves, and palm leaves, and branches of leaf trees to make booths as it is written. And the people went forth and fetched them and made themselves booths, every one upon his roof, and in their courts and in the courts of the house of God and in the place of the water gate and in the place of the gate of Ephraim. And all the congregation who had returned from the captivity made booths, and they dwelt in the booths; for since the days of Joshua, the son of Nun, unto that day the Israelites had not done so. And there was very great gladness. And he read in the book of the law of God day by day from the first day unto the last day, and they kept the feast seven days and on the eighth day there was a solemn assembly, according to the rule (Neh. 8,13-18).

In this account the use of booths has quite lost its connection with the ancient vineyard festival, and, as in the Priestly Code, there is not the least hint of a connection with the grape harvest. A decree is quoted according to which bearers are to be sent to gather branches in the mountains, a command which does not occur in any of the law codes transmitted to us, from which it follows that none of them can be identical with Ezra's law. The law treats the branches as a sort of adornment. The booths have become a kind of separate institution with an independent significance. People are to live in them, not in their houses, so as to remind them of their earlier conditions of life. The statement that the Israelites "had not done so" since the days of Joshua (v. 17) cannot mean that the feast had never before been celebrated with booths. For Ezra's purpose is precisely to reintroduce the ancient custom. The remark probably refers to the view that the booths were the habitations of the wilderness period in which they had not normally dwelt since the days of Joshua, hence they must live in them during the feast in order to be reminded of the time when the nation was founded.

After the exile there developed in course of time definite forms of the feast, which was now no longer conducted by the king. We know fairly well what the feast was like at the beginning of our era. All lived in booths. On the first night the precincts of the temple were illuminated by lamps and torches. On the stairs between the outer court and the temple stood the temple singers singing the "song of degrees" (Ps. 120-134) to the accompaniment of music, and a torch-dance was danced in a wild rapture. In the morning three blasts of the trumpet were heard, after which the congregation left the sanctuary. On every feast day many sacrifices were offered, regular or voluntary. On the last day a jug of water was fetched from the brook of Siloah. It was received with trumpet blasts and the high priest poured it out as a libation at the base of the altar, clad in his holy robes, surrounded by his sons, while the priests blew trumpets and the congregation fell on their faces. Then the priests went seven times in a procession round the altar which was decorated with branches. Each participant bore a branch *(lūlāb)* and a fruit *('ethrōgh)* in his hands, and the temple singers sang a *hallēl* hymn (Psalm. 118). Finally the high priest blessed the congregation from the altar [1].

The water libation is hardly any fresh feature for it accords well with the ancient tradition of the feast. The feast takes place just at the beginning of the rainy season, and the sanctification of the water means that its blessing is created anew for the coming year, the produce of which is dependent on it. "At the feast (of the tabernacles) they are judged in respect of water," says the Mishnah. [2]

That a great and real importance was attached to the festival in post-exilic times appears from a prophetic utterance dealing with the enemies who at the end of the long struggle subordinate themselves to the Jewish city: And every one that is left of all the nations that attack Jerusalem shall go up from year to year to prostrate themselves before the king, Yahweh of the hosts, and to go on a pilgrimage, and to keep the pilgrimage feast of the tabernacles. And whoso of all the families on the earth doth not go up to Jerusalem to prostrate himself before the king, Yahweh of the hosts, over them the rain shall not fall (Zech. 14,16 f.). It is added that the Egyptians, who, as we know, are not dependent on rain, shall be subjected to other plagues if they do not go up to celebrate the feast of the tabernacles.

We may probably see an indication that rain had come to play a leading role at the feast in the fact that precisely the absence of rain was meted out as a punishment. It is not implied, however, that rain is obtained by sanctifying the water at the feast. It is the reward of those who by participation in the feast show their subjection to the God of Israel. Of the old peasant festival by which the grape-harvest was sanctified there is hardly a trace left.

The ancient festivals of the farmer and the stockbreeder were equally distributed over the year because they were connected with the growth and ripening occurring in nature. They formed natural focal points in time at which what had been acquired was sanctified, and the blessing of the future created anew. The exact dating which must be required by the temple could not but withdraw the feasts from their natural basis. But there were other festivals the exact dating of which was given by their character, associated as they were with the movements of the celestial bodies.

The connection between the celestial bodies and time with all its happenings was evident to everybody. The changes of the sun were associated with the seasons, but the moon was constantly changing at brief intervals. The Israelites attached a special significance to its movements. Each new change meant a fresh beginning. The days on which it occurred were set off against the others, and a special importance was attached to what happened on them. This was given a natural expression by the Israelites sanctifying them as festal days and thus making them focal points in time.

In the form in which we know the day of the *new moon* and the *sabbath* it is only the former which has any direct connection with the moon. The sabbath is kept every seventh day regardless of the changes of sun and moon; and how these artificial seven-day periods came into existence we do not know. They are decreed in all the laws and were established at any rate in the monarchical period. But the holiness of the sabbath must once have had a living background, and then it must have been associated with the moon, for it is of the same type as new-moon day, and they are often mentioned side by side (Isa. 1,13; Hos. 2,13; Am. 8,5). Out of the ancient moon-feast day there was then by systematisation formed a mechanically fixed holy day. Whether the Israelites had a moon feast of this kind in pre-Canaanite times, or how much they have adopted from the Canaanites, and how much influence Babylonian customs may have had — these are all questions to which we can only give unsatisfactory answers. In post-exilic times the Jewish sabbath acquired a new and special character as an institution peculiar to Jews in contradistinction from other peoples [1].

The new moon and the sabbath were celebrated as holy days *(mō‘ₐdhīm)* by abstention from the normal work of agriculture and trade (Ex. 34,21; Am. 8,5). These days were especially suitable for visiting holy men (2 Kings 4,23). On the day of the new moon Saul partook of a festival meal with his men on his farm, and at Bethlehem they celebrated a great sacrificial feast on the same day (1 Sam. 20,4 ff. 24 ff.). Hosea likens the day of the new moon and the sabbath to the great festivals with their rejoicing (Hos. 2,13). They must, then, have been common feast days in Israel both in the south and the north, and we have evidence of various kinds that they were celebrated as temple feasts in Jerusalem in the monarchical period.

In the 9th century when a revolution made Joash king, this happened on the sabbath when the guard were entering the temple. It may perhaps be interpreted to mean that the king normally went in a procession to the temple to conduct the ceremonies there (2 Kings 11). The observance of the sabbath also brought with it the establishment of a special kind of structure in the temple (2 Kings 16,18). A festival calendar decrees a "holy assembly" on the sabbath as on the great feast days (Lev. 23,3). Isaiah attests that such solemn assemblies took place in his time, c. 700. He says: The new moons and sabbaths, the calling of assemblies — I cannot endure sin and festive assemblies (ʿ*aṣārā*, Isa. 1,13). Yahweh hates their new moons and feasts (*mōʿadhīm*), he says, it does not please him that they tread down his courts (vv. 12.14). Expressions such as these show that we are here concerned with feasts in which great throngs of people take part.

The ordinances of Ezekiel confirm that on the aforementioned days there were great festivals in which the people took part under the leadership of the king. He states that the prince is to take charge of the sacrifices on the pilgrimages, the new moons and the sabbaths (Ez. 45,17). He himself is to participate in these feasts. On the sabbath and the new moon in contrast to the procedure on week days the eastern gate of the inner court is to be left open. The prince is to stand at the inner threshold of the inner gate while the priests offer his sacrifices. Then he is to fall on his face across the threshold and again leave by the gate. In the meanwhile the people are in the outer court. Certain sacrifices which are to be made on the two feast days are also mentioned (Ez. 46,1-7). These rules faintly reflect the old days when the king went to the temple in a solemn procession amid the throngs of the people, as the central figure in the holy ceremonies. We do not know what more happened. One of the psalms (Ps. 92) is stated to belong to the sabbath but it is an ordinary hymn of praise without any distinctive feature.

The frequent repetition of the sabbath gave to it a special position among the festivals. "Yahweh hath caused feast (*mōʿēdh*) and sabbath to be forgotten on Zion" is the cry we hear after the fall of the temple (Lam. 2,6). The sabbath and the new moon are mentioned separately among the obligations, the maintenance of which Nehemiah made the Jews take upon themselves (Neh. 10,

34). They had their special offerings (Num. 28,9 ff.); on the day
of the new moon as well as on other feast days trumpets were
blown during the sacrifices (Num. 10,10), a heritage from the
brilliant temple feasts of the monarchical period. But in post-
exilic times the sabbath was important not so much because of
what happened in the temple as by the character it gave to the
life of the Jewish people.

Our consideration of the feasts shows us throughout the same
main historical feature, from the sanctification on the farms or
at the small sanctuaries of the families as also of the world
of nature, or from the holy meals and festival rites of the smaller
city communities, to the taking over by the royal temple of the holy
acts under a priesthood trained for the purpose. The great temple's
absorption of the festivals did not exactly mean that they were
withdrawn from the families, for the people visited the temple by
families. But the families had no longer any independent
significance, they had been torn from their environment, and it
was not on them that everything rested. They were "laymen" who
trod down the outer courts and were important by their numbers
only.
    They were "called" to the great festal assemblies (Isa. 1,13;
Lam. 1,15, cf. Lev. 23,2.4). A king could at any time summon
people to a holy convocation, as may be gathered from the history
of Jehu (2 Kings 10,18 ff.). The laws for the temple of Jerusalem
show that the people were summoned to a solemn assembly at the
feast of weeks, at the new moon, and on the sabbath, as well as
the first and last days of the spring and autumn festivals,
which lasted for several days[1]. At these large convocations the
lay population filled the temple court as spectators or supernumer-
aries, while the priests performed the holy rites. At the Passover, a
common festival from the earliest times, the families only retained
their active significance because of its disintegration as a common
feast, part of it being transferred to private houses.

In this development we see the radical importance of *the king*. For the king and the royal temple were intimately associated. The king was the nucleus from which the people drew their power. Cities and families looked to him for sanctification and a re-creation of the blessing, hence they could not but recede into the background and subordinate themselves to him. We have seen that the Paschal legend shows traces of the influence of the kingship, though it is not demonstrable in detail. Altogether, it is difficult to say what was the king's part in the temple cult, because it was without interest at the time when the old traditions were collected. There are, however, sufficient traces to show the profound difference between the part played in the cult by the chief of early days and the king of the later period. In the book of Samuel we see Saul on his farm at the feast of the New Moon. His men and his family are gathered around him; their blessing is centred in him. Later sources show us a glimpse of a similar feast in the royal temple, where the king comes in a procession amid trumpet blasts, and the offering is made on his behalf, while the people look on, glad to receive a share of the strength concentrated and again renewed in the king.

This position in the cult was not achieved by the king at one stroke. David, the creator of the monarchy, appeared as the leader of a cult festival described in the book of Samuel, when the Ark was transported to Zion, first on the unsuccessful journey to Obed Edom's house, and then at the final transference to Zion. On this latter journey the Ark was carried in a procession; after six paces a halt was made to sacrifice an ox and a fatted calf, by which procedure a holy atmosphere was secured for the Ark. The people followed in a procession with a great outcry, *t⁻rū‘ā*, and the blare of horns. And before Yahweh i. e. before the Ark, David performed such a violent dance that the linen ephod he wore was flung from about him. When the Ark had reached its destination, David offered fresh sacrifices, and finally he blessed the people, bestowed gifts on them, and allowed them to return home (2 Sam. 6,13 ff.).

David is the active factor, he dances the cult dance before the Ark, dressed in an ephod which gives him a priestly char-

acter. He takes the lead in creating the holy sphere around the
Ark, he sacrifices, blesses the people, and is the great giver. The
people flock around him and take part with noise and shouting;
for noise, as well as stillness, belonged to an assembly dominated
by holiness, whether on its way to war or to worship. The story
gives us an account of how processions with the Ark generally
took place, and it seems natural to suppose that it describes
conditions in the monarchical period. But whether there was
actually a royal cult under David is uncertain.

Solomon created a new basis for the cultus by building his
magnificent temple. Its close association with the kingship is
strongly accentuated in the narratives, where it is mentioned as
an essential part of the covenant between Yahweh and David,
a pledge of the maintenance of the royal house (1 Kings 8,18 f.,
cf. 2 Sam. 7). From the book of Kings we can see that Solomon
conducted the worship and renewed it for the glorification of his
kingship. But we do not know in what his worship consisted. His
speech of inauguration was given its present form in post-exilic
times; it even mentions the temple merely as the place in which
the God of Israel is invoked, not as a real cult-place.

The chief traces left to us of the special position occupied
by the king in the cult are found in a series of psalms which
have been preserved because they were constantly used in the
post-exilic period. It is a matter of course that the royal psalms,
and indeed other psalms also, acquired a different meaning during
that period from what they had originally had. And the order
in which they have been collected exhibits no internal sequence,
though the collection was made at a time when the temple cult
was in full progress. We have already seen that these psalms
show how high the king soared above the people in holiness,
right up into the divine sphere. Such a position could only be
maintained through the cult, and this seems indeed to be
implied in some of the psalms. One of them opens thus: Yahweh
saith unto my Lord: Sit thou at my right hand, that I may lay
thine enemies as a footstool at thy feet. Yahweh sendeth out the
rod of thy strength from Zion, rule thou in the midst of thine
enemies! (Ps. 110,1-2). The text goes on to say: Yahweh sweareth

without repentance: Thou art a priest forever after the way of the king of justice [1]. The Lord is at thy right hand, striking kings in the day of his wrath! (vv. 4-5).

In these lines the king is represented primarily as the man who asserts himself against his enemies and puts down foreign kings. He obtains the strength to do so because Yahweh joins forces with him. This is expressed in different ways. Yahweh makes him a priest never to be conquered by time, as is a true king when he has a well established royal house. That he is a priest means that he is filled with the holiness of the God, precisely as it is active in the temple. Therefore he is near Yahweh, in the battle Yahweh fights at his right side. The same thing is expressed in another way by the command to the king to seat himself at the right side of the God, when his enemies will be laid at his feet as a footstool, prostrated in the dust before him. It is the aim of the psalm to show that the work of the God and the king cannot be distinguished from each other. Their common power is rooted in Zion, that is to say, in the temple, thence they shall prevail over all enemies, and the king and Yahweh may with equal justice be said to accomplish the work.

It would be natural to suppose that the first line, which must be conceived as being recited by a priest, invites the king to assume royal honours by seating himself in the temple on a throne at Yahweh's side. We have no information, however, that there was a seat for the king in the temple beside Yahweh's seat, which must have been next to the Ark.

Another, similar, psalm (Ps. 2) is dominated by the contrast between the king and his enemies. But here dominion over the peoples is the point of departure. Thus an imaginary state of things is implied, that in which the Judaean king rules the world. The nations rebel and try to break away from "Yahweh and his anointed". But Yahweh mocks them, saying: And I have set my king on my holy hill of Zion. The king himself says: I will declare the decree of Yahweh. He said to me: Thou art my son, I have given birth to thee this day. Ask of me and I will give thee the nations for thine inheritance, the uttermost parts of the earth for thy possession! (vv. 6-8). The psalm ends with a proclamation of the universal dominion of the Judaean ruler and a call upon the kings to submit.

The expression "I have given birth to thee this day" would seem to point to a definite act in the temple by which the king was consecrated. Through this rebirth he becomes Yahweh's son. The greatness of which he thus obtains a share gives him the prerogative of supremacy over all other kings and dominion over all the earth, because Yahweh is stronger than other gods. Thus closely are Yahweh and the king allied. This is primarily the reason why the petty Judaean prince could lay claim to universal rule. The reason why the Israelites were able to take over this ideal of a deified king which they knew from their neighbours and give it such a wide significance, was that the kingdom, owing to the conquests of David, had been established as an extensive realm with vassal kings of a similar kind to the strong neighbouring kingdoms. The last part of the hymn promises the king that the claim based on his and Yahweh's combined strength shall be realised through events to come. But what thus appears as a claim, is a reality in the cult ritual. This is expressed by the independence of the kings being regarded as a revolt against the ruler of Zion.

It is highly probable that a consecration of the king took place at an annual festival [1]. "The shouting for a king", *t⁽e⁾rū‘ath melekh*, a manifestation of the people's exultation (Num. 23,21), belonged to this day, and that exultation showed itself in all kinds of ways. "In the day of our king princes are sick with the heat of wine" says Hosea (7,5) in a passage whose context is otherwise obscure. "The king" may here just as well be the god.

When Yahweh calls the king his son, he expresses the same thing as when he offers him a seat by his side. The king may call Yahweh his father (Ps. 89,27); he is a first-born son (v. 28). He is even called God (Ps. 45,7) in a song of praise, which, however, may not be of a ritual nature. By calling the king God and a son of God the Israelites, like their neighbours, described him as the man whose strength of soul penetrates right down to the depths from which all strength springs. The king is inferior to the God, but there is no fixed line between them; they are of the same kin.

A series of hymns and prayers show how it was attempted to assure this greatness of the king in the temple. All power is concentrated on making him great; for if this can be done, all others can obtain the blessing from him. One of the psalms (Ps. 72) is a prayer that the king may actualise the royal ideal. He is to be full of righteousness, "judge" his people, help the weak, and put down evil-doers, so that peace and justice may prevail, and fertility fill the mountains[1]. He is to rule from ocean to ocean (v. 8), i. e. over all the earth (cf. Zech. 9,10); the peoples from the coasts of the Mediterranean and the Red Sea will bring him gifts of homage. His name shall live forever, elevated above the vicissitudes of time; all the nations of the earth shall seek to obtain the blessing from him, for he possesses it in a higher degree than any one else. We do not know on what occasion this prayer was recited, but it would be well suited for the day of the king's consecration, for it mentions all the essential characteristics which were to be strengthened in the king through the cult.

Dominance was what was always desired for the king. All the will to rule of the people was concentrated in him, hence there was a constant endeavour to secure victory for him, to fulfil his desires. This is very conspicuous in a psalm which we presume to be part of the ritual preparation for victory in a coming war (Ps. 20). The king is addressed, presumably by priests, with the prayer that Yahweh may send him help from his sanctuary. They beseech Yahweh to accept the offerings with good-will and fulfil the king's desire and plans by bestowing victory on him. Suddenly the certainty of success sets in: Yahweh will give his anointed victory. The enemy, who has only external instruments of war to rely upon, will fall before him who has the entire divine power of Zion behind him.

Another psalm has a similar theme (Ps. 21); it exalts Yahweh because he has given the king strength and victory, fulfilment of his desire. He has been given all that belongs to a king: life without end, glory and honour. Against this back-

sary to demand more power for him, which again came to mean fresh demands for Israel. It was David who founded and Solomon who developed this institution. The resulting conception of the relation of the king to his people and of his claim to universal power did not arise spontaneously in Israel but was the result of influences from without. We know it from the great empires, but nowhere was the cult so strongly concentrated on the sanctification and deification of the king as in Egypt, which, as we know, had the greatest influence on Canaan in the earlier monarchical period. How great the direct influence of Egypt was on this point we cannot, however, say, for we know very little about cult conditions in Israel. And there is presumably as great a possibility of influence from the East, where the position of the king was much the same. But the Psalms show that Israel did not quite superficially adopt from without the old oriental ideas about the kingship and its claims. They created a cult in some form or other, which realised the king's powerful position and pretentions. They assimilated the foreign element and created a special Israelite kingship, around which a special cult grew up. It is, therefore, easily understood that it came to exercise a strong influence on the cultus as a whole.

As among other peoples, *processions* were often a feature of the festivals. Doubtless such holy pageants took place on many occasions in the course of the year. When Nehemiah had had the walls of Jerusalem rebuilt, he arranged a big procession. At the head of it went the leaders of the people and the priests, and it proceeded to the temple with singing and dancing, offering sacrifice there. The echoes of the joyous shouts could be heard far away (Neh. 12,27 ff.). By this procession the walls were "purified" (12,30). That means that they were sanctified and appropriated. Exactly the same custom is recorded from numerous other peoples; it was not, of course, a new custom introduced by Nehemiah. We may take it for granted that in the monarchical period, also, the city was regularly sanctified by similar processions. Thus it was, properly, defended and fortified by Yahweh as his, the great king's, city [1].

The journeys of the pilgrims going to attend the festivals are sometimes described as processions. They are wanderings in "the way of holiness on which no unclean person is" (Isa. 35,8). Of those who are travelling to the temple it is said, therefore, that "they go from strength to strength to appear before God on Zion" (Ps. 84,8), and we are told about a "gladness of heart, as in him who goeth with a flute to proceed to Yahweh's mountain, to the rock of Israel" (Isa. 30,29). The procession is a holy act, the participants are sanctified by it and filled with strength.

It is preferable that some holy treasure should be carried at the head of the procession. We have heard of the procession in which the Ark, surrounded by a sphere of holiness, was carried to Zion with the king dancing before it, with the offering of sacrifices and amid the shouting of the people. The story of how Jericho fell when a procession with the Ark went round it shows the great power attributed to holy processions, when the mightiest of Israelite treasures was at the head of them. Through this treasure Yahweh himself was present and led the procession.

Such a divine procession is described in a psalm running thus: They see thy processions, Elohim, the processions of my God, my king, in holiness (or in the sanctuary). The singers go before, next the players of instruments amid damsels playing with timbrels. In unison they bless Elohim, the Lord, Israel's ... (Ps. 68,25-27). The maidens playing timbrels, and no doubt moving in rhythmic measures to the music, are familiar to us from the Passover festival; but there is reason to believe that such processions often took place in Jerusalem. In another hymn we learn of a procession in which Yahweh proceeds to the entrance of the temple (Ps. 24). First Yahweh is praised in general terms as lord of all the earth. Then the condition for entering the temple is mentioned: a clean heart and abstention from sin; and finally the text goes on to say: Lift up your heads, O ye gates, be ye lift up, ye eternal doors, that the king of glory may come

praised as the God who assumes sovereignty, wins honour among the peoples, terrifies the gods, gains glory in his sanctuary, comes to judge the earth righteously, while the heavens, the earth, and the sea rejoice (Ps. 96). But while all the peoples tremble before him when he ascends the throne of the cherubim, he listens graciously to the great men of the history of Israel who keep his law (Ps. 99).

In these psalms we find the temple and Israel to be the central themes. The holiness of the temple forms the background of the throne, and Yahweh's possession of it means the assertion of the power of Israel, the people of righteousness. The maintenance of this power is due to the might of Yahweh. His power extends over all the world, because he is its maker; all foreign nations prostrate themselves before him and submit to Israel. Thus we see a very close connection between the consecration of the king and Yahweh's kingship. Both mean universal dominion. The universal power of the king is due to that of Yahweh, and Yahweh rules the whole cosmos, because he has created it.

Only very few traits suggest that ritual ceremonies underlie this series of hymns, ceremonies consisting partly in the regeneration of the king, partly in the regeneration of the god, while both represent the creation of universal dominion. We do not know how the two things were combined, but to the Yahweh feast there belonged a procession, which ended in Yahweh's ascent of his throne. This meant that he put down all his enemies, secured victory for Israel, and bestowed his strength on the righteous. When a king comes to the throne we likewise hear of processions and a solemn enthronement; but this refers to the throne in the palace [1].

It has correctly been pointed out that such festal customs did not arise independently in Israel, but through influences from without. They were not, however, adopted as mere imitations, but acquired their special Israelite stamp. In the two large cult domains of civilisation which essentially influenced Canaan, that of Egypt and Assyro-Babylonia, such a ritual regeneration partly of the king and partly of the God, played a leading role. The renewal of the kingship is most prominent in Egypt. Here the king had to go repeatedly to the sanctuary where he was purified, invested with the symbols of power, and crowned, whereupon he ascended the throne for his two kingdoms, by which acts he became the son of the God. This gave him the power on his part to resuscitate the God when the latter annually died, and to help him to assume universal power. We find the same interaction between the king and the god in the East, even though the independent regeneration of the king here seems to be less important. There, too, the king and the God must annually renew themselves; to them both it means the creation of power over the world, and security for the new year. As in Egypt the regeneration of the God takes place amid hard struggles with the hostile demoniacal powers, represented dramatically, and the feast is connected with large processions. The people take part, expressing their grief or joy, while they watch the performers of the actual drama. In the Ras Shamra texts we have a complete cult drama centring round the death, conflict, and resurrection of the god, and his ensuing taking over of the kingship when he seats himself on the throne. The texts do not show clearly what part the king played at this feast.

If we compare the Israelite festivals here concerned with those just mentioned, the connection will at once be evident, but also the difference. In both places there is a new beginning for the God and the king; and it is of the greatest importance to the people, for it means new life and new blessedness from the God, with the demand for universal dominion. It is obvious, however, that the renewal is not radical in Israel as in the other countries. The death of the God, a well-known phenomenon among essentially agricultural peoples, means that life begins all over again, and is created from the very beginning by ritual acts. The God and the king are the two principal powers on which everything turns. The king must be regenerated through the God, and the God receives new life through the king. Everything depends on their strength, hence it is for them that dominion is created.

If we view the Israelitish customs against this background, it is clear that they have come into existence under the influence of the neighbouring cultures, but also that they have not been

that we hear of Yahweh's fight with the dragon, Rahab or Leviathan, and its helpers; in this fight he conquered chaos and the untamed water, created order out of lawlessness, and blessedness instead of darkness and the curse. The destructive waters were changed into life-giving rains and springs. The victory was won in primeval ages but it had to be constantly renewed [1].

We have seen that the fight against the dragon was used at the Passover as an expression of Yahweh's victory over hostile Egypt. The connection with the creation, and the association of the creation with Yahweh's dominion over all the earth naturally suggests that there is a connection between these events of primeval ages and the renewal of Yahweh's sovereign power. That such a renewal took place at a cult festival is probable in itself and is supported by the circumstance that the proclamation of Yahweh's assumption of the royal power was connected with processions. We have no description of such a festival, and it is always difficult to establish what lies behind the allusions in the psalms. But Yahweh's occupation of the throne was not a regeneration of Yahweh, but a renewal of the covenant and the promise of power for Israel. Hence it is questionable whether we may assume that there was a real regeneration of the world in the cult, or whether the regeneration of the world did not rather consist in a mere glorification of Yahweh's creative work in primeval ages and an assurance of his constant maintenance of the order of the universe, as denoted by the fact that he "judges" [2]. There is, then, a strong presumption that the whole glorification of Yahweh's occupation of the throne and everything appertaining thereto did not constitute a special feast, but formed part of a feast. The question then arises as to what feast it was.

Every feast is a fresh beginning, an act of sanctification from which the future springs; but a feast at which the sovereign power of God is renewed must be so in a special degree. It belongs naturally to the beginning of the new year. We have not, however, any certain knowledge as to when the year began in early Israel. The year "expired" (Ex. 23,16) or "turned" (Ex. 34,22) at the time of the fruit-harvest, but this means that it dies only to "return" in the spring (2 Sam. 11,1; 1 Kings 20, 22.26) [1]. From this point of view the year may be considered to begin either with the spring when it comes to life again, or with the autumn at the beginning of the rainy season, which lays the foundation for the growth of the new year, the first seed being sown shortly after. It is not to be wondered at that Jewish scholars might disagree as to whether the world had been created in Nisan (c. April) or in Tishri (c. October) [2].

All festival calendars begin with the spring feast and end with the autumn feast, and there can be no doubt that, at any rate after the exile, Nisan was regarded as the first month of the year. In the books of the Kings the deliverance from Egypt is taken as the starting-point of the national history (cf. 1 Kings 6, 1), and this creative event has its background in the Passover which is celebrated in Nisan. We have seen that the Passover, the only Hebrew festival of which we have some knowledge, aims at glorifying Yahweh as the god who defeats Israel's enemy and asserts his power; he is extolled in the psalm associated with the Passover as the god who does royal deeds (Ex. 15,18) [3]. We have likewise seen that this creation of the nation is identified in various prophetic and poetic utterances with the battle against the dragon which, as we know, was associated with the creation of the world. It occurs so frequently that it can hardly be a casual poetic conceit. All these features agree perfectly with the glorification of Yahweh who ascends the throne as king, puts down the foreign gods, and seizes the power over the world; judges the unrighteous, and creates happiness for those who rightly call themselves his people, while he renews the blessing which is to give life to the coming year. The whole character of the Paschal feast would seem to indicate that it continued to be what it undoubtedly was from the beginning, the main festival of the Israelites. Hosea says: What will ye do about the festal day, in the day of Yahweh's pilgrimage feast? (9,5). His question is due to the fact that he sees the people being destroyed, when it is partly carried off to Ashur, partly returns to the bondage of Egypt (vv. 3.6). What sense is there, then, in celebrating a feast which commemorates the deliverance from Egypt? Thus it

itself the greatest of benefits, but the association of the blessing with regeneration made it a source of strength in daily life. The *blessing* was a regular component of the feasts. The father and the chief pronounced it in their circle, and at the great feasts the leader blessed the people in the name of Yahweh. We hear this about David or about Solomon when he stood before the altar in his new temple (2 Sam. 6,18; 1 Kings 8,14.55).

It was not only at the feasts that the blessing was pronounced in the temple. The strength of the blessing was sought at all times, and it became the business of the priests to communicate it to the people. The priests were to "stand before Yahweh to minister unto him and bless in his name" (Deut. 10,8, cf. 21,5). They were sanctified so as to be able to "produce sacrificial smoke before Yahweh, to minister unto him and to bless in his name forever" (1 Chron. 23,13). After the exile the high priest took the place of the king as the person who blessed the people in the temple after the offerings had been made (Lev. 9,22 f.); he did this with hands uplifted. We know the form of the priestly blessing pronounced in the temple: Yahweh bless thee and keep thee, Yahweh make his face shine upon thee and be gracious unto thee, Yahweh lift up his countenance upon thee and give thee peace! (Num. 6,24-26). The light of the divine countenance means life, stronger than that which comes from the glance of any chief. Life, blessedness, and peace are the values which Yahweh bestows on the visitors to the temple through the priest. The form of the blessing shows that the values of life are obtained in the temple through the holiness created there.

The strength given by the temple and the cult could also be used for other purposes than that of conferring blessedness. A *curse* emanating from the holy place had a particularly strong effect. From the old days we hear of Balaam who was obliged to sacrifice in order to be able to curse Israel emphatically, but who, while in the holy condition, was compelled by Yahweh to bless (Num. 22,40; 23,14.29 f.). If an Israelite had been exposed to molestation by an unknown person he could strike at the delinquent by letting a curse be pronounced on him before the altar. That such curses for private purposes were common in the temple of Jerusalem may be gathered from the fact that this usage is emphasised as a general custom of the temple in the inauguration speech ascribed to Solomon (1 Kings 8,31 f.). And the law prescribes a sin-offering to purify such persons as by any knowledge of the matter may be affected by such a curse (Lev. 5,1). We even have a fairly detailed ritual by which a husband who suspects his wife of infidelity may make her punishable by the curse if she proves guilty (Num. 5). And just as the people was blessed in the temple, curses were also pronounced on its enemies, and such curses could be directed against the enemies of a private individual. This is evidenced by several psalms, doubtless used in the temple. An execration formula has come down to us. The Levites are to pronounce it and the people are to acknowledge it item by item (Deut. 27,14-26). This means that it is a ritual used in the temple on occasions unknown to us. Something similar underlies the statements about the blessing and the curse which were communicated to the assembled people (Deut. 27,1-13; Josh. 8,30-35). [1]

Altogether, words acquired a wonderful power by being pronounced in the sanctuary. The psychic content to which they gave form was given a deeper meaning, they were strengthened and established by being pervaded with holiness. The god in whose sanctuary they were pronounced became a party to them; if they were not kept, the person who had uttered them not only made a breach in his own psychic integrity, i. e. committed a sin, he also offended the God who was concerned in the promise. Hence *covenants* of any importance were made in the holy place; we hear this about the covenant of friendship between David and Jonathan (1 Sam. 23,18), about the covenant between the king and the people, and of course about the covenant between Yahweh and the people, which, as we know, was renewed at all the great ritual functions. [2]

Through the covenant the two parties create something outside and higher than themselves, and its holiness appears from the fact that the divine power takes part in it and watches over it. Yahweh "is between" the parties. But it is the same when a private individual pronounces a word which he fills with his entire soul, so that he stands or falls by the keeping of it. This is done by the *oath*. Everything that forms the essence of his soul, and which it draws with it when it reaches its highest tension: honour, the fathers, the God; all this fills the word with a concentrated strength, making it just as holy as that spoken by the prophet from the depths of his soul; the oath is pronounced out of the strength of the God and with him as a participant. Hence the uttering of an oath is a holy act, and it accords well with its nature that it is to be pronounced in the holy place, perhaps in connection with an offering or contact with holy objects.

The holy words of the oath were of the greatest importance in the Hebrew community. They gave coherence to the acts of men and created confidence among them mutually. Obligations must constantly be fortified by holy words; they afforded the security which held together the community. When Jephthah became chieftain, "he pronounced all his words before Yahweh at Mizpeh" (Judg. 11,11). These words contained promises of exploits he intended to carry out for the benefit of the people. Binding oaths appertained to visits to the holy place. Hosea says: Come not ye unto Gilgal, neither go ye up to Beth-aven, nor swear 'by the life of Yahweh' (Hos. 4,15), and Amos refers to the oaths of the various sanctuaries among the ritual sins he condemns because they mention strange gods (Am. 8,14). [1] The oath was so important a part of the cult, because the community was made up of psychic values, and the legal procedure of which it formed a part was largely associated with the temple and the priesthood. [2]

The laws prescribe that the Israelites are to "show themselves before Yahweh" or "see Yahweh" [3] at the main festivals, but any one could go to the sanctuary at any time to obtain strength. When David came to the sanctuary of Nob, Saul's Edomite chief shepherd Doeg was shut up *(ne'ṣār)* there (1 Sam. 21,8, cf. Neh. 6,10). Visitors sat still, in contemplation, while the power of holiness filled their mind. Many people came into the royal temple of Jerusalem every day "to prostrate themselves before Yahweh" (Jer. 7,2).

Many psalms express the happiness of sitting in the temple of Jerusalem. One day there is better than a thousand others, longing consumes him who lives afar (Ps. 84), in a hostile environment he yearns for God in the temple as a hart pants for the water brooks (Ps. 42; 43,3 f.). He bends towards the temple (138,2); when there, he rejoices in sharing with his brethren the blessing of Yahweh (122; 132). It would be best to dwell there forever. "I will dwell [1] in Yahweh's house for many days of my life" (23,6). "One thing I beseech of Yahweh, I wish for myself; that I may dwell in the house of Yahweh all the days of my life, to behold the graciousness of Yahweh and to enquire [2] in his temple" (27,4, cf. 61,5). Happy the man whom Yahweh chooseth to be near him, who liveth in his courts and is satisfied by the richness and holiness of his temple [3] (65,5). To live and to dwell *(gūr, yāshabh, shākhan)* are expressions for the shorter or longer stay in the holy place of the visitor to the temple; it is to the outer courts that he has access, there he is sated with the psychic richness which holiness gives him.

All who come to the temple must be righteous and purified (15,1; 24,4; 26,6). If they are, they will always get something of what the temple feasts give in abundance. Here there is fellowship with friends (55,15), every man can here "behold God" (63,3), and all who are tortured by harrowing thoughts attain peace and understanding here (73,17). Inspiration and peace proceed from the sanctuary.

The altar fire in the temple court burnt forever (Lev. 6,5 f.). Besides the prescribed offerings, private offerings were constantly made, to which we frequently find references in the psalms (54,8; 56,13; 65,2; 66,13 ff.; 76,12; 96,8; 107,22; 116,14 ff.). The people who visited the temple had very often votive offerings to make. They were promised in an emergency, and the sacrificer loudly proclaims the mercy which delivered him from his distress (66,13-17.19). All distress meant psychic weakness, and in no place could one fight better against it or for the blessing than in the sanctuary. Hence any one suffering from disease or other weaknesses goes to the temple, or at least turns towards it praying to be saved. [1]

Up to the time of Hezekiah there was a special cult for any one who sought to be healed in the royal temple of Jerusalem. We are told that Hezekiah "broke the brazen serpent which Moses had made, for until those days the children of Israel had burnt incense to it, and it was called n^ehushtān (2 Kings 18,4). What this means we learn from a kind of cult legend in the Pentateuch.

Yahweh once punished the Israelites in the wilderness by letting them be bitten by venomous śārāph snakes. Then they went to Moses, confessed their sins and asked him to save them. Moses turned to Yahweh. "And Yahweh said unto Moses: Make thee a śārāph serpent and set it upon a pole. And any man who hath been bitten, let him recover (literally: live) when he seeth it. And Moses made a serpent of brass and put it upon a pole. When the serpents bit a man, if he looked upon the serpent of brass, he recovered" (Num. 21,4-9).

According to the more recent finds there can be no doubt that we are here concerned with a purely Canaanite cult. [2] This was why Hezekiah abolished it. People sacrificed to the serpent, thus strengthening its species and entering into a covenant with it, so rendering harmless its attacks. The importance of the śārāph serpent in the cult at the royal temple is evidenced by the vision of Isaiah, in which Yahweh is surrounded by these serpents, and they act as Yahweh's ministers to Isaiah. This means that the śārāph had become Israelitish. That is the case, too, in the ancient cult legend which has been connected with Moses. Here the form is changed, it is true, so that no actual worship takes place any longer; the serpent of brass is an arbitrary means used by Yahweh to heal the people. The legend gives us some insight into the history of a foreign cult in Israel.

When sickness and other impurity was over, a purification had to take place; it was generally accomplished by sanctification in the temple. This was essential to the return to normal life. Women in childbed were to sacrifice (Lev. 12), men or women who had had an issue were to undergo certain purifications and washings and finally to sacrifice (Lev. 15). The treatment of lepers shows plainly what the cult meant in private and in public life. If there appeared a rash on the skin, the priests were to examine it (Lev. 13; Deut. 24,8 f.). If their diagnosis was leprosy, the patient was a "stricken man", who was cast out of the community, behaved like a man performing the death wail, rent his clothes, covered his beard, neglected his hair, and kept people at a distance by the cry: Unclean! (Lev. 13,45 f.). If he recovered, the priests must gradually lead him back into men's society by a long series of purifications, until he was finally fully restored by sacrifices (14,1 ff.). For the purifications were used cedar wood, scarlet cloth and a bunch of hyssop dipped into living water in an earthen vessel, over which a bird was slaughtered; the water was sprinkled on the person, another bird was dipped in it, and then set free with the uncleanness. These rites show a distinct relationship with Babylonian and Hittite methods.

So as to be able to be the great source of purification to the people, the temple itself must have its cleanness and holiness carefully maintained. Men's presence in it produced a certain danger of pollution, hence it had to be purified. In the latter part of the monarchical period, this probably happened twice, prior to each of the great festivals (Ez. 45,18-20); in post-exilic times it was once a year, on the Day of Atonement (Lev. 16). The rites are characteristic of the ceremonial which developed at the temple of Jerusalem in the later regal period.

The high priest bathes and puts on sacred robes. Then he brings a bullock for a sin-offering to make atonement for himself and his house. From the people he receives two male goats, and after casting lots is to divide them according to the lots between Yahweh and Azazel, a demon of evil. After sacrificing his sin-offering bullock, the high priest is to put a censer full of burning incense into the inner cell so that it is filled with smoke and the holy object in the cell is veiled. He then takes some of the blood and sprinkles it in the direction of the holy object, "the instrument of atonement" *(kappōreth)*. He is to do the same with the sin-offering goat of the people, and finally he is to put the blood on the horns of the altar for burnt-offerings, and sprinkle blood from both sin-offerings on it. In this way he will procure atonement for the sanctuary, for his family and the people; uncleanness and sin are dissolved and vanish. Now Azazel's goat is brought forward. The high priest lays his hands upon its head and by a confession he transfers the sins of the Israelites to it. A man who stands ready then takes the goat into the wilderness, and thus the sin is carried to the place to which it belongs; only after purifications can the man return. The high priest in the meanwhile enters the sanctuary again, takes off the sacred robes, bathes and puts on his ordinary apparel. Finally he sacrifices a ram for himself and one for the people, the fat from the sin-offerings is burnt on the altar, while the remains are burnt outside. Then the atonement has been accomplished.

This rite shows the intimate psychic connection between the sanctuary and the Israelites. The uncleanness of the temple and the sins of the people have the same effect; they are removed together and by the same means. The special position occupied by the high priest, whose responsibility is as great as that of the whole people, shows that he had inherited the position of the king, but doubtless he performed a good many of the rites even in the time of the monarchy. The special removal of the sin of the people by transferring it to an animal which is turned out into the wilderness, again shows how much of their cult ceremonial the Israelites had learned from foreigners. Assyro-Babylonian exorcism was based on such methods, and both the Babylonians and the Hittites had rites reminiscent of the Israelitish ritual. [1]

The Israelites went to the sanctuary to be strengthened by its holiness, but also to honour Yahweh by prostrating themselves before him (1 Sam. 1,3) as in the western Asiatic countries people fell on their faces before princes. The Canaanite Israelites did homage to the God by a kiss (1 Kings 19,18; Hos. 13,2). At the altars Yahweh's name was remembered or invoked (Gen. 12,8; Ex. 20,24), for the offering was accompanied by a direct appeal. A prayer accompanying the presentation of first-fruits has been preserved (Deut. 26,4 ff.). At the festivals the people stood with lifted hands addressing their prayers to Yahweh (Isa. 1,15; Ps. 88,10). Any one coming to the temple in distress brought his complaint before Yahweh. A sanctuary may thus be called a house of prayer. It is an expression of hopeless misery when it is said that "Moab shall go to his sanctuary to pray, and he cannot" (Isa. 16,12).

Any one who was in doubt and needed counsel was from early days accustomed to go to the temple to consult Yahweh *(dārash* or *shā'al* Ex. 18,15; 1 Sam. 9,9; 22,13; 1 Kings 22,7 et al.), and whether the answer was given by the oracle or by a priest or a prophet, it was "Yahweh's mouth" (Josh. 9,14) that spoke. Yahweh was not consulted to obtain abstract knowledge. If Yahweh gave counsel, he would also bestow blessedness.

There is no antagonism between the psychic effect of holiness in man and the intervention of Yahweh for which the worshipper prays. [1] When man obtained holy strength and blessedness at the feast, it was the gift of Yahweh; when the offering purified his soul and blotted out his sin, it was Yahweh who forgave, just as it was Yahweh who was active when the prophet or the chief was overcome by a holy ecstasy. There was the same interaction when man offered his prayer with a vow. This was to influence Yahweh's will and dispose him to be gracious, but the effect was not of an outward kind. The vow consecrated the soul of man with a holy strength which was concentrated on what the soul desired, and in this holiness Yahweh himself was in harmony and in fellowship with man. This relation between God and man may have many grades, and in Israel there was a strong tendency to accentuate Yahweh's self-glorious work. The tendency might become so strong that it almost threatened to disrupt the old psychic law governing man's actions and make him quite passive.

How this tendency might act on an ancient holy custom and give it a new character may be gathered from a story about David.

We know that sanctification caused a certain removal from normal life, from food and from sexual intercourse, but also that the same thing was the rule for any person upon whom the curse had fallen, in the shape of disaster and death, because the totality demanded that the normal and the abnormal should be kept apart. When Bathsheba's son had fallen ill, "David sought the God for the boy", he fasted and spent the night on the bare ground, no one could induce him to eat. On the seventh day the boy died, and David's men who had tried in vain to make their master eat during his son's illness, were afraid to tell him. However, he understood from their behaviour what had happened, and at once he rose up, washed and anointed himself, put on ordinary apparel and went to the house of Yahweh to prostrate himself before him; then he went to his own house and ordered food. His men were amazed at this conduct and did not conceal their amazement. "And his servants said unto him: What is this that thou art doing? Thou didst fast and weep for the boy while he was alive, but now the boy is dead thou risest and dost eat. But he said: While the boy was yet alive I fasted and wept for I thought: Perhaps Yahweh will have mercy on me and the boy will recover. But now that he is dead, wherefore should I fast? Can I bring him back again? I shall go to him, but he shall not return to me" (2 Sam. 12,15 ff.).

The narrator tells this little story in his concise and clear way, like an anecdote one might almost say, without revealing himself at any point. The story shows David's love of his son, but its most important point is David's relation to ancient Hebrew customs. According to these he should have felt his uncleanness after the death of the boy, and should have brought himself in an abnormal condition by means of fasting, mourning raiment and what appertained to them, but he did the opposite. He anointed himself, ate and drank and sacrificed, which means that he went back to entirely normal intercourse with other people.

David's conduct was a gross breach of Israelite custom, all the more remarkable because the consequences must be most severe to himself and his house. By the side of this, his zealous humbling of himself prior to the death of the boy seems peculiar. If he had gone into his temple and had made a vow to Yahweh to do this or that if the boy recovered, then from the old point of view there would have been good sense in fasting and abstention. But this was not the case. David behaved *before* the death of the boy as a normal man would do after it, thus reversing the mourning customs. This is what is noticed by his men, who represent the common Israelite view of life.

David proffers the explanation himself, clearly and without beating about the bush. To observe mourning rites after the death is absurd, for they cannot call back the dead. On the other hand, they are in place during the illness, for then there is still some hope that by the king's great humbling of himself Yahweh's mercy will be awakened and make him keep away death.

In this way David in fact takes the ground from under the early Hebrew view of life and death. The spontaneous display of grief, the consequences which the uncleanness of death bring into the life of man, are unknown to him. He merely judges actions by their results. How far he is from the tradition may be gathered from the fact that he does not fear a breach with it which, according to the old way of thinking, would mean destruction to himself; whenever he feared such a danger, he generally showed extreme caution. And yet he was so closely bound up with the traditional customs that he found it natural to use them; he merely gave them a new character. They were not spontaneous manifestations, but they could be used to impress Yahweh.

This outlook must lead to a change in the view of the sacred customs. In early times the invocation of Yahweh acted in unison with the holy strength which man created in himself through asceticism and other psychic training; these were two aspects of the same matter. David's view breaks up this coherence. The ascetic striving has no effect of immediate importance on man's soul. It merely acquires significance as a humiliation which influences Yahweh and induces him to act so that man can receive a gift from him.

The brief story shows a quite revolutionary new attitude in the psychic history of Israel; the evidence it affords is all the more important because it entirely agrees with the picture of David which we have from other angles. David and his men represent two different types, but David's type could not exist without the others. He uses the same forms of life as they do, but uses them in his own way. This does not mean of course that the old order is abolished then and there. But a new element has been introduced, and it is bound to spread and affect religious life. It implies a fresh conception of man, which is connected with the social conditions that developed in Canaanite Israel. David's view of ritual customs corresponds entirely with the changed ideas of honour and the other values of life which were gradually spreading in Israel; it agrees with the tendency to emphasise the eulogy of Yahweh at the festivals, and it is noticeable not least in its view of Yahweh and his work.

———————

From early times lamentation and humiliation formed part of the Canaanite cult; they belonged amongst other things to the rites connected with the death of the god. We know an early Israelitish feast of lamentation at which the young women bewailed Jephthah's daughter, who was not allowed to live the normal life of a woman.

When great disasters had happened, a public fast might be held which, in the monarchical period, was proclaimed like other feasts; the occasion might be that a great landowner was to be charged with having "blessed" God and the king (1 Kings 21, 9-13). We hear of such feasts, too, in tales of the earliest times. We are told that the Israelites went out to fight Benjamin; but first they gathered at Bethel where they sat before Yahweh weeping and fasting, after which they sacrificed (Judg. 20,26). A preparation for war of this kind is hardly conceivable, however, in earliest Israel; and here as in a similar account of the earliest times (1 Sam. 7,6) it is most likely the voice of later ages that speaks. In the latter part of the monarchical period feasts of atonement became a frequent necessity. Baruch in Jehoiakim's days read the speeches of Jeremiah in the temple at a fast that had been proclaimed throughout the town and the whole people (Jer. 36,9). In the last disastrous days of the kingdom a band of men came from the central regions of the realm with their garments rent, their beards shaven, and their skin gashed to offer sacrifices in the house of Yahweh, which was perhaps already destroyed at that time (Jer. 41,4 ff.).

These men, then, come in a state of mourning to sacrifice, a mixture of two conditions which is most remarkable and would hardly have been conceivable in early times. But it agrees with the character of the ordinary feasts of atonement, as we see from the book of Joel.

The background of Joel's speeches is the unhappy condition of the country. Grasshoppers have eaten the crops, all sacrifices have ceased and all energy is relaxed. The prophet then invites the priests to perform mourning rites (sāphadh), to dress themselves in mourning clothes and lament. They are to sanctify a fast and proclaim an ʿaṣārā, the term for the festal assembly at the temple, the people is to gather and invoke Yahweh in the temple (Jo. 1,13 f.). The whole feast is to consist in lamentations; by fasting, weeping and wailing they are to turn Yahweh's mind, so that he regrets the evil he has sent and bestows his blessing on the people. The priests especially are to weep and remind Yahweh of what his honour demands of him (2, 12-17).

We have seen how holiness and its opposite could gradually become fused because they had in common a segregation from everyday life. Fasting with what belongs to it affords an example of such a fusion. For it is necessary both to sanctification and under the curse, and it is an old idea that Yahweh could be influenced by it. But when this aspect of it is one-sidedly emphasised, the decisive distinction between the two quite different reasons for fasting falls away, and the mourning rites acquire precisely the importance which David ascribed to them. They become the expression of the humbling of one's self before Yahweh, and hence a means of winning his goodwill. [1] During the social and political disintegration of the later monarchical period this view became so common that it was almost the normal thing to approach Yahweh with grief and fasting. Fasting and lamentation are mentioned together with sacrifice as means of winning Yahweh's goodwill (Jer. 14,12). A story about Hezekiah is characteristic. When he received a provocative letter from the As-

syrians, he put on mourning raiment and, going to the temple, he
spread the arrogant letter before Yahweh in order to awaken his
jealousy (2 Kings 19,1.14). Now the mourning raiment was quite
compatible with what was holy. It was in this period the sin-
offerings became a necessity.

In post-exilic times religious life was dominated by this mood.
During the exile, days calling to mind the destruction of the
temple had been dedicated to fasting and lamentation (Zech. 7,3.5,
cf. 8,19); the re-establishment of the congregation was based on
continual fasts and confessions of sin (Ezr. 8,21; 10,1; Neh. 9),
and so it continued to be. In this spirit Solomon's speech at the
inauguration of the temple was composed. According to it the
temple is the place where the people humbles itself with confessions of sin and beseeches God for help when disasters befall it
from enemies, drought or famine (1 Kings 8,33 ff.). The temple
became a house of weeping, where the altar was covered with
tears (Mal. 2,13). In the book of Jonah it is a matter of course
that a menacing disaster must be averted by feasts of atonement
with mourning rites, fasting, confession of sins, and lamentation,
and the book of Esther (4,16) tells of three days of unbroken fast
to ensure the success of an undertaking. Fasting has acquired a
value in itself, and the next step is to enquire whether it is done
in the proper way; not in the old sense, i. e. whether the requirements of cleanness and holiness are fulfilled, but in the sense
that it must be prompted by the proper spirit. This reduces fasting
to nil, and indeed, the enquirer's answer to himself is that the
proper fast consists in acting righteously (Isa. 58,6).

The numerous lamentations in the book of Psalms belong to
the cult growing up at the royal temple in the later monarchical
period and after the exile. Some apply to the people, others to
individuals, some have doubtless been employed in large cult
assemblies, others at private visits to the temple, when some
one sought a cure for a sickness of the soul which included a
sickness of the body. In these lamentations all self-control and
restraint is abandoned. The worshipper pours out his soul, ex-
posing it in all its misery and disintegration. The sensations of
the soul are given free scope, they move heaven and earth, but they

come from an impotent soul; therefore they culminate in a distressful cry for help, the soul giving itself entirely into the hand of a stronger being. When these cries of distress are sent up to Yahweh in the temple, they may, in the time-honoured way, be accompanied by a vow to make a sacrifice (Ps. 22,26; 50,14; 56,13; 61,6.9; 66,13; 116,14.18).

If the worshipper has been granted his desire, his soul overflows with songs of thanksgiving and praises of Yahweh. He abandons himself to joy as he did to grief. It is Yahweh who puts the new song of praise into his mouth (Ps. 40,4), it is recited when the votive offering or praise offering is made (50,14.23; 56, 13; 107,22; 116,17).

The temple always had visitors enough, both at the festivals and on ordinary days. They came to consult the priests, listen to the prophets, offer sacrifice, beseech Yahweh for help, or give thanks and praise because they had received it. Or perhaps they would merely sit there, allowing the holiness of the place to fill their souls. The temple was the home of all peace of the mind and blessedness.

Nothing conveys so strong an impression of the heterogeneous and composite history of Israel as its cultus. But out of the chaotic multiplicity there gradually developed a fixed form which became the only Israelite form.

The sanctification of nature and man with his history at the feasts made them points at which the future was created. By this means the Israelites in Canaan combined the new and the old. The old feature was their history, the new feature was the assimilation of the nature of the agricultural land, and it was about the latter that a fight was fought in early Israel. In this fight the monarchy interfered, introducing fresh elements into the cult. They were adopted from without but given a specially Hebrew character. In this way the king created a centre for the people, a cult which united them, and whose fixed points were the great festivals. In spite of the division of the people, the cult at Jerusalem retained its central character, because it was associated with the monarchy that founded the nation, with David and his house; and this character was further established upon the fall of the northern kingdom. We cannot follow the history of the cult at the royal temple, but we can see that under some kings foreign cults flourished there, under others they were abolished, but behind them all the purely Israelite cult which gradually grew up was retained.

The temple created by the king, under his leadership and supported by a steadily increasing priesthood, grew to be the mainstay of the spiritual life of the people. But during its growth the whole institution changed its character. The firm coherence of the families became looser, the relation to nature fell into decay, and at the same time political disasters made all life uncertain, men became different from what they had been. The ancient feasts were not enough to maintain the blessing, it was necessary to find stronger means of wiping out sin and keeping away the curse. The sanctification of nature through the sacrifices recedes into the background, their power of expiating and obliterating sin has to be utilised to the utmost, new kinds of offerings are found, sin-offerings useful for that purpose; and the greatest weight is attached to the rites being performed with the greatest accuracy in all details. The ancient means of sanctification, fasting and other deviations from normal life, become a kind of self-torture, humiliations supporting the miserable sinners' cry for help.

The focal points of the year are no longer the focal points of life in the old sense, they merely serve to intensify what is done daily all the year round. For the entire cult, the daily as well as the periodical worship, aims at maintaining a holy centre which can make life safe. This gives to the priesthood a quite superhuman significance. The cult has become a technique, and the priests alone master it. But also the priests alone have the privilege of performing it. They only have the holiness necessary to maintain the cult.

The development which took place at the temple of Jerusalem was peculiar to that sanctuary. Hence it became isolated from all the others, which had preserved the character of the ordinary

Israelitish sanctuaries of Canaan in earlier times. It is only natural, then, that the fight against the latter should become more violent in the last days of the monarchy; for viewed from Jerusalem they must seem non-Israelite and purely Canaanite. The movement was consummated by the exile. Whether this terminated the fight against the other sanctuaries or whether the final blow was struck after the return, we cannot say. The returned exiles, who had to begin over again, were bound by conditions as they had developed before the exile at Jerusalem, and to them the other sanctuaries must be entirely foreign. It is quite possible that the vehemence which marks the Deuteronomic fight against these sanctuaries finds its explanation in the ill feeling nourished by the returned exiles against those who lived on, content with the old forms of worship, outside the capital.

A peculiar fate befell the kingship while all this was happening. It was the king who had created the temple and its cult, and it was he who made it the centre it became. But the rites which after the foreign pattern grew up around the king did not make of him such a deeply rooted, indispensable institution as in the countries whence they were derived. The Israelite tradition was too strong to assimilate the foreign customs in their entirety, therefore the king could not become the pillar on which everything rested. The growth we can observe in the temple institution did not exalt the king and still less did it establish his position. The centre of gravity was transferred to the priesthood. At the fall of the kingdom, the king could be abolished from the cult without its being greatly noticed. The priests were ready to take over all the work and all the responsibility. We see from Ezekiel that already shortly after the fall of the kingdom they had got so far as actually to regard the king as a usurper who had unlawfully interfered in the cult.

When the returned exiles re-established the cult at the temple of Jerusalem they did not act blindly as people who were merely to fulfil the commandments of an arbitrary law. The temple was still an indispensable part of the totality of the people. It was the very thing it had striven to be in the last days of the monarchy: a holy centre, whose holiness was maintained by the priesthood, an institute of atonement, which could constantly purify the people from sin and avert the curse. The various days of expiation, formerly designed for the purification of the temple prior to the great festivals, were united into the Day of Atonement which was given prominence as an independent principal feast characteristic of the whole cult, because its aim was to maintain holiness by a grand atonement of the sins of the Israelites, and to renew the sanctuary by a radical purification of it.

History records instances in which a priesthood has grown so strong by the side of the kingship that it has seized the reins of power, and its high priest has become king. We know other instances in which the monarchy had to give place to other forms of government, but where the king's position was so firmly rooted in the cult that a special king had to be maintained in the cult under the new forms, such as the *rex sacrorum* of the Romans or the *basileus* of the Greeks. In both cases there was a split in the functions of the monarchy. The cult aspect grew strong and became independent. In Israel no cultus king was required after the fall of the kingdom. For the temple cult had become so highly developed that the high priest could take over the main part of the ritual functions of the king. And it was unnecessary for the priesthood to depose the king, for this was done by the Babylonians just as the priesthood had become strong enough to stand alone. But here also the balance between the two functions of the king was upset, and the priesthood combated his cult function in history, so that we can merely gain by inference some idea of his former importance.

After the exile the temple cult retained the independence it had acquired, and the leadership in other departments of communal life was as a rule assumed by others than the leaders of the cult. But no hard and fast line could ever be drawn between cult life and social life, because all forms had developed on the assumption of their unity.

Nor did the king vanish entirely from remembrance in the cult for which he had provided the foundation. The organisation of the cult which was reintroduced after the exile was still ascribed to David and Solomon (Ezr. 3,10; Neh. 12,45 f.), and as late a book as the Chronicles makes David the founder of that organisation of the temple servants and especially of the musical service which prevailed in its time (1 Chron. 24-25; 2 Chron. 7,6; 35,15). This survived side by side with that which made Moses, the chief at the birth of the nation, introduce the entire cultus of Israel.

It was of even greater importance that the king, after his disappearance, lived on as an ideal figure whose coming was hoped for. He had disappeared from the cult, but the ideal which had been created and nourished in the royal cult survived. Post-exilic Israel never gave up the expectation of a happy time, in which Israel was to be the centre of all nations, and the ideal king the centre of Israel. The dominion thus to be won for Israel was identical with the ideal dominion created and maintained in the royal cult at Jerusalem, and here we must seek the root of the hope of later Israel. This hope was perhaps the most precious gift which the monarchy bestowed on Israel through its cult.

FOREIGN CULTS

THE greater part of the Israelite cult was determined by the influence of foreigners. This applies to the worship centring round the king, and primarily to everything belonging to Canaanite agricultural life. The adoption of a peasant life meant a psychic transformation, which was reinforced by the sanctification that bound together the Israelite soul and that of the Canaanite agricultural world.

The sacrifices and the feasts show us the vital relation between the Israelites and nature in the early days, but the dissimilar conditions under which the Israelites lived in Canaan caused a great difference in the degree of assimilation of the Canaanite psyche as manifested in the cult. Some Israelites became entirely Canaanite, some who still lived as nomads with flocks were able to preserve the early Israelitish manner of life, and between the two there were many variations. The fight between them filled the history of Israel. Only when one temple dominated would there be a possibility of one definitely Israelite cult, but even the temple of Jerusalem harboured an abundance of Canaanite and other foreign cults through the ages.

However, from the nomadic period the Israelites had a special character, preserved for instance in the Paschal feast, and this gave rise to a special instinct in Israel which distinguished between what could and what could not be assimilated; but only the violent combat made it a perfectly sure instinct, so that a definite Israelite cult could develop out of the assimilated material.

We have seen how the cult connected with the monarchy was moulded so as to accord with the fundamental conception of the Israelites. Notably, everything connected with the death of the God had to be excluded if the feasts were to be Israelitish. The worship of the serpent, the animal whose life was associated with the life of the Canaanite soil, was for a time introduced at the temple of Jerusalem; later we hear partly about an abolition, partly about a modification of this cult. The agricultural rites, in so far as they meant the sanctification and appropriation of the produce of the field, could be adopted by the Israelites, and yet there were forms of this cult which those who adhered to Hebrew tradition could not accept.

Unfortunately we have in the O. T. only attempts at descriptions of purely Canaanite feasts. An arbitrarily summoned holy convocation took place under Jehu. We learn that the participants filled the temple building, and to each was given a garment from the wardrobe. Jehu, who wished to exterminate the cult of Baal, was so familiar with it that he could conduct the worship, and he offered sacrifice and burnt offerings, but afterwards he caused the whole assembly to be murdered (2 Kings 10,15 ff.). Thus we are not told what it was that characterised a feast of Baal. Nothing is said as to why the participants were furnished with robes, whether it was merely necessary on account of their sanctification, or whether a special kind of garment was needed for the performance of the rites. Other narratives, however, provide us with more definite particulars.

At the great offering arranged by Elijah on Mount Carmel, the participation of the priests of Baal consisted in their performing dancing or jumping movements [1] around the altar, while they gashed their skin with swords and spears until the blood flowed, in the meanwhile beseeching the God for help (1 Kings 18,26.28). The functioning priests are called prophets, and they were in a state of prophetic frenzy from noon till the time of the *minḥā* offering (v. 29).

Their ecstasy is an expression of their intensified psychic condition which in early Israel, too, belonged to holiness. There it was known in the *hillūlīm* of the grape-harvest and the behaviour of the prophets in the temples. Its connection with violent mourning rites points to the regeneration feasts of the eastern countries, at which lamentations over the death of the God formed a part: but they might acquire an independent and signal

importance which left its impress on the cult, even outside the
great feasts. This, however, is not always the most conspicuous
trait.

The Pentateuch gives an account of an Israelitish festival of
a Canaanite type, a Yahweh-Baal feast, which is assigned to the
making of the covenant on Sinai, namely in the story of the
golden calf. It shows how extensively the Canaanite cult had invaded Israel. The leader of the feast is Aaron, the chief priest
at the temple of Jerusalem. We must take this as evidence that a
similar cult also entered the royal temple, and this is abundantly
confirmed by the book of Kings. What happened was that Aaron
made a gold image of a bull, which he declared to be Yahweh;
then he built an altar and proclaimed a feast for the next day.
The day began with burnt-offerings and peace-offerings, and the
people sat down to eat and drink. Then they rose to abandon
themselves *(leṣaḥḥēḳ)*. A noise was heard as from a singing
people, which reached the ears of Moses and Joshua, and when
they approached they saw the people abandoning themselves to an
ecstatic tumult [1] without restraint or self-control (Ex. 32,3-6.
17 f. 25). Then Moses intervened and abruptly put an end to the
feast.

This story is intended to strike a death blow at the Canaanite
cult of Yahweh. It is most harmful to the covenant, the greatest
danger to its existence, hence the story of its denunciation is directly
associated with the fundamental making of the covenant. The main
point is the representation of Yahweh as a bull, which makes the
entire feast a sin. But the character of the feast, also, is of an evil
kind, the licentiousness of the people may make them an object of
derision to their enemies (v. 25). Such an idea is not very natural
in ancient times when both Israel and her neighbours regarded
free self-abandonment as a sign of the workings of holy strength.
Probably we may here trace post-exilic Israel's judgment of such
phenomena. But it is likely that the narrator in talking of
licentiousness is thinking of an ecstasy connected with erotic excitement, as was the case in *hillūlîm*.

Both in Egypt and in Babylonia, the marriage of the God,
accomplished in the person of the king, formed part of the

fertility rites. Just as the rites appertaining to the death and resurrection of the God acquired an independent character in special cults, thus also the holy marriage was not restricted to the annual feast or limited to the king alone. Bands of priestesses were attached to the Babylonian temples, whom men could visit. We do not know according to what rules, but sexual intercourse with the hierodules in the holy place contributed to strengthen fertility, i. e. the blessing, for the participants and the community. [1] The very exercise of sexual intercourse in the holy place acquired an independent value, however, and even men or boys, sometimes eunuchs, could supply the place of the "sacred women".

In Canaan the sexual cult played a similar part as in the East. In the early Canaanitish myths from Ras Shamra we find the holy conception of gods described, evidently in connection with a meal and wine-drinking. Of course such myths correspond to ritual acts in the temple. This cult penetrated deep into Israel. The women who were in its service were holy women in the most literal sense, their name is ḳedhēshā. In the books of Samuel we are told that in Shiloh there were women who served at the temple, and Eli's sons had intercourse with them (1 Sam. 2,22); it is the only hint we have of such a thing in this book, and it is doubtful how valuable it is. But we have other evidence of a sexual cult at Israelitish sanctuaries. Amos quotes Yahweh as saying: And a man and his father go to the woman to profane my holy name, and upon clothes laid to pledge they stretch themselves at every altar, and they drink the wine of the raped in the house of their God (Am. 2,7 f.). Various charges are accumulated here, but they would seem to indicate that men could visit the cult women in the temples without any special rules and have intercourse with them there in connection with a sacrificial meal and the drinking of wine.

Of the connection between wine and the sexual cult we saw a glimpse at the grape harvest feast. Hosea says: Fornication, wine and cider take away the heart (4,11), thinking of the Canaanite -Israelite cult. And in a subsequent passage he condemns the association of the sexual cult with sacrifices: They sacrifice on the tops of the mountains, and light the fire of sacrifice on the hills, under oaks and poplars (?) and terebinth, for its shadow is good! And then your daughters commit fornication and your young women commit adultery. I will not afflict your daughters because they commit fornication, nor your young women because they commit adultery. For they (viz. the priests) ... [1] with the harlots, and sacrifice with the sacred women. But foolish people fall (Hos. 4,13 f.). Here we are told that the sexual cult is practised with the $k^e dh\bar{e}sh\bar{o}th$ by the priests, but it is not stated whether it is a festal custom or a daily habit. But it was not the priests alone who practised this cult. Micah says that all the holy images and asherahs of Samaria are derived from the wages of harlots (Mic. 1,7), from which we may infer that men who visited the hierodules paid a due to the temple. [2]

The importance of the mourning rites in the cult of Baal, which plays such a conspicuous role in the sacrificial feast on Carmel, is also attested by Hosea who, in an utterance otherwise obscure, speaks of how the people and the priests mourn over the calf (Hos. 10,5). [3] And we hear of a direct connection between the sexual cult, the Baal, and the mourning rites in Jeremiah's lamentations over Jerusalem. He gives Yahweh's words as follows: Thy children have forsaken me and swear by a non-God. I fed them, but they committed adultery, in the house of the harlots they gash themselves (Jer. 5,7). Here again we meet with the ancient cult of the dying God in connection with fertility rites. Just as Hosea calls the sacred women harlots, Jeremiah brands the holy houses in which the cult takes place as houses of harlots. He also charges the prophets with committing fornication with the women of their people (29,23), just as Hosea makes the same accusation against the priests. All Israel has behaved like a harlot "under every green tree" (Jer. 2,20), on all hills fornication is committed, Jerusalem will never again be clean (13,27). Ezekiel's accusations are even more vehement (Ez. 16,20.22 f.). We receive the impression that sexual rites dominated the Israelite cultus throughout the monarchical period.

From Jeremiah's words we understand that Jerusalem, also, had plenty of these cults. Doubtless there were not a few sanctuaries in monarchical Jerusalem where the sexual cult was practised, and it was likewise countenanced in the royal temple. Curiously enough, the book of Kings only speaks of "holy men" *(kādhēsh)* not of "holy women". They are also called "dogs" (Deut. 23,19). Such temple servants, we are told, practised the same abominations under Rehabeam as were practised among the peoples inhabiting Canaan before the advent of Israel (1 Kings 14,24). It is stated that both Asa and Jehoshaphat expelled them (15,12; 22,47); nevertheless in the time of Josiah they had special chambers in the royal temple (2 Kings 23,7). Of course there is all the more reason to suppose there were cult women in the temple; a reminiscence hereof may perhaps be found in the account of the women who performed cult rites *(ṣōbhᵉōth)* at the entrance to the wilderness sanctuary (Ex. 38,8). Possibly, like the "holy men", they were removed by certain kings, but otherwise they practised their cult unmolested. Was the sacred marriage, too, celebrated by the Israelite king as part of his cult? If this was the case, every trace of it has disappeared.

According to the story of Judah and Tamar, these "sacred women" were not only to be met with in the temples, they might sit by the roadside, lying in wait for men like common hetæras (Gen. 38,14 f.). It is not easy to decide whether such was really the case in earlier times; but it is understandable if it gradually came to be so, and it is then likely that the feeling of the sacred character of this cult was thrown much into the background.

That the Israelites adopted the Canaanite sexual rites is not very strange. For, as we have seen, they took over the Canaanitish concept of man and nature, sanctified it and achieved an intimate psychic relationship with it. The sexual rites were a traditional part of the intimate intercourse with nature of the agriculturists, and of their striving to maintain its blessings. There appeared to them to be a unity in the creative power which made its activity in the life of man during sanctification strengthen its effectiveness in the world of nature also. [1] And the Israelite view of the sexual relation, as we know, was not of such a nature that a man was regarded as an adulterer because he had sexual intercourse with other women than his wife. From the point of view of the Israelite man there was no reason to reject just this part of the Canaanite peasant custom, when he adopted the rest. Hence these cults penetrated far into Israel and were probably also recognised at the temple of Jerusalem, as was the cult of the serpent.

Nevertheless the speeches of the prophets show that not all Israelites were ready to adopt or recognise this Canaanite cult. It is possible that this was in some degree due to the fact that the sexual rites constantly occurred in connection with the lamentations over the dying God, which the Israelites, with their traditions from the nomadic period, always regarded as militating against the nature of their God. The utterances of the prophets would seem to indicate, however, that the sexual cult in itself struck them as un-Israelitish, and inimical to their traditions. They regarded it as a sin that Israelite women, who were to serve the purity of the race, gave themselves to any man who visited them. Hence they call it all fornication and adultery; and even though they did not condemn men's intercourse with women other than their wives, they could not reconcile it with the character of their ancestral God that such acts should be considered holy ones. Precisely because the sexual rites affected the most intimate part of their nature, they could not on that point allow themselves to be transformed by the customs and feelings of Canaanite agriculturists. The sexual cult was not only useless, it was sacrilegious.

The view of the matter represented by the prophets found expression in the denunciation of the cult that appears in the law of holiness and in Deuteronomy. For an allusion to this is undoubtedly found in the passage: Thou shalt not offend thy daughter by making her a prostitute (Lev. 19,29), and even more plainly: There shall be no cult women among the daughters of Israel, and there shall be no cult man among the sons of Israel. Thou shalt not bring the wages of prostitutes or the prices of dogs into the house of Yahweh thy God for any vow, for both are an abomination to Yahweh thy God (Deut. 23,18 f.). This passage attests that a due was paid on such visits to the temple, and that such might take place by virtue of a sacred vow. The law sems to show that it was a common custom in "Yahweh's house" also, i. e. at the royal temple.

The legends of the wanderings contain a denunciation of the sexual cult, though in an indirect form. We are told that the Israelites at Shittim committed fornication with the daughters of Moab, who invited them to sacrifice to their God, and thus they joined in the worship of Baal Peor. Then Yahweh's anger was kindled, and Moses commanded that those who had sinned were to be killed (Num. 25,1-5). Here the account is interrupted and the sequel is a similar story about an Israelite who brought a Midianitish woman to the sanctuary in the sight of all the Israelites who were weeping at the entrance. While they were in a tent Phinehas came and stabbed them both through her belly. Then the plague stopped, but 24,000 people had succumbed to it. By this act Phinehas won the priesthood (v. 6 ff.).

Both the first and the last part of the narrative undoubtedly has the Canaanite sexual cult as its background, but it is only described as the seducing of Israelites by foreign women, which means at the same time apostasy from their own God; the actual sexual cult seems but remotely connected with the story. Both at the beginning and at the end a plague has been mentioned which befell the Israelites as a punishment from Yahweh, and it is characteristic that the privilege of becoming an Israelite priest is won by fighting against such things. This is the judgment pronounced in post-exilic times when the struggle had in the main come to an end. The Midianites are mentioned as an ancient enemy people who had dealings with Israel in the earliest times; but it is highly improbable that this nomadic people should have had cults of such a kind. [1]

When the Israelites so largely adopted the sexual rites as a natural component of the agricultural cult complex, it is natural to suppose that they adopted them in great part as Yahweh rites. But they also adopted other phases, especially that which was associated with the death of the God, as a purely foreign feature. The cultivation of small holy gardens, Tammuz gardens, is attested by Isaiah (niṭʿē naʿᵃmānīm, Isa. 17,10, cf. 1,29). [2] Immediately after the abolition of the monarchy Ezekiel speaks of

women who sat at the northern gate of the temple weeping for
Tammuz, while others prostrated themselves before the sun. In
a room there were images of animals and "abominations", and
Israelites with censers stood there (Ez. 8,10 ff.). ¹ Yahweh had
deserted the temple, and we receive the impression that eastern
cults at once took possession of it.

For, in addition to the cult which the Israelites adopted together with the rest of their culture through their intercourse with
the Canaanites, many foreign cults were in the course of time
introduced through their dealings with other peoples. Foreign
colonies naturally brought with them their own cults. Round
Jerusalem there were Moabite, Ammonite, and other alien cults
which had been introduced under the patronage of Solomon for
his foreign wives (1 Kings 11,7 f.). With his Phoenician wife
Jezebel Ahab brought in the cult of the God of Tyre (16,31 f.).
The political connection with the eastern states from about 700
caused new cults to be introduced. Manasseh introduced the cult
of "the host of heaven" (2 Kings 17,16; 21,3). In the royal
temple there were horses and chariots for Shamash and perhaps
even an imitation of his temple at Sippar or Larsa. ² In the
book of Isaiah we are told that Judah has introduced foreign
customs both from the east and the west; foreigners overrun the
country, their trade brings gold and silver into the land and
fills it with foreign gods which are worshipped (Isa. 2,6 ff.).
Jeremiah speaks of the cult of the queen of heaven at Jerusalem.
Sacrificial cakes ³ were baked and libations poured to her (Jer.
7,18, cf. 44, 19), just as to the Babylonian Ishtar; but, as a matter
of fact, it was an early Canaanite cult. It was in the same period
that Molech exacted his numerous infant sacrifices in the vale of
Hinnom (2 Kings 23,10; Jer. 7,31). From the last years of the
kingdom Zephaniah gives some hasty impressions of the invasion
of foreign elements into the customs and the cult. In Jerusalem we
find Baal and his special priests (kᵉmārim). On the roofs people
bow down to the host of heaven. The higher ranks wear foreign
dress; they follow foreign customs, thus they jump across the
threshold; the city is filled with foreign "people of Canaan" and
traders (Zeph. 1,4 ff.).

This means that Jerusalem developed in the normal way into a great international city. The Israelites did not give up their own God Yahweh because they adopted foreign customs and cults; we hear, too, that in such circles men swore by Yahweh (Zeph. 1,5). At Elephantine the Jews swore both by Yahweh and by other gods, and yet they were good Israelites. The main thing was that Yahweh's nature should remain the same, whatever cults gathered round him, and this it probably did. We have seen how it set its stamp on the Yahweh feasts at the royal temple, at the same time as foreign cults accumulated in his temple. This distinctive stamp, which is vigorously stressed by the prophets, was the expression of a spiritual peculiarity of the people, who preserved it all through the exile, and it formed the nucleus around which the new Israel grew up at the restoration.

What the Israelite cultus in Canaan was like during the exile we do not know, but it is probable that the local Canaanite cults were carried on as hitherto. In post-exilic times we again hear of people who make offerings in a state of sexual excitement near the leafy trees, and who also sacrifice children (Isa. 57,3 ff.); they sit in graves and eat the flesh of swine (65,3 f.), but they also practise cults in which they eat mice, kill dogs, and do other things of which we have heard nothing in pre-exilic times (66,3. 17). [1] Feasts of lamentation are held for Hadad-Rimmon as for Tammuz (Zech. 12,10 f.). In one of the latest prophetic books we see that there is still a connection between agriculture, ecstatic prophecy, mourning rites, and a sexual cult. It is said that the prophets will one day be ashamed of the visions they have during their ecstatic frenzy. Then they will no longer don the hairy mantle, and the prophet will say: I am no prophet, I am a man who tills the soil; a man has made me the owner of land from my youth (but not Baal). "What are those wounds on your breast?" He shall say: Wounds I have received in the house of my lovers (but not in the house of a god) (Zech. 13,6). Though the meaning of this utterance is not certain in detail, it is, at any rate, concerned with apostasy from the traditional Canaanite cult.

In post-exilic times all these cults were not, however, as important as they had once been. The struggle had come to an end, the peculiar Israelitish character had developed and taken root, and it had again obtained its strongest citadel in the temple of Jerusalem. The dividing line between the Israelite and the foreign element was now so deep and definite that foreign cults could no longer threaten to transform Israel.

GOD AND MAN

THE strength within men was renewed by the cult re-creation of holiness; so also was the force of their covenant, as far as it reached. The bond between the individual members of the covenant was strengthened, but the effect extended to all the invisible upholders of the fellowship.

It was in the first place the family which was fortified, as well as the city community and the people. But these units did not consist merely of their contemporary members. The family was rooted in its ancestors, and the blessing bestowed on the family could not be strengthened without the ancestors being included in the fellowship. At the Passover it was the happiness and salvation of the forefathers which was re-experienced. How the presence of the fathers found expression in other cult acts has not come down to us; probably a blessing was pronounced on them. That there was a living connection with the departed results from the whole nature of the case.

In the book of Job we may find utterances which seem to exclude any link with the dead. He says: For the tree there is yet hope if it be cut down. It can still sprout and its tender branch will not fail. Even though the root thereof wax old in the earth and the stock thereof die in the ground, it putteth forth buds through the vapour of the water, and bringeth forth boughs like a cutting. But man dieth and is devoid of strength, man giveth up the ghost and vanisheth (Job 14,7-10). And the text goes on to say: As stones are hollowed by water and the dust of the earth is washed away by its showers, thou hast quenched the hope of man. Thou crushest him forever and he perisheth, thou changest his countenance and spurnest him. If his sons gain honour, he knoweth it not; if they are brought low he heareth not of it. Only his own flesh will feel pain, only his own [1] soul suffer grief (14, 19-22). In another connection we hear him say that Sheol is his house, darkness his bed, the grave his mother, decay his sister (17,13 f.); the grave is the meeting place appointed for all the living (30,23), where the righteous lieth among the stones of the valley (21,32 f.); he vanisheth like the cloud that returneth not (7,9) and goeth to the darkness whence he came (10,18 ff.), in virtue of the law also expressed in Genesis: Man was taken out of dust and shall return unto dust (Gen. 3,19).

Job's description of the hopeless emptiness of death corresponds to Bildad's representation of the lot of the wicked, when he speaks of death as a mythical being, whose first-born stretches out his hands after the unfortunate to devour their limbs and draw them down to the king of terror (18,13 f.). But Job also speaks of the kingdom of death as a home of peace where all tribulations are over, and where kings, princes, and slaves have become equals (3,13 ff.).

Job's words must not be regarded as intended to instruct us about the realm of death. In his passionate grief he draws those pictures of death which his mood induces him to form according to the current Hebrew conception. All Israelites are agreed in fearing death, because it robs man of his vital strength and makes him a shadow. [2] There is no remembrance of Yahweh in Sheol (Ps. 6,6). The mourning rites express that the family has been smitten by its worst enemy and has come into contact with the world of uncleanness and the curse. When Job says that the dead man merely feels his own pain (Job 14,22), this is a strong expression of the isolation of the dead: he can no longer take part in the weal and woe of the family, but is left to his own corruption.

The reason why Job expresses so strongly the terror of death is that he has been deprived of the values of life. Family, friendship, fellowship, all has been dissolved and the blessing lost. No one will deny the cruelty of death, and the transition is always painful for the dying as well as the survivors. But if death is normal, it does not mean that the blessing is lost. If a man dies at a ripe old age, surrounded by his family, he passes precisely to those forefathers who are the upholders of the blessing. For him as for the family it is then important that the normal fellow-ship should be preserved, and this takes place through the burial.

"I will sweep out completely after the house of Jeroboam, as a man sweeps away dung" (1 Kings 14,10), we read as an expression of the extermination of the race. When this is carried out, the dead will lie about to be devoured by the dogs of the town and the birds of the field (v. 11), nobody shall be buried. The same threat is pronounced against Baasha and Ahab (1 Kings 16,3 f.; 21,23 f.; 2 Kings 9,9 f., cf. v. 35), we also meet it in the form that the dead shall be as dung upon the field (2 Kings 9,37; Jer. 16,4). It was from this fate that Rizpah so bravely defended her sons by protecting their hanged bodies from the attacks of birds and beasts (2 Sam. 21,10). One so cruelly flung away is treated no better than an ass that has died from disease. He is entirely expelled from the family, he is without peace; he is like the man for whom the family do not lament (Jer. 22,18 f.). It is the relation to the family which is the decisive factor. Every disaster befalls the man who is not buried in the grave of his fathers (1 Kings 13,22).

It follows that the family grave was to be as close to the family as possible. Samuel was buried in his native city of Ramah "in his house" (1 Sam. 25,1, cf. 28,3), and Joab was buried in his house on the plain (1 Kings 2,34). [1] The dwelling of the dead formed part of that of the living. Those who had no family could not of course have any family grave, but for them there was a public grave in Jerusalem, "the graves of the children of the people" (2 Kings 23,6; Jer. 26,23; cf. Isa. 53,9).

Even though the members of the family obtained occupation elsewhere, they returned to their native place at their death. David conferred a benefit on Saul and Jonathan and the other members of the family by moving them to Saul's father Kish's grave which was probably situated at Gibeah. [2] The men belonging to David's circle were also buried in their own city. Asahel, who was one of David's men at Hebron, was carried to his father's grave at Bethlehem after he had been killed (2 Sam. 2,32), and when Ahitophel saw no other alternative than to take his own life, he went to his native city to put his house in order and to be buried in his father's grave (17,23). The aged Barzillai declined going to David's court on the plea that he wanted to die in his own city by his father's and mother's grave (2 Sam. 19,38).

The custom, however, did not follow any rigid law. Those who had made a great beginning as founders of a family could be buried where their life-work had been, i. e. among their posterity but not with their fathers. It is doubtful whether this was the reason why Joab was buried in his own house and not at Bethlehem like his brother Asahel. But David himself, whose home was also at Bethlehem where, as a young man, he was expected to appear at the family festivals, had his grave in "the city of David" which he founded himself at the same time as his monarchy (1 Kings 2,10). It was a matter of course that his descendants, the kings of Judah, were buried "with their fathers in the city of David" (1 Kings 11,43; 14,31; 15,8.24; 22,51 etc.). Only Hezekiah and his descendants were buried in another place outside the town, though of course on royal land (2 Kings 20,21, cf. 2 Chron. 32,33; 2 Kings 21,18.26 et al.). [1] In the grave one was "gathered to one's people" (Gen. 25,8.17; 35,29; 49,29.33; Num. 27,13; Deut. 32,50 et al.), or "to one's fathers" (Judg. 2,10). One "went to one's fathers" (Gen. 15,15) and about a king who dies it is constantly said that "he slept with his fathers".

The royal tombs in David's city constituted a family grave of great importance, because the house to which they belonged was the one on which the blessing of the people depended. But the family formed by Israel had its forefathers also, whose graves were guarded with no less care. At Hebron, the first home of David's monarchy, was the sepulchral cave with Abraham and Sarah, Isaac and Rebecca, Jacob and Leah (Gen. 23; 25,9; 49,31). Near Ephrath and Ramah was the grave of Rachel, the ancestress of the Benjaminites (Gen. 35,19; 1 Sam. 10,2; Jer. 31,15.17), while Joseph's grave was at Shechem (Josh. 24,32), Deborah's near Bethel (Gen. 35,8), and Joshua's at Timnath Serah or Timnath Heres in Ephraim (Josh. 24,30; Judg. 2,9). These ancestral graves were found scattered throughout the country, probably furnished with massebahs which established their importance

(Gen. 35,20). The stories about the patriarchs show the great importance attributed to their graves. It is carefully related how the family grave at Hebron was acquired with full proprietary right by the first ancestor of Israel. And Jacob and Joseph, when in Egypt, attach much weight to the bringing of their bodies to their ancestral soil (Gen. 49,29 ff.; 50,5 ff. 13). In the Passover legend we are told that the Israelites, when they emigrated, carried with them the bones of Joseph, in order to take them to Canaan (Ex. 13,19).

The relation between the living and the dead was mutual. The forefathers upheld the name by remaining with the descendants. And the family secured the right to their land and their blessing and that of the land by having their forefathers buried in the family soil. This was not a peculiarly Hebraic notion. Nehemiah knew that the king of the Persians would understand him when he spoke of his grief because "the city, the place of my fathers' sepulchres, lieth waste" (Neh. 2,3).

In the relation to the dead there is, however, always a duality. The dead are unclean, and yet as fathers they are maintainers of the blessing; they are without strength, and yet strength flows from them to the survivors. A conflict arose in Israel between these points of view, the same conflict which was later carried on in the Christian world and in Islam.

According to the book of Samuel the struggle was already in progress under Saul, for he put away out of the land those who procured oracles and prophecies by means of the dead (1 Sam. 28,3). But when the fight against the Philistines approached its climax and Saul was left without counsel and in distress, being without a word from God, he went as a last resort to "a woman who had a spirit" *(ba'alath 'ōbh),* and he found her at Endor. In the narrative of this visit we learn how the Israelites could seek help from the dead (1 Sam. 28). Disguised, accompanied by two men, Saul came in the night to the woman, saying: Divine unto me by the spirit *('ōbh),* and bring me him up whom I shall name unto thee. The woman excused herself with Saul's prohibition, but when Saul swore that no harm should come to her, she was willing. He asked her to bring up Samuel. At that moment the woman discovered that it was Saul, but he reassured her and enquired what she saw. She replied: I see a god *('elōhim)* ascending out of the earth. When she described his appearance and Saul understood that it was Samuel, he fell on his face. Samuel asked: Why hast thou disquieted me to bring me up? Then Saul stated his great distress to his one-time adviser, but the only reply he received was the merciless sentence that all was over.

We have no certainty that this description, which is formulated with such great art, entirely reproduces conditions in Saul's time, but at any rate it gives us some insight into the relation of the Israelites to the dead. Samuel, the recently departed leader, has not lost his personality. He can be brought up in his old shape, easy to recognise, and he speaks of the future with the same authority as previously, or rather with even greater authority. He now belongs to the holy beings who are called divine; for the departed soul belongs among the holy (Job 36,14). The woman's art consists in her ability to conjure up the dead man. It is said that she is to divine *(ksm)* by "the ghost" *(bā-'ōbh* v. 8).

We continually meet with the two terms *'ōbh* and *yidh'ōnī* in conjunction (Lev. 19,31; 20,6.27; 2 Kings 21,6; 23,24 et al.). They denote departed souls who speak to the living. Their whispering voices can be heard from the ground (Isa. 29,4), but most frequently they speak through a man or a woman who understands how to make them active. This spirit is said to *be in* the man or woman in question (Lev. 20,27). That means that it enters their soul and unites with it. Therefore the person through whose mouth the departed speaks can also be called *'ōbh* and *yidh'ōnī* (2 King 23,24), words used too about all dealings with the dead (2 Kings 21,6).

People "enquire of" or "consult" the departed spirits in the same way as they consult Yahweh in the oracle (Lev. 19,31; Deut. 18,11). The behaviour of those who bring up the dead is very like that of the prophets; a divine voice speaks in their souls, only it is not that of Yahweh.

The Israelite laws unanimously denounce appeals to the departed spirits, and in that respect they agree with Isaiah, who at the same time shows how common a custom it was. People say: Seek unto the ghosts and the spirits that whisper and mutter. Should not a people seek unto its gods *('elōhīm)*, to the dead for the living? (Isa. 8,19). But instead Isaiah refers them to the law as the true guide. The denouncing of these customs is justified by the fact that they are alien to the nature of Yahweh, i. e. to the nature of the Israelites. In times of stress the Egyptians seek "idols and conjurers and ghosts and spirits" (Isa. 19,3), and they belong to all the Canaanitish things that Josiah fought against (2 Kings 23,24); in Deuteronomy we are told that it was precisely such abominations which made Yahweh drive the early inhabitants out of Canaan to give place to Israel (Deut. 18,11 f.). Hence the Israelites must not defile themselves with them, it is directly in conflict with the sanctification they are to seek. Anyone who has dealings with such things is to suffer the dishonourable death of stoning and his "blood" shall be upon him, i. e. he is himself responsible for his death (Lev. 19,31; 20,6.27).

The narrative about the calling up of Samuel shows that people did not invoke the departed of their own family only, they also consulted those who had held an authoritative place in life. But other customs, showing us the nature of the relation to the dead, are in the main connected with the family to which the departed belongs.

Jeremiah speaks of the disastrous times when some people die without being buried: And men do not lament for them, do not gash their skin for them, nor make themselves bald for them. And men do not break bread for a mourner to comfort him for one who is dead, nor do they pour out the cup of consolation to him for his father and for his mother (Jer. 16,6-7). Here there is an allusion to what was customary when some one died. The usual lament was made, the skin was gashed (as Jer. 41,5; 47,5), and the head was shaved. The latter trait is often mentioned (Isa. 15,2; 22,12; Ez. 7,18; Am. 8,10; Mic. 1,16). We have already become acquainted with these mourning rites putting the person humiliated by sorrow into a condition corresponding to

31*

his state of misery; it is from this condition that his friends seek to rescue him and give him back to life again by offering him the normal bread and the cup of consolation. [1]

But many ideas might be associated with the mourning rites. The person who practised them would feel himself in fellowship with the deceased through them, and the rites must be felt as something done in honour of the departed. The shaving of the head might become a kind of sacrificial gift to the dead person; and self-torture, with the gashing of the skin till the blood flowed, was a pledge of love, an ascetic act for the sake of the dead. Thus the mourning rites acquired the character of a cult; the deceased was honoured by them, and the bond with him strengthened, and these two factors acquired a special character by the fact that they recalled cult customs connected with the Canaanite agricultural festivals at which the death of the God was a prominent feature. This is probably the reason why they are emphatically forbidden in the laws. "Ye are the children of Yahweh, your God. Ye shall not cut yourselves nor make any baldness between your eyes for the dead" (Deut. 14,1). The reason given is that they are to be a holy people before Yahweh, exactly as in the law of holiness (Lev. 19,27 f.; 21,5 f.). The interdictions are proof that the customs were fairly common; and this is no wonder, for they expressed the duality of the view of the dead.

That the covenant with the dead was also strengthened by giving them some of the produce of the fields may be seen by the declaration prescribed by Deuteronomy upon the giving of tithes. The giver is then to declare that none of it has been in contact with uncleanness, "and I have not given ought thereof to a dead person" (Deut. 26,14). This custom seems so natural that one is surprised to find no more evidence of it.

The dead kings were honoured in a special way by kindling a fire to them; it is said to be a common custom observed for the kings who died in time of peace (Jer. 34,5; 2 Chron. 16,14). It is expressly stated about Joram in Judah that a fire was not kindled in his honour, as had been done for his ancestors (2 Chron. 21, 19). It is difficult to say what this custom meant since it is quite isolated and of it we learn nothing more. It may perhaps be a burning of incense. [1]

The above-mentioned customs show how vital the relation to the deceased continued to be. The dead had passed over into another form of existence, they were *'elōhīm,* divine beings, and men benefited by their power by invoking them and strengthening the connection with them. Those especially who had received the great blessing in the present life became divine at death. This was a common view among the settled nations of western Asia, and the Israelites adopted it in Canaan. But the opposition it evoked showed that it was not quite in agreement with the ancient traditions of Israel, and no wonder. For nomads do not live in such intimate fellowship with the dead as do agricultural peoples who are firmly bound to the soil in which their dead lie buried.

In their relation to the dead the Israelites took the same stand as in the fertility cult. They accepted most of it but shrank from adopting it in its entirety. The dead passed into the great holiness and became participators in the divine world; there can be no doubt about this as to the earlier period. But their holiness must be compatible with the nature of Yahweh, or his jealousy would prepare to fight. Prophecies emanating from a divine soul other than that of Yahweh could not be tolerated any more than a cult that recalled the divine mourning rites. Gradually Yahweh laid claim to all divinity for himself, and henceforth he was bound to demand that no one else should receive any worship resembling his cult. This tendency in Yahweh further involved the absence of anything but approximations to divinity for the king. Yahweh intended to assert his nature, and tolerated no approaches.

The eagerness to expel the dead from the divine world was connected with the increasing strength of the holiness of the temple and its sensitivity to all uncleanness. The uncleanness of death became more accentuated and it still adhered to the grave and the bones of the dead (Num. 19,16). These, indeed, came to be regarded as especially unclean, well fitted for desecrating altars and rendering them useless for worship (2 Kings 23,14.18.

20). Ezekiel draws the conclusion that the nearness of the royal tombs to the temple is a sacrilege. We read: The house of Israel shall no longer defile my holy name, they and their kings, by their whoredom nor by the carcases of their kings when they die [1] (Ez. 43,7). The fact that the kings lived next to the temple was bad enough in itself, but now there must be an end of the defilement, the Israelites must remove their whoredom and their royal corpses from Yahweh (v. 9).

Thus the dead bodies of the kings are just as objectionable to Yahweh's holiness as the sexual cult and, like the latter, must be removed from the temple of Jerusalem. Here one aspect of the conception of the dead is carried to its extreme, and we hear nothing of the sustaining power and the blessing of the dead. This was of course connected with Ezekiel's endeavour to reduce the king and reserve the sphere of holiness for the priests, nor did it mean that the ancestral tombs were henceforward desecrated in Israel. Nehemiah's words to the king of the Persians show their importance. Even though later Israel could no longer call the dead divine, they were still the maintainers of the people's blessing. Their graves were still the best guarantee of their presence, and by keeping up the connection with them the survivers claimed their share in the blessing bestowed on them by their own and their fathers' God.

The early Israelite relation to the dead shows that in older times there was no gulf between the divine and the human. Like the king, the dead of men themselves reached the divine world and constituted a transitional form between the human and the entirely divine. The divine was not, indeed, any strictly bounded domain. It formed the source of all that acted with the strength of life, because it was identical with perfect holiness. Just as the vitality of the root is felt in the farthest twigs, thus the divine strength was felt wherever there was life.

The Israelite conception of spiritual life always presupposes a divine power behind all human action. Man accomplishes his work through the blessing that fills his soul. If he is a man of humble condition he owes his blessing to that of the chief and the strong men, but the blessing of all is derived from that of the ancestors. The progress of the family depends on its acting in harmony with all the rest of the spiritual power active in the world around it, the same that is renewed in the holy festivals and which is of divine foundation and origin. If the strong man rejoiced in his strength it was not because this was something peculiar to himself; on the contrary, he felt the common strength active in him, which came from the great divine source of strength. God was with him, as it is constantly said about the man who possesses the blessing and succeeds. [1] Yahweh loves him (2 Sam. 12,24).

The divine strength acts through the human soul, just as kinsmen, and especially the great ones, act in their fellows. If a man cannot act, it means that God has withdrawn himself from him (1 Sam. 28,15). In the little daily acts there is no reason to think especially of the divine power. But if a man is to accomplish some great deed he must "encourage himself in Yahweh, his God" (1 Sam. 30,6), and the man and the God may then with equal right be said to have acted. When the ancient heroes fought they were filled with the soul of God, and when, for instance, Gideon won his victory it was both his and Yahweh's deed. When Elisha, the man of God, had cured Naaman, it was a proof that there was "a prophet in Israel" (2 Kings 5,8), but also a proof that there was no God like the God of Israel (v. 15). All great deeds were from God. Nehemiah built Jerusalem because God had put it into his heart to do so (Neh. 2,12; 7,5).

The divine power unites with that of man, but it is not merged in it, because it goes infinitely deeper. It is associated with a divine will independent of man. Samson entreated Yahweh to give him the gift of strength (Judg. 16,28), a psychic strength within himself and yet a spirit of Yahweh. Hannah prays for a son and means by this prayer the blessing which will enable her to give birth. Man may be an instrument which the God uses by working in his soul. Samson desired to marry Delilah, but his parents objected because she belonged to the hostile Philistine people. "And his father and his mother knew not that it was of Yahweh, because he sought an occasion against the Philistines" (Judg. 14,4). Nor did Samson himself know that his wishes and projects were inspired by the God as part of his own plans. David thought that Saul's enmity against him might be caused by men or be inspired directly by Yahweh, and then the whole affair could be terminated by a sacrifice (1 Sam. 26,19). The God inspired ideas, plans, wishes in order to promote his counsel.

In the souls of the blessed the God worked for the increase of strength and the fulfilment of counsel; but in those who had lost the blessing he caused disaster. Saul perished because an evil spirit from God took up its abode in his soul (1 Sam. 16,23; 18,10; 19,9). Yahweh made Ahitophel's advice useless by charming Absalom's soul (2 Sam. 15,31; 17,14). And when he desired to deprive Rehabeam of the northern kingdom, he inspired him with the harsh answer which turned its inhabitants against him (1 Kings 12,15). It was a divine dispensation *(sibbā)*.

The divine activities in the souls of men are a mystery which can never be fully cleared up. Because they are entirely united with the human will, they cannot always be distinguished. They may act in friend and foe, and there is no certainty as to where they will lead them, but as events develop they reveal it. When David roamed the country as a raider he took his parents to Moab "until I know what God will do with me" (1 Sam. 22,3). Saul endeavoured to seize him and put an end to his career, "but God delivered him not into his hand" (1 Sam. 23,14), because God was with David and gave him good counsel, at the same time confusing Saul's soul more and more. When the struggle between Adonijah and Solomon — carried on openly or by intrigue — ended in the victory of Solomon, Adonijah explained what had happened to Bathsheba in the following words: Thou knowest that the kingdom was my due and that all Israel set their faces on me, that I should be king; but the kingship was transferred and fell to my brother, for it fell to him from Yahweh (1 Kings 2,15).

The history of David shows what it meant that God was with

a man. It meant, amongst other things, that he influenced the wills of other men, making them act for the benefit of David. When David was on his way to Nabal to take a sanguinary revenge for his mortifying words, and Abigail came and soothed his anger by her good gifts, David blessed Yahweh because he had sent Abigail, and he blessed her and her shrewdness which had prevented him from bringing blood upon his head; he also blessed Yahweh because he had kept him from doing her harm (1 Sam. 25,32-34). When Nabal had died, David blessed Yahweh who had fought his ignominious fight with Nabal (v. 39). Abigail acted entirely on her own responsibility; it was her wisdom which impelled her to act; and Nabal died from fear of the disaster that had threatened him. And yet both Abigail's idea and act as well as Nabal's death were the work of Yahweh.

Behind the acts of man there may always be divine plans of which man himself does not know. But a prophet may come and reveal Yahweh's plan and so prevent the disaster, when Yahweh has inspired a man to act for his own ruin (1 Kings 12,22 ff.). Yahweh has started the disaster through the king and stops it through the prophet. For what Yahweh inspires in a man he must in all cases bear the responsibility and its consequences. Therefore if Yahweh means to destroy a man he lets sin arise in his soul and allows evil to consume his blessing. When Yahweh meant to punish Israel, he made David conceive the sinful idea of numbering the people. The presupposition of the story is that the people is responsible for what David does, and David suffers from the consequences of what Yahweh inspires him to do. His heart smote him, and he acknowledged that he had sinned, having done what Yahweh egged him on to do (2 Sam. 24,1.10).

The God's independence of man offers him the possibility of acting through man without man's will being entirely implicated in the act. The law considers such cases. It says: If any one slays a man, he shall surely be put to death. But if he doth not intend it, God letting it happen at his hand, I will appoint thee a place whither he can flee (Ex. 21,12 f.). It is, then, taken into account that God may act by a man's hand, without he himself having his heart wholly in the act. This does not free the man from responsibility, but it gives him an opportunity of escaping from it, because he has been impelled by a stronger power over which he had no control.

Behind everything that happens the Israelite sees this stronger power. When Eli's priesthood lapses, it is Yahweh who has taken his blessing and his promise from him (1 Sam. 2,30). As long as events are in their development, men can never be sure where Yahweh will let his power come into play.

The divine action is both identical with the deeds of man and goes beyond them, because it is displayed through countless other souls in the world of man and nature. It extends from man's inmost soul right out to what befalls him as his fate. "I went out full, and Yahweh hath brought me home again empty. Why then call ye me Naomi, seeing Yahweh testified against me and Shaddai hath afflicted me?" says Naomi (Ruth 1,21), referring to the association with prosperity expressed in her name. She describes her evil fate saying that "the hand of Yahweh hath struck me" (1,13). "The hand of Yahweh" often denotes the fate that befalls those who are not in harmony with him, while "the finger of God" (Ex. 8,15) is seen in acts in which a definite divine will is recognised. [1]

Therefore Jacob can say: Elohim hath taken away the cattle of your father and given them to me (Gen. 31,9), when he had taken possession of Laban's herd by ingenious arts. And, on the other hand, Joseph's brethren call out in terror when they find the money they have paid for the corn at the bottom of their sacks: What hath Elohim done unto us? (42,28). If they themselves had secured the money as a gift from Joseph, it would also have been an act of God, but then they would have known what it meant; now they did not know what God's act implied. When they returned to Egypt again Joseph comforted them, telling them that he had received his money, it was the God of their fathers who had given them what they found in their sacks. This settled the matter, and no one asked how it had been done. Coming from a divine power with which they were in harmony, the gift could not entail any disaster.

Joseph's words imply that man may meet with differing divine powers, and this was always taken into account in early Israel. But the greatest power with which man could meet was the God of the people; all the strength and holiness by which the people lived were gathered in Him. Just as the Philistines cried: Our God hath delivered our enemy into our hands (Judg. 16,24), so also Israel gave honour to Yahweh for all their victories and their good fortune. Yahweh said during one of their wars: Behold all the great multitude out there; this day I will deliver it into thine hand, and thou shalt know that I am Yahweh! (1 Kings 20,13). The Israelites were to acquire the victory, but it was their God who bestowed it on them, because all their strength came from him. Thus the people is faced by the divine power in the same way as the individual. The conflicts of peoples were the conflicts of gods. Each people invoked its God, strengthened him and urged him on, in order to gain power from him, and those who won the battle praised their God for it.

All then depended upon who had the strongest God. But even the people whose God was strong could never feel quite secure any more than the individual. For in each situation they could never tell whether they were in perfect harmony with their God, or where his will would lead them. Thus, in spite of all the greatness of the God there was always room for the uncertainty of life. Through oracles, prophets, and the interpretation of dreams and signs men sought to get into touch with events and learn what the divine purpose was and whether "the thing was established by God" (Gen. 41,32). In the first place they sought to strengthen themselves and the God to the utmost and at the same time the covenant with him. But the arbitrariness of the will of the God constantly kept alive the suspense of life.

Just as the divine power was manifold, so also men met with it in manifold forms in early Israel. The dead belonged to the divine world, as a kind of transitional form between God and man. Whenever a man sanctified himself to become, for instance, a Nazirite, he entered into the divine sphere; he became akin to

God, because the holy strength which filled his soul was the same that gave the divine soul its special character.

Wherever holiness was present, God was. The particular Israelitish holiness might be present in so concentrated a form in a place or in an object that it was Yahweh who revealed himself through the place or the object. The Ark, the ancient sacred treasure of the people, acted as a fully valid form of revelation for Yahweh, identical with his power and will.

When the Ark was carried into the battle with the Philistines and the enemy saw it, they were struck with terror and cried that a God had come into the camp. And what a God! He had conquered the Egyptians and delivered Israel out of the hand of that mighty people! (1 Sam. 4,5 ff.). When the Ark had been placed in the temple of Dagon at Ashdod, Dagon was compelled to fall on his face before it, and wherever it went the hand of Yahweh lay heavy on the city, because it was amongst enemies who tried to dominate it (1 Sam. 5). Where no honour was given to it, it slew people, and it was Yahweh who did it (6,19). We know its honour was outraged by well-meaning souls who tried to support it (2 Sam. 6,7), and how it was finally carried to Zion with divine reverence, while David danced "before Yahweh", when he danced before the Ark (v. 16). During the wanderings in the wilderness, which were organised as a military expedition, it was the Ark that led the way. When it started, the people cried: Arise Yahweh, when it stopped, the call was: Return Yahweh (Num. 10,35 f.).

All the narratives about the Ark show that it was identified with Yahweh. His thought and his will, his power and his jealous demand for honour are embodied in this chest. But this does not prevent Yahweh from simultaneously being and acting in many other places, in the sanctuaries and in holy men.

When ordinary men were sanctified, they only obtained a small share of the divine psychic power. It was otherwise with those who became entirely filled with it and thus enabled to do great deeds. When the spirit of Yahweh "embodied itself in Gideon" and stirred in Samson (Judg. 6,34; 13,25), these heroes had a divine soul; hence they were divine .The battle was "for Yahweh and for

Gideon" (Judg. 7,18.20), because there was a firm unity in their action. The soul of God was in the hero and outside him at the same time. The hero strengthens his own soul in which the God is, and simultaneously he prays to the God outside him for help, like Samson, who, when he was filled for the last time with the strength, cried: Lord Yahweh, remember me, I pray thee, and strengthen me only this once, O God! (Judg. 16,28). Thus he appealed to the God whose soul was within himself.

As the hero is himself both a representative and an instrument of the divine power, thus also the prophet. Both perceive the presence of the God in their ecstasy, when the strength and the impressions rise from the depths of the soul. The prophet feels it within him, and yet as something coming to him from without. Both these things are combined in the expression that Yahweh speaks *in* the prophet. "I stand upon my watch and set me upon a fortress and watch to see what he will say in me, and what answer I shall have to my complaint. And Yahweh answered me, saying: Write down a vision". (Hab. 2,1 f.). Yahweh's *rūᵃḥ*, the divine soul was in him and spoke.

Jeremiah, who has told us more than any of his fellows about the experiences of the prophets, himself describes his condition at the moment of inspiration as similar to that of a drunken man, whom wine has overcome, on account of Yahweh and his holy words (Jer. 23,9); and he hears Yahweh say that he was sanctified already before his birth, because he was ordained to be a prophet (Jer. 1,5). Jeremiah's fight against his opponents is Yahweh's fight, it is Yahweh who revenges himself when he smites Jeremiah's enemies (Jer. 11,20; 15,15; 20,12). Thus the prophet is Yahweh's mouth (Jer. 15,19). He reveals God to men. "The Lord Yahweh doth nothing but he revealeth his secret to his servants the prophets", says Amos (3,7).

But though the prophet is filled with the divine soul and knows the secrets of God, he never identifies himself with God. Just as the hero has God in him and yet outside and above him, even so the prophet. We have records of several colloquies between the prophets and the God who inspired them. Yahweh speaks to Amos of his visions (Am. 7,8), and Jeremiah in particular has told us of converse he has held with his God. We know this well from the mystics, but there is a difference between the prophets of Israel and mystics such as those of Islam. The mystic, too, describes his experience as an intoxication. Self-consciousness is lost and the soul is filled with a power that is divine, because it is experienced as intensified life. Therefore the mystic may say that his soul is God, and the whole world is transformed for him. Afterwards he may use the current conception of God to give expression to his experiences. All within him is concentrated in the experience, it gives everything; and what he says afterwards is merely the conversion into external forms of the inner experience.

It is difficult to say how deep the Israelite prophets' inner experience goes. But it is not as among the mystics an aim in itself, it is a means by which the prophet is inspired to outward action. Like the mystic the prophet also feels a stronger power seize upon him; but while the mystic applies all his energy to killing the self and his will, till he becomes entirely merged with that which fills his soul, the experience of the prophet, as far as we know it, means a strengthening of the will, an incentive to action, in order that he may influence others by what has inspired him. Thus the experience of the prophet, despite much similarity, is different from that of the mystic. The world does not fade away from him, and he does not feel himself changed into God. Hence the prophets of Israel create no new idea of what God is. They experience the ancestral God as power and will.

There is good reason to believe, however, that this matter has not always been regarded in the same light in Israel. The classical prophets were sent by Yahweh with a message to their fellow men, and yet Yahweh was in their souls. It was he who spoke through their mouths. There is nothing to prevent these two points of view coming very near to each other, but the more Yahweh became a clear-cut personality who withdrew himself from men, the further must the two sides of the character of the prophet be removed from each other, and the idea of the prophet as a messenger must come into prominence.

The intensity with which the great prophets constantly feel the spirit of Yahweh within them would, however, seem to indicate a tradition from a time when the union of the divine and the human in the prophet was more pervasive, and what we know of the prophetism of the earliest times does not conflict with this. The change corresponds entirely to that by which a distinction was drawn between the deceased and the divine world.

Hence in earlier times when people spoke of "a holy man of God" (2 Kings 4,9), we may imagine that they were thinking of a divine man rather than a man who had been sent by God; the linguistic expression covers both shades of meaning. That such was really their idea agrees with the fact that the Israelites believed in the existence of men of God who were exclusively a manifestation of God, having no other personality than that of Yahweh. Such a man of God who suddenly appeared and then disappeared was Yahweh's *mal'ākh* who in some respects recalls the Northern "fylgja".

We are told (Judg. 13) that Yahweh's *mal'ākh* appeared to Manoah's childless wife at Zorah, promising her a son who was to live as a Nazirite. Then the woman went to her husband, saying: A man of God came unto me and his countenance was like that of a *mal'ākh* of God, very terrible; and I asked him not whence he came, neither told he me his name (v. 6). She went on to tell him what had been said, and Manoah prayed Yahweh that "the man of God which thou didst send come again to us and teach us what we shall do unto the boy that shall be born" (v. 8). And thus it came to pass. God's *mal'ākh* reappeared to the woman while she was sitting in the field alone (v. 9), and she hastened to her husband and said that the man who had appeared the other day had shown himself to her again. Manoah then returned with her to the field and the man affirmed that he was the same who had made the strange promise to the woman (v. 10 f.). And when Manoah asked what they were to do, Yahweh's *mal'ākh* repeated what he had said to the woman (v. 14). Manoah then invited him to a meal off a kid; but he answered that he would not eat, but they might offer a sacrifice to Yahweh (v. 15 f.). Manoah had not yet understood that it was

Yahweh's *mal'ākh* and asked him his name, but received an evasive answer. Then he put his offering on the rock. "And it came to pass when the flame went up to heaven from the altar, Yahweh's *mal'ākh* ascended in the flame of the altar, while Manoah and his wife looked on it, and they fell on their faces to the ground" (v. 20).

In exactly the same way Yahweh's *mal'ākh* appeared to Gideon in Ophrah, summoning him to do great deeds among his people. He spoke with divine authority and promised Gideon his help. "I send thee". And when Gideon fetched a meal for the guest, the latter bade him put it on the rock, whereupon he touched it with his staff; the holy altar flame rose up out of the rock and consumed it, and Yahweh's *mal'ākh* disappeared (Judg. 6,11 ff.).

These narratives show how the personalities of the man of God and of Yahweh are merged in one another. Manoah's wife saw a man of God. His countenance was of such power that he might well be a *mal'ākh* of God, but it was impossible to decide, there was no difference in their natures. The sudden appearance proved nothing, for ordinary men of God could also be suddenly transported and in other ways overthrow the order of nature. This man of God could even address Gideon with full divine authority without disclosing his real identity, for ordinary men of God also spoke with the same authority. It was only when he ascended in the holy flame that it became clear that he was a manifestation of Yahweh himself, not merely a man of God, but a *mal'ākh* of God. The appearance of the God was so manifold that he could equally well reveal himself in the shape of a holy man and a holy flame.

It was as a man that Yahweh's *mal'ākh* generally revealed himself, and the narratives show us that he was identical with Yahweh himself. When Yahweh found Hagar in the desert and spoke to her, it is now Yahweh, now his *mal'ākh* who is said to speak (Gen. 16,7.11.13). Jacob says both that the God and his *mal'ākh* has protected him (Gen. 48,15 f.; cf. 24,7.40; 31,11. 13). As soon as Yahweh appears among men it is his *mal'ākh* they see. He can cry from heaven (21,17; 22,11.15), but most frequently he appears among men and in human shape. He barred the way to Balaam and his ass with a drawn sword in his hand, and the story tells us that the dumb beast became aware of the figure at once, while Balaam only had his eyes opened when Yahweh gave the animal a voice (Num. 22,25 ff.). He might appear as a punisher and killer on an inhuman scale, as when he destroyed a whole host of Assyrians (2 Kings 19,35); or when he smote the Israelites with the plague as a "destroyer" (*mashḥith*) (2 Sam. 24,16 f.; cf. Ex. 12,23). Sometimes he approaches a prophet, touches him and converses with him, as we hear in the case of Elijah (1 Kings 19,5.7; 2 Kings 1,15). A prophet can say that he has received his word of God from a *mal'ākh* (1 Kings 13,18).

It is entirely in the old spirit when we are told that it was Yahweh's *mal'ākh* who went in front of Israel and led her on her expedition from Egypt through the wilderness, just as it was he who started from Gilgal and led the Israelites onward in Canaan (Ex. 14,19; 23,20 f.; 32,34; 33,2; Num. 20,16; Judg. 2,1). This does not conflict with statements that it was Yahweh who was the leader (Ex. 13, 21; 14,24). The relation between Yahweh and his *mal'ākh* is not an immutable identity. There is nothing to prevent Yahweh from addressing his *mal'ākh* and bidding him stop his work (2 Sam. 24,16); but later, when Yahweh's personality and unity became strongly accentuated, a change occurred in the conception, and Yahweh's *mal'ākh* became an independent divine personality, subordinate to Yahweh, the highest heavenly servant or angel. This conception is expressed in some of the above-mentioned utterances about him as the being who is to lead the Israelites. The Israelites are enjoined to obey him, because Yahweh's name is in him (Ex. 23,20 f.), and the later view is expressed even more clearly when Yahweh explains that he can only send his *mal'ākh*, because he would be obliged to destroy the people for their obstinacy if he were in their midst himself (Ex. 33,1 ff.).

The change is analogous to the one that took place in the conception of the prophet and the man of God. This appears plainly from the fact that the designation Yahweh's *mal'ākh* can be applied to one of the later prophets viz. Haggai (Hag. 1,13), and the very last of the prophets known to us is merely called Malachi, "my mal'ākh". Here the word simply denotes a man who has been sent on a mission from Yahweh.

It is probably the result of a later conception of a mal'ākh as a subordinate being of a certain divine character that the stories of the patriarchs sometimes mention mal'ākh's of Gods instead of gods. Yahweh visited Abraham accompanied by two mal'ākh's (Gen. 19,1), Jacob saw a number of God's mal'ākh's wandering up and down the ladder to heaven at Bethel (28,12), and at the entrance to Canaan he met with a throng of these beings (32,2). Here, at any rate in the first example, we can trace the beginning of the conception that a mal'ākh is a divine being acting in the service of Yahweh.

———————

The statement in one of the psalms that man is but a little lower than a God (Ps. 8,6) should hardly be taken too literally. But in early Israel there was not, any more than among other peoples, an impassable gulf between the human and the divine world. For the native element of the latter was holiness, which was to be found throughout the world of man and of nature. The men of God belonged to the divine world, and there was a tendency to regard the king as a divine being. Men and gods had much in common, not merely the pleasure they take in wine and oil which Jotham mentions in his fable (Judg. 9,9.13). This kinship was manifested in myths about primeval times, about Enoch who walked with the gods and was suddenly transported (Gen. 5,24), or about a generation of giants, men of renown, begotten by the sons of God with the daughters of men (Gen. 6,1 ff.). But there is not much left to us of these kind of narratives, which were bound to seem foolish to Judaism.

A divine figure might appear anywhere within the world of holiness. "Call now. Will he answer thee? To which of the holy ones wilt thou turn?" Eliphaz asked Job (Job 5,1), and Job answers: I have not denied the words of a holy one (6,10). They agree that life is full of "holy ones", divine souls that dominate men and maintain life. The dead are among such holy souls (Job 36,14), together they constitute a host that gather around the ruler of all the holy, who surpasses them all in power (15,15). They form as it were an intimate assembly (Ps. 89,6.8) accompanying Yahweh as his followers (Deut. 33,3; Zech. 14,5).

Where holiness has a fixed and durable character it is concentrated in some divine being. This is what is called *'ēl* in Hebrew, an almost common Semitic term, related to the much commoner plural word *'ĕlōhīm* and *'ĕlōªh*.[1] In early Israel the plural *'ĕlōhīm* frequently denoted "the divine", the divine power taken as a whole or as it is revealed in a more casual or vague form without any idea of a clear-cut, divine person. The prophet is an *'ĕlōhīm*-man; the king is as an *'ĕlōhīm-mal'ākh* (2 Sam. 14, 17), and is solemnly addressed as *'ĕlōhīm* (Ps. 45,7); the departed soul that ascends from the deep is an *'ĕlōhīm* (1 Sam. 28,13); and Moses is called an *'ĕlōhīm* as compared with Aaron because he imparts inspiration, power, and authority to him (Ex. 4,16; 7,1). When a man rises above others in wisdom and power to do right, it is because he has something of the soul of *'ĕlōhīm* in him (Gen. 41,38; 1 Kings 3,28). In *'ĕlōhīm* is embodied all the holy strength that lies beneath the surface from which life and events spring forth. "Am I *'ĕlōhīm* to kill and to make alive?" asks an Israelite king who is requested to bring about a recovery through one of his men of God (2 Kings 5,7). The divine element in the man of God is the strength to act, and it is present in its strongest form in the powers that are all holiness. Therefore only Elohim can interpret dreams and tokens; what happens is what has been decided by the powers (Gen. 40,8; 41,32). When Joseph's brethren call out in terror: What hath Elohim done to us? (Gen. 42,28) it means, according to the old view, that they are not thinking actually of the ancestral God, but of the divine powers in general.

In ancient legal language the powers are sometimes designated by this name. He who unintentionally slays a man, his hand is led by Elohim (Ex. 21,13). In legal disputes the case is brought before these powers to be settled (Ex. 22,7 f.), and in certain instances the matter is then settled by the parties swearing an oath by the principal power, the oath by Yahweh (v. 10).

Everywhere throughout nature Elohim is felt. The regular growth comes from the powers, but Elohim is especially felt in all that is mighty. Thunder is the roaring of Elohim (Ex. 9,28); a paralysing fear is a terror of Elohim (Gen. 35,5); even the struggles of two women for honour and happiness may be called Elohim struggles (30,8) on account of their violence. Now the voice of God is heard, as at Sinai, in the roaring of the thunder, now the prophet hears it as a still, small voice (1 Kings 19,11 ff.). When the people were awaiting the coming of the God to strengthen them in battle, his steps could be heard in the tops of the trees (2 Sam. 5,24).

The various Elohim beings had their special character. The practised prophet could distinguish Yahweh's voice from other sounds (1 Sam. 3,7). Each generation constituted a psychic whole with a deep root among the ancestors and possessing peculiar and holy powers. Hence the Israelite families of earlier times had their own Elohim. These household gods were called *t^erāphim*. We hear of them not only in the story of the Aramæan, Laban, where they are mentioned as playing a part during Jacob's flight when Rachel stole them (Gen. 31,19.30.32), but also in David's history, which shows that David had teraphim in his house (1 Sam. 19,13).[1] When we are told that Jacob buried the strange gods he had brought with him at Shechem (Gen. 35,2.4), it is, we may suppose, especially teraphim of which the narrator is thinking, and the statement is an outcome of the hatred of later times for everything divine outside Yahweh.

One of the laws perhaps describes a holy ceremony before the household god. A Hebrew slave was to be liberated after 6 years' service, but he might stay with his master if he so desired. The law then says: Then his master shall bring him to *hā-'^elōhim* and lead him to the door or unto the door post, and his master shall bore his ear through with an awl, and he shall serve him forever (Ex. 21,6). Deuteronomy describes a similar procedure (15, 17), and here it is clear that it takes place in the home, but nothing is said about the man being brought before the God, which is a natural consequence of the fact that Deuteronomy only recognises a presentation before Yahweh on Zion. But a comparison between the two laws renders it natural to suppose that in earlier times the slave was brought before the household god in the house, and by being nailed to the door-post was admitted as an obedient member to the father's house. [1]

The family always dominated Israelitish thought. The relation of the Israelites to their God was determined by their ancestors. But the ancestors constituted a family, and the Israelites regarded their God as the God of this family, the God of Abraham, Isaac, and Jacob. This ancestral God, Yahweh, towered above all divine souls as the greatest and strongest, because all Israelite holiness was concentrated in him, from him flowed the strength and the blessing on which the life of Israel depended.

The God of the people was not the centre of a neutral colourless power, for the blessing always had its own special character. The God of the Israelites was the God in whom the Israelite blessing and holiness were rooted, and it was determined by the Israelitish character and usage, *mishpāṭ*. The nature of the God may be said to be formed according to the psychic character of the people, but the Israelites were not in doubt that the reverse was the case. They were Yahweh's children, brought up by him. Their psychic content took its special colouring from the source whence it flowed, and all their *mishpāṭ* was derived from Yahweh. This applied not only to the holy acts which Yahweh demanded, but also to the feelings of the heart and all the work of daily life, for all Israelite action was an expression of Israelite *mishpāṭ*. When the farmer cultivated his soil, sowing the different kinds of corn in the proper way, this too, was the *mishpāṭ* which his God had taught him (Isa. 28,26).

Every psychic change which took place, for instance when covenants of a more serious nature were made, acted throughout the whole family, right back to the ancestors and the God, who had to enter into it in order to give it strength and unity. The history of the people in which its soul manifested itself and of which it was created and formed, was the history of its God; he was active in it, and it was his power which moved in it. At the

ancient Passover festival the people fortified itself by commemorating its history. It meant at the same time a sanctification
and thus a strengthening of the God of the people and of their
mutual covenant.

The relation between the people and its God obtains its most
characteristic expression in the fact that Yahweh is called the
Holy One of Israel. For this implies that he is holier than other
holy beings, and that all the holiness of Israel is derived from
him. This firm covenant between Yahweh and Israel persisted
throughout its history. When the people subsequently avoided
covenants with foreign people, it meant that both the people and
its God defended themselves from subjecting their nature to any
outside influence. This was the result of a conflict in which
Yahweh was in the foreground. During this conflict his personality was exalted and became complete, and he claimed all divinity
for himself alone. When the Israelites now spoke about Elohim,
they no longer vaguely meant "divine beings" as would often be
the case in ancient times. There was only one divine person, therefore Elohim came to be a paraphrase for Yahweh. The struggle
for Yahweh's self-assertion came to be identical with the history
of Israel.

YAHWEH AND BAAL

WHEN the Israelites invaded Canaan they were led by their own God, and now it became their task to take possession of a country with foreign gods. The stories of the patriarchs, describing the conquest of the country in the form of the family history of the forefathers, contain a record which in a more condensed form shows us how the first ancestor of the people fought his way into the land of the foreign gods.

When Jacob arrived at the river Jabbok with his wives and children and all his property, he had before him his settlement with Esau, and his entry into Canaan. In the night he then took his wives and children and all his property and conveyed them across the river. At last he alone was left. "And a man wrestled with him till the coming of the dawn. And he saw that he could not prevail against him, and he touched the hollow of his thigh; and the hollow of Jacob's thigh came out of joint as he wrestled with him. Then he said, Let me go, for the dawn cometh. And he said, I will not let thee go except thou bless me. He then said unto him, What is thy name? He answered: Jacob. And he said: Thy name shall be called no more Jacob but Israel for thou hast fought with gods and men and prevailed. And Jacob asked him and said: Tell me, I pray thee, thy name. But he said: Wherefore askest thou after my name? And he blessed him there. And Jacob called the name of the place Penuel, "for I have seen a God (*'elōhīm*) face to face, and my soul was saved". And the sun rose upon him when he passed Penuel, and he halted upon his thigh" (Gen. 32,25-32). It is added that this was the origin of the Israelite custom not to eat the sinew of the hollow of the thigh.

The story is unusually brief, but nevertheless it gives a clear and very significant picture of the Israelite ancestor as the man who won the right to the country for himself and his offspring. He is at Jabbok, which in certain periods was probably regarded as a boundary river (Num. 21,24), and at any rate according to the covenant with Laban flowed near the frontier of Aram. On the other side of the river he is to meet Esau and after the reconciliation with him he is to head for Canaan proper, west of Jordan. In the course of the night he takes his family and property across, which must no doubt be understood to mean that he himself has to cross several times. When finally at the end of the night he was left behind alone, the mysterious man came and wrestled with him.

This man has quite the same character as the Yahweh-mal'ākh's we know from the book of Judges. Like them he appears suddenly, and he absolutely refuses to disclose his name; but he quite frankly tells Jacob that he has wrestled with a God. Hence the man is a God or a mal'ākh of God, one of those whom Jacob has seen encamped in the neighbourhood, near Mahanaim (Gen. 32,2). He came to wrestle with Jacob, but Jacob was too strong for him, so that he only saved himself by resorting to irregular practices, putting Jacob's hip out of joint. And even then Jacob was strong enough to keep hold of him and demand his blessing. The strange God had to give Jacob all the honour due to him. He admitted himself defeated and gave expression to the fact in the name he gave to Jacob; and he blessed him as he had demanded. Thus Jacob wrestled with a God and escaped merely with a limp; he had won fresh honour and renewed blessing.

The story is pervaded with the greatness of the first ancestor. The man of God is so strong that by a single stroke he can put Jacob's hip out of joint, a feat impossible to a man. And yet the first ancestor was still stronger. In a lame condition, in which an ordinary man would not be able to move, he could retain his hold of the man of God and force him to give him the blessing. But who is the God?

It is excluded that it can be Yahweh's mal'ākh. How could any Israelite say that Jacob had defeated him? And was there any sense in Yahweh attacking Jacob at the entrance to the land he had himself promised him? Further, the fear of the dawn which the God displays is not in accord with the appearance of the Yahweh-*mal'ākh*, which generally takes place in the daytime. The reason why the God comes to wrestle with Jacob is that the latter intends to enter Canaan and take possession of it. The gods encamped here at the entrance to the country represent the divine powers ruling in the land which Jacob wants to take over. Hence the God wants to bar the entrance to him, and Jacob, who has gradually felt during the struggle with whom he is dealing, forces his divine antagonist to pronounce the blessing, the blessing in virtue of which he could take possession of the land.

The brief legend which forms a firm unity [1] describes in the form of a myth Israel's relation to the gods of the country. It is not even Yahweh's *mal'ākh* who fights to wrest the country from the alien gods. The first ancestor, in virtue of Yahweh's protection, prevails over the alien God himself and obtains his blessing. That settles the matter and the land is appropriated. When Joshua found himself at the entrance to the country he, too, encountered a divine being. But that was Yahweh's *mal'ākh*, and he carried a drawn sword, for his purpose was to dedicate the people to the battle in which he intended to lead them (Josh. 5, 13 ff.). In the tales of the patriarchs we hear nothing of harrowing fights between Israel's and Canaan's gods. Protected by his God Jacob and his family, the Israel of early times, wander among the inhabitants of the country who, being struck by a terror coming from God, are prevented from touching them (Gen. 35,5). Of the fight with the gods nothing remains but the narrative mentioned here. A wrestling contest with the God who appeared in the border country settled the matter, and everything was then put into the hands of Jacob.

The stories about the forefathers almost make the appropriation of the country an idyl which recalls the spirit pervading the book of Ruth. They only know of the country as the land in the possession of Israel and have quite forgotten the fighting. This has not prevented them from preserving many genuine traits of the inner life of early Israel. But the historical narratives and the prophetic speeches testify to the fighting. And the struggle between the cults of which we have already heard was a struggle about and between gods. In our sources it is described as a fight between Yahweh and Baal.

In a land with such a complex civilisation as Canaan we must expect to find many gods. And as a matter of fact the inscriptions have handed down to us a number of names of gods, some of which recur in the names of places and men. As a rule we do not obtain much information as to the nature of these gods, so far as they are not gods who belong to the neighbouring countries. The finds at Ras Shamra on the coast of northern Syria have provided us with a number of texts which give us not only information about the cult in an early Canaanite community, but also about the part played by various gods in it. In this connection we are only interested in the Canaanite pantheon in so far as it has a determining influence on the development of Israel. [1] In the Old Testament the Canaanite gods are termed Baalim (Judg. 2,11; 3,7; 8,33; 10,10; 1 Sam. 7,4; 12,10 et al.). In Egyptian texts, too, Baal is often mentioned. He was worshipped by the Canaanite foreign colonies at Memphis; he is described as a strong and warlike god who puts down his enemies and excites terror when he roars in the heavens or strides across the mountains. In the Ras Shamra texts he is the god of life and fertility, identical with Hadad (Haddu). We know both from the Amarna letters and from numerous inscriptions, that this name of Baal was actually a common Canaanite name for a God. It is used especially by the Canaanites and the Aramæans, but is found among all Semitic peoples.

The designation *ba'al* was in its real sense no proper name for a definite God. We know that it was not even any specific name for a God, but was also used in the human world, and this gives us a hint as to the character of the Baal god. The word denotes the dominant will in a psychic whole, [2] and it is, therefore, especially applied to the master of the house as husband and owner. That the word can also be used about divine beings is connected with the Semitic conception of nature.

Everything is living, that is to say, animated. If we take a tree such as the palm, the individual palm is a form of the palm species, of the life or soul of the palm. The soul is the tree as a whole, but it is also something separate, an organon from which palm life flows. This soul is the *ba'al* of the palm; we know the name, *ba'al tāmār*, as a place name (Judg. 20,33). We are not here concerned with a meaning of *ba'al* adopted from its use in human life, with one or the other aspect of the concept as the starting point. The use in both cases is quite original. The Baal of the palm is the dominant will in, or rather the upholder of, the psychic whole constituted by the life of the palm.

Therefore there exist an infinite number of Baalim who reveal themselves in nature. The plants of the field with all their life constitute just as many Baalim. It is with them the farmer has to do. Job solemnly denies having done violence to his land, by which he would have "extinguished the soul of its Baalim" (Job 31,39).

It is more or less a matter of chance what Baalim we hear about. We are told of the female Baal of a fountain, *ba'alath be'ēr* (Josh. 19,8, cf. perhaps 2 Sam. 5,20); *ba'al zebhūbh* is the Baal of the flies (2 Kings 1,2.3.6.16). A calf Baal seems to have been named in the 'Aglibol of the Palmyrenes. A Baal may be the Baal of a holy object, as *b. hammān*, known in Palmyra, Carthage, and on several of the islands in the Mediterranean where the Phoenicians traded (Malta, Sicily, Sardinia); or it may be the Baal of a sanctuary, as recorded from the southern Arabs and the Punic peoples. The Baal may be the Baal of a mountain, as b. Tabor, b. Hermon, b. Carmel, b. Peor, b. Lebanon etc., or the Baal of a district or a city, as b. Meon (Num. 32,38), b. Hasor (2 Sam. 13,23), b. Sidon, b. Tyrus, b. Judah, b. Gad etc. A Baal for the north, *b. ṣāphōn*, is recorded both from Lebanon, from Tyre, and from the Canaanite colony at Memphis, and is found in Egypt as the name of a city near the Red Sea (Ex. 14, 2.9; Num. 33,7). The name is known in Ras Shamra, where *ṣpn* is the mountain where the gods dwell. In many parts of the Semitic world mention is made of the Baal of heaven, *b. shāmēm*, a mighty Baal; for from heaven came the rain; and the sun, moon and stars which ruled over light and time belonged to it. As mentioned above, he is the Baal referred to in the Ras Shamra texts. Just as there are Baalim for holy objects and places, thus also there is a *b. markōdh* for the holy dance, and a *b. marpē'* for healing; and there is a *b. bᵉrīth*, the maintainer of the covenant on which the community of Shechem was based.

If men were to find their bearings and secure their position in the world, it could only be done by getting into harmony with this innumerable swarm of Baalim. Eliphaz says when he speaks about happiness: With the stones of the field is thy covenant, and the wild beasts of the plain have been brought to peace with thee (Job 5,23). It means that his field will thrive and his race prosper. Great deeds must be done in harmony with the whole of the cosmos. Some Aramæan chiefs, presumably in the 8th century, made a covenant in the presence of a number of gods who are mentioned, and further of "the gods of the open space and the earth, [and in the presence of Ha]leb and of Sbt and of... El and 'Alyān, and of [the] heaven[s and the se]a, and the primal sources, and of the day and the night, who are witnesses of everything". [1] The forces of the cosmos, as we know, took part in Israel's fight in the Deborah battle.

Philo of Byblos says that people worshipped the plants with libations and sacrifices because men derived their life from them. [2] In saying this he has mentioned something central in the cult, for the aim of the cult is precisely to strengthen the life of nature and man's covenant with it. But what is done to the plant, is done to the Baal of the plant. The treatment of the vine and the fruit trees is an example of this. They were first allowed to develop freely for three years, whereupon the fruit was consecrated in the fourth year, and only profaned by being used by human beings in the fifth year (Lev. 19,23; cf. Deut. 20,6; 28,30; Jer. 31,5). The whole of this procedure shows what it means to respect the souls of the Baalim, as Job says he has done (31,39), and at the same time enter into a covenant with them and obtain a share in their strength.

Man had to sanctify the whole of his world, but this did not mean that he was obliged to appeal to a special Baal for each

species of plant or animal. The cohesion brought about by the
cult between the souls of men, plants, animals, and the rest of
the world manifested itself in the fact that their life and strength
could be concentrated in some few gods. In Canaan the Baal most
frequently had the shape of a bull, as we learn from the Old
Testament. This was natural because the ox was the most important animal of Canaan; all agriculture was dependent on it.
It is probably accidental that we have no record of any Baal
named after the ox on Canaanite soil, while we have a calf Baal,
'Aglibol, in the Aramæan area. *The* Baal, the chief God of the
Canaanites, was determined by the nature of the ox, as is shown
by its figure. So it was in Ras Shamra, as well as in the Canaan
of the Israelites. But the Baal appearing in the shape of a bull
could at the same time be a Baal of heaven; his power was displayed in thunder and lightning which were connected with the
rain on which the field subsisted. And if it was also the Baal
of a certain city, the life, law and customs of that city were
determined by it. When Jeroboam set up his bull gods, he said
that it was the God who had brought Israel out of Egypt (1
Kings 12,28). The peasant life of Canaan and the history of
Israel sprang from a common source.

Hadad, identical with the mighty Baal of western Asia, is
sometimes represented as a warrior with a bull and a thunder
bolt, [1] which shows his importance for the people's self-disclosure
and for agriculture. But these attributes merely indicate his most
striking characteristics. When every city or district had its own
Baal, their common character might show many special shades
of significance. Just as thunder and lightning acquired an essential
place in the nature of Hadad, thus also the sun and the moon
might acquire predominant importance in the character of a God
or be worshipped as independent deities who absorbed other
elements; but in this they did not differ from other souls that
formed the life of nature.

By the side of the male Baal there existed the female Baalath. Two names are found in the Old Testament for the female deities of Canaan, viz. Asherah and Astarte.

We know Asherah as the name of the tree trunk standing in the place of worship, as the sanctified soul of the tree. It became of great importance beside the Baal as a female deity. We learn this from the fact that the Asherah or Asherahs and the Baal or Baalim are mentioned together as the Canaanite gods (Judg. 3,7; 2 Kings 23,4; 2 Chron. 19, 3; 24,18; 33,3), they formed the central point of the cult and inspired the prophets (1 Kings 18,19). We hear once or twice about some external adjuncts of the Asherah cult (1 Kings 15,13; 2 Kings 21,7). [1]

Why precisely a female deity was associated with the tree is obscure. But the nature of the Canaanite cult was such that the female element was bound to acquire great importance in the pantheon. The numerous small images of goddesses which have been discovered and which vividly denote female fertility, show that the goddess meant a great deal in the household worship of the family.

The Canaanite goddess was frequently called Astarte ('ashtōreth), a designation which, like Baal, recurs among all Semites, among the southern Semites in a masculine form. Just like the Asherah, Astarte is mentioned with Baal as a representative of the whole Canaanite cult (Judg. 2,13; 10,6; 1 Sam. 7,3 f.; 12,10). Together they formed the soul of the sexual cult. Like Baal the goddess might assume a special character in different localities, thus we hear of the Astarte of the Sidonians (1 Kings 11,5.33; 2 Kings 23,13). An Astarte temple is mentioned at Bethshean (1 Sam. 31,10) and the excavations have shown that Egyptian kings built several temples to the Canaanite goddess in that city.

In the earliest of these temples we see the goddess represented with a peculiarly distinctive character, as an Egyptian woman with two horns. The Egyptian quality is derived from the colony that worshipped her. The horns are ram's horns curving downward as seen also in a statuette found at Gezer. [2] This "double-horned" Astarte has given her name to a city in the land east of

Jordan (Gen. 14,5; Deut. 1,4; Josh. 9,10 et al.). The representation shows that this great Canaanite goddess, who together with the Baal was the maintainer of the fertility cult associated with agriculture, was by nature a goddess of the flocks, just as the Baal was a god of the herds. This connection with the flocks is confirmed by an expression such as "Astartes of the small cattle", which denotes the increase of the flocks of sheep and goats (Deut. 7,13; 28,4.18.51). We understand the expression best if it denotes the young that are sanctified and given to the Baal of the species from whom it draws its life. Astarte, then, was a Baalath, of the kind who also sustained the vitality of the human species.

Other animals might be dedicated to the same goddess, such as the pigeon, which was also found at Bethshean, as well as the pig and the serpent. Like the Baal she might assume different characteristics. She might be war-like and motherly, the finds show her with various attributes of alien origin, Egyptian, Ægæan, Hittite, and Babylonian, as might be expected in a land of the nature of Canaan. The women of the sexual cult, the Kedeshas, were no doubt dedicated to her.

In one of the temples of Bethshean, built by Rameses II, where Astarte is represented as a warlike figure, she is called "the queen of heaven, the ruler of all gods". Under this name the goddess was worshipped down through the ages, and the cult was especially practised by women, just as the worship of Baal devolved on men. Jeremiah testifies to the signal importance of this popular cult in Israel in his time. He says: Seest thou not what they do in the cities of Judah and in the streets of Jerusalem? The children gather wood, and the fathers kindle the fire, and the women knead dough to make sacrificial cakes for the queen of heaven [1] and to pour out drink offerings unto other gods that they may vex me (Jer. 7,17 f.).

A controversy between the prophet and the Judæan women in Egypt because of this cult affords some information as to what the mighty goddess meant in Israel. The women declare that they will go on kindling sacrificial fires and pouring out libations to the queen of heaven as they, their fathers, their kings and chiefs had always done in Judah and in the streets of Jerusalem. As a reason for their fidelity to this cult they say that, as long as they kept it up, they had bread and happiness in full measure, but when they discontinued it, disaster and misery befell them. And they refer to the fact that their husbands have been fully cognisant of their baking sacrificial cakes and their libations to the goddess (Jer. 44,15 ff.).

Thus the women regard the cult as based on early Israelite traditions even among the leaders; it was this cult which secured the blessing and gave them bread and happiness. They aim a special shaft at the prophet who is so zealous for reform, by stating that disaster came as soon as they complied with the demands of the reformists and discontinued the cult. Against this sure logic Jeremiah has no answer except *his* assertion that the disaster was due to Yahweh's anger at their cultus, and he gives special emphasis to it by overwhelming the outspoken women with the most violent curses.

To secure bread and happiness was, as we know, the aim of the greater part of the Israelitish cult, especially that associated with agriculture. But the purpose was so wide that one could not do enough for it, and the scene here described shows what an important place the gods originally alien to Israel occupied by the side of Yahweh throughout history in the struggle to support life.

Baal and Astarte embody in themselves the world of deities which the Israelites found when they settled in Canaan. The God under whom Israel took possession of the land differed as much from these gods as did Israel from the people of Canaan. He was far removed from peasant life and its customs, he was a God of nomads and the keepers of flocks, he was the soul of the history of the people, the guardian of its will to live and its self-disclosure; and therefore a war-like god, as we become acquainted with him in the Song of Deborah. The people's covenant with him was strengthened by the Paschal feast; through it the life of the flocks was preserved and Israel's life under the leadership of their God was strengthened.

Previous immigrants into Canaan had adopted the customs of the country and with them its gods; this was likewise done by Aramæan nomads who settled in the civilised countries. The Israelite tribes also were bound to adopt Canaanite customs, as actually happened; hence it was only natural that they should adopt the foreign gods too, and that their own God should become changed and assume a different character. Both these things happened to a great extent, and to large parts of the population Yahweh became a Baal. But from the story of the cult we have seen that the tranformation did not take place without demur, there were aspects of the nature of the Baal which Yahweh could not adopt. This was felt in the cult at the royal temple, and it was preached with vigour by the same circles who opposed the social innovations.

There cannot be any doubt that from the beginning the name of Israel's God was Yahweh. The Passover is associated with Yahweh, and he is the God under whom the people fights in the Deborah battle shortly after the immigration into Canaan. The origin of the name is unknown to us, [1] nor would it tell us much as to the character of the God; this is revealed through history. In the holy places throughout the country the Israelites would call the God active there Yahweh or merely "the God" or "God", *'ēl*, *'elōᵃh* and *'elōhim*, as we have seen by many examples. The designation Shaddai also occurs; it is the name prevalent in the book of Job. No great weight attaches to the name, for the personality of the God was not very prominent at the local sanctuaries. People sought "the God" there. Yahweh at Shiloh must have had a special character, for he was there associated with the Ark, the earliest sacred treasure of the Israelites. But "Yahweh at Hebron" to whom Absalom made a vow (2 Sam. 15,7), had hardly any very special character, any more than Yahweh at Gilgal, Bethel, Beersheba, Nob etc. These were ancient sanctuaries, and when the peasants there offered animals and the produce of the field, as had always been done, it made no difference whether they were offered to the Baal or to Yahweh. Thus Yahweh must necessarily acquire the nature of a Baal, and the same held good if a dispute was to be settled at a sanctuary and the judgment was passed according to the traditional Canaanite custom.

Where the adoption of the Canaanite cult and Canaanite custom took place imperceptibly, the transformation of the Israelite God into a Baal was bound to follow as a matter of course. Where the contrast was not felt, no conflict could arise. As among other people, strangers could be admitted to the cult community and approach Yahweh. The Edomite Doeg sat in a consecrated condition "before Yahweh" in the temple of Nob, as if he were an Israelite (1 Sam. 21,8). The books of Samuel are full of the struggle between Saul and David and between Israel and her external enemies, but we hear nothing there of the fight of Yahweh to assert himself against the Canaanite gods.

Hence it was only natural that Yahweh, like Hadad and other Canaanite gods, should be called a Baal. That this was the case appears from a proper name such as *Ba'alyā*, "Yahweh is Baal", but also from the names of prominent Israelites in which the name of Baal is incorporated, as *Jerubba'al* and *Merība'al*, "Baal's man"; *Be'elyādhā'*, "Baal knows", the name of one of David's sons. It is probable that the Israelites had the name of Baal as a designation for a god before the immigration into Canaan. But in Canaan this designation acquired its particular importance, because the Canaanites had given it a special character. Thus the above-mentioned names show a peaceful relation to the Canaanite pantheon, whether it actually was Yahweh who was called a Baal, or whether Israelites, besides naming themselves after Yahweh, also named themselves after Baal.

Thus it continued to be down through the ages. In the northern kingdom Yahweh was worshipped in the guise of a young bull (1 Kings 12,28), i. e. entirely as a Baal; in the blessing of Jacob Yahweh is called "the bull of Israel" (Gen. 49,24). Among Ahab's men one had a name meaning "Yahweh is a calf", [1] and names with Baal were adopted just as well as names with Yahweh. All this shows that the development in Israel proceeded along natural lines, Yahweh assuming a great deal of the nature of Baal, while other gods flourished beside him. Along with this current, however, there flowed another which led to conflict. And it became all the more bitter because Yahweh had come to resemble Baal so much.

In the Song of Deborah we read the obscure statement: He chooseth new gods (Judg. 5,8), in which we sense a hint of that change of culture which began immediately after the immigration. But the people's will to assert itself was centred in Yahweh; those who took part in the battle "came to the aid of Yahweh" (5,23). Here we meet with a God ready to fight, prepared to defend his own and his people's nature against the inroads of the alien element. That there actually was a fight between Yahweh and Baal in the early period of the settlement we learn from a story about Gideon.

We are told that Gideon, after his meeting with Yahweh's *mal'ākh,* built an altar in the place. But another story has it that he first pulled down his father's altar to Baal with its asherah. When the inhabitants of the city wanted to kill him in consequence, he was protected by his father Joash who said that Baal must fight his own battles (Judg. 6,25-32). Gideon's name Jerubbaal is explained in the story by the fact that he fought Baal which, however, it cannot mean; the meaning is "Baal fights". Altogether it is questionable how much importance can be attached to this quite isolated narrative. But that Joash who bore the name of Yahweh *(yō)* had an altar to Baal, and that his son who bore the name of Baal built an altar to Yahweh, would probably be in good agreement with the mixture of cults in the earliest time.

We have no certain evidence of the conflict until the monarchical period in the 9th century. It is true that the book of Kings tells us of prophets who already under Solomon and Jeroboam came to announce Yahweh's punishment for the non-Israelite cults. But these narratives leave a strong impression of having come into existence after the conflict had reached its climax, on the view that all misfortunes came from the Canaanite cult, and that this had been predicted from the beginning by prophets. Just as the adoption of the cult of Baal and the transformation of the nature of Yahweh took place by imperceptible degrees, thus also it is natural that the reaction against it should only mature gradually

33*

and that it should break out in full force at a time when the transformation had progressed very far. It must then come from circles that had lived in comparative isolation and preserved the ancient Israelite traditions. Naturally we hear nothing about the preparation of the whole of this movement, before it suddenly breaks out and unfolds itself in all its vigour.

The stories of Elijah describe these events as a cult-fight and a struggle between gods. We are told that Elijah came from his native place Tishbe in Gilead, and announced to Ahab in the name of Yahweh that there would be a drought for several years (1 Kings 17). It appears from the sequel why the drought was to come. Ahab and his house "followed the Baalim" (18,18), therefore Yahweh intended to punish him. Partly he "imitated the sins of Jeroboam, the son of Nebat", which consisted in worshipping Yahweh in the shape of a bull, partly he built an altar to Baal in Samaria because his wife Jezebel was the daughter of a Phoenician king (1 Kings 16,31 f.). We are even told that Jezebel had caused Yahweh's prophets to be exterminated, but Ahab's trusted minister Obadiah had hidden a hundred of them and thus saved their lives (18,3 f. 13).

When the country had long suffered from the drought Elijah came once more to the king. Ahab greeted him with bitterness as the destroyer of Israel, but Elijah answered that it was the king who was destroying Israel by his conduct. And the prophet then proposed that there should be a contest between himself and Jezebel's 450 prophets of Baal on Mount Carmel, and the proposal was accepted. When the people were assembled on Mount Carmel Elijah came forward, saying that he was the only Yahweh prophet left, but he would take up the contest with the 450. The people were now to stop their cult processions both for the one and the other. [1] It would then be decided which of them was God, Yahweh or Baal, and they were to follow him who won. The ordeal was to consist in himself and the prophets of Baal each sacrificing a bull, and that party should be the victor whose God kindled the altar flame. They all agreed to this. Hence we are here concerned with an ordeal, in which the contest is between two kinds of men of God and between two gods.

It is then recorded how Baal's prophets prepared their sacrifice and went round the altar they had built making the movements peculiar to the cult and crying: Hear us Baal; gashing their skin till the blood flowed, abandoning themselves to ecstasy in the Canaanite way. But their ritual efforts were all empty, their God made no sign. Elijah mocked them, sure of his victory; their God could not hear them, perhaps he was asleep, or occupied in some other way. Their frenzy increased, the blood flowed, with noonday they reached the climax, but by the time of the after-noon sacrifice it was over, their cause was lost.

Then Elijah came forward. He rebuilt Yahweh's altar with one stone for each of the tribes of Israel and dug a trench round it. He arranged the sacrifice, and three times he caused water to be poured over it so that it flowed into the trench. Then he said: Yahweh; Abraham's, Isaac's, and Israel's God! Let it be known this day that thou art God in Israel and that I am thy servant and have done all this at thy bidding. Hear me, Yahweh, hear me! And this people shall know that thou Yahweh art the God since thou turnest their hearts back again. — Then the fire of Yahweh descended and consumed the holocaust and the wood and the stones and the earth, and licked up the water that was in the trench. And the people fell on their faces crying: Yahweh is the God, Yahweh is the God. There was a sequel to the contest for the prophets of Baal were taken down and "slaughtered" by the brook Kishon, all at the command of Elijah. Shortly after the rain came (1 Kings 18).

This was not the end of the fight. Jezebel sought the life of Elijah, and he fled to Horeb, the old mountain of God. During the drought he had drunk of a brook in the land east of Jordan, and the ravens had brought him food (1 Kings 17,5 f.). Here in the desert south of Judah Yahweh's *mal'ākh* himself gave him bread and water.

On Mount Horeb Yahweh appeared to him. We are told that first there came a storm that burst rocks, then an earthquake, then a fire, but Yahweh was not in any of these. Then, as sometimes happened, the prophet felt the presence of Yahweh in a still and small voice (Job 4,16). During all this Elijah had been sitting in a cave, but now he rose and took his stand at the entrance to the cave with his head covered. A voice asked him what he was doing there, and he answered: I have been jealous for Yahweh, the Lord of hosts, for the Israelites have forsaken thy covenant. They have thrown down thine altars and slain thy prophets with the sword so that I alone am left, and they seek to take my soul (1 Kings 19,14). Elijah is then commanded to anoint Hazael at Aram and Jehu in Israel. Both of them will become an affliction to the people, but 7000 have not bowed down before Baal nor kissed him. They shall be saved.

The stories about Elijah for the first time depict clearly the fight between Yahweh and Baal. They give no colourless report of long past events but draw a series of pictures of highly condensed content. In this way persons and events are idealised, and the contrasts are brought out in sharp relief.

At the centre of events we have Elijah as the type of Israelite who is faithful to the God of his fathers and a watcher over the covenant. He belongs to the prophets, the natural guardians of Israelite psychic life because it is concentrated in them. But the legend describes him as a lonely man. It is true that we hear of 7000 who have not bowed down to Baal, but the worshippers of Yahweh have to hide; Jezebel has killed their prophets; Elijah alone is left. Thus the legend raises him to be the man in whom all fidelity to Yahweh is concentrated, everything depends on him. His home was in the land east of Jordan; there he lived in the lonely valleys. As the man who represents the real Israel he goes to Mount Horeb whence comes all that is truly Israelitish.

Opposed to Elijah we have Jezebel, the Phoenician princess, as the enemy of Yahweh and the real Israel. It is her priests and prophets who are associated with Baal; for her sake the king builds a temple to Baal at Samaria. It is all Canaanitish; Elijah is active in the Phoenician region exactly as in the rest of Canaan (1 Kings 17,7 ff.). Jezebel represents the Canaanite element, but she is not content to work for her own cult, she also persecutes the cult of Yahweh and exterminates his prophets.

Between Elijah and Jezebel we have Ahab, who is subject to pressure from both sides. He appears as a passive instrument in the hand of the Phoenician queen, he supports her in her zeal for the foreign cult, and calmly allows her to fight his own. On the other side Elijah treats him as a man without authority. It is Elijah who conducts the whole ordeal, and causes his opponents to be slain without Ahab raising a hand. The king is an indifferent spectator, when it is all over he returns home at the command of the mighty prophet, only to denounce him to his wife. It is she who threatens to take Elijah's life, just as it was she who drove Ahab to the rupture with Naboth which again brought down the prophet's judgment on him. Jezebel is not merely the scheming woman playing her own game with the man. She has become the embodiment of the fight against Yahweh, hence she takes all power into her own hands, and Ahab becomes a type of the passive Israelites.

It is not difficult to see that the actors in the drama have been formed according to the nature and purpose of the legend. Ahab was no shuttlecock bandied about between a woman's schemes and a prophet's authority, even though both these powers of course may have exerted their influence over him. He was a great and powerful king, who set himself great aims and attained them. As king of Israel he was a worshipper of Yahweh, his sons Ahaziah and Joram bore the name of Yahweh. According to the legend itself the chief of his household, Obadiah, was the protector of the prophets of Yahweh, and prior to the war with the Aramæans he sought the aid of a band of Yahweh's prophets (1 Kings 22). This does not agree with Elijah being as isolated as the legend would have it, nor with the king allowing Jezebel to exterminate the prophets of Yahweh. That Ahab, like Solomon, provided for the cult of his wife is a matter of course, but that she should have persecuted the God of her royal consort and his cult is not very probable. Everything would seem to indicate that Ahab and his wife held the current opinion that the various cults were to be allowed to flourish together. But this very thing was an abomination to Elijah, hence he was bound to become the aggressor. The legend which originated in circles of the kind to which Elijah belonged took another view. According to it the stranger Jezebel was the aggressor, Elijah the victim.

The story of the ordeal is akin to the cult legends that show
the origin of a sanctuary to be due to Yahweh's accepting
sacrifice in it. The question is to which God the Israelite owes
worship, and naturally the ordeal is intended to show which of the
two gods is able to take the offering. The scene describes plainly
the relation between men and their God. The ordeal is a psychic
contest between two kinds of worshippers. We see the Canaanite
priests put forth all their strength. By the concentrated psychic
power manifesting itself in their ecstasy they strive to compel the
completion of the sacrifice, this being the same as the victory of
their God; and simultaneously they entreat his aid: he is to act,
to intervene, and to secure their victory. If they failed it meant
that they had not the power, or that the God had not the power,
which was the same thing.

Elijah had only to beseech Yahweh to assert himself, then
Yahweh's fire fell down and consumed the offering, because he
possessed the power. But Elijah combined something else with
this. He consecrated water by having it poured over the altar, in
this way he procured the desired rain. Yahweh had taken away
the rain, through his man of God he created it again. Yahweh's
divine power had prevailed.

Thus the legend centralises in one event, in which Yahweh and
Baal fought each by his men, that conflict between the Israelite
and the Canaanite cult which covers the whole period. The conflict was settled by the victory of Elijah and Yahweh, Baal had
no longer any right, he had demonstrated his lack of divine
power. Hence his worshippers, too, had lost their right, and after
this psychic defeat the priests of Baal could be cut down without
ceremony.

The exterminatory campaign against Baal which the legend of
Elijah shows us in a special light, was continued by Jehu, who
was anointed by a prophet from Elijah's circle. He killed Ahab's
family and Jezebel, and we know how he sent out invitations to
a festival for Baal where the priests and prophets were gathered
together, and had them cut down in the middle of the feast. Afterwards Baal's temple at Samaria was pulled down and desecrated.
Thus "Jehu destroyed Baal out of Israel" (2 Kings 10,28). But

this did not mean that the Canaanite cult was stamped out, as is testified by the later prophets. And as a matter of fact, the story goes on to say that Yahweh was still worshipped as a bull.

The legends of Elijah have preserved moods and conceptions prevalent in certain prophetic circles in the days of the Northern Kingdom. They do not represent all prophets of Yahweh, for we know that many of these gathered round the king. But if we ask what Yahweh cult it was for which Elijah and his fellows fought, we obtain no answer; it is taken for granted that this is a familiar matter. They cannot, like the later prophets, have detested the cult in the "high places". As we know, Elijah complains of the very fact that the altars of Yahweh have been pulled down, and he rebuilds one of them himself on Mount Carmel. And Jehu whose work was so pleasing to the Yahweh for whom these prophets fought, worshipped this God in the shape of a bull, i. e. as a Baal, just like the other Israelites who had adopted Canaanite culture.

Hence, in reality we do not know what the conflict was about, because there were so many different grades in the Israelite adoption of Canaanite customs, and none of the Israelites had entirely avoided them. But Elijah's chief grievance was that Baal was tolerated side by side with Yahweh. Even though Yahweh was changed, he was still Yahweh, the ancestral God from Horeb, and he was the only God Israel had a right to know.

As already mentioned, the reaction that took place against the merging of Israel in the Canaanite culture was to a certain extent due to an isolation of the Israelites. Israelitish tribes had immigrated simultaneously in such numbers that they were not gradually absorbed by the population of the country, and in the highlands large parts of the people long lived a life not very different from that of their fathers. Through the Paschal feast they continually re-knit the tie that bound them to their history. Thus there was established a nucleus of the population which did not follow suit when the spreading of the people over the plains gave an impetus to the transformation in the Canaanite spirit. It was in these parts of the populace that the reaction was prepared.

There were Israelite circles which were so remote from the

Canaanite transformation that they strove to preserve intact the original Israelitish manners and customs. When Jehu was waging his sanguinary war against Ahab's house he met Jehonadab, the son of Rechab. The new pretender to the throne knew what kind of a man he was, and asked if his heart was with Jehu, as Jehu's with him. Jehonadab answered in the affirmative, and gave him his hand, after which he entered Jehu's chariot to witness his zeal for Yahweh (2 Kings 10,15 ff.). They were united in their common hatred of Ahab's Baal cult; this is all that we know about Jehonadab from the books of the Kings.

Towards the close of the history of the kingdom of Judah, however, we hear of a community who regarded Jehonadab as their progenitor, namely the Rechabites. They say that their first ancestor's law was that they must never drink wine, neither build houses, nor sow seed, nor plant or own vineyards; but they were always to live in tents in order that they might live long in the land in which they dwelt as gērīm (Jer. 35,6 ff.). Jeremiah met these people in Jerusalem and gave them full recognition; which is easily understandable for the Rechabites realised the ideal towards which all prophets half tended. With them the reaction against Canaanite life is so complete that it cannot really be called a reaction; they have not yet adopted anything that is Canaanite, except presumably the language. Farming, viticulture, fixed abodes, all that constitutes the Canaanite mode of life is denied to them. They live in tents and have no feeling of possessing the land, they are merely gērīm. They have preserved the pre-Canaanite way of living as nomads or semi-nomads, that which was still retained by the earliest immigrants in the southern highlands. Their genealogies would seem to connect them with the Kenites (1 Chron. 2,55), and these were precisely a semi-nomadic people of the plains who lived on the southern borders of Canaan.

The Rechabites throw light on the history of Israel, because they realise in its purest form the tendency with which we continually meet in Israel, the attraction towards the past and towards pre-Canaanite life. It is this tendency which makes the wilderness period the ideal time in which all Israelite law came into existence; it is this that inspires the prophets' fight against the

THE RECHABITES 523

Canaanite practices; it is this we feel in the representation given in the patriarchal stories of the life of the forefathers as nomadic or semi-nomadic. The Rechabites show that all varieties were represented in Israel from the people that detested all Canaanite forms of life to those who became entirely Canaanite. At what point of this extensive scale Elijah and his circle were to be found we cannot say with certainty, but they tended towards the ideal represented by the Rechabites, it was the ancestral God they wanted to maintain in Israel.

The conflicts of the period of Elijah were superseded by other struggles to keep Israel free from a cult that would estrange it from its traditions. A decisive factor in the struggle was the cultus founded by David's royal house at Jerusalem.

YAHWEH ON ZION

AMONG the many political achievements of David the greatest was perhaps that of getting the Ark of the Covenant safely installed on Zion. By that act he appropriated the whole history of Israel for the new monarchy and established the identity of its God with that of the ancient God of the people. And yet it is a matter of course that a God who was the ruler of a great monarchy must differ both from the God that was active in a tribal union of nomads and the God who displayed his activity at the various sanctuaries which were the centres of the peasant communities and their chieftains.

In a great state like that of Egypt which is entirely based on the monarchy, the God is the king's, not the people's God. In Israel the immediate relation between Yahweh and the people was so firmly established by tradition that it could not be given up. Yahweh continued to be the God of Israel. But when the monarchy was introduced, it was attempted to make it the intermediary between Yahweh and the people, and the cult created around it could not fail to influence the nature of Yahweh. The Yahweh worshipped on Zion was David's God (2 Kings 20,5 = Isa. 38,5). He chose the royal house to live before him forever.

The relation of the monarchy to Yahweh is established in Nathan's speech to David, though it is true that it has been given its present form in later times. It reaches its climax in these words: When thy days be fulfilled and thou sleepest with thy fathers I will set up thy seed after thee which shall proceed out of thy bowels and I will establish its kingdom. It shall build a house for my name and I will establish the throne of its kingdom forever. I will be a father to it and it shall be my son so that when it commits sins I will chasten it with the rod of men and with the stripes of men. And my love shall not depart from it, as I let it depart from Saul whom I removed for thee. And thine house and thy kingdom shall be secure forever before me. [1] Thy throne shall be secure forever (2 Sam. 7,12-16). Here the unique relation between Yahweh and the kingship in David's house is plainly designated as a relation between father and son which cannot be destroyed by the vicissitudes of time. And preceding this passage we have the following: I will secure for thee a great name like the name of the great in the earth and appoint a place for my people Israel and plant it, and it shall dwell in its place and be in motion no more, neither shall violent men continue to afflict it as before (v. 9 b f.). This tells us that now Yahweh is acting for the people through the king.

These utterances show the position the monarchy came to assume in relation to Yahweh, and David becomes the type of the true king. The other kings are compared with him, and praised or blamed according as they walk in his ways or not. For his sake Yahweh upheld the blessing in Jerusalem (1 Kings 15,4), and Yahweh saved the city from its enemies for his own and for David's sake (2 Kings 19,34; 20,6; Isa. 37,35).

The Yahweh who was worshipped on Zion was so intimately connected with David that we must needs ask whether David's own relation to Yahweh brought anything new into the history of Israel. That it was actually so appears from the books of Samuel.

We have seen that the books of Samuel, like many other narratives of Israel, embody in a peculiar way subject-matter representing both early and later views which it is impossible to separate mechanically. There can be no doubt that the stories about Saul and David are more in sympathy with David than with Saul, and that the tales transmitted have been given a new colouring from ideas foreign to the ancient subject-matter. But we have seen with what a sure touch the profound difference between Saul's and David's characters is drawn. And it is done indirectly, by means of their words and deeds, so that we scarcely know whether we have to do with a naive narrator or an artist who knows quite well how penetrating his characterisation is. Of course we

have no guarantee that David actually did and said what has
here been handed down to us, and we have no external means of
ascertaining anything about it. But the very fact that all the
many small things together form clear coherent pictures shows us
that the whole matter cannot be without foundation. Saul and
David represent different types, each identifiable with trends in
Israel that we know. Any other "proof" that they correspond to a
historical reality we have not. If we sum up the features which
throw the strongest light on David's character, we shall see that
they point to a definite conception of divinity.

When David was standing with his men in the cave in which
Saul had taken refuge, the men said to David: This day it will
happen as Yahweh hath said unto you: I deliver thine enemy
into thine hand and thou mayest do unto him as it seemeth good
unto you ... But David answered his men: Yahweh forbid that I
should do this unto my master, Yahweh's anointed, to stretch forth
mine hand against him. He is Yahweh's anointed! (1 Sam.
24,5a. 7).

David's words do not mean that he wishes Yahweh's anointed
to live, but merely that he fears the consequences of raising his
hand against him. He says quite frankly that he wishes Yahweh
would smite Saul and he even hopes that the restraint shown by
him will procure so much added favour for him with Yahweh
that it will induce Yahweh to intervene. He says: Yahweh shall
judge between me and thee; Yahweh shall avenge me of thee, my
hand not being upon thee (24,13); and further: Yahweh shall be
judge, and judge between thee and me, and he shall watch and
fight in my cause, and obtain justice for me against thee (24,16).

David's view appears just as plainly in the parallel narrative.
David says to Abishai who wants to kill Saul: Destroy him not,
for who hath ever stretched out his hand against Yahweh's
anointed and gone free? And he goes on to say: By the life of
Yahweh, Yahweh shall surely smite him; or his day will come
that he dieth; or he will go to the wars and he will perish. Yahweh
forbid that I should stretch out mine hand against Yahweh's
anointed (1 Sam. 26,9 ff.). And to Saul David says: Yahweh re-

quites every man for his righteousness and his faithfulness, Yahweh who delivered thee into mine hand today, but I would not stretch out mine hand against Yahweh's anointed. And as thy soul was great today in mine eyes, thus my soul shall be great in the eyes of Yahweh, and he shall deliver me out of all tribulation (26,23 f.).

David's conduct is part of his policy towards Saul. By giving Saul his life he humiliated and defeated him. But it is equally an expression of his policy towards Yahweh; in this way he reveals the gulf between himself and Saul.

Both for Saul and for David Yahweh is a power which is felt in all events, and lies behind their own acts, because it is the wellspring of the blessing. In Saul as in the other ancient chiefs this power works directly in their souls. A man can act with confidence according to the law of his nature, trusting that the divine power will work in harmony with the healthy soul. If this is not done, it means that a breach has occurred, if not otherwise then by some error in the cult. Thus in our narratives. Saul lost the blessing because he had committed a cult sin and provoked Yahweh's anger.

David acted on that assumption and defeated Saul because Yahweh was with him. But the striking difference in the actions of the two men is connected with the fact that Yahweh's self is much more prominent in David's thoughts than in Saul's.

Had Saul been confronted by an opponent of his own type, both would have filled themselves with the strength of Yahweh and fought to see who possessed most of the blessing; and if the anointed chieftain was slain, it simply meant that Yahweh no longer gave him the strength that he had previously given. Against Saul's instinctive self-expression David opposed his plotting, and he avoided direct combat because there was something about Saul that he dared not fight against, viz. the consecration to Yahweh he had achieved by his anointment. Through the fight with David Saul strove to preserve himself and thus the blessing of Yahweh; but David had always two factors to take into account, Yahweh and Saul. Yahweh was behind it all and could settle the matter according to his own pleasure. He was a significant personality who had his special demands which it was necessary to consider in one's calculations.

When it became clear to Saul that he had been in David's power and yet had been spared, he could only understand it as a generosity which showed David's greatness and thus his own defeat. "Blessed art thou, my son David! Thou shalt surely act, thou shalt surely prevail" (1 Sam. 26,25). And yet David himself has said quite plainly that he merely acted as he did for fear of offending Yahweh by stretching out his hand against his anointed. And when he hopes that Yahweh will requite him for his righteousness, it does not mean that the blessing follows upon his great generosity, but the meaning is that by being careful not to interfere with what belongs to Yahweh, he expects to win his favour, thus inducing him to make return by slaying the chief spared by David.

Thus David's act had a double sting; it affected Saul according to the law both of Saul's and of David's God. The same was the case when David killed the man who brought him the message of Saul's death and thought to ingratiate himself by pretending that he had killed him. David took over the near kinsman's claim for revenge as part of his policy, and at the same time he avoided Yahweh's anger by freeing himself from guilt in regard to the life of his anointed.

In all circumstances we see David facing Yahweh as one person another, and Yahweh is like a ruler whose demands for honour must above all receive consideration. When David fled before Absalom, and the priests had brought the Ark with them, David bade them take it back. "If I find favour in the eyes of Yahweh, he will bring me back and show me himself and his habitation; but if he say thus: I have no delight in thee, then let him do to me as seemeth good in his sight" (2 Sam. 15,25 f.). He was entirely in Yahweh's hands, and he would not risk offending him by carrying the Ark with him on his flight. It is distinctly implied in his words that the Ark would be of no use to him, Yahweh would do with him as he pleased even without it.

So great was the distress to which Absalom brought David

that he could not be sure whether Yahweh had not abandoned him. When Shimei cursed him, crying that Yahweh had given the kingdom to his son to avenge his conduct towards Saul's house, David could do nothing with him. If it were true, David would be fighting Yahweh by fighting him. Therefore he forbade the sons of Zeruiah to slay Shimei for his cursing. "Yahweh hath commanded him", says David (2 Sam. 16,10.11). And again we have the same curious argument as when he met Saul: "Perhaps Yahweh will look on mine affliction, [1] and Yahweh will grant me prosperity to requite me for his curse this day" (v. 12). If Shimei is in the wrong, Yahweh will have mercy on David because of the injustice he has suffered, and take the vengeance for him which it would be imprudent and risky for himself to take.

This does not settle his account with Shimei. When David returned in safety, Shimei came to him asking for mercy. Now the sons of Zeruiah thought they were on the safe side. Shall he not be put to death? asks Abishai, adding in the true spirit of David: For he hath cursed Yahweh's anointed! (2 Sam. 19,22). But again David goes his own way. It is his day of victory and he does not want his good fortune exposed to defilement by unnecessary bloodshed. Hence he saves Shimei's life, taking his oath to spare him. Here, too, it is not magnanimity. David had safeguarded himself against defilement by the killing of Shimei. Yet the curse rankled as a threat against his house: Shimei must be exterminated. We have seen how Solomon succeeded in accomplishing this without violating his father's oath. [2]

The dread of interfering in a way that might provoke Yahweh's anger is the leading motive in the whole of David's conduct. When Nabal had offended him, he and his men went out to take vengeance as any Bedawin would have done. But David did not reason like a Bedawin. When he met Abigail who brought him a number of good things and thus satisfied his demands, he exclaimed: Blessed is Yahweh the God of Israel, who sent thee to meet me to day, and blessed be thy wisdom, and blessed be thou who this day prevented me from shedding blood and seeking victory by mine own hand (1 Sam. 25,32 f.). And again Yahweh is praised for fighting for David himself and avenging him on

Nabal, but at the same time preserving him and freeing him from doing evil (v. 39). Always we meet with this fear of doing something that might offend Yahweh through natural self-assertion; coincident with it is the satisfaction that Yahweh himself undertakes the revenge which the man desires but dare not carry out himself for fear of Yahweh.

While the early chiefs made straight for their goal, filled with the spirit of Yahweh, David makes life a political game and turns the wisdom of life into calculating art. And the art consists in venturing as little as possible into the foreground, but influencing Yahweh to act in one's interest. Yahweh is in the background, mighty in his majesty, but by wise conduct one may provoke his vengeance, rouse his desire for honour or his pity: that is the way to achieve the proper end. This view of life stamps David's actions throughout. He employs the covenant as a means of achieving his own ends, and makes use of the holy customs in the same way. His fasting for the sick boy was not a spontaneous act evoked by the condition to which he was brought by grief and humiliation, it was merely a means designed to win Yahweh's favour (2 Sam. 12,22). The sacrifice was made in order to conciliate Yahweh hence the chief importance attaches to what it cost the man who made it (2 Sam. 24,24). When Nathan has promised David's house the kingship, David forms his answer thus: Who am I, Lord Yahweh, and what is my house that thou hast brought me hither? And this was yet a small thing in thy sight, Lord Yahweh, and thou hast spoken also of thy servant's house for a great whiie to come! (2 Sam. 7,18 f.). This utterance is entirely in David's spirit. It is Yahweh's personal favour which has brought him all his prosperity.

David's view of life does not of course subvert the laws of life. Not only does the power of God lie behind everything, it also acts through men, animals, objects, and other souls that fill the world. David, too, knew how to fortify himself through Yahweh, his God. But the divine did not unfold itself freely to him in all its multiplicity, and the stream flowing between God and man was not spontaneous and unchecked. This was due to the fact that at its source the divine power was concentrated in a firm will, emanating from a significant personality. David's Yahweh is so personal that he stands apart from the life of man and nature. His influence in nature and in man does not become weaker on that account, quite the contrary. But he cannot be merged with other souls, he is self-contained and acts from afar. The soul of animals and plants has no part in his nature, the character of his soul is throughout like that of man. He demands honour and more honour as an Israelitish ruler. He is almost an Israelite among other Israelites, only he is so mighty that all must give way to him.

David's relation to Yahweh presupposes a firmly rooted cult tradition. Sacrifice and the ascetic holy customs are something handed down by which Yahweh may be influenced, hence they can be used as a means to determine his acts. The sanctification of the prince is a mighty fact. As the anointed of Yahweh he is under divine protection, no one can touch him with impunity. The Ark is like the honour of Yahweh, everything must be staked to win it, and no care is too great in regard to it. That David could disregard a holy custom such as fasting after a death was not due to want of reverence for what was holy. To him the power of the holy had rather increased incalculably owing to its isolation and direct relation to Yahweh's person.

The whole of this change in the conception of what is holy and divine would, if sustained, knock the ground from under the old cult acts. The death rites have no inner necessity, the dedication of the chief is no confirmation of the fact that he is filled with the spirit of God. The sacrifice is not a necessary sanctification of nature and at the same time a gift to the God in whom the same psychic power is concentrated as that which acts in nature. David's view does not create any new cult, but he utilises the cult as it stands. The cult creates a holiness which can be led into the channels of normal life, though not organically connected with it. Therefore the wise man can employ it as a legalist operates with his legal system.

David's view emphasises the arbitrariness of the relation between God and man. Man does not attain harmony with Yahweh by freely unfolding all his power in his actions. By giving honour to Yahweh, by obeying his will, and duly venerating him by cult

actions he wins Yahweh's favour. Yahweh prefers to protect those
who leave everything to him. On those who give all honour to
him he bestows blessedness and success in their work. In the story
of Goliath David says to his enemy: Thou comest to me with a
sword and with a spear and with a javelin, but I come to thee in
the name of Yahweh of the hosts, the name of the God of the
armies of Israel, which thou hast mocked (1 Sam. 17,45). These
words are quite in harmony with David's way of thinking. Of
course they do not mean that weapons are of no importance in war,
but they have no power to slay in the hand of the man who has
offended Yahweh. When Yahweh intends to uphold his honour,
he may bless quite inferior weapons so that they prevail against
the stronger.

David stands out clearly in the narratives as a very distinct
type. Again and again we see that his immediate entourage does
not understand his way of thinking. This is emphatically expressed
in the scene in which he refuses to do harm to Saul, in the story
of his fasting for his son, and in the tale of his leniency to
Shimei. As previously mentioned, David belonged to circles in
which the line between Israelite and foreign began to be vague,
and in this we must probably see an important presupposition for
the origin of his type. But in the marked personification of
Yahweh features are emphasised which were of early origin in
Israel, for Yahweh had always been characterised by power and
will. The ancient God of the Israelite nomads, who was extolled
in the Paschal feast, was a powerful personality, and the contrast
with the dying and resurrected God of the Canaanites will probably have contributed to make his personality stronger and accentuate its firmness still more. The partial adoption of Canaanite
customs without any links with their original causes forms the
natural background of David and his curious relation to his
powerful God. And from whatever point of view we regard his
special character in relation to those about him, we find cohesion
in his ideas, which all centre round his conception of Yahweh.

When the presentation of a historical view shows abrupt
ruptures with the old and clear new lines it is usually due to a
simplification of what has happened. Between the marked con-

trasts there nearly always runs a web of connecting threads even
if they may be difficult to see. Thus also in Israel, where the
numerous gradations were interwoven. Even though David represented a new conception of God, Israelitish culture was not
suddenly transformed. But his ideas and his psychic nature,
formed through the meeting of the Canaanite and the Israelite
spirit, cannot have existed quite isolated in him: there must have
been circles in which the soil was prepared for that type. And
the fact that a man of his kind founded the monarchy in Israel,
brought his type into prominence, and in many ways we see the
future unfold itself in harmony with it.

The Yahweh who was worshipped on Zion throughout the
monarchical period could rightly be said to be David's God. The
aggrandising cult of Yahweh's firmly established personality
under the monarchy was bound to emphasise and intensify the
characteristics peculiar to the Yahweh served by David. However
much foreign cults gathered round him, David's God was still
reverenced as the Lord of Zion, essentially different from Baal.

The immediate sanctification of nature through the cult was
not therefore destroyed. The history of the sacrifice shows us
that it could still flourish and put forth new shoots. But gradually
as Jerusalem became a great city whose inhabitants were removed
from nature, the cult became more and more detached from the
life of nature, and this meant a steady growth of the spirit of
David. It was combined with a marked development of the holiness
of the cult as something quite independent, by which holiness became withdrawn from daily life, and that again meant the unfolding of ideas which lay fully formed in David's mind. And the
development which we have noticed in the conception of God, the
sharp line drawn between God and man, which excluded intermediate forms and removed the dead from the divine world,
which raised Yahweh above the world of man, and which made
the prophet a messenger instead of a man of God, all this merely
meant the consistent application of the conception of the divine
represented by David. It created an Israelitish type which spread
more and more. It was through it that the transformation occurred
of the fundamental psychic values, with which we have met in all

domains. Indeed, we may say that David's view of life points directly towards the form of spiritual life which is designated late Judaism.

In the domain of the cultus this current is felt, not only in the praise-giving cult associated with the royal temple. If we compare the cult ecstasy of the priests of Baal on Mount Carmel with Elijah's passionate but sober appeal to Yahweh who is now to show himself as the God of the fathers, of Abraham, Isaac, and Jacob (1 Kings 18,36 f.), we have a picture of the difference between the purely Canaanite and the Israelite-Canaanite conception of the cultus and the relation between God and man. The spontaneous abandonment, the cult ecstasy, was suppressed in favour of the exaltation of the mighty God, who alone was all-powerful.

By creating the monarchy, David, the greatest figure in the history of Israel, also became a founder and renewer in the domain of the cultus, though he had passed entirely beyond the spontaneity of the culture, and his view of the divine rather contained the germs of the drying up of the cult than of its growth. When the central feature of the cult was to praise Yahweh and win his favour, then there was no great step to declaring everything superfluous which went beyond praise and invocation. In reality the prophets in their fight for what was truly Israelitish were driven in that direction. During this fight Yahweh on Zion tended more and more to become the victorious ruler.

THE PROPHETS' FIGHT FOR YAHWEH

WHILE the monarchy established a new centre for the cult of Yahweh on Zion, the cult at the various sanctuaries of the country was continued. David did not fight the Canaanite cult, but his God differed widely from the Canaanite Baal. Elijah who fought against Baal in the 9th century does not seem to have had anything to do with Zion, at any rate it does not appear so from the narratives. In these we may, however, trace a relationship between the powerful God of the fathers for whom he fought and the Yahweh for whom David secured a seat on Zion.

From the middle of the 8th century we may again follow the fight through the speeches that have come down to us from a number of prophets. Of course the campaign had not ceased in the meanwhile. There is a connection between the dislike of the earlier and the later prophets for the purely Canaanite cult, and their fight for the God of their fathers must be due to the fact that down through history there were still sections of the populace who retained more of the Israelite tradition than others. But a difference arises between the two generations of prophets on account of the later prophets' revolt against social life as it developed in the cities, and their new conception of the whole cult activity.

The cult at the sanctuaries, "the high places", is subject to constant attack from a number of prophets. The fullest picture of the state of affairs, though somewhat one-sided in character, we obtain from Hosea, who flourished in the middle of the 8th century. He gives us a clear view of his own conception of Yahweh and the proper worship of Yahweh.

Hosea takes us to the very heart of the question as to Yahweh's relation to the agricultural life of Canaan, that which formed so great a part of the nature of Baal. We see, then, that Yahweh has entirely taken possession of Canaan. Outside it the Israelites cannot offer sacrifice to Yahweh, and they cannot eat anything but unclean food (Hos. 9,3 f.). The country is called the land of Yahweh (9,3), and possibly Yahweh's house (9,15). From numerous utterances it appears that the Israelites whom Hosea was addressing worshipped Yahweh (4,15; 5,6; 8,13; 9,4 f.), on the other hand they are violently blamed for having forgotten Yahweh and worshipping Baalim. This shows that conditions were just as complicated as in the time of Elijah. Yahweh has more or less become a Baal, and other Baalim are worshipped in company with him. Sometimes Hosea speaks as if the Israelites worshipped Baalim alone, their worship of Yahweh being a delusion.

Hosea is not in doubt that his Yahweh is the true God of Israel, the other gods worshipped have obtained a place that does not belong to them. Since the land is Yahweh's land, its growth and life belong to him; the Baalim, the old gods of the country are usurpers. He represents it thus: Yahweh — and by this is always meant Yahweh as the prophet conceives him — is the true husband of Israel, but the people has become unfaithful to its consort and has kept lovers.

The representation of the relation to Yahweh as a marriage seemed natural to the Israelites. The Canaanite conception of the God as a Baal meant that he held a similar relation to them whose Baal he was, as a husband to his wife, and since the fertility rites seemed to Hosea and his circle to be fornication and adultery, it resulted that the relation between the Baal and the people was a distorted marriage, a life in unbridled adultery, whereas Yahweh was the true husband. Expressions denoting adultery are therefore continually used about the non-Israelitish cultus (Ex. 34,15 f.; Lev. 17,7; 20,5; Jer. 2,20; Ez. 16,15 et al.). [1]

To Hosea the two relations seem so much alike that he does not use one as a metaphor for the other. Yahweh is the husband who supports his unfaithful wife, the Baalim are lovers; and the impression is strengthened by the fact that the prophet realises the relation in his own life by his marriage to an unfaithful wife, just as Isaiah went naked and barefoot for three years and Jeremiah wore a rope and a yoke on his neck to actualise what filled their souls. It is true that it is not possible for us to distinguish what the prophet experienced as reality observable by others and what he experienced in imagination, for both were equally real to him. Yahweh says in Hosea that His wife, the mother of the Israelites, i. e. Israel, went after her lovers, thinking that they gave her bread, water, wool, flax, oil, corn, and wine; and she made sacrifices to the Baalim. They appeared at the feasts to Baal decked with rings and chains, both at the New Moon, the Sabbath, and other feasts (2,4 ff.). They turned to foreign gods and practised their cult (3,1), offered sacrifices to Baalim and graven images (11,2). Notably Samaria's calf is mentioned, an image of Baal of the usual type, made of gold and silver (8,4-6). The people and priests of Samaria are filled with fear of Beth-Awen's calf. [1] The calf is said to be the cause of their grief and joy (10,5), and the obscure text doubtless refers to the feeling at the annual disappearance and reappearance of the God. But the places of worship upon which the curse falls are numerous.

In all threshing-places they seek the reward of a whore, says the prophet (9,1); by which he again expresses that the produce of the field is regarded as something that belongs to the domain of the Baal, and the more produce, the more worship. "The richer the fruit, the more altars; the more his land prospered, the finer massebahs they made" (10,1). The sacrifices are made on the tops of the mountains and in the high places, under oaks, poplars, and terebinths (4,13), in Gilead, Gilgal, Beth-Awen (4,15; 12,12). The Israelites worship idols made by craftsmen, sacrifice to bulls and reverently kiss calves (12,12; 13,2). Amid all this we hear that they sacrifice oxen and sheep to Yahweh (5,6), but the sacrifices offered to him do not please him (8,13).

The most characteristic feature of this cult is the sexual rites, which make the whole thing seem an indecent frenzy to the prophet, and the priests, the advisers of the people, are chiefly responsible for this (chap. 4). It has made the soul of the Israelites a "lewd spirit" (5,4), which together with the wine drunk at the feasts steals people's hearts (4,11). All this is something foreign. The Israelites have begotten strange sons (5,7), and strangers devour their strength (7,9). Such strangers have they become that when the many commandments of the torah are written down, they are regarded as a strange thing (8,12).

This means that the cult militates against Israelite custom, against the torah of Israel's God and the understanding of his will (4,4 ff.), the whole thing is complete apostasy from Yahweh (4,10), a breach of his covenant and his torah (8,1). This corresponds to the breach of good custom which the prophet finds in social life. There is a want of love and truth, people swear falsely, murder, steal, and commit adultery (4,1 ff.; 10,4), ever since the days of Gibeah they have sinned, it says (10,9), with an allusion to events unknown to us. In short, there is a want of mishpāṭ, which is necessary for the existence of a normal community (5,11), and to the prophet there is a close connection between the cult and the social defects, both mean unfaithfulness to the ancestral God.

When the prophet regards the life and cult of his people in this light, it is impossible for him to find anything but disaster and evil therein. And in fact, wherever he turns he finds that the blessing is failing. The land is in distress (4,3), and Israel is as a worthless tool among the peoples (8,8). And yet it is but a slight beginning. The people's cult is a poison which is bound to consume it and bring about its fall (5,5).

The people accepts corn, wine, and fruit as if it were all the outcome of its cult, but experience will teach it that this is a delusion. "The threshing-place and the wine-press shall not provide for them, and the new wine shall fail them" (9,2). Vines and figs, which the unfaithful wife thought she owed to her lovers, shall be destroyed by Yahweh and be transformed into a deserted thicket for wild animals (2,14). The entire foolishness of the cult becomes evident when they cannot eat till they are satisfied. When they "commit fornication" they shall not be able to multiply (4,10); the very things they wanted to attain by the cult, blessedness and fertility, are taken from them. Thus Ephraim loses her honour and decays; the women cease to give birth; and if any children grow up, they are taken away (9,11 f.).

In the first place the desecrated altars are to be pulled down (12,12). The unlawful gods shall be carried away as spoil, the high places shall be destroyed, and the altars be overgrown with thorns and thistles, a terror which shall make people pray that the mountains may hide them (10,6-8). Thus the feasts in which the people rejoiced cease of their own accord (2,13). Ephraim and Judah are consumed from within as by vermin and rottenness. It is Yahweh himself who calls down misery upon them, he attacks the vicious people as a lion his prey; there is no consolation in turning to strangers (5,11 f.). We are also told that Yahweh will withdraw from them till they seek his face again (5,15).

This is an indication that there is still hope. The root of the evil, the strange Canaanite cult and its gods, will be removed of itself through the punishment; but the source of the blessing, the true Yahweh, the people must seek by reassuming the true Israelitish attitude. Who then is Yahweh, and what is demanded of the Israelites?

All the prophet's speeches are pervaded by the idea that Israel is the same people as that which once left Egypt, only she has adopted foreign customs. And Yahweh is the same as he who brought Israel up from Egypt, but the people has gone astray after foreign gods or has sought Yahweh as a foreign god. What must be done is that Israel must abandon foreign customs and return to her early God. This is all the easier because the old God is in reality still near. It is he who has been in the background and bestowed on the people what it thought it had received from another Yahweh or from the Baalim; it is he whom the prophet preaches, and in whose name he speaks.

The starting-point, then, is the Yahweh who was commemorated at the Paschal feast. "I am Yahweh, thy God, from the land of Egypt, I will again let thee dwell in tents as in the festal days" (12,10). This means that the people is to start all over again and become as at the beginning of its history. For then the relation was as it ought to be. "When Israel was a child, then I loved him, and called my son out of Egypt" (11,1), but it was not long before the apostasy began. "I found Israel as grapes in the wilderness, I saw your fathers as the first-fruits of a fig-tree with its first produce; they came to Baal-peor and dedicated themselves unto infamy" (9,10).

The identity with Yahweh of the Paschal feast is again established: I am Yahweh, thy God, from the land of Egypt, and thou knowest no God but me, nor any other saviour besides me. I did know thee in the wilderness, in the land of drought. When they grazed, they were filled; when they were filled, their hearts became arrogant; therefore have they forgotten me (13,4-6). Here we see Hosea's view of history. Israel belongs to the lowly life of the desert, there Yahweh took care of her; but the rich life of Canaan made her forget the God who saved her in her humble days, and yet she is by her nature indissolubly bound to him.

In spite of all apostasy Yahweh continued to be Israel's God. "I strengthened [1] their arms, and yet do they plot mischief against me" (7,15). It was Yahweh who was the true husband, who gave the people the riches of Canaan. But for a time he will take it all away from the wife and let her return to the wilderness once more (2,16). Later their relations shall again be as in the days of her youth when she came up out of Egypt, and she shall call Yahweh her husband, while the Baalim shall disappear from her (2,17 ff.). Then Yahweh will make a covenant for them with nature, with the wild animals, the birds, and the creeping things. War shall be abolished, they shall dwell in security. Righteousness, truth, and love shall make the covenant with Yahweh a lasting one (2,20 ff.).

Thus Yahweh is still with Israel. She shall seek him and return to him (6,1; 10,12; 12,7; 14,2), giving up the foreign customs which are sinful (14,2). "Return to thy God, be constant in love *(hesedh)* and righteousness *(mishpāṭ)* and wait always for thy God" (12,7). Love and righteousness are the prerequisite for the maintenance of a normal community. The idea is that when the Israelite obeys these commands so that the community is kept in order, he must confidently wait for Yahweh to do the rest.

By *mishpāṭ* is understood what is fitting for an Israelite community. That there was a dispute as to what this was, we know, and Hosea shows us that a number of written laws must have been regarded as un-Israelitish, though in the prophet's opinion they were the very laws that should be observed (8,12); *ḥesedh* is the feeling of fellowship between the Israelites themselves and between them and their God. The maintenance of the Israelitish community by right Israelite conduct and fellowship is the decisive point. What Hosea meant by this in detail does not appear from his work. That the breaking of covenants, blood-guilt, and murder must be avoided in the Israelite as in any other community is a matter of course (6,7.8.9). To this must be added what Hosea calls whoredom *(zᵉnūth)*, i. e. the Canaanite sexual rites of the cult (6,10); and when Israel built palaces in the cities and Judah built fortresses, it was a sign that they had forgotten their creator (8,14). Right conduct meant a knowledge of God, because it was subordination to Yahweh's will, and everything turned on that. Nothing can affect the covenant in a similar way; this puts the cult in the second place. Hence the well-known words uttered by Hosea: I desire love and not sacrifice, and the knowledge of God more than burnt offerings (6,6); those who seek Yahweh with their herds shall not find Him (5,6).

It would seem probable that Hosea, as a consequence of his way of thinking, must wish for a return to the Nomadic existence in the wilderness as the proper way of living for the people. He did not, however, draw this conclusion. Hosea has the Canaanite view of the desert. It is the "land of drought"; to return to it would be a punishment, just like a return to Egypt or an expulsion to the unclean land of Ashur (8,13; 9,3.6). Yahweh and Canaan are inseparably bound up together, and Hosea does not go so far as the Rechabites who wanted to continue the Nomadic life in Canaan; but he shows a somewhat similar tendency.

When the Baalim are taken from the Israelites, and they turn again to the God of their fathers, Yahweh will give them fertility throughout the country. He will then make a covenant for them with the beasts of the field, the birds, and the creeping things and will break the bow and the sword so that warfare ceases, and they can live in safety (2,20). Then he will take charge of the heavens, and the heavens will take charge of the earth, i. e. by giving it rain, and the plants will grow (2,23). This is the true marriage covenant between Yahweh and Israel (2,21 f.), of course contrasted with that which the sexual rites created with Baal. It should be noted that the covenant with nature is made with hostile creatures, and therefore has a purely negative character. Animals which consume the corn shall no longer be allowed to do damage to Israel, and enemies who rob her shall be paralysed. Growth follows from Yahweh's command to the sky to give its goodly rain. In this there is not the least psychic relation to nature. The Israelites derive benefit from it, they take its produce, but they have no covenant with its life. Yahweh is outside and above nature, and Israel shall receive the gifts of nature from his hand.

We are here confronted with a main point of the prophet's conception of Yahweh. He has liberated the people from Egypt, he is a living power in its history, and the guardian of its psychic character. He has made Canaan his land without changing his own nature by entering into a covenant with its nature. The duty of the people is to preserve the covenant with him by observing Israelitish *mishpāṭ*, otherwise receiving everything from him. Then he will give it the produce of the land and free it from its enemies. Yahweh of the wilderness has appropriated the country and preserved himself. Israel must do the same.

Of course there must be some uncertainty as to what should be recognised as Israelitish custom, if the Israelites do not, like the Rechabites, reject everything that is Canaanite. It could, therefore, become a matter of controversy, and the various communities acquired what was Canaanite in different measure, as is, indeed, shown by the extant laws. Unfortunately we do not know the written laws which Hosea mentions, and which were rejected by people as foreign. Hosea's mention of them shows us that laws were written to express the view of certain circles as to what was the proper custom, without having any external authoritative character. That even those laws which the prophet regarded as Israelite bore the impress of the people's life in Canaan through centuries is a matter of course, although the prophet could not know anything about it. He thought that the people, merely by discontinuing some bad habits, might again become what they were in the wilderness period and "return" to Yahweh.

It appears from various allusions that it is the life of the humbler class that the prophet regards as the truly Israelitish custom. Prosperity has estranged the people from its God (13,4-6). When it forgot its creator, it built palaces (8,14), and its participation in the politics of the great through the building of fortresses makes it walk in its own ways, and prevents it from receiving peace from Yahweh. By Yahweh, not by the sword, shall Judah be saved (1,7).

Hosea stands between those who had become completely Canaanite and the Rechabites who entirely rejected Canaanite customs. He shows us that the reaction against the transformation of the people had constantly had its stronghold in certain circles, for it cannot have arisen suddenly as the casual idea of an individual. As a matter of fact, Hosea feels that he is a link in a chain of prophets who have worked to preserve the people by their warning speeches, ever since the people was brought out of Egypt by a prophet (6,5; 12,11.14). It is he and the other prophets who have preserved true Israelitish custom. These circles were remote from the large cities and their cultural life; they were in contact with the small farmers and the shepherds.

It is not difficult to see that the Yahweh whom Hosea preaches is closely related to David's God. Man's relation to Yahweh is the same in both cases as well as the relation to nature. The living relation to nature is outside the horizon of both, but man derives benefit from nature. Therefore sacrifice is not a sanctification of the growth of the soil, but merely a tribute to Yahweh, and when Hosea says frankly that Yahweh does not care for sacrifice, he merely draws the conclusion from presuppositions already present in David's faith. The relation to Yahweh is purely personal and is maintained by the Israelites actualising the type of man that bears the impress of Yahweh himself, the Israelite type.

This affinity between such different types as the prophet Hosea and David points to something of a common Israelite character, which is not unaffected by Canaanite influence, but which must be rooted in the earliest history of the people. And there can be no doubt that Hosea regarded David's God as the Yahweh for whom he was fighting.

Hosea utters many words about the kings of Israel. The house of Jehu shall decay, consumed by its blood-guilt (1,4). Ephraim has constantly taken kings and chiefs in whom Yahweh had no part (8,4) ; therefore they have all failed and shall render no aid in the time of disaster (7,7; 13,10); the kings shall entirely disappear (8,10; 10,15). On the whole, Hosea speaks mostly to and about Ephraim; however, Yahweh has also a "controversy with Judah" (12,3), who so eagerly fortified her cities (8,14), but there is a difference in tone. Judah shall not incur the same guilt as Ephraim (4,15), she shall seek to be saved by Yahweh, and not by bow and by sword, by battle, by horses and horsemen (1,7). Judah's special position is due to the fact that she has the kingship of David, but the Israelites must give up the Baalim and seek Yahweh their God and David their king (3,5 ,cf. 2,2). The genuineness of these utterances has been doubted, and it is impossible to say whether this or that word has been uttered by Hosea himself. But the view of David and Yahweh on Zion which is implied in them, is the very view which might be expected from the prophet.

Hosea gives us a clear picture of the God in whose cause he is fighting, for he constantly describes the nature of the Baalim as a contrast to him. Other prophets show us a similar picture but with other significances, and thus testify to the strength of the movement represented by Hosea.

In some of the other prophets it is clearly seen that they look upon Zion as the dwelling-place of the true Yahweh. Hosea's contemporary, *Amos,* who was a keeper of flocks and tended sycamores near the Dead Sea, pronounced stern judgment on the sanctuaries in Ephraim and Judah; but he does not speak against the temple of Jerusalem ,which was the nearest within his range of vision, and he hears Yahweh roar from Zion (Am. 1,2).

Actually his God is, indeed, the same as the mighty ruler who sat enthroned in the temple of Jerusalem. When Yahweh passes over the earth, it trembles and shakes, the hills billow like melted wax, expressions reminiscent of the Song of Deborah (Judg. 5,4 f., cf. Mic. 1,4). But we are also told that the pastures wither, and the forests of Carmel dry up when he appears (1,2; 9,5). He is the creator of nature, and she is his obedient servant. He is the creator of the stars, of day and night, and he pours rain upon the face of the earth (5,8). He is the mighty judge of the peoples, and he shall smite Israel's neighbours. But he does not do so simply because they are the enemies of Israel. Here we meet with a new idea in the conception of Yahweh, but it is implied in the history which we know already.

Yahweh's judgments are those of a God of a pronounced Israelite type. The ruling God on Zion is the same as the old God of the people, the guardian of Israelite *ṣedhākā* and *mishpāṭ*. As in Hosea, so also in Amos, we hear complaints that the people have quite abandoned Israelite custom. Social conditions especially are brought into prominence. One class has usurped all the power and all wealth. They live in palaces and houses of hewn stone in un-Israelitish luxury, satisfied and secure, especially in the two great cities Jerusalem and Samaria (5,11; 6,1,4 ff. 8). This position they have gained for themselves by oppressing other Israelites, poor people who are actually the righteous that can claim to be protected. These they sell, cheating them in trade and turning aside their right, passing judgment according to bribes. The *mishpāṭ* which as Israelites they ought to love and practise they have thus changed into a poison, and they have thrown justice to the ground (2,6; 4,1; 5,7.11 f. 15; 6,12; 8,4 ff.). All this shows a contempt for Yahweh's *tōrā* and his laws, and accords with the fact that they have allowed themselves to be led astray by foreign gods, by "lies", and have adopted their foreign cult (2,4. 6.8); which cult at Bethel, Gilgal, Beersheba, Samaria, and Dan is all sin (4,4 f.; 5,5; 8,14).

Altogether Yahweh is displeased with their feasts and sacrifices. He hates and despises their pilgrimages and cult festivals, he will not look upon their offerings, nor will he hear their music and singing. "But righteousness *(mishpāṭ)* shall pour forth as water, and righteousness *(ṣedhākā)* as an ever-flowing stream" (5,24). To possess the right character is what is most important, the cult consists merely in giving praise, and Yahweh does not care for it in the usual forms. He points to the wilderness period, the period in which the people had not yet become changed, and says that at that time they offered him no sacrifices (5,25).

Amos draws the same conclusion from these conditions as Hosea. Yahweh will send a fire upon Judah, the palaces of Jerusalem shall fall, and even the strongest shall not be able to save Ephraim (2,5.14 ff.). The altars and palaces of Bethel shall be overthrown (3,14 f.; 9,1), their riches shall fail (5,11). The people shall perish with its sanctuaries (3,2; 5,1-3.11.16 f.; 6,9 ff.; 7,1 ff.; 8,9 ff.). The people who expect that a day of Yahweh will come with victory, will be deeply disappointed. Yahweh shall come with gloom and darkness, not with light, and they shall flee from disaster to disaster (5,18-20).

The idea of a day of Yahweh takes us to fixed ideas of the relation between Yahweh and Israel, and of the intervention of Yahweh in the fate of the people. Isaiah, too, mentions that a day of Yahweh will come against all who exalt themselves (Isa. 2, 12 ff.), Zephaniah expects the day of Yahweh to come very soon, when all Israelite apostates shall be punished (Zeph. 1,7 ff.). On the other hand, Zephaniah also expects Yahweh to gather together the peoples one day, to smite the foes of Israel, and rule as king in their midst (3,8.15), just as Obadiah preaches that the day of Yahweh is near for all the peoples, and after it he shall be king of Israel (Ob. 15.21). This line of thought can be followed through a number of prophetic utterances down through the ages (Isa. 27; 33-35; 52; Zech. 14 et al.). It recalls so vividly the form of praise with which Yahweh was extolled in the cult of the royal temple that there must be a connection. What is celebrated as a reality on Yahweh's festal day in the temple is, according to the teaching of the prophets, something which shall be revealed at some future day. It seems natural to suppose, then, that an anticipation of the future has detached itself from the annual cult, a hope that what is taught every year through the praise given in the temple of Jerusalem will one day become history. [1]

Thus the contemporaries of Amos conformed to a tradition which was probably rooted in the royal cult of Jerusalem. But

Amos makes the day a day of disaster, because he sees it in the light of Yahweh's relation to the people as a whole. Yahweh will be kind to his people. He has brought them up out of Egypt, led them through the wilderness for 40 years and conquered the country for them; and since then He has constantly let prophets and Nazirites arise out of their midst (2,9-11). Israel was the only people Yahweh knew (3,2).

But the Israel known to Yahweh was a people of a certain character, of a special nature, which Yahweh still demands of his people but which he does not find any longer among the Israelites. Therefore, if the people would have life from its God, it must seek Him, that is to say, live according to his commands. "Seek me and live"! (5,4.6.14). If they will love righteousness, Yahweh will perhaps have mercy on the remnant of Joseph, on what is still left of ancient glory. Yahweh has tried to lead them back into the right way by punishing them with drought, famine, and the plague in such a way that they could not but notice it. One city was given rain, another was not (4,6-11).

It will be seen how the old conception of the sinner being the prey of the curse has acquired a special meaning by the strong accentuation of Yahweh's personality and its might. Nature is an instrument in his hand, by which he can reveal his arbitrary will for the chastening of the people. Hence to punish them he can suddenly let the sun set in the middle of the day and envelop all the world in darkness (8,9). This self-glorification of Yahweh is of importance for his whole relation to Israel.

When the Israelites try to create greatness for themselves by their display of power, and when they build themselves magnificent palaces, it is an expression of arrogance which offends their God (6,8). If they do not alter this and everything else that conflicts with Israelitish custom, they are not true Israelites and are therefore no nearer to Yahweh than other peoples such as the Kushites, Philistines, or Aramæans (9,7), and Amos mentions that greater peoples than his have perished (6,2).

Two lines of thought lead Amos to this radical conclusion. Yahweh on Zion is glorified as the ruler of all the world; he rules not only over Israel but over the other peoples as well. Amos has taken this idea seriously, regarding Yahweh as the God who also controlled the fate of the neighbouring peoples. He had brought the Philistines from Kaphtor and the Aramæans from Kir. Parallel with this runs the line of thought represented by the prophets, that Israel is no longer Israel; only those who observe Israelitish customs, in the first place of course the prophets (2,11), are Israelites. Hence they alone belong to the God of Israel. Thus the people whose God Yahweh is becomes in a way an ideal quantity not characterised by birth, but by nature and manners. Yahweh is in some degree independent of his own people, and on the other hand, he has a certain connection with other peoples.

Their dislike of the transformation of the people in conjunction with the excessive aggrandisement of Yahweh carried the prophets to this point. But the judgment which fear and indignation led Amos and those equally-minded to pass on their countrymen must not make us forget that Yahweh was still the God on Zion, an altogether Israelite God, who exacted the observance of Israelite customs; and to magnify Him was in the strictest sense a glorification of the Israelite nature. But can an Israelite ideal survive without Israelites? Or expressed more in accordance with the spirit of the early Israelites: When the God of Israel is mightier than everything else, how, then, is it possible that his people, those who embody his nature, can entirely disappear? The sting of this question was felt for centuries in the history of Israel.

How strongly Amos felt it we do not know, but it is hardly conceivable that he reckoned with the extinction of Israel as the last stage. Most probably he expected Yahweh to create a new kingdom on Zion by raising up "the falling tabernacle of David" (9,11), but in the speeches that have come down to us, this is not very apparent, because they are entirely concerned with contemporary conditions and the dangers that lurk behind them. And we have absolutely no guarantee that the general hopes for the future expressed at the end of the book of Amos have been formulated by him.

Thus in the two prophets known to us from the middle of the eighth century we find a peculiar combination of an aggrandisement of Yahweh based on David's kingship with the simple, plain mode of living which separated the earliest Israelite communities from the city and peasant community of the Canaanite culture. From this combination there arose a definite Israelitish type, represented by the two above-mentioned prophets, and its importance appears from the fact that we find it again and again in other prophets who had their activities in Judah as long as it still existed as a kingdom. In these prophets we find exactly the same conception of Israel and Yahweh as we found in Hosea and Amos.

Isaiah, whose speeches may be assigned to the period from about 736 to about 700, was a native of Jerusalem. This determined his outlook. He was closely associated with the temple. He knew thoroughly its festal assemblies (1,11 ff.), and it was in the temple that he received the consecration for the special activity that characterised him as a prophet. He took for granted that Yahweh belonged to the temple of Zion. Here he saw him at his consecration, sitting on a throne surrounded by seraphim, while his train filled the sanctuary (6,1), and the God and the prophet talked about the vocation of the latter. Yahweh is called "Yahweh of the hosts, who dwells on Mount Zion" (8,18, cf. 2,3) ; around Zion, therefore, a new world shall grow up (28,16). Here justice and righteousness had their home in the old days (1,21). The prophet is no doubt thinking of the time of David. For Ariel, a name for the cult-place Jerusalem, is to him, in accordance with history, the city where David pitched his camp (29,1). It is the God of David he is serving.

Although Isaiah belongs to the great city, he takes the same view of its social life as the shepherd Amos. He is quite outside the ruling circles, and has only hostile denunciatory words for them. Like Amos he accuses them of oppressing the humbler class and filling their houses with stolen goods; therefore Yahweh is at war with them and takes action against them (3,13 f.). They take bribes and distort the law and enrich themselves at the expense of those whom they ought to protect, the poor, the widows, and the fatherless (1,23; 5,23; 10,2).

The prophet is talking to the class of influential men who grew up in the shelter of the kingdom. They do not respect the old rights of the families, but appropriate their land and thus make for themselves large landed estates, while the others become destitute of property (5,8). This unscrupulousness as regards ancient Israelite tradition marks their entire way of living. They build themselves magnificent houses (9,9), they accumulate hoards of gold and silver, and fill the land with foreign gods and foreign customs (2,6-8). They live in luxury, holding splendid banquets, at which they revel in wine and listen to music (5,11 f. 22; 28,1.3), a description quite similar to that given by Amos of the social life in the towns of his time (Am. 6,3-6). Like Amos (4,1) Isaiah is shocked at the ladies living in lighthearted security, walking the streets of Jerusalem with mincing steps and wanton eyes (3,16. 18 ff.; 32,9).

All this is non-Israelitish; and thus a violation of righteousness and justice, a result of holding Yahweh's *tōrā* in contempt (5,24). Just as Hosea speaks of good law codes which are rejected by the Israelites, so Isaiah directs his lament against people who make wicked laws and set down in writing their grievousness (10,1). He also speaks of those whose fear of Yahweh consists in "precepts taught them by men" (29,13). This shows how deliberately the struggle was waged in the 8th century. The various circles had each their own set of written laws about which they fought.

Isaiah has made clear his view of the relation between Israel and Yahweh in the parable of the vineyard. Yahweh planted a vineyard, cleared away the stones, and formed it in every way, and after all it bore wild grapes (5,1-7). This means that Israel has become estranged from her God, that she has abandoned his *ṣedhākā* and *mishpāṭ*. The Israelites were sons of Yahweh, fostered by him, and then they forgot him and deserted him, a thing not even done by domestic animals (1,2-4). The expressions we know from Hosea also recur here. Jerusalem has become a harlot, and yet she used to be so faithful (1,21).

We see that Isaiah takes quite the same view of Israel's relation to Yahweh as the two somewhat earlier prophets. Israel has changed her nature and thus failed her God. We may take for granted that Isaiah also thinks that the true Israelite nature is that of the people in the wilderness period, but it does not appear in his speeches: his interests and horizon are bounded by Jerusalem. It is Jerusalem of the early days which he holds up to his contemporaries. In the time of David the Israelite ideal was realised; the assumption is no doubt that this period was in harmony with the original history of the people.

Isaiah also takes the same view of the temple cult as his predecessors. Yahweh abhors it and will have none of the festal assemblies and sacrifices; he will not hear the prayers they offer at their gatherings because their hands are full of blood. If they do not conform to Israelitish custom, their cult is useless and abhorred by Yahweh. Isaiah does not say that offerings are always evil, and it does not occur to him to doubt that Yahweh dwells in the temple. But his entire conception of Yahweh has, as with the other prophets, cut the ground from under the cult. The maintenance of the Israelite nature is the chief demand, without its fulfilment all other magnification of Yahweh is worthless. But if this demand was fulfilled, the prophet would not probably think of any deviation from the traditional way of glorifying Yahweh.

More and more forcibly Isaiah maintains that the conduct of the Israelites is a manifestation of arrogance. They set themselves against Yahweh's *tōrā* and try to secure happiness in their own way. Therefore their actions are an insult to Yahweh's honour, and Yahweh's amour propre demands that they should be punished. Isaiah's discourses announce the punishments awaiting the people. For the most part they are concerned with the Assyrians, whom Yahweh calls in to chasten the people; and the prophet's speeches show that the procedure of an Assyrian army was not unknown to him (5,26 ff.; 7,18 ff.; 8,5 ff.; 10,28 ff.). But the Egyptians, too, and the neighbouring peoples are mentioned as the castigators. In some speeches we hear that disaster has already come, the land is a wilderness and foreigners consume its substance (1,7). It is all Yahweh's work. He strikes so as to humble all that exalt themselves and are arrogant, in order that his honour may be

supreme; it is his assertion of his honour, his *kin'ā*, that causes it
(1,31; 2,9 ff.; 5,15 ff.; 9,8 f.; 10,33).

Isaiah has just as strong expressions as Amos about the
complete destruction of the people. Jerusalem and Judah shall
fall, the city being left a widow (3,8.25). This comes most into
prominence in the words by which Isaiah is consecrated to his
mission. Quite ruthlessly Yahweh says that the teaching of the
prophet shall have the effect of rendering the heart of the people
dull so that it neither hears, nor sees, nor understands, that
Yahweh may not be able to heal it. And when the prophet asks
for how long, the answer is: Until the cities be wasted without
inhabitants, and the houses without men, and the land made
desolate (6,11, cf. 29,9 f.).

The violent threats are, however, accompanied by a steady
conviction that something must survive, since it is connected with
Yahweh. Zion was the seat of Yahweh, how could it possibly
perish? The last words of the consecration say that a stump shall
be left which shall be a holy seed (6,13). And as a matter of fact,
despite the hopeless words of the consecration, we see that Isaiah
tries to persuade people to "learn to do good" and apply themselves to *mishpāṭ* (1,17). Yahweh will clean out the dross, crush
the sinners who have turned away from his *mishpāṭ*; then
Jerusalem shall have judges and leaders as in the old days; it
shall be called the city of righteousness, and Zion shall be saved
by *ṣedhāḳā* and *mishpāṭ*, only those who return to Yahweh being
able to survive (1,25-28).

No doubt the relation between the two lines of thought has
been subject to some variation, changing with the moods of the
prophet in the varying situations. That Ephraim was to perish was
certain (8,4; 9,7 ff.; 17,1 ff.; 28,1 ff.), and the prediction was
confirmed before the prophet had been active for very many years.
But Isaiah's interest was in the Yahweh of Zion. When the leaders
of the people wanted to increase their power by an alliance with
Egypt, this was an insult to Yahweh which would lead to dis-
honour (30,1 ff.; 31,1 ff.), and the prophet can then say that
Yahweh is fighting against Mount Zion as a lion falls on its prey
(31,4). But when enemies turn towards Zion, the other idea comes

up, and the prophet says: Yahweh has founded Zion and the miserable in his people trust in it (14,32). This view was the strongest, because it was connected with the prophet's most elementary conception of Yahweh. In two historical situations Isaiah showed that his belief in Zion was unshakeable.

When the kings of Ephraim and Damascus were gathering forces against Ahaz in Judah (734) and the latter was full of fear, Isaiah met him and told him that the counsel of the two kings should not persist. Ahaz was to keep quiet. "If ye do not believe *(ta'**minū)*, ye shall not be upheld *(tĕ'āmēnū)*", says Isaiah (7,9), and he boldly offers any sign that shall confirm his words. But Ahaz declines, being unwilling to tempt Yahweh. Then the prophet is filled with indignation, and declares that a sign shall nevertheless be given, for "the young woman is with child, and she shall bear a son, and she shall call his name God-With-Us (Immanuel)". While the boy is young, the land [1] shall be wasted and disaster shall befall the house of the king and the people, the like of which they have not seen since Ephraim departed from the house of David. The Assyrians shall be summoned and shall waste the land, the precious vineyards shall become desolate, and thorns and thistles, the growths of the curse, shall spread over the cultivated hills. Immanuel and those who remain shall live with a cow and a sheep and eat of curds and honey (Isa. 7).

The long series of speeches associated with the meeting between the king and the prophet does not at once make things clear. To begin with, it expresses confidence, and it finishes with threats, and yet it all comes within Isaiah's sphere of ideas. Isaiah first declares that the two hostile kings can do nothing. For they are fighting against Yahweh; the Judæans have merely to believe in him, and he will see to their security and self-assertion. This is the prophet's point of departure, therefore he ventures to offer a sign. The reason why Ahaz rejects this offer is, according to his own words, that God is so mighty a ruler that man must beware of everything that implies a doubt as to his power. We hear no other utterance from Ahaz during the meeting. It shows that he has the same conception of Yahweh as the prophet, only he draws another conclusion from it. The difference is connected with the prophet's conviction that he has been sent by this mighty God, whose sign was to confirm his mission; and he understands the king's words as a token of indifference to his prophetic utterance, as indeed they are. Then his anger flares up. The king, who would not offend Yahweh, has offended the prophet; but in this way he has not only annoyed a man, he has also annoyed the prophet's God (7,13), Yahweh. Then the prophet opens up a new prospect of the future.

In this it is Assyria, not the two minor kings, that plays the main role, and she is to strike greater terror to the heart of Ahaz than that aroused by the two kings. Does this mean, then, that the prophet, offended at the king's refusal, suddenly changes his mind and threatens with destruction the royal city, the rescue of which he has just announced, with the sole difference that another people than those now threatening it is to bring about its fall?

It is clear that the king's insult to the prophet has evoked the threats, but this does not imply that the threatening prospect of the future was produced by the momentary wrath. And even while uttering his threats Isaiah does not say that Jerusalem is to perish; this would not accord with his belief in the God of Zion, or in Yahweh's power to assert himself. The belief in the survival of Zion appears again and again in Isaiah. The envoys of the Philistines were told that the miserable in Yahweh's people put their trust in the fact that he had founded Zion (14,32), and to the careless wine-drinking inhabitants of Jerusalem Yahweh's word is: On Zion I lay for a foundation a stone, a tried stone, a precious cornerstone. He that believeth doth not make haste. [1] And I will lay judgment to the line and righteousness to the plummet (28,16 f.).

Zion survives and forms the foundation of a new building, that which is built with *mishpāṭ* and *ṣ^edhāḳā* and which is the refuge of him "who believes". History also records that Isaiah announced the impregnability of Zion to Sennacherib's attack in 701 (Isa. 37,5 ff. = 2 Kings 19,5 ff.). As likely as this is true, so is it as unlikely that Isaiah should have prophesied the fall of Zion before the Assyrians, after having first announced that it should be saved from the two neighbouring kings.

And, indeed, Isaiah only said the same thing to Ahaz as he had said on other occasions. The land shall be wasted, but something shall survive, for the judgment is a cleansing which removes sins (1,25 ff.), a tree stump shall remain (6,13). The prophet expresses his belief that a remnant shall carry on the history of Israel by giving his son the name *Sheʾār yāshūbh* "a remnant returns". This very son was with him when he met Ahaz (7,3). The new sign given to Ahaz is in good accord with this, for the name God-With-Us says something similar to the elder son's name.

The image of the future is obscured by the birth of Immanuel being associated with the destruction of the land. But his existence points towards a future with the residue. Hosea wanted to send Israel into the wilderness to begin life over again. But Isaiah sees the country turned into a desert where Immanuel and the remnant are to live the life of the past, the simple existence of the shepherd, after the hated city life has perished. Vineyards and wealth are now replaced by poverty and plain living. Through this life Zion's survival in a regenerated state is secured.

The new Israel was to be the true Israel, and like the other prophets Isaiah found it in his own circle. Just as Shear-yashub was the prophet's own son, there is every reason to suppose that the young woman who is to give birth in the future to the important child is the prophet's own wife, and Immanuel, therefore, the prophet's son. These children with the significant names and the disciples whom the prophet gathered around him constituted a circle which he regarded as the nucleus of the new Israel, who "returned" to Yahweh and strove to attain his righteousness. It is said quite plainly: Roll up the testimony, seal the lore among my disciples. And I will wait for Yahweh who hideth his face from the house of Jacob, and I will wait for him. I and the children whom Yahweh hath given me shall be as signs and warnings in Israel from Yahweh of the hosts, who dwelleth in Mount Zion (8,16-18).

Isaiah demands that his countrymen shall observe Yahweh's custom and further humble themselves before Him, recognising that man can do nothing, only Yahweh can act. Therefore man shall keep in the background, remain passive and wait for Yahweh

(7,4; 8,17), give honour to Him and trust in his strength. This is the "faith" which Isaiah constantly demands (7,9; 8,13 f.; 28, 16; 30,15). It is no fresh demand he is making. "Faith" in its upholders and most of all in the God of the Covenant has always been necessary to the community. The reason why faith only is demanded, is because a gulf is fixed between God and man, so that man can give nothing else. And this is due to a conception of Yahweh which had prevailed in large circles of Israel since David's time.

The God who exacts this faith is a definite, well-known God, Yahweh of Zion. Isaiah is in no doubt that he is the same as the God speaking in him; therefore he exacts the most absolute respect for his prophetic words. According as people hear him or not Yahweh becomes a holy refuge or a stumbling-block which shall cause the prophet's countrymen to fall (8,13 f.).

Isaiah's interest centres entirely round Judah and Jerusalem, but he takes for granted in his speeches — as does Amos — that Yahweh is able to summon at his pleasure either Ashur or Egypt as taskmasters. Just as the clouds must send down rain or keep it back according to his command (5,6), thus the people must obey his will. Ashur is not meant to destroy Yahweh's people and take over the power herself. When she has served as the scourge of Yahweh's wrath, it is enough; if she goes beyond the mark, she will incur punishment for her arrogance (10,5 ff.; 14,24 ff.). In the same way Yahweh will paralyse Egypt, making her Gods tremble before him and the heart of her people melt in his presence (19,1 ff.). Yahweh will remain calmly in his dwelling, looking upon the war of the Ethiopians; when the time comes he will check them (18,1 ff.).

In Isaiah the different aspects of the prophecy are very conspicuous. Yahweh on Zion surpasses all in holiness; his honour fills the earth (6,3), therefore everything turns upon him. His people have deserted him and are to be punished, but a remnant worthy of him shall survive together with Zion. Other peoples are instruments in his hands, but as soon as they rise in arrogance against him, they shall be struck down. Isaiah has only some few references to the foreign cult (1,29), about which Hosea and

Amos are so much concerned, he is preoccupied with Jerusalem and the political situation. He does not hint, like Amos, that foreign peoples may be as near to Yahweh as Israel. He is sure that Yahweh's people cannot perish, and the idea of the remnant is met with several times in the writings that have come down to us under his name (4,2; 10,20-22; 11,11.16; 28,5). It is hardly likely that he whose thoughts were so largely determined by the influence of Zion, should fail to imagine a regeneration of the house of David, transformed according to the demands of David, as part of the future Israel. It is probable, therefore, that the descriptions of the ideal king of the future are derived from Isaiah or his most intimate circle (9,5 f.; 11,1-10). The transformation of nature which is associated with the rule of this ideal king is completely in the spirit of Isaiah.

Still it is very difficult to point out what is derived from Isaiah in the book named after him. Numerous utterances point to a later historical background, and many passages are prosaic additions to the original pronouncements. It may be taken for granted that many utterances are derived from his circle of disciples or from their disciples again. The constant augmentation of his book is a testimony to his great importance.

———

In the time after Isaiah, when the Assyrians ruled over western Asia, the prophetic tradition lived on; no essentially new features were added. *Micah,* a contemporary of Isaiah, from Moreshet, one of the small cities of the Mediterranean plain, reminds one both of Amos and Isaiah. He speaks of the guilt of Samaria, of its idols acquired for a "harlot's hire" (1,7), the contagion spreading to Jerusalem (1,9.12). This implies that Jerusalem, as Isaiah thinks, was originally faithful; but unrighteousness has usurped the power, evildoers prevail (2,1-5; 3,1-4.9-11), prophets lead the people astray (2,6-11; 3,5-8). Zion has been built with blood and violence, and the prophets declare that no evil can happen because Yahweh is present there (3,11). Micah, like Isaiah, knows that Yahweh is on Zion, he goes forth from its temple, and the earth trembles under his steps (1,2-4). The whole country shall suffer punishment. Provoked by those who think that the temple will shelter them from all evil, Micah does not shrink from saying that "Zion shall be ploughed up like a field, Jerusalem fall into ruins, and the temple hill become wooded heights" (3,12). What Micah then thought would happen, is difficult to say. He declares himself that it is a manifestation of his strength and rectitude that, unlike other prophets, he pronounces the doom of the people (3,8). But Zion was nevertheless the dwelling-place of Yahweh. Should Micah think otherwise than Isaiah who expected a re-generation of a true Israel around Zion?

In the middle of the threats there occurs an utterance which says that Israel and Judah shall be united, under the leadership of Yahweh and the king (2,12 f.). It is indeed natural for Micah to have thought so, but we have no certainty that this utterance is due to him. A number of utterances belonging to the book of Micah contain similar thoughts, but they are very different from Micah's style and can scarcely be referred to him, though they cannot be said to conflict with his ideas. Here Zion is the centre of the earth, where all men seek to be taught what is right, so that all war shall cease of itself (4,1 ff. = Isa. 2,2 ff.). Yahweh shall rule on Zion over his "remnant", the enemies that gather against Zion shall be crushed (4,6-10.11-13). A king of David's house shall collect his people [1] and with Zion as the centre and Yahweh as God establish a world-wide dominion, Israel shall defeat all her enemies and rule without instruments of war and without idols merely by Yahweh asserting his power (Mic. 5). These are the main ideas contained in the utterances, which reflect sentiments of the last days of the kingdom.

Similar ideas are put forward by other contemporary prophets. *Nahum* announces Yahweh's cruel revenge on the Assyrian op-pressors. *Zephaniah* preaches that judgment shall befall Jerusalem for all foreign things admitted during the Assyrian period both in the cult and in everyday life. The day of Yahweh shall come, all that is foreign shall be exterminated, judgment shall smite the nations, Jerusalem shall be chastised, but finally a kingdom shall be founded on Zion where Yahweh shall be king of the remnant of

Israel and even distant nations shall submit. In *Habakkuk* we hear the old complaints of violence and injustice, and it is announced that Yahweh will call in the Chaldæans to inflict punishment, but the righteous shall live by his truth (2,4).

The prophets continued to play the same part in popular life as long as the kingdom existed, and as late as its last days a prophet acted in the spirit of Amos and his successors. *Jeremiah* does not differ from his predecessors by new ideas; his prophecies are the same as theirs but refer to other situations. Like Hosea he is much preoccupied with the cult of the numerous sanctuaries, and like Isaiah he observes life in the capital and undertakes to interpret world-events to people and rulers. He has not the forceful personality of Isaiah, his nerves are sensitive, and none of the prophets has revealed more of his own sensations than he. His utterances are full of heart-rending anguish concerning the vocation of the prophet. He turns like a wounded animal upon those whom he regards as enemies, and flings Yahweh's curses at them. His style is forcible, more verbose than that of the earlier prophets. He cries in agitation: O land, land, land, listen to the words of Yahweh! (22,29). His utterances are full of indignation, but also of grief at the misery in store for his people. Some of his speeches are given in their typical rhetorical-poetical form, others are re-told in prose, and it may thus be difficult to say whether they render Jeremiah's thoughts.

Jeremiah was a native of Anathoth in Benjamin. According to the tradition he began to appear in 627 B.C. His home lay outside Judah but near Jerusalem. Like all the other prophets he regarded Zion as the dwelling-place of Yahweh. Its temple was Yahweh's true sanctuary, in it Jeremiah moved as in a home, and here he delivered some of his prophetic discourses. "A throne of glory, a high place from the beginning, is the place of our sanctuary" (17,12), he says about Zion, and in times of distress his words are: Is not Yahweh, then, in Zion? Hath it no king? (8,19, cf. 3,14; 14,19; 26,18; 31,6.12). Yahweh, Zion, and the king belonged together. Like everybody else Jeremiah lived by the tradition that was founded by David and established through the royal cult. It comprised all Israel; Ephraim, which had perished as a kingdom a hundred years earlier, was unreservedly included by Jeremiah in the Israel whose God is Yahweh on Zion. The same is demanded of it as of Judah, and one day it shall seek out Zion and Yahweh who is to be found there (31,6.12). In a prose discourse we are told that Judah behaves even worse than Ephraim (3,11).

Yahweh on Zion is the same as the God who was the leader throughout the history of Israel. Like Hosea, Jeremiah mentions that Yahweh betrothed himself to Israel in the wilderness. Then the people was consecrated to Yahweh and therefore protected against her enemies (2,2-3). Now the land of Israel is becoming a wilderness plundered by foreigners, and yet Israel, always in vain, turns to Egypt and Ashur (2,18.36). Their misery is due to their apostasy from Yahweh. Jeremiah characterises the situation by a parable known to us from Isaiah. The people had been planted as a noble vine but had become degenerate (2,21). Even with lye its filth cannot be washed away (2,22). By the apostasy Jeremiah means in the first place the sexual cult at the numerous sanctuaries in honour of the Baalim (2,23); like the earlier prophets he calls it harlots' service; it took place in every high place under the green trees (2,20). He constantly varies his accusation that the people behaves like a harlot who has failed the lover of her youth, or even like animals in heat (2,23 f. 32 f.; 3,1 ff.; 13,27). The misery already present shall be increased manifold by the fresh disasters that threaten from a savage and mighty people of the north (4,5-31).

In these earliest speeches, possibly delivered at Anathoth, Jeremiah shows that he takes the same view of Israel and Yahweh as the previous prophets. Since Israel came into the land she has abandoned her God. Her altars and asherahs under the green trees on the hills are a sin (17,1 f.). She calls trees and stones her father and mother, and yet these offer no help in her distress; Yahweh has constantly tried to open the people's eyes by his punishments, but in vain (2,27-30). Only one is the true Yahweh.

Characteristic of the strongly personal view of Yahweh is this utterance: According to the number of thy cities are thy gods, O Judah (2,28; 11,13).

The gist of Jeremiah's teaching is, then, that the people must return to their God, whose sons they should be; they must understand that he alone can save them, while the hills were "for lies", and the sacrifices to Baal, "the abomination" *(bōsheth)*, were in vain (3,22 ff.). The hope implied in this invitation is in a prose piece given the shape of a promise that a new Israel shall arise out of Ephraim and Judah on Zion under righteous kings; even the ancient sign of unity, the Ark, shall be entirely superfluous, Jerusalem shall be the throne of Yahweh, round which all the nations shall gather (3,14-18).

When Jeremiah came to Jerusalem and wandered about its streets and marketplaces, he noticed that conditions were here as in the other cities. People swore false oaths by Yahweh or swore by other gods, by a "non-god" (5,2.7). The city was full of violence (6,6 f.), of treachery and lewdness (9,1). Jeremiah describes it as a society in dissolution, where one man did not trust another; where fraud and lies prevailed; where all were against all (9,2-11); that is to say, exactly as it is recorded in the Psalms. We hear the customary complaints that the orphans and the poor are deserted (5,28), but Jeremiah is not only the champion of the poor against the mighty. None of the earlier prophets would have said as he did that at first he thought only the poor lacked judgment, but he quickly discovered that the great, too, had burst the bonds of Yahweh (5,4 f.). All seek unrighteous gain, high and low alike, (6,13); the shepherds themselves have become as cattle in judgment (10,21). And amidst all this, priests and prophets serve falsehood, saying that there is peace and peace again (6,13 f.).

Jeremiah returns several times to the agricultural rites. Yahweh sends winter rain, early rain, and late rain, all in due season, just as it is he who observes the order of the harvest weeks. That nevertheless the crops have failed, is due to the people's sins alone, which have disturbed the proper order of things (5,24 f.). They have deserted Yahweh for a non-god by adopting a Canaanite cult; when he fed them to the full, "they committed adultery, gashing their skin in the house of the harlots" (5,7). The apostasy of the people makes Yahweh despise their offerings. He does not care for the costly incense from Saba and other distant countries, he takes no pleasure in their burnt-offerings and sacrifices (6,20). Their fasting and sacrifices make no impression on Yahweh (14, 12). One of the prose passages makes Jeremiah, like Amos, allude to the fact that they were not ordered to sacrifice in the wilderness period (7,21 f.); it is doubtful whether this passage is by Jeremiah.

Like the earlier prophets, Jeremiah invites the people to look back upon their past history. Yahweh told them to ask for the ancient paths and walk in the way that led to goodness, and he raised up prophets for watchmen to warn them, but in both cases they refused to follow Yahweh's directions (6,16 f.), just as they always declined to return to him despite his punishments (5,3). While animals keep to the habits prescribed by their nature, Israel has abandoned Yahweh's mishpāṭ. They have neglected his law (tōrā), therefore misfortune must come (6,19); all this is caused by their defiance and obstinacy (5,23, cf. 9,13; 16,10 ff.). It appears from Jeremiah, as from Hosea and Amos, that there was a dispute about the right laws. People say to him that they possess Yahweh's tōrā and hence true wisdom. But Jeremiah answers them harshly: Truly, the lying pen of the scribe hath worked for falsehood. The wise are disgraced, dismayed, and tricked; they reject Yahweh's words, what wisdom is there in them? (8,8). The latter words must mean that they do not heed Jeremiah's revelations, but we cannot of course tell to what objectionable laws he is alluding.

In the usual prophetic way Jeremiah varies his accounts of the people's sin, of what is non-Israelitish in their conduct, as well as his description of the punishments awaiting the wicked people. First they were threatened by the Scythians [1] and Medes (5,10 ff.; 6,22-30; 8,10-22; 9,12-21); later, after the battle of Carchemish in 605, by the Chaldæans. Through symbolical acts Jeremiah kept the danger before them. He vividly portrays how disaster ravages the country (Jer. 13-14; 16; 19; 21). Like Isaiah, Jeremiah spoke plainly to the kings of the calamities to come; even when the enemy was besieging the capital he still intervened with his speeches, based on his idea of Israel and Yahweh.

Of special interest is a speech which Jeremiah delivered in the temple to induce the people to mend their ways and thus avert disaster. Yahweh bid him say that if they did not keep his law and obey the words of the prophets' message from God, "then I will make this house as Shiloh, and make this city a curse to all the nations of the earth" (26,6). In a report of the temple speech it says: Do not trust the lying words: Yahweh's temple, Yahweh's temple, Yahweh's temple is here! (7,4). This recalls Jeremiah's style, but it is doubtless a later construction. The result of the prophet's words was that he was seized by the other prophets and the priests and brought before the authorities as a man who deserved to die. Another man, Uriah, had been killed by Jehoiakim for a similar speech about the temple, but Jeremiah insisted that he had been sent by Yahweh, and it was pointed out that Micah had once spoken in a similar way. Jeremiah was, in fact, saved by a patron (Jer. 26).

Jeremiah was just as convinced as all the others that the temple was the dwelling-place of Yahweh; his life was devoted to the service of the God of Zion. But the temple was not merely the seat of Yahweh. It was the place where he met with the Israelites. And when they were corrupt with sin, Yahweh must withdraw from them. They polluted the sanctuary, and this sealed its fate. Yahweh's nature was still that of the God of Zion, and for that very reason he rose to such heights that he left his original basis. This is the same thing that appeared so clearly in Amos, and in reality it is a natural consequence of David's and the prophets' notions of Yahweh, just as natural as the prophets' conception of the temple cult, which is also to be found in Jeremiah. The decisive feature in this conception of Yahweh is that he is quite distinct from nature, and, human himself in essence, raised high above human beings, but in both worlds his will alone prevails.

This conception of Yahweh comes out strongly and clearly in Jeremiah. Yahweh set the sand as a limit to the sea and thus made an eternal law for the powerful element of chaos, then

36*

should not Israel fear him? (5,22). He alone sends rain. "Are there raingivers among the shadowy beings of the nations (i. e. their gods), and can the heavens themselves send down showers? Is it not thou, Yahweh, our God? Therefore we wait for thee, for thou hast created all" (14,22). Yahweh is the creator. This idea, which recurs again and again in the praises of the temple hymns, expresses his power and thus his very nature. By virtue of this the God of Israel dominates all. He fills heaven and earth, therefore nothing can hide from him; he is always near, not a God far off (23,23 f.).

Nothing characterises his nature as well as the parable of the potter, employed by Jeremiah, though the more extended form is presumably due to his successors (18,1-12). The great potter makes of his material what he pleases, and the material is humanity. He can raise up or overthrow nations and kingdoms. Therefore Israel has only to obey his will, nevertheless she prefers to follow her own stubborn heart.

Man has only to fear Yahweh and do honour to him before the darkness falls (5,22; 13,16). He who relies on man shall end in a cursed condition, only those who trust in Yahweh shall be blessed (17,5-8). Thus Jeremiah says the same thing as Isaiah. Yahweh rewards man with the fruits of his conduct (17,10). The judgment again and again passed on Israel by Yahweh through the mouth of his prophet is a kind of revenge, an expression of personal affront (5,9.29), for the least sin is an insult to his honour and produces a reaction from him.

And yet, in spite of his might, he is still the God of Israel, the God on Zion. Not only those who are secure say that Yahweh's temple is a shelter. From Jeremiah, too, there is an appeal to Yahweh to assert himself: We acknowledge, Yahweh, our iniquity and the guilt of our fathers, that we have sinned against thee. Do not reject us for thy name's sake, do not abandon the throne of thine honour, reflect, break not thy covenant with us (14,20-21). Jeremiah recognises the unity and common responsibility of the people and knows that it must lead them to the gulf of destruction. But they have still their covenant with the mighty God; he must maintain it, he must not let his honour be sullied by abandoning his throne, his temple. Thus two aspects of Yahweh's self-expression contend with each other, his unique might as the creator, which raises him above all creation, and his fellowship with his people through his covenant and his sanctuary.

It is the same problem which we find in different forms in all the prophets. It was a consequence of their God being detached from all that was earthly, and yet being the God of Israel. Jeremiah felt that it might give rise to painful problems to have so exalted a God who at the same time guaranteed the maintenance of what the Israelites understood by justice. For we see that he underwent the same experience as Job: Just art thou, O Yahweh, when I plead with thee; yet would I talk with thee about righteousness. Wherefore doth the way of the wicked prosper? Wherefore do all those thrive who deal treacherously? Thou plantest them and they take root; they grow and they bring forth fruit. Thou art near in their mouth but far from their reins (12, 1-2). Jeremiah demands of Yahweh that he shall slay them.

However, Jeremiah was not, any more than the other prophets, turned from the main tenets of his teaching. The Israelites were to do justice, i. e. live according to the rules which the nature of their God demanded, and then as to all the rest trust in Yahweh. It is characteristic that just when disaster was at its worst, during the siege of Jerusalem, Jeremiah showed his conviction that there was a future for Israel by purchasing a family property at Anathoth (Jer. 32). This hope finds expression in a number of utterances which, however, can hardly all be ascribed to Jeremiah himself (Chaps. 30-31).

His hope is constantly based on the expectation that the Israelites will turn to Yahweh. It is not enough for them to abandon the Baalim and extol Yahweh. Both Isaiah (29,13) and Jeremiah (12,2) complain of those who honour Yahweh by lip-service, while he is far from their hearts. They must practise Yahweh's righteousness, and external acts are not sufficient. They must come from the soul, it is the soul, therefore, that must be transformed. The farther it has strayed from the Israelite character, the stronger becomes the demand for the transformation of the "uncircumcised heart" (Jer. 9,25). If the law has not sprung directly from the soul, then it must be learnt with all the strength of the heart. The demand that the people shall "return" *(shūbh)* to the God and the character which was its original mark, implies a demand for a psychic transformation. When all the attention is concentrated on the latter, the term "return" is deprived of its original background and acquires the sense of an intense change of disposition, a conversion.

We hear of such a conversion in the book of Jeremiah, perhaps not in words he has spoken himself, but in words giving his ideas. Yahweh will renew his covenant, and it shall be more enduring than the one made when he brought Israel out of Egypt, for under the new covenant the Israelites shall have Yahweh's law written in their hearts (Jer. 31,31-33).

The reactionary prophets that developed from the ancient prophets' guilds were a powerful factor in Israelite popular life as long as it existed, and remain as a mighty testimony to the disharmony of Israelite culture. They interpret events and point to the soil from which these spring. The basis of their interpretation is their conception of Yahweh and Israel.

The prophets are representatives of the circles in which the Israelite psyche of the traditional type especially survived. They work to maintain it and think that Israel is not Israel if it cannot actualise it. Righteousness, the expression of the soundness and rectitude of the soul in the Israelite sense, therefore becomes greater than the Israelites. They are tested by their ability to practise it.

The prophets were determined to fight for the ancient God of Israel, the God who had delivered her from Egypt. There is a difference between Elijah's Yahweh who fought with Baal and conquered, and the exalted lord of the later prophets who ruled over foreign nations as well as Israel. But it is only a difference of degree. The God of the prophets is the powerful God of the Passover who is raised above nature and man. It becomes more and more conspicuous that he is identical with the God who was worshipped on Zion as the creator of the world and the ruler of the nations.

Through this mighty God events and the course of history are simplified. History was not an interplay of the life of souls, or rather, this interplay was a drama the threads of which rested in one hand, that of Yahweh; and his standard was the righteousness which was his own essence and which he demanded of his people. Other nations must submit to be used as instruments for the chastisement of the unrighteous Israelites, this was the explanation of their victories and world power.

If some few utterances seem to indicate that foreigners may be just as near to Yahweh as the wicked Israelites, they must be interpreted to mean that he cares as little for the Israelites. But if consistently applied the idea is absurd. For the righteousness demanded is Israelite righteousness, and Yahweh is the God of Israel. Therefore the connecting link between Yahweh and Israel could never be broken. Israel alone could actualise his righteousness; however much he was exalted, he could not abandon his own people, which was his own foundation.

Thus relations between Yahweh and Israel become subject to a tension that finds expression in the alternate words of doom and of expectation which we hear from the prophets. As far back as the prophetic writings we trace the tendency to fix both kinds of predictions in stereotyped forms from which Jewish eschatology later formed its schematic prophecies of the future.

The aim of the prophets' endeavour was to counteract certain forms of culture, but it rose in their view to be a battle for what was good against what was evil. And since they expected everything from the almighty will of Yahweh, they demanded the complete extermination of evil. This gave to their conflict a passionate violence which intensified the disharmony.

Their conception of Yahweh became of dicisive importance for the relation between God and man. There was no organic relation between the sanctification of nature by sacrifice and Yahweh who was exalted high above nature. For man it was important to be in harmony with the will of Yahweh, obedience and praise was what Yahweh demanded. In this way the entire sacrificial cult actually became superfluous, or at any rate of secondary importance; the prophets worked on in the spirit of David. By stressing the demand for righteous conduct and a humble heart, they gave an independent importance to the observance of the law; the law was identical with the will of Yahweh, to observe it was to maintain the Israelite character and to obey Yahweh. The change in culture to which this gave rise meant that popular life became divorced from nature. By carrying things so far the prophets made their people capable of maintaining an Israelitish society outside the land in which it had grown up and taken shape.

REFORMS, EXILE AND RESTORATION

I F the prophets had been isolated representatives of some extreme
school they would hardly have acquired much importance.
Their strong point was that in their fight against the foreign
element, they could appeal to history, to the traditions of which
the Israelites were attached by strong ties, for through the
Passover they were continually bound to Yahweh who had brought
Israel up out of Egypt. Hence it was not only the prophets who
defended themselves against the cult practices which could not be
reconciled with the traditional Israelite character and ways.
Among the very leaders of the Israelitish cult, i. e. the kings, we
can trace the familiar conflict as to which cult the Israelites could,
in their view, adopt.

It appears in the books of the Kings, where, among the stereotyped phrases about the kings of Ephraim who did what was evil
in the sight of Yahweh, we hear now and then about kings of
Judah, who did what was right in the sight of Yahweh, and the
reference is always to the cult.

Asa, one of the first Davidians, sent all the "holy men", the
male servants of the sexual cult, out of the country, "and removed
all the idols that his fathers had made" (1 Kings 15,12). Further,
he burnt in the valley of Kedron an asherah-cult object which his
mother had procured, and even deprived her of the dignity of
queen mother (gᵉbhīrā, v. 13). Asa's son Jehoshaphat acted in the
same spirit, also attempting to exterminate the "holy men" (1
Kings 22,43.47).

Then followed some Davidians associated with the house of
Ahab, who adopted its cult, viz. Joram, his son Ahaziah and,
after he had been killed, his mother Athaliah. When she was killed,

and Ahaziah's son Joash, who had been brought up secretly in the temple, was made king, the temple to Baal which had belonged to Ahab's house was destroyed (2 Kings 11,18). The book of Kings records that Joash did what was right because the priest Jehoiada instructed him (2 Kings 12,3). But no concrete features are mentioned. It is said, however, that "the high places" did not disappear (12,4). This statement must probably apply to sanctuaries in and about Jerusalem as well, apart from Athaliah's special temple which must have belonged to the Baal of Tyre. On Amaziah, Uzziah, and Jotham a similar judgment is pronounced as on Joash; even if they did not act exactly like David, they were nevertheless on the whole pleasing to Yahweh (14,3; 15,3.34).

The kings who displeased Yahweh were Solomon and his two successors, who are blamed for their adoption of the cults of the neighbouring countries, also the kings related to Ahab, who introduced the Phœnician cult from Samaria; and under them all "the high places" survived. With Ahaz (734-15) begins the Assyrian rule in western Asia, and this involves the introduction of the cult from the east. We learn that Ahaz became an Assyrian vassal, and that he introduced a new altar after a model from Damascus. But his condemnation takes the general form that he walked in the ways of the kings of Israel, to which is added the remark that he passed his son through the fire according to the abominations of the people whom Yahweh had cast out for the sake of the Israelites, and that he sacrificed in the high places (16,2-4).

A complete revolution occurred with Ahaz' son Hezekiah, who reigned for 29 years. He, and later Josiah, are the only kings who are considered to be on a level with David, and are said to have done what was right in the sight of Yahweh (18,3). Hezekiah renounced all connection with Assyria. Normally this must mean that he also gave up the eastern cult practices. But here again the judgment passed on him is confined to what was specially Canaanite. Hezekiah removed the bamahs, broke the *maṣṣēbhās*, cut down the asherahs, and destroyed the brazen serpent which Moses had formed and to which the Israelites had sacrificed (18,4). He trusted in Yahweh, the God of Israel, and adhered to him, observing his commandments, which Yahweh had enjoined on Moses (18,5-6). Thus Hezekiah must have removed some cult objects from the temple of Jerusalem, and differs from the earlier reformers by attacking the "bamahs", i. e. sanctuaries other than the temple of Jerusalem. According to the story of the siege of Jerusalem by the Assyrians, the Assyrian leader must have known of Hezekiah's activities, and he says that Judah and Jerusalem were bidden to bow down to "this altar" only at Jerusalem (18, 22), which would mean that worship outside the royal temple was prohibited.

The reforms were, however, abolished by Hezekiah's son Manasseh who was king for 55 years. He, too, behaved like "the people whom Yahweh had cast out before the Israelites" and did "as Ahab, the king of Israel had done". He rebuilt the bamahs which his father had destroyed, erected altars to Baal, made an asherah, and worshipped all the host of heaven. This refers to the Assyrian cult of Shamash, the sun and all his host. He introduced this cult into the royal temple, in the two courts; further he passed his son through the fire, practised soothsaying, and consulted the spirits of the dead, all of which offended Yahweh. Amon followed in his father's footsteps, but of him we are told that he worshipped "idols" (2 Kings 21).

Then, after Amon, came the king who is commended as the greatest reformer, viz. his son Josiah, who "walked in all the ways of his father David" (2 Kings 22,2). The story of the reform of Josiah differs from the others by the fact that it is inspired by the finding of a law code. In the year 622 the king sent Shaphan with a message to Hilkiah the high priest who received him with these words: "I have found the book of the law ("the book of the *tōrā*") in the house of Yahweh". Shaphan took it to the king and read it to him. Then the king rent his garments and sent some men to a prophetess to hear Yahweh's word about the threats which the lawbook contained. The answer was that Yahweh would bring down disaster on the city and its inhabitants, because they had abandoned Yahweh and sacrificed to foreign gods, "the work of their hands". But seeing that the king had become alarmed and rent his clothes and wept and humbled himself on hearing the

words of the book, Yahweh promised that he should be gathered
to his fathers in peace, and his eyes should not behold the coming
evils. Then the king gathered the people in the temple, had the
book of the law, or as it is also called with the same meaning,
the book of the covenant, read aloud, and the king made a
covenant, which the people joined, all pledging themselves to
keep the commandments of the lawbook just found (2 Kings 22,
3-23,3).

After this the king proceeded to introduce reforms. He had all
the cult objects belonging to "the Baal and the asherah and all
the host of heaven" removed from the royal temple, burning them
outside the city in the fields of the valley of Kedron (23,4). [1] He
burnt the asherah in the same place and spread its dust on the
graves of the poor (23,6). He pulled down the cells of the "holy
men" in the temple (v: 7), and he removed the horses of the
Shamash cult standing at the entrance to the court, and likewise
the chariots belonging to the cult, and burnt them (v. 11). Thus
was exterminated the Assyrian Shamash cult which must have
had processions of chariots imitating the course of the sun and so
establishing a connection with the heavenly powers that governed
the day. The altars of Manasseh in the courts, and the altars on
the roofs, were likewise pulled down by the king (23,12). Just
outside Jerusalem he polluted *tōpheth* in the valley of Hinnom
where the children had been passed through the fire for Molech
(23,10). And he also polluted the bamahs southeast of Jerusalem
which Solomon had erected to Phœnician, Moabite, and Ammonite gods (v. 13). Further he broke down the maṣṣebahs and
cut down the asherahs and filled their places with human bones
(v. 14), by which means they were polluted. And he pulled down
the "bamahs of the gates", [2] sanctuaries situated near one of
the gates of Jerusalem (v. 8 b.).

We hear twice about the priests at the various sanctuaries of
Judah. The king put down the "idolatrous priests" *(kᵉmārim,*
only used about "illegitimate" priests) which the kings of Judah
had installed at the bamahs in the cities of Judah and around
Jerusalem, and those who sacrificed to the Baal, to the sun and
the moon, and all the host of heaven (23,5). And he brought

hither all the priests of Judah and polluted all the bamahs of Judah (v. 8 a.). The priests of the bamahs did not, indeed, go up to Yahweh's altar at Jerusalem, but they ate unleavened bread among their brethren (v. 9), i. e. at the Passover.

These activities in Judah were now extended to the area of the old realm of Ephraim. The altàr at Bethel was polluted with particular thoroughness and interest. It was the altar by which Jeroboam had brought Israel to sin. For this pollution the ashes of the objects from the Baal cult had been preserved (23,4). The altar was pulled down, and the bamah and the asherah were burnt (v. 15). We are further told that Josiah took bones from the graves and burnt them on the altar, all according to the account of a man of God in the days of Jeroboam (1 Kings 13). It is then reported that Josiah also removed all bamah temples in the cities of Samaria which the kings of Israel had erected as an outrage to Yahweh, and he did to them as to the bamahs of Bethel; and he cut down all the bamah priests there. After this deed he returned home to Jerusalem (2 Kings 23,19 f.) and celebrated a Paschal feast the equal of which had not been seen since the days of the judges (23,21-23). Finally, he is also said to have abolished the raising of the dead and teraphim, idols, and the like at Jerusalem, in accordance with the law book found by Hilkiah (v. 24). Neither before nor after was there any king who like him turned to Yahweh with all his heart in accordance with the *tōrā* of Moses (v. 25). — Of his son Jehoahaz it is reported that he did what was evil in the sight of Yahweh, just as his forefathers had done, and the same judgment is passed on Jehoiakim, Jehoiachin, and Zedekiah (2 Kings 23,32.37; 24,9.19).

Before we attempt to estimate the historical importance of these communications, we must look at the nature of the utterances on the cult conditions found in the book of Kings. The books of the Kings, as they have come down to us, are based on earlier more detailed documents, to which reference is made in them. There was "The History of Solomon" (1 Kings 11,41), "The History of the Kings of Israel" and "The History of the Kings of Judah", which are mentioned under most of the kings. The latter is last mentioned under Jehoiakim (2 Kings 24,5), who died in 597, shortly before the first capture of Jerusalem. Whether the two last kings were included in it we do not know, but the book must have been written during or just before the exile, probably during the exile, since it seems most reasonable to suppose that it was concluded after the completion of the list of kings. The perpetuation of the cult being the chief task of the king, this work, just like the other two, no doubt contained much information about cult practices. Further there must have been a collection of narratives about the prophets comprising the stories of Elijah and Elisha.

Our work, then, is an adaptation. The adaptor's, or as we may call him, the author's contribution consists in the combination of the above-mentioned two works, in which he must no doubt have made very extensive abridgments, but he has also furnished positive contributions, determined entirely by personal viewpoints. From these he has framed speeches such as Solomon's temple address, set his impress on stories such as that about Solomon's dream, and established judgments by which the kings are described as evil or good, all events being thus seen in a certain light.

The author starts from the assumption that there is only one temple "to the name of Yahweh", namely the royal sanctuary in Jerusalem (1 Kings 3,2). There is a difference in principle between this and all other so-called sanctuaries; the latter, therefore, have their own name, viz. bāmā. The temple of Jerusalem is the temple of Yahweh, and he alone is God, as indeed all the nations of the world shall acknowledge (1 Kings 8,16.60). He alone, therefore, is to be worshipped by the Israelites; they shall keep his commandments and honour him, not acknowledging foreign gods (3,14; 9,1-9). It is from this standpoint that the author takes a retrospective view of history and reviews its events. His conception of history is quite schematic. Israel took possession of Canaan, Yahweh expelling its population. But some remnants remained and they seduced the Israelites (1 Kings 9,20 f.; 14,24); for this disobedience Yahweh continually punished the people by disasters, and one after another of the kings led the way. The fall of the northern kingdom was such a disaster. The author makes some reflections on it, also taking into consideration the Babylonian exile of the Judæans (2 Kings 17,20); and the temple speech of Solomon, too, takes into account the experiences of this exile (1 Kings 8,46 ff.).

We know these points of view in all essentials from the prophets; they are determined by the reaction against the foreign element. The author who drew upon the earlier works, parts of which, as we have seen, were only finished during the exile, may himself have carried out his work during that period. But it is more probable that he belongs to the period after the restoration, when Israel looked back upon her early history across the gulf of the exile. The importance of the kings for the cult appears from the fact that the full responsibility for cult undertakings is laid at their door, but the author sees them from a remote distance, prophets and priests take precedence of them. It is mentioned as a sin by Jeroboam that he appointed priests who did not belong to the family that gradually came to be the ruling one, the Levites (1 Kings 12,31; 13,33). But otherwise it is the prophets who take the lead in the history of Israel.

In the stories of Elijah, which seem to be preserved without essential alterations, we see a prophet appear in the strength of Yahweh as rebel against a king; just as in the history of Ahab and other kings, we see the rulers exploiting the prophetic power. But, under the impression of the great prophets of doom, the author of the books of the Kings has formed an idea of history according to which the prophets appear as the chastisers of the kings, who give them conduct marks and regularly keep them informed of how events will develop, always as a reward or a punishment for their behaviour.

Through Ahijah Jeroboam is promised his kingship owing to the sins of Solomon, even over as many as ten tribes, in accordance with the post-exilic theoretical view of the tribal conditions (1 Kings 11,29 ff.). Later on the same prophet informs him of the fall of his dynasty because of his cult sins (1 Kings 14). After the rupture Rehabeam gathers a mighty force of 180,000 men in order to regain the power, but he sends it home again because a prophet forbids him to fight; what has happened has been the will of Yahweh (12,21-24). Josiah's desecration of the altar at Bethel is predicted to its founder Jeroboam (1 Kings 13). Thus the fate of the dynasties was predicted to Baasha (1 Kings 16,1 ff.), Ahab (21,20 ff.), and Jehu (2 Kings 10,30; 15,12) with appropriate rebuke. Isaiah goes to the palace of Hezekiah, questions the king because he has received foreign embassies, and informs him of the exile of his successors as a suitable but moderate punishment (2 Kings 20,12 ff.).

In his estimate of the kings the author takes no account whatever of their ability or importance. They are judged exclusively by their obedience to the law and the prophets, and this obedience is displayed in the cult. The author takes the same view of the cult as the prophets. Everything connected with the Canaanite cult is evil; Yahweh is raised above nature, he is not connected with it. It is a matter of course to the author that a correct cult can only be practised in the temple of Jerusalem. Therefore the "bamahs" are merely sin. That Elijah, the man of God, nevertheless offered sacrifice on Carmel is an inconsistency which the author has retained from the early stories of the prophets.

Solomon, the builder of the temple, was in the main regarded as a prototype; but he made offerings at the bamahs, not considering his chief temple as the only one possible. That he did so before this temple was built was not so sinful (1 Kings 3,3), but he went on building bamahs, even to foreign gods. The author says, half apologetically, that it was not until he grew old that his foreign wives lured him to do this (1 Kings 11,4-8), but it gives the motive for his son's loss of Israel, and he was only allowed to keep Judah out of consideration for David and Jerusalem, which Yahweh had chosen (vv. 9-13).

From his standpoint the author must condemn all the kings of Israel, as indeed he does. But to the general denunciation of the bamahs is added his indignation because Jeroboam set up two calves at Bethel and Dan and declared them to be Yahweh who brought Israel out of Egypt (1 Kings 12,30). This making of an image of Yahweh, and even in the shape of an animal, is "the sin of Jeroboam". It caused the fall of his own house (1 Kings 14,9 f.; 15,29), and because of it the succeeding kings of Israel are condemned (1 Kings 15,30.34; 16,2.13.19.26; 2 Kings 3,3; 10,29; 13,2.11; 14,24; 15,9.18.24.28). But to this must be added Ahab's sin which consisted in his prostrating himself before Baal and Astarte (1 Kings 16,32 f.). The cult of Baal and the Canaanite cult of Yahweh, which seemed one to the prophets, are thus two different sins. It is said expressly about a king that he committed both Jeroboam's and Ahab's sin (1 Kings 22,53 f.), about another that he only committed Jeroboam's sin (2 Kings 3,2 f.). Jehu exterminated Baal, but did not give up Jeroboam's sin (10,28 ff.). The kings related to Ahab in Judah committed Ahab's sin (2 Kings 8,18.27), but it is never said about the kings of Judah that they imitated Jeroboam's sin; on the other hand, it is said in a more general way about Ahaz that he acted like the kings of Israel (2 Kings 16,3). The judgments must be due to the information drawn from the adapted writings and are tinged accordingly, as when we are told about Israel's king Hosea that he did what was evil in the sight of Yahweh, though not as the kings who preceded him (2 Kings 17,2). Unfortunately our author thought it better for posterity to know his own judgments than the facts on which they were based. Hence we merely possess information of a vague and general kind.

The bamahs are always a sin. It is the author's notion that after the ideal period of David and the incipient decay under Solomon they spread under Rehabeam with their massebahs and asherahs and even with "holy men" (1 Kings 14,23 f.). Then, throughout the history of Judah kings succeed each other which alternately please or displease Yahweh; but on most of those who are pleasing to Yahweh, i. e. the line of kings down to Hezekiah, there is the comment that the bamahs did not disappear (1 Kings 15,14; 22,44; 2 Kings 12,4; 14,4; 15,4.35). The author must, then, base his favourable judgments on information drawn from the earlier work, from which it appeared that these kings counteracted the foreign cult in the temple of Jerusalem.

The reforms of Hezekiah and Josiah, though recorded at greater length, must not, therefore, be regarded as isolated, decisive events. The Israelite dislike of Canaanite and other foreign cults also, according to the book of Kings, had its representatives in the earlier kings. And the activities of the two above-mentioned reformers did not result in the abolition of the foreign cult in

Israel. On the contrary, Jeremiah and Ezekiel testify that it still filled the capital and the country (Jer. 13,23.27; Ez. 5,11; 6; 7,9.20.24; 8; 16; 20; 23). Jeremiah gives no sign that any complete change occurred in his lifetime. After the death of Josiah he still preaches against the high places and their "abominations".

The constant spreading of the foreign cults and the violent reforms were equally manifestations of the uncertainty prevailing among the people, of which Jeremiah's conflict with the women is such a typical sign (Jer. 44,15 ff.).

It is only natural that there should be a connection between the reforms of the two kings and their attempts to free themselves from their dependency on foreign powers. Hezekiah refused to subject himself to Sennacherib and came successfully out of the contest. Josiah must have emancipated himself from his grandfather Manasseh's policy and broken away from the great Assyrian empire, for it was the latter's ally Necho, the king of Egypt, who slew him at Megiddo. Thus Josiah's abolition from his temple of the Shamash cult was in good agreement with his policy. [1] But the chief point in the reforms of the two kings was something different from political liberation. They were part of a current which we can follow throughout the history of Israel, the conflict between the specially Israelite and the foreign element. And the foreign element was in the first place the Canaanite element, for this was the cult with which the Israelites were in closest contact, and which was even adopted under the name of Yahweh. The reforms of Hezekiah can therefore be described as an abolition of the altars of Yahweh (2 Kings 18,22), and Josiah can be described as a second Jehu who destroys the bamahs of Samaria and cuts down their priests. Doubtless this description is idealised in accordance with the author's view. But we have no reason to doubt that Hezekiah and Josiah were guided in their reforms by the same incentive as other, earlier kings and many in Israel besides the reactionary prophets, viz. the magnifying of the God of Israel who dwelt on Zion, as opposed to all the foreign elements that obtruded themselves on the people, especially in the cult.

Notably the reform of Josiah acquires a special position because of the detailed description and the comprehensive character given to it in the account. It is further stressed by being connected with the finding of a law book. It is not expressly stated that the law book caused the reform, and Chronicles mentions the reform before the finding of the law book (2 Chron. 34). But the author of the book of Kings undoubtedly wanted to convey the idea of a connection. According to the statement of the high priest, the lawbook was found in the temple. The contents are not given, but the story shows that it was full of threats against the Israelites because they had fallen away from Yahweh. At the making of the covenant in the temple the king and the people promised to keep its commandments. The making of the covenant expressed that the people accepted the book as Yahweh's will. How much it meant is doubtful. In the days of Zedekiah, the king and the people made a similar covenant in the temple to observe ancient Israelite law and set free the Hebrew slaves and slave women (Jer. 34,8 ff., cf. Ex. 21,2; Deut. 15,12 ff.); but that covenant came to mean very little, and, as already mentioned, the covenant made under Josiah likewise came to mean little for the permanent extermination of the foreign cult.

_____

If there was an increasing tendency to reforms among the Judæan kings, we cannot wonder at it. We see that the author of the book of Kings distinguishes between the abolition of sanctuaries outside the great temple and the abolition of idols and of other foreign cult practices. But behind both demands there is actually one, viz. the demand for the autocracy of Yahweh on Zion.

The ancient God of the Paschal feast, the God of David and the God of the prophets, was essentially the same ruling God, unfettered by nature, ruling over it and over man. His strong and pronounced personality must make it more and more impossible to seek his dwelling in more than one place. Thus, not only did the royal temple become something apart, eclipsing other temples, but its God alone became the God of Israel and therefore the sole God who could claim to be worshipped. The reforms of Hezekiah and

Josiah, which turned both against foreign cults and bamahs, were
natural manifestations of the struggle to maintain Yahweh on
Zion.

This of course does not preclude the possibility that one of the
reforming kings may have been prompted by the finding of a law
book. We know from the prophets that the various circles gave
expression to their demands in laws by which they fought each
other. At the outset it is not very probable that precisely the law
that came to light under Josiah should have come down to us.
Several of the codes transmitted to us, as we might expect, bear
the impress of the struggle against the foreign element, especially
the Law of Holiness and Deuteronomy, as well as Ezekiel's draft;
and all these consider Jerusalem the only sanctuary. But in
Deuteronomy this appears as a demand of a similar kind to that
indicated in the book of Kings; therefore this law has throughout modern times been regarded as the law found under Josiah.
The code represents the reforming tendency and is, therefore, in
any case of interest in this connection.

Deuteronomy, as handed down to us, contains a collection of
laws reflecting Israelite popular life as it shaped itself in the cities
under the influence of the laws of the surrounding communities.
Numerous examples have shown us this in the most varied fields
of culture. But the laws of the code have been partly rewritten and
renewed, adapted to new demands which can in the main be
gathered under two heads: a campaign against everything foreign
and a prohibition against worship outside the temple of Jerusalem,
i. e. the same tendencies that we know from the author of the book
of Kings. Where the ancient Deuteronomic laws were in force we
do not know, but they were not one-sidedly determined by
Jerusalem. The law of deliverance from blood-guilt on finding a
person slain in the open land (Deut. 21,1-9) implies that it was
in force for a large territory. When these old laws were formulated
we cannot possibly say, but they must have arisen gradually as a
result of common practice. In this connection it is, however, the
completed Deuteronomy, with its special tendency and character,
which is of interest.

The intention of the author, whom we may call D, must have

been to present a law valid for Israel as a whole, with Jerusalem as its centre. He has adopted the ancient custom of formulating the laws in the name of Moses. In this way their whole milieu is presented as something of the future. Jerusalem is not mentioned by name but as "the place Yahweh shall choose". Israel becomes an ideal quantity, and the old concrete laws are incorporated in a corpus of an abstract character. The fathers of Israel are addressed, and the experience of the wilderness period, which is described in an historical introduction, is used to exhort Israel to observe Yahweh's law (1-4,8).

The concrete laws (12-26) are often presented in connection with general admonitions, and they begin with circumstantial instructions and rebukes in the same style and language as the historical introduction. The address does not progress smoothly. Several times there are remarks meant to lead on to the actual laws (4,1; 4,44-48; 6,1-13; 12,1), but new speeches are continually inserted, and they are all in the same style and spirit, so that a formal literary division does not yield results of much real interest. It is explained that the laws, apart from the 10 commandments (5,1-22), were announced to Moses alone (5,23-33).

The fundamental ideas of D appear plainly from these speeches. Everything centres round the notion that Yahweh, the God of Israel, is one (6,4; 10,17). Therefore Israel is to love him alone and fear him. The Israelites must keep his *tōrā*, carry his commandments in their hearts (6,6), they must have them bound to their hands and foreheads, affixed to their door-posts (6,8; 11, 18-20). They must not make themselves any image of Yahweh under any form whatsoever (4,9-40), and they must not worship the heavenly bodies which Yahweh has allotted to other nations (4,19), or they will be scattered among other peoples and will have to worship gods of wood and stone. It is true that they shall then return to Yahweh, and he will again receive them.

When the people enter the rich land of Canaan, they must not forget their God who brought them out of the land of bondage, but must fear and serve him, and swear by him (6,10-13; 8,10 ff.; 10,20). Through the humiliation of the wilderness period they were brought up to such obedience (8,1-5). They must not obey any of the gods of the neighbouring peoples, or Yahweh will show his jealousy and destroy them (6,14 f.; 7,4; 8,11-20; 11,16 f. 28); but if they keep his covenant he will bless them (6,2; 7,12-15; 11,9). From this D infers that the Israelites are to exterminate all the Canaanite peoples. Covenant and marriage with them are excluded, since this would seduce the Israelites to worship foreign gods; they are to show that they are Yahweh's holy chosen people, by pulling down altars, *maṣṣēbhās*, asherahs and images (7,1 ff.). Yahweh will destroy the Canaanites because of their wickedness, and in order to maintain his covenant with the fathers of Israel; not because of the righteousness of the people (9,1-6), for they have always been obstinate; now however, they must consider how to secure the blessing by shunning other gods and loving and fearing Yahweh (9,7-11,31).

This striving to destroy everything that is un-Israelitish sets its stamp on the concrete laws as they have been formed by D. It applies especially to all Canaanite cults. The destruction of the Canaanite people is taken for granted (12,2.29; 20,16-18), but after that the Israelites are to destroy "all the places where the peoples whom you expel served their gods, on the high mountains, on the hills, and under every green tree", with their altars, *maṣṣēbhās*, asherahs, and images (12,2 f.), and Israel must not make *maṣṣēbhās* or asherahs (16,21 f.). They must not worship Yahweh thus, they must only seek and offer sacrifice to him "in the place that Yahweh, your God, shall choose from all your tribes to put his name there" (12,5.11.14). There they shall come and eat their sacrificial meals with their sons, daughters, slaves, and slave-women, and the Levites from their towns (v. 12). This is the law providing that the temple of Jerusalem shall be Yahweh's only sanctuary. In this connection D establishes that while sacrifice is only allowed at Jerusalem, the slaughtering of cattle may take place anywhere, as long as the blood is not consumed (12,15 ff.).

Thus D takes it for granted that the temple of Jerusalem is the only Israelitish sanctuary, while all others have been taken over with their cult from the Canaanites. And it is strictly prohibited, when these have been destroyed, to enquire how they worshipped their gods in order to imitate their practices, for they did before their gods what Yahweh abhorred, they even burnt their sons and daughters (12,29-31). In connection with this, stern commands are given as to the destruction of those who seduce people to worship foreign gods. A prophet who speaks words to that effect is to be killed (13,2-6), nay, one must kill even one's nearest relatives if they try to lure one to worship any of the gods of the surrounding peoples, near or far (13,7-12). And if it is recorded that a city has been led to worship other gods, the city is to be captured, the inhabitants killed, and the city with all that is in it is to be burnt "as a holocaust to Yahweh" and must never be rebuilt (13,13-19). D reverts to this again and again. Those who worship other gods or the sun, the moon, and the host of heaven are to be killed (17,2-7).

There is also a special interdiction against "holy men" and "holy women" (23,18 f.). All foreign customs which have any connection with the cultus must be abhorred, thus certain mourning rites (14,1) and all kinds of soothsaying, for among their own people there will always arise prophets who can tell them what is right and who can claim obedience (18,9-22).

Behind the utterances of D we see a very self-contained society, fighting convulsively to preserve its individuality from the foreign innovations threatening it. Notably it endeavours to keep free from the gods of the foreign peoples and what belongs to them. A strong clannish spirit is necessary within the community. In the year of release claims on countrymen are to be remitted, but foreigners may be pressed for payment (15,3). Interest must not be taken from countrymen, though it may be taken from strangers (23,20 f.). Goodness to all weak members of the community is enjoined. The old demand for liberation of a Hebrew slave after seven years (Ex. 21,1 ff.) is supplemented by an admonition to furnish him lavishly with cattle, corn, and wine, and the reason given is that the Israelites themselves were once slaves in Egypt and were liberated by Yahweh (15,13-15). From the same motive leniency is inculcated towards orphans, widows, gērīm, the partly incorporated "sojourners" of foreign, especially of Canaanite origin. They are to possess their rights and are to be allowed to glean in the fields the remains of corn, olives, and grapes (24, 17 f. 19-22), and they are to be taken to the feasts in Jerusalem in company with slaves, slave women, and Levites (16,11 f.). In other respects D takes the same view of the *gēr* as the other law codes (Ex. 22,20; 23,9; Lev. 19,34).

Not every one can be admitted to this closed community. Ammonites and Moabites must never be admitted, Israel must not work for their peace and happiness. Edomites and Egyptians may be admitted, but not until the third generation (23,4-9). Amalekites are to be entirely exterminated, like all Canaanite peoples (25, 17-19). That the *gērim* were descended from these very peoples D has not called to mind. They had once for all been admitted to the community and their origin had been forgotten.

The law compilers' but especially D's view of the community is the same as that of the prophets. According to this view Israel proper consists of people in humble circumstances. Her whole nature is determined by this fact, therefore to assert herself she must maintain the humbler class. The Passover feast extols Yahweh as the god who showed his strength by saving his people, from this D draws a moral as to the nature of the people. Israel was saved from the lot of foreigners and *gērim*, so this was the class she had originally belonged to. Hence it is un-Israelitish to rise above others in power and wealth. This view finds its most peculiar application in the precepts relating to the king, who must not be chosen out of foreigners, must not live like a great man, must not procure riches and not acquire horses by giving up men to Egypt. ¹ Altogether, he must not let his heart exalt itself above his brethren, but is to bow down to the Deuteronomic law which he is even to copy out and read over daily (17,14-20).

The ideas and demands of D tell us nothing strikingly new. They point clearly to the fight of the prophets for a community of easily contented people in humble circumstances, for the ancient Israelite customs in contrast with the fertility cult of the arable land and other foreign elements, and for the mighty God of Israel, whose unity was linked with his personality, the strength of which is so prominent in David. D then has his place in a well-known line in the history of Israel.

Since the beginning of the 19th century the general view of the origin of Deuteronomy has been that it is the law book which was found under Josiah and that it was compiled in the 7th century. The possibility that D shaped his work in the 7th century cannot be denied, but it is not probable. Through the struggles of the 7th century the ground was prepared for such a self-contained Israelite community as D takes for granted, but it did not come into existence before the exile. From that time the difference between the Israelite and the foreign element acquired its absolute character.

When the prophets preached against the foreign element, they had definite things in view. They intervened in questions of immediate importance and protested against the transformation of Israel by foreign customs. But the prophets did not demand that the Israelites should be the sole inhabitants of the country. That is a purely abstract consequence of their ideas. Theoretically it was indeed natural. If Canaan was the land of Yahweh, and Yahweh's people polluted themselves by adopting the customs of other peoples, then the idea does not seem remote that Israelites alone should live in the country. It was this conclusion which D drew and which he claimed should be reduced to practice. But this means that D treated the question quite in the abstract. In the 7th century the Judæans lived in natural companionship with strangers, both Canaanites and foreigners, and those Judæans who were bound by strong traditions carried on just as natural a war with them, but more especially with the Israelites who had adopted their customs. The reason why D now puts forward the purely doctrinaire demand that the country should be cleansed of all non-Israelites can only be that he views facts from a distance. During the exile a compact and self-contained Israelite community was formed. To this community the ideal right of Israel to the whole of Canaan must appear as a fundamental truth, and it is natural that this truth should be transformed into a claim for the extermination of the completely foreign people with which the Israelites found the country filled when they came back to Canaan.

Thus it seems most probable that D dates from the postexilic period and the reference to the king points in the same direction. The reference to him is purely negative, the king is merely a tolerated person. "The breath of our nostrils", "he in whose shadow we thought to live among the peoples" (Lam. 4,20) must not rise above others, he is merely to be the obedient pupil of the priests and the author. This means that he cannot be king. It is probable that throughout the monarchical period there existed circles constituting the extreme opposition, which regarded the kingship with distrust as an un-Israelitish institution, and prophets could speak frankly in the presence of the king, with the authority of inspiration. But not even the castigating prophets regarded the kingship as un-Israelitish, quite the contrary. And it cannot be said to be probable that the Deuteronomic view of the kingship should have found legal expression in priestly circles of the 7th century, least of all when the law was to be carried into operation by a king. The clause referring to the king is best understood if the king had disappeared from real life, the direction of the community having been taken over by the priests. This supposition is strengthened by the strong stress laid on the injunction that the king must not be chosen among strangers. The idea of choosing an alien to occupy the throne of David can hardly have come within the horizon in the days of the kings, when the son regularly succeeded his father by virtue of his birth. But after the exile, when Jerusalem was under a foreign ruler and the question of an Israelite king must constantly come up, a warning against foreign rulers is quite natural.

Finally D regards Yahweh from another angle than might be expected in the 7th century. Yahweh has not become mightier than in the cult hymns of the temple of Zion or in the teaching of the prophets, for to them, too, he was lord of the gods and the nations. But the conflict in the people was between concrete cults, the Israelite cult of Yahweh and the Canaanite or other foreign cults. In Deuteronomy the conflict has been made to turn upon a choice in point of principle between the absolute Yahweh on the one side and all the vain gods of the surrounding nations on the other. Here we are only concerned with a slight displacement, but it corresponds to the new relation into which Israel entered towards foreign peoples through the exile, as we learn, also, from Deutero-Isaiah. Thus several facts would seem to suggest that Deuteronomy was compiled on the basis of extant laws in the time shortly after the exile. The smooth and verbose style characteristic of the long speeches accords well with such a late origin; their force lies in the forced strength of the conviction, not in the rich subject-matter, as in the pithy prose of the old popular writings.

If these considerations are correct, Deuteronomy cannot be the law book brought to light under Josiah. Either it must have been a law book unknown to us, which has disappeared like so many others, or it must have been our law book in an earlier form. The latter supposition is beset by the difficulty that those parts of Deuteronomy which might have been of importance in Josiah's reform form part of the views which, according to what we have shown here, should be due to the later author. It must then be assumed that there was an earlier adaptation, but it would be difficult to demonstrate this, and the whole matter would lose interest, for the old laws that form the nucleus of Deuteronomy have nothing to do with the cult reforms.

The entire question, however, is not so simple. Deuteronomy represents an earlier material written according to later views, but so also does the book of Kings. And as we have seen, the author of the book of Kings holds, on essential points, the same views as the author of Deuteronomy. The resemblance is not limited to standpoints. Numerous portions of the book of Kings have the same style and choice of words as Deuteronomy, conveying the impression that they were written by the same man. [1] This would seem to indicate that the adaptor of the book of Kings was either identical with the adaptor of Deuteronomy, or since this point of view cannot easily be consistently applied, was closely associated with him and was his pupil. And there is no reason to believe that his own contributions should have been restricted to the general considerations, the style of which is so easy to recognise. Amongst other things he probably enlarged the account of Josiah's reform and gave it a wider scope than it originally had.

The great difficulty, if we assume that the adaptor or author of the book of Kings is identical with the author of Deuteronomy, is that he no doubt thought of Deuteronomy himself as the law book found under Josiah. In the account of Josiah's reform there is an allusion to one of its provisions (2 Kings 23,9) saying that the priests were brought up to Jerusalem from the sanctuaries, but without being allowed to ascend the altar (cf. Deut. 18,7). And when Amaziah took revenge on his father's murderers, we are told that he did not kill the children, with the addition that this was "according unto that which is written in the book of the law of Moses, wherein Yahweh commanded, saying: Fathers shall not be put to death for sons, nor sons be put to death for fathers, but every man shall die for his own sin" (2 Kings 14,6). This note probably originates from the adaptor of the book, and it is to Deuteronomy (24,16) he is referring. That law, then, is to him the "Law of Moses", hence it is probable that he also thought that it was the "law book" found under Josiah. That the law found under Josiah should already have been in operation under Amasiah is of course an inconsistency on the part of the author. It shows how little weight can be attached to his own view of the facts.

Whatever the historical relation between Deuteronomy and the reform of Josiah, the law is an independent expression of the greatest importance of the reform movement. It denotes its climax, because it demands the extermination of everything that conflicts with the recognition of Yahweh as the only God, and especially of all worship other than that offered to him on Zion. In this respect it became decisive for post-exilic times, and its whole spirit led directly to Judaism.

The increasing importance which the royal temple of Jerusalem acquired down through the ages as the dwelling-place of Yahweh, made the blow all the more painful, when it was destroyed by the hand of an enemy. Nebuchadrezzar twice captured the city, in 597 and 586 or thereabouts, and each time sacked the temple. On both occasions he deported large numbers of the citizens, among them the greater part of the priests; on the last occasion the temple was burnt down and the monarchy abolished (2 Kings 24,10 ff.; 25). Some years later some more citizens were deported to Babylonia (Jer. 52,30). Thus Judæan communities arose in the East. They were placed in certain towns, such as Tel Abib, Tel Melah, Tel Harsha (Ez. 3,15; Ezr. 2,59), but they also lived in the large Babylonian cities and took part in the business life there. It was not the first time Israelite colonies had grown up abroad. In the time of Ahab, in the 9th century, there were Israelite quarters in Damascus (1 Kings 20,34); and in the 8th century, after the fall of Samaria, Israelites were settled in northern Mesopotamia (2 Kings 17,6). In 701 Sennacherib, according to his own account, carried a band of Judæans eastward. In Upper Egypt we know the 5th century Jewish military colony from the Elephantine papyri, but doubtless there have been Israelite communities in Egypt much earlier; many fled to this country after the fall of Jerusalem (Jer. 41,17; 43,7; 44,1, cf. Isa. 19,18 ff.).[1] Like the Phoenician colonies the Israelitish ones probably kept up the connection with Canaan, though we know nothing about any regular form of communication. Jehoiakim could have a prophet, Uriah, fetched from Egypt to be put to death because he had spoken against the temple. The Jewish colony at Elephantine appealed to Jerusalem when it was in distress, and Jeremiah and Ezekiel testify to the communication kept up between the recently deported and those who were left. In foreign countries strangers lived as clients, still belonging to their own community. But when the kingdom and the temple had fallen, the people had lost the centre round which it was to rally. Yahweh on Mount Zion had no temple, while the other sanctuaries prospered.

The moods engendered by this misfortune are recorded in *Lamentations,* which is doubtless based on personal experience. The lament centres entirely round Zion, which stands desolate, deprived of its bands of pilgrims, bereft of its people. In the days of disaster they suffered the pangs of famine, women devoured their children (Lam. 1,11.19; 2,11 f. 20; 4,5.10). Priests and elders perished, no one helped (1,19), palaces and fortresses were destroyed (2,2.5.8 f.). But the deepest anguish is felt at the desecration of the temple. Strangers invaded it, the enemy murdered priests and prophets and made a noise in the sanctuary as of a cult assembly (1,10; 2,7.20.22). Feasts and sabbaths had ceased, the king and the priests had been cast out, the altars and the sanctuary had been desecrated (2,6-7). The king, Yahweh's anointed, who had been as the breath of the people's nostrils and in whose shadow they were to take their place among the nations, is now caught in the net (4,20). He sat with his chiefs among strangers, where no prophets came with words from Yahweh, and where it was not possible to live according to the *tōrā* of Yahweh (2,9). Thus the life of the people came abruptly to an end.

The poet admits that the disaster had been caused by the sins of the people which surpassed even those of Sodom (3,42; 4,6). The sons reap the fruits of the sins of the fathers (5,7). With dislike he remembers the prophets whose visions were vain and shallow (2,14). Prophets and priests actually shed innocent blood, hence they have been smitten (4,13 f. 16). He is in no doubt that Yahweh has caused their downfall.

The poet regards the relation of Yahweh to Zion and Israel in the same light as the prophets of doom. That the disaster is a defeat inflicted on Yahweh, does not enter his mind. Yahweh himself invited the enemy to the feast of the grape-gathering in Judah, and himself trod the press (1,12-15.17). It was he who raged like an enemy against Jacob, who destroyed the city and gave up to destruction his sanctuary with its cult (2,1-8.17.20; 3,1 ff.; 4,11).

With all these things Jeremiah had threatened the Israelites, and yet he was in no doubt that Yahweh dwelled in the temple of Zion. The poet has exactly the same ideas. Yahweh has forgotten his foot-stool (2,1). Mount Zion has been destroyed, and yet Yahweh sits forever on his throne. His association with Zion is not broken, therefore he must bring back his people (5,18-21), i. e. back to Zion, or he will break the bond uniting him with it (v. 22). Here again as in the prophets there is a germ of hope. Yahweh remains forever the God of Israel, and even if this means that he is the mighty upholder of Israelite righteousness, who chastises the evil and adulterous people, yet it unites him with Israel by an indissoluble bond. Yahweh is just, therefore he has punished the defiant people (1,18); but he also wishes men to trust in him, then he will help them. In its distress the people has been given another possibility of exciting the pity of Yahweh. The more Israel is defeated, the greater is the prospect that Yahweh will intervene to rescue her. He does not mean to let her perish entirely, she acquires a new right through excessive suffering, a claim to be helped. Thus Israel can appeal to Yahweh both in the guise of the great God who takes pity on his children and in the character of the mighty guardian of justice, who procures for the wronged their rights.

Therefore the poet calls for the help of Yahweh, pointing to the pitiable condition of the people (1,11.20; 2,18 ff.), because strangers have taken their inheritance (5,1 f.). He constantly varies his main theme, Yahweh decides what is to happen. Therefore the people must humble itself, give its cheek to him who smites it, and sit alone waiting for Yahweh's pity (3,28 ff.). And the wickedness of the enemy is to be kept before Yahweh so as to provoke his revenge (1,22; 3,59 ff.).

The fall of Jerusalem was no great external event, for its political authority did not reach far. But the monarchy and the royal temple formed the ideal foundation of the culture founded by David, its fall meant the end of this cultural period. And yet it did not perish utterly, for David had already, by his conception of Yahweh, detached the God from the cult, and thus from the cult place, and this conception may ever after be traced in the prophets. By virtue of it Lamentations can regard the destruction of the temple as a thing that does not offend Yahweh or affect his nature, but rather as an event that serves to glorify him. And in the appeal to Yahweh's pity and in his raising of those who take refuge with him we meet with a view of the relation to Yahweh which was current in Israel from the time of David.

In Canaan life continued in the normal way, apart from Jerusalem. Whether worship took place in the royal temple during the exile we do not know. Some priests were left behind (Lam. 1,4), and at any rate during the first period people still made offerings there (Jer. 41,4 ff.). Outside the capital the cult was carried on as usual. This was the case under Zedekiah, as testified by

Ezekiel, and there was no reason to interrupt it. The reformers' party had been weakened, therefore life went on with a more or less peaceful cooperation between Israelites and foreigners who came in from Edom ,Moab, and other adjacent territories, or who had been brought from the east by the Assyrians when they captured Samaria. This can be inferred from conditions in the period of the return.

For colonies of foreigners it was natural to maintain the cult of their own God, and also to carry on a certain cult of the gods to whose country they had been admitted, as for instance the Egyptians did at Bethshean. Indeed we know from Jeremiah that the Israelites in Egypt sacrificed to "other gods" (Jer. 44,8); at Elephantine the Jews had a temple to Yahweh, and they also worshipped some few other gods, probably Canaanite. Of a cult of Egyptian gods we hear nothing, but oaths are taken by them in court. [1] A prophecy that Egypt shall one day worship Yahweh with an altar in the middle of the country (Isa. 19,18-22) means that the Israelites shall be the leaders in the country, not tolerated clients.

Those who were deported to Babylonia in 597 had expectations, excited by prophets and soothsayers, of soon being able to return. But Jeremiah said that it would take a generation, 70 years, and exhorted them to make a normal life for themselves among the strangers, whose peace was their peace (Jer. 29,1-14, cf. 25,11). It was the rule for the future life of the Jews: to associate with the strangers in the hope of returning one day to Canaan, the home of true Jewish life. It became of decisive importance for the future that the dislike of foreign elements had grown so strong before the exile, the type had been fixed, and the priests from the temple of Jerusalem who were learned in the law were the leaders who saw to it that it was preserved. The most vigorous representative of it was Ezekiel.

The speeches of *Ezekiel*, which like those of Jeremiah have hardly all come down to us in their original form, [2] show us the ideas of the critical prophets in a new shape. Some of them date from the time between the two captures of the city. He was then staying in northern Mesopotamia, but still kept up a connection with Jerusalem, which always filled his thoughts, and the final downfall of which was reported to him by fugitives (33,21). In a series of visions the prophet sees Jerusalem fall in the midst of her sins, her contempt of Yahweh's law, and the pollution of his sanctuary (Ez. 4-5). He utters the well-known accusations against the bamahs and against the foreign cults of Jerusalem; but this does not include all, Jerusalem is utterly depraved. She has committed blood-guilt and worships false gods (15 f.; 22,1-4), but to this must be added contempt of parents; cruelty to the weak, gērim, orphans and widows; breaking of the sabbath; meals in the high places and whoredom, adultery, bribery and injustice (22,7 ff.), all as in the earlier prophets. Priests break the law and desecrate what is holy; the rulers are ravenous wolves; the prophets divine falsehood and "daub with whitewash", the kings shed blood and the common people practise oppression when they can (22,6.26 ff.).

This conception of Jerusalem and the people is expanded into an historical vision. Jerusalem is called the daughter of an Amorite father and a Hittite mother, an utterance more profoundly true than Ezekiel could know (16,3.45). It is described how she grew up, Yahweh made a covenant with her and gave her all loveliness. But she became a harlot and committed whoredom in the high places with all strangers who came to her, Egyptians, Assyrians, and Chaldæans. She made images of men, decked them with gaily coloured garments and sacrificed oil, incense, and bread to them, nay, even her own children (16,15 ff.). At every street corner and in every market place she built high places for worship (16,23-25), a picture which accords with Jeremiah's descriptions of Jerusalem. With bitter irony we are told that Jerusalem did not receive a harlot's hire of her lovers, but had to pay them herself (16,33 f.). Sodom and Samaria, her sisters, were less guilty (16, 48 ff.). The punishment is unavoidable, but finally we are told of a renewal of the covenant by which the two sisters are to be adopted as daughters. Jerusalem and Samaria are also on another occasion set side by side as sisters, Oholah and Oholibah, who were first violated in Egypt and since then have constantly sought lovers, so they shall suffer the same doom (Ez. 23).

It is the parable expressing the relation to Yahweh known from the time of Hosea, which recurs here. There is still a reference to the sexual cults, but with a new shade of meaning, originating from the changed historical outlook. The foreign lovers are no longer the Canaanite gods but the surrounding great powers into whose political game Israel had entered. The contrast to Yahweh is no longer the Canaanite Baalim with whom He is fighting for supremacy in the soul of the Israelite, but all foreign gods, who are merely impotent blocks of stone or wood.

It is this mighty Yahweh who has chosen Israel, but they have constantly rebelled against him. This is described in a special speech which passes in review the history of the people. It began in Egypt where Yahweh revealed himself to his people and swore to lead them to a land that flowed with milk and honey, if only they did not pollute themselves with the abominations of Egypt (*shikkūṣ*). But they did not care. For the sake of his name, however, he took them into the wilderness and gave them his life-giving laws and sabbaths, but they defied them. Then Yahweh swore to disperse them among the nations, and he was slow in taking them to the promised land, and gave them bad laws. Yet for the sake of his name he led them into the land, and they built high places for sacrifice. And they defiled themselves with whoredom, and abominations, and the offering of children. Israel would be like the nations and worship wood and stones. But, we are finally told, Yahweh will take the Israelites from Babylonia and Egypt into the adjoining deserts. There he will judge them and purge out the recalcitrant from among them. Then Israel shall no longer offer sacrifice to idols, but serve him with worship on his holy mount (Ez. 20).

Thus we meet again the old prophetic ideas but in the form they must take during the exile. Yahweh rises as the unique god among all gods, and Israel has been chosen to be his people, but she is always refractory and follows her own heart. Therefore Ezekiel, in the period before the final downfall of Jerusalem, had

continually to announce what was to come in many strange similes
(Ez. 4-5; 7; 12; 15; 21; 24). Notably King Zedekiah's defeat is
prophesied (Ez. 17). A single speech is of special interest. The
prophet sees in his vision how Yahweh orders all the depraved
inhabitants of the city to be slaughtered, but first a man is sent
out in linen clothes to "set a mark on the foreheads of those men
who sigh and complain of all the abominations done in it" (9,4),
in order that they may be spared. Here it is clearly stated that
there was a party in the town which regarded the foreign customs
in the same light as the prophets. And in the book of Ezekiel we
find several passages expressing that justice shall be done to
every one individually (Chap. 18). Yet a number of the depraved
shall save their lives and be carried into exile, in order that they
who are already there may see their conduct, and recognise that
Yahweh did well in destroying the others (14,12-23).

There are other statements about the relations between the
community in Jerusalem and the exiles. The leading men at
Jerusalem say that Jerusalem is the caldron and they are the
flesh in it (11,3). The exiles "are far from Yahweh, and unto us
is this land given in possession" (11,15). But the prophet says
that these leaders are to perish, whereas the exiles are to return
and be given a new heart, and exterminate all the abominations.
This utterance, which is shaped according to the events in 586
(11,11,cf. 2 Kings 25,6 f. 21), shows that the exiles are regarded
as Israel proper, from which regeneration is to come. After the
fall of Jerusalem a similar note is struck. Those who are living
among the ruins say that the land is theirs, but they are unworthy
of it. For they eat blood, worship idols, commit violence, and
adulteration, therefore they shall all perish (33,23-29). But the
exiles are not all of them righteous either. Among them, too,
there are many who set up idols in their hearts, and Yahweh will
not answer them when they appeal to the prophet (14,1-11, cf.
20,1 ff.); they sacrifice to foreign gods (20,39).

The exiles have been cast out precisely as a punishment for
their sins. But since their humiliation among the nations is a
desecration of Yahweh's holy name, he will again turn their fate.
He will remove their uncleanness and change their stone hearts

38*

into human hearts, and then the people shall be restored (36-39), Israel and Judah shall again be united under David (37,15-28, cf. Chap. 34), and by a mighty judgment Yahweh shall conquer all the foes that rise up against him and his people (38-39), and thus exercise the power that was created for him by the royal cult at Jerusalem. In the book of Ezekiel there follows a draft of a law for the temple and the life gathering round it, based on the surviving traditions.

Comparing Ezekiel with the earlier prophets we find that the same ideas recur, but in a sharper form. The conflict in the midst of which they were was history to him, and the disaster they predicted was his daily life. Thus to Ezekiel the events must be as a confirmation of that view of Israel and Yahweh which he shared with his predecessors. Israel has not fulfilled the righteousness that Yahweh demanded, her whole history is a chain of sins, and the sins may be gathered under one head: disobedience, rebellion against Yahweh. The prophet is firmly convinced that Yahweh directs the events, and precisely because of the people's character the destruction of the temple and Jerusalem does not become offensive to Yahweh, but on the contrary a triumph for him. It is Yahweh himself who calls in the most cruel and depraved of the foreign peoples that they may desecrate the temple, his treasure (7,21 f.). When the people is humiliated and scattered, it is to learn that "I am Yahweh" (6,7; 7,4; 12,15 f.; 33,29), for it is Yahweh's outraged honour which asserts itself through the punishment (16,42; 21,1-12). And yet Zion is still the seat of Yahweh, the temple is his hoarded treasure. But he prevented its destruction becoming offensive to himself by turning away his face (7,22). Yahweh's honour (kābhōdh), which dwelled in the temple, left it before the destruction. First it went to the threshold of the temple, then it was carried away, dwelling as usual above the cherubim, who had now become beings that moved of themselves, and it took up its abode outside the gates of the city, on the mountain east of the city (9,3; 10,4.18 f.; 11,22 f.). Thus the difficulty which might arise from Yahweh's temple being destroyed was solved by Ezekiel.

Yahweh, then, passed over the destruction of his temple as one who celebrates a triumph. But this did not mean that Yahweh was no longer the God of Zion, quite the contrary. It is implied in the whole account that the temple is Yahweh's temple, and that he leaves it to dwell in the vicinity for a time. We cannot decide whether any fact underlies the idea that Yahweh took up his abode on the mount of olives, or whether it is only an idea the prophet falls back upon. At any rate we do not meet with it again.

The higher Yahweh was raised above his own sanctuary and his own people, the more did the people become a sinful mob. In the eyes of the early prophets Israel had abandoned her ancient God, she ought to return to him and he would again be her god. The gulf which the earlier prophets had set between the people and the God had been deepened so much by Ezekiel that he presents the relation between them as something purely accidental, and even as the result of an unfortunate choice on the part of Yahweh. The history of Israel is one great sin.

In one of his accounts of the history of the sinful people it is clearly said that Yahweh's relation to Israel is due to the fact that he chose her and revealed himself to her in Egypt, promising by an oath to lead her to Canaan (20,5 f.). If Yahweh did not again repudiate her, though she would not give up the gods of Egypt, it was exclusively for the sake of his own name, because the other peoples had seen that he had revealed himself to Israel (20,9) and he would then be dishonoured if he did not keep his promise. Thus the whole history of Israel is a chain of rebellions on the part of the people, and of undeserved help on the part of Yahweh. But this is exclusively due to his care for his name, his honour, because he has once for all associated Israel with himself, yet he has also given her bad laws such as those relating to the offering of children, that she might not live (20,25 f.). For the same reason Yahweh will now again take charge of the people. For the sake of his name he will regenerate them (20,44). This is explained more fully to mean that the dispersion and humiliation of Israel offends Yahweh's holy name, for people say: These are Yahweh's people, and they are gone forth out of his land (36,20). He will avenge this offence by regenerating and restoring the people.

The old prophetic demand for a repudiation of the foreign

element recurs in Ezekiel in a new and stricter form, the exclusion of it becoming identical with the fulfilment of the demand for holiness made on them who desire to belong to Yahweh. The other side of this demand is the strong feeling of the sinfulness of the people which dominates the book of Ezekiel. And this feeling is again connected with the circumstance that Yahweh is raised so high above the people that the bond between them seems on the point of breaking. But every time the tie is about to break, the breach proves impossible.

It is true that Yahweh is the God of Heaven and Earth, to whom other gods are as nothing. But in nature he is still Israelite. Ezekiel comes near to inferring that Yahweh's law is quite arbitrary, but apart from a few exceptions he does not go so far. The laws are demands according with the holiness of Yahweh. But if Yahweh's demand for holiness is Israelite law, then he cannot be severed from Israel, only Israel can be his people entirely. This means that Yahweh's exaltation high above men and all other gods is an expression of the fact that the Israelite soul at its highest eminence is the greatest and strongest thing in the world. Mankind, and not least the Israelites are humiliated; but in Yahweh Israel embodies all her strength and all her ideality and realises for them a remarkable personal form.

Ezekiel gives us the most clear-cut picture of the harrowing character of Israelite history. The people was so divided that what was life to one was death in the eyes of another. And what was un-Israelitish to Ezekiel and those of his mind had, nevertheless, penetrated so deeply into the hearts of the people that even Ezekiel admitted that it had become the law of Yahweh. Much of what we read in the book of Ezekiel is the opinions of an individual mind, but in the main the book is typical, for it develops the ideas of the monarchical period in the shape they were bound to take in the exile. In Ezekiel we see a new Israel take shape as a self-contained community. In order to assert themselves in their exile the Israelites ardently maintained their psychic characteristics which found expression in the law of Yahweh. An imitation of the cult at Jerusalem was excluded, so the people must live in hopes of its restoration, at the same time maintaining the traditions which could be observed outside the temple. And the greatness of Yahweh was to be maintained under all circumstances.

Whenever the early prophets mentioned Yahweh's relation to foreign gods, Yahweh was the strong God as against the weak. But when Yahweh's position as a ruler and the creator of heaven and earth became a claim to be maintained with all its consequences, this meant that he alone was in possession of divine qualities. If the exiles had not upheld to the utmost this claim for Yahweh, he would have become reduced to a small people's defeated God. Hence it is not by chance that we find the strongest expressions for Yahweh's power in the two prophets who taught during the greatest humiliation of his people, viz. Ezekiel and *Deutero-Isaiah.*

The Israelites saw how the gods of the foreign nations were worshipped in the form of images. In this they differed from Yahweh, and the prophets of the exile saw in this a difference in principle which actually explained all. The other gods were mere stone and wood, says Ezekiel, and Deutero-Isaiah makes this the starting-point of a violent controversy.

The great part played by this controversy in Deutero-Isaiah shows that the exiles were constantly confronted with the problem of the relation between Yahweh and other gods, and presumably he is contending against vacillation in his own circle. Like the temple hymns and the earlier prophets, he starts from Yahweh's creative activity as evidence of his unique divine power. All the world and its nations are but as a mote to him. Over against him are the other gods who are made of wood and covered with gold. With ironical circumstantiality he describes how such a god comes into existence. The tree grows up, is felled, and worked by various master craftsmen, part of the wood is burnt, people bake bread and warm themselves at its fire, and another part of the wood is made into a god to whom they kneel down (Isa. 40,12 ff.; 41,7; 44,9-20; 45,20; 46,1 f. 5-8). These are the gods they mention in the same breath with Yahweh.

The whole body of speeches by Deutero-Isaiah are intended to proclaim that Yahweh will now assert himself and gain renown all over the earth by restoring his people, who are again to gather round Jerusalem. It is Yahweh, not the idols, who has decreed this and predicted it through his prophets. The speeches of Deutero-Isaiah are another testimony to the way in which the prophets of Israel interpret the course of events to the honour of Yahweh. Kyros had started on his victorious career, and the fall of Babel was imminent. Yahwistic prophets in Babylonia evidently saw the importance of his expedition and prophesied his victories. Now the prophet says that Kyros is an instrument in the hand of Yahweh, who directs the events of history. Kyros shall conquer Babylon, and he shall set free the Israelites, who are to go to Jerusalem and once more lay the foundations of Israelite national life.

The prophet proves that this is so by referring to earlier prophetic utterances from Yahweh, and thus the display of power with which Yahweh intends to surround his name becomes at the same time a proof that he alone has divine power as the ruler of the course of history. With great assurance the foreign gods are challenged to bring forward proofs that they have taken an active part in the events, so that they can claim recognition as gods. But they have nothing to show. The predictions have come from Yahweh, it is he who has called Kyros, just as in primeval ages he raised up the generations (Isa. 41; 43,8-13; 44,6-8; 48, 3 ff.). Thus the prophetic utterances are to Deutero-Isaiah just as real utterances from God as they were to the early prophets.

Just like the other prophets Deutero-Isaiah regards the exile as a punishment for the sins of the people imposed by Yahweh because they did not keep his law (42,24 f.; 43,27 f.; 47,6; 50,1 f.). But the sin has now been doubly paid for (40,2), and the prophet paints with impressive rhetoric how Babylon shall fall, and the liberated people return to the expectant Zion. It is Yahweh who wipes out the sins and brings home the people, the people itself has made no effort, during the exile it has not tried to win Yahweh's favour by offerings (43,22-44,5); for the sake of his name and his honour Yahweh will restore his people (48,9.11;

52,5 f.). The people that bears Yahweh's law in its heart shall be renewed, they that revile the subjugated people shall perish like garments eaten by moths, but Yahweh's righteousness, which is displayed in his assertion of himself, shall persist forever (51,7 f.).

The view taken by the prophet of the victories of Kyros is of great interest. It is an ancient prophetic notion that the victorious great powers were instruments in the hand of Yahweh to punish his apostate people. But now there appears a rising ruler of the world, who is said to be merely an instrument for the reunion of the small Israelite people, and the glory of its mighty God. Kyros is Yahweh's shepherd (44,28), the ancient oriental designation for kings, and it is Yahweh's purpose that he is carrying out. It is Yahweh who takes him by the hand and allows him to conquer countries and capture their treasures, all for the sake of his servant Israel (45,1 ff.). He is the bird of prey from the East, called hither to fulfil Yahweh's counsel (46,11). Kyros himself does not know Yahweh (45,4), and yet he is Yahweh's friend who performs his pleasure. Yahweh alone has called him and given him victory (48,14 f.). For Yahweh is the sole creator of everything, there is no God beside him (45,5 f. 14.21 f.; 46,9 et al.).

The prophet never wearies of describing the glory which Yahweh purposes to give to his people. Eternal salvation awaits it (45,17), it shall enjoy righteousness and honour, and it shall rejoice at Yahweh's victories (45,25; 46, 13 et al.). When it listens to the commands of Yahweh, peace and happiness shall flourish (48,18 f.). The whole people shall be restored under the rule of Yahweh, Jerusalem shall arise in a new and glorious shape (49,8-50,3; 51,1 f.). The return shall be a triumphal procession, led by Yahweh, while other nations look on in wonder (52,11 f.).

The prophet is carried away by his anticipation of the greatness of the events, his eloquence rises to the highest pitch. What is going to happen is in the strictest sense world events, because the fate of Israel is involved in them; the prophet expects to see in them the realisation of the great works with which the cult in the royal temple of Jerusalem was concerned. When Yahweh leads home his people, it is a recurrence of that struggle with the dragon in which he vanquished Chaos, the fight which was repeated when he led his people up out of Egypt (51,9 f., cf. 43, 16 f.; 52,4). Then it shall be spoken to Zion as at the royal temple feast: Thy God hath taken over the kingship (52,7). The exile was a time of deluge as in the days of Noah when Chaos ruled, now the oath of those days shall be restored (54,9). The primordial events shall not only be experienced again, they shall be thrown entirely into the shade, when Yahweh intervenes and transforms the desert to fertile land in order to regenerate his people (43,18 f.).

It will appear from the speeches of Deutero-Isaiah that Canaan and Jerusalem seem much remoter to him than they were to Ezekiel. Jerusalem is glimpsed in the distance as the ideal home-land of the Jews, but we receive no impression of its being po-pulated, the population is in exile, mostly in Babylonia, while their native land is merely a land of ruins. There are few con-crete features, the temple is not mentioned; on the other hand, the restoration of the monarchy is referred to, but not in direct terms. Yahweh will make an everlasting covenant for the people, the sure mercies of David (55,3), he who was a chief of nations (v. 4). This can only mean that the Davidic monarchy shall be revived, and in virtue hereof Israel shall exercise world power, extending to peoples she does not know (v. 5).

Thus the small subjugated Israelite people becomes the centre of the nations. In the last parts of the book of Isaiah, of which Deutero-Isaiah is hardly the author, [1] though they bear the im-press of his ideas, this is given the form that Jerusalem is sought by her children from all countries, the treasures of the earth are brought to her, strangers toil for her, kings must serve her, the splendours of Lebanon ornament her temple (60; 61-62; 66), while her enemies are trampled down by Yahweh on the day of retribution (63,1-6). But this power, which makes Israel the centre of the world, is based on an ideal strength. Righteousness and peace, the two poles in the fundamental values of Israel, dominate Zion; in virtue of them Yahweh becomes the light of

Israel and gives the power to it as his holy people (60,17 ff.; 61, 3.8 ff.; 62,12). These are ancient ideas known from the prophets and the cult hymns, and they are given direct expression in other bodies of prophetic utterances (Isa. 2,2-5; Mic. 4,1-5); yet they contain a new shade of meaning.

Now that the monarchy did not exist any more with the temple as an actual centre uniting the whole of Israel with Canaan, it acquired a purely ideal existence, and the same applied to a certain extent to Israel. At the same time as she was uprooted from her own soil, her law was raised above her and acquired an independent value. The consequence was that, in spite of the isolation of Israel, strangers could associate themselves with her by subjecting themselves to her law. This is expressly mentioned. The stranger who wishes to associate himself with Yahweh shall not be excluded from His people. If the stranger is willing to keep the sabbath and the rest of the covenant, he is to be admitted to the temple, which should, if possible, become a house of prayer to all nations (Isa. 56,3.6-8). The gēr of the old days joined the community in order to share in its benefits. Now a gēr becomes a proselyte, drawn to the congregation by its law.

To Deutero-Isaiah life in Canaan with its struggles centring around the Canaanite cults had receded into the distance. The people had sinned, but they had paid for it. What preoccupied his mind was the position of Israel among other peoples; she was lowly and held in contempt, and yet she was the people of the only God, upholder of his law; she was the people of suffering but no longer of sin. Between the descriptions of the future power for Israel and her mishpāṭ are inserted a number of poems about Yahweh's servant, who performs Israel's task among the nations, as the upholder of the true law (Isa. 42,1-7; 49,1-7; 50,4-11; 52,13-53,12). Deutero-Isaiah often mentions Israel as the servant of Yahweh, a characteristic expression of his conception of the position of the people as Yahweh's instrument and witness (41,8 f.; 42,19; 43,10; 44,1; 45,4; 48,20). In the poems we seem to see the servant in varying forms, because the poet regards him as the embodiment of the Israelite ideal.

Yahweh has called his servant to establish his mishpāṭ and

law on earth, and diffuse it among the peoples, who are looking forward to it; and he fulfils the task of winning non-Israelites for the law of Israel with quiet meekness. In this way he becomes a light to these peoples, the upholder of a great covenant (42,6). Thus Yahweh speaks of the servant. And the servant himself describes in a poem (49,1-7) how Yahweh called him, Israel, to be his servant, who was to plead his cause with a ready tongue. First his mission was to be that of regenerating Israel, but now he, the despised one, has been given the task of being a light to the nations of the world, that all the kings may rise before him, and the chieftains prostrate themselves before him (49,7). He only acts because he relies on Yahweh's help (49,4; 50,7 ff.); from him he daily receives instructions, trusting in him he endures scorn and stripes, for he knows that the enemies shall be consumed like moths; they who "kindle a fire" shall be marked by Yahweh's hand (50,11).

The climax is reached in the last poem, which gives an account of the sufferings of the servant. It begins with Yahweh's utterance that the servant shall have his rights and be raised up after suffering his greatest humiliation. The description of the latter is given by witnesses, who saw him as a despised outcast, tormented by pain, till he was led to the disgraceful death of a criminal. But Yahweh wished him to suffer, for if he gave his soul, he should live long and have offspring by which Yahweh's will should be fulfilled. And those who describe his woes acknowledge that he suffered the pains they should all have suffered, for he had to bear their sins (53,4-6.12).

The description is extremely personal. It is of a man who is suffering, just as an earlier poem describes how he is spat upon and has his beard pulled out (50,6). It is Israel embodied in a person who endures the fate of Israel, with the sufferings of the weak, and yet realises the true law given by the only God. The prophet, in this account, surely had actual examples in view, men in whose life and fate he saw a typical realisation of the nature of the true Israel, as it appeared among the peoples. And just as the description has been most personal, we see that it does not apply to a single chance individual. The wretch dies and is buried, and yet the servant shall for that very reason live on in renewed strength. The true Israel perishes in those who embody her, but is awakened by their death to new life. This is a new idea in Israel, but it was the natural concomitant of Deutero-Isaiah's view of the people as formed through the experience of the exile. The servant was Israel, who yet had a task among the Israelites and the strangers. Hence it is difficult to say whether it is the Israelites or the other nations that appear (in Chap. 53) as witnesses to his fate and acknowledge that he suffered it for them. The words of the poems about the servant fit so naturally into Deutero-Isaiah's view of Israel that the question as to whether they are from his hand is only of a purely formal literary interest. [1]

Ezekiel and Deutero-Isaiah, who lived each at an extreme limit of the exile, show us how this came to form the foundation of a new Israelitish life. The exiles had been uprooted from their own soil, but in order to preserve themselves they had to try to keep up the tradition, and this was entirely determined by Jerusalem and its temple. Thus their life acquired a certain unreal character, the law survived without its natural background, as the manifestation of Yahweh's will. The exalted position of Yahweh made it possible for the old order of things to persist as an idea, his will was not determined by the events of the earth. But Canaan was still his country, the temple of Jerusalem the ideal centre of the world, and Israel was his people. She was to work in the world among the peoples for his will, that is to say, for his law, and for the sake of his honour he must again bring his people back to its home and his temple. A new Israel developed as a result of the exile, an isolated community, elected from Jerusalem. Its God was the only God; thus it was raised to a higher sphere as an intermediary between God and man; all the nations shall be taught by it. With this background we understand both the idea that Canaan, the land of Yahweh and his people, shall become the goal of all nations, and also the idea that all foreign peoples shall be expelled from Canaan, because their nature is in conflict with the spirit of Yahweh. Thus ideas embodied in the reform movements of the monarchical period matured in the Jewish community in Babylonia.

———————

The Babylonian Jews shaped the type that became determining for the future. It was implied in their ideas that they must strive to re-establish the old centre. The first attempt was made when Kyros had conquered Babylon (538) and permitted their emigration. There was, however, no enthusiasm among the Israelites of Canaan. They could do without the temple at Jerusalem, but Haggai proclaimed (520) that poverty and bad harvests should cease when it was built. When the foundation stone had been laid, the same prophet talked of the riches that were to be collected in it, and he proclaimed that blessedness would soon spread (Hag. 2,1-9,15-19, cf. Zech. 8).

A re-establishment of the monarchy was impossible, but the Persians had generously made Zerubbabel, a descendant of David, governor of Judah; and with the high priest Joshua he laid the foundation of the temple and finished it (Hag. 1,1.12 ff.; 2,2 ff.; Zech. 4,6 ff.). The prophets saw in him the man who was again to realise the monarchy, which had survived as an ideal, with its demand for world-wide dominion. Empires shall fall and thrones be overthrown while heaven and earth shake, says Haggai, when Yahweh makes Zerubbabel a signet (Hag. 2,20-23). Zechariah says that when Yahweh again takes up his abode on Zion, Israel shall be served by the peoples for which she is now toiling, and many nations shall join Yahweh (Zech. 2,13-15). We know both ideas from Deutero-Isaiah; and in cryptic words Zerubbabel is mentioned as the person who builds Yahweh's temple and occupies the throne with honour, while Joshua stands at his side as high priest (Zech. 3,8; 6,9-15). This of course did not come to pass, and the temple cult had to be carried on without the king.

The belief that conditions from the monarchical period were to be revived in an idealised form found little foothold in events. People asked how it was that succour did not come, and received the old answer that it was due to their sins (Isa. 59); they

anxiously enquired what was the right conduct, and were given
the reply that right fasting consisted in helping the weak and
thus preserving the community (Isa. 58, cf. Zech. 7). We still
hear of foreign cults of a sexual character on hills and under
green trees (Isa. 57,5 ff.), of strange mystery cults and sacrificial
meals to the gods of fate (65,3 f. 11; 66,17). Gradually there are
also complaints that the priests neglect the cult at Jerusalem;
the people do not pay tithes and they marry foreign women
(Mal. 1-3). Thus Israel in Canaan is again about to lose its
special character during the intercourse with the strangers. But
the exiles in Babylonia, now Persian, demanded that this special
character should be maintained and fixed with the temple as a
centre, that thus they might have a centre. Therefore the old
reform movement was continued in a new and more practical
form by the exiles, through Ezra and Nehemiah.

Ezra probably occupied a leading position in the Jewish
community of the Persian empire, and Nehemiah a position of
trust as cupbearer at the Persian court, which shows that their
isolation did not prevent the Jews from taking part in the life
of the foreigners. The two men were hardly active at the same
time at Jerusalem, but whether Ezra came before or after
Nehemiah is difficult to decide, though the arguments for Ezra
coming after Nehemiah seem the strongest. [1] When Nehemiah
came to Jerusalem with the authority of a governor (Neh. 5,14),
Sanballat, the governor of Samaria, was the leading man. By
his side were the Ammonite Tobiah and the Arab Geshem (Neh.
2,10.19; 3,33 ff.; 4,1; 6,1 ff.), and these representatives of neighbouring peoples lived on friendly terms with the Judæans, who
married Ammonite, Moabite, and Ashdodite women whose
language their children learnt (13,23 ff.). One of the sons of
the high priest had married a daughter of Sanballat (13,28);
Tobiah was related to the priest Eliashib and had a cell in the
temple court (13,4 ff.); he was the friend of leading Judæans
(6,17 ff.). There was distress in the Judæan community, but the
wealthy Judæans, in part priests, only supplied the poor with
corn on being given securities on their property, and after taking
their children as slaves (5,1 ff.). The Judæans did not, any more

than before the exile, constitute a compact community, but in the early days they had the monarchy as their fixed centre.

Nehemiah's purpose was to transform the community gathered round the temple in accordance with the form its offshoots in the exile had taken. Against him were the leading foreigners, but so also were the leading Judæans, who had prophets assisting them (6,10 ff. 17 ff). Nevertheless he carried through his plan. The walls of Jerusalem were rebuilt and consecrated and the city populated by a suitable number of Judæans (7,1 ff.; 11,1 f.). He ransomed Judæans from slavery, he gave loans which he remitted, and made the wealthy promise to do the same (5,6-13). He separated the foreigners from the Judæans, saw to it that the sacred dues were paid, and had the gates closed on the sabbath, so as to prevent trading with foreigners; and he reproached and chastised those who had foreign wives, referring, not very logically, to the fact that even Solomon who was beloved by God, took foreign wives (Neh. 13). Nehemiah, whose activities according to the text were interrupted by a visit to the Persian court (13,6), transformed Jerusalem with a firm hand into a city with a closed Jewish community after the ideal of the Babylonian Jews.

When Ezra went to Jerusalem he had authority from the king to lead a caravan in which there were many priests, further to enquire into conditions in Juda and Jerusalem on the basis of the law he had with him (Ezr. 7,11 ff.), also to deliver a temple gift from the king and his council as also from countrymen in the Persian empire, in addition to the offerings he was going to make himself. Everything was to be performed according to the commands of "the God of heaven" in his temple at Jerusalem, that disaster might not befall the king; and Ezra was to appoint judges to administer justice according to the law of his God. We may take it for granted that this law was the same that was recognised among Babylonian Jews, and his authority then means that Ezra was allowed to carry out reforms in Jerusalem in accordance with the law and custom of the exiles. But it also means that the great king acknowledged the God of the Jews to be the God of heaven, whose cult was of importance for him and his dynasty. In the same way Kyros had maintained the cult of Marduk, and the authority given by the King of the Persians does not mean that he defers to Deutero-Isaiah's view of the matter; but we find here the beginning of a conception of the gods of the individual peoples which came to prevail in the Hellenistic period.

The story of Ezra which we owe to the Chronicler but which is partly based on Ezra's own reminiscences, is not coherent, and does not give us any clear picture of the whole. Mention is continually made of "the exiles" *(hag-gōlā)*, as if only Jews who had returned from the East were regarded as constituting the true Israel in Jerusalem (Ezr. 8,35; 9,4; 10,6.7.16, cf. 4,1; 6,19 f.), and yet they had mixed with the population and taken foreign wives; this applied even to leaders and priests (Ezr. 9,1 ff.). This mode of expression is probaby due to the fact that the leaders in the Jewish community were Babylonian Judæans who had gone to Jerusalem and there had followed the general custom. Ezra was appalled at these conditions, and made contrite confession, during which people flocked around him; and a meeting was fixed during which they acknowledged their duty of isolating themselves and putting away their foreign wives. Without any connection with this, and in the middle of the narrative about Nehemiah (Neh. 8-10), we are told that Ezra, upon request, came forward with his law and read it aloud from a high place in an open square, while some Levites interpreted it piece by piece to the people. The leaders, the temple staff, and those who agreed to the isolation, then pledged themselves on Ezra's law. At that time the feast of the tabernacles was celebrated as it had not been celebrated since the days of Joshua (Neh. 8; 10). In this connection (Neh. 9) a detailed confession of sins is reported to have been made by Ezra at a penitential feast on the 24th of the 7th month. The story of Israel is described therein as a continued disobedience on the part of the people, and a chain of benefits on the part of Yahweh.

Ezra's activities went in the same direction as those of Nehemiah and are best understood as a continuation of his fundamental work to transform the community of Jerusalem according to the ideas of the Eastern Jews. The main claim was the recognition of the law of the latter, with the demand for isolation in its forefront. The demand for isolation plays a great part in the laws transmitted to us, as we have seen in the case of Deuteronomy (cf. Ex. 34,11 ff.; Lev. 18,24 f.27 f.; Deut. 7,1-3; 23,4 ff. et al.). Altogether there must of course have been a close agreement between the law book of Ezra and the laws transmitted to us, as will, indeed, appear from the special laws mentioned (Neh. 10). But entire agreement there is not, and we have no reason to believe that the law of Ezra was identical in its formulation with our Mosaic law or any particular part of it. [1]

Nehemiah and Ezra laid the foundation of an isolated Jewish community at Jerusalem. When the distinction between what was Jewish and what was foreign was again becoming vague in the Hellenistic period, it was this which stirred the Maccabees who started the ancient feud against what was foreign. The fight against the Greek element was a continuation of the movements in Canaan, which had been directed against Canaanite, Assyrian, Babylonian, and Persian manners and customs down through the ages. That the campaign was continued in Palestine was due to the community which had been transported to Babylonia from Jerusalem and its environs. The restoration was a necessity to the Babylonian Jews, because Jerusalem with its temple formed the foundation of their ideal world. They made the Jews a separate people, isolated from all others, at the same time as their God was the mighty ruler of all the world. They once again made Jerusalem the centre of Israelitish psychic life, but at the same time they made the law so strong that the temple acquired its chief importance by virtue of it.

It was natural that this spirit should grow up in the exile as a result of the reform movements in the monarchical period. We can trace their roots back to the earliest history of the people, and they continually put forth new shoots down through the ages in types like David and the long series of the prophets of doom.

YAHWEH AND ISRAEL

DURING the changes in the history of Israel the name of the people assumes varying meanings, reflecting their history. First it denoted the union of tribes which had immigrated from the plains and settled in the central and northern parts of Canaan. Thus it is recorded in the Song of Deborah. Judah only acquired importance under David when he united it with the northern tribes; it became part of Israel, and at the same time the most important part, because it possessed the kingdom and the royal temple. Under the division of the kingdom we see the name of Israel used, both about the northern part, as prior to David, and about the whole people, comprising Judah. This usage we know amongst other things from the prophets, but at the same time the latter were preparing a new division of the people. By their excessive assertion of Israelite tradition as against foreign manners, they show a tendency to exclude from the people those who entirely assimilated Canaanite customs. Israel became an ideal, determined entirely by conduct, by the law of Yahweh, and its centre was Jerusalem, because it was Yahweh in Zion that the prophets looked to. Early Israel, the northern tribes, receded into the background, especially after the fall of its monarchy; it was the relation to Yahweh on Zion and his law which was decisive. This view, through the exiles, became the determining one for the future.

Yahweh's history is deeply rooted in the history of the people. We know him as the leading will in the united tribes, as the God who lived in the various places of worship, as the mighty royal ruler in Zion, creator of heaven and earth, as the guardian of Israelite law and tradition. When his people had become reduced to a community of small citizens in a foreign country, he had become so great that he claimed to be leader of all the world, and the God whose law all were to obey. The most apt expression of the relation between Yahweh and Israel is the covenant, *b*^e*rīth*. This denotes the psychic communion and the common purpose which united the people and its God. It is also expressed by saying that the peace of Yahweh reigns in Israel (*shālōm*, Jer. 16,5); therefore the relation between them is characterised by love, the feeling of fellowship among kinsmen. The covenant finds expression in the nature and customs of the people. By observing this *mishpāṭ* Israel maintains the covenant, but a departure from true custom, to which in the first place would belong intercourse with other gods, is a breach of the covenant. Yahweh maintains the covenant by acting as the God of Israel. ¹

This relation between the people and its God finds expression in many ways. Yahweh is the father of Israel, who has begotten or created the people. Israel is his son, the Israelites are his sons. Israel is called his first-born to express its preferential position. Yahweh is the creator of Israel. It can be varied in different ways. Yahweh has planted the people as a proper vine, though later, it is true, it became a wild growth. He has chosen Israel, we are also told, a new way of expressing the fact that it is a privilege for Israel to have him for their God. ² The relation of the owner and the husband we know from the designation Baal. It is also expressed in the statement that Israel is the lot and inheritance of Yahweh, his own people; ³ therefore his yoke is laid upon it, even though generally the people refused to bear it.

Like the related peoples, Israel called their God "Lord" and "King", names the explanation of which is not far to seek. For Yahweh occupied the same position in the covenant as the king in the western Asiatic communities; and the authority of the king was due to the fact that it was rooted in that of the God. Like the king and the chief, Yahweh is a saviour *(mōshī^a^c)* who secures victory and progress to his people. If the people has suffered any injury, it is Yahweh who intervenes as the strong protector and heals the wound. During their bondage in Egypt and during the exile Yahweh was the *gō'ēl* of Israel, he heals it and secures to it redress by vengeance. He is called a rock because his strength and will to uphold the covenant is unshakable. [1]

Yahweh asserts himself in avenging Israel, because they have a covenant with each other. The history of the war shows how the self-realisation of the two parties coincides in earlier times. The Israelites come to the aid of Yahweh, and the wars of Israel are the wars of Yahweh, their enemies his enemies (Judg. 5,23.31; 1 Sam. 18,17; 25,28). Participation in war is a duty for Yahweh and Israel (Num. 32,22). Yahweh gives the warriors strength from the Ark, he or his commander is the leader of the expedition (Josh. 5,13-15); the god-inspired heroes have his soul in them, the holiness of the warriors means that they fight before his countenance (Num. 32, 22.27.32) and that it is he who delivers the enemy into their hands (Num. 21,3; Judg. 7,15), therefore the Israelites are the hosts of Yahweh (Ex. 7,4; 12,41). Both in the old days and in the monarchical period people acquired strength for the fight through the cult; through it Yahweh is active, and he bestows victory. The king says that Yahweh teaches his hands war, fortifies him, so that he forces the enemy to his knees. "Thou givest me my enemies as a neck (i. e. to tread upon)", "thou makest me the head of peoples"; it is the God of his salvation who gives him revenge (Ps. 18,35 ff.). Yahweh is an avenging God, who strikes down the foreign peoples in order to assert himself (Jer. 46,10; 50,28; 51,56).

From the period of conquest and through the monarchical period Yahweh has a very warlike character which set its mark, too, on the account of the wilderness period, when he led the Israelites as an ordered army on the march. He is called a warrior and a war hero (Ex. 15,3; Isa. 42,13; Ps. 24,8), he appears with a large and a small shield, with a spear and a battle axe (Ps. 35,2 f.), or as an archer, who bends his bow and sends out his shafts (Ps. 18,15; Lam. 2,4). He is called "*yahwe 'elōhē ṣebhā'ōth*", a name frequently contracted to "Yahweh of the hosts" *(yahwe ṣebhā'ōth)*, which in the course of time came to be a proper name for Yahweh, and in which his divine power was expressed.

The royal cult on Zion strongly emphasised the war-like character of Yahweh, glorifying him as the ruler who subjugated all. But, as we have seen, the ruling god was also exalted above and isolated from his own people. Thus David's view of the divine activity became the established one and the whole power and action was shifted to the divine sphere. Yahweh's warfare became a perfectly independent activity, independent of the people, nay, even excluding their participation. This view is often implied in stories of how Yahweh fought the wars of Israel in the old days.

In the narrative of Gideon, who first sends home the timorous and then those who drink in the usual way, we find the motive that there should only be few warriors in order that they may not become arrogant and imagine that they have gained the day by their own strength. Yahweh wishes to conquer alone (Judg. 7,1 ff.). The story of the fight with the Amalekites in the wilderness period also gives us an old war story presented in the light of Yahweh's sole power. Joshua is to fight with some few chosen men, but their strength is not the decisive factor. Moses stands on a hill near by with the rod of God in his hand, and when he lifts it Israel is victorious. The victory is won because Aaron and Hur support the arms of Moses (Ex. 17,8-13).

That the rod of Moses possessed a divine power which might become active in a battle quite agrees with the old spirit; but in the form the narrative has been transmitted to us the rod has become a purely arbitrary means for Yahweh to accomplish his intention of completely wiping out the Amalekites (v. 14), exactly as when Yahweh sometimes lets Moses procure water from the rock by his rod, sometimes by a word (Ex. 17,1-7; Num. 20,1-13). In the same way, in the story of the fall of Jericho, we see the Ark act quite alone, without the Israelites fighting.

Isaiah blames his people because they put their trust in fortified walls, while they forget him who created all the world (Isa. 22, 11), an utterance highly reminiscent of the same prophet's admonition to the king only to believe in Yahweh when he went in fear and trembling of the disaster threatening him from his enemies. We perceive in Isaiah's utterances a distinct separation between divine and human activity. Whatever men may try by means of their instruments of war, it is Yahweh who secures victory, independently of these. "Horses are prepared for the day of battle, but victory is with Yahweh", says the Jewish proverb (Prov. 21,31).

In this there is implied not only a strong feeling of the uncertainty of all human activities, but also the conviction that there is a fixed point in the life of Israel, namely Yahweh; if the people can make him side with it, there is no limit to what it can achieve. When the people became powerless, this idea grew and found sharper expressions. Amos' strong stressing of the fact that it was Yahweh who brought Israel out of Egypt, and he who exterminated the Amorites (Am. 2,9 f.), need not mean a depreciation of human activity. But in Hosea we read: I will not save them by bow nor by sword, nor by battle, nor by horses or horsemen (Hos. 1,7), but it is doubtful whether this utterance was shaped thus by Hosea. On the other hand, the idea appears with clarity in Deuteronomy. Here it is said that Israel shall not fear horses, chariots, and a multitude of warriors, for it is Yahweh alone who secures victory, and this shall especially be so at the conquest of the country (Deut. 7,17 ff.; 20,1-4). The same view, that Israel received the country as a gift from Yahweh, "neither by the sword nor by the bow", has also found expression in other writings (Ex. 23,27 ff.; Josh. 23,3.10; 24,12), and in the Psalms we hear that it is fear of Yahweh, not armies and horses, that gains victory for the king (Ps. 33,16-18).

The altered view of Yahweh's action in war is typical of the whole development undergone by his relation to Israel, as we have been able to trace it through the varying times and in the divers circles of Israel. It became deeply imprinted on Yahweh's inmost nature.

———

Like any other soul, the soul of Yahweh has its honour, identical with its content, which fills it, gives it weight, and constitutes the basis of its claims. Yahweh's honour, his *kābhōdh*, is determined by his power and activity. Yahweh himself and his sanctuary are Israel's glory, which she was not to change for any other; when Israel lost Yahweh's Ark, his glory had departed from the people (1 Sam. 4,22, cf. Jer. 2,11; Ps. 106,20). Conversely, the people is Yahweh's glory, because he has created it himself and called it by his name (Isa. 43,7). All his ways, his *mishpāṭ*, constitute his glory, most of all the exploits he performs for the benefit of his people as its mighty king. Other peoples see his deeds and recognise the greatness of his *kābhōdh*, his glory and his name are feared in the east and in the west; his glory is exalted above all nations and above the heavens, because all the fullness of the earth enters into it. [1]

Yahweh has acquired for himself this great glory as the God of his people. But it is due to the circumstance that he has defeated all other gods, and in the end to the circumstance that none other is God. "I am Yahweh, that is my name, and my glory I give not to another" (Isa. 42,8; 48,11). This unique glory Yahweh possesses as the maker of heaven and earth, that which played so great a part in the cult in Zion; therefore the heavens declare his glory, which is raised above all time, for he can forever rejoice in his works (Ps. 19,2; 104,31).

The idea of the divine creation originated from the fundamental idea of holiness and divinity. All life is upheld by the holy strength behind it, but the Israelites see all holiness centring in their great God; he is active in all living things and maintains them; his hand directs the interplay of all souls.

Many testimonies express this view of the relation between the God of Israel and the life of the universe. Job describes how God knows of everything in the world. The inaccessible, mysterious Sheol lies uncovered to him, he keeps the earth suspended above the abyss, he gathers the waters into clouds, and separates light from darkness (Job 26). His glance reaches to the ends of the earth, he weighs the wind and measures out the boundless water, he sets a law for rain and thunder; therefore he alone knows wisdom (Job 28,23-26). He lets thunder and lightning fare forth under the heavens; snow and storm, rain and cold come at his command; the wild beasts remain in their dens at his bidding. He makes the vault of the heavens firm as a mirror; he gathers the clouds and spreads them (Job. 37). In God's powerful speech the greatness of the world is described with its manifold life, the sea with its springs, the earth with its pillars, the heavens with their stars, the animals of the air and the earth; all these are evidence of the greatness of Elohim, because they exist and act as he decrees (Job 38). This agrees with the homage paid to Yahweh in the Psalms. The earth is Yahweh's and the fulness thereof, and all that dwell in it, for he has founded it upon the primeval sea (Ps. 24,1 f.). Heaven and its hosts came forth at his command; he gathers the waters of the ocean as in a leather sack; he lays up the primeval seas in stores (33,6 f.); he establishes the mountains, stills the roaring of the seas and the tumult of the peoples, blesses the land with water, makes the corn shoot, wets the furrows of the plough, blesses the seed, clothes the country with crops and grazing sheep (Ps. 65). The maintenance of life through the blessing is an expression of Yahweh's constant creative activity. He is the great giver to whom all living beings look. One Psalm lets us see Yahweh as the lord of a great estate who generously supplies the wants of every one. He sets boundaries to the waters and establishes the earth; he sends streams in which the wild beasts can quench their thirst; he gives pastures to the cattle and bread to men; bestows wine and oil on them; plants trees for birds; places the wild beasts in the mountains; sets the moon to mark the festivals; regulates darkness and light; looks after animals and men. By his hand they are sated: from the strength of his soul they obtain life; if he hides, they are terrified; if he takes away his spirit, they die (Ps. 104).

Jeremiah describes Yahweh's relation to nature by saying that he has a covenant with day and night and has set laws for heaven and earth (Jer. 33,20.25), a characteristic Israelitish way of expressing the fact that the phenomena of life are in psychic contact with Yahweh, and that he is their lord. It is he who gives rain in the winter, autumn, and spring, all in due season; he watches over the lawful harvest weeks (Jer. 5,24). All the life which the Israelite meets with in nature bears witness to the strength of his God which passes all understanding, for everything is the result of his power. Jeremiah says that the rain is neither due to the gods of other peoples nor to the sky itself, but exclusively to Yahweh (14,22). Nature works neither of itself nor through other gods, but only through Israel's God, and its stupendous order gives the Israelite every reason to fear his might. Therefore there is a close connection between the law of nature and the law of Israel. Nature fails the Israelites if they sin and offend against the law of Yahweh (Jer. 5,23-31).

The identity of the divine force and the force of nature is seen among Israel's neighbouring peoples in their cult, in which the God and all life is normally renewed and regenerated. And this regeneration is described mythically as an action which was performed by the God or Gods in primeval ages from which time flows forth. In Israel too the cult means a regeneration of nature, but we have seen that this point of view combined with another which prevented it from being consistently carried through. Yahweh was outside and above ordinary life, separated from nature, and it was not necessary for him to be radically renewed. Thus the creation in primeval ages does not become the mythical expression of what is annually repeated in the cult, it becomes an event in time, which once took place at its beginning. Herein we find the germ of a change in the old view of time. But by being detached from the cult the creation becomes a dogmatic postulate without any organic connection with reality. It means that what exists has once been established and received its law by the decision of Yahweh; but then the relation between the act of creation and the continued maintenance of life is obscured.

The creation becomes the concentrated expression of Yahweh's power over nature. His might is, on the other hand, manifested in the fact that all the earth totters, trembles, and melts like wax when he appears (Judg. 5,4 f.; Mic. 1,2 ff.; Hab. 3). It was this power over nature which especially assured the Israelites that Yahweh could demand submission from all nations, and it provides the background for the view that Yahweh's relation to Israel is due to his free choice, and so can be dissolved again, a view which was constantly elaborated, but in the nature of the case it could never be consistently maintained.

As the God of Israel Yahweh always wins glory whenever Israel is successful and prosperous; thus he makes a name for himself and gains honour among the nations (Jer. 33,9). Therefore, even though Israel is unworthy, she shall nevertheless be upheld for the sake of Yahweh's name and glory. It is this idea which we have found so much stressed in Ezekiel and Deutero-Isaiah, and in the song of Moses we are told that Yahweh would have exterminated Israel if this would not have made her enemies think that they were the stronger, and Yahweh powerless (Deut. 32,27). Therefore the Israelites appeal to the honour of Yahweh when they are in distress. Before the immigration Moses reminds Yahweh of the renown he has won by leading Israel out of Egypt. If now he lets his people perish in the wilderness, the nations will say that he was unable to bring it into Canaan (Num. 14,11 ff.). During the conquest, when the Israelites suffered defeat at Ai, Joshua turned to Yahweh, asking him what he would do about his great name, if the Canaanites wiped Israel's name off the face of the earth (Josh. 7,7-9). "Why shall the foreign nations say: Where is their God?" cried the psalmist during the exile (Ps. 79,10).

It is especially during the last years of the monarchy and the exile that we hear these cries of distress. We are taken back to the days of Hezekiah by the story of the Assyrian commander's letter, which warns the Israelites not to think that Yahweh, better than other gods, is able to vanquish the Assyrians. Hezekiah put the letter before Yahweh in the temple to challenge him to uphold his honour (Isa. 37,9 ff.). Yahweh's susceptibility in that respect was regarded in a purely human way. Jeremiah endeavours to rouse Yahweh to action for the sake of his name, in spite of the sins of the people, and he tries to egg him on by saying outright that he is like a metic or a traveller who does not belong to the community of Israel, or even as a fool who can do nothing (Jer. 14, 7-9). The care to fight for his glory *(ḳin'ā)* is no less strong in Yahweh than in Israelites jealous of their honour. He rouses it, puts it on as a cloak (Isa. 42,13; 59,17); by means of it he defends his people, his city, and the royal house of David (2 Kings

19,31; Isa. 9,6; 37,32; Zech. 1,14; 8,2). Jealousy is a fire because it burns in the soul and makes the cheek glow. Yahweh speaks with the fire of his *ḳin'ā*, it devours the whole earth (Ez. 36,5 f.; 38,19; Zeph. 1,18; 3,8). In Yahweh, too, the sting of mortification stirs the bowels (Isa. 63,15).

But Yahweh's jealousy is a two-edged sword. It is not only aroused by the enemies of his people, but by the people itself. This is because the pith of Yahweh's honour as of man's is righteousness, and because he hates sin. All righteousness is rooted in him, therefore he defends every breach in it. From the earliest times he has maintained the law of retribution, and those guilty of bloodshed were strung up before him (2 Sam. 21,1.6.9). He visits with disaster the man of violence who breaks the law of the family (1 Kings 21). He who has been wronged appeals to him as a judge (Gen. 16,5; Judg. 11,27; 1 Sam. 24,16), he demands his help by virtue of his righteousness, for "Yahweh renders to a man his righteousness and his faithfulness" (1 Sam. 26,23). We know the problems with which the Israelites were confronted because they invariably expected their God to support righteousness, and we know that it led to a breach in the ancient conception of the action and its fruits. We can now see that this change in the fundamental concepts of life is connected with the view of Yahweh which we can trace back to David.

Yahweh's hatred of sin is in its essence based on the fact that sin is inimical to life. It creates disaster in the soul, but at the same time it is a breach in Yahweh's will, a disobedience which offends against his honour. This applies not only to the cult sins which are aimed directly at the holy life (1 Sam. 2,25), or false oaths which fill the name of God with lies (Lev. 19,12). Sin sets up a wall between Yahweh and the sinner (Isa. 59,2), it kindles his jealousy and wrath (Deut. 29,19). The wretch feels the anger and *ḳin'ā* of Yahweh like a fire (Ps. 79,5). Ezekiel describes how Yahweh turns his jealousy to Jerusalem (Ez. 5,13; 16,38.42; 23,25), and it only abates when it has raged for some time. In the wilderness it nearly consumed the Israelites (Num. 17,10; 25,11), and the prophets are constantly pointing out that Yahweh's wrath comes upon the people because of their sins. Israel's distress

shows that Yahweh has set their sins before him (Ps. 90,8). Down
through the family sin carries on its destructive work, because
Yahweh is a jealous *(ḳannā')* God, who visits the sins of the
fathers on the children (Ex. 20,5; 34,14; Deut. 4,24; 5,9; 6,15,
cf. Ps. 109,14). Sometimes we meet with the idea that sin does not
cause disaster until remembered and found out by God (Gen.
44,16; 1 Kings 17,18). The jealousy which the Israelites so often
tried to arouse was turned against themselves when sin gained
the upper hand.

Since the Israelites gradually felt more and more dominated
by sin, the question might arise how it was possible that the
world and mankind could survive at all. But then the Israelites
put their trust in their God. He knows that man is evil from his
youth (Gen. 8,21), therefore excessive demands cannot be made
on him. If God were always to be wroth, the souls would fail,
and yet he himself made them (Isa. 57,16). Even though he is
a jealous God, he is also merciful and long-suffering to those
who love him. He flings sin into the sea and shows love towards
the fathers, so as to keep his oath to them (Ex. 20,6; Mic. 7,18 ff.).
This covenant with the patriarchs becomes the support of the
Israelites. It is emphasised in the many confessions of sin from
the later history of the people. In view of it Yahweh is bound to
forgive. It is owing to this that not only wrath but mercy, too,
may become an expression of Yahweh's justice to the sinful people,
and a means of maintaining his glory.

The removal of sin is necessary, because a sinful soul cannot
exert itself, and no one can live under the wrath of God. The
ancient remedy, sacrifice, still worked both for the purification of
the soul and to obtain the forgiveness of Yahweh. A worshipper
offering sacrifice says in the same breath "judge me", i. e. secure
my rights to me, and "purify my reins and my heart" (Ps. 26,1 f.).
Another worshipper prays that Yahweh will mercifully wipe out
his sins, and purify his guilty soul, but he also entreats Yahweh
to conceal his face from the sins, i. e. disregard them (Ps. 51,3 f.
11). The miserable sinner seeks deliverance from his sin, healing
of his soul, and Yahweh's favour in the cult. But the cult element
may recede into the background, for the chief object is to win

Yahweh's forgiveness. The sinner's relation to him is purely personal, as if he were facing a human ruler. "Against thee and thee only have I sinned, and done that which was evil in thy sight, that thou mayest be righteous in thy speech, pure in thy judgment" (Ps. 51,6). That sin has been committed against Yahweh alone means that all other considerations become as nothing compared with the outrage to his honour. Utterances of this kind are heard again and again in the Psalms. The chief object is to win Yahweh's favour and avoid anything that will affect his glory.

Therefore the confession of sins is a means of winning forgiveness. In this way the sinner shows that he does not intend to deceive Yahweh, nothing is concealed, but the entire credit for the forgiveness is given to Yahweh. "He who hides his sins shall not prosper, but he who confesses and forsakes them, shall have mercy" (Prov. 28,13). In the Psalms the worshippers constantly say that they confess their sins without reserve (Ps. 32,5; 38,19; 51,5), and in the same degree they acknowledge Yahweh's righteousness both during their sufferings and after their deliverance. Job's friends also advise Job to confess his sins and beseech forgiveness, and for a moment Job himself recognises the possibility that he may have sinned, but then God may simply forgive his sin and let his guilt disappear (Job 7,20 f.).

When Yahweh has forgiven the sin this means that it has actually been wiped out; the soul is again sound. "Blessed is he whose transgression is forgiven, whose sin is covered. Happy is the man to whom Yahweh imputeth not guilt and in whose spirit there is no laxity" (Ps. 32,1-2). Though it is merely said that the sin is forgiven, covered, not imputed to him, this means the regeneration of the strength of the soul. "Thou hast kept my soul from the pit of corruption, for thou hast cast all my sins behind thy back. For Sheol doth not praise thee, death doth not glorify thee..." (Isa. 38,17 f.). Yahweh's forgiveness of sins is identical with the curing of the man, and Yahweh has given it him that he may not lose one of his votaries, an idea also met with elsewhere (Ps. 6,6; 30,10). In a prophetic vision of the future we are also told that "no inhabitant shall say: I am weak. The people that dwell there have had their sins removed" (Isa. 33,24); this says that the forgiveness of sins means the increase of strength.

The Israelites may use the strongest words to express that Yahweh alone can secure strength and happiness and that he can do so whenever he likes, but they are loth to disrupt the connection between the nature of the soul and its fate. Therefore we come across the idea that Yahweh, when he desires a man's welfare, prevents him from committing a sin. When Abimelech had taken Sarah, God revealed to him what he had done, but he adds that since it was done in ignorance, God had hindered Abimelech from sinning against him by violating Abraham's wife, and he could avoid disaster by sending her back (Gen. 20,6 f.). And on the other hand we find this strange utterance dating from the period towards the end of the exile: "Why hast thou made us to err from thy ways Yahweh, making our hearts too hard to fear thee. Return for thy slaves' sake, for the tribes of thine inheritance" (Isa. 63,17). The connection between sin and disaster is firmly established, therefore the intervention of Yahweh is associated with the will of man, by which his fate is determined. It is the same idea which we come across in its inverse form when enemies are cursed, with the prayer that Yahweh will add more sin to their sin (Ps. 69,28).

Thus there is no limit to the power of Yahweh over men. He penetrates to the inmost depths of their souls and determines the will by which they incur responsibility. All are in his hand, one day he will cut them all off by death, none of them can pay a ransom and redeem his brother from him (Ps. 49,8). Yahweh is so mighty compared with men that they shrink to nothingness before him. No living being is righteous in his presence, man is dust and ashes (Gen. 18,27; Ps. 143,2; Job 4,17 f.).

The Israelite is always filled with the feeling of the might of his God. He feels it everywhere, in the world of nature surrounding him, in the events that happen, in the commands of the law, and most of all in his own soul. Therefore he fears Yahweh as he fears everything divine.

The part played by fear *(yir'ā)*, and especially by the fear of Yahweh *(yir'ath yahwe)*, in the Old Testament is deeply rooted in the psychic nature of the Israelite. Fear, of course, is not peculiar to the Israelite. When man is confronted with what is strong and incalculable, he feels his inferiority; then fear will easily arise, and he will wish to fly, unless his inner firmness is so great that he prefers to stop and fall. ¹

But in the relations between men as they developed in Israel, fear was bound to play a considerable part, the more the superior person claimed all honour for himself and complete subjection from others. It became natural to the Israelites to describe any relationship of authority as implying fear. One must fear one's father and mother (Lev. 19,3), and when Joshua was raised among the Israelites by Yahweh, "they feared him as they had feared Moses" (Josh. 4,14), just as it is a matter of course that men fear the prophet who speaks with real authority (Deut. 18,22; 1 Sam. 12,18). Even though fear in such circumstances may sometimes be less dominant, it is characteristic that it is the word "to fear" which is used, and that at any rate means that in the given case complete submission is necessary.

That what is divine is stronger than men is implied by its very nature, and everywhere among the peoples it is a danger to men to be directly confronted with it. But in Israel the divine is so mighty compared with men that danger gains the ascendancy, and the divine being who shows himself spreads terror around him. This has been so from the earliest times. The *mal'ākh* of Yahweh who appeared to Samson's mother struck terror at once (Judg. 13,6), and when she and her husband had understood whom they had before them, her husband said: "We shall surely die, because we have seen God" (Judg. 13,22); and we feel the same terror in Gideon's cry when Yahweh's *mal'ākh* had appeared to him (Judg. 6,22). When Jacob felt that his God was present at Bethel where he was lying, he was struck with terror and exclaimed: How terrible *(nōrä')* is this place

(Gen. 28,17). He even calls his God the Fear of his fathers *(pahadh,* Gen. 31,42.53). [1]

The divine awfulness pervades the whole of the Old Testament. The revelation in Sinai is one great terror, and Yahweh appears in order that the fear of him may overwhelm the Israelites, so that they may not sin (Ex. 20,20). But it is a miracle that they have heard his voice and yet preserved their lives. His glory appears as a consuming fire (Ex. 24,17; Deut. 5,26). His name is dreadful, great and holy, he is terrible when he comes from his sanctuaries (Ps. 68,36; 99,3; 111,9), and the very sanctuary is and is meant to be an object of fear to the people (Lev. 19,30; 26,2). Everything which is associated with what is divine makes the Israelite tremble. "My flesh trembleth for fear of thee, and I am afraid of thy judgments" says a pious worshipper (Ps. 119,120). It is a matter of course, therefore, that man stands in the presence of God as a slave before his master. It is expressly said in a psalm: Behold, as the eyes of slaves look unto the hand of their masters, and the eyes of a slave woman unto the hand of her mistress, so our eyes are turned towards Yahweh, our God, until he have mercy upon us (123,2). Everywhere man calls himself a slave *('ebhedh)* before God — and yet the distance between God and man is infinitely greater than between a slave and his master.

The fear of Yahweh enters in a remarkable manner into the Israelite view of life. We know that all blessedness comes from the divine power working in the soul, but harmony with Yahweh is obtained by fearing him. Therefore the fear of Yahweh enters as a necessary component into the psychic nature of the blessed, it becomes inseparable from righteousness. The fear of Yahweh is wisdom or the first fruits of wisdom (Ps. 111,10; Prov. 1,7; Job 28,28). "Perfect and righteous and fearing God" are synonyms (Job 1,1.8; 2,3), just like "men of strength *(hayil),* fearing God, men of security" *('emeth* Ex. 18,21). As the true ruler must be righteous, thus also he must act in fear of Yahweh (2 Sam. 23,3.; Isa. 11,2 f.; cf. 33,6). It is the fear of God which makes men act in the right way, therefore it is inculcated by the laws (Gen. 20,11; 42,18; Ex. 1,17, cf. Lev. 19,14.32; 25,17 et al.).

This does not merely imply that men should act in the right way for fear of the consequences, even though this also is implied. The spontaneous awe of God's might goes through man's marrow and bones and bends his will. And this unreserved submission to Yahweh's will must create blessedness, because it is the true righteousness (Ps. 25,12 f.; 128; Prov. 10,27; 14, 27). Yahweh can claim to be feared, because it is a recognition of his greatness. Therefore the fear of Yahweh becomes a virtue in itself and rises above time.[1] Through it true knowledge of Yahweh is indeed gained, therefore every leader must have "knowledge and the fear of Yahweh" (Isa. 11,2).

What makes fear a good thing is the consciousness of the Israelite that it is his own God of the Covenant who instils it into him. It is to pervade the Israelites so that they close round their God in a community which is holy because he is holy. Fear is to unite this community in love and in affection for him.[2] He is like a strict father who shows his love of his son by chastising him, because this will result in the humbleness best suited for his life conditions as a human being (Prov. 3,12). And if all pride is obliterated in Yahweh's presence, then everything in life is received as a gift from him; he returns what a man has relinquished. He is the redeemer, the avenger, the saviour, and the counsellor; to him the Israelite submits his cause and waits for him. Yahweh is his salvation and his honour (Ps. 62,8).

Thus the fear of Yahweh leads to the disappearance of all other fear. "Yahweh is my light and my salvation; whom shall I fear?" (Ps. 27,1). Thus, despite all fear and weakness, the Israelite is secure, because he feels that he is in the hand of the Almighty. When he believes (he'emīn) and relies on Yahweh (bāṭaḥ), he wins that 'emūnā, that firmness and security which he has not in himself. In the Psalms we find a long series of expressions for the security which the Israelite feels under his God as his shepherd, in the shelter of his wings (Ps. 23; 36,8;

91,4). The night loses its terrors, as also the fatal arrow; even
Chaos he fears no more, because he knows that the creator is
behind all; he that watches over Israel neither slumbers nor
sleeps (46,2-4; 91,5; 121,2 ff.). The Israelite constantly oscil-
lates between fear and security in his relation to life, and the
two opposite feelings are closely associated because they both rest
in a power outside and above man. Their association finds its
paradoxical expression in Eliphaz' words to Job: Is not thy fear
thy trust? (Job 4,6, cf. 22,4).

When the Israelite is entirely pervaded by the nature of
Yahweh, feeling it in fear or in affection, he is irradiated with
happiness. He prospers greatly in the light of Yahweh, but
is terrified when Yahweh hides his countenance (Isa. 1,15; 2,5;
Ps. 30,8; 36,10; 119,105). Yahweh is a value in himself; he who
knows how it is to feel him near is thrilled by him and overwhelmed with happiness on feeling his favour. He calls Yahweh
his portion, the portion of his inheritance and his cup. [1]

The Israelite seeks trust in his fear and strength in his
weakness. It is implied in the whole relation between God and
man in Israel that Yahweh prefers to care for the miserable. He
is their gō'ēl, he who gives their eyes light; he who wrongs them
must remember this (Deut. 24,15; Jer. 20,13; Prov. 23,10 f.). To
oppress them is an outrage to him, for he is their creator, therefore he rewards him who helps them (Prov. 14,31; 19,17). Just
because he avenges gērim, orphans, and widows, a worshipper
beseeches him with the words that he is a gēr and a tōshābh before Yahweh, a wretch with no resort (Ps. 39, 13; 1 Chron. 29,
15, cf. Ex. 22,20-23.26; 23,9; Ps. 68,6.11; 146,9). This is a
feature found throughout the Old Testament. In the story of the
patriarchs we see how Yahweh looks after the slighted wife and
gives her children, while the preferred wife must remain childless
(Gen. 29,31).

We have previously considered utterances of this kind in which
different ideas meet. In the first place there is the idea which we
know so well from the prophets, that Israel is a people in humble
circumstances, as shown by its history, since it was a people of

gērim in Egypt. Hence it is just as much against its nature to oppress the lowly as to have dealings with the mighty (cf. Ez. 23,5.12). Further the law of retribution comes into play, for it gives to the wronged person a claim which Yahweh intends to uphold. But most of all Yahweh loves the weak because he can unfold himself entirely to them, giving them everything. A broken and contrite heart is most pleasing of all to him, because he heals it (Ps. 51,19; 147,3). On the other hand, he loves nothing that is strong. The ancient legend of the builders of Babel, who wanted to build as high as heaven and make a great name for themselves, shows us Yahweh on guard against those who want to rise against him. And in the Psalms we read: He delighteth not in the strength of the horse, he taketh not pleasure in the strong legs of the man. Yahweh taketh pleasure in them that fear him, in those that wait for his mercy (Ps. 147,10 f.). These are sentiments with which we are familiar from the prophets. Nothing is so hateful to Yahweh as arrogance; and it is even a challenge to him to put one's trust in fortresses, chariots, and horses. We are told, therefore, that Yahweh has a day against all that exalts itself; it shall be humbled, and Yahweh alone shall remain exalted (Isa. 2,9 ff.; 23,9). It is true that wealth is a man's happiness, but the righteous man does not put his trust in it, and does not take pleasure in what he earns himself (Ps. 52,9; Prov. 15,16; Job 31,24 f.). But Yahweh exalts the poor, and humbles the great (Ps. 107,36 ff.); he lays low the high, raises up those that mourn, destroys the thoughts of the crafty, and saves the miserable from the mighty (Job 5,11 ff.). Unscrupulously he attacks those who will not humble themselves. He scorns the scorners, but is gracious to the humble (Prov. 3,34). To the affectionate and just he is affectionate and just, but crafty with the crafty; he saves the afflicted, but he brings down high looks (Ps. 18,26-28).

These ideas appear with special clarity and strength in a Psalm which, curiously enough, is attributed to the childless Hannah. Its conclusion shows that it dates from the monarchical period: "My heart rejoiceth in Yahweh, mine horn is exalted in Yahweh. My mouth mocks at mine enemies, because I rejoice in thy salvation. There is none holy as Yahweh, nay, there is none besides thee, and no one is a rock like our God. Be not babblers with arrogance, let not audacity come out of your mouth. For Yahweh is a God of knowledge, he establishes what is done. The bows of heroes are broken, but the stumbling gird themselves with strength. They that were full hire themselves out for bread, but the hungry cease... The barren beareth sevenfold, but she that hath many sons repineth. Yahweh killeth and maketh alive, sendeth down to Sheol, and bringeth up. Yahweh maketh poor and maketh rich, bringeth low and lifteth up. He raiseth up the oppressed out of the dust, lifteth the poor out of the dunghill to seat them among the nobles, and make them occupy seats of honour. For the pillars of the earth are Yahweh's, he set the world upon them. He watcheth the feet of his votaries, but the wicked are flung into the dark. For a man shall not gain power by force. The adversaries of Yahweh are amazed, he roars at him in heaven. Yahweh judgeth all the earth; he giveth strength unto his king, he letteth the horn of his anointed be exalted" (1 Sam. 2,1-10).

It is possible that this Psalm was among those used in the royal cult at Jerusalem; but it mentions not only Yahweh's fight against strangers, it celebrates his whole activity in life. He makes life and death, lays low the great and exalts the humble, turns everything upside down. The most important thing is to belong to his votaries. He who does so can say that his horn is exalted, which means that his strength and his honour are augmented. Thus though the great are humbled, there is still a power left. The Israelites say, however, that it is not gained by force, but by the action of Yahweh.

When Yahweh lays low those that exalt themselves and lifts up the weak that take refuge with him, then his honour swells and he secures *kābhōdh* for himself. Thus he secured honour (*nikhbadh*) by Pharao when he vanquished him (Ex. 14,4.17 f.), just as he secured honour by Sidon (Ez. 28,22). The substance of his soul being holiness, he is also said to sanctify himself when he displays his strength in great deeds. He sanctifies himself in his righteousness and sanctifies himself in his honour (Ex. 29,43 LXX; Isa. 5,16). If any one rises against him, he sanctifies himself through them by punishing them (Lev. 10,3; Num. 20,13), and he sanctifies himself before the nations when he lifts up his people (Ez. 20,41; 28,25; 38,16; 39,27); he sanctifies his great name (Ez. 36,23).

_____

The Israelites may contribute to this increase of Yahweh's honour and holiness in the first place by subordinating themselves entirely to his will and thus acknowledging his greatness, exactly as before a human ruler. And those who honour Yahweh are honoured by him, just as he sanctifies those who sanctify him (1 Sam. 2,30, cf. Lev. 20,8; 22,32; Deut 32,51). But to give praise to Yahweh is also a reality by which man can increase Yahweh's honour and make him great, if only it is not by lip-service and empty words which do not emanate from the inmost soul, as in those who praise him, but defy his laws (Isa. 29,13). Therefore the Israelites praise Yahweh as the king of honour (Ps. 24,7 ff.), they pray to him to give honour not to them but to his own name. Numerous Psalms praise him, give him glory and honour (tehillā and kābhōdh, Ps. 66,2, cf. 22,24), fill his name with honour and strength ('ōz, 29, 1 f.; 96,7). Even the foreign nations shall give him kābhōdh and tehillā (Isa. 42,12);[1] heaven and earth and the sea, all the world unites in praising him (Ps. 69,35).

The giving of praise is the natural form of the relation of man to Yahweh as he was known in Zion and from the prophets. Of course he is also honoured by the sacrifices and the rest of the temple cult, and Deutero-Isaiah says expressly that the people did not honour him in their exile by sacrifice; from this it may be seen that Yahweh restored it entirely of his own accord (Isa. 43, 23). But the whole view of the relation between Israel and Yahweh, as we have become acquainted with it here, was bound to lead on to the idea that sacrifice was not a necessary or natural expression of the relation. This conclusion was, as we have seen, drawn by some of the prophets and by others.

The world of nature was remote to them, its sanctification meant nothing in their relation to Yahweh; it was of importance only as a manifestation of his great creative power. And if sacrifice was regarded as a gift made to Yahweh, well then, all animals belonged to him already (Ps. 50,8-12). That is why we are told that Yahweh takes no pleasure in sacrifice, but in righteousness (*mishpāṭ* and *ṣᵉdhāḳā* Am. 5,22-24), in love and the knowledge of God (Hos. 6,6), in rectitude, love, and "walking humbly with your God" (Mic. 6,6-8). Feasts are worth nothing to him compared with doing good (Isa. 1,11 ff.). To listen to Yahweh is better than sacrifice; to listen is better than the fat of rams (1 Sam. 15,22). To do Yahweh's will, to observe his *tōrā*, to give honour to him is better than sacrifice (Ps. 40,7-11). Sometimes we hear that Yahweh exacts obedience to his will, but has not demanded offerings (Jer. 7,21-23, cf. 6,20; Am. 5,25; Ps. 40,7). Praise is dearer to him than sacrifice (Ps. 69,31 f.); the sacrifices in which he takes pleasure are a broken spirit, a broken and contrite heart (51,19).

All this scarcely means that prophets and those similarly disposed wished that the sacrificial cult should disappear. It belonged to the order of daily life, but the sacrifices were to be put in their proper place (cf. Ps. 50,5; 51,21). It is, however, of great interest that this opinion of the sacrificial cult is put forward. It shows how deeply the view of Yahweh that came to prevail had penetrated into the life and thought of Israel.

Israel placed all her values and all her self-confidence in her God. The Israelites deprived themselves of everything, but they won it all again through their God. He was outside and above the world, but he held it in his hand with its life and its values. What was divine had been removed from the world, but this involved a risk of the forces which kept it together falling asunder, and the ground being cut from under the whole culture. The cult, which sanctified life and created the forces by which life was to be lived, lost its vital power. The distrust of human abilities, and the aversion to all that exalted itself undermined social life and threatened to remove the foundation of human activity. When wealth and heroic deeds did not result immediately from a man's growth and create honour for him, then the view of man and his relation to his environment which had formed the basis of the culture had begun to decay. It would not have been strange if all this had led to the consequence that life in this world was without value. And we do, in fact, find such a scepticism expressed in Ecclesiastes.

The revolutionising element did not, however, as a rule give rise to any denying scepticism, nor any revaluation attempting to replace the ancient ethos by purely inner values. Wealth and power in the world remained what they had always been in Israel, the life and happiness of a man. The only difference was that man must not arbitrarily take possession of this happiness by virtue of the greatness of his soul, he was to take all as a gift from his God, humbling himself before him, bowing down before his will, and giving him all the honour. Only through Yahweh did man acquire a right to live. This entire view of things was not attained by any rupture, but by a change in the proportion of these elements which had always been present in Israelite culture. The Israelite who kept to the covenant thus acquired confidence in his rights and his progress, because he knew that his mighty God was with him.

We only know Yahweh as a jealous God, violent in his self-expression, of which we have also seen that an increase can be demonstrated. This will appear with all clarity if we review Yahweh's relation to other gods.

In early Israel as in any other people it was a matter of course that the other nations, each by itself, lived their lives with their gods. To deny that Moab's God was active would be the same as to deny the psychic reality of Moab, a downright absurdity. And as a matter of fact, we find evidence in the narratives of the Israelites of a natural recognition of the gods of the neighbouring peoples within their own domain.

A well-known account is that of Jephthah's negotiation with the Ammonites about the right to the region situated east of Jordan on the borders of the two peoples' lands, and which Israel had once taken from the Ammonites. It is not easy to say at what period this curious discussion obtained its present form. But

Jephthah's arguments are to the effect that Yahweh has given his people this piece of land in a lawful war, and so he asks: Wilt thou not take possession of that which Chemosh thy God letteth thee acquire? Thus we also take possession of all that Yahweh, our God, driveth out before us (Judg. 11,24). The name of the God, Chemosh, points to the Moabites, to whom perhaps the whole story actually relates. Be this as it may, the narrative points to a view according to which the peoples of Yahweh and Chemosh recognise each other's rights and the activity of their gods each within his limits, according to the same law.

This conception of the gods was far more general in early Israel than we gather from the Old Testament with its stamp of Judaism. That the book of Kings describes as apostasy Solomon's institution of cults to neighbouring gods represented by their peoples in Canaan (1 Kings 11,3 ff. 33), is of course due to the later author's interpretation of old narratives about proceedings that were quite natural. David also regarded expulsion from one's native country as identical with the necessity of serving alien gods (1 Sam. 26,19, cf. Cain Gen. 4,14). We have also evidence that an Israelite king appealed to a foreign God, Baal Zebub in Ekron, when he thought that he could best be answered by him in a certain situation (2 Kings 1,2).

In the book of Kings we have evidence of how the two national gods Chemosh and Yahweh met in war, even though the narrator does not say so directly, all the more so since Chemosh was victorious. The kings of Israel and Judah went with their troops into Moab, and the king of the Edomites joined them. Yahweh let Elisha, his man of God, help them; he deceived the Moabites by means of a red stream of water, making them believe that their enemies had quarrelled and were killing each other; they fell without order on the supposed prey, and suffered a great defeat which Mesha, the king of Moab, in vain sought to retrieve. Then it goes on to say briefly: Then he took his first-born son that should have been king in his stead, and offered him for a burnt offering upon the wall; and there was great wrath against Israel, and they departed from him and returned to their country (2 Kings 3,27).

This can only mean that Chemosh was incited by the offering to bestow such strength on his people that they defeated the Israelites. Thus Chemosh defeated Yahweh. The author has avoided mentioning the name of Chemosh, but he has not reinterpreted the event in the light of later times, and so he has preserved a valuable relic of the earlier view of Israel. In the story about the Assyrian commander's address to Hezekiah the enemy points out that no other people's God has been able to stop the great king, how, then, should Yahweh be able to do so? This speech induces Yahweh to drive out the hostile army (2 Kings 18 f. = Isa. 36 f.). This is a narrative in the old spirit, though it is not related entirely in accordance with it. Thus the statement is inserted in the speech of the commander that it is Yahweh who has called him in to destroy the country (2 Kings 18,25; Isa. 36,10).

Among the utterances directed against the neighbours of Israel we find expressions like the following: Woe to thee, Moab, thou art undone, O people of Chemosh. He giveth his sons as fugitives and his daughters into captivity to Sihon, the king of the Amorites (Num. 21,29, cf. Jer. 48,46). Or: Why hath Milcom [1] inherited Gad and his people settled in his cities? ... Milcom shall go into exile and his priests and his princes together (Jer. 49,1.3). Even a very late prophet calls foreign women the daughters of a foreign God (Mal. 2,11), and similarly we hear in the book of Ruth of a Moabite woman who comes to Canaan that she has come to seek shelter under the wings of Israel's God, and her Israelite mother-in-law has returned to her own people and her own God (Ruth 1,15; 2,12).

Parallel with this view of the divine in Israel and among other peoples we have, however, the opinions that led to the great exaltation of Yahweh, which involved altered conceptions of the foreign gods. During the struggle between Yahweh and Baal the aversion to what was foreign arose and became intensified, especially towards foreign cults. It is highly probable that already in laws from the monarchical period there were formulated interdictions against the worship of foreign gods, as we know them from the book of the Covenant; commandments such as these: He that sacrificeth to the gods save to Yahweh only shall be banished

(Ex. 22,19) or: Thou shalt have no other gods before me (Ex. 20,3), a commandment which is even given the strict form that the names of other gods must not so much as be mentioned (Ex. 23,13).

Yahweh in Zion was exalted precisely as the God who was stronger than other gods, who defeated and judged them. He is constantly praised as the God who is greater than all the gods; a great King over all gods; terrible over all gods. No one is like him among the gods; he is the God of gods, the Lord of lords; he is judge in the assembly of gods; before him they prostrate themselves (Ps. 82,1; 86,8; 95,3; 96,4; 97,7.9; 135,5; 136,2 f.). And repeated reference is made to his great deeds, especially the creation of the world and the deliverance of his people from Egypt. By these deeds he has shown that none is like him among the gods; he is greater than all the others (Ex. 15,11; 18,11). The Paschal legend is framed on this theme.

Yahweh fights not only the various popular gods, but also everything which exalts itself and claims to be divine. The sun and the moon, which meant so much for the maintenance of order in life, often became independent gods among the neighbouring peoples or became part of the nature of other gods. Job expressly denies having kissed his hand to these mighty beings (Job 31, 26 f.), and in a judgment prophecy it is said that Yahweh will visit all the host of heaven on high, and the kings on earth, and the sun and the moon shall be put to shame, when Yahweh shall reign in Zion (Isa. 24,21.23).

In this struggle with the other gods there is a conviction that Yahweh is the strongest; he can be most active, as evidenced for instance in Yahweh's fight with Baal on Mount Carmel. But in earlier times there is a balance between the various national gods which corresponds to the proportion of their peoples. The words of the Aramæan Naaman, that there is no God in all the world except in Israel (2 Kings 5,15), merely mean that Yahweh is an unusually strong God. Therefore Naaman takes with him Israelitish earth on which he can sacrifice to Yahweh, but this does not prevent him from worshipping Rimmon also (v. 18). This corresponds to the early Israelite view. But gradually this became quite different, Yahweh claiming all divinity for himself.

We know the main points in the development of this conception which attained its climax during the exile. The root of the idea may perhaps be found in the bitterness which characterised Yahweh's fight with the Canaanite gods about the power over the soul of Israel, for in its keenness the fight was bound to lead to an alternative which would make Israelites deny all divinity to Baal. The Yahweh of the Paschal feast was ready to assume more and more power, and as the cult in Zion celebrated him as the conqueror of all gods and the creator of all things, the prerequisite was present for denying the divinity of other gods. The conclusion was finally drawn by the prophets of the exile. The development of this idea comprises two important domains: the relation of Yahweh to foreign peoples, and Israel's view of foreign gods.

The early view, that Yahweh fights the foreign peoples and their gods as a victorious warrior in order to assert his superiority, acquires its intensified form owing to the growing claims of Yahweh. And the more unclean and unsanctified the foreigners became, the stronger became the claim for their subjection to Yahweh. But if Yahweh was Lord of heaven and earth he could not be merely a destroyer of foreign nations. All the prophets agree that Yahweh leads the nations and he does so for definite purposes, using the great kings as instruments for the chastisement of sinful Israel. But in Amos we also meet with the idea that Yahweh chastises foreign peoples for special sins (Am. 1,3 ff.), and that he has directed their wanderings (Am. 9,7). The prophet even goes so far as to put them on the same footing as Israel in regard to Yahweh. This is the extreme consequence of the world dominion of Yahweh. That view of course did not prevail, but the idea of a positive relation between Yahweh and the foreign peoples was bound to recur from time to time. The Psalms say that all the kings of the earth shall praise him (Ps. 138,4); because he is the leader of all nations, all peoples shall fear him and praise him (67; 113,3 f.). That Yahweh should have ordered the internal affairs of foreigners and given them their laws is an idea which would never occur to any Israelite. On the other hand, during the exile Deutero-Isaiah draws the conclusion from Yahweh's absolute rule that foreigners must subordinate themselves to Yahweh by accepting his law. The same idea is expressed in utterances ascribed to earlier prophets. Thus the nations are to constitute a great community led by the Israelites gathered around the temple in Zion and characterised by their law, ruled by their God as the sole God (Isa. 2,2-4 = Mic. 4,1-4). This idea we meet with again after the exile, when Zechariah says that Yahweh in Jerusalem shall found a kingdom extending all over the earth, and all nations shall submit to him by joining Israel and keeping her feast of tabernacles (Zech. 8,21 ff.; 9,7; 14,9-19). Another prophet says that those who do not serve Yahweh shall perish (Isa. 60,12). An echo of such tones is heard in the temple speech ascribed to Solomon (1 Kings 8,60).

We have seen evidence that the Persian king accepted the idea that Yahweh was the king of heaven, whose cult must not be neglected. The chronicler explains this to mean an acknowledgment on the part of the ruler of the world empire that he owed his power to Israel's God (Ezr. 1,2). Altogether, the Israelites take it for granted that Israel, at any rate the true Israel, is nearest to Yahweh as an intermediate link between him and the nations, and in this idea may be more or less incorporated the other point of view claiming the subjugation of foreign peoples. One prophet expects foreigners, when the temple becomes the centre of the world, to carry their treasures to it; the Israelites shall consume their wealth, and the foreigners shall be shepherds and labourers to them (Isa. 61,5 f.).

This view of Yahweh prevented Israelites from having any relations with foreign gods, as David recognised that an exiled Israelite was bound to have. In the Psalms we find assurances that the worshipper has no dealings with foreign gods, does not raise his hands to them or prostrate himself before them (16,1 ff.; 44,21; 81,10). These utterances mean not merely that the true Israelite refrains from foreign cults because they are un-Israelitish and profane, but also that gods other than Yahweh are not real gods.

What they are we are told in the Song of Moses (Deut. 32), which deals with Yahweh, Israel, and the gods. When the earth

was divided among the nations the bounds were set according to
the number of "the sons of God" (v. 8). [1] This implies a certain
recognition of the early view of the peoples and their gods. It is
then recounted how Yahweh found his people in the wilderness
and gave it a glorious land. "But it forsook the God which made
it and lightly esteemed the rock of its salvation, and they provoked
him to jealousy with strangers, angered him with abominations;
they sacrificed to the demons which are not God, to Gods they
did not know . . ." (vv. 15-17). Then Yahweh grew angry and
said: They have moved me to jealousy with a non-God, have
angered me with their delusions *(hebhel)*, then I will provoke
them to jealousy with a non-people, fret them with a foolish nation (v. 21). The other peoples' "rock is not as our rock" (v 31).
When later Yahweh secures redress to his people "he will say:
Where are their gods, the rock in whom they trusted; who did eat
the fat of their sacrifices, drank the wine of their drink-offerings?
Let them rise up and help you and be a protection to you! See now
that it is I, even I, and there is no god by my side! I kill and I
make alive, I smite and I heal, and no one can deliver out of my
hand" (vv. 37-39). Then Yahweh swears to render vengeance to
all his enemies.

Here we are concerned both with the gods that some Israelites
worshipped and with other peoples' gods, and they are all on the
same line. They take the sacrifices which are offered to them,
but real gods they are not. Not only are they foreign to the
Israelites, they are demons who may indeed apparently be regarded as belonging to the world of gods, but in reality they are
delusions which lack that which should make them gods, the
great strength, the power of creating life and death. [2] This is
reserved for Yahweh.

It is probable that the Song of Moses dates from the time
after the monarchical period, but its view of Yahweh and the gods
hardly differs from the general opinion of the prophets. Characteristic of the conception is the pronounced personal character
ascribed to the God. The direct connection between the God and
the psychic life of the world is broken. A God is a person of a
human kind, but with unlimited power; he stands behind existence

and directs it according to his will. But since Yahweh has appropriated all power, the others have been deprived of their force. This agrees entirely with the whole character of the God of Zion.

_____

The fight against foreign gods was gradually connected with the fight against *idols,* the two things becoming inseparable. The main features in the history of this fight, of which we have already seen some aspects, may again illustrate the evolution of the nature of Yahweh. We know of a fight against images from periods of Christian and Moslem culture. Each time it begins with a fight against certain images and ends with general principles. It was no different in Israel.

In the earlier period of the history of the Israelites holy images were common in the cult as among other peoples.¹ During the first struggles on record between Yahweh and Baal, in the time of Elijah and Elisha, we hear nothing of images playing any part whatever in the fight. From the book of Kings we know that in the northern kingdom, under all its kings, the people had images of Yahweh in the shape of a young bull. This was "the sin of Jeroboam", since this first king in Ephraim set up his two calves of gold in Bethel and Dan (1 Kings 12,28), and from this presumably is derived the name "Jacob's bull" for Yahweh (Gen. 49,24; Ps. 132,2.5). The image of the bull denoted that Yahweh's nature was associated with the ox which formed the centre of Canaanite life and worship. In addition, there were, as we have seen, probably human images.

Besides these images the Israelites had a holy object with which Yahweh was associated, the most important of all, namely the Ark. It probably contained a holy object or several such, treasures from the pre-Canaanite period, and thus hardly anything that could be called an image, which, indeed, it would be absurd to put away in a chest. It was the Ark which was Yahweh's chief revelation in Zion.

It is quite possible that Solomon, who, as we know, lived in the style of a great Canaanite prince and proposed to found a

Canaanite-Israelite cult, set up a bull image of Yahweh in his temple. There is even a temptation to draw that conclusion from the fact that Jeroboam set up his bulls to compete with Jerusalem, as is expressly mentioned in 1 Kings 12,28. But if this was the case, that rival of the ancient holy object of the people, the Ark, was soon removed again, perhaps by Asa, who is mentioned as the first reforming king. [1] We may conclude this from the fact that the book of Kings never accuses the kings of Juda of "Jeroboam's sin", and even more from the fact that it militated against the nature of Yahweh in Zion as we know it from the Psalms and the prophets. On the other hand, in the course of time other images collected in Yahweh's temple and in other temples in Jerusalem.

We meet with the first denunciation of images in Hosea, who speaks of the kings and chiefs of Ephraim, which she has set up without consulting Yahweh, and in this connection he mentions that "they make their silver and their gold into idols *('a ṣabbīm)* that they may be exterminated" (Hos. 8,4, cf. 4,17; 14,9) ; and he says: And now they go on sinning and making themselves molten images *(massēkhā)*, of their silver idols *('a ṣabbīm)* in their skill, all of it the work of craftsmen. They say to them ... Men that sacrifice kiss calves (13,2). The Israelites are accused of offering sacrifices to the Baalim, burning incense to images *(p e sīlīm* 11,2).

Hosea's denunciation of images is directly connected with his campaign against the Canaanite cult with which they are closely associated. They make Yahweh into an ox. This is also the case in Micah who says about the images that they are derived from harlots' hire, that is to say, from the temple treasure obtained through the sexual cult; therefore Yahweh will destroy them, and they shall again be reduced to what they actually were, viz. harlots' hire (Mic. 1,7).

But Hosea also indicates that the idols which the Canaanitish Israelites include in their cult are the work of man, produced by craftsmen. And gradually this idea comes to prevail. All other gods but Yahweh are images made by men. "Its land was filled with non-gods, he prostrates himself before the work of his own hands, that which his fingers have made, "says Isaiah (2,8);

what Yahweh has done to Samaria and her non-gods he will do to Jerusalem and her images (*'aṣabbīm*, 10,10 f.). This point of view is very conspicuous in Jeremiah when he blames his contemporaries for calling the tree "my father" and saying to the stone "thou hast brought me forth", whereas they turn their backs on Yahweh (Jer. 2,27). In this way the question of idols has been made a question of the relation between the divine and the world of nature.

In the cult of the ancients, idols are of the same nature as all other holy objects. Their significance depends on their power to embody a psychic content. The pole of the sanctuary has the life of the tree in it, but it can absorb all the holy force of the place, and the large holy objects of the people have in them the holy forces which uphold its life. The Ark was precisely such a holy treasure. It made no difference whether it was a box, an unshaped stone, or an image with animal or human features, which was to express dominant traits in the nature of the God in question. But when the God was detached from the life of nature, and his relation to it consisted only in the creator's display of power, then the psychic strength was removed from nature, it became merely an instrument for the creator, a means for him to display his power. Then it would be absurd to seek divine life and holy strength in the things of this world. And if idols were formed in the shape of animals or men, it could only be understood as a ridiculous attempt to degrade the creator by ascribing to the imitations of creation that power which He alone possessed.

Thus all images, whether of Yahweh or of other gods, become the greatest of all delusions, because they are aimed directly at the honour of Yahweh, He alone possessing divine power as the maker of heaven and earth. This consequence of Yahweh's unique divine power is thus on a line with the result that all worship is actually useless, and that all human activity only acquires a value by being executed as a gift from Yahweh. It is only natural that we should also hear the judgment that altars are man's handiwork on which, in contrast with Yahweh, one cannot rely (Isa. 17,7 f.).

The various consequences of Yahweh's greatness did not

develop at the same time and were not carried to extremities. If this were to be done, there would be no limits to what might be disrupted in normal Israelite life. But the absolute rejection of images meant to represent gods was doubtless most clearly displayed within Israelite circles in the Assyrian and particularly in the exilic period, when Yahweh was faced by the gods of prepotent nations who were all represented by images.

In the Psalms we are told that worshippers of images and idols shall be confounded (Ps. 97, 7). The gods of the nations are powerless images, non-gods of silver (cf. Isa. 31,7); they have mouths, eyes, ears, a nose, hands and feet, and yet they cannot use one of their limbs (Ps. 115,4 ff.; 135,15 ff.); and by these worshippers of images the Israelites allowed themselves to be taught, they whose God had created heaven and earth! (Ps. 106, 36). They changed their glory for an image of an ox that feeds on grass (v. 20).

Deutero-Isaiah especially, who lives in the midst of the Babylonian cults, does not weary of pouring out his scorn on the gods who are merely images of wood and stone, whose coming into existence he describes from the planting of the tree (Isa. 40,12 ff. etc.). [1] We find the same mockery in the book of Jeremiah where there is a description of how an idol is made by the united efforts of the carver and other workmen, and is clad in garments of red and violet purple — and then it is all merely juggling and delusion (Jer. 10,1-16, cf. 50,2; 51,15-19.47.52; Hab. 2,18; Zech. 13,2). In Ezekiel we find not mockery but a glowing indignation when he describes how the temple is filled with *gillūlīm* and images of all sorts of reptiles, and especially an image which provoked Yahweh's jealousy *(semel hak-ḳin'ā,* Ez. 8,3.5). When the Israelites lived among strangers the question of the relation of Yahweh to the other gods subsequently came into the forefront again, and it always remained a question of the relation to images. [2]

The war against the Canaanite cult found expression in the story about the golden calf which we have already considered; [3] but it is written in such a form that it contains a denunciation of images. The narrative is as follows (Ex. 32): While the people were waiting for Moses whose stay with Yahweh in the mountain proved lengthy, they came to Aaron, saying: Stand up, make us gods which shall go before us, for we know not what is become of this Moses, the man who brought us out of the land of Egypt (v. 1). Aaron then let them bring their golden ornaments and made of them a molten calf, and they said: These be thy gods, O Israel, which brought thee up out of the land of Egypt. Then Aaron built an altar before the calf and proclaimed a feast *(ḥagh)* to Yahweh the next day. Early on the morrow they offered sacrifices and peace offerings; the people ate and drank and began to abandon themselves *(ṣaḥḥēḳ)*. — Then we are taken up into the mountain. Yahweh tells Moses that the Israelites, the people that he has brought out of Egypt, have done ill and turned aside from the path he had commanded them to follow, having made themselves a molten calf, prostrated themselves, offered sacrifice to it and said that these were the gods that had brought Israel out of Egypt. Further Yahweh says to Moses that he has seen that they are a stiff-necked people, "and now, therefore, leave it to me, and let my wrath wax hot against them, and let me do away with them, but of thee I will make a great nation" (v. 10). But Moses mollified Yahweh and advised him not to let his anger blaze against the people which he had with such mighty power brought out of Egypt; the Egyptians would then say that out of mischief he had brought them out to slay them in the mountains. Therefore he should turn from his wrath and remember his oath to Abraham, Isaac and Israel that he would multiply their seed as the stars and give them the land. Then Yahweh repented of what he had said. — Moses descended from the mountain with the two tables of the law, which were made by God and written on both sides by Him. When the noise of the people was heard, Joshua thought it was a noise of war, but Moses said that he could hear singing. When they came and saw the calf and the dancing Moses' anger blazed, and he broke the tables against the rock. He took the calf, burnt it up, and ground it to powder which he put into water and made the Israelites drink. Then he turned to Aaron who explained how he had been forced, "and I cast the gold into the fire, and there came out this bull calf". —

When Moses saw the people in unbridled abandonment which exposed them to the mockery [1] of their enemies, he went and stood by the gate to the camp and asked: Who is on Yahweh's side? Then the Levites went with him through the camp, cutting down the people; therefore they were consecrated as priests and the blessing for this task was bestowed upon them. — The next day Moses again went into the mountain to Yahweh, entreating forgiveness for the sin of the people, the making of a god of gold, and begging to be blotted out of the book of life if Yahweh did not forgive. Yahweh answered that he only who sinned against him should be blotted out of his book, and he bid him lead the people to the place he had told him of, adding that he would visit their sins on them when the time came.

This story is a typical example of an ancient cult legend renarrated in the spirit of exilic or rather post-exilic Judaism. We catch a glimpse in it of traits which give a picture of the Israelite-Canaanite cult and its destruction by Moses, judgment being thus pronounced in the great struggle which dominated the history of Israel. It is remarkable that Aaron, the high priest of the royal temple, is made co-responsible for the Canaanite cult with the young bull, the festal offerings, the dances and the ecstatic abandonment. It is possible that we may here have reminiscences from a time when there was the image of a bull in the temple of Jerusalem; for the people of post-exilic times it could only appear as a sad testimony to weakness even in the best. With refined irony Aaron is characterised by his answer to Moses that he merely cast the gold into the fire and this bull calf came out — entirely of its own accord. The introduction of the Levites as Moses' fellow fighters who thus win their right to be priests, a feature appearing in another form in a corresponding legend (Num. 25,6 ff.), might in itself belong to the original narrative, but this would bring in a deliberately introduced contrast between Aaron and the Levites, which is hardly conceivable.

There are other irregularities showing that the story has not been remoulded into a firmly coherent whole by the writer who formed it; but he has set the stamp of his time upon it. The people's appeal to Aaron is full of the Jewish ironical feeling towards the gods. The people expressly demands "gods" (vv. 1.4.8), though the plural form which is emphasised in the verbs corresponds badly with the single image; it is the belief in several gods which is the delusion that is to be branded as the foolishness that it is. And when the people demands that such gods should be "made", it expresses the Jewish conception of the absurdly simple way in which other gods come into existence; but this scene, and that in which Moses meets the Israelites on coming down from the mountain, are those in which we must seek the early material.

There is not complete coherence between Moses' conversations with Yahweh and the rest of the story. First Yahweh grows angry, but Moses mollifies him. But this scene does not seem to have any influence on the next, in which Joshua suddenly appears and creates an introduction in which Moses seems to be quite astonished to discover what has happened, and gives free vent to his indignation without regard to his talk with Yahweh. He asks Yahweh to forgive the people without any connection with the first scene in which Yahweh gives up his purpose of destroying it. But both scenes between Yahweh and Moses show evidence throughout of exilic or post-exilic Judaism.

The way in which Moses ascends the mountain and confers with Yahweh is remote from the early conception of the meeting of man and Yahweh. We find in the tale that mixture of respect and frankness with which Judaism lets the great men of the past parley with their god as man to man. Yahweh has now found out that the people he had chosen and brought up out of Egypt was a refractory people which was inclined to evade his precepts and make idols, and he consults Moses about it; the latter appeals to Yahweh's honour: What will the other peoples think and what will become of his oath to the patriarchs? Feature by feature leads us into the atmosphere of Judaism. And when Moses again goes up to speak to Yahweh and ask forgiveness for the people which has made a god of gold, Yahweh answers that he will punish him who sins against him by blotting him out of his book. Here we see Yahweh as the great keeper of accounts, who treats every one according to his conduct, an idea which belongs to exilic and post-exilic times.

The hatred and contempt of later Israel for other gods than Yahweh and for all idols has been unambiguously expressed in the various law codes. The Decalogue says: I am Yahweh, thy God, who brought thee out of the land of Egypt, out of the house of bondage. Thou shalt have no other gods before me. Thou shalt not make unto thee any graven image *(pesel)* or any likeness of any thing that is in heaven above, or that is in the earth beneath or that is in the water under the earth. Thou shalt not prostrate thyself before them nor serve them, for I Yahweh thy God am a jealous God ... (Ex. 20,2-5; Deut. 5,6-9). The book of the Covenant has: Ye shall not make beside me gods of silver, neither shall ye make unto you gods of gold (Ex. 20,23), and its laws end in admonitions not to bow down to the gods of Canaan, but to destroy their massebahs and only worship Yahweh (Ex. 23,20-33). Similar commandments are repeated about breaking down the altars of the Canaanites, avoiding any covenant with them, and kneeling to their gods or making images (Ex. 34,11-17).

Deuteronomy repeats the same admonitions over and over again, inculcating the worship of Yahweh alone. And there is an elaborate command against making images of anything whatever for the purpose of falling down and worshipping it, be it male or female, beast, bird, reptile, or fish. The reason given is that Israel at Horeb heard only Yahweh's voice but saw no shape (Deut. 4,9 ff.). In all the law codes we find the same thing: Ye shall not make unto you false gods, neither rear you up idols or massebahs, neither shall ye set up any stone with images in your land to bow down to them. I am Yahweh, your God (Lev. 26,1, cf. 19,4). Therefore the images and bamahs of the Canaanites shall be exterminated (Num. 33,52).

It is a common feature of all these laws that the assertion of Yahweh and the rejection of images is the same thing to them. They give the sum and substance of the struggle waged at the close of the monarchical period and during the exile.

In the history of the prohibition of images the aversion to seeing Yahweh as a bull played its considerable part. The conception of Yahweh that came to prevail was entirely determined by his human character. His soul is built like a human soul, only that it is inconceivably great and strong. He looks after his children like a father, he chastises his enemies like a mighty king. He is angered when resistance is made to his will, but he can be mollified again when the sinners repent. He is affectionate to the affectionate, cunning with the cunning (Ps. 18,36 f.). Both in threats and promises it is said that Yahweh is not like a man that he should lie or repent (Num. 23,19; 1 Sam. 15,29; Isa. 55,8 ff.). This means that the strength of his soul is just as much greater than that of men "as the heavens are raised above the earth", which again means that his purpose and actions are not changed by petty human considerations. But we often hear that Yahweh "repents" or "turns away from" the evil he intended to work among the Israelites, when they on their part give up the evil they do to him. Yahweh, like men, has his own personal life, he is provoked and "roused" to action, and in all his might he acquires fresh psychic strength by resting on the Sabbath (Ex. 31,17). The raising of Yahweh above the world did not mean that he was made into an abstraction.

As the reason for the prohibition of images it is said in a single passage that the Israelites did not see Yahweh's shape at Horeb. This does not mean that he has no shape. Every soul is active in a bodily shape, and Yahweh's body resembles that of a man. We hear of his face, his eyes, his nose, and his mouth. When he appears in all his might, there is smoke from his nostrils, fire from his mouth (Ps. 18,9). His lips are full of wrath, his tongue is like a consuming fire, his breath is like a tidal flood (Isa. 30, 27 f.). His arm executes great deeds, with his finger he wrote on the holy tables (Ex. 24,12; 31,18; 32,16). Isaiah saw him on a throne, clad in a mantle. [1] He made man after his likeness (Gen. 1, 26 f.; 9,6), a direct proof that his shape is of the same kind as that of man.

In the old days the cult order gave fixed rules how men could go to the temples to meet Yahweh and "see his face". When he was exalted above men and things, it became impossible for men to see him. But at the same time Moses, the founder of the people, was raised to a special position. He spoke "mouth to mouth" with Yahweh and saw Yahweh's similitude *(t͞munath yahwe)*, while a story tells us that the prophets only received Yahweh's communications in dreams and visions (Num. 12,6-8).

These questions were revolved in the imagination, when they had become disassociated from the cult tradition after the destruction of the old life of the people. In connection with the narrative about the golden calf Yahweh and Moses are mentioned again.

Yahweh commanded Moses to go to Canaan with the people. A *mal'ākh* was to accompany him and drive out the Canaanites, but Yahweh would not go with them himself, for then he would have to destroy the people. Moses asked Yahweh to tell him who was to accompany them, and was then told that Yahweh's face would go with them and take them to the land. Moses now asked to be allowed to see Yahweh's honour *(kābhōdh)*. Yahweh answered that he would let his glory *(ṭūbh)* pass by Moses and at the same time cry out Yahweh's name. But "thou canst not see my face, for man cannot see me and live" (v. 20). But Yahweh would see to it that Moses only saw the back of his *kābhōdh*. Moses then went up the mountain with fresh tables. He saw Yahweh pass and called out to him, and Yahweh made a covenant with him by which he bid him keep away from the Canaanites and their cult and their gods, after which a number of ritual laws are communicated (Ex. 33-34).

This story does not quite agree with another interwoven one where we are told that Moses pitched a tent outside the camp where Yahweh spoke face to face with Moses as one man to another (Ex. 33,11). It is probable that there is early material behind this tale, [1] and the cult laws (34,18-26) actually describe Israelite cult life. But the main story bears entirely the stamp of the unreal speculations of the time after the fall of the kingdom. We find the well-known abstract conception of the relation to the Canaanites and their gods. The narrator makes the utmost effort to raise Yahweh completely above Israel and yet include him in their expedition. He decides to send a *mal'ākh* (33,2, cf. 23, 20 ff.), from early times the term for the shape in which Yahweh appeared to men, now a servant sent by him. The question asked by Moses: Whom will Yahweh send with him (33,12), would have been impossible in earlier times — for whc should go with Israel if not its God? The author finds a way out by saying that "Yahweh's face" goes with them (v. 14 ff.) — and yet no one can see Yahweh's face without dying.

This is illustrated in the scene which is of special interest to us here. With great plastic power Yahweh's solemn passing by Moses is described. Moses has desired to see Yahweh's *kābhōdh*, but even Moses is too lowly for that, he sees as it were the shadow of it, as he turns his eyes towards its back.

We know that in the opinion of the Israelites the face, the name, the honour, were all an expression of the soul. Yahweh's name works and acts and the Israelites put their trust in it. [1] When we are told that Yahweh's name is in Yahweh's *mal'ākh* (Ex. 23, 21) this would be a tautology according to the early view, because according to this both were forms of revelation of Yahweh himself. Yahweh's honour is the greatness of his soul as well as that in which it reveals itself. "Thy honour *(kābhōdh)* and thy power *('ōz)*" are in the sanctuary (Ps. 63,3, cf. 26,8). Yahweh is there with all the contents of his nature. But in later Israel there is a tendency to let these terms for Yahweh's soul come into the forefront, so as to avoid a direct appearance of Yahweh's person.

There was a shrinking from letting Yahweh appear; but Ezekiel saw his glory, and he witnessed how Yahweh's *kābhōdh* left the temple, just as he also saw it return and fill the temple (Ez. 3,23; 8,4; 10,18 f.; 11,22 f.; 43,2.5; 44,4); it was like a brightness (1,28). It appeared wherever Yahweh was, in the holy tent; in the temple; and in Sinai (Ex. 24,16, cf. 16,7.10; Ex. 40,34; 1 Kings 8,11). It was seen in the altar flame when Aaron offered the first sacrifice, in the cloud that led the people, and in the tent when Yahweh spoke to Israel (Ex. 16,10; Lev. 9,6.23 f.; Num. 14,10). It can all be understood in the old sense, but the authors prefer to say Yahweh's glory instead of Yahweh himself, just as they prefer to say that his name dwells in the holy place rather than that he does so himself (Deut. 12,5.11; 16,11 et al.), and gradually they also avoided all mention of his name.

The question as to where Yahweh dwelt was not difficult to answer in earlier times. Yahweh was present wherever there was Israelite holiness, and the many holy places were just as many abodes of Yahweh.

Apart from Sinai which only lived in the people's memory, holiness was restricted to Canaan. This was Yahweh's land, whereas other countries were unclean (Hos. 9,3, cf. Josh. 22,19; Am. 7,17). Its cities were Yahweh's cities; they were his property, like the people (2 Sam. 10,12; 14,13.16; 20,19; 21,3). Here the Israelites could live in the land of man, and any one kept outside it was removed from Yahweh and had to serve other gods (Gen. 4,14.16; 1 Sam. 26,19). The Israelites, and thus Yahweh, had taken over the land. This is expressed in a condensed form in the story about Jacob's fight with the foreign god, and in the narrative in the book of Joshua about the occupation of the country under the leadership of Yahweh's commander (Josh. 5,13 ff.).

The soul of Yahweh and that of the country pervaded each other. Aramæan assailants once called him a mountain God (1 Kings 20,23), a reminiscence from the time when Israel still lived in the highlands and bore the impress of its character. The nature of Yahweh and the country belonged together, therefore people could not live in the country without obeying Yahweh's commandments, or the country would spue them out (Lev. 20,22). The foreign colonists entering the land after the fall of Samaria were made to feel this; without knowing the mishpāṭ of the God of the land they could not stay there (2 Kings 17,24 ff.). Israelites living among strangers were asked the question: Where is thy God? (Ps. 42,4.11), and they learned that it was difficult to sing the songs of Yahweh on foreign soil (Ps. 137,4) Canaan was the "land of the covenant" (Ez. 30,5), because it constituted the foundation of Israel's covenant with Yahweh.

That Yahweh could thus pervade the whole country with his nature was due to the fact that blessedness from the strength of his soul radiated from all his sanctuaries spread throughout the land. When after the exile the temple on Zion was the true and only temple to Yahweh, Yahweh's relation to the whole land was no longer a living thing, but history had set up the claim that the whole country should be Israelitish, dedicated to Yahweh, and this claim the Israelites maintained after the exile, as is evidenced by the Pentateuch.

That Zion was Yahweh's abode was held to be certain both during and after the exile. But when Yahweh was detached from the world and raised above all that is in it, the question must arise whether Yahweh did actually dwell in any place on earth. The question is, indeed, raised in the speech, ascribed to Solomon, at the inauguration of the temple: Does God actually dwell on earth? The heaven and the heaven of heavens cannot contain thee, how much less this house that I have builded! (1 Kings 8,27). The answer is, as in Deuteronomy, that Yahweh lets his name dwell there (v. 18 f. 29). And he turns his eyes towards the place and looks after those who go there as if he dwelt there entirely — which, however, he does not.

That Yahweh dwells in heaven it not an idea which arose late in Israel. In this respect Yahweh may be the inheritor of the Canaanite Hadad or Aliyan Ba'l, whose death and uprising formed the nucleus of the chief annual festival. He was the rider of the clouds and the ruler of heaven as giver of rain and fertility. [1] In the days of King Ahab, Micah, the son of Imlah, appeared among the prophets. He had a vision in which he saw Yahweh seated on his throne surrounded by the host of heaven (1 Kings 22,19). Thus Yahweh was enthroned in heaven as a king surrounded by his court. Among the souls around him is mentioned the "spirit" that is to descend and enter into the prophets as a lying spirit. It is the primal prophetic soul from which the inspiration issues.

Of such strong souls there were many among those around Yahweh. They are those whose strength and substance are holiness throughout, therefore they belong to the divine circle. They are called "the Holy ones" or "the sons of God" (Deut. 33,3; Job. 1,

6; 2,1; 5,1; 6,10; 38,7); they praise Yahweh and are ready to
serve him, they are entirely subservient to him (Job 25,2). They
form his intimate council when he sits in their assembly as a king
with his men (Ps. 89,6-8). Isaiah saw winged serpent-like beings
that hovered around him crying: Holy, holy, holy is Yahweh of
the hosts, all the fullness of the earth is his glory *(kābhōdh)* (Isa.
6,2 f.).

Yahweh's abode in the heavens is a temple or a palace, his holy
temple, where everything cries "praise" (Ps. 11,4; 29,9). There
stands his throne, and thence he looks down upon the children
of men (2,4; 14,2; 93,2; 103,19); therefore the heavens are his
holy heavens and his only abode (Jer. 25,30; Ps. 20,7; 102,20).

The fact that Yahweh's abode was in heaven became to the
Israelites an expression of his relation to the world as its mighty
creator who was outside and above the whole creation. The idea
became significant during the exile, when Yahweh's temple was in
ruins and all his institutions had perished. Deutero-Isaiah
describes how he alone meted out and produced the entire world,
which is all merely as a mote to him, and in this connection he
says: He sitteth enthroned above the circle of the earth, and its
inhabitants are as grasshoppers; he stretcheth out the heavens as
a cloth, spreadeth them out as a tent to dwell in (Isa. 40,22). The
clouds and the stars provide a standard by which Yahweh's might
can be measured (Job 22,12 ff.). In poetical style one of the
Psalms lets the entire universe subordinate itself to Yahweh as
the God who sits enthroned above all creation. Above the mighty
ocean of heaven he has arched his hall; the clouds are his chariot
as they were Aliyan Ba'l's before him; he walks upon the wings
of the wind; the light is his garment; the wind and the flaming
fire are his messengers and ministers. He has fixed the earth;
made order out of chaos; and all life looks to him to receive
everything from his hand. If he looks at the earth, it trembles, if
he touches the mountains, they smoke. His honour alone is eternal
and unshakable (Ps. 104).

It is owing to these presuppositions that the Israelites could
ask, as Solomon is made to do in the narrative, whether Yahweh
dwells on earth. Not because the earth is too remote for him;
Yahweh is God in heaven and God on earth; no one can hide

from him, for he fills heaven and earth (Josh. 2,11; Jer. 23,23 f),
but because the earth is too insignificant to be his dwelling-place.
That the question acquired importance may be seen from a
prophetic utterance from the close of the exilic period: Thus saith
Yahweh: The heaven is my throne and the earth is my footstool.
What is the house ye will build unto me, what place is my
dwelling-place? All this hath mine hand made, so that all this
came into being, saith Yahweh (Isa. 66,1 f.). Thus the later Israelitish conception not only cut the ground from under the
sacrificial cult but also from under the temple. What Yahweh
desires, it is added, is humble contrite souls that tremble upon his
word (v. 2).

As in other domains, here too, the full conclusion was only
drawn sporadically. But the early view of the temple as the abode
of Yahweh had, nevertheless, become changed. In the Lamentations Yahweh's rejection of his sanctuary is deplored (2,7); his
work of destruction came from on high (1,13; 2,1), for he is the
God of heaven. He has hidden in the clouds and is entreated to
look down from heaven (3,41.44.50). But his temple was
nevertheless his seat in so far as it was his footstool (2,1, cf.
Ps. 132,7). This view, which of course links up with the idea that
the Ark is his footstool (1 Chron. 28,2; cf. Ez. 43,7; Ps. 99,5),
meets with the view that the whole earth is his footstool. We also
find an utterance stating that Yahweh descends to review his
hosts on Zion, which he fills with righteousness (Isa. 31,4; 33,5),
his actual habitation being heaven. But besides this we further
find, in the post-exilic period, statements to the effect that Yahweh
dwells in Jerusalem (Zech. 8,3). It is these different points of view
which Deuteronomy attempts to reconcile by saying that Yahweh
let his name dwell in the temple. His strength and essence are
there, but it is hinted that he is not entirely bound to the place.

———

The Israelites' view of themselves and their relation to their
God was bound to be reflected in their *conception of their history*.
The Preacher, to whom life resolved itself into emptiness, complained that "what has happened is remote and far, far away,
who can find it?" (Eccl. 7,24). This lack of a living contact with

history was characteristic of a sceptic to whom what happened seemed to be chance manifestations of a capricious will without any psychic content. The normal Israelites did not lose their contact with the past, but their view of history was characterised by their conception of the activity of their God.

The life of the Israelites in Canaan was related in stories, relics of which have come down to us in three collections succeeding each other in chronological order: the book of Judges, the books of Samuel, and the books of the Kings. Each of them has its peculiar character. The book of Judges gives us a small remnant of legends about tribal warfare and the feats of heroes from the time of the foundation, hence also legends about the founding of sanctuaries; a series of vidid pictures of the Israelite tribes' penetration of the country. The books of Samuel with the histories of Samuel, Saul, and David give an account of the men that denote the transition from the chieftainship of tribal life to the monarchy at Jerusalem. The work has its own peculiar style and occupies a special position by its acute characterisations of Saul and David as persons and as types. It differs widely both from the book of Judges and from the books of the Kings, even though it is joined on to the latter by the close of David's life being incorporated in the books of the Kings as an introduction to the history of Solomon; the books of the Kings give an abstract of tales about kings and prophets down to the fall of Jerusalem.

In the material which forms the foundation of the above-mentioned works we have the direct expression of the life of the Israelite people as it was lived. Out of it there arose in the mind of the Israelite a fixed point, viz. David. He had founded the monarchy and with it a new relation to Yahweh; the temple cult belonging to the monarchy had grown out of his work. He made a unity of the disunited tribes and gave to his dominion the extent which later formed the basis of the ideal claims of Israel (Gen. 15,18; Ex. 23,31; Deut. 1,7; Josh. 13,1 ff.). David gave an entirely new trend to the history of Israel, thus giving Israel new ideals and claims, but also renewed confidence.

All this found expression in the Israelite view of David. His success was due to his covenant with Yahweh, and on this covenant

Israel based its faith that the life and power which the monarchy had maintained for the people would not be lost. David became the ideal king, not only in the sense that he was the true king, but also that he was the person in whom the blessing of the kings had its origin. Both these views appear in the books of the Kings, where the kings are judged by comparison with David, and where Jerusalem is said to be preserved from destruction for the sake of David (2 Kings 8,19; 20,6).

The maintenance of the monarchy as the upholding power in the life of the people thus became identical with the maintenance of David's blessing and his covenant with Yahweh. Therefore a Psalm celebrates this covenant: I have made a covenant for my chosen, I have sworn unto David, my servant: Thy seed will I establish forever, I will build up thy throne for generation after generation (Ps. 89,4 f.). Later it is described how Yahweh found David and anointed him, promising him that his enemies should not defeat him but be beat down before him: My faithfulness and my loving-kindness is with him, and in my name shall his horn be exalted. I set his hand in the sea and his right hand in the currents of the ocean (v. 25 f.). [1] He calls Yahweh his Father, God and the Rock of his salvation, and Yahweh makes him his firstborn, exalted above the Kings of the earth. The covenant with him shall stand fast, his house shall keep the throne forever; if it forsake Yahweh's law, it shall be punished, but Yahweh will not break his covenant (vv. 27-38). All this is the background of a prayer to Yahweh that he will restore the anointed whom his foes have defeated. Another Psalm also recalls Yahweh's oath to David, and entreats him not to cast off his anointed considering all that David did for Yahweh when he carried the Ark to Zion (Ps. 132). These ideas were constantly kept alive by the royal cult in Jerusalem.

David is no remote person, he lives in the monarchy as the king who can claim dominion over all the earth within the ocean that surrounds it, exalted above all kings. Therefore David is also like a landmark showing the beginning of a new period in the life of Israel, or like a well-spring giving its history a new direction and another content.

The Israelites of exilic and post-exilic times, who considered the acknowledgment of anything divine other than Yahweh as a capital sin, regarded their history from the immigration into Canaan till the fall mainly as a chain of sins and apostasies, which must give them all the more reason to humble themselves before their God. This view of their history, which falls into line with the judgment of the prophets, is displayed in the great confessions of sin from post-exilic times and finds expression in the adaptation of the book of Judges and the books of the Kings. But on this view, too, David stands pre-eminent as the man who gave himself wholly to Yahweh, and on whom therefore great happiness was bestowed (cf. Ps. 78,70).

The strange thing, then, is that Israel in an essential degree came to deny her real history. The ancient heroes, from whom the tribes had gathered strength in the old days, because they found their own strength in them, lost interest or seemed merely examples of presumptuous self-confidence. The books of the Chronicles are a characteristic instance of a much abridged and transformed history of Israel on these lines.

The covenant with David was only an indirect manifestation of Yahweh's relation to Israel. The people found the historical expression of it in another place, viz. in the glorification of Yahweh's deliverance of the people from the bondage of Egypt in the Paschal legend. This was at the same time the founding of the people and the inauguration of its relation to its God, and the Paschal legend shows us how Yahweh's greatness through the changeful times manifested itself in this event. Through the annual festival the deliverance from Egypt was made something still living and present, and therefore the firm foundation above which the historical horizon of Israel rose. It was the event in primeval ages (*kedhem*) from which the people and its life had issued. It coincided with the mythical wars of Yahweh in which he defeated his foes and created the order of the world. Therefore this event fills all the history of Israel, as we learn from the prophets and the Psalms; it constituted so great a part of the nature of Yahweh that the Israelites swore "by Yahweh who brought Israel out of Egypt" (Jer. 23,7).

No event in the life of the people came to characterise Israel's relation to Yahweh as the emigration from Egypt. The whole history of Israel was *a divine dispensation.* [1] Its God was enthroned "from eternity to eternity", because all time, i. e. all history, flowed from him, but he acted in time, choosing Israel among all the nations of the world and leading her to Canaan for the purpose of making her the centre of all nations. Only, the Israelites were to bow down to him and obey his will as recorded in the law. All the stories of the wanderings in the wilderness and the conquest of the land are dominated by this view.

The stories of the wanderings form the necessary sequel to the Paschal legend. But the stories of Yahweh's revelation in Sinai are also closely connected with it, because they establish the relation between Yahweh and Israel through the giving of the law. This gives to the whole wilderness period its great importance as the period which forms the foundation of the life of Israel, and numerous examples have shown us how social and ritual questions that arose among the people through the ages are reflected in the narratives dealing with the wilderness period. Thus the Paschal legend gathers to itself the historical material, and Israel obtained a history from which it could gather strength, because it was entirely dominated by Yahweh, with the great men of the past as his instruments. Though the life of the people was exclusively determined by Canaan, and the desert was in their view a wilderness where lawlessness reigned, they still sought their history, so to speak in a condensed form, in the desert. It is understandable that in this way an artificial element must creep into their conception of their history. The most striking example is the conversion of the temple of Jerusalem into a portable sanctuary.

The Israelite laws gave the norm of the covenant between Yahweh and Israel. It is natural, therefore, that together with the giving of the law in Sinai the Israelites are told of the covenant between Yahweh and Israel, an act by which the normal relation between the people and its God is established. The story of the making of the covenant (Ex. 24) forms part of an account of the appearance of Yahweh and the giving of a number of laws.

We are told (Ex. 19) that the Israelites came to Sinai and camped before the mountain, whereas Moses went up to God (1-3a). And Yahweh called to Moses out of the mountain that he was to remind the people of what he had done for them in Egypt, and if henceforth they would keep his covenant, they were to be a peculiar treasure to him, a holy nation. Moses submits this to the elders, and the people agree to it, of which Moses informs Yahweh (3 b-8). Now Yahweh tells Moses that he will come and speak to him from a thick cloud in the audience of the people that they may believe Moses (9). And Yahweh bids Moses go to the people and let them sanctify themselves until the third day, for then Yahweh will descend upon Mount Sinai: but bounds are to be set round the mountain, and any one who merely touches it, man or beast, shall be put to death, though without being touched by any other man's hand (10-13). Moses descended and let the people sanctify themselves until the third day (14-15). On this day in the early morning a dense cloud settled on the mountain, there was thunder and lightening, and a loud trumpet blast was heard so that they were seized with terror. And Moses took them to the foot of the mountain. And the mountain was enveloped in smoke as from a furnace, for Yahweh descended upon it in fire (16-18). The sound of the trumpet grew louder and louder while Moses spoke and God answered him amid the noise (19). When Yahweh had descended upon the mountain, he called Moses up to him and bid him warn the people not to break through to gaze, or many of them would perish. The priests, too, who approached the presence of Yahweh were to sanctify themselves, lest Yahweh break forth upon them. Moses answers that bounds have been set around the mountain, but he is commanded to fetch Aaron, whereas the priests and the people are to keep back. Then Moses descended to the people (20-25).

Now God spoke the ten commandments, a brief summary of laws of a more general character (20,1-17). But the thunder, the trumpet blast, and the smoking mountain frightened the people, so that they kept at a distance; and the people asked Moses to speak to them instead of God, that they might not die. And they kept far away while Moses approached the dark cloud in which

God was concealed. And Yahweh let Moses say to the Israelites that now they had experienced how he had spoken to them out of heaven (18-22).

Next a number of laws are given (Ex. 20,23-23,19), and Yahweh further tells the Israelites that he will send a *mal'ākh* to lead them to Canaan, whose population Yahweh will exterminate; and Israel must not bow down to their gods or enter into any covenant with the people (23,20-33).

Yahweh then told Moses to come up with Aaron, Nadab and Abihu and 70 elders. Only Moses was allowed to approach Yahweh, not the others, and the people were forbidden to ascend the mountain (24,1-2). Moses repeated Yahweh's word and commandments to the people, and the people declared that they would obey them. And Moses wrote them down. The next morning he built an altar and a massebah for each of the twelve tribes. And he let the young men offer burnt offerings and peace offerings of bulls to Yahweh; and Moses took half of the blood in a bowl, with the other half he sprinkled the altar. He read aloud the book of the covenant, and the people said that they would do as Yahweh bid them. Then Moses sprinkled the blood on the people, saying: This is the blood of the covenant which Yahweh maketh with you on these terms (24,3-8). Moses, Aaron, Nadab, Abihu, and 70 elders went up the mountain and they saw Israel's God, under whose feet there was a work of art of sapphire stones, and something like the sky in its clearness. And God did not turn his hand against the nobles of Israel, so they saw God, and did eat and drink (9-11). Yahweh then bid Moses ascend into the mountain, to receive the stone tables with the law and the commandment which Yahweh had written. Moses and Joshua ascended the mountain, letting the elders remain with Aaron and Hur. Moses went up, and the cloud in which Yahweh's honour was, rested on the mountain for 6 days, and on the seventh day Yahweh called from the cloud to Moses; and Moses went into the cloud and remained 40 days on the mountain, but to Israel Yahweh's *kābhōdh* seemed like a devouring fire (12-19).

As a sequel to this we are told of the golden calf, of how Moses broke the two tables written by God himself, and later

42*

made fresh tables on which he wrote. When Yahweh passed by Moses who saw his back, Yahweh declared that he would make a covenant in the audience of the people. Yahweh promised to drive out the Canaanites, Israel must not make any covenant with them, not prostrate themselves before other gods, and not make images. To this is added a brief abstract of Israelite laws, and finally Yahweh bids Moses write down these words for on these terms he intends to make a covenant with Israel. Moses remained 40 days in the mountain, "and he wrote on the tables the words of the covenant, the ten words". It is said that Moses' face shone when he left Yahweh. So he veiled his face, every time he came down from Yahweh (Ex. 32-34).

There is no proper coherence in the whole of this story, and it contains many obscurities which it has been impossible to remove by the various attempts to distinguish between "the sources". [1] What is of interest to us is to find the realities behind the story. That the small groups of laws that enter into the story are such realities is clear, they give rules for early Israelitish social life and ritual, but what we are here concerned with is the stories that form the framework round them. A covenant between Yahweh and Israel is mentioned, and this covenant is connected with the giving of the laws.

The making of the covenant (Ex. 24,3-8) consists in a sacrificial act; to this is added the reading of the "Book of the Covenant" which must contain the laws that give the norm of the covenant, and the covenant is then made by the holy blood being sprinkled on the people. When we are told that a massebah is set up for each of the twelve tribes, this is a natural consequence of the entire view of the people as found in the wilderness stories. But the holy act itself must reproduce a cult custom which the people knew. It is obvious that such a covenant ceremony, including pledging on the law, must have taken place at one of the annual festivals, but the sources say nothing about it.

We hear of the making of a covenant in the temple when the Law Book was found under Josiah (2 Kings 23,3), but we hear nothing else about the procedure except that the law was read aloud. And we learn of the making of a covenant concerning a certain precept, with a sacrificial act which, however, differs from the incident in the Kings (Jer. 34,8 ff.). But we have evidence in Deuteronomy of such a general covenant ceremony with sacrifice and the proclamation of the law. Here the people are commanded to set up stones at Shechem with the law written on them, and there an altar is to be erected on which burnt offerings and peace offerings are to be made, and the blessing and the curse are to be pronounced (Deut. 11,26-29; 27). We are told that this commandment was complied with (Josh. 8,30-35), and it is said about Joshua that at Shechem he let the people pledge themselves on the law and make the covenant (Josh. 24). These utterances, which militate against the demand of Deuteronomy for the centralisation of the cult, would seem to point to festivals with the making of covenants and pledging on the law. [1] Though they give us no clear picture, and appear to have been told at a time when the whole thing was no longer vivid, they seem to indicate that the story of the making of the covenant on Mount Sinai, which thus tells us about the institution of the whole relationship between Israel and her God, is actually based on a cult custom.

If we ask what "Book of the Covenant" is referred to in the story about the covenant made in Sinai, we are faced by one of the many obscurities of the tale. It would seem natural to think of the law code given immediately before, which, indeed, we generally call the Book of the Covenant. But we have no certainty, for there is no inner coherence between these laws and the account of the covenant, and it is risky to attach weight to the place of the laws in the narrative, which is interrupted by other laws irrelevant to it (Ex. 25 ff.). To this must be added that the story after the breach by the worshipping of the golden calf is continued with an account of the renewal of the covenant, and here it is said expressly that it is founded on another abstract of early Israelite laws (Ex. 34). And in between comes the story of the ten commandments which God spoke directly to the Israelites (20,1-17), as if these were the foundation of the covenant, but which Moses had

to go up the mountain to fetch as written with God's own finger
on stone tables (24,12-19), and which he later had to get renewed,
this time on tables he had made himself (34,1.4.28.29).

This would seem to indicate that the story, as transmitted to
us, has an artificial character, and that alterations have been
made in it, though not consistently carried through.

We have seen that that part of the story which deals with the
worshipping of the golden calf and Yahweh passing by Moses is
coloured by a later view. The same applies to the whole first part
of the narrative which deals with the appearance of Yahweh in
Sinai. The central point in this part is the description of Yahweh's
descent upon the mountain (19,16-19). From this account it has
been thought possible to locate Sinai as a volcano, and a search
has therefore been made for volcanoes in the regions to the east
of the Red Sea. A search might with equal justice be instituted
for the mountains that melted like wax when Yahweh passed over
the hills of the earth. The author has done all that he could to
convey an idea of the might of Yahweh. The dark cloud, the
thunder and lightning, the trumpet blast, the smoke, are all meant
to express Yahweh's power over the world of nature. He causes
noise and revolutions when he touches it, as we know from
numerous descriptions of Yahweh's procedure. We can find a
similar view of Yahweh's relation to the earth in the prophets,
but there is no evidence of an old tradition in the description.

That the story has an artificial character appears from the
ease with which the narrator lets Moses pass up and down the
mountain again and again, sometimes quite superfluously, about
a matter that has already been arranged (19,20 ff.). We have not
before us a clear and connected story founded on realities. And
yet there are realities embodied in the separate parts of the story,
the same as we meet in the narrative about Dathan, Abiram, and
Korah, and of which we catch a glimpse in the vacillation in
the Paschal legend wherever it is concerned with the relation
between Moses, Aaron, and the people, viz. in the question as to
the authority among the people and the access to Yahweh.

Moses occupies a special position. He who "carries the people
like a nurse" (Num. 11,12), has in his position features of the

king as he was during the prosperous days of the monarchy in Jerusalem. But he cannot simply be regarded as the archetype of the king, as Aaron is of the high priest. Partly his figure had doubtless, as the leader in the wilderness period, a form and character independent of the monarchy, partly it must affect again the picture of him that the king disappeared, and that in later Israel there was no living head of the nation in whose light Moses could be viewed. He was something apart, a leader in primeval ages, who spoke directly with Yahweh (Num. 12,8).

The figures mentioned besides Moses are the people and its elders, Aaron, i. e. the high priest, the other priests, and among them representatives of certain families of priests, Nadab, Abihu, and Hur. In one section Moses is the intermediary between Yahweh and the elders, the representatives of the people (19, 3 b-8). The object is, as during and after the exile, to make the people a holy people rallying round Yahweh. The section describing Yahweh's theophany (19,9-25; 20,18-22) is written in the same spirit. The mountain is a holy domain like the temple of Jerusalem, and the sanctuary has acquired that overstressed holiness which we know from the later Jerusalem period. Just as the people were not allowed to enter the sanctuary proper, so they must not even touch the mountain, and if any one offends, nobody must pollute himself by touching him when he is put to death. The people and the priests must sanctify themselves and keep back, for the mountain is like the inner sanctuary of the temple where God is present himself. Only Moses must go there, and, as is added later (v. 24), Aaron. And Yahweh let the people hear that he spoke to Moses, that they might believe him (19,9). This result was indeed achieved, for the people recognised that they could not tolerate the presence of Yahweh themselves, so they asked Moses to be their intermediary, and it is strongly emphasised that now the people have tried it for themselves (20, 18-22). It is the position of the lay people in later times which is thus established. Entirely coloured by exilic or post-exilic times is the talk about the relation to the Canaanites and their gods which is joined on to the law code (23,20-33).

As a frame round the story of the making of the covenant we

are informed that Moses was called up into the mountain with Aaron, Nadab, Abihu, and 70 elders. But only Moses is allowed to go to the top, the others keep at a distance, and the people must not approach the mountain. Here Moses appears in perfect isolation, while Aaron is put on the same footing as the other priests and the representatives of the people. This is hardly rooted in facts, therefore it is expressly pointed out that God did not smite the nobles of the people. When it says that they saw the God of Israel with sapphire stones under his feet, we have travelled far from the early view of the God connected with the cult, into the Judæan imaginings of the splendour of the divine heavens (24,1-2.9-11), which we do not trace till we come to Ezekiel. Finally we hear (24,13) that Moses and Joshua, i. e. the leader and his successor, ascend the mountain to fetch the tables, while Aaron and Hur remain with the people.

It is difficult to find any order in the ideas expressed in our story concerning the relation of the various persons to what is holy, and their access to Yahweh. But the reason why the story has become so obscure is precisely the continual alterations made in it owing to its central position in the history of the people, since it is the account of how the foundation was laid for the relation between Yahweh and the people.

David and Moses became the main pillars in the two views of history which formed the background of the Israelite confidence in life, but to later Israel their importance seemed less due to what they did than to what they received. In the covenant which they both had with Yahweh the people saw a guarantee that its God would continue to bestow his blessing on it. It gave self-confidence to the people in a peculiar way, not by achievements which they could regard as theirs, but by the consciousness of being chosen by the Almighty.

Besides the two kinds of history mentioned here, the Israelites had a third, viz. *the patriarchal history*. It gives us a new form of the ancient history of Israel, the tribal experiences expressed in the lives of the forefathers. In it we get a series of pictures of the life of Israel in earlier times, which would otherwise be unknown to us. We become acquainted with the Israelites as shepherds and semi-nomads who wander about the country with their tents (Gen. 13,3; 25,27; 46,34; 47,3), we are carried far away from the world of towns and even from that of the peasant. The shepherd is superior to the peasant, as shown by the story of Cain and Abel; and the towns are derived from the lawless Cain (4,17); Jerusalem is insignificant. This is the view of the world which we know from the Rechabites, and by which the prophets, too, are influenced.

As the stories have been transmitted to us, they give us ample insight into early Israelite psychic life, but there can be no doubt that they would have done so still more, if we had known them in their earlier form. We may conjecture that the individual figures have in olden times been associated with difinite groups of the people and with definite sanctuaries. The God is the God of the patriarch and is sometimes called Yahweh and sometimes by the more general name of Elohim, sometimes El Shaddai or other names. These different names of gods may contain reminiscences of diverse divine personalities in early Israel; [1] but as we know them they are all revelations of the same God of Israel.

Shaddai, whose origin is unknown, is mentioned in several writings down through the ages as another name for Yahweh (Gen. 49,25; Num. 24,4.16; Ps. 68,15; 91,1 et al.), and in the book of Job it is the common designation for the God besides Eloah and Elohim; perhaps the term was common in communities outside Jerusalem. In later times it was felt as an archaic name for Yahweh; therefore one story lets Yahweh reveal himself to Abraham as El Shaddai (Gen. 17,1), and one part of the Paschal legend even lets Yahweh say to Moses that he was only known to the fathers by that name (Ex. 6,3). Here we are merely concerned with speculations as to names without any real substance, but even behind them may lie old traditions. The whole history of the patriarchs, as we know it, presupposes that the patriarchs are the progenitors of all later Israel, and that the God who revealed himself as the God of their race was identical with the later God of Israel. Their importance is due to the promises made to them, and they have become ideal types of the Israel that does nothing of its own accord, but receives everything as a gift from Yahweh. In that way their life has become an idyl, widely different from what we learn in the history of the wanderings and the history of the conquest, or in the early histories of the heroes.

What Abraham was to the Judæans who in the earliest times of the history of the people gathered around the sanctuary at Hebron is quite unknown to us. As we know him he is the father of the people who, in return for his obedience and righteousness, won the covenant with Yahweh by which the people later lived. In obedience to Yahweh he left his family to take over the land which Yahweh proposed to give him. It was in that remote past when there were still Canaanites in the country (Gen. 12,6), but they are entirely without importance. Abraham traverses the country in every direction, and the whole of it is given to him and his offspring (12,7; 13,14-18). He takes possession of it by building altars in the north and the south (12,7; 13,18). In everything he showed his faith in Yahweh, and Yahweh repaid him by promising him numerous offspring and making a covenant with him by which he was promised the land for his descendants to the extent it should attain under David (Gen. 15). This was given him on account of his righteousness, but his righteousness showed itself in obedience, which stood the test when he did not refuse to sacrifice his only son, the very son by whom the promises were to be fulfilled (Gen. 22). All the main features of the stories about Abraham are coloured by the time after the regal period. The stories about the sanctuaries reveal nothing as to a living relation to the cult, they are preoccupied with the dominant purpose of the stories, to prove the right of Israel to Canaan. No one disputed this right in pre-exilic times, we never see this problem arising in the prophets, it was a matter of course that Israel owned her land with which she had become one. The question only came up when the nation had ceased to exist and desired to re-establish a right for themselves.

Isaac was the founder of the altar at Beersheba (Gen. 26,25), but alle the material which might have given independent life to his figure has vanished, only his name remains as the inheritor of Abraham's covenant and the man who carried on the blessing and the right to the country (Gen. 26,2-5.24).

Jacob is the true progenitor of the people, the man from whom the historical tribes were descended. The stories about him afford us ample material, a series of pictures rich in matter from the early life of the Israelite people. These stories, too, have been coloured by the main view of the histories of the patriarchs. It is the blessing of Abraham and Isaac which Jacob carries on, and it is stressed as an essential part of it that the land is promised to him and his house (28,13 f.). He made the sanctuary at Bethel Israelite when he learned that his God was there; and at Shechem he abolished all the foreign gods of his family (35,2.4). The wanderings of Jacob were part of the same divine purpose as those of Abraham. He received it all as a gift, being too humble for all the mercy shown to him (32,11); at his death he acknowledged that he had been guarded by the God before whose countenance his fathers, Abraham and Isaac, had walked (48,15). We cannot single out such individual features from the stories and regard them as "later additions". They fall naturally into line with the whole exposition and fit into the stories, because Jacob has his character from that Israel which, like David, preferred to keep back in order to let Yahweh act.

The account of the life in Canaan found in the patriarchal stories has been linked up with the ancient history of the people. It is linked with the Paschal legend, by being assigned to the time before it, and the history of Joseph is its intermediate link. Through it the tribal ancestors are brought into Egypt, and thus Israel obtains a continuous history from Abraham to Moses. This emigration to Egypt, too, is part of Yahweh's purpose with his people. "Not you sent me hither, but God", says Joseph to his brothers (Gen. 45,8, cf. 50,20). Thus the patriarchal history shows from first to last how the people was chosen and led by its God, that he might fulfil the promises he had made to it. [1]

The historical horizon created for Israel through David, through the Paschal legend with the associated stories about the covenant of Sinai, and through the patriarchal stories gave the people fixed bearings and a background for their claims and their faith. The more the self-confidence of the people was shaken, the more it clung to its history. The prophets saw in the history of the people one great sin. The earlier prophets saw the root of it in the life in Canaan, but Ezekiel included the whole history of the people in his judgment, and the time during and after the exile abounded with confessions of sin, to which also corresponded the continuous tales about rebellion and disobedience in the period of the wanderings. Thus the deep chasm between the people and its God was traced back through its history. The promises of Yahweh and the fathers to whom they were given were made the positive content of the history, that in which Israel put its trust, because the promises had been transmitted to the descendants (Neh. 9,7).

The promises to Abraham, Isaac and Jacob were incorporated in the legend about the deliverance from Egypt (Ex. 2,24; 3,6.16). The patriarchs are given great prominence by the prophets from the exilic period and later. Abraham was the friend of Yahweh, and Israel is his house (Isa. 41,8); he was but one and yet he was given the great blessing, how much the more, then, would it be given to his descendants (51,2; Ez. 33,24). One prophet prays for faithfulness to Jacob, love of Abraham; that is what Yahweh swore unto them in the days of old (Mic. 7,20, cf. Jer. 33,21.26). Another prophet says in despair that Abraham and Israel do not know their descendants, Yahweh is their father and must intervene (Isa. 63,16); it is not the fathers who give strength; but through them Yahweh has bound himself to his people. In Deuteronomy the Israelites are constantly reminded of Yahweh's oath to their forefathers, and it is said expressly that the covenant was not for them alone but also especially for their descendants who were to take possession of the land (Deut. 4,31; 5,3; 7,8; 9,5.27, cf. Lev. 26,42; 2 Kings 13,23; Ps. 105,6.9.42). It was Yahweh's mercy from of old ('ōlām, cf. Ps. 25,6), by which he had bound himself; therefore he must uphold the people for his own honour's sake.

In the relation of Israel to her God there is a constant fluctuation between two goals: on the one hand, the eagerness to exalt Yahweh above everything and free him from constraint by what is found on earth, and on the other hand, a passionate endeavour to bring Israel into more and more intimate relations with him. In the Hellenistic time, when the various civilisations mixed and men tried to find a common God behind all the individual gods, the Jewish effort to free their God from all earthly limitations had fitted him for taking the place of the desired common God. However extensive his power became, he still retained his character of the God of Israel. When new religious communities made Israel's God their own, they therefore acquired something of the Israelite spirit, and Israelitish psychic life became active through the ages far beyond its original limited circle.

NOTES.

P. 2 [1]. *bipherōaʿ peraʿōth* is one of the obscure expressions of the song of Deborah. Nowadays it is often interpreted: "because they wore their hair hanging loose in long locks", referring to a common custom in war, since *pāraʿ* may mean "loose", and *peraʿ* in the sense of lock of hair occurs in Num. 6,5; Ez. 44,20 (cf. Ass. *pirtu* and Arab. *farʿ* about long hair). Or, according to a version of LXX: "because the princes behaved like princes", since Arab. *farʿ* may denote "a prominent man", and the verb may mean "to be prominent". The meaning "to revenge" has been taken from Aram., and the translation "to gain liberty" has been inferred from the sense "loose" occurring in Arab. The meaning attaching to *prʿ*, partly of long hair, partly of a prominent man, can be referred to a basic sense of being subject to no restrictions, unfolding oneself freely. Therefore the verb is used in Hebrew about leaving to itself, e. g. letting the hair grow or hang loose, Lev. 10,6; 21,10; Num. 5,18. It is used in Niph. (Prov. 29,18) and Hiph. (2 Chron. 28,19) about acting licentiously and in the passive participle Qal (Ex. 32,25) about the cult ecstasy. This latter use corresponds exactly to the sense given in this translation, viz. the psychic abandonment or ecstasy that occurs in war; *peraʿōth* may be interpreted as a nomen actionis in the plural. It is hardly exactly the same sense that is implied in the term *hithnaddēbh* (from which *nādhībh*, chief) occurring twice (v. 2.9). This means to let oneself be led by one's own inner impulses, hence to be self-glorious, noble. It has entirely come to denote voluntary action, but it probably meant something more violent in the old days. — As regards the various conceptions, see the commentaries by Budde, Nowack, Moore and Burney, where more literature is quoted.

P. 2 [2]. For *nāṭāphū*, *nāmōghū* or *nāmōṭū* "tremble" has been suggested, according to a version of LXX, but M. T. is just as good.

P. 2 [3]. *ze sīnay* seems to be an explanatory gloss. Albright reads *ze* as *d* in Ras Shamra: "the one of Sinai", Bull. of the Amer. Schools of Or. Res. No. 62, 1936, p. 30.

P. 2 [4]. Here we read *perāzōth* with 4 mss., a Syriac version, and Targum, i. e. the open villages, without walls and therefore defenceless, Ez. 38,11; Zech. 2,8; Est. 9,19. In the earliest times the Israelites lived in such towns or camped in tents in Canaan. — The form *ḳamtī* may be the 2. pers. fem. or the 1. pers.

P. 2⁵. *lāḥem* or *lāḥēm* seems to be the word from which *milḥāmā* "war" is formed. It is used as a verb in Niph., and some few times in Qal; here Pi. seems to be the nearest. The view given in the translation that the fight will now centre round the settled towns makes good sense. The interpreters generally alter the text, even the very clear "new gods are chosen", a characteristic expression from the time of transition.

P. 2⁶. No certain translation can be given of *meḥaṣṣesīm*. The meaning "divide booty" is inferred from *ḥēṣ*, which is used about the arrow employed in the casting of lots; see Burney's Comm. and Ges.-Buhl. The emendation *meṣaḥᵃḳīm* (Budde) or the corresponding fem. (Burney) "joking" does not agree well with the ecstatic earnestness of the poem. The preceding *mikḳōl* cannot be translated under these circumstances.

P. 2⁷. *pirzōnō*, same word as *perāzōn*, v. 7, is unknown.

P. 2⁸. *yeradh* is unintelligible; here we read *yāradh* "descends". *sārīdh* "fugitive" is also unintelligible. V. 13 a might be conceived to be a description of a fugitive coming from the first skirmish "to the mighty"; and v. 13 b might be what he said: Yahweh's people, come down to aid me among the heroes; *yeradh* in v. b must then be the imperative.

P. 3¹. After "their root" the words "in Amalek" are left out; perhaps both expressions are due to a corruption of the text. "After thee, Benjamin" is a war-cry, Hos. 5,8, which must mean that Benjamin is to go first. Cf. Burney's Comm. — Montgomery in Journ. of the Amer. Or. Soc. 58, 1938, p. 138, quotes as a parallel Arab. *warā'aka* "(look) behind thee", which must mean "take heed".

P. 3². *sōphēr* is used about functionaries, both civil and military. It is interesting to note that it is employed in Israel at this time to denote a ruler.

P. 3³. The text has: And my chiefs in Issachar...; in the translation *b* has been transferred to the foregoing and altered to *k*. In what follows *kēn* is interpreted as a faithful, devoted person, just like the corresponding *'āmūn* in 2 Sam. 20,19; Ps. 12,2; 31,24; Arab. *ṣadīḳ* may be quoted as a parallel. In this passage many interpreters read Naphthali, to which Barak belongs according to 4,6, see Comm.

P. 3⁴. This utterance is repeated in v. 16; some interpreters omit it in v. 15; others in v. 16; but the repetition may perhaps be intentional. The prepositions *bi* in v. 15 and *li* in v. 16 are equally good. On the other hand, *ḥiḳrē* in v. 16 is surely better than *ḥiḳeḳē* in v. 15; the latter must be understood as equivalent to *ḥuḳḳē* and means decrees, resolutions.

P. 4 [1]. For *ta⟨ⁿnennā* (sing.) "answers her", read *ta⟨ⁿnenū* (plur. without suffix).

P. 4 [2]. Read *lᵉṣawwā'rī, shālāl* is either an error for another word, or it begins a new strophe the rest of which is lost.

P. 8 [1]. H. S. Nyberg, however, takes *mᵉlākhīm*, v. 19 ff., as used about gods. See Studien zum Hoseabuche, p. 47 [Uppsala Universitets Arsskrift 1935, 6].

P. 9 [1]. Read *yāmēs*, actually melt. Cf. I—II p. 150.

P. 12 [1]. This implies a characteristic limitation in the recognition of the absolute value of food. There are even said to be peoples who deny the value of food for the maintenance of the organism, see Malinowski, The sexual Life of Savages in North-Western Melanesia, London 1929, p. 371 f.

P. 12 [2]. Cf. the expression "anoint for war" in Sanhedrin XIII, 3.

P. 13 [1]. The special sense of *yᵉdhashshᵉne* is obscure.

P. 16 [1]. See I—II, pp. 141—144.

P. 17 [1]. See I—II, p. 168 f. (Isa 20,2-3 here referred to, says that the Assyrians shall drag away the Egyptians and Ethiopians, not that the Assyrians shall be dragged away).

P. 20 [1]. In the narrative in Josh. 6 there is obscurity as regards the blowing of the trumpets and the clamour of the warriors. In vv. 2-5 Yahweh issues his command to Joshua that for 6 days the warriors shall go once daily round the city, while 7 priests carry the rams' horns in front of the Ark. But on the 7th day they are to go 7 times round the city and the priests are to sound the horns. When the people hears the noise of the horns they are to raise up a great shout and the city will fall; v. 5 it would seem may also be interpreted to the effect that the people are to shout when they hear a *long* blast from the horn. In vv. 6-11 we are told of how Joshua gives the order partly to the priests partly to the people, 6-7; to this is added the information that Joshua commanded the people to be silent until he ordered them to raise the war cry (v. 10), and we hear of the procession on the first day (v. 11). A description of the order of the procession is inserted, corresponding to Yahweh's command in v. 4, in which it is said that the priests went along blowing with the horns, vv. 8-9. Then the procession on the second day and on the rest of the six days is described, vv. 12.14, and an account of the procession with the priests sounding the horns is inserted (v. 13) as in v. 8 f. Next follows the description of the seventh day in v. 15 ff. They went round the city as usual, only on this day seven times. The seventh time the priests sounded the horns and Joshua commanded the people to raise the war-cry, "for Yahweh gives you the city" (vv. 15-16), to which he adds a lengthy warning to ban the entire booty (vv. 17-19). The text then goes on to say: And the people raised a war-cry and they sounded the horns, and it came to pass: when the people heard the sound of the horns they shouted with a mighty war-cry and the wall fell down etc. (v. 20). Here are two beginnings. According to the one the war-cry follows upon Joshua's speech in accord with his command in v. 10. In the other it follows the sounding of the horn in accord with Yahweh's speech in v. 5, but in both cases the sounding of the horns only sets in at the seventh round on the seventh day. Thus it is only the descriptions inserted (as repetitions of v. 4) of the procession in 8-9 and 13 which have the continual sounding of the horns during all the processions, in contrast with the rest of the narrative. If these are omitted no other obscurity remains but that in v. 20, and that disappears if 20 a is left out (to *hash-shōphār*). — Wellhausen (Composition p. 121 f.) and the commentators distinguish between two co-ordinate accounts. But a division of the narrative into two co-ordinate stories has not been possible. Behind the division lies the desire to segregate a simpler and more natural tale (cf. Kittel, Geschichte I 5.-6. ed., 1923, p. 414 f.). It is reasonable to suppose that other stories of another character have preceded ours. But a separation of the sources implies that such a story existed in a written form and was then mechanically combined with the other one, and there is no sign of this. Literary criticism here goes beyond its natural limits as also in the treatment of the story of the passing over the Reed Sea, see Additional Note I. It is just as objectionable to attempt to reconstruct the historical event on the basis of the details found in the account, as done in Garstang's otherwise instructive work: Joshua, Judges, 1931.

P. 21 [1]. This translation of *shālīshīm* is quite uncertain.

P. 23 [1]. Read *he-'ādhām*.

P. 27 [1]. See I—II, p. 250 f.

P. 30 [1]. Here we may recall that the Romans not only dedicated captured objects to the temples but also burned part of the spoil before the gods of war, see Livy XLV, 33; Appian, Rom. Hist. VI 57; VIII 48. Appian thinks that it was the poorest part which was thus burned.

P. 33 [1]. *nāśi'* Ex. 22,27; Lev. 4,22; Num. 1,44 etc.; *nāghīdh* Job 29,10; 31,37 et. al.

P. 36 [1]. *pa'am* inf. Piel, literally to set in restless motion, cf. in Niph. Gen. 41,8; Ps. 77,5; Dan. 2,3; in Hithp. Dan. 2,1.

P. 38 [1]. On this view of *berū*, see the author's Der Eid bei den Semiten p. 44 f. A similar story about single combat between two rulers taking the place of fighting between their armies occurs in Ṭabarī, ed. de Goeje, I 2639; Abū Nu'aim, Gesch. Iṣbahāns, ed. Dedering I 25.

P. 40 [1]. See I—II p. 421 f.

P. 44 [1]. See I—II p. 251.

P. 47 [1]. Apart from the earlier treatment of the literary question we may refer the reader to O. Eissfeldt, Die Komposition der Samuelisbücher, 1931, and to the minute investigation of the history of the legend in J. Hylander, Der literarische Samuel-Saul Komplex, 1932.

P. 48 ¹. Read *lū* 1 Sam. 13,13.

P. 48 ². The meaning of *nēsaḥ* is doubtful.

P. 52 ¹. The consecutive perfects in 1 Sam. 16,23 must, according to ordinary usage, be understood as a continuation of the invitation expressed in v. 22.

P. 55 ¹. Read *beyādhī*.

P. 58 ¹. See I-II p. 295.

P. 59 ¹. LXX ἐνώπιόν μου "to my eyes", from which it appears that LXX has not understood David's train of thought.

P. 59 ². On the difficult text see S. R. Driver, Notes on the Hebrew text of the Books of Samuel, 1890, and the commentaries of H. P. Smith and of Budde. One might read *be῾ārē hā῾ēmeḳ* "in the cities of the plain" and then keep "in Transjordania", which must then mean the nearest cities in Transjordania.

P. 64 ¹. 1 Kings 9,26 f.; 10,11.22. It is hardly probable that only one ship is concerned, thus Kittel, Gesch. II 251. On the whole question cf. Th. H. Robinson, A History of Israel I, p. 256 f. It was the old trade route through the Red Sea and the route from Egypt to Asia Minor and the north-eastern countries which Solomon used, see 1 Kings 10,26 ff. where we should probably read Egypt and Koa. The introduction of horses and chariots means a change of the earlier methods of warfare. By way of the Red Sea gold, silver, fine woods, precious stones, ivory, and other contributions to a more refined civilisation were imported, 1 Kings 10,11 f. 22.

P. 64 ². Fortresses at Tamar to the south and more westward: Gezer, Baalath, then Beth-horon, Megiddo, Hasor, besides renewed fortification of Jerusalem, 1 Kings 9,15 ff.; war chariots 10,26. At Megiddo Guy has excavated in 1928—29 Solomon's stables with room for 300 horses besides chariots and men, see Oriental Institute Communications No. 9, 1931.

P. 66 ¹. On Egypt where the Israelites had themselves worked as bondmen, see Erman, Aegypten, 1885, p. 180 ff.; 2. ed. by H. Ranke, 1923, p. 139 ff. Among the Babylonians Hammurabi caused Sippar's wall to be built by labour gangs from his people. Otherwise partly prisoners of war, partly the humbler classes are employed both among the Babylonians and the Assyrians. We are told that Sargon imposed tasks on the inhabitants of the city of Assur as proletarians, see Meissner, Bab. und Ass. I pp. 113.123 f. 129.139.145. In the Assyrian law code a punishment frequently employed is work for the king as a bondman for a month.

P. 69 ¹. The Amarna letters, ed. Knudtzon, 4,8 f.

P. 69 ². See I—II p. 81 ff.

P. 70 ¹. In Ez. 45,14 the text is corrupt, see Comm. Among the Syrians the Romans also took a share of the grazing for their horses, see Rob. Smith, Religion of the Semites, 3. ed., p. 246 ¹.

P. 70 ². Samaria's Ostraca are published in Reisner's Harvard Excavations at Samaria, p. 227 ff. For the Judaean see Chabot, Répertoire d'Épigraphie sémitique III, p. 47 ff.; these also give the names of the cities in which the tax was collected (Hebron, Socoh, Ziph, Mamshath). Albright no doubt correctly dates them to 750—590, see his close investigation of the whole question in Journ. of the Pal. Or. Soc., 1925, pp. 17-54. Following him Jack, Samaria in Ahab's Time, 1929, Chap. V. Prior to Albright A. Alt has thrown fresh light on the list of Solomon's districts in Alttestamentliche Studien Rud. Kittel gewidmet, 1913, pp. 1-19; cf. I—II, p. 38 f.

P. 72 ¹. See on this subject Erman, Aegypten p. 113 f., 2. ed. p. 85 f. and Meissner, Bab. u. Ass. I s. v. Königin-Mutter. Among the Hittites the king's wife plays a conspicuous part, even in the cult. See Götze, Kleinasien [W. Otto, Handb. d. Altertumswiss. III, 1,3], 1933, p. 87 f.

P. 72 ². In LXX it is changed into his kissing her.

P. 73 ¹. n⁽ˢū' must no doubt be regarded as an active kātūb form just like zākhūr, yādhū⁽ etc., see I—II, note 2 on p. 199.

P. 74 ¹. See Erman, Aegypten p. 110 f., 2. ed. p. 84 f. In Egypt it was a title given to functionaries, while in Israel it seems only to have been employed about a single person.

P. 78 ¹. 2 Sam. 12,30 et al. ⁽aṭārā is used, denoting here a crown of great weight. It is of interest to note that among the Fatimides too we hear of a crown of great weight which may perhaps have been hung up over the head of the ruler, see Kahle in Z D M G 89, 1935, p. 336. The crown is also called kether. The relation between the use of the diadem and the crown is not quite clear. On the diadem and staff among the Egyptians, see Erman, Aegypten p. 94 f. 314 f., 2. ed. p. 64 f. Invocation of the crown was part of the coronation ritual, see H. Kees' Egyptian texts p. 41 in Bertholet, Religionsgesch. Leseb. 2. ed. 1929. On the Ass. and Bab. royal crown (with fillet of metal) see W. Reimpell, Gesch. d. bab. u. ass. Kleidung, ed. Ed. Meyer 1921, pp. 41-43.

P. 79 ¹. Judg. 5,14 speaks of a shēbheṭ worn by the "scribe", an old term for a functionary, administrator. See the note p. 3². The chief is called m⁽ḥōkēk, cf. v. 9; Isa. 33,22, the same word that denotes the staff in Gen. 49,10; Num. 21,18; Ps. 60,9; 108,9. The Arab khaṭīb "orator", who had the character of a chief, appeared with a lance or staff in his hand.

P. 80 ¹. A treatment of the throne in the ancient East is a desideratum. Thrones with many steps were used in Christian times for the patriarch or bishop in the churches. In St. Sophia at Constantinople there were 8-9, elsewhere even 15 steps, see Daremberg, Saglio & Pottier, Dictionnaire des Antiquités V, p. 283 s. v. thronos. Otherwise the throne is generally a chair, mostly an armchair with a foot-stool which may have the character of a step, thus among the Egyptians and Babylonians, likewise the Aramaean Barrekub of Sam'al from about 730, see the illustration Garstang, Hittite Empire, 1929, p. 238; and the Phoenician Ahiram before the 10. century, see Benzinger, Hebr. Archäologie, 3. ed. p. 106. In Egyptian pictures we find in some few instances a king on a throne with many steps, thus 4 in Flinders Petrie, The Royal Tombs of the First Dynasty I, London 1900, Pl. XV No. 16, and 9 in Quibell, Hierakonpolis I. Egyptian Research Account, 4 mem. I 1900, Pl. 26 B. Lions as a foundation or at the sides are common. Ahiram's throne has winged lion-like animals, see above; similarly Phoenician thrones of gods, see Contenau, Civilisation phénicienne, p. 178 f. and the figure p. 112 f.. For Egypt see Gressmann, Texte u. Bilder, 1. ed., Fig. 227 after Dibelius, Lade Jahwes, 77. At Megiddo has been found an ivory relief of a prince on a throne with sphinxes at the sides and a foot-stool, Ill. London News 23 Oct. 1937, p. 708.

P. 85 [1]. Weber, Aufsätze zur Religionssoziologie III mentions Shechem and Shiloh as the seats of such "Amphictyonic" gatherings, see p. 98. The same view in A. Alt, Die Staatenbildung der Israeliten in Palästina, 1930, p. 11, and further developed in M. Noth, Das System der zwölf Stämme Israels, 1930; see also Mowinckel, Psalmenstudien V, p. 101 f. and B. Luther & Ed. Meyer in Die Israeliten und ihre Nachbarstämme, p. 542 ff., cf. Ewald, Gesch. d. Volkes Israel II, p. 282 f.; 336 f. It plays a significant part in the important book: Königtum Gottes, 1932, by M. Buber who rightly in such gatherings sees a continuation of the covenant of Sinai. In Ex. 24 he sees an historical account of the covenant between the people and Yahweh as it was actually made at Sinai. Yahweh is king of the tribe, hence he is also called by the ancient Semitic term for a god, *melekh*. The contrast between the kingdom of Yahweh and the human kingdom Judg. 8 and 1 Sam. 8 would then be an old Israelitish idea. This point of view is adhered to with great stringency, but I doubt whether we can take for granted such an uncorrupted tradition from the wilderness period in a cult communication in the Pentateuch, just as I think that too much stress is laid on the designation of Yahweh as *melekh* in the old times. Cf. on this subject J. Hempel, Gott und Mensch im A. T. p. 136 f. — Federation feasts such as these took place not only among the Amphictyonic tribes of Greece; thus at the feriae Latinae the Latin tribes celebrated a similar feast on the Alban mount and according to Tacitus, Germania

§§ 39.43 various Germanic tribes too had certain common cults. See further p. 160; 382 f.; 661.

P. 90 [1]. A similar conflict between the ideas of the chief and the great king of course occurs in many other places. Thus in Italy and Greece in imperial times there was opposition against the idea of the divine emperor from those that rallied round the lowly leaders of the community of the old times. See A. Alföldi, Die Ausgestaltung des monarchischen Zeremoniells am römischen Hofe [Mitt. d. deutsch. Arch. Inst., Röm. Abt. 49, 1934].

P. 90 [2]. I. e. conqueror of spoil, cf. the Arab. use of *abū*.

P. 91 [1]. *geza'* in Isa. 40.24 is a living stem of a plant and the word has most likely the same meaning in Job 14,8, which indeed agrees with Arabic and Syriac. The expression therefore does not presuppose the fall of the house of David.

P. 91 [2]. On the use of '*al* for psychological phenomena see I—II p. 160[1].

P. 91 [3]. Read '*āriṣ*, see the Commentaries.

P. 92 [1]. On this emendation of the text see Comm.

P. 92 [2]. The construction is reminiscent of Isa. 21,1; 38,20.

P. 94 [1]. A. Causse, Les dispersés d'Israel, 1929, shows the extent and importance of the Israelite emigration before the exile.

P. 105 [1]. The narrative in Num. 11 is of the same kind as the others dealing with the assigning of authority and responsibility and, on the other hand, the constant disobedience and rebellion of the people. On this depends the connection between the want of meat and the appointment of elders. Of course it may be conjectured that the mention of the elders in vv. 16-17 and 24-30 originally had nothing to do with the rest of the tale. But as it stands the latter part provides the motive, and there is nothing whatever to indicate that the two parts should originally have existed as independent stories which were parts of consecutive tales mechanically worked together (see Wellhausen, Composition p. 99, and the commentaries).

P. 109 [1]. It has been thought that in *nāyōth* or *n^ewāyōth* 1 Sam. 19,18 f. 22 f.; 20,1 we had a term for prophets' monasteries.

P. 111 [1]. The uses in other languages quoted in Ges.-Buhl s. v. *nb'* point to the ecstatic sound rather than to the more elaborate speeches the prophets utter outside their ecstasies.

P. 112 [1]. See I—II p. 168 f., cf. note 1 to p. 17. In the usual discussion as to whether Hos. 1-3 concerns a "real" marriage which the prophet has contracted, or whether it is an allegory, the question is treated as a purely literary one without reference to the special prophetic experiences in which a "prophetically" experienced marriage is a real marriage. Precisely in such a psychically experienced marriage there may appear features that do not quite agree with each other.

The problems in the book of Hosea are treated by Joh. Lindblom, Hosea literarisch untersucht, Åbo 1927.

P. 117 [1]. *śar ham-maśśā'*, see S. Mowinckel, Psalmenstudien III p. 17 f.

P. 125 [1]. See Jer. 27,9; 29,8; Ez. 13,6.9.23; 21,34; 22,28; Mic.3,7; Zech. 10,2.

P. 125 [2]. See I—II p. 139 f. In 1 Sam. 28,6 the three methods are mentioned, cf. v. 15.

P. 127 [1]. See Mowinckel, Psalmenstudien III.

P. 150 [1]. Accounts of the history of the priesthood will be found in the various treatments of Israel's archaeology, history and religious history. The history of the priesthood played an important part in the books of Graf and Wellhausen (Prolegomena, 5. ed. p. 118 ff.) about the dating of the writings of the O. T.; see also Kuenen, Gesammelte Abhandlungen, übers. Budde 1894, pp. 465-500. To this may be added Baudissin, Die Gesch. d. alttest. Priesterthums, 1889; various parts of Ed. Meyer, Die Israeliten und ihre Nachbarstämme, 1906. The pre-exilic foundation of the priestly laws and thus of the picture they give of the priesthood is pointed out by Eerdmans, Alttestamentliche Studien IV, 1912. An account with references to Indian analogies is found in Max Weber, Gesammelte Aufsätze zur Religionssoziologie III, 1921, p. 173 ff. A careful analysis is given in G. Buchanan Gray, Sacrifice in the Old Testament, 1925, pp. 179-270 and, with discarding of the usual dating of Deuteronomy, by G. Hölscher in Pauly-Wissowa, Realencyclopädie d. class. Alterthumswiss. ed. W. Kroll, vol. XII,2 (Halbb. XXIV) art. Levi. In a fresh investigation in the "Festskrift" of the University of Copenhagen 1931 Aage Bentzen reviews the history of the priesthood of Jerusalem point for point, strongly stressing the interests reflected in the various literary evidences.

P. 150 [2]. "Fill the hand" Ex. 28,41; 29,9; Judg. 17,5.12 et al., is an expression taken from Ass. for giving authority to the priest.

P. 152 [1]. I. e. we have a common enemy, viz. Saul. It would seem more natural to interchange "mine" and "thine", we then get a regular formula for a covenant. See the author's Der Eid bei den Semiten p. 27, note 3; 59.

P. 153 [1]. The names Abiathar and Ahimelech have been interchanged in the text 2 Sam. 8,17.

P. 153 [2]. See p. 10 of the work of Bentzen mentioned in note 1 on p. 150, with reference to Hall and Mowinckel.

P. 154 [1]. It is said partly that the house shall become weakened, only one person being left to continue the priestly duties (v. 33), partly that it shall later beg a place in the priesthood of Jerusalem, partly that it shall perish. The implication underlying the whole account is that Eli's priesthood at Shiloh was once the only true one which received "all the offerings of the Israelites" (v. 28). This shows that the utterance has been shaped after the exile. 1 Kings 2,27 sees in the deposition of Abiathar a fulfilment of the threat of the destruction of the Elides. Here it is implied that Abiathar, the son of Ahimelech at Nob, belonged to the Elides. It is doubtful, however, whether Ahimelech was an Elide, see p. 152. If 1 Sam. 2,27-35 is based on an earlier form of the denunciation of the Elides, the allusion to the person saved as priest for the family (v. 33) may be to Ahitub and his son Ahijah, see p. 152. V. 36 shows how the country priests who lost their means of subsistence went up to the sanctuary.

P. 155 [1]. According to Jer. 41,5 Shiloh which is mentioned under Jeroboam in 1 Kings 14,3 was inhabited after the destruction also. The Danish excavations do not seem to confirm this. See H. Kjær, The Excavation of Shiloh 1929, Journ. of the Pal. Or. Soc. X, 1930, pp. 87—174, and Pal. Expl. Fund Qu. St., 1931, pp. 71—88; Albright, The Archæology of Palestine and the Bible, p. 160 f.

P. 157 [1]. kōhēn in Arab. about the soothsayer, kāhin; kōmer from a root meaning heated, excited. The former is Canaan., perhaps a loanword in Arab.-Ethiop., the latter in the main Aram., see Gray, Sacrifice p. 183 f.

P. 161 [1]. Se I—II p. 353.

P. 166 [1]. See Gray, Sacrifice p. 185, cf. khnt in Lidzbarski, Handbuch p. 294.

P. 170 [1]. See further Ed. Meyer, Israeliten p. 79 ff.; Hölscher, art. Levi in Pauly-Wissowa's Dictionary XII (Halbband XXIV) Col. 2170. In southern Arabic inscriptions from al- 'Ulā in Northern Arabia the forms lw'n and lw'tn have several times been found. The editors translate "priests" and "priestesses". The Isr. designation would then like kōhēn have a corresponding word in Arabic, and it would thus be proved that the word meant priest. See D. H. Müller, Epigraphische Denkmäler aus Arabien [Denkschr. Wien. Akad. phil. Cl. 37, 1889]; J. H. Mordtmann, Beiträge zur minäischen Epigraphik, 1897; Jaussen & Savignac, Mission archéologique en Arabie 1—2, 1909. 1914. A review of all the texts is found in an article by H. Grimme in Le Muséon 37, 1924, pp. 169—199; he quotes as a parallel lāwā "borrow" and translates (temple-) pledge; he too here sees the background for the Israelite Levite priesthood. If the etymology is disregarded a meaning such as "consecrated to the temple" would seem most natural, so that a connection with Isr. usage seems possible.

P. 170 [2]. 1 Sam. 6,15; 2 Sam. 15,24; 1 Kings 8,4 seem to originate from the post-exilic conception of the Levites. 1 Chron, 24,3 does not prove that the Elides were later regarded as Levites, since it is doubtful whether Ahimelech is an Elide.

P. 171 [1]. Nyberg (see p. 8[1]) p. 43 f. interprets gedhūdhīm as "travellers", which then becomes the obj. of *ḥakkē* instead of part of the subject "wie ein Mann auf Reisende lauert..."

P. 172 [1]. The text adds "and his mother".

P. 172 [2]. See Wellhausen, Prolegomena, 5. ed., p. 348; Meyer, Israeliten p. 55. It would be tempting to understand *massā* as "oracle", but it would have to be *maśśā*'.

P. 174 [1]. See p. 170 [2].

P. 177 [1]. No certain explanation of the difficult passage can, however, be given. See Comm. and Ges.-Buhl.

P. 178 [1]. Thus tractate Sukkah fol. 56 a, quoted in Levy, Neuhebr. u. Chald. Wörterbuch s. v. *mūkhar;* for the rules for priests in Deuteronomy, see also the explanation of the relation between Deuteron. and the book of Kings p. 580 ff.

P. 182 [1]. Libni perhaps from Libna, Korah a Judaean family, son of Hebron 1 Chron. 2,43, also Edomite 1,35; Gen. 36,5.14.18 et al., see Hölscher, art. Levi, Pauly-Wissowa XII, Col. 2183.

P. 183 [1]. I cannot enter into the literary and critical problems in Ez.-Neh. In spite of the ingenious criticism previously put forward by Wellhausen and others, later especially by Mowinckel and Hölscher, I am of opinion that the reasons for referring the list Ezr. 2 = Neh. 7 to the first return are weightier than the opposite. Cf. Kittel, Geschichte III, 1929, § 44, and Schaeder, Esra der Schreiber 1930, p. 15 ff.

P. 185 [1]. Cf. Josephus, Antiquitates VII, 14,7.

P. 186 [1]. For the various genealogies see Hölscher's article in Pauly-Wissowa. That Abiathar is counted among the Ithamarides in 1 Chron. 24,6 is not mentioned in the text, but is inferred generally from the fact that he and Zadok (who is the representative of Eleazar) are mentioned together as the two priests, see Comm.

P. 188 [1]. See p. 117 and the note.

P. 189 [1]. On the incomes of priests see Deut. 18,3 f.; Ez. 44,28-31; Lev. 5,13; 6,9 ff.; 7,6 ff.; 10,12-20; Num. 6,19 f.; 18,8 ff. and add to this Lev. 27,30-33. See further the detailed accounts in Wellhausen, Prolegomena, 5. ed. p. 149 ff. and in the archaeologies.

P. 192 [1]. See Ed. Meyer, Israeliten p. 450 note 1. Meyer mentions and accepts Redslob's presumption that the name Aaron should be derived from the Ark, *'ārōn*, see op. cit. p. 93.

P. 195 [1]. See the author's Der Eid bei den Semiten p. 43. This assumption is surely also possible without altering *mal'akh* to *melekh*.

P. 196 [1]. I am thinking of the role played by the high priest in Lev. 16 cf. 6,12-16, see p. 353.

P. 198 [1]. Sinai Judg. 5,5, hardly, however, belongs to the original text, see p. 2 [3]. On Sinai see I—II p. 17 [1].

P. 201 [1]. *mō'ēdh* and probably also *'ēdhūth* belong to the root *w'd.* Their meaning has contacts with Arab. *shahāda* and *ḥaḍra* or *maḥḍar* (the first and the last words are used in Arab. translations of *'ōhel mō'ēdh)*, but likewise with the very important *'ahd,* which also coincides with *berīth,* see the author's Der Eid bei den Semiten pp. 7—11.

P. 202¹. See Vincent, Canaan Chap. 2; on caves see p. 138 f.; G. Contenau, La Civilisation phénicienne, p. 127 ff.; Watzinger, Denkmäler Palestinas I, 1933, p. 64 f. A natural sanctuary with open altars on rocks has been excavated at Bēt Sha'ār south-west of Jerusalem, Arch. f. Orientw. XI, 1936—37, p. 397.

P. 202². See the preliminary reports by Alan Rowe in Palestine Explor. Fund Quart. St., 1927. 1931.

P. 202³. See Sellin's reports in Zeits. d. deutsch. Pal. vereins, 1926. 1929. So long as the whole site has not been excavated it cannot of course be said with certainty whether it is the temple of El Berith which has been found. See Zeits. f. d. alttest. Wiss., 1932, p. 78. 306. The most recent excavations have brought to light new temples. There is reason to mention the two uniform temples at Ras Shamra from the 1st half of the 2nd millenium, one of them to the god Baal. They consist of two rooms. In a corner of the inner room there is a platform for an idol or the like, in front of the temple a court with an altar before the entrance, see Schaeffer, Syria, 1931. 1932. 1935. In Palestine proper must especially be mentioned Ai, now et-Tell, where three temples have been found one above the other, the oldest from the beginning, the youngest from the close of the 3rd millennium. The middle sanctuary had one large room, the upper one, three rooms; see the Quarterly of the Dep. of Antiquities in Palestine IV, 1935; V, 1936; and the report by Judith Marquet-Krause and R. Dussaud in Syria XVII, 1936. Further the three superimposed Canaanite temples in Lachish, now Tell ed-Duweir, see J. L. Starkey in Pal. Expl. Fund, Qu. St., 1934. 1935. 1937. At Megiddo a small one-roomed temple has been found dating from about 1500, but rebuilt several times up to the 13th century, as also one from the 11th or 10th century, see Illustr. London News, May 1934, June 1936; H. G. May and R. M. Engberg, Material Remains of the Megiddo Cult [Chicago Or. Inst. Publ. XXVI], 1935, p. 8 ff.

P. 206¹. The position of *Ḳādēsh Barnēᵃ* is uncertain. When I wrote note 1 on p. 17 in I—II I was not acquainted with the decisive criticism of Trumbull in Woolley and Lawrence, The Wilderness of Zin [Pal. Explor. Fund, 1914], Chap. IV.

P. 207¹. For this point of view see Gunkel's commentary on Genesis and A. Alt, Der Gott der Väter, 1920.

P. 211¹. There is no reason to insist on a distinction of the sources in Gen. 28,11 ff. If the alternating use of the name Yahweh and the more general Elohim is not considered decisive, there are neither contradictions nor repetitions. In v. 20 we must probably on account of the last sentence in v. 21 read *yahwe* for *yihye* as do LXX and Trg. It may then be understood thus: If God Yahweh is with me... or If Yahweh is God with me... Nor is there any break in the unity in 35,1-15, and the defective state of the text is not done away with by distinguishing two sources. The narrator has allowed two traditions as to Jacob's change of name to stand side by side, one according to which he obtained the name of Israel when he obtained by fighting the right to take possession of the land, and one according to which it took place when Yahweh appeared to him at the northern Israelitish sanctuary.

P. 215 [1]. See p. 27, cf. I—II p. 250 f. We may here recall that Alexander, according to Arrian, Alexander's Anabasis V, 29 at the place in India where here turned back, raised 12 altars of immense height as thanksgiving gifts to the gods and memorials, $\mu\nu\eta\mu\varepsilon\tilde{\iota}\alpha$, of his exertions. The contribution of archaeology to the question of the massebahs is naturally uncertain, see the article by Burrows in Journ. Pal. Or. Soc. XIV, 1934, p. 42 ff.

P. 217 [1]. As Budde remarks in his Commentary, it is difficult to interpret *way-yibhen* in 1 Sam. 14,35 about the raising of a single stone in the way Rob. Smith does (Rel. of the Semites, 3. ed., p. 202), but it also seems difficult to me to accept Budde's interpretation that Saul first sets up a stone for instant use (v. 33) and later an altar. Possibly *'ebhen gedhōlā* may not mean one stone only, but several stones, hence: "Roll big stones up to me today" (v. 33). Then *hay-yōm* v. 33 will correspond to *hal-laylā* v. 34, and the words need not be changed. In the course of the afternoon the big stones were rolled together, and in the evening people made their offerings; *way-yibhen* v. 35 must then be understood as a summary, in the same way as the cons. imperf. is used e. g. in Gen. 23,17: "Thus Saul built an altar to Yahweh" etc. That *'ebhen gedhōlā* in 1 Sam. 6,14.15 denotes a single stone there can hardly be any doubt, but this is not decisive since it may mean both one and several stones.

P. 217 [2]. See Sellin in Zeits. d. deutsch. Pal.vereins 49, 1926, p. 312 ff., though it is not certain. On altars see Galling in Biblisches Reallexikon s. v. Altar.

P. 218 [1]. *bekhol ham-māḳōm* may mean "in every place", cf. Gen. 20,13; Ex. 1,22, but is not very good language. The most obvious sense is "in the whole place" i. e. in the whole sanctuary, but it is not very probable. Possibly the use of the article is due to a scribal error.

P. 218 [2]. H. M. Wiener has very energetically emphasised the difference between the two kinds of altars in OLZ. Beiheft 3, and Monatsschr. f. Gesch. u. Wiss. d. Judent. Bd. 71, p. 353 ff., but draws rather too many conclusions from the fact. On altars with horns in Phoenicia see Contenau, La civilisation phénicienne, Paris 1926, p. 178. On Shechem see Sellin in Zeits. d. deutsch. Pal.ver. 49, 1926, p. 232 f. In Megiddo too horned incense altars have been found, see May & Engberg's work, mentioned p. 202[3], p. 12 f. For a general treatment see Cook, Rel. of anc. Pal. p. 30 f.; Vincent, Canaan p. 124, note 3, and more fully Galling, Der Altar in den Kulturen des alten Orients, 1925; see also Realwörterbuch der Vorgeschichte s. v. Göttersymbol and Altar. The horned type of altar in Canaan seems to be derived from Crete where the horns are conventionalised as a kind of pinnacles, but where their origin as cow-horns can still be seen. About these "horns of consecration" see A. Evans, The Palace of Minos I p. 443 ff.; II, 1 p. 336 f. and fig. 189; II, 2 p. 608 and fig. 381 a; p. 614, fig. 386; p. 619, fig. 388. On Paphos see Blinkenberg, Le temple de Paphos [Vid. Selsk. Hist.-fil. Medd. IX, 2] København, 1924, p. 10.21. — Further Journ. of Hellenic Studies 21, 1901, pp. 101—193; Dussaud, Les civilisations préhelléniques, 2. ed., 1914, p. 343.

P. 220 ¹. The son does not quote the curse which might befall him.

P. 221 ¹. Judg. 17,3 must be regarded as the solemn dedication formula. The sanctification takes place in favour of the son, ʾashibhennū has been translated "I hand it over", Hiph. of shūbh often expressing the concept "transference" without any element of a rendering back, thus Num. 18,9; 1 Kings 22,26; 2 Kings 3,4; 17,3; Ps. 72,10; "to thee" must refer to Yahweh.

P. 221 ². This sentence may be understood to mean that Micah already had a house of gods, but it more probably means that he obtained it under the circumstances indicated.

P. 221 ³. shaʿar is used about large entrance gates such as city gates and temple gates; on the latter see the author's Der Eid bei den Semiten, p. 146 note 3. In both cases the word is difficult here since we receive the impression that the place is not a large closed city, and that the sanctuary also is too insignificant to have a shaʿar.

P. 221 ⁴. The story is of quite another kind than the one that follows and has a quite genuine character. The obscurities relate to details and do not affect the context as a whole, which is clear; hence they are not solved by assuming two sources, an assumption that cannot be adhered to.

P. 222 ¹. Deut. 27,15; Isa. 42,17; Nah. 1,14; Hab. 2,18. Sometimes it may be understood as hendiadyoin; thus it must probably be understood in Judg. 17,3 f.; 18,14, if the two expressions had not been separated in 18,17.18. This may perhaps be due to secondary reasons, however. Pāsil too is often used, see Ges.-Buhl.

P. 225 ¹. Ephod and teraphim have been the subject of many conjectures and discussions, see Gressmann, Die Lade Jahwes, p. 29 ff. On teraphim see Vincent, Canaan p. 153 ff. A synonym of ʾephōdh is ʾaphuddā used precisely about the garment of an idol, Isa. 30,22, cf. 40,19; Jer. 10,9; Ez. 16,18. The view of the ephod as a garment for a god or a priest which has also been put forward by Sellin in Journ. Pal. Or. Soc. XIV, 1934, pp. 185—93, has been strongly supported by an extensive archaeological material set forth by H. Thiersch in Ependytes und Ephod, Gottesbild und Priesterkleid im alten Vorderasien [Geisteswiss. Forschungen ed. W. Mitscherlich] Stuttgart 1936. The gazelle skin mentioned here on p. 147 f. from the Thebes of Thutmosis IV would agree well with the designation apron, see Pl. XLVIII, 2. In Ugarit the priests used masks, Illustr. London News 27. 2. 1936, p. 310. And in a text 1* AB I 5 Virolleaud (Syria XV, 1934) and others (see Hempel, Götting. Nachr., Phil. hist. V, NF I, 1936, p. 16) read 'pdk as the word ephod. I, however, here read a verb, pdy.

P. 225 ². See Macalister, Excav. of Gezer II, p. 425. At Shechem (Balāṭa) a house altar has been found which is referred to the 8th—7th century. It is 60 cm high, 36 cm broad, with 4 projections at the upper corners. Likewise another 90 cm high, see Sellin in Zeits. d. deutsch. Palästinaver. 49, 1926, p. 232 f.

P. 226 ¹. The alternation of the sing. and the plur. in Am. 3,14 may be understood to mean that the singular denotes the principal altar, cf. 9,1, which was outside. The plural is generally regarded as a textual error.

P. 228 ¹. See Blinkenberg in Arch. f. Rel. wiss. 28, p. 157, cf. Thiersch in Zeits. f. d. alttestl. Wiss. 1932, p. 80.

P. 228 ². With the reading leshōrīm. 'ashērū is understood as a living tree in Mishnah 'Abodah Zarah, III 7.

P. 229 ¹. On the political significance of 'Abd al-Malik's building enterprise see Le Strange, Palestine under the Moslems p. 115 f.

P. 230 ¹. The pronouns in 1 Sam. 4,8 show that the forms must be regarded as real plural forms.

P. 233 ¹. Of course a smoother text can be obtained by altering it, e. g. to 'el ribhṣē, "to the camping places of the tribes of Israel", but we have no authority for such an emendation.

P. 233 ². lō in v. 7 may without straining be taken as a dativus ethicus, see the examples in Jouon, Grammaire de l'Hébreu Biblique, § 133 d.

P. 234 ¹. Especially Am. 5,26 if we read sukkōth, see Sellin, Das Zelt Jahwes, p. 178 [Beitr. z. Wissensch. v. alt. Test., ed. Kittel Heft 13] Lpz. 1913.

P. 235 ¹. Problems concerning the Ark are discussed in various publications besides that referred to at p. 234¹; they are mentioned in Benzinger's Archäologie, 3. ed. 1927, p. 312. R. Hartmann, Zelt und Lade in Zeits. f. d. altt. Wiss. 37, 1917—18, pp. 209—44, has given a clear account of the material and pointed out Arabian analogies to the tent. Very full particulars concerning the Arabian holy tent kubba, as a rule a pyramidal leather tent, have been published by H. Lammens, Le culte des bétyles et les processions chez les Arabes préislamites in Bull. de l'Inst. Franc. d'Arch. Or., 17, le Caire 1919, pp. 39—101; reprinted in his L'Arabie occidentale avant l'hégire, Beyrouth 1928, pp. 101—179.

Amongst other things L. attempts to show that the two goddesses, according to the tradition carried into the battle of Uḥud, were conveyed in such a *ḳubba*, see p. 54 ff. Cumont has called attention to Syrian representations of two goddesses on a camel saddle of the same kind in his Études Syriennes, 1917, pp. 263—76. The word *ḳubbā* also occurs in Hebrew, Num. 25,8, where it may mean a tent, perhaps even one used for the cult. The word has also recently been found in Palmyrene by Ingholt, Berytus III, 1936, p. 85 ff. The Assyrian gods, too, had travelling tents, according to Perrot & Chipiez, Hist. de l'art, II, p. 202, figs. 68 and 70. Cf. also M. Buber, Königtum Gottes, 2. ed., p. 78 and note. Of another kind are the tabernacles used for Egyptian gods, see W. B. Kristensen in Mededeel. d. Kon. Akad. v. Wetensch. Afd. Letterk. Deel 56, ser. B. No. 6, Amsterdam 1923 (a paper on the Ark by the same author is found ibd. Deel 76, ser. B., No. 5, 1933). Light huts such as P.'s tabernacle, of wood covered with hangings, were used in Greece as sanctuaries in which spoils were hung and sacrificial meals eaten, see Euripides, Ion 1122 ff., cf. Daremberg et al., Diction- naire des Antiquités V, p. 117. According to Diodorus XX 65 the Phoenicians carried holy tents with them in war, cf. R. Pietschmann, Gesch. d. Phönizier, p. 168 f. — From Hellenistic times we also have evidence on coins of portable chests in Phoenicia; a Tyrian type of such chests contains a stone, see S. A. Cook, Rel. of Anc. Pal., 1925, p. 164 f.; Gressmann, Die Lade Jahwes, 1920, thinks that Ark and ephod belong together, so that there was an Ark for each ephod (p. 34). This conjecture must, in spite of 1 Sam. 14,18, be regarded as un- founded. A similar conjecture has been put forward by W. R. Arnold, Ephod and Ark, in Harvard Theol. Studies III, 1917. He thinks that it was a small chest which contained oracular lots and which was found, therefore, at several sanctuaries. Where ephod means something other than a priestly garment, he thinks that it has been inserted instead of *'arōn*, a conjecture for which there is no evidence whatever.

P. 239 [1]. The name has come down in different forms; in Chronicles it is *'ornān*. Perhaps it is not Semitic, see comm. to 2 Sam. 24,16.

P. 240 [1]. Similar conditions with regard to private ownership of holy places are found in Arabia, see Wellhausen, Reste arab. Heid., 2. ed., p. 130. The same applies to mosques. — A holy threshing-place is known among other agricultural peoples, cf. Farnell, Cults of the Greek States III, p. 145 (Triptolemos' holy threshing-place on the Carian plain). The Thalysia festival was celebrated on the threshing- place where there was an altar, see M. P. Nilsson, Griechische Feste, p. 331.

P. 241 [1]. Good arguments have been brought forward to show that the rock, as stated in Jewish tradition, lay in the Holy of Holies. See Galling, Zeits. d. deutsch. Pal. Ver. 55, 1932, p. 247; Hertzberg in

Journ. Pal. Or. Soc., 1932, p. 32 ff., Hollis in Myth and Ritual, ed S. H. Hooke, 1933, p. 101 ff.

P. 242 [1]. 2 Kings 16,14 f. must be understood to mean that the ancient altar was removed from its place and was temporarily erected between its old place and the temple; on the new altar the priest was to sacrifice, but the king would consider what was to be done with the old one (lᵉbhakkēr, v. 15).

P. 242 [2]. The copper altar of Solomon was probably hollow and filled with earth, like several Assyrian altars (thus already Wiener, Realwörterbuch, s. v. Brandopferaltar), i. e. it was not unlike the altar of the Priestly Code which as we know was a box mounted with copper. The model of Ahaz' altar was probably Assyrian. On Ass. altars see Meissner, Babylonien und Assyrien II, p. 73 ff. Unger in Reallexikon d. Assyriologie s. v. Altar; brick altars were frequent; they were used in Israel at any rate for foreign cults, Isa. 65,3. The altars to Astarte in the temple of Amenophis at Beisan were of bricks, see Pal. Explor. Fund, Qu. St., 1927, p. 69.

P. 242 [3]. The details of Ez. 43,13-17 are very difficult to understand, see especially Bertholet's Comm. and Joh. de Groot, Die Altäre des Salomonischen Tempelhofes [Beitr. z. Wiss. v. A. T., ed. R. Kittel, N. F. 6, 1924], p. 45 ff.

P. 242 [4]. The altar in the first post-exilic temple (that of Zerubbabel) is mentioned in 1 Mac. 4,44 ff. On top of this Antiochus Epiphanes built his altar "the desolating abomination" in 168 B. C., 1 Mac. 1,54, cf. Dan. 11,31; 12,11. After their victory the Maccabees removed "the stones of pollution" again, and after some hesitation the old altar was pulled down. The stones were laid on the temple mount; when a prophet came he was to say what was to be done with them (1 Mac. 4, 43-47). The altar demolished by the Maccabees must be identical with that mentioned in Isa. 27,9, and to which Hekatæus refers: a square altar of unhewn stones, 20 cubits long on each side, 10 cubits high, corresponding to 2 Chron. 4,1. Hekatæus, a contemporary of Alexander the Great, is cited in Josephus, Contra Apionem I, 22. That this and other post-exilic altars in spite of the adherence to the law as to natural altars, was to a certain degree artificially made, perhaps by means of mortar, appears partly from the accurate measurements, partly from the fact that they are provided with horns. — The altar in Herod's temple is described by Josephus in Bellum V, 6 (in Antiquitates XV, 11,5 it is referred to without any description). According to this it was 15 cubits high, 50 cubits long and broad, and a gradual ascent led up to it from the south, hence not from the east like the stairs in Ezekiel. Other measurements are given in Mishnah, Middoth III, 1; according to this the altar consists of steps like Ezekiel's, the lower one of which is 32 cubits in length and breadth, the superimposed ones being respectively 30, 28, 26, and 24 cubits, i. e. there are 5 breaks, while Ezekiel has 4. Here also the corners have "horns" and a slope leads up to the altar from the south, III, 3. We are told that the unhewn stones of the altar were gathered at Beth-Kerem, III, 4, and that they were white-washed twice a year, III, 4. An account of the history of the altar is given in G. Buchanan Gray, Sacrifice in the Old Testament, Oxford 1925, pp. 96—147. W. Robertson Smith has a curious conception of the history of the altar in Jerusalem. He considers the information about Solomon's burnt-offering altar untrustworthy; Ahaz would then be the first to build a permanent fixed altar in Jerusalem. The account in 2 Kings 16,14 of his altar being substituted for the copper altar is removed by a textual emendation. He thinks, indeed, that there was a copper altar, but this he identifies with one of the two copper columns Jachin and Boaz, a notion which, however, can hardly be called well founded; see Lectures on the religion of the Semites, 3. ed. by Stanley A. Cook, London 1927, pp. 379. 384 and Additional Note pp. 485—489. Conversely de Groot maintains in his above-mentioned work that from the very first there were two altars in the temple court: the altar for burnt-offerings and the copper altar. He bases this on 2 Kings 12,10, according to which Jehoiada, the priest, set up a money chest "by the side of the altar to the right as you enter Yahweh's house". From this he infers that there was an altar to the right of Yahweh's house and interprets 2 Kings 16,12 ff. in accordance herewith. But 2 Kings 12,10 may just as well mean that the money chest stood to the right of the altar for any one entering the temple — hence not "right" in the frequent sense of "south". He identifies this altar with *kiyyōr* 2 Chron. 6,13. That Solomon's copper altar is identical with his principal altar is the natural view, which is also found in Josephus, Antiquitates VIII, 3,7; 4,1.

P. 243 [1]. See Josephus, Antiquitates VIII, 3,5-6. Chariots with vessels like Solomon's have been found in Larnaka and Enkomi on Cyprus, see R. Kittel, Studien zur hebr. Archäologie u. Religionsgeschichte [Beitr. z. Wiss. v. A. T., 1], 1908, p. 189 ff., and I. Benzinger, Hebr. Arch., 3. ed., 1927, p. 219. Holy lakes are common at temples, but in Babylonia where water played a special part in the cult, there were sometimes in the temples large water basins or bowls called "oceans" *(apsû, tâmtu)*, see Meissner, Babylonien und Assyrien II, p. 77 f. A basin resting on bulls has not, we think, been found. In Hittite temples too a cult ocean was found. See E. Forrer in Glotta, 1938, p. 186.

P. 243 [2]. The placing of two columns at the entrance to the temple seems to be derived from Canaanite tradition; thus at Shechem, see Sellin in Zeits. d. deutsch. Pal. Ver. 49, 1926, p. 313; 51, 1929, p. 120;

on Cyprus, see Guthe, Bibelwörterbuch, p. 655; at Byblos see S. A. Cook, Religion, p. 166 f. A temple at Medum with two columns in front of it is mentioned by Flinders Petrie, Ten Years' Digging, p. 140 f., cf. Watzinger, Denkmäler Palästinas, I, 94 f. The two columns being disengaged, they do not support the roof of the forecourt as in the Syrian-Hittite Hilani style. W. Andrae, Das Gotteshaus und die Urformen des Bauens im alten Orient, Berlin 1930, p. 41, maintains this, thinking that the architrave was fastened under the column-heads. It is difficult to see how this can be reconciled with the description in the book of the Kings, and furthermore it militates directly against Jer. 52, 21 f. and Ez. 40,49.

P. 244 [1]. There is much evidence in favour of the supposition that the inner room, the cella, was on a higher level; notably this would explain that the ceiling was lower than in the hall. Thus, with references to Amenophis' and Rameses' temples at Bethshean, K. Galling in Journ. of the Pal. Or. Soc. 12, 1932, p. 43 ff., and Möhlenbrink, Der Tempel Salomos [Beitr. z. Wiss. v. Alt. u. Neu. Test., ed. Alt & Kittel, 4. Folge Heft 7], 1932, p. 138 ff. agreeing with Alt; cf. also Watzinger, op. cit. I, 90. It is remarkable, however, that no stairs are mentioned.

P. 244 [2]. While the plan with a detached altar and a temple building lying behind it is a common Canaanite one, see above p. 201 f., the excavations have not brought to light any one temple which can be called the direct model of Solomon's. In an article "Ein altmediterraner Tempeltyp" in Zeits. f. d. alttest. Wiss., 1932, pp.73—86, H. Thiersch has called attention to a common Canaanite type of temple consisting of a wide forecourt and a main court only slightly longer than broad, divided by columns into three naves, the middle one being a little broader than the others. The cult statue had its place in the latter, probably in the middle. Thus in Tell el-Naṣbe, though the character of its large building as a sanctuary has been doubted (see Hempel, op. cit., 1929, p. 69), in Tell el-Djemme, the ancient Gerar (cf. again Hempel, p. 65); at Shechem; in the sanctuary of Astarte at Megiddo in Rameses' temples to Astarte and Dagon in Bethshean (whose temples are for the first time shown in reconstruction by Alan Rowe and Vincent in Pal. Explor. Fund. Qu. St., 1931, pp. 12—21). He compares this type with the type with three naves demonstrated by Blinkenberg (Vid. Selsk. Hist. fil. Medd. IX 2, København, 1924, Le Temple de Paphos), known from Cyprus and Crete, from which it spread to other places; but Solomon's temple was not built on this model. W. Andrae, Das Gotteshaus p. 21 f.; 25; 30 seeks its prototype in Assyria where from the middle of the 2nd millennium long-house temples are found with a front hall, main hall, and in the background "the Holy of Holies", viz. an idol on a platform, perhaps in a niche. Möhlenbrink arrives at a similar result in the work cited in the preceding note, while he also points out the near connection between the royal palace and the temple as a point of similarity with Ass. and Bab. conditions. Whereas the likeness is striking as regards the long-house type, this can hardly be said to be the case with regard to the Holy of Holies. According to Andrae, the platform with the idol constitutes part of the main hall itself. He supposes, indeed, that a curtain covered it, and therein sees a resemblance to Solomon's temple. But he does not mention on what he bases his conjecture, and the characteristic feature of Solomon's temple is not the curtain, which the later descriptions mention, but the partition-wall, which makes the inner room a separate chapel. Its closed unlighted character later acquired great importance in the cult and the ideas associated with it. Such a closed adyton in the background is found in other types of temples, partly in Babylonia and especially in Egypt. This would seem to indicate that various types have been mixed in Solomon's temple. Cf. Watzinger, op. cit., I, pp. 89—95.

P. 244 [3]. On incense altars found during excavations, see Vincent, Canaan, p. 181 f.; Cook, Rel. of anc. Pal., p. 61 f.; Albright in Zeitschr. f. d. alttestl. Wiss., 47, 1929, p. 13 (house altars in Tell Beit Mirsim); May & Engberg, Material Remains of the Megiddo Cult, p. 12 (cf. p. 218[2]). Wellhausen, on the basis of purely literary critical considerations, thought that the incense altar in the temple of Jerusalem was post-exilic. Of course we cannot know whether it was there already in Solomon's time, but that such an altar, which is even mentioned in Ez. 41,22, should be something new dating from post-monarchical times is not very probable. Cf. B. D. Eerdmans, Alttestamentliche Studien, IV, 1912, p. 28 ff.; Max Löhr, Das Räucheropfer im alten Testament [Schriften der Königsberger Gelehrten Gesellschaft, Geisteswiss. Kl. Heft 4], 1927; H. M. Wiener, The Altars of the Old Testament, Lpz. 1927. Wellhausen's view is subscribed to by Gray, Sacrifice, p. 142 ff., who points out that the Jewish incense altar was different from the clay altars found, and by Albright in his notice on Wiener in Journ. of the Pal. Or. Soc., IX, 1929, p. 53, and in his Archæology of Palestine, 1932, p. 108. A. refers to the fact that Ingholt at Palmyra found the word ḥammānū as a designation for an incense altar; and ḥ. is condemned by the prophets, from which it may be inferred that incense altars belong to foreign cults. A sense such as the above-mentioned of ḥ. seems very natural and comes near to Littmann's translation "firealtar", πυρεία, in agreement with Grotius and Rob. Smith and in contrast with the current translation "sun-column", see E. Littmann, Nabataean Inscriptions [Publ. of the Princeton University Arch. Exped. to Syria], Leyden 1914, nos. 27 and 97. But this can hardly be of decisive importance for the question as to whether there was an incense altar in the principal temple of the monarchical period. *Hammānīm* are mentioned in Isa. 17,8; 27,9; Ez. 6,6 in conjunction with altars, asherahs, and stone gods that are to be destroyed. Lev. 26,30 f. mentions them along with bamahs and sanctuaries to be demolished if the people is refractory, since Yahweh does not accept its offerings. In 2 Chron. 14,4; 34,4.7 they are mentioned in connection with bamahs, foreign altars, images, massebahs and asherahs, removed either by Asa or by Josiah, and we learn that they stood on the altars (34,4). The latter fact would seem to indicate that they need not be large separate altars, but may be smaller erections, i. e. a kind of censers, but it must be assumed that they differed in size. In the above-mentioned places *hammūnīm* are not denounced separately but as part of the foreign cult, and this does not exclude that they could be used in Yahweh's cult just as well as altars and massebahs. The sources, however, do not quite agree as to the existence of the incense altar in post-exilic times, see Eerdmans, op. cit., p.31 ff. and Löhr, op. cit., p. 35 f.

P. 247 [1]. *kappōreth* is probably, like *pārōkheth*, a *katābat* form — here connected with Piel — a feminine of *katāb*, which really means the action as such (in Hebr. the abs. inf.). The feminine form in the various conjugations is very frequent in Aram. dialects. That the place or means of the action is expressed by the action itself is quite natural to Israelite logic, cf. I—II, p. 110 f.

P. 248 [1]. On empty thrones of gods see Reichel, Über die vorhellenischen Götterkulte, Wien, 1897; S. A. Cook, Rel. of anc. Pal., p. 21 f., and Daremberg etc., Dictionnaire des Antiquités, V, 279 b. In the discussion about Yahweh's throne the Ark was previously considered to be a throne of a god, see especially Dibelius, Die Lade Jahves, 1906. Budde has rightly disputed this on the view that the Ark was a chest, not a throne. The opinion here put forward of the relation between cherub, throne, and Ark comes very near to that advanced by H. Schmidt in the Commemorative Publication to Gunkel [Forschungen zur Religion und Literatur des Alt. u. Neu. Test., ed. Bultmann u. Gunkel, N. F. 19,1], 1923, pp. 120—144. The above reconstruction of Ezekiel's throne is taken from this work. On the other hand, the same author has no doubt in his paper Mose u. d. Dekalog, ibd., pp. 78—119, been too optimistic both in his consideration of the Pentateuch as a source for the wilderness period and in his attempt at a reconstruction of the ten commandments.

The word cherub is derived from Ass. where *kuribu* is used about mythical animal figures, see Meissner, Bab. u. Ass., II, 50. Here beings will often be found which are made up of several different animals and sometimes combined with the human figure, as in Egypt the sphinx. As regards the Hittite world, see Ed. Meyer, Reich u. Kultur der Chetiter, 17; 24 ff.; 49; 77; for Sendjirli see the illustration in Garstang, The

Land of the Hittites, 2. ed., p. 258, and Pl. XLIX; L. On the bronze bowl from Larnaka a number of different cherubic beings are represented, Contenau, La civilisation phénicienne, fig. 67, p. 178; further Dussaud, Civilisations préhelléniques, pp. 313. 328. Of similar composite beings on Canaanite soil see S. A. Cook, Rel. of anc. Palestine, p. 55. On the Israelite cherubs see especially Dibelius, op. cit., p. 72 ff.; Gressmann, Die Lade Jahves, p. 8 f.; 45 ff.; S. Landersdorfer. Der Βααλ τετραμορφος und die Kerube des Ezekiel, Paderborn, 1918. — As to thrones flanked by composite animals see Contenau, Civilisation phén., figs. 27,33.34. For thrones of gods flanked by similar figures in the Syro-Hittite area see Garstang, The Hittite Empire, 1929, pp. 304. 305.

P. 250 ¹. The Ark is believed to have disappeared in 586, but it may have happened earlier. S. Lønborg has made reference to Joash's plundering, 2 Kings 14,8-14, and in this connection conjectures that the Ark was carried back to Shiloh, to which Gen. 49,10 is then referred; see Arch. f. Religionsw., XXVII, pp. 369—84. On substitutes for the Ark see S. A. Cook, Religion of ancient Pal., p. 215.

P. 250 ². Josephus, Bellum, V, 5,5; Mishnah, Yoma, V, 2.

P. 251 ¹. miphleṣeth 1 Kings 15,13 is unknown. Some rabbis thought it was a phallos. Abodah zarah, 44 a, thus also Hieronymus, but there is hardly any basis for this. The reference might be to another sanctuary in Jerusalem, but in any case it is strange that nothing is said about Asa removing the asherah itself.

P. 251 ². Concerning images of serpents see p. 452².

P. 252 ¹. On asherah as a goddess see p. 510. A large number of images of Astarte have been found in Canaan, e. g. in Tell Beit Mirsim, see Albright in Zeits. f. d. alttestl. Wiss., 1929, p. 7; 15; at Gezer, see Macalister, Excavations, I, 52; II, 403; 411 ff.; at Megiddo, see May & Engberg, Material Remains etc., p. 28 ff. See further Vincent, Canaan, the Index.

P. 252 ². 2 Kings 23,11 is difficult. It may perhaps be translated: "and he stopped the horses which the kings of Judah had presented to the sun from entering Yahweh's house (and put them) in the eunuch Nethanmelech's chamber in parwārīm". The reference must then be to images of horses. Oestreicher, Das deuteron. Grundgesetz, p. 54, identifies parwārīm with ē-barbar (babbar), a name for the Shamash temple at Sippar, Larsa, Lagash, and Babylon, so that it must have been a real Shamash chapel which stood by the temple of Jerusalem. This would seem to be possible linguistically, cf. the form parbār in 1 Chron. 26,18; but the meaning has at any rate been forgotten in the O. T., and in New Hebr. the word means an extension built on to a house. The building remained, probably on the western side of the

temple, see 1 Chron. 26,18 and Ez. 41,12, as an addition to the temple.
— In 2 Kings 23,12 such an exact description as "Ahaz' upper chamber"
should not be removed as a gloss; either it is a more precise definition
of *hag-gāgh*, or this word must be read without the article in st.
constr. — On sacred chariots see Stanley A. Cook, Rel. of ancient
Pal., p. 165 f.; 207; 214. As to chariot wheels of clay at Megiddo, see
May & Engberg, op. cit., p. 23 f.

P. 253 [1]. Möhlenbrink, in his publication cited on p. 244[1], insists
that these were only added to the temple of Zerubbabel. Some of his
archaeological arguments would seem to favour this, but they are not
decisive. Possibly these extensions were added later in the monarchical
period.

P. 255 [1]. Many temples had an inner and an outer court, thus in
Egypt; likewise at Ur, see Woolley, Ur of the Chaldees; at Byblos, see
Archiv f. Orientf., XII, 1937, p. 91. The two courts may be
conceived to have come into existence by the southern wall of the
temple site being lengthened eastward, but then the outer court would
be "the new one", contrary to 2 Chron. 20,5. Chronicles implies that
the bipartition existed in Solomon's time (1 Chron. 28,12).

P. 255 [2]. Josephus, Antiquitates, XIII, 13,5.

P. 257 [1]. *makkūr*, 2 Kings 12,6, in New Hebr. and Targ. means
"acquaintance", properly perhaps client, in the sense of a person with
whom one has a commercial connection. Here it is used almost like the
Arab. *ṣāḥib* about the person applying to the priest in question.

P. 259 [1]. For altars in the streets, see Unger in Reallexikon der
Assyriologie, art. Altar; cf. 1 Mac. 1,55.

P. 260 [1]. See p. 318[1]; 320[1].

P. 263 [1]. Cf. also Ex. 15,17. According to the Islamic tradition
the building on al-ḥaram came from the angels and was founded by
Adam, see Ibn al-Firkāḥ, ed. Matthews, Journ. Pal. Or. Soc., XV, 1935,
p. 53 f. In Egypt the temples were often built according to the projects
of the gods, see Moret, Du caractère religieux de la royaume pharaonique, 1903, p. 131. Gudea and a number of his successors in Babylonia
built temples after dreams, see Meissner, Bab. u. Ass., II, p. 245. At
Ras Shamra the gods themselves conducted the building of Ba'l's
temple.

P. 263 [2]. See I—II, p. 475 and note. The expression "the navel of
the earth" occurs in Judg. 9,37.

P. 265 [1]. See the author's Der Eid, p. 119 ff.

P. 266 [1]. The translation of *zāgh* is uncertain.

P. 266 [2]. *pera'* in Num. 6,5, same word as in Judg. 5,2 where
it has also been supposed to refer to the hair.

P. 269 [1]. *shūmeṭū* 2 Sam. 6,6 is obscure, perhaps "glided out".

P. 278 [1]. *ḥalālā* in connection with *zōnā* possibly means a violated woman, perhaps one who has taken part in the sexual cult; the word would then be a kind of travesty of *kedhēshā*.

P. 279 [1]. *yiḳreḥū ḳorḥā* Lev. 21,5 may mean: produce a bald spot or merely: crop the hair; Ez. 44,20 seems to indicate the latter meaning. In Lev. 19,27 it appears to apply especially to the temples and the ends of the beard; whereas in Deut. 14,1 it refers to the hair on the forehead.

P. 281 [1]. Reading *ḳiddashtīkhā*.

P. 286 [1]. The different elements in Num. 16—17 are usually grouped in two "sources" JE and P, the latter of which has two components. Thus Kuenen in Theol. Tijdschr., 1878, p. 139 ff., and Wellhausen, Composition des Hexateuchs, 3. ed., 1899, p. 106 note; 340 —42; after which without essential alterations commentaries by Dillmann, Holzinger, Baentsch, Gray and various introductions, thus also Gressmann, Mose, p. 261. The three components are then 1) The Reubenites Dathan and Abiram with 250 men revolt against the rule of Moses and the bad life conditions in the wilderness; they are swallowed up by the earth near their tents with their kin and property (16,1b.2a.12-15.25-26.27b-34). 2) Korah with 250 prominent men rise against Moses and Aaron because they exalt themselves above the congregation, though it is holy in its entirety. They then appear with incense pans in company with Moses and Aaron, but the rebels are consumed by fire. Now the congregation complain to Moses and Aaron, Yahweh comes down upon them, but is stopped by Aaron's incense. The pre-eminence of Levi's tribe is then proved by the flowering of Aaron's rod (16,1a.2b-7a.18-24.27a.32b.35; 17,6-28). 3) Korah leads a rising of 250 Levites against Aaron because they are not content with the subordinate priestly service, but they are burnt up at an ordeal as they are offering the priestly incense offering (16,7b-11.16-17; 17,1-5). The last story, the beginning of which is missing, is merely an emendatory addition to 2) which is referred to P, while 1) is attributed to JE. 1) deals with a revolt against the authority of Moses, 2) with the rebellion of the lay population against the priests, 3) with the revolt of the Levites against the real priests. In 2) Korah is regarded not as a Levite but as an ordinary Israelite. — This distribution of the subject matter emphasises the various elements contained in the story, but the difficulty lies in demonstrating the existence of independent stories quite mechanically combined by a redactor. This would imply various adaptations with insertions for the purpose of making the stories cohere, but under such circumstances a purely literary solution of the difficulties will be very problematic. It is true that Moses' activity as leader is especially stressed in the relation to Dathan and Abiram 16,12-15; but this does not imply any purely "secular" consideration which was altogether foreign to the ancients. Moses occupies the same position as in the other post-exilic traditions, e. g. Num. 12,1 ff. He is Yahweh's elect, a quite special instrument with which Yahweh enforces his will with the people, as seen clearly in 16,28. Therefore he does not represent any definite institution or figure from the historical time of the people. But revolt against him is revolt against the holy authority. Dathan and Abiram are specially addressed because they as laymen have a special character. The awkward way in which the address to them is inserted in the story in 16,12-15 would seem to indicate that this passage has been introduced separately. The same thing may apply to the special address to Korah in 16,8-11, which similarly states exactly what were the claims put forward by Korah. But Korah, Dathan, and Abiram cannot be separated from each other, they appear together from the very beginning. And Korah cannot at any stage have been anything but the ancestor of the well-known family of subordinate priests. It is they and the lay population who form an alliance against the leaders who lay claim to holiness and leadership. The ordeal first takes place by Korah and his followers standing with incense in company with the whole congregation at the sanctuary; here Yahweh intends to isolate Moses and Aaron and strike down the congregation, but he gives up his project upon the intercession of Moses and Aaron, 16,18-22, a situation that recalls others of a similar kind Ex. 32,31 ff.; Num. 14,11 ff.; 17,10 ff. Then the delinquents are isolated and Korah, Dathan, and Abiram are swallowed up by the earth with their kin, 16,23-34, and fire consumes the other 250 Israelites who joined in the revolt, 16,35; 17,1 ff. Thus it is also understood in Num. 26,8-10. It cannot be denied that there is something remarkable about the double way of death, and it might be anticipated that all who would wrongfully be priests would be consumed by a holy fire like Nadab and Abihu, Lev. 10,1 ff. Thus the story is long-winded and badly told. But the existence of a separate story about Dathan and Abiram cannot be proved from our story; nor is it proved by the fact that only Dathan and Abiram are mentioned in Deut. 11,6 and Ps. 106,17. Korah may here be left out accidentally or out of consideration for the well-known Levite family. The greatest formal obscurity is caused by the special addresses to Korah and to the two others in 16,8-15. As already mentioned, they may have been inserted later on but it must be accentuated that in reality they merely serve to make clearer the special standpoint of the two parties, the subordinate priest and the layman.

P. 288 [1]. See I—II, Index. The year is characterised by the crying of d^{e}rōr. This, which also comprises the liberation of slaves (Ez. 46,17), must mean something like sh^{e}miṭṭā (Deut. 15,1.2.9; 31,10), to let loose or the like, viz. from normal conditions, cf. Isa. 61,1; Jer. 34,8.15.17.

P. 294 [1]. In primitive Christianity this aspect of holiness became very prominent, see A. Fridrichsen, Hagios-Qados, Kristiania 1916 (Videnskapsselskapets Skr.), and still more in Protestant Christianity. It is Robertson Smith who has first emphatically pointed out the importance in the history of religion of holiness among the Semites. But it must be viewed in connection with these peoples' view of the psychic totality. R. Otto has coined a word, "das numinose", which is thought to be especially suitable to denote holiness.

P. 300 [1]. Cf. I—II, p. 486.

P. 300 [2]. In Lev. 19,25 *lehōsīph* must be understood in close connection with v. 24. The reason why Deut. 20,6 uses the word *ḥillēl*, profane, about beginning to use the grapes of a vineyard is that the fruit has before that been holy as in Lev. 19,24. — Deut. 22,9: "Thou shalt not sow thy vineyard with two kinds of seeds lest the fulness thereof (i. e. the whole of it) become holy, the seed thou sowest and the fruit of thy vineyard", must be understood to mean that the holiness of the vines will act on the corn, for the brief growth of which other laws are in force, lest it make the whole crop useless to men. The basic idea is here different from that in the externally similar Lev. 19,19.

P. 300 [3]. The decrees about first fruits and tithes are dealt with in Wellhausen's Prolegomena, in Rob. Smith's Religion of the Semites, in the various archaeologies and in the careful work of O. Eissfeldt, Erstlinge und Zehnten im Alt. Test. [Beitr. z. Wiss. v. A. T., ed. Kittel], Lpz., 1917. Since *bikkūrīm* means the first ripened, cf. *bekhōr*, first-born, it it chiefly used about the raw crops, while *rē'sīth* means the first and therefore most essential in a more comprehensive sense. Wellhausen thinks that the first-fruits in Deut. are taken from the tithes as the part assigned to the priests, and bases this opinion on Deut. 26,12 ff. Eissfeldt thinks that the demand for tithes is already present in the claim for the first of the corn, wine, and oil in the book of the Covenant; he holds the same view as Wellhausen as to the tithes in Deut., and thinks that it has been so in earlier times too.

P. 303 [1]. The day after the sabbath, Lev. 23,11, is understood by Dillmann, Bertholet, and Baentsch in their commentaries, and Nowack, Archäol. II, 176 f. as the Sunday in harvest-time, which would be the first Sunday of that period, cf. Deut. 16,9. It would then stand in a strange relation to the *maṣṣōth* feast, which also came in the time of the barley-harvest. In later Judaism the passage was sometimes understood to refer to the sabbath of the festival week, but then there appeared the interpretation that *shabbāth* does not denote the weekday but the first *maṣṣōth* day, the 15. Nisan, because it was a day of rest. Hence the sheaf was brought on the 16. Nisan, see Josephus, Antiquit., III, 10,5; Mishnah, Menaḥoth, X. After having become part of the Paschal ritual the sanctification of the sheaf lost its old significance.

According to the above-mentioned tractate only a small measure of flour was offered from corn cut with a sickle by men chosen for the purpose in some place near Jerusalem where they found ripe corn.

P. 311 [1]. Concerning the Babylonians and Assyrians see Meissner, Bab. u. Ass., I, pp. 125. 127. 130 and Eissfeldt's investigation in the Commemorative Publ. to Baudissin [Beihefte z. Zeits. f. d. altt. Wiss., 33, 1918] pp. 163—174. Baudissin refers to several people round the Mediterranean in his Gesch. d. altt. Priesterthums, p. 53 note. Rob. Smith too one-sidedly believed the tithe to be derived from a state tax.

P. 312 [1]. It is called *lehem hap-pānīm*, the bread of the presence of the "countenance", i. e. of Yahweh, or *lehem ham-maʿᵃrekheth*, and on one occasion *lehem hat-tāmīdh* "the permanent bread", Num. 4,7. What the bowls and jugs of the table have been used for cannot be said with certainty. In some cults cakes of clay were used, see p. 474[3].

P. 313 [1]. The form *tizzākhār* Ex. 34,19 is meaningless; as a rule the reading *haz-zākhār*, "the male" is substituted, "and" being omitted, this part of the sentence will then be appositional:. all thy male cattle, the first-born etc.

P. 318 [1]. Conditions among the Phoenicians and the Phoenician Punians are elucidated by information in later Greco-Roman authors as well as by an inscription and archaeological discoveries at Carthage, see M. Mayer in Roscher's Lexikon, II, 1501 f. (s. v. Kronos = Moloch; Menschenopfer) and Baudissin in Herzog-Hauck, Realenzyclopädie, XIII, 269 f.; Dussaud, Les origines cananéennes du sacrifice Israélite, 1921, p. 163 ff.; Contenau, La civilisation phénicienne, 1926, p. 137 ff. In Palestine the mass of children's skeletons found together at Gezer and the finds at Taanach and Megiddo would seem to show evidence of the sacrifice of children, see the publications of Macalister and Sellin as well as Vincent, Canaan, p. 188 ff.; S. A. Cook, The Religion of ancient Palestine, pp. 79.82 ff. It is true that this interpretation of the archaeological finds has been disputed, see P. Thomsen, Palästina und seine Kultur, 1931, p. 50 ff. The same tendency is shown in O. Eissfeldt, Molk als Opferbegriff im Punischen und Hebräischen und das Ende des Gottes Moloch [Beitr. z. Rel. gesch. d. Altertums, 3], Halle, 1935. He makes reference to Punic inscriptions where he thinks *molch* must be interpreted as a term for offering in the sense of "Versprechen". He insists on the same meaning in the O. T. where he would read throughout, without the article, *lᵉmōlekh*, so that Molech, Melech as the name of a god drops out. The arguments in favour of this interesting conception do not, however, seem to me convincing as far as the O. T. is concerned, cf. M. Buber, Königtum Gottes, 2 ed., 1936, pp. 211—25.

P. 319 [1]. In the redemption an idea is implied which may develop into the idea of the sacrificial animal as a substitute. This does not appear in the O. T. but is expressed in the Punic formula "anima pro anima, sanguine pro sanguine, vita pro vita", which recalls the doctrine in which the development of blood revenge ended, cf. I—II, p. 392 ff. See p. 3 of Eissfeldt's work cited p. 318[1]; A. Alt in Zeits. f. d. altt. Wiss., N. F. ii, 1934, p. 303 ff.

P. 319 [2]. Lev. 27,1 ff. and Num. 18,15 ff. mention all first-born, the earlier laws and the Paschal legend, Ex. 13,13, merely speak of sons.

P. 320 [1]. If the archaelogical finds really show remains of child sacrifices they do not point to a rite with burning. Such a rite is probably denoted by the expression he‘ebhīr bā’ēsh though the meaning of "passing through the fire" is not quite clear. Dussaud, Les origines cananéennes, p. 164, thinks that it indicates the transition to divine life; but it is strange, then, that the transition to the holy sphere only in this special instance is given this expression. It is possible that the sacrifices in the vale of Hinnom are due to Phoenician influence. Diodorus, XX, 14 speaks of a Tyrian Melkart at Carthage, whose statue received the children who then passed down into a furnace.

P. 324 [1]. Or "without leaven" since both interpretations can be deduced from mēhāmēṣ.

P. 325 [1]. pillē’, Lev. 22,21; Num. 15,3.8 and the Hiphil Lev. 27,2 may also be thus interpreted; Num. 6,2 must then likewise be interpreted in this way, see above p. 265.

P. 328 [1]. Especially the tractate Nedharim. See the author's "Der Eid bei den Semiten" p. 200 ff.

P. 330 [1]. The word, which also occurs in Phoenician (mnḥt), is most probably derived from nāḥā "to lead, conduct". The gift is what is conducted to the place, just as ḳorbān is that which is brought near. It has rightly been considered a parallel to Arab. hadīya.

P. 331 [1]. See especially Num. 7,3 ff. The Aram. form ḳurbān is used in Neh. 10,35; 13,31 about the delivery of fire-wood to the sanctuary. The verb hiḳrībh is employed both with an ordinary gift and a sacrifice as the object, see the examples in Ges.-Buhl; higgīsh, which also means to "bring near", is used in the same way.

P. 331 [2]. Most probably we must read ḥamūdhōth Hag. 2,7.

P. 332 [1]. See p. 256 f.

P. 335 [1]. In the O. T. the word occurs in the plural with or without zēbhaḥ, see Ges.-Buhl. The corresponding singular form is shelem, which only occurs in Am. 5,22. The word is found in Phoenician, Corp. Inscript. Sem., I, 86 B, 4, where the meaning, however, is uncertain; and ibd., 165,3 ff. (the Massilia inscription) in connection with kll, that is to say, about burnt offerings. Cf. Lidzbarski, Handbuch, p. 376, and other treatments of the Massilia inscription, as also Dussaud, Les origines cananéennes etc. p. 142 ff., further in the Ras Shamra lists of sacrifices (Bauer's edition 1 and 3). A direct derivation from *shūlēm* (Dussaud, p. 100 f.) is not possible; that would be *sheʾlēmīm*, and such a use of the adjective would be peculiar. An emendation of Am. 5,22 does not seem well-founded. The Hebr. *shelem* bears about the same relation to *shālōm* as Arab. *silm* to *salūm*.

P. 336 [1]. It should, however, be noted that the name Ramah is not mentioned in 1 Sam. 9; but it appears from 1 Sam. 1,1; 16,13; 19,18 ff., and especially from 25, 1 that Ramah is Samuel's native city.

P. 339 [1]. In v. 34 read *ʿal had-dām* with many mss., as in vv. 32.33. It is generally interpreted "with the blood in it", LXX συν; this interpretation of *ʿal* is not reasonable, for the blood was also poured out in the people's way.

P. 339 [2]. Some read with LXX *ʾasher beʾyādhō* "what he had".

P. 343 [1]. Mishnah, Sukkah IV, 9.10.

P. 344 [1]. Rob. Smith, Religion of the Semites, 3. ed., p. 376 and adjoining pages. He bases his opinion on various evidences among the Semites that human victims were burnt outside the city; but possibly the reference may be to sanctuaries extra muros.

344 [2]. The Phoenicians have the three kinds of sacrifices *kalil*, *shelem-kalil*, *ṣawʿat* (vocalisation arbitrary), Corp. Inscr. Sem. I, especially 165.167; cf. treatments by Cook, Lidzbarski, and others in epigraphical works; Dussaud, Les origines cananéennes du sacrifice Israélite, p. 142 ff.; Lagrange, Études sur les religions sémitiques, 2 ed., p. 471 ff. In Ras Shamra all the common forms of sacrifices occur: burnt offerings, libations, meals etc. Several terms are uncertain, a provisional treatment of the matter has been given by Dussaud in Rev. de l'Hist. d. Rel. CV, 1932, p. 285.

P. 346 [1]. Besides in the sacrificial laws *ʾishshe* is mentioned in Deut. 18,1; 1 Sam. 2,28. The derivation from *ʾēsh*, fire, is obvious, even though the ending is unusual. Bauer & Leander, Hist. Gramm., p. 456 note 2, conjecture a dialectic e (ä) = ā. A derivation from *ʾnsh* "be familiar" is less probable according to the meaning. On the derivation and use see Ges.-Buhl and Gray, Sacrifice, p. 9 ff. In Ras Shamra we have probably the corresponding *ʾitt*, evidently with the feminine ending.

P. 346 [2]. *zēbhaḥ* continued to be used particularly about meal offerings, because the slaughtering here played a very prominent part. The two kinds of offerings are mentioned side by side Ex. 18,12; 24,5; 32,6; Lev. 17,8; Num. 15,3; 1 Sam. 13,9; 2 Sam. 6,17; Isa. 1,11; Jer. 7,22; Hos. 6,6; Ps. 40,7; 50,8.

P. 346 [3]. This is Rob. Smith's view, Religion, 3. ed., p. 367 ff. It is connected with his whole idea of the sacrifice, according to which this properly consists of a meal taken with the God on a related animal (Totemism) which is like a fellow member of the tribe; but in the case of a human being, the participants refuse to partake of the meal but destroy it by fire, and this is the origin of burnt offerings. Cf. p. 344[1]. It is superfluous to point out the narrowness of this theory, which has nevertheless been of such great importance in showing that the offering cannot be interpreted as a gift in the modern sense. Hubert & Mauss in Mélanges d'histoire des religions, 1909, base their explanation on sacralisation and desacralisation, but keep somewhat one-sidedly to rites developed later. A careful treatment of the various Israelite kinds of sacrifices is found in R. Dussaud, Les origines cananéennes du sacrifice Israélite, 1921, which especially draws comparisons with Phoenician material; further in G. Buchanan Gray, Sacrifice in the Old Testament, 1925; Ad. Wendel, Das Opfer in der altisraelitischen Religion, 1927; W. O. E. Oesterley, Sacrifices in ancient Israel, 1937.

P. 348[1]. Read "a three-year old bull" instead of "three bulls".

P. 348[2]. See Vincent, Canaan, p. 50 f. 192. 196. 199 f.

P. 354[1]. *tāmīdh* in v. 13 shows that it is a daily offering, so that the expression "on the day he is anointed" cannot belong to this law. See the Commentaries and Schürer, Gesch. d. jüd. Volkes, II, 4. ed., p. 347 f.

P. 355[1]. That the dove was also in pre-Israelitish times dedicated to Astarte has been proved by the excavations in Bethshean, see Palestine Explor. Fund., Qu. St., 1926, p. 210; 1927, p. 74, and S. A. Cook, Rel. of ancient Pal., 1930, Index s. v. dove, cf. May & Engberg, Material Remains of the Megiddo Cult, pp. 15.21.

P. 357[1]. To this must be added the reference in the Elephantine Papyr., Cowley 30,21.25; 31,21; 32,9; 33,11. The reference to 1 Sam. 2,28; Isa. 1,13 (v. Hoonacker in Revue Biblique, 1914, p. 161 f.) cannot be considered decisive, since the allusion may be to smoke from the sacrifice. Löhr in his thorough study, Das Räucheropfer im A. T., p. 167 ff., reckons with the possibility of keeping distinct two Hebr. roots *ktr*, corresponding to Arab. *ktr* "drip", and *ktr* "exhale fragrance". The Ras Shamra texts show that incense was used for offerings in Phoenicia in the middle of the 2. millennium, see La légende de Danel, I, 112. 126 f. 140 f. It is of interest to note that it was used in connection with funerals, cf. p. 485[1].

P. 359[1]. See I—II, p. 399.

P. 361[1]. Zimmern, Akkadische Fremdwörter, p. 66, mentions for Assyr. both the sense "bestreichen" and "abwischen"; in the cult language it occurs pretty frequently in a sense analogous with the Hebr. Dependency of the Hebr. word is probable, but it is doubtful whether it goes so far that the Hebr. can be called a loanword. The relationship between the later Hebr. cultus and the Bab.-Ass. with its incantations and preventive rites is obvious, cf. p. 375. 454. It also appears in a certain uniformity in the character of the prayers, see A. Falkenstein, Die Haupttypen der sumerischen Beschwörung, 1931, and Walter G. Kunstmann, Die babyl. Gebetsbeschwörung, 1932, both in Leipziger semitist. Studien [Neue Folge, 1—2].

P. 366 [1]. A single exception Lev. 22,23.

P. 366 [2]. In Lev. 1,11 the slaughtering takes place "by the side of the altar, towards the north, before Yahweh". In the temple plan of Ezekiel the platforms for the slaughtering of burnt-offerings, sin-offerings, and trespass-offerings are found in the eastern gate hall of the inner court; similar platforms are found in the outer corners, probably for the slaughtering of shelāmīm offerings, Ez. 40,39.43.

P. 367 [1]. Ex. 29,22; Lev. 7,3 f.; 8,25; 9,19 also forbid the eating of the fat tail. It is therefore a doubtful improvement to insert the fat tail (hā-ʾalyā) in an emendation of the text in the story of the sacrificial meal in 1 Sam. 9,24.

P. 367 [2]. This interpretation is the most natural one, see on this subject Dillmann's Commentary.

P. 368 [1]. The sanctification by tenūphā may be conceived to have developed from the sprinkling of blood on the altar which is done by similar movements, and this again was a natural result of the circumstance that the altar had become so high that it would have been difficult to pour the blood over it. It is not clear to what extent tenūphā is used. According to Ex. 29,26 f.; Lev. 8,27; 9,21; 10,15 the breast and the shoulder are to be "waved", but Lev. 7,30 only mentions the breast, and the terms the terūmā shoulder and the tenūphā breast would seem to indicate that strictly the waving was only characteristic of the breast. The shoulder appears to be the old share of the priest, cf. Deut. 18,3. The priest having also been given the breast which was habitually waved, the waving was then extended to the whole of the priest's portion in good agreement with the increasing holiness of the priest, but it was not consistently carried through. "The waving" may according to the above be regarded as a substitute for the transference to the altar, but also as a mark of the sanctification accomplished by this transference. In the latter case it would seem less necessary, nor do we find any consistency in the practice. Ex. 29,24; Lev. 8,27 demand tenūphā of fat and the rest which is brought to the altar, but in other sacrifices it is not mentioned; see Lev. 7,11 ff. In the purification trespass-offering for lepers the sacrificial lamb is "waved" before being slaughtered before Yahweh, and likewise the oil, but this is not said about the other offerings Lev. 14,12.21.24. The sheaf of the first crop is to be waved, Lev. 23,10 f.; at the feast of weeks the sin-offering and the sacrifices are to be waved with the first loaf and thus to be sanctified, Lev. 23,20. The same applies to the jealousy flour offering,

Num. 5,25, and to parts of the Nazirite offering, viz. the shoulder of a ram and unleavened cakes, which are then given to the priest "besides the *terūmā* shoulder and the *tenūphā* breast", Num. 6,20. The "waving" would seem to be a custom which has gradually gained ground but has not been quite generalised. The rabbis regard *terūmā* as analogous with *tenūphā*, consisting of an upward movement, see Wiener, Bibl. Realwörterbuch s. v. Weben (und Heben). There can hardly be any doubt, however, that this word is merely a comprehensive term for a due.

P. 368 [2]. *'azkārā* is an Aramaic form of Inf. Hiph. and probably means "call to mind", cf. Ex. 20,24. Others: quod odorem spargit, see König, Lehrgebäude II, p. 181, cf. Ges.-Buhl and Dussaud, Sacrifice, p. 93 ff.

P. 374 [1]. Wellhausen, Prolegomena, 5. ed., p. 72 f., and many after him think that sin- and trepass-offerings in the pre-exilic time consisted of a fine, 2 Kings 12,17, cf. 1 Sam. 6, to which must be added that Deut. 12,6 does not mention these offerings. This is only done by Ezekiel and it is he, then, who has converted the fine into offerings. This argument which, incidentally, is characteristic of the literary critical method, rests on a quite unrealistic conception of the way in which ritual customs arise. The sanctifying and purifying sin-offering cannot arise out of a fine to the priests, even though this may as in blood-revenge be considered to "cover" the offence. The statement in 2 Kings 12,17 that the priests were to have silver for *'āshām* and *ḥaṭṭā'ōth* without it being taken to Yahweh's house cannot be an exhaustive definition of what this institution was. No safe solution of the difficulty can be given. The purchase of sacrificial animals has been suggested. A more reasonable suggestion would be a fine *accompanying* the animal victim; this would be specially suitable in the case of the trepass-offering and could then have been transferred to the sin-offering. But an even more obvious suggestion would be an extra payment which the priests had the right to demand when they were to officiate at these new sacrifices. Hos. 4,8 does not prove the use of the special sin-offering at the time of Hosea, but shows that it was already then a purpose of the sacrifice to expiate sin. See Dillmann and Bertholet on Lev. 4; Benzinger, Archäologie, 3. ed., p. 367 f.; Dussaud, Sacrifice, p. 156 f.; Gray, Sacrifice, p. 57 ff.; Wendel, Opfer, p. 77.

P. 379 [1]. After *way-yāḳom yehōnūthān* in v. 25 the main verb has dropped out.

P. 379 [2]. Add "day".

P. 379 [3]. Cf. also Lev. 15,16.

P. 380 [1]. It is a remarkable fact that guests are so easily admitted to the sacrificial meal. In later ages the sacrificial meal could actually acquire the character of a social function, cf. Prov. 7,14, as among the Greeks; cf. in Greek the connection between φιλοθύτης and the term for hospitality, see Plutarch, Themistocles, I 5; Aristophanes, Vespæ 82.

P. 381 [1]. It will certainly make the cult legend clearer if the story about Jephthah's daughter is interpreted as the foundation legend of a feast at which young women dedicate themselves to a sexual cult, as has been well shown by G. Boström, Proverbialstudien [Lunds Universitets Årsskrift, N. F. I, 30,3], Lund, 1935, p. 115 ff. But it requires extensive emendations in the text.

P. 382 [1]. See p. 84 f. and note 85[1].

P. 383 [1]. An accurate definition of the meaning of the word ḥūgh cannot be given. Wellhausen, Reste arab. Heid., p. 110. 141 thought that the basic meaning was "der heilige Reigen", for which reference may be made to ḥūgh "circle" and "to circle". But this meaning has in that case quite disappeared both in Hbr., Syr., and Arab., cf. Nöldeke in Zeits. d. deutsch. Morgenl. Ges., 41, 1887, p. 719 note 3.

P. 384 [1]. The expression is analogous to 1 Kings 18,1.15, cf. 1 Sam. 1,22; textual emendation is unnecessary.

P. 385 [1]. See the preceding note.

P. 387 [1]. See p. 384[1].

P. 387 [2]. A connection with Deut. 15,19-23 dealing with the sacrifice of the first-born is conjectured by Guthe in Baudissin-Festschrift [Beihefte zur Zeits. f. d. alttest. Wiss., 33], 1918, p. 227. It is not, however, suggested by the text.

P. 388 [1]. In this connection it may, however, be pointed out that during the Passover and maṣṣōth feast the Samaritans live in a tent camp on Garizim. See J. Jeremias, Die Passafeier der Samaritaner [Beihefte z. Zeits. f. d. alttestl. Wiss., 59], 1932, pp. 7. 73 and Petermann, Reisen im Orient, I, 1865, p. 288. The former work, which gives good photographs of the feast, states that the tent camp is pitched already 10 days before Passover. Whether the Samaritan custom, which is natural enough for feasts outside the home, is due to an ancient tradition can hardly be said with certainty. Tents or booths for the participants were also common in the great Greek festivals such as the pan-Ionian, pan-Amarian and other feasts, see M. P. Nilsson, Griechische Feste, p. 189 note 1; likewise at Latin feasts, see Daremberg, Saglio & Pottier, Dictionnaire des Antiquités, vol. 5, 1905, p. 117 s. v. tentorium.

P. 391 [1]. Cf. Pesaḥim VI, 3.4.

P. 393 [1]. Viz. in the computation of the payment for the lamb.

P. 393 [2]. Ex. 12,9 is difficult. Dillmann in his Comm. "seinen Kopf nebst seinen Beinen und seinem Innern", i. e. "ganz"; for this use of ʿal he quotes Ex. 35,22; Num. 9,11; 1 Sam. 14,32; Baentsch in his Comm. "so dass der Kopf noch mit den Füssen und Eingeweiden zusammenhängt". According to the above translation the text would mean that the animal was to hang with the head uppermost, but this translation cannot be regarded as certain. It is not supported by Samaritan custom, according to which the animal hangs with the head downward, see the work of Jeremias cited p. 388[1] with the illustrations pp. 25.32. 33. Dillmann's conception of *'al* is somewhat forced, cf. p. 339[1]. The Jewish and Samaritan interpretations stress the fact that the animal is roasted whole, but it is difficult to see that it is merely this idea that is to be conveyed in v. 9; on Jewish tradition see Jeremias, op. cit., p. 94.

P. 397 [1]. The expression "between the two evenings" as the time for the Paschal sacrifice also occurs in Lev. 23,5, while Deut. 16,6 has "at sunset". According to the Samaritans and the Karaites the former expression denotes the time between sunset and darkness, according to the Pharisees the time from the beginning of the sunset till the complete disappearance of the sun; see the commentaries on Ex. 12,6 and Ges.-Buhl s. v. According to Num. 28,4 the *tāmīdh* sacrifice of the evening is to be offered "between the two evenings". At the time of Christ it was offered at about 3 o'clock, in earlier times somewhat later, see Schürer, Geschichte II, p. 347. According to Pesaḥim V, 1 the Paschal victim was to be killed immediately after the *tāmīdh* offering. The corresponding Arabic expression *baina l-'ishā'aini* results from the fact that the word does not mean a point of time but a period of time, namely from sunset to the disappearance of "the whiteness remaining in the horizon after the redness appearing after sunset", cf. al-Makkī, Ḳūt al-Ḳulūb I, pp. 19,12 ff.; al-Ghazālī, Iḥyā', Cairo 1322, I, 235 infra; 243,3. The last limit was called al-'ishā' al-āḥira "the last (part) of the evening" I. Hishām 158,11 f.; Bukhārī, mawāḳīt al-ṣalāt, bāb 20; Baiḍāwī to Sur. 2,183. The dual form then denotes the two extreme limits of the period. The Hebr. expression may be interpreted in a similar way.

P. 398 [1]. See Curtiss, Ursemitische Religion, p. 206 ff.; Jaussen, Coutumes des Arabes, p. 337 ff.

P. 399 [1]. The texts only speak of lambs of last year's young. Whether young of the same year were originally sacrificed must be left open.

P. 399 [2]. Burckhardt, Notes on the Bedouins and Wahábys I, 1831, p. 58; Burton, Pilgrimage to al-Madinah and Mecca, London 1913 [Bohn's Library] I, p. 245 note 4; A. Musil, Arabia Petræa III, p. 148; Jaussen, Coutumes des Arabes au Pays de Moab, p. 61 ff.; cf. also Dillmann's commentary on Ex. 12,20.

P. 400 [1]. Of great interest is Dalman's communication in "Arbeit und Sitte in Palästina" I, p. 416, according to which it is the custom to bake unleavened bread in the field during the barley harvest, of which the reapers eat. At the end of the harvest, on the other hand, some fresh corn is roasted. At p. 419 he says that the bread eaten by shepherds and labourers in the field is often unleavened. A wider folkloristic basis for the avoidance of leaven which is supposed to injure the soul of the corn during the harvest time has been pointed out by B. D. Eerdmans in the Nöldeke-Festschrift, pp. 671—679. That the *maṣṣōth* feast was originally a special harvest feast is the commonly accepted view. Wellhausen, Prolegomena, 5. ed., p. 84 f. regards it as the beginning of the harvest festivals, while the feast of weeks is their termination. Deuteronomy's interpretation of the *maṣṣōth* meal as a remembrance of the rapid exodus, with which we may compare the story of the legend, has been renewed in a curious manner by Wellhausen who thinks that the loaves were unleavened because they were to be baked in a hurry.

P. 401 [1]. Mishnah Pesaḥim II, 5.

P. 401 [2]. Beer, Pascha oder das jüdische Osterfest, Tübingen, 1911. p. 16 f. and in his edition of Pesaḥim p. 13 f. thinks of a fertility rite for the animals, "Widdersprung". This meaning might perhaps be the original one, and might then have changed. — A description of a typical commemoration feast among the Romans, Kapratinai or Quintiles, is found in Plutarch, Romulus 29, Camillus 33. The Shi'itic Ḥusain feast on the 10. Muḥarram is celebrated as a commemorative feast with the roles cast as in drama, cf. p. 411. We are here concerned with a feast in which we can follow the transformation by the legend of the historical events, because we know these from old texts. The Christian mysteries are of the same kind. They are no different in nature from the dramatic feasts of "primitive" peoples.

P. 402 [1]. Thus Pesaḥim X, 5.

P. 407 [1]. See Additional Note I on the Paschal legend and the crossing of the reed sea.

P. 409 [1]. Cf. I—II, p. 476 f.

P. 410 [1]. See above p. 302 f. and the tractate Rosh hash-Shanah I, 2.

P. 413 [1]. Pesaḥim V; VII, 13. At Hierapolis the pilgrims only presented the sacrificial animal before the altar, then they led it to their dwellings where they killed it, see Lukian, De dea Syria § 57. The Samaritans have several statements to the effect that the Paschal offering was not bound to any particular place, neither to priests, temples, nor altars. See Jeremias, Die Passafeier, p. 68 ff.

P. 414 [1]. The letter is found in Sachau's ed., No. 6, Ungnad, No. 6, Cowley, No. 21. Unfortunately the extant text is very fragmentary. The date from the 15th to the 21st is mentioned (l. 5) and it is said that they are to be clean, they must not have anything leavened by them, and they must not drink [beer, as is no doubt rightly conjectured by

Strack in his edition of Pesaḥim p. 7*, beer being forbidden as a fermented drink, cf. Pesaḥim III, 1]. This shows plainly that the feast of unleavened bread is meant, but since "..... sunset to the 21st Nisan" is also mentioned (l. 8), the Passover has surely also been mentioned; it is indeed referred to on an ostracon from Elephantine, Sachau, Taf. 64,2 l. 5. Many think that the writing is an edict from the King of the Persians, in which he, of course under Jewish influence, interferes in the inner rites of Judaism and gives definite commands about the festival, the observance of which he demands. Ed. Meyer, Der Papyrusfund von Elephantine, 3. ed., 1912, p. 91 ff. thinks that we are concerned with the introduction of the Jewish maṣṣōth feast after the postexilic Jewish law, according to which the Paschal sacrifice must only be offered in Jerusalem, so that it was discontinued in the Diaspora. Hence Darius' Edict is said not to mention the Passover at all, though this does not agree with l. 8, see above. — On the contrary, Beer, in his edition of the tractate Pesaḥim, p. 42, thinks that the fresh injunctions of the Edict concern the unification of the Passover and the maṣṣōth feast, "die von Ezechiel eingeleitet und in den jüngeren Paschaperikopen von P vollzogen ist". Cowley, Aramaic Papyri, p. XXIV f. maintains that a general observance of the Passover was only decreed by Deuteronomy in 621, and then fully introduced by Ezra; therefore it was previously unknown to the colony. All these reflections, more or less assailable in detail, are based on the common belief in the decisive importance of written laws for cult customs. But the text lends no support whatever to the contention that the Persian king wanted to reform the Jewish cult. The document is a letter from a Jew to Jews in which he exhorts them to fulfil their cult duties, and refers to the king's letter to the governor, but there is no reason to believe that this contained anything but a permission to celebrate the feast according to the common Jewish custom (l. 4a), with orders to remove the difficulties in the way of this. Hananiah, one of the Jews who had influence at court, informs his countrymen of the order given and adds his admonitions (from kʿt, l. 4). Hananiah himself went to Egypt (Sachau 11,7, Ungnad 11,7, Cowley 38,7) but his activities led to a conflict with the priests of Chnum, presumably on account of the sacrifice of lambs. These disputes led to the destruction of the temple at Elephantine (Sachau 1, Ungnad 1, Cowley 30) in the 14th year of Darius, i. e. 410. In this connection it is interesting to note that Moses in the Paschal legend utters a fear of the Egyptians revenging themselves on the Israelites because they sacrifice what is an abomination to the Egyptians (Ex. 8,22). If the Paschal legend should have received its form on foreign soil, the familiarity with Egyptian customs suggested by it would seem to indicate that Egypt was the country in which it was formed. — On the Passover and other Jewish feasts observed outside Jerusalem in later times, see Beer in his edition of the tractate Pesaḥim, p. 76 f., and Schürer, Gesch. d. jüd. Volkes III, 4. ed., p. 143 f.

P. 414 [2]. Josephus, Bellum VI, 9,3 mentions for the year 66, when Cestius Gallus came to Jerusalem, 256,500 offerings of Paschal lambs and estimates the number of participants at 2,700,000, figures which do not seem possible. It appears from the context that the sacrifices were offered in the temple.

P. 414 [3]. De decal. § 30, cited by Beer in Pesaḥim, p. 49.

P. 414 [4]. See Beer, Op. cit., p. 76 f. Some attempts were made to keep up the ritual slaughtering of the Paschal lamb. It persisted among African Jews at the time of Augustine, and in our day, apart from the Samaritans, among the Falashas in Abyssinia, see the references in Jeremias, Passafeier d. Sam., p. 1 note 2; 67 note 4; 72 note 1, and the works mentioned in 414[1].

P. 418 [1]. "Over two lambs" Lev. 23,20 hardly belongs to the text.

P. 419 [1]. "Festive rejoicing" is undoubtedly the essential meaning of hillūlīm. Thus also Wellhausen, Reste, 2. ed., p. 110 f., and Rob. Smith, Religion, 3. ed., p. 432. The Arab. hilāl "new moon" probably belongs to another root, as indicated by the Ass., see Ges.-Buhl s. v. hll. The verb hillēl is related to the present word, but also the verb which means to be mad, beside one's self, for the "festive rejoicing" was of an ecstatic kind, and in the ecstasy mentioned here the erotic element played a great part, see Additional Note II.

P. 421 [1]. It is a peculiar feature that though the feast, in Lev. 23,34. 39, is said to last 7 days, vv. 36.39 mention a festive gathering on the 8th day, while at the Paschal feast it is to be on the 7th day, Lev. 23,8.

P. 422 [1]. See Additional Note II.

P. 423 [1]. M. T. "and in order that".

P. 424 [1]. A description of the feast at the time of Christ is found in P. Volz, Das Neujahrsfest Jahwes, 1912, p. 2 ff. The sources for the later period are found in the Mishnah Sukkah; the gospel of S. John 7 and 2 Macc. 10,6 f., which speaks of an inauguration feast of the temple in which the feast of tabernacles was imitated and the Jews carried branches and rods wreathed with leaves. Further, Josephus, Antiquitates, III, 10,4 (according to which the use of booths originated from Moses' injunction to the tribes to make such in order to protect themselves against the oncoming cold of winter); IV, 8,12; XIII, 13,5; XV, 3,3; according to Bellum II, 19,1 Cestius found Lydda empty because all the inhabitants had gone to the feast of tabernacles in Jerusalem.

P. 424 [2]. Rosh hash-Shanah I, 2.

P. 426 [1]. Notably after F. X. Kugler's investigations it must be considered very unlikely that the Babylonians had the continuous 7-day week. On the other hand, in the time of the Hammurabi dynasty the days of the new moon, the waxing half-moon, and the full moon were celebrated, viz. the 1st, 7th, and 15th, and further the 28th, the day it disappeared. The day of the full moon was called the *shabattum* or *shapattum*. Of the 21st we hear nothing in the old days. Among the Assyrians the 7th, 14th, 21st, 28th and further the 19th day of the month are mentioned as unlucky days. Here a system has been introduced, but not so far as to dispense with the month in the calculation of the days. At the same time the significance and fatality of the days developed one-sidedly, so that they became "evil days" on which all undertakings, and among them especially sacrifices, must be avoided. By the side of this division we also find a division of the month into periods of 5 days. On these questions see B. Landsberger, Der kultische Kalender der Babylonier und Assyrer [Lpz. semitist. Studien, VI] 1917, p. 98 ff., 119 ff., 131 ff.; B. Meissner, Babylonien und Assyrien II, pp. 92. 395 f. — It is a probable presumption that the Hebr. *shabbāth* is derived from the east, and that on Canaanite soil too it originally meant the day of the full moon. It may have had this sense still in earliest Israel, but it is difficult to see whether the two half-moon days were then also sanctified. But at any rate the transition from moon-days to the continuous 7-day periods is surely due to a special Israelitish systematisation. By its complete detachment from the movements of the moon it is much farther-reaching than the systematisation that took place eastward. The urgent demand for rest from work marks a special feature of the holy day and gradually affords a basis for fresh motives for it. This development recalls that in Assyria, but here the Israelites do not go so far as the Assyrians, as they have never regarded the sabbath as a day of ill omen. On the whole subject see inter alia J. Meinhold, Sabbat und Woche, 1905; H. Webster, Rest Days, 1916, and the archaeologies. See further above p. 288 ff.

P. 428 [1]. There are two terms for these large temple gatherings, one is *mikrā' (ḳōdhesh),* Ex. 12,16; Lev. 23; Num. 28,18.25 f.; 29,1.7.12; Isa. 1,13; 4,5; the other is *ʿaṣārā* or *ʿaṣereth,* the meaning of which is related to Arab. *ḥarām,* so that in itself it means a cult gathering. Thus 2 Kings 10,20 about the assembly at a Baal festival, Isa. 1,13; Joel 1,14; Am. 5,21 at a Yahweh feast. It is used in particular about the gathering on the last day of the spring and autumn feasts Deut. 16,8 and Lev. 23,36; Num. 29,35; Neh. 8,18; 2 Chron. 7,9; in Jer. 9,1 it is used in a more general sense. See Ges.-Buhl s. v. Josephus uses ἀσαρθά especially about the feast of weeks, see Antiquitates III, 10,6.

P. 431 [1]. The expression indicates both "as it befits" and "because you are" a true king; *malkī* is conceived as st. constr. with the old ending *ī* just as in *dibhrāthī.* Of course it is also possible to read it as a proper name Melchizedek. But partly it is remarkable to meet with this non-Israelitish figure in an Israelitish cult poem, partly it is doubtful whether there is any old Israelitish tradition behind Gen. 14, the only passage in which Melchizedek is mentioned.

P. 432 [1]. In Babylonia the reign of a king was reckoned from the annual festival. If he acceded to the throne in the middle of the year, the period between his accession and the first annual festival was not included in his reign; it was called *rēsh sharrūti* "the beginning of the kingship", cf. Meissner, Bab. u. Ass. I, p. 63 f. If *rē'shīth mamlākhā* Jer. 26,1 were to denote the king's annual festival, see Mowinckel, Psalmen-studien II, p. 7 f., the meaning would not coincide with the Babylonian expression.

P. 433 [1]. The association of the "judgment" of the ruler who helps widows and orphans with his securing of fertility also takes place in ritual form in Ugarit, see Danel, ed. Virolleaud, I, 25, cf. 18; II, 5,8.

P. 437 [1]. We may here recall that a procession whereby the king appropriates the capital is one of the features of the Egyptian king's consecration festival, see Additional Note III. For the processions in Egypt people had small idols which were carried in a naos of wood. Processions for the purification of cities and walls played a prominent part among the Greeks and Romans.

P. 439 [1]. Whereas Gunkel and Gressmann believed the Royal Psalms to be glorifications of the Israelite king by a literary imitation of Egyptian and Babylonian patterns, S. Mowinckel in "Kongesalmerne", Kristiania 1916, and in his "Psalmenstudien" II, 1922, p. 6 f. maintains throughout that they are Israelite cult poems. Only thereby do they acquire real importance. In the same way he would see in the hymns that mention Yahweh's enthronement a reality pointing to the ritual practices of the cult; he attempts to reconstruct these in the main on the basis of the Psalms by comparison with similar feasts especially among the Babylonians; thus in an article "Tronstigningssalmerne og Jahves Tron-stigningsfest" in Norsk teol. Tidsskr., 1917, and in the above-mentioned "Psalmenstudien" II: Das Thronbesteigungsfest Jahwäs und der Ur-sprung der Eschatologie. Here important elements of the Irsaelite cult have been pointed out, which have been overlooked before. The difficulty of a consistent reconstruction of the festival ritual lies on the one hand in the fact that the parallels from foreign peoples cannot quite be made to fit Israel, on the other hand in the circumstance that the Israelitish material, in the main hymns of praise, only in a few instances contain unambiguous allusions to a definite feast. Yahweh's enthronement psalms are also treated as cult psalms by H. Schmidt, Die Thronfahrt Jahves am Fest der Jahreswende im alten Israel [Samml. gemeinverst. Vorträge], Tübingen, 1927. Gunkel in the introduction to his com-mentary on the Psalms maintains that these Pslams are eschatological. See Additional Note III.

P. 440 [1]. See p. 76 ff.

P. 443 [1]. The Bab. and Ass. mention certain gods as judges whereby they are chiefly conceived as the administrators of justice. See Tallquist, Der assyrische Gott, p. 63 ff. We now find the Israelite range of ideas recurring at Ras Shamra, see p. 433[1].

P. 444 [1]. I—II, p. 472 ff. A similar fight with "the sea" is now also known from the Ras Shamra texts.

P. 444 [2]. I—II, p. 348 ff., cf. above p. 443[1].

P. 445 [1]. I—II, p. 489 f.

P. 445 [2]. Rosh hash-Shanah, fol. 10b. 11a.

P. 445 [3]. It may be noted that it says Yahweh *yimlōkh*, not the perfect, i. e. without reference to any definite finished act.

P. 446 [1]. The tractate Rosh hash-Shanah I, 1. The term for New Year's Day in the O. T. only occurs in Ez. 40,1, but here probably only in the sense "the beginning of the year". It does not appear from this when the year began according to Ez., but 45,18 ff. shows that the Paschal month is also the first to him. In the Gezer inscription the year begins with the fruit harvest, i. e. with the autumn; thus also an agricultural inscription in Tosephta, ed. Zuckermandel, p. 215,15 ff. quoted under Lidzbarski's treatment of the Gezer inscription, Ephemeris III, p. 43. An account of the discussion on the beginning of the year is found in Ginzel, Handb. d. Chronol., II, p. 22 ff. For Israel reference may be made especially to Mowinckel, Psalmenstudien II, p. 81 ff. who regards the autumn as the beginning of the year and the time of the principal festival and sets forth in detail his grounds for this view. Cf. also his article on the chronology in Acta Orientalia, X, 1932, p. 173 ff. In prayers on New Year's Day Yahweh was in a later period given praise as a king, according to Fiebig in the tractate Rosh ha-Shanah, p. 49 ff. This may be interpreted as remains of the feast for the king, see Mowinckel, Op. cit., p. 82. It should be noted, however, that something similar takes place on other new moon days, Fiebig, p. 27. The view that the autumn feast was the principal festival and New Year's feast has been advanced by Wensinck, The Semitic New Year and the Origin of Eschatology, Acta Orientalia I, 1923,p. 158 ff. He also regards the Feast of Tabernacles as a New Year's feast. Just like Mowinckel, then, he sees a feast as the background of eschatology, and this is no doubt right. On the relation to the Babylonian festival see F. M. Th. Böhl, Nieuwjaarsfeest en Koningsdag in Babylon en in Israël. Den Haag, 1927.

P. 446 [2]. Morgenstern, Amos Studies II [Hebrew Union College Annual, vol. 12—13, Cincinnati 1937—38], p. 1 ff. sets forth arguments to show that the time is the same as in Jerusalem and that "the 8th month" only refers to the 1st day (the New Year's Feast) when the king ascended the altar and offered incense, cf. 2. Chron. 26,16 ff.

P. 449 [1]. On the curse in connection with holy places and sacrifices, thereunder Num. 5, see the author's Der Eid bei den Semiten, p. 94 f. 104; on cursing psalms see I—II, p. 450 f. On ritual cursing and blessing see Mowinckel, Psalmenstudien V, 1924; J. Hempel in Z. D. M. G. 79, 1925, pp. 20 ff. In the mosques the cursing of enemies and hostile parties belonged regularly to the cult.

P. 449 [2]. See I—II, p. 308 f.

P. 450 [1]. Namely Samaria's Ashima, Dan's god, and Beersheba's Daud, after some textual emendations, see the author's Der Eid, p: 159.

P. 450 [2]. See above p. 160 ff. and the author's Der Eid, p. 145 f. H. Schmidt in the collection: Old Testament Essays, London, 1927, p. 143 ff. thinks that various psalms of lamention originate from people who were subject to legal prosecution in the temple.

P. 450 [3]. Ex. 23,15 has: my face must not be seen *(lō' yērā'ū pānay)* empty-handed. Corresponding to this we must, despite Mass., read: see my face, Isa. 1,12; Ps. 42,3, where there is no preposition. At the same time we find Niph. with *'el* Ex. 23,17, with *'eth* Ex. 34,23 f.; Deut. 16,16; 31,11; 1 Sam. 1,22, "show oneself to". This is generally altered to Qal "see", but this is dubious, since Niph. with *'el* is used in 1 Kings 18,1.15 about appearance before the king, Hoph. with *'eth* Lev. 13,49 before the priest.

P. 451 [1]. Read *weyāshabhtī*.

P. 451 [2]. *lebhakkēr* as in 2 Kings 16,15. The expression may belong to the cult, but it may also be interpreted according to Ps. 73,17.

P. 451 [3]. *kōdhesh* instead of *kedhōsh*.

P. 452 [1]. See I—II, pp. 443. 467 f.

P. 452 [2]. Images of serpents have been found at Gezer, see Macalister, Excavations II, Index, cf. Vincent, Canaan, pp. 117. 174 f.; Cook, The Rel. of Anc. Palestine, 1930, p. 82; further at Shechem, see Zeits. f. d. altt. Wiss., 1932, p. 77; at Bethshean, see Alan Rowe i Pal. Explor. Fund, Qu. St., 1926, p. 210; 1927, pp. 69. 74, cf. Vincent in Rev. Bibl., 1929, p. 105 f. and Cook, Religion, p. 98 ff.; at Tell Beit Mirsim a snake goddess has been found, see Albright in Zeits. f. d. altt. Wiss., 47, 1929, p. 6. The same author has treated the whole question as to snakes in Amer. Journ. of Sem. Lang. and Lit., Vol. 36, 1920, p. 258 ff.; further Baudissin, Studien zur semit. Religionsgesch. I, 1876, p. 257 ff. and Adonis and Esmun, 1911, pp. 325—39, as also in the Nöldeke-Festschr., p. 729 ff. A winged serpent as in Isa. 6,2 is probably seen in Cook, Rel. of Anc. Pal., Pl. IX, 16, see p. 53 f. and Lidzbarski, Ephemeris I, p. 12. For images of serpents in Southern Arabia see Grohmann in D. Nielsen, Handbuch, p. 175; in Petra see Dalman, Petra und seine Felsheiligtümer, 1908, p. 76; in Phoenicia, see Contenau, La civilisation phénicienne, p. 185 f.; at Tell Halaf, see v. Oppenheim, Der Tell Halaf, p. 188. In Crete the well-known snake

712

goddess from Knossos, Gurnia and Prinia, see Evans, The Palace of Minos, I, 1921, p. 495 ff. 523, figs. 359—362. 365. 377; III, p. 439 ff., figs. 304– 307. 318; G. Glotz, La Civilisation Égéenne [l'Évolution de l'Humanité] 1923, p. 286 ff., figs. 43. 44. 62. In Greece holy snakes are associated with various deities, thus with Demeter, see Nilsson, Griechische Feste, p. 348 f., but especially with Asklepios, just like healing, as among the Israelites, see e. g. E. Rohde, Psyche I, 2. ed., 1898, p. 141 ff. At Rome there was in Bona Dea's temple on the Aventine a herbarium with healing herbs and snakes, see Fowler, Roman Festivals, p. 104. A cult of the snake for healing purposes was, then, probably common in the Mediterranean countries.

P. 454[1]. At the Babylonian New Year's feast the Esagil temple was purified inter alia by the head being cut off a ram, whose body was then used to smear the temple room with. Then the whole animal was thrown into the river by the two officiating persons and they were not allowed to enter the temple throughout the festival. See Zimmern, Das bab. Neujahrsfest [Der alte Orient, 25,3], 1926, p. 10 f. Somewhat similar but yet different is the ceremony in Hittite incantations, at which a ram is sent into the enemy's land to prevent visitations from their gods, see J. Friedrich, Aus dem hethitischen Schrifttum [Der alte Orient, 25,2], 1925, p. 10 ff. At the Thargelion feast in Athens the city was purified by processions, and the evil was transferred to two men, *pharmakoi*. A similar use of "scape-goats" is known elsewhere, see Farnell, Cults, IV, p. 268 ff.

P. 455[1]. The connection of prayer with other forms of worship is reflected in the language: *'āthar* "pray", Arab. "sacrifice"; *hithpallēl* a common term for praying, actually means "procure a decision" as from the oracle, as seen by Piel which means "decide, judge", Gen. 48,11; 1 Sam. 2,25; Ez. 16,52; Ps. 106,30. A careful account of the kinds and forms of prayer is found in A. Wendel, Das freie Laiengebet im vorexilischen Israel, Lpz., 1931.

P. 459[1]. On the significance of grief and weeping in the cult see Wensinck, Some Semitic Rites of Mourning and Religion [Verh. Kon. Ak. v. Wet. Amsterdam, Afd. Letterk., nieuwe reeks, XVIII, 1], 1917, especially p. 78 ff. A Danish work on this subject by F. Hvidberg based on the Ras Shamra texts is to be published in German.

P. 467[1]. *wa-yᵉphassᵉḥū*, a verb of the same root as *pesaḥ*, see p. 401.

P. 468[1]. *pārūaᶜ* Ex. 32,25, see p. 2[1]. On the use of *'annōth*, about cult song, see C. Peters in Kahle Festschrift, p. 29 f.

P. 469[1]. On the Babylonians see Meissner, Bab. und Ass. II, p. 68 ff. 435 f., but similar customs are common among agricultural peoples, as shown by numerous examples in Mannhardt's and Frazer's works. Often the cult act itself was merely imitative. On Greek soil the sexual temple cult was especially found on Cyprus in the service of Aphrodite, M. P. Nilsson, Griech. Feste, p. 364 ff., see further Stengel, Kultusaltertümer, p. 86; N. Nilsson, Études sur le culte d'Ichtar [Archives d'Études Orientales, 2]. In Rome there were games of a sexual character at the floralia; see Wissowa, Rel. u. Kultus d. Römer., 2. ed., 1912, p. 197 f. See further Additional Notes II and III.

P. 470 [1]. *y^ephāredhū* Hos. 4,14 is uncertain; the usual sense is "separate". Hos. 7,4.6 mentions the sexual aberrations of the Israelites which cause barrenness and thus are a parody on the sexual cult. Cf. Nyberg's treatment of the text in Studien zum Hoseabuch, Uppsala, 1935, p. 51 ff.

P. 470 [2]. Such a due, aphrodisia, was common in temples with a sexual cult; on the Babylonians see Herodotos 1,109; Strabo XVI, 1,20; on Byblos, Lukian, De dea Syria, 6; cf. W. Otto, Priester und Tempel im hellenistischen Ägypten, I, 316 [3].

P. 470 [3]. Nyberg, Op. cit., p. 73 f., reads *l^e'eghlath* Hos. 10,5 and translates "Kalbsgemeinde", believing that the grief is due to a political defeat. I consider it defensible to read *l^eēghel* with LXX and Syr., since *wt* may be dittography of the next word's *yt*. I would suggest the following translation: The inhabitants of Samaria go on pilgrimages to the calf of Beth-Awen when its people grieve over it (viz, at its death) and its priests rejoice over it (viz. when they announce its resurrection), on account of its honour — when this has disappeared from it. The latter remark is ironical; people worship the calf at the feast just when its honour as a god is proved to be nil. Hvidberg (Københavns Universitets Festskrift, Nov. 1938, p. 83) reads *'eghlath* and refers it to 'Anat, who takes part in the lamentation over Baal, as in Ugarit.

P. 471 [1]. To this is due the frequent comparison between a wife and a field pointed out for the Greek world by Dietrich, Mutter Erde, 1913, p. 107 ff. and still found in the Koran Sur. 2,223. The same is the case among the Egyptians, see A. Volten, Studien zum Weisheitsbuch des Anii [Det Kgl. Danske Videnskabernes Selskab, Hist. fil. Medd., XXIII, 3] Copenhagen 1937—38, p. 47. Further in the Amarna letters 74,17 f.; 75,15; 81,37; 90,42; in the Ras Shamra hymn to Nkl l. 21 ff. [Syria XVII, 1936], cf. Goetze in Journ. Amer. Or. Soc., LVIII, 1938, p. 305, note 199.

P. 473 [1]. Num. 25,1-5 is quite coherent and should not be divided between two sources. The tale has been interrupted to give place to the story about Phinehas, which was important for the later priesthood.

P. 473 [2]. This meaning of *na'^amān* is now confirmed by the Ras Shamra texts, cf. *n'my* "my favourite" about the disappearing god, I AB II, 19; D VI, 6 and the name *n'mn* in Danel and Keret.

P. 474 [1]. In v. 17 perhaps there is a hint of a phallos cult in the word *z^emōrū*, see Ges.-Buhl s. v. and Hölscher, Hesekiel, p. 74.

P. 474 ². True, this conjecture is only based on an etymology, viz. that mentioned on p. 252² (by Oestreicher).

P. 474 ³. *kawwānīm*, as in Bab. see Ges.-Buhl. Rowe recalls these in connection with the clay cakes found in Bethshean, see Pal. Expl. F., Qu. St., 1928, p. 81; cf. p. 511 f.

P. 475 ¹. On these cults see Rob. Smith, Rel. of the Semites, 3. ed., p. 290 f. 621; Hölscher, Die Propheten, p. 376 f. refers them to an Egyptian descent. The sacrifice or ritual killing of dogs often occurs among the Greeks as a link in special rites, especially for purification, cf. M. P. Nilsson, Griech. Feste, p. 404 f.; thus also among the Hittites, see A. Götze, Kleinasien, in W. Otto, Handb. d. Altertumswiss. III, 1,3, p. 153 f. The remarks about the Israelites are too few to give any idea of conditions among them.

P. 478 ¹. *'al* here as so often denotes the maintainer of the psychic sensations, see I—II, p. 160 ¹.

P. 478 ². On the dead souls see I—II, p. 180 f.

P. 479 ¹. Graves in the houses, well known from the excavations of Woolley in Ur, are also found in Ras Shamra, see Illustr. London News, 22. Febr. 1938, pp. 308. 344; Claude F. A. Schaeffer, The cuneiform texts of Ras Shamra-Ugarit, London, 1939, p. 18.

P. 479 ². In 2 Sam. 21,14 Rizpah's sons have undoubtedly also been mentioned originally, as appears from v. 13. V. 14 says: And they buried Saul's and Jonathan, his son's bones in Benjamin's land *beṣēlā'* in his father Kish's grave... The Hebr. word may mean "in a side-chamber", which makes good sense. Most investigators, however, take it as a place name; if so ,Kish's family property would not be Gibeah; Kish's native place in Benjamin is nowhere expressly mentioned, but it appears from 1 Sam. 11,4 that Saul already before he became a prominent man lived at Gibeah and it would agree with his whole position that he lived on the family property.

P. 480 ¹. 2 Kings 20,21 says nothing about Hezekiah's funeral but merely that he slept with his fathers; according to 2 Chron. 32,33 he was buried "by the ascent to the graves of David's sons". Manasseh was buried "in the garden of his house, in 'Uzza's garden", 2 Kings 21,18, and 2 Chron. 33,20 has had "in [the garden of] his house". Amon was buried "in his grave in 'Uzza's garden", 2 Kings 21,26 (Chron. nothing), Josiah "in his grave", 2 Kings 23,30, "in his fathers' graves", 2 Chron. 35,24. About Jehoiakim it is said 2 Kings 24,6 only that he slept with his fathers; in 2 Chron. 36,8 M. T. there is nothing, but in LXX as in Kings, and further "and was buried in 'Uzza's garden (γανοζαη, interpreted as a place name) with his fathers". There is every reason to believe that all these kings were buried in the same place, hence in a garden below the old royal tombs. "The ascent to the tombs of David's sons" is probably identical with "the steps leading down from the city of David", Neh. 3,15; 12,37, near the gate of the fountain and Siloah. And the royal gardens were actually close to this place, 2 Kings 25,4; Neh. 3,15, in the area south-east of the hill; cf. R. Weill, La cité de David, 1920, p. 57 ff. 'Uzza's garden must have formed part of these. — Despite Ez. 43,7 the royal tombs were hardly removed. David's tomb was shown at the time of Christ, Acts 2,29. According to Josephus Hyrkan I and later Herod broke into the tomb and stole its treasures without reaching the grave itself, Antiquitates VII, 15,3; XVI, 7,1. In the Talmud it is discussed whether it would have been permissible to remove the royal tombs. See Weill, La cité de David, p. 38 ff.

P. 484 [1]. Jer. 16,7 should be read with Duhm, Giesebrecht, Volz *leḥem 'al- 'ābhēl*, cf. LXX; further *'ōthō for 'ōthām*. Schwally, Das Leben nach dem Tode, 1892, p. 22, keeps *lāhem* and interprets "they do not break (bread) for them", viz. for the dead, by which meals for the dead would be directly proved, but the continuation would then be very far-fetched. On the sarcophagus of Aḥiram women are seen making rhythmic movements with their bodies, two of the figures with their hands above their heads, cf. 2 Sam. 13,19; Jer. 2,37. Illustr. inter alia in Cook, Rel. of anc. Pal., pl. VI.

P. 485 [1]. Perhaps this is what is indicated in 2 Chron. 16,14 where the burning is mentioned just after the reference to the fragrant substances put into the grave. Perhaps it is this custom that is referred to in 1 Sam. 31,12. The burning of fragrant wood for the dead is testified to in Arab. literature, see Wellhausen, Reste arab. Heid., 2. ed., p. 177 f. and the author's article Masdjid in Enc. of Islam III; cf. for Ras Shamra, p. 357[1]. Cutting of the hair is common in Arabia, the hair cut off being put on the grave, see Wellhausen, Reste, p. 182; Goldziher, Muhammedanische Studien, I, p. 247 ff. — Apart from Egypt and Babylonia we have evidence of the dead kings' divinity among the neighbouring peoples. In the Aramaic Hadad inscription l. 17.21 f. King Panammu expresses his expectation that his successors will say when sacrificing to Hadad that Panammu's soul is to eat and drink with Hadad. It is uncertain whether sacrifices to the dead king are mentioned in the Panammu inscription l. 21. — Among the Hittites the king was deified at his death see F. Hrozný, Hethitische Keilschrifttexte aus Boghazköi [Boghazköistudien, ed. Weber, Heft 3, Lpz. 1919], p. 164 f., and at certain feasts sacrifices were offered to the previous kings; see E. Forrer, Gesch. Texte aus Boghazköi [Wiss. Veröffentlichungen d. deutsch. Orientges., 42] Nos. 24.25.27-29.

P. 486 [1]. Read *beṃōthūm*, but perhaps the word is dittography of the next.

P. 487 [1]. See I—II, p. 194 f.

P. 490 [1]. The expression may perhaps originate from omens in which the god shows his will by moving his finger. There is probably a reference to this in one of the Taanach letters (the goddess Ashirat's finger), see Gressmann, Altorientalische Texte und Bilder I, 1. ed., p. 128.

P. 499 [1]. All three Hebr. forms occur in the Ras Shamra texts, cf. Bauer's article in Zeits. f. d. alttestl. Wiss., 1933, p. 81 ff. *'il > 'ēl* occurs in all Semitic languages except Abyssinian, see Baudissin, Kyrios III, p. 8 f. 167, and further Littmann's Nachtrag IV, p. 18. It occurs in South Arabic, cognate with Æthiopian; see D. Nielsen, Handbuch der altarabischen Altertumskunde I, p. 217 f. A review of the various conjectures concerning *'l* and *'lh* is found in Lagrange, Études sur les religions sémitiques, 2 ed., p. 79 f. If we start from *'il* as a primitive Semitic designation for a divine being, there is of course no sense in tracing its origin to a verb, but a relationship with *'ūl* "be strong" seems obvious. The relation between *'il* and *'ilāh* (Hebr. *'elōᵃh*) is not clear. Wellhausen suggested taking *'ilāh* as the plural of *'il* after the analogy of other plural formations with *h*, making *'elōhīm* a pluralis pluralis, see Zeits. d. deutsch. morgenl. Ges., 55, 1901, p. 699 f.; Vollers, however, in Zeits. f. Ass., 17, 1903, pp. 305—12, and H. Bauer in Z. d. d. m. Ges., 69, 1915, p. 561 regard *'ilāh* as the vocative after the analogy of Arab. forms. Fischer starts with the form *'ilāh* and considers *'il* an abbreviated form developed from the use in proper names, Z. d. d. m. Ges., 71, 1917, p. 445. A verb *'aliha* in Arab. only occurs as a variant of *waliha*. The meaning "instil fear (of God)", Wellhausen, Vakidi, p. 356, is due to an erroneous reading, see Fischer in Islamica, I, p. 390 ff. The difficulty is that both *'il* and *'ilāh* are primitive Semitic, hence Nöldeke gave up the attempt at a solution, see Sitzungsber. d. preuss. Akad., 53, 1882, p. 1175 ff.

P. 500 [1]. See p. 225. The plural form in *terāphīm* seems to express something of the same kind as in *'elōhīm.*

P. 501 [1]. It is not said expressly in Ex. 21,6 but may be inferred from Deut. 15,17 that the slave's ear was nailed to the doorpost. Ex. 21,6 might refer to the sanctuary of the town (thus Dillmann), but the close connection of the two sentences as well as the testimony of Deut. renders this improbable. In later Israel it was the custom to have amulets fixed to the door-post, *mezūzā*, Ex. 12,7; Deut.. 6,9; 11,20; Isa. 57,8.

P. 505 [1]. The reasons for splitting up Gen. 32 into two sources are not more weighty here than in the other stories about Jacob. Investigators refer to repetitions in v. 23 f., but they are of a purely stylistic character. In 26a Jacob's hip is put out of joint by a blow, in 26b owing to the wrestling, but there is nothing contradictory here. The assertion that the change of name in v. 28 f. is in itself a kind of blessing which would exclude the words "and he blessed him" in v. 30 has no greater weight. The sentences are linked quite naturally together to a unity. See Comm. of Dillmann, Holzinger, Gunkel, Skinner and others concerning the separation of the sources. W. Max-Müller, Asien und Europa, p. 163 note 1; B. Luther in Zeits. f. d. alttestl. Wiss. XXI, p. 66; Ed. Meyer, Die Israeliten u. ihre Nachbarstämme, p. 57, and Gunkel think that in 26a it is the god who is struck on the hip by Jacob and then asks to be allowed to go. But there is no reason to introduce another meaning here than in the rest of the tale, according to which Jacob prevails, but receives a certain injury. — Hosea knew a story like this with a few different features. Curiously enough the prophet uses it as an accusation against the people. "In his mother's womb he deceived his brother, and in his prime he fought with a god. He fought with a *mal'ākh* and prevailed, and he (the *mal'ākh)* wept and made supplication to him. At Bethel he found it and there he spake with it" (Hos. 12,4 f.).

P. 506 [1]. The material concerning Canaanite gods known before the finds of Ras Shamra is to be found in S. A. Cooke, Rel. of Anc. Pal., p. 104 ff. For Ras Shamra the texts are published by Virolleaud in "Syria" 1929 and following years. Handy editions in transcription have been given by Bauer 1936, by Ginsberg 1936, and of the mythological texts by Montgomery & Harris in 1934. A new series of publications, "Mission de Ras Shamra" has been started in 1936 with fresh texts published by Virolleaud, tome I: La légende phénicienne de Danel, tome II: La légende de Keret. The mythology has been treated by Dussaud in Rev. de l'hist. d. rel., 1931—32, and in his Les découvertes de Ras Shamra et l'ancien testament 1937; by H. Bauer in Zeits. f. d. alttestl. Wiss., 1933, pp. 81 ff.; by D. Nielsen (Ras Šamra Mythologie und biblische Theologie) 1936, and others: cf. bibliographies in the text editions. The principal myths are mentioned below, Add. Note II.

P. 506 [2]. See I—II, p. 62 f. The whole question as to Baal has been treated by Rob. Smith in Religion of the Semites, 3. ed. by S. A. Cook, p. 93 ff. 532 ff.; Lagrange, Études sur les religions sémitiques, 2. ed., p. 83 ff.; Baudissin occasionally in Studien zur semit. Rel. gesch., 1—2, 1876. 78 and in Adonis und Esmun, 1911, p. 24 ff. as also in Kyrios, 1929, III, pp. 20—44. An instructive review of the whole Semitic material is furnished by L. B. Paton in Hastings, Encyclopedia of Rel. and Ethics, art. Baal. The Egyptian material has been collected by Gressmann in the art. "Hadad und Baal" in Beihefte z. Zeits. f. d. alttestl. Wiss., 33 ("Festschrift" Baudissin), 1918, pp. 191—216. Concerning the Canaanite material see the preceding note. See also Buber, Königtum Gottes, 2. ed., p. 66 ff. In the Ras Shamra texts we become acquainted with Al'iyan Ba'l or Hadd as the king of gods who governs fertility and "rides on the clouds". — On "Balsamem" see Lidzbarski, Ephemeris f. sem. Epigraphik, I, pp. 243—260, who, however, erroneously thought that this Baal appeared late. It is mentioned in Asarhaddon's treaty with King Ba'l of Tyre from the 7th cent., see Winckler, Altorient. Forschungen II, p. 10 ff. 192, (cf. Ephemeris II, p. 122), and in the Zkr-inscription from the 8th cent., see on this subject

Ephemeris III, p. 1 ff. It is especially the Canaanites and the Aramaeans who have retained the typical use of *b.* as a designation for divine beings. Among the eastern Semites the use of it has become very limited, in northern Arabia and Æthiopia there are only relics of the old usage, but in Arabic, both northern and southern, the same thing is expressed by *dū*, fem. *dāt.* Rob. Smith started from too narrow a conception when he thought that B. was properly speaking the god of the naturally well-watered and therefore fertile land.

P. 508 [1]. See the inscription from Sudjīn published by Ronzevalle in Mélanges de l'Université St. Joseph, Beyrouth, XV, 1931, p. 241 f. and the corresponding text, Face A. Fragm. ant. L. 70 *rḥbh w'dm*[*h*] may be the open uninhabited area and the inhabited earth, or space and the earth as a whole. H. Bauer in his analysis of the inscription in Archiv f. Orientforschung, VIII, 1932, p. 5 does not read *w'dm*[*h*] l. A, a, 10, but suggests *wḳdm hdd ḥlb* "and before Adad from Haleb". See also Dussaud in Comptes rendus de l'Acad. d'Inscr. et de Belles-Lettres, 1931, and J. Cantineau in Rev. d'Assyriologie et d'Arch. Orient., vol. 20, No. 4. The inclusion of the cosmos in oaths also occurs in Hittite documents, see also Der Eid bei den Semiten, p. 225. In a Greek inscription a slave woman calls Zeus, the earth, and the sun to witness that she has been freed; see Farnell, Cults of the Greek States, III, p. 8. The '*alyān* mentioned in l. 11 is of course identical with '*elyōn* in the O. T.

P. 508 [2]. Fragmenta Historicorum Græcorum, III, ed. Müller, p. 565, piece 4. The passage referred to by Paton, cf. 506[2], runs as follows in translation: But these were the first to sanctify the shoots of the earth and consider them as gods, and they worshipped them from whom both they themselves and their successors and all who went before them drew their life and they arranged libations and sacrifices. — Philo adds that this agreed with their weakness and the folly of their souls.

P. 509 [1]. Hadad-Ba'l is often represented in relief or in figurines at Ras Shamra as a warrior with a club and a pointed cap furnished with horns; see the various illustrations in Syria and Schaeffer, The cuneiform texts of Ras Shamra-Ugarit, pl. XXXIII and XXXV, fig. 1. In the Hadad statue from Sendjirli Hadad is represented as a bearded man with a horned cap, see Sachau, Ausgrabungen in Sendschirli, I, Berlin 1893. On representations from the time of the Cassitic Babylonians Hadad is represented as a calf with a thunderbolt; see Lagrange, Études, p. 92 f. In later representations from the west he is seen as a man on a throne with an ox on either side; see Gressmann, Altorient. Bilder, 2. ed., No. 364, later as Jupiter Dolichenus standing as a warrior with an axe and with a thunderbolt on a bull, see ibd., 1. ed., no. 141. 142, 2. ed., nos. 355. 357; Garstang, The Hittite Empire, 1929, p. 302. In an Assyrian procession of gods he figures as a warrior with an axe and a thunderbolt and with two pairs of horns projecting from his head, ibd., 1. ed., no. 90. The bull was worshipped throughout western Asia, in Egypt, Canaan, Asia minor, the Ægæan. A reproduction of *'il shōr* "the bull El" as a bearded god with a pointed cap sitting on a throne is found in the Illustrated London News for Febr. 20. 1937. For peculiar earlier representations of bulls on cylinder seals see Contenau, La glyptique Syro-Hittite, figs. 5.6.15.22.24.44 and S. A. Cook, Rel. of anc. Pal., Pl. V, 9-12.14. — Resheph is represented as a purely human figure, a warrior of Semitic type; see Gressmann, Altor. Bilder, 1. ed., no. 128; Cook, Religion, Pl. XXIV, 2; also of Egyptian type, see Gressmann, 1. ed., no. 131; Cook, Pl. XXIV, 3; XXV, 2; and probably as the god at Bethshean, see ibd. at the beginning of the book. A bronze statuette of Resheph in Tell Duwēr is shown in the Illustrated London News for Oct. 1936.

P. 510 [1]. Cf. note 1 to p. 251. In the Amarna letters the goddess appears in the names 'Abd-Ashirti and 'Abd-Ashrāti; the goddess is mentioned in one of the Taanach letters, see Gressmann, Altor. Texte, I, 1. ed., p. 128; in the Ras Shamra texts Athirat is a mother goddess. Here she is connected with the sea. See also Ges.-Buhl and the literature mentioned there; and further Cook, Rel. of anc. Pal., p. 123. — The femininity of the tree may be due to the prominent part played by the fruit on it.

P. 510 [2]. Cf. note 1 to p. 252. In the Ras Shamra texts the masculine form occurs just as in southern Arabic. The horned Astarte from Bethshean is mentioned by Rowe in Pal. Explor. Fund, Qu. St., 1927, p. 69. Illustration in Rel. of Anc. Palestine, Pl. XXVII, 2; from Gezer, ibd., Pl. XXVIII, 1.2; Vincent, Canaan, p. 164, and Macalister, Gezer, II, p. 419, fig. 504. Sheep and goats were often sacrificed to Astarte on Cyprus and in other places, see Rob. Smith, Rel. of the Semites, 3. ed., p. 469 ff., note G. Astarte is sometimes depicted with cow-horns, thus in Gezer; see Macalister, Gezer II, p. 413, fig. 498, and especially in Phoenicia, like the Egyptian Hathor, thus in the Byblos inscript., Zeits. d. deutsch. morgenl. Ges., 30, 1876, p. 132. An enormous number of figurines of Astarte have been found at Hamah during the Danish excavations. — The dove is found in connection with Astarte at Bethshean, see Pal. Explor. Fund Qu. St., 1926, p. 210; 1927, p. 73 f.; in Tell el-Naṣbe, ibd. 1930, p. 12 f. and in Tell Beit Mirsim, see Albright in Zeits. f. d. altestl. Wiss., 1929, p. 13; for the goddess with dove in Crete see Evans, Palace of Minos, II, 1, p. 339; on Cyprus, see Guthe, Bibelwörterbuch, p. 54, as also much later on coins from Askalon. — For the serpent see note 2 to p. 452. — For the pig's head in the Astarte temple at Bethshean see Pal. Ex. F., Qu. St., 1927, p. 72. — Near the sea or near rivers the fish might be dedicated to Astarte, and she is represented with the body of a fish, see Hogarth, Hittite Seals, no. 170; Cook, Rel. of anc. Pal., p. 172; Lagrange, Études, p. 130 f.; see Lukian, De dea Syria, 47, on Hierapolis. — For the various

Astarte types see Vincent, Canaan, p. 158 ff. The queen of heaven at Bethshean is a warlike goddess, see Pal. Explor. Fund., Qu. St., 1927, p. 76. For models of her sacrificial cakes see ibd., 1928, p. 81. See also concerning Astarte Ges.-Buhl s. v. and the literature mentioned there. On the Canaanite goddesses 'Anat and Ḳadesh see Cook, Rel. of anc. Pal., p. 104 ff.

P. 511 [1]. Read *lᵉmalkath;* cf. for this cult p. 474.

P. 513 [1]. On the name of Yahweh see Ges.-Buhl. G. R. Driver, in the collection "Old Testament Essays", 1927, pp. 18—24, thinks that an earlier pronunciation Yā has later been superseded by Yahweh. The name, however, seems to occur already in the 15th century in northern Canaan in the form Yaw, viz. in the Ras Shamra texts, see Virolleaud in Rev. de l'Hist. d. Rel., 1932, I, p. 247; Bauer in Zeits. f. d. alttestl. Wiss., 1933, pp. 92—94. This would seem to indicate that the name was not originally specifically Israelitish; in that case the previously known names Ya'ubidi and 'Azriya'u for princes in Syria acquire renewed interest. See the later treatments by Kuhn in Littmann-Festschrift (Orientalist. Studien, ed. Paret), p. 25 ff. and by Schleiff in Zeits. d. deutsch. Morgenl. Ges., 90, 1936, p. 678 ff.

P. 514 [1]. *'glyw,* no. 41 in "Harvard Excavations at Samaria", 1924; see also the brief survey in Jack, Samaria in Ahab's Time, 1929, p. 101. Of 52 names 11 are compounded with *yw,* 6 with *ba'l,* cf. Jack, p. 157.

P. 516 [1]. *pōsᵉḥīm* is the same word that is used about the Paschal feast and about the procession of the priests of Baal around the altar in v. 26; see note 1 to p. 467. Unfortunately the other word "on the two *sᵉ'ippīm"* is quite unknown. — The sharp contrast between the nomadic traditions and the peasant culture is also found among other Semites. Diodorus Siculus, XIX, 94 says of the Nabataeans that their law forbade them to sow corn, to plant any fruit-bearing plant, to use wine and to build houses. They thus hold the same views of agriculture as the Rechabites in Israel mentioned at p. 522 f.

P. 525 [1]. Thus instead of "thee".

P. 529 [1]. Read *bᵉʿonyī.*

P. 529 [2]. See I—II, p. 382 f.

P. 536 [1]. See the references in Ges.-Buhl s. v. *zānā.*

P. 537 [1]. See p. 470[3].

P. 540 [1]. Omit *yissartī* as in LXX.

P. 546 [1]. This point of view forms the main content of the latter half of Mowinckel's Psalmenstudien II to which the reader is here referred. Wensinck too has put forward this view, see note 1 to p. 446; cf. Kraeling in Journ. of Bibl. Lit., 1928, pp. 133—59.

P. 553 [1]. The sentence "whose two kings thou dost dread" must have got in by mistake, thus Buhl's Danish commentary.

P. 554 [1]. Of course it would also make sense to read with LXX *yēbhōsh* "is not confounded".

P. 558 [1]. A pronouncement of this kind need not imply the exile; partly the people was not united in Canaan, partly there were many Israelites in exile before the Babylonian exile, cf. A. Causse, Les dispersés d'Israel, Paris, 1929.

P. 562 [1]. Cf. Zeits. f. d. alttestl. Wiss., 1924, p. 157.

P. 572 [1]. According to Gressmann, Zeits. f. d. alttestl. Wiss., 1924, p. 322 ff. the reference in 2 Kings 23,4 is to Assyrian gods, Ashur and Ishtar, whose images stood in the temple hall, while the Canaanite asherah pole is not mentioned till v. 14. Ahaz' altar is supposed to have been dedicated to the Assyrian cult. It is doubtful, however, whether so much can be implied in the text. Jer. shows that the cult of the queen of heaven, which was old in Canaan, see p. 511 f., was very widespread in the 7. century, but it need not have been the Bab.-Ass. Ishtar. — Model chariots of clay as votive objects used in the Shamash cult are found at Megiddo and elsewhere. See May & Engberg, Material Remains of the Megiddo Cult, pp. 23—25.

P. 572 [2]. The reference must be to sanctuaries at the entries, but the passage is obscure, since the "bamahs of the gates" are first mentioned and then a single one. In the description of the situation, too, there is some obscurity. The emendation to *śeʿīrīm* is no improvement.

P. 578 [1]. The political significance of the reforms is strongly emphasised in Oestreicher, Das deuteronomische Grundgesetz, 1923. New light has been thrown on the policies of the great empires in J. Gadd, The Fall of Nineveh, 1923, which describes the campaigns against Assyria in 616—609. Nineveh was captured in 612 by Babylonians and Medes, while the Egyptians supported the Assyrians. The new chronicle shows that Assyria was feeble at the time of Josiah and thus gives the background for his independent activity. See Gressmann in Zeits. f. d. alttestl. Wiss., N. F., 1 (42), 1924, p. 157 f.; Welch, ibd., N. F., 2 (43), 1925, pp. 255—260.

P. 584 [1]. Cf. p. 96. About the surrendering of men to the Egyptians see Ed. Meyer, Der Papyrusfund von Elephantine, 1912, p. 32 ff.

P. 587 [1]. See especially 1 Kings 2,1-4; 3,14; 6,12 f.; 8,14 ff.; 9,1-9; 11, 1-13.29-38; 2 Kings 17,7-20; 21,5-15. On Deuteronomy see Additional note IV. Deuteronomy indeed implies that the Israelites carry on international transactions as money-lenders, Deut. 28,12.

P. 589 [1]. On the early colonies and their importance see A. Causse, Les dispersés d'Israel, 1929.

P. 592 [1]. The other gods are 'Anathbethel and Ashimbethel, 22,123 ff. (Cowley's ed.), 'Anath-Yahu, 44,3 a goddess connected with Yahweh;

further Harambethel, 7,7, cf. Haramnathan and Bethelnathan, 18,4. Oath by Sati, 14,5.

P. 592 [2]. Hölscher, Hesekiel, 1924, attempts to follow out this point of view in a literary analysis.

P. 602 [1]. See on this subject Mowinckel's survey of the more recent works in Acta Orientalia XVI, 1937, pp. 1—40.

P. 605 [1]. Concerning the question as to Yahweh's servant which acquired renewed interest by Duhm's comm., see the commentaries and S. Mowinckel, Der Knecht Jahwäs, 1921; O. Eissfeldt, Der Gottes-knecht, 1933; Sellin in Zeits. f. d. alttestl. Wiss., 1937, p. 177 ff. On the question as to the individual and the people cf. I—II, p. 275 f. An interesting conjecture has been put forward by J. L. Palache in The 'Ebed-Jahveh Enigma in Pseudo-Isaiah, Amsterdam 1934, who, basing on 42,19, thinks that the servant is Meshullam, Zerubbabel's son. In the death and resurrection of the servant we may find reminiscences of old cult traditions as described above.

P. 607 [1]. Thus Mowinckel in his Norwegian books about Ezra and Nehemiah from 1916, and Oesterley in Oesterley and Robinson, A History of Israel, II, 1932, Chap. X. Conversely Schaeder in Esra der Schreiber, Tübingen, 1930, p. 11 ff., and Kittel, Gesch. Israels, III, 2, §§ 61—63. Like Torrey they place Neh. 8 (and 9) after Ezr. 8.

P. 610 [1]. In Ezra's time there was as yet no strict observance of the letter of the law. It is characteristic that Ezra, 9,11 f., speaking of isolation from the polluted country population refers to the prophets, not to a command from Moses. Nevertheless the demand is of course an expression of "the commandments of our God" and the *tōrā*, Ezr. 10,3. — Nehemiah 1,8 f. quotes a message from Yahweh to Moses that the Israelites shall be scattered if they transgress, but if they turn to Yahweh and keep his commandments, they shall be gathered to the place Yahweh has chosen to let his name dwell in, even though they are at the uttermost part of the heavens. This word to Moses is not found in our texts, but it vividly recalls Deuteronomy, Ezekiel, and altogether utterances from exilic and early post-exilic times. In Ezra's "law which Yahweh had commanded by Moses" there was a written command about the feast of tabernacles which is not found in our law codes (Neh. 8,14 f., see p. 423). Among the duties the con-gregation undertook at the instance of Ezra the following are not mentioned in the law codes known to us: the duty of not buying corn of the people of the country on the sabbath and on holy days (Neh. 10,32); the rendering of of a shekel as a temple gift (v. 33), while Ex. 30,11-16 claims ½ shekel; the decree about the supplying of fuel (v. 35). It is not possible to say what is the literary relation between Ezra's law and our laws.

P. 612 [1]. For special expressions of the idea that the covenant with Yahweh is pervaded by love see 1 Kings 8,23; Jer. 16,5; Ps. 89, 29.34; for Israel's maintenance of *mishpāṭ*, Ps. 25,10; 103,18 and the stories about the making of the covenants in Ex. and Deut.; breaches of the covenant, 1 Kings 19,10.14; Jer. 11,10; 14,21; 22,9; Hos. 6,7; 8,1; Ps. 44,18 et al.; Yahweh's maintenance of the covenant, Jer. 14,21 et al.

P. 612 [2]. Yahweh the father of Israel, Deut. 32,6.18; Isa. 63,16; creator, Deut. 32,15; Isa. 43,1; 44,2; elector, Deut. 7,6; Isa. 41,8 f.; Israel his son, Hos. 11,1, first-born, Ex. 4,22, sons and daughters, Deut. 32,19; Isa. 1,2; Hos. 2,1; vine, Jer. 2,21, cf. Isa. 5.

P. 612 [3]. *ḥēleḳ, naḥᵃlā*, Deut. 32,9; Zech. 2,16; *sᵉghullā*, Ex. 19,5; Deut. 7,6; 14,2; 26,18; Ps. 135,4; yoke, Jer. 2,20.

P. 613 [1]. Yahweh *mōshīᵃ*, Judg. 6,36; 1 Sam. 14,39; Isa. 45,15; Hos. 13,4; *gō'ēl*, Gen. 48,16; Ex. 6,6 15,13; Isa. 41,14; 43,14; 44,23; f.; Ps. 19,15; 103,4; Job 19,25 et al.; healer, Ex. 15,26; avenger, Isa. 47,3; 63,4; Jer. 51,6.24; Ps. 94,1; rock, Deut. 32,15.18; Isa. 26,4.

P. 616 [1]. Yahweh's *mishpāṭ* and his ways are his *kābhōdh*, Ez. 39,21; Ps. 138,5, likewise his miracles, Num. 14,22, his kingship, Ps. 145,11 f.; the nations shall acknowledge his honour, Isa. 40,5; 66,18 f.; Ps. 96,3; 97,6; 102,16; fear it, Isa. 59,19; Ps. 102,17. His honour is exalted above heaven and earth, Ps. 57,6.12; 108,6; 113,4; the fullness of the earth his *kābhōdh*, Isa. 6,3; Ps. 72,19, cf. Num. 14,21.

P. 624 [1]. According to Plutarch, Vitæ, Cleomenes 9, the Lacedaemonians, who gained renown for their courage, had yet a temple dedicated to fear.

P. 625 [1]. In the author's Der Eid bei den Semiten, p. 151, another original conception of *paḥadh* is mentioned, suggested by Arendonk. In the present text there can hardly be any doubt that it means terror.

P. 626 [1]. Gen. 22,12; 2 Kings 4,1; 17,32; Isa. 50,10; Jon. 1,9; Ps. 15,4; 19,10; Job 1,4 etc.

P. 626 [2]. Holy as Yahweh, Lev. 19,2; love him, Deut. 6,5; 11,13; 19,9; 30,16; fear and love, Deut. 10,12.

P. 627 [1]. *ḥelḳī*, Ps. 73,26; 119, 57; 142,6; Lam. 3,24; cup, Ps. 16,5. For similar expressions about Israel in relation to Yahweh see p. 612, note 3.

P. 630 [1]. See I—II, pp. 235. 238.

P. 634 [1]. *malkām*, v. 1.3 is plainly an emendation made on the basis of later views.

P. 638 [1]. Thus in LXX; this reading is necessary instead of M. T. "Israel's sons".

P. 638 [2]. It is expressed in the term *hebhel* which means the same as *shāw'*; on this, also used about the gods, Jer. 18,15; Jon. 2,9; Ps. 31,7, see I—II, p. 413[2]. The same thing is probably expressed by *'ᵉlīl*, which also denotes the powerless, inefficient, Jer. 14,14; Zech. 11,17; Job 13,4. It is used about a false god in Isa. 10,10, often in the plur.,

Isa. 2,8.18.20; 10,10 f.; Hab. 2,18 et al., see Ges.-Buhl. The idol and the false god are designated by the term *gillūl;* it is found in Lev. 26,30; Deut. 29,16; 1 Kings 15,12; 21,26; 2 Kings 17,12; Jer. 50,2 and often in Ez.

P. 639 [1]. See p. 221 f.

P. 640 [1]. It is said in 1 Kings 15,12 that he removed the *gillūlīm* that "his fathers" had made. On images in the royal temple cf. Mowinckel in Acta Orientalia VIII, 1930, p. 257 ff.

P. 642 [1]. See p. 599.

P. 642 [2]. On a coin in the British Museum which is believed to be from Gaza, c. 400 B. C., is seen a Zeus-like god with an inscription generally read *yhw,* see inter alia S. A. Cook, Rel. of anc. Pal., pp. 147. 186, Pls. XXXII and XXXIV, 30.31. This interpretation would indeed seem natural. However, Sukenik, referring to other coins, thinks that it should be read *y h d,* see Journ. of the Pal. Or. Soc., XIV, 1934, p. 178 ff.; XV, p. 341 ff.

P. 642 [3]. See p. 468.

P. 644 [1]. *shimṣā* must be connected with *shēmeṣ* "whisper", Job 4,12; 26,14, cf. *dibbā.*

P. 647 [1]. The psalms speak of Yahweh's wings, 17,8; 36,7; 57,2; 61,5; 91,4; see on this subject S. A. Cook, Rel. anc. Pal., p. 52 f., which quotes many instances of winged gods. It is hardly probable, however, that the Israelites imagine Yahweh to be winged. They might be thinking of the wings of the cherubim, but more probably it is a conventional expression adopted from outside. In the image of Yahweh mentioned at p. 642[2] he is sitting on a winged wheel.

P. 648 [1]. This also applies to the fragmentary story of the holy gifts of gold ornaments given by the Israelites, Ex. 33,5 f.

P. 649 [1]. See I—II, p. 245 ff.

P. 651 [1]. Stade, Bibl. Theol., I, 291 thought that it was not until Ezekiel that Yahweh became a heaven god proper, and that the Persians had an important influence in the development of this notion (p. 325). See, however, above p. 506 with note 2. In Assyria Ashur and several other gods were gods of heaven; see Tallquist, Der assyrische Gott [Studia Orientalia, IV, 3], Helsingfors, 1932, pp. 46. 48.

P. 655 [1]. This means that his power reaches beyond the world-embracing ocean, cf. the Ras Shamra texts according to which El's hand is as wide as the ocean.

P. 657 [1]. On the relation between the human and the divine activity in history see J. Hempel, Altes Testament und Geschichte, Gütersloh, 1930.

P. 660 [1]. Cf. the criticism in B. D. Eerdmans, Alttestamentliche Studien, II, pp. 61—98. Gressmann, Mose, p. 180 ff., would see in Ex. 19-24; 32-34 both in a literary respect several sources, and in the matter various "Schichten". His criteria for these seem strange, see especially pp. 182. 185.

P. 661 [1]. See p. 85 and the note.

P. 665 [1]. A fresh attempt to find the underlying material in the stories of the patriarchs is found in A. Alt, Der Gott der Väter [Beitr. z. Wiss. vom A. T., 3 Folge, Heft 12], 1929. Just as Nabataean and other inscriptions mention the gods of definite persons he thinks that Abraham's god is the god who, without belonging to a certain locality like the 'ēlīm, has revealed himself to a person, Abraham, and is then worshipped by him and his group. On the relation between El, Eloah and Shaddai see B. D. Eerdmans, Studien in Job, Leiden 1939. The name 'lyn ('elyōn) is found among the Aramaeans see p. 508 [1]. It is of interest to note that El in Ras Shamra occupies the same position towards the country as later Yahweh. In the O. T. El amongst other names for gods becomes the name for Yahweh.

P. 667 [1]. It does not come within the scope of this work to give an account of the literary genesis of the Pentateuch, and it is perhaps questionable whether a certain and complete account can ever be given of it. The work of the last generations has yielded as the certain result that the Pentateuch is composed of heterogeneous elements, and that its final compilation was not carried out before the exile. The numerous analyses made in the present work have, however, shown that the usual "source hypothesis" in the form given to it by Graf-Kuenen-Wellhausen cannot be regarded as the final solution but must undergo alterations. The natural point of departure is Deuteronomy, which forms a separate unit. It has been mentioned at p. 580 that it is based on an earlier law code later amended and provided with admonitions and historical abstracts with a definite tendency, probably pointing to the time shortly after the exile. Closely allied to Deuteronomy are the stories of the book of Joshua about the conquest of the country and with the lists of the Israelitish areas. In these stories also the ancient subject matter cannot be segregated by means of formal literary criteria, as we have seen in the analysis of the stories about the capture of Jericho and about the deception of the Gibeonites. — In the middle portion of the Pentateuch, Ex., Lev., and Num., the various law codes form natural units, partly the laws of the Book of the Covenant Ex. 20,23-23,19 and the parallel collection in Ex. 34, partly the "Law of Holiness" Lev. 17-26, and the groups usually comprehended under the term "the Priestly Code". Many examples have shown us how ancient matter and later constructions have been combined in these law codes which can hardly be supposed to have received their final form until the post-exilic period, although the substance of the laws has of course come into existence during the growth of Israelite manners and customs in the old chieftain period and the regal period. There has been too great an inclination to regard the law codes as purely literary products of authors who worked in succession, each of them further developing his predecessors' work. On this view the laws and the prose narratives are placed on an equal footing, as originating from the same authors, whose works run parallel throughout the whole Pentateuch. On this view the laws of the Book of the Covenant would originate from the same "author" as some of the stories in Genesis.

The central part of the narrative matter is made up of the description of the distress of Israel in Egypt, the growing up of Moses, Yahweh's struggle with the Egyptians, and the deliverance of Israel. We have seen that this description (Ex. 1-15) is the cult legend of the Passover reflecting the annual re-living of historical events, as it took shape down through the ages. We have seen the inequalities of the text which cannot be explained by a literary analysis that divides the subject matter between parallel "sources". A ritual background must probably also be assumed for the revelation legends from Sinai, which are closely allied to the whole material of the laws and connected with other traditions of the wanderings in the wilderness. It applies to the revelation legends that they are strongly dominated by the post-exilic view of Yahweh and Israel, just as also other of the wilderness stories (e. g. Ex. 16) and the description of the sanctuary in the wilderness most probably have the post-exilic temple as their background.

Before the Paschal legend, in direct coherence with it, are placed the stories about the forefathers. Here we find the fresh tribal legends about Jacob and his sons, giving us Israelite history in the condensed form of ancestral history, illustrating the relation to Edom and Aram with vivid features of the life of the populace and a penetrative characterisation of the forefathers of the people and the individual tribes. To this are added the adventures of Joseph, who became grand vezier in Egypt and prepared the way for that power for Israel which was to cause the later oppression and the events of the Passover. Just as Moses made the covenant with Yahweh which was associated with the Passover and the law, thus the patriarchs founded the local places of worship and in connection herewith the covenant with Yahweh which secured to Israel the blessing and the right to Canaan. By the incorporation of foreign cult myths as an introduction, the history of Israel acquires a cosmic background and we see a development of the world with Israel as the goal which terminates in the description in Joshua of Israel's conquest of Canaan. Thus we get a consistent plan throughout the Pentateuch and the book of Joshua. It is the common view that such a plan has existed from the beginning of the genesis of "the sources", the "Yahwist" and the "Elohist" having already been extant in the early monarchical period, each comprising in the main this plan, according to which the priestly sources were then again formed. This view is based on the observation of duplications and contradictions in the stories. Through these investigators have been led to find the continuous interwoven sources, the unity of which it is thought possible to demonstrate throughout. That the subject matter is made up of unequal elements is clear. There are two conceptions of the genesis of the world, two stories of the flood which are interwoven, etc. The matter in Genesis which is attributed to the priestly source is not difficult to isolate but it cannot be regarded as certain that it constitutes an independent coherent book. As regards the rest, which is supposed to be made up of the works of the Yahwist and the Elohist, we have seen again and again that the importance of the repetitions has been greatly exaggerated, and that the narratives as a rule are naturally coherent. The alternation of the divine appellatives is often rather arbitrary and therefore no reliable criterion. It is doubtful, therefore, whether we can accept the Yahwist and the Elohist in Genesis as two separate sources.

The analysis of Ex. 1-15 in Additional Note I will show that we have here a cult legend forming a separate whole and which has not been formed by the mechanical combination of independent parallel expositions. The rest of the subject matter in Ex.-Num. comprises laws, cult legends, and traditions of the wanderings of the Israelite tribes. Such a summary is not peculiar to Israel, we know it also from Greek and Roman authors' tales about the earliest history of their peoples. In Islam all rules of life were for a couple of centuries referred to the founder, but the Israelites continued referring such rules for the administration of the law and the cult to the founder as late as exilic and post-exilic times. Our analyses have shown that a series of laws and legends having their origin in the cult, among these the legends associated with Sinai, did not receive their present form until that time and are thus influenced by the special development in Jerusalem. These analyses have also shown that the common view of the literary genesis of the subject matter does not hold good. Literary criticism has limited itself to purely formal characteristics and drawn greater conclusions from them than they can maintain. It has not only been supposed that the tribal legends of Genesis and the laws and cult legends of Exodus could be referred to the same original authors, but even that these could be shown to reappear further on in such different material as the stories in the book of Judges and in the books of Samuel. — It would seem natural to ask: When, then, has all this material existed as a continuous unity? The only reply that can be given is that possibly there may at one time or another during the monarchical period have existed literary compilations with a coherent exposition of laws, cult legends, tribal legends, myths and history, but nothing compels the supposition that this learned work was composed before the exile. And a penetrative analysis of the individual groups of the continuous story available to us shows that we cannot by a separation of this exposition in its components succeed in reproducing earlier works which have been of the comprehensive character of our Pentateuch.

ADDITIONAL NOTE I.

THE CROSSING OF THE REED SEA AND THE PASCHAL LEGEND.

In forming an opinion of the story about the crossing of the reed sea it must be kept in mind, as we have remarked above, that this story, as well as the whole emigration legend, though inserted as part of an historical account is quite obviously of a cultic character, for the whole narrative aims at glorifying the god of the people at the paschal feast through an exposition of the historical event that created the people. The object cannot have been to give a correct exposition of ordinary events but, on the contrary, to describe history on a higher plane, mythical exploits which make of the people a great people, nature subordinating itself to this purpose. The hymn of triumph is indeed on the same plane as the rest of the legend. In the literary criticism this character of the legend of the crossing of the sea, has not been sufficiently considered, and the narratives have been treated in a quite formalistic way. Usually three linked-up accounts are distinguished. The point of departure is essentially as follows: 1. Ex. 13,17-19 states that God led the Israelites round by way of the desert, not directly through Philistaea, lest they should be scared by the fighting, but another motive is set forth in 14,2-4, according to which Yahweh lets the Israelites turn back to Pi Ha-Hiroth by the reed sea, so as to induce Pharaoh to pursue them. 2. In Ex. 14,5-7 Pharaoh regrets that he has set free his bondmen, but in 14,4 it is Yahweh who hardens Pharaoh's heart in order to exalt himself at his expense. 3. Ex. 14,19 shows a dualism, for it is said both that God's *mal'ākh* and that the pillar of cloud stationed themselves behind the Israelites. 4. In Ex. 14,21 the water is driven back by an east wind blowing all the night, but according to the same verse the water stands in walls on both sides; now Moses is to stretch out his hand, now his rod. By combining these observations three accounts are elicited: According to J Yahweh dries up the sea by an east wind (v. 21) and the Israelites march across, the Egyptians pursuing them to the opposite bank. At the morning watch Yahweh confounded the Egyptians from the pillar of cloud and fire

(v. 24), and checked the advance of their chariots. Therefore the Egyptians decided to fly (v. 25). But in the morning the sea returned, the Egyptians fled towards it and perished (v. 27). According to P Moses, at the command of Yahweh, stretches out his hand over the waters which then divide. After the Israelites have crossed, Moses again stretches out his hand, while the Egyptians are in the middle of the sea; the waters return and submerge the Egyptians. Into this account are introduced parts of E, who is said in the main to have had the same exposition as P, but in E it is the rod of Moses which is stretched out over the waters. Thus, with various small divergences, the different histories of Israel, introductions, and commentaries on Exodus.

The most important point is the crossing itself. Wellhausen and others attach significance to the fact that in the exposition assigned to J we have a more natural account which on the whole might reproduce historical events. To this we must reply that an ordinary easterly gale could not possibly dry up a body of water such as the one here concerned. This must happen by the water being driven from the coast and from such depths that an army could be drowned in it; but such an effect would at best be conceivable with a north wind, since the sea in question extends from south to north. And the water must have been driven very far back, for otherwise it would have been more natural for both parties to have gone northward round the coast. It must also be asked whether an east wind which could dam up such water masses would not prevent the Israelites from crossing in the face of the wind. Such "realistic" considerations, however, must not be brought to bear on the legend which aims throughout at showing that Yahweh does with the enemy and with the forces of nature what he likes so as to save Israel and gain honour for himself. Nothing is said about the wind driving the water back from the coast. On the contrary, the narrator means to convey that the Israelites faced a body of water that quite shut them off; from this position Yahweh saved them. The east wind, ḳādhīm, is to the Israelites a violent destructive wind. Just as Marduk in the Babylonian myth of the creation sends the cyclone, the violent south wind, against Tiamat, thus Yahweh uses this mighty instrument to make a way for his people through the sea. It is possible that now one, now another motive for leading the Israelites to the sea has been incorporated, but these irregularities are not sufficient to warrant the inference that several complete co-ordinate stories have been pieced together. Everything takes shape according to the idea of the legend. Yahweh hardens Pharaoh's heart, therefore he must act as he does; his soul is unfree and without strength, he must regret that he has let the Israelites go, he must be enticed into the water so as to perish. The keynote of the whole story is that Israel as well as her enemies is entirely in the hands of her God. He does not let the Israelites proceed direct to Canaan lest they should be scared by the Philistines. He leads them to the reed sea that he may accomplish his memorable deed against Pharaoh. When the Egyptians approach the Israelites lift up their voices in lamentation, a feature merely designed to intensify the impression of the greatness of their salvation. Yahweh then shows Moses what he is to do: he is to lift his rod and stretch out his hand over the water, then it will divide and they can cross on the dry bottom. The pillar of fire and cloud, in which the might of Yahweh dwells, now moves between the two hosts, hindering the Egyptians from falling upon the Israelites at once. "And Moses stretched out his hand over the sea; and Yahweh stirred up the sea by a strong east wind all that night and he made the sea dry land, and the waters were divided. And the Israelites went on dry ground in the middle of the sea, and the water was a wall unto them on their right hand and on their left" (14,21-22). In the morning watch *('ashmōreth hab-bōker*, v. 24) Yahweh confused the Egyptians from the cloud so that they could not go on in the sea. The implication is that the Israelites have now gained the other bank. Upon Yahweh's command Moses again stretches out his hand and the waters return to their usual bed. The Egyptians who had turned to flee when they felt Yahweh against them, ran up against the water everywhere and Yahweh threw them pell-mell *(wayᵉnaʿēr)* into the waves (Ex. 13,17-14,31).

The legend purposes to describe the mythical fight between Yahweh and his enemies and this purpose dominates the narrative to such a degree that it is impossible to show what were the events that have been transformed into this grand drama. It is through the feast that the events have been condensed and exalted to the dimensions they have assumed in the sacred story. Therefore it is only conceivable that they have acquired the form we know through the practical cult. Here the events have been re-lived in the Paschal night by the whole of the festival legend being reviewed. Therefore the night that is passed in the crossing of the reed sea is for the participants identical with the Paschal night itself, the night they experienced in the holy place, and which was not of course different from its archetype in Egypt. This holy night which opens with the killing of the Paschal lamb is "a watch night *(lēl shimmūrīm)* for Yahweh to lead them out of the land of Egypt; this very night is a watch for Yahweh, valid for (i. e. re-lived by) all the Israelites in their generations" (Ex. 12,42). At the time of the morning watch *('ashmōreth hab-bōker)* the Egyptians have been defeated (Ex. 14,24). In these expressions we may see allusions to the arrangements of the festival night in the cult. By the morning watch the contest of the night in the renewed experience in the cult has been brought to an end, and the song of triumph forms its termination.

The usual separation of the sources of that part of the festival legend which relates to the departure and the crossing of the reed sea is due to a misunderstanding of the whole character of this story. The narrative is no report but a cultic glorification. Something similar applies to all the rest of the Paschal legend. It is impossible to form any definite notion as to how such a festival legend has come into existence. Of course it has constantly been altered and enlarged in the course of time, and it would be quite unreasonable to believe that all the holy words and acts of the Paschal night have come down to us in the legend transmitted.

As we have tried to show, there is a unity in the whole legend which is dominated by the contest between Yahweh and Pharaoh, the aim of which is the deliverance of Israel while at the same time it has the Paschal feast in view, to the contents of which there are constant allusions. There are, however, as is only to be expected in such a legend, internal incongruities and irregularities. It must at the outset be considered more likely that these are due i. a. to additions and alterations made in the course of time than that they should be caused by parallel tales having been divided and put together like a mosaic.

One of the principal points is the relation between Moses and Aaron; it is clear that there is some uncertainty here. That Moses is the principal character appears from the whole introduction to the legend, from the story of his birth, his first appearance, his flight to Midian and his calling, just as it is he alone who brings the people out of Egypt. Already in the story describing how he is called, Ex. 3-4, Aaron comes forward. Moses is reluctant to take the part of a leader and alludes to his lack of eloquence. Then Yahweh gives him the Levite Aaron by his side to speak on his behalf (4,14 ff.). The sole object is to appear before the Israelites and convince them. Moses has his rod with which he is to work wonders before the Israelites, but it is also suggested that he is to work wonders before Pharaoh (4,21). The story of the meeting of Moses with Aaron and their joint action towards the Israelites corresponds entirely to the arrangement made in the preceding part of the tale (4,27-31). And the sequel is in good accord with this. It states that Moses and Aaron go to Pharaoh together and beg that he will let the people go (5,1-6,1), but here it seems to be Moses who speaks to Pharaoh (5,23). All this hangs well together. Moses is the leader and appears as such before Pharaoh, though he has Aaron by his side, and to the people he lets Aaron speak on his behalf.

But the sequel (apart from 6,2-27) shows further developments. Yahweh commands Moses to give his message to Pharaoh, but Moses excuses himself on account of his slow speech and is allowed to have Aaron as his spokesman before Pharaoh. And now Aaron's rod is to be the powerful rod that is to be changed into a serpentlike creature in the presence of Pharaoh — but the magicians are able to imitate this (6,28-7,13). Here, then, Aaron is the spokesman also in the presence of the foreign ruler, and it is his rod that works wonders. Moses only possesses the formal superiority which is expressed by Aaron acting upon his orders. This might be regarded as a new departure in the story if it were consistently adhered to in the sequel, but that is not the case.

If we consider first the fourth plague (the flies, Ex. 8,16-27), the account is as might be expected according to Ex. 3-5: Yahweh bids Moses apply to Pharaoh, bringing him Yahweh's command to let Israel go, and threatening that in the opposite case all Egypt will be filled with flies except the part Goshen which is inhabited by the Israelites. This is done to make Pharaoh recognise that it is Yahweh who holds the power in the country. The plague sets in. Pharaoh sends for Moses and Aaron and after some negotiation he promises to yield. Moses leaves Pharaoh, at his bidding the plague ceases, and again Pharaoh hardens his heart. — Here Aaron is only introduced into the tale when Pharaoh wants to negotiate (8,21), but at the end of the same scene he has been forgotten (8,26); there is no question of the rod in this tale.

The seventh plague (hail, Ex. 9,13-35) is described in the same way. Moses threatens to call forth hail to show the might of Yahweh. It comes when Moses lifts up his rod. Here again Pharaoh sends for Moses and Aaron (9,27), but Aaron is left out at the end of the scene (9,33). It should be noted that the Egyptians are expressly advised to take shelter with their animals. The purpose is to make the people respect Yahweh who has the power.

The account of the eighth plague (grasshoppers, Ex. 10,1-20) shows quite the same features as the seventh. Only upon the urgent entreaties of his men does Pharaoh send for Moses and Aaron to negotiate before Moses calls down the plague by stretching out his rod (10,7-8), and though it is Moses who speaks and acts all the time, nevertheless we are told from the beginning that Moses and Aaron go to Pharaoh (10,3).

The fifth plague (murrain, Ex. 9,1-7) is described in a similar way to 4.7.8 but much more briefly. Yahweh lets Moses go to Pharaoh and ask for leave or threaten him with a murrain which shall befall the cattle of the Egyptians but not of the Israelites. This came to pass, but when Pharaoh learned that no Israelite cattle had died, his heart grew "heavy" and he refused to let them go. Here there is no talk about Aaron nor of how the plague was brought about. It is a peculiar feature that Pharaoh grows refractory on learning that the cattle of the Israelites is exempted. Would it not be supposed that this was the very thing to convince him? The fact is that the phenomenon which was to convince him irritates him and makes him still more foolish.

If now we turn to the first and second plagues we shall see that they are in the main recounted like 4.7.8.

It is Moses who threatens Pharaoh with the first judgment (the turning of water to blood, Ex. 7,14-25). He asks that the Israelites may be allowed to go to the festival; he declares that Yahweh will reveal himself by letting Moses strike the water of the Nile with his rod, when it will turn to blood, the fishes will die, and it will become undrinkable. But instead of an account of Moses striking the waters with his rod and bringing the plague to pass, we have the statement that Aaron stretched out his rod over all the waters of Egypt and all water turned to blood (7,19 f.). It is added that the Egyptian magicians did the same thing, so Pharaoh did not take it to heart — a strange trait, since the changing of all water to blood could not of course be repeated.

The second judgment (the frogs, Ex. 7,26-8,11) is recounted in a somewhat similar way. Moses asks for leave to go and threatens Pharaoh with a plague of frogs. Then quite unexpectedly comes the item that Moses lets Aaron stretch out his rod, whereupon all the waters teem with frogs, but the magicians did the same thing (8,1-3). As in 4.7.8 Moses and Aaron are now sent for by Pharaoh, who promises amendment if the frogs are removed. Moses gives Pharaoh his promise, he and Aaron go away, and upon the entreaty of Moses Yahweh removes the plague, whereupon Pharaoh again hardens his heart.

The third, sixth, and ninth plagues remain. A feature common to them is that they are introduced without any preceding threat or negotiation. The third judgment (gnats, Ex. 8,12-15) is introduced by Yahweh commanding Moses to let Aaron strike the dust with his rod whereupon it is turned to gnats. The magicians were unable to imitate this and said that it was the finger of God, but Pharaoh hardened his heart. The sixth judgment (boils, Ex. 9,8-12) is brought to pass by Moses taking some soot which he throws into the air; a plague of boils sets in which also attacks the magicians, but Pharaoh hardens his heart. The ninth judgment (darkness, Ex. 10,21-29) is introduced by Moses alone who lifts his hand towards the sky. Then Moses alone (in 2 Mss., however, with Aaron) is called into the presence of Pharaoh who offers to negotiate, but at last turns out Moses. The legend has now come to the final decisive judgment which is closely connected with the whole purpose of the festival legend: the death of the first-born. This is made known to Pharaoh by Moses as a last fatal greeting (Ex. 11).

If we consider these stories en bloc we shall see that not two of them are quite identical in structure. In particular the part played by Aaron is obscure. In the fifth plague (murrain, 9,1-7) we hear only of Moses who is to go to Pharaoh, but this story seems to be abbreviated. In the ninth plague (darkness, 10,21) it is Moses alone who acts, is sent for by Pharaoh, and sent away by him. In the sixth plague (boils, 9, 8-12) Yahweh speaks to Moses and Aaron, but Moses alone is active. In contrast with this we have the third plague (gnats, 8,12-15) in which Yahweh bids Moses stretch forth his rod and thus work the wonder. This is the only plague brought to pass as in 7,9 ff., whereas the feature that Yahweh bids Moses let Aaron work the wonder with his rod is introduced into 1 and 2 (water to blood, 7,19 ff.; frogs 8,1-3) together with the magicians, but it is inserted in the tales in an inorganic way. Similarly Aaron has been introduced in No. 4 (flies, 8,16-28) and No. 7 (hail, 9,13-35) though only in the way that he is sent for by Pharaoh with Moses when the plague takes effect (8,21; 9,27); but in both cases this does not affect the story, Moses alone speaks, and about him only is it said that he left Pharaoh. In No. 8 only (grasshoppers, 10,1-20) is Aaron there from the beginning to threaten Pharaoh (10,3) and is later called to Pharaoh with Moses (10,8.16). Pharaoh addresses them both (10,8 ff.), but it is Moses who speaks and acts, and on their departure after the uttering of the threat he alone is referred to (10,6).

As will be seen, there is an endeavour to give Aaron more influence as the helper or equal of Moses, or even as the person who possesses the real power. This tendency is not without interest. For Aaron, as we know, is the chief priest at the temple of Jerusalem, while Moses, as the primeval chieftain in certain respects corresponds to the king. That Moses is God to Aaron and that the latter is his mouthpiece to the people is a fairly accurate reproduction of the relation we must assume to have existed at the temple between the king, the chief priest, and the people. That the chief priest is also to appear before the foreign ruler goes far beyond what is implied in that relation, and in this feature and altogether in the tendency to bring Aaron into the foreground, we may venture to see an expression of conditions at the post-exilic temple, though this cannot of course be shown in detail, any more than Moses can be regarded simply as a representative of the king. We have seen that the endeavour to bring Aaron into notice has been manifested in very different ways. It is only quite consistent and clear in the story about the transformation of Aaron's rod (7,1 ff.) and about the plague af gnats (8,12 ff.), otherwise it appears in more or less consistent additions. We can catch a glimpse of a very good realistic foundation for these changes in the growing influence of the high priest's position among the people, but there is nothing to suggest that they are derived from a continuous, parallel, independent source.

Another obscurity in the legend is connected with the magicians. They appear with Aaron in the transformation of the rod 7,11; of the water of the Nile 7,22; in the plague of frogs 8,3; in the plague of gnats, 8,14 f.; but they are also present when the plague of boils sets in (9,11) which is brought to pass by Moses alone. This shows that they cannot be referred to a literary source in which only Aaron is active. They give to the plagues another character than that of being merely judgments. They make them ordeals deciding which is the stronger. This point of view comes in, too, in the other plagues. Yahweh sends the plagues not only that his people may be delivered, but also that his power may be recognised. This purpose dominates the whole legend and is strongly accentuated in the description of some of the other plagues: 8,18; 9,16.20. But it acquires a distinctive character in the above-mentioned stories in which we evidently have a contest between the Egyptian and the Israelite holy men of a similar kind to that fought by Elijah with the priests of Baal, a procedure also known from other places. Thus the tribe Tamim submitted to Islam after a contest between their "speaker" and poet and the prophet's (Ibn Hishām, pp. 934—938). It is possible that this element has been pushed somewhat into the background in the legend familiar to us. This creates a presumption that such contests belonged to the sacred customs of the Paschal night for the re-living of Yahweh's victory. Among the Hittites we find a typical example of cult contests of this kind. Two parties fight at a festival; one party is called after the ruling people Hatti, the other Māsha after another people of Asia Minor. The first party wins. See Götze, Kleinasien [in W. Otto, Handbuch der Altertumswissenschaft III 1,3], 1933, p. 152. Altogether such contests are common at cult festivals.

As already mentioned, Aaron with his rod does not appear throughout in the same parts of the tale as the magicians. Nor do the formal deviations in the construction of the stories link up with other characteristics to form a whole which indicates separate sources. Without any introduction, negotiations or threats the gnats, the boils, and the darkness are mentioned. The first are called forth by Aaron's rod and convince the magicians, the second by Moses and attack the magicians, the last one by Moses alone. Our survey above shows that not two of the stories have quite the same construction, but in pairs blood and frogs, gnats and boils, hail and grasshoppers resemble each other very much in character. The commonly accepted separation of the sources is not well founded, and the ascription to J, E and P must be said to be quite unsatisfactory as an explanation of the irregularities. The Paschal legend has a character of its own, and this is very different from the old tribal legends collected in Genesis. If we have really here in some form or other the cult legend which was used at the temple of Jerusalem, bearing the mark of conditions both in the monarchical period and in post-exilic times, it is clear that there is no close inner kinship with the old tribal legends of Genesis. And in all respects this is the most likely.

We will discuss quite briefly the introduction to the legend. Ex. 6,2-27 gives a message from God and a series of genealogical tables. Both of these have the character that is peculiar to the "Priestly Code". The message corresponds closely to Gen. 17, which is also combined with another communication about a divine revelation. But the whole story of the revelation Ex. 3-4 and the first application to Pharaoh, Ex. 5, is closely identified with the whole plan of the legend. The reason why the story about the sudden circumcision of Moses, Ex. 4,24 f., has been incorporated in the Paschal ritual is presumably that circumcision is emphasised as a prerequisite for participation in the Passover. In the story about Moses' flight to Midian his father-in-law is called Reuel in 2,18; but in 3,1 and 4,18 he is called Jethro, while in Num. 10,29; Judg. 4,11 he is called Hobab. This points to different traditions, still here also it must be said that the hypothesis of parallel sources is not well founded. Gressmann in "Mose" p. 1 ff. points out that the different strands of the narrative in Ex. 1 do not run on, and imposed labour does not denote an aggravation. Imposed labour and the killing of boys are irreconcileable contrasts, for the taskmaster is interrested in preserving labour. Therefore the birth legend is supposed to be younger than the other elements, and Gressmann reconstructs it in accordance with the story of the murder of the innocents. This use of logic would seem rather bold. These stories also are not meant to cohere in natural progression, but are intended to convey a strong feeling of Pharaoh's oppression.

The central part of the legend, which deals with the Paschal night, has also in the course of time been subject to alterations. It is possible that the part played by the houses is an ancient feature transformed according to conditions in Jerusalem in post-exilic times or perhaps even according to conditions in a foreign country. Various special provisions concerning the observance of the Passover have been introduced (12,43-49), and an entire compendium on the nature and significance of the Passover, in the style of Deuteronomy, has been inserted (Ex. 13). A remark on the route of the Israelites (12,37) fits the whole legend into the coherent tale of the journey to Canaan.

If the above remarks are correct, the Paschal legend reflects the various important periods of the history of Israel. The Paschal sacrifice itself and the foundation of the feast points to the nomadic period, the troublous times in Egypt and the deliverance. The spirit prevalent in the legend derives its character from the God who ruled from the royal temple in Zion. Some few features of the legend are likewise characterised by conditions in the monarchical period. The festival hymn in Ex. 15 is entirely a hymn to the royal temple and its God. Moses is not the king, but as the primeval chief he has certain traits of the idealised king, who acts as the instrument of Yahweh in dealings with the foreign ruler and saves his people, whose leader he is. Aaron, high priest of Jerusalem, is his helper and to a certain degree the intermediary between him and the people. A feature denoting post-exilic times is the not quite consistent endeavour to bring Aaron into the foreground. The significance attributed to the houses, not to the temple, in the legend may be due to conditions in post-exilic times, either as they developed in Jerusalem in accordance with ancient custom, which it was not possible to suppress entirely in spite of the attempts at centralisation, or as the expression of customs in Jewish colonies outside Jerusalem which continued the practices of the monarchical period as well as it could be done in their communities. We cannot say anything quite definite about these conditions as we only know what can be inferred from the legend itself which by no means shows us a complete picture of the festival. The features here pointed out cannot be established by a literary division of the legend; such a division cannot be carried out at all in a satisfactory manner.

For the separation of the sources the reader may be referred to Wellhausen, Die Composition des Hexateuchs, 3. ed., 1899, p. 61 ff.; the various introductions, particularly Driver's (ed. 6, 1897) and Steuernagel's, 1912, p. 146 ff., the commentaries by Dillmann, Baentsch, Holzinger and others; R. Smend, Die Erzählung des Hexateuch, 1912, p. 112 ff.; H. Gressmann, Mose und seine Zeit, 1913. A criticism of the separation of the sources is found in Eerdmans, Alttestamentliche Studien, III, 1910. See the author's article "Passafest und Passalegende" in Zeits. f. d. alttest. Wiss., N. F. II, 1934, pp. 161—175.

ADDITIONAL NOTE II.
THE ISRAELITE-CANAANITE AUTUMN FESTIVAL.

As will appear from the account given, few features of the old autumn festival can be established as certain. These are: Picking of the grapes with pressing in the vineyards; dwelling in booths of green boughs while the feast is in progress; a special performance by the women with dances and the ecstatic *hillūlīm* by the vineyards; with which is associated a story of the abduction of brides, and the men's meal in the temple of the city. We cannot fit these features into any ritual and the picture they give of the festival is only obtained by a combination of Israelite and Canaanite traits. If we disregard the special character which the Israelites may have given to the feast, and which at any rate they gave to it in Jerusalem, there can be no doubt that it must be viewed in connection with the common Canaanite fertility cult designated above as a foreign cult, and the chief elements of which are the lament at the death of the God; the rejoicing at his resurrection; the violent ecstasy which has partly the effect of prophetic enthusiasm, partly of sexual excitement, to which belongs the ritual performance of sexual intercourse. We know all these features from the comprehensive ceremonial for royal feasts which is mentioned in the next additional note. But the separate items may acquire independent importance and can be displayed in different forms. The principal features of these festivals are common among agricultural peoples all over the world. A large material, particularly of the remains of European peasant customs, was collected by Mannhardt and later by Frazer who incorporated material from a number of extra-European peoples. Notably these customs are known from the *Osiris* festivals in which life perishes with Osiris and is resurrected with Horus with whom the king is identified. The same is expressed in the elaborate ritual of the principal Babylonian festival, see Additional Note III. The death of the God is not only a mythical expression of the decaying of plant life. The growth of the fields is decisive for the peasant's whole life, it is one with the life of man, of the whole world. To him therefore, the cessation of growth means the destruction of all life. Death threatens the human and all other communities, but through the festival the divine regeneration is brought about and with it the renewed growth of all forces. This all-pervasive significance of the disappearance of the God is expressed in Sumerian and Babylonian laments for *Tammuz*, see Zimmern, Sumerisch-Babylonische Tamuzlieder [Ber. d. sächs. Ges. d. Wiss., 1907], examples in Gressmann's Altor. Texte, p. 93 ff.; an analogous effect is that of Ishtar's disappearance in the myth of her journey to the underworld. The eastern Tammuz cult is recognised again in the Adonis feasts of Syria which encountered the related Osiris cult and again had affinities with the Phrygian feasts to Kybele and Attis; see Frazer, Adonis, Attis, Osiris, 1-2, 3. ed., 1914; Baudissin, Adonis und Esmun, 1911. The death of the God was marked by lamenting, the worshippers beat themselves with their hands, cut off their hair, and offered sacrifices to the God as to the dead. Ritual sexual intercourse in Syria took the peculiar form that the women sought cohabitation with strangers, and gave the pay for this to the temple. See Lukian, De dea Syria § 6, something similar to what Herodotos tells us about Babylon.

The *Ras Shamra* texts show us a cult drama in Canaan already in the 2nd millennium, of the same kind as that of the neighbouring countries. The cosmic forces are represented by various gods under the leadership of El, the father of the gods. Al'iyan Ba'l is "the Ba'l of the earth", I AB III, 3.9.21; IV, 29.40; "the Ba'l of the springs", I AB IV, 27.38, son of Dagan (corn), I AB I, 6; I* AB VI, 23. He reigns in heaven, the home of the rain, and "rides on the clouds", I* AB II, 7; II AB III, 11. 18; III AB, 8, but at the beginning of the drama he descends into the underworld, taking with him cloud, wind, *mdl* (presumably the heavenly water reservoir, cf. Job 38,37), rain, attendants. The pig too, which often belongs to these cults, is mentioned. Then not only fertility but all vitality disappears. The goddesses Anat and Shapash (the sun) descend into the lower world and entreat its ruler Mot (death) to set free Ba'l, but he refuses (I AB II, 6-14). Then it is said, probably by Anat, that she will go and seek him. "Soul (life, *npsh)* has become wanting among men, soul has forsaken the earth, the earth has been forsaken by my favourite *(na'miya,* cf. *na'mān,* Danel II, 6,32.45; III, 1,14 and Isa. 17,10), the luxuriant pasture has come to be a wilderness to the lion which slays its prey" (1.15-20). At last she "seizes Mot, son of the gods, with a sword she splits him in half, with a sieve she winnows him, in the fire she burns him, in the mill she grinds him, in the field she sows him, his flesh, that the birds may eat his parts..." (1.30 ff.). This shows that Mot is identical with the ripe corn. Then it is said that Al'iyan Ba'l is living and "heaven will rain oil, and the valleys will cause honey to flow" (I AB III). Ba'l who is now called the son of Athirat (I AB V, 1) makes his way to the throne by force, but first there is a description of a fight between him and Mot which results in Mot descending to his domain in the underworld where he reigns over *rephā'īm* and death gods (I AB VI). Other texts describe Ba'l's fight with "devourers", ox-like demons, in which he is overcome by fever and lies like one dead for 88 days (BH), or with the master *(zbl)* of the sea, who subjects himself to him (III AB). In connection with the uprising of Ba'l the myth describes the building of a temple to him (II AB). Flames of fire are set in the temple for seven days (i. e. in sacrifices), Ba'l places a lattice in it corresponding to a rift in the clouds, that his voice (i. e. thunder with rain) may be heard. Ba'l takes the seat as King and judge and gives a feast on meat and wine to the gods and goddesses in the temple. He declares: "I alone shall reign over the gods in order that gods and men may become fat, in order to satisfy the multitudes of the earth" (VII, 49 ff.). This means that after the rites of mourning the new creation of order and fertility is celebrated by a feast for seven days after the dedication of the temple. Cf. the author's article in Acta Orientalia vol. XVIII, 1939, pp. 1—14. — In "La légende de Danel" we partly meet with rites of a similar meaning.

From *Asia Minor* we now know from earlier times the Hittite myth of the agricultural god Telepinush, the disappearance of whom has the same consequences as we heard of in other places. All vitality

47*

vanishes. The fire will not burn, no plants will grow, animals and humans will not pair nor look after their offspring, springs dry up, gods and men die of hunger, food does not satisfy, drink does not quench the thirst. Various messengers are sent to Telepinush, but only the bee is successful. It is commanded to wake him by stinging and to cleanse and sanctify him with wax; this would seem to indicate that the cultic use of the products of the bee, perhaps also the fact of its hibernation determines its role. See the survey in Götze, Kleinasien [W. Otto, Handb. d. Altertumswiss. III, 1,3], pp. 134—136.

The cults of Asia Minor encountered the *Greek* cults and influenced some of them. The myth of the beautiful youth Adonis whom his beloved Kypris loses upon his unhappy death was in Hellenistic times a suitable subject for sentimental Greek poets, as Bion of Smyrna; see Willamowitz-Moellendorff, Bion von Smyrna, Adonis. Berlin, 1900. But the agricultural feasts of the Greeks were of the same character as the aforementioned from the eastern countries. This applies not only to the feasts to Demeter and Kore-Persephone but also to the cult of Dionysos who taught men agriculture and to whom the bull and the he-goat as well as certain plants were dedicated. Of special prominence here is the violent ecstasy, particularly among the female participants, with attendant erotic excitement and prophetic inspiration. A sacred marriage was celebrated by Dionysos with the Basileus' wife at the anthesterial feasts; see Farnell, The Cults of the Greek States V, 1909, p. 85 ff. (the last feature p. 217) and Martin P. Nilsson, Griechische Feste, 1906, p. 258 ff. — E. Rohde, Psyche, 2. ed., II, p. 38 ff. especially emphasises the ecstatic and prophetic element. The fertility cult reappears in different forms at several other Greek festivals.

The use of *booths* in the cult is no specially Israelite feature but on the contrary constitutes part of the above mentioned common fertility cults. Adonis gardens were used, mentioned inter alia in Isa. 17,10, i. e. jars or baskets in which grew forced plants which were displayed during the festival as representatives of the flora, while fruits and branches were hung up as "Laubeinkleidung" and "Laubumkleidung", see Mannhardt, Wald- und Feldkulte, 2. ed., I, 1904, p. 316 ff.; II, 1905, p. 259 ff.; 273 ff.; Frazer, Adonis etc., I, p. 236 ff. Mannhardt quotes some, later oft-cited, extracts from the idylls of Theocritus XV, according to which the Adonis feast was celebrated at Alexandria under Ptolemy Philadelphus, Aphrodite's and Adonis's images being placed each on its bed with fruits, cakes, Adonis gardens and booths of green boughs. Their marriage was celebrated, the next day came the death of Adonis and his image was cast into the sea, with songs saying that he would come again; see Op. cit. II, p. 277; cf. Frazer, Op. cit., I, p. 224 f. The cultic use of the booths differs.

Sometimes they may be tents for gods or kings, see the work by W. B. Kristensen mentioned in Additional Note III, cf. Nilsson, Gr. Feste, p. 300[1], sometimes the worshippers live in them, or we hear nothing of their use. In Rome booths were used at Feriæ Annæ Perennæ March 15; see Fowler, The Roman Festivals, under that date. In Greece there are especially three festivals at which the use of booths together with other features recall the Israelite-Canaanite autumn feast.

The Laconic *Tithenide* feast to Artemis Korythalia was a feast for fertility in nature and among mankind. Branches of olive and laurel are placed in front of the doors, booths are built, and nurses bring the little boys to the goddess. Dances of an ecstatic and sexual character performed by women, sometimes also by men in women's attire, play a prominent part. At the feast a suching pig was sacrificed, as to Demeter; see M. P. Nilsson, Griech. Feste, pp. 182—189. At the *Karneia* festival in Sparta which was celebrated in honour of Apollo for 9 days in August, a man was draped with garlands. He prayed down a blessing on the town whereafter he ran away pursued by youths carrying branches with grapes, *staphylodromoi*. Such races, a form of contest, are also well known, and the overtaking of the fugitive means the securing of the year's blessing for the growth of everything. The worshippers then lived in booths distributed in groups and organised in a military way. Dances executed by naked men and boys were associated with the feast; see Nilsson, Op. cit., pp. 118—129; Farnell, Cults, IV, p. 259 ff.; V. Chapot in Dictionnaire des Antiquités, V, 117 s. v. tentorium. *Hyakinthia* was a Spartan feast associated with Hyakinthos and Apollo. Sacrifices were offered to the former at his grave, a meal was consumed by ungarlanded worshippers without singing in booths on couches of branches; no bread was eaten, but figs and beans. The sources are not quite clear, but there seems to be here the well-known connection between death rites and mourning rites; a meal with a festal hymn to Apollo, which is also mentioned, perhaps belongs to the latter part of the feast. In a procession to Amyklai, maidens drive in chariots; singing, flute-playing, and dancing take place. A special nocturnal dance is performed by the women; see Nilsson, Op. cit., pp. 129—140; Farnell, Op. cit., IV, p. 264 ff. At the festival to Aphrodite at Korinth booths of green boughs were also erected, Nilsson, p. 378.

Here we find certain features indicating the death of the God, but the most prominent trait is the union with nature by the use of green boughs and the booths, and the dance of the women in an ecstasy of a sexual character. The object of it all is to maintain the vitality of nature and man, and the corresponding features in the Israelite-Canaanite autumn feast had the same significance. There can now be no doubt that in its Canaanite form the feast also celebrated the death and resurrection of the God. Among the Israelites the festival gradually lost its association with nature. The use of booths became a duty, the special importance of which came to be that one must not live in one's usual dwelling. Thus the same point of view appears as among the Arab Hums, who for a certain period did not live under the shelter of roofs, a point of view which has been brought to notice by Wensinck, Arabic New Year and the Feast of Tabernacles [Verh. d. kon. Akad. v. Wet. Amsterdam., Afd. Letterk., nieuwe reeks, XXV, 2] 1925, p. 25 ff.

The dance of the women seems to have survived, though presumably in an altered form, for it says in Mishnah Taʿaniyyot IV, 8 that before the day of Atonement the maidens of Jerusalem danced in the vineyards that the youths might watch them and select the proper brides. A connection between the ecstatic dances of the women and marriage customs seems natural, the object of the dances being to strengthen fertility and the power of propagation. We are then led to the question as to how the tale of the *abduction of women at Shiloh* is to be understood. In Judg. 20 we are told how the whole tribe of Benjamin was exterminated by the other Israelites. Without any connection with this another story is given in Judg. 21. The Israelites, it says, had taken an oath at Mizpeh that they would not give their daughters in marriage to the Benjaminites. At an assembly at Bethel they wept and made lament because one of the tribes of Israel was doomed to perish. They found out, however, that the Jabeshites had not been at Mizpeh and taken the oath; they then carried on a war of extermination against them and carried off 400 maidens to the Benjaminites. As this was not enough, they advised the Benjaminites to lie in ambush in the vineyards of Shiloh at the annual feast and carry off the brides they needed among the women dancing at the feast. Before their fathers and brothers they could then maintain that the young women had not been seized in war, nor had the men broken their oaths since they had not given their daughters to the Benjaminites.

While the preceding tale told us of a complete extermination of Benjamin, in which the men must be the chief victims, we now hear of how the men of Benjamin procure women to marry by two abductions, one of which is associated with the feast at Shiloh. This narrative recalls in character the Roman tale of the rape of the Sabine women. Of this Livy says (I, 9.10.13) that when Romulus had founded and strengthened Rome his people suffered under the scarcity of women. An application to their neighbours concerning an alliance and connubium was refused. Romulus then celebrated the Consus feast and at his invitation the neighbours came as spectators to the feast. While it was in progress the Romans made a sudden sally and carried off the women. One of the most beautiful of these was carried off to the house of a certain Thalassius. When asked to whom she was being taken the abductors cried: To Thalassius! This then became a wedding cry. The maidens' parents fled, complaining that the law of hospitality had been broken. The abducted maidens, too, complained, but Romulus went about consoling them with the promise that they should obtain full marital rights. Now war broke out with three peoples. Romulus won, killed the hostile king, and laid his armour by the holy oak on the Capitol whereafter he founded the temple of Jupiter. We are then told that preparations were made for war but the Sabine women interceded, with flowing hair and rent garments they entreated their kinsmen and their husbands to make peace. This they did, forming one state divided into curiae named after the Sabine women.

The story forms part of Livy's accounts of the earliest time of Rome. But that it is no ordinary tale appears from various features. A cry at the wedding feasts takes its origin from the event, the founding of the main temple is associated with it, and it forms the basis of the Roman federation of states, as well as its division into curiae and the names of these. We have here then the condensed history we know from foundation legends and myths. Plutarch (Romulus 14.15.19.21) tells essentially the same story. Since many men would not stay in the newly founded Rome because they could not get wives, the rumour was spread about that an altar belonging to the God Consus had been found; a feast was celebrated with contests and sacrifices, and at a given sign 30 Sabine women were abducted, one for each curia, in order to strengthen the bond between the two peoples, one being Hersilia whom Romulus wedded. From this event several marriage customs are derived, thus the cry "to Thalassius". And because the women were then abducted and carried away, brides are carried over the threshold, and their hair is parted with the point of a lance. This took place on the 18th of August when the consualia were celebrated. Now followed fights between the two peoples, first single combat between their kings, in which Romulus won, but later when the armies stood facing each other, the women led by Hersilia made peace. The Romans and the Sabines were now to live together, the women were to manage the house and only be obliged to do wool work. Certain feasts were held in common, as the Matronalian Feast where the settling of the conflict was celebrated.

Finally the close connection with Roman festivals appears from Ovid's Fasti III, 167 ff. Here we are told that Mars bid his son Romulus hold a feast for Consus and there the Romans were to capture wives for themselves since no one would marry them. When the women were with child they appeared in the temple of Juno, and now the reconciliation followed between the armed hosts. Therefore in commemoration hereof the 1st of March (the Matronalian Feast in honour of Mars and

Juno) is dedicated to the Sabine mothers, at the season when everything is beginning to shoot, and the cattle pair, and Juno Lucina is worshipped who delivers women in childbed.

Consus was the God of the fertile soil; his altar at the Circus maximus was covered with earth except at the feast; this took place in the middle of August after the harvest, but also on the 15th of December after the sowing of the seed. We see its origin in the different tales connected with the rape of the women. The legend about this is, then, what is generally called an aetiological legend, not a very apt term, for the legend is not artificially formed in order to furnish a motive for the feast. It is the direct expression of the ancient view of history, according to which the most important events of life, especially those appertaining to the cult, can be traced back to the condensed history of the earliest times. The fact that the Sabines came to watch the feast would be curious as an ordinary historical communication, but it merely means that they came so that one of the features of the feast, the rape of their women, could be accomplished. There can be no doubt that the legend gives expression to a part of the festal rites.

The different forms of the festival legend express certain marriage rites. That these are associated with the Consus feast is not to be wondered at since it is concerned with the fertility of the earth. But Ovid's Fasti shows that it also belonged to the fertility feast for corn, cattle, and men on the 1st of March. One tradition says, therefore, that the abduction of the women took place in March. It must be supposed, then, that the rape of the women has been celebrated at two feasts, the Consus feast and the Matronalian feast, as an expression of the renewal of human fruitfulness. This means that at these two feasts the contents of the legend have in whole or in part been reproduced in the cult.

If we wish to understand the contents of the legend we must view it in connection with popular marriage customs as known to us from the most different parts of the world. An element in these is often the rape of a bride. At a stated time she disappears and must be searched for and carried off by the bridegroom, or he seizes her after a pretended fight. Since the appearance of Mc. Lennan's work on marriage (Primitive Marriage, 1865, see I—II, p. 78[1]) this has often been regarded as a relic of an original abduction marriage, of which then of course stories such as that about the rape of the Sabine women is said to furnish weighty evidence. The whole of this view is based on the conception that there is only one culture and prior to that chaos. In no community has the arbitrary abduction of women formed the normal basis of marriage (a criticism of the theory is given in Westermarck, The History of Human Marriage, II, 5. ed., 1925, p. 240 ff.). The abduction of the bride at marriages is a ritual act which marks the passing of the bride from one family to another, a passage which also finds expression in many other ways, e. g. in acts which are meant to conceal and obliterate it. Thus in Sparta the bride was abducted but at the same time she had her hair cut and was dressed in male garments and at first the man visited her secretly (Plutarch, Lycurgus, 15). It is a similar rite on a large scale we have in the legend about the rape of the Sabine women. It celebrates the Roman marriage as a foundation for the community and its prosperity, but also the marriage connection brought about by a pact between the Romans and the Sabines. Surely such an abduction has been performed in the course of the festal rites, and the reason why the Romans represent the men, and the Sabines the women, is that it is a Roman feast. It must be supposed, then, that it is such a festal custom which is expressed in the legend.

Among other peoples, too, we hear of the abduction of women at feasts. The Messenians had a sanctuary to Artemis at Limnæ on the Laconian frontier, where they celebrated a festival in common with the Laconians. Here they are said to have violated Laconian maidens (Strabo VIII, 4,9; Pausanias IV, 4,2; 31,3) which led to a war, and a story is referred to the latter part of this war, according to which the Messenian Aristomenes carried off some Laconian maidens who were dancing at a festival in honour of Artemis at Caryæ (Pausanias IV, 16,9) or at the Hyakinthia, see P. M. Nilsson, Griechische Feste, p. 137, who refers to Euripides, Helena, 1465 ff., and a quotation from Hieronymus. But it is difficult to see what is implied, and of course stories about the abduction of women have not all the same contents.

The comparison with the Roman legend strengthens the presumption that the narrative of the Benjaminite abduction of women is of a cultic character. As at the Roman fertility festival there was then at Shiloh associated with the dance of the women which was to strengthen the human power of propagation, the custom of carrying off some of the women during the dance. In this the Benjaminites have played their special part and the custom meant a strengthening of marriage which was naturally associated just with this feast, and at the same time of the connubium between Benjamin and its northern neighbours. A further explanation of details is, however, impossible. What the connection was with Jabesh we do not know, any more than we can point out what historical elements are implied in the preceding story about Benjamin's fight with the other tribes. The condensed history of the early beginnings is not kept apart from the general history as a separate whole. There is no sharp line of demarcation between the general history, the condensed history, and pure fiction; to find out "the historical nucleus" which we are apt to look for is therefore as a rule a hopeless task. This is a common feature of the peoples, and the Greek and Roman stories of the earliest times afford ample evidence thereof.

ADDITIONAL NOTE III.

PRINCIPAL ROYAL FEASTS.

In *Egypt* the king, on his enthronement, is made a god and called Horus. This deification is renewed at the *sed* feast which takes place on the 1. Tybi after the inundation, which is coronation and New Year's day. This regularity is not, however, quite established. The principal point in the festival is that the king ascends two thrones, each in its naos; these are made like booths with life-giving boughs (see W. B. Kristensen, De loofhut en het loofhuttenfeest in den egyptischen cultus, in Med. d. kon. Akad. v. Wet., Afd. Letterk., deel 56, ser B. no. 6., Amsterdam, 1923). The thrones are those of the north and the south; on both he is seen with the corresponding crown, carrying Osiris' crook and flagellum. Then follows *sma tawi*, the "union of the two countries" in which the king is seated with the royal insignia between goddesses of Upper and Lower Egypt, over lotus and papyrus, which represent Upper and Lower Egypt, united by bands from a pillar held by two gods. Then follows a procession round "the white wall" which is identical with Memphis. The principal God gives the king all lands within the orbit of the sun, that is to say universal dominion. This is expressed in various ways, thus by the shooting of arrows in 4 directions and the sending out of 4 birds. The gods of other cities take part in the processions, and the population join in with cries and rejoicing. To the *sed* festival belongs the raising of the *sed* column and preceding games and contests. The king receives "millions of years" at the festival. On account of his deification he is enabled to perform similar acts to Osiris who dies, is resurrected, and filled again with divine strength. The death and resurrection of the God, well known from the Osiris legend, is accomplished through a dramatic ritual with mourning rites and fighting of enemies. An item in the rites carried out by the king is the marriage of the God to his consort.

See A. Moret, Du caractère religieux de la royauté pharaonique [Annales du Musée Guimet. Bibliothèque d'Études, XV] Paris, 1902; same author, Le Nil et la civilisation égyptienne [L'Évolution de l'humanité, ed. H. Berr] Paris, 1926, p. 142 ff.; 451 ff.; A. Erman, Die ägyptische Religion, 2. ed., 1909, p. 62 ff.; K. Sethe, Beiträge zur ältesten Geschichte Ägyptens III, 1905, p. 121 ff.; the same, Urgeschichte und älteste Religion der Agypter [Abh. f. d. Kunde d. Morgenlandes XVIII, 4) Lpz. 1930, §§ 121. 128. 168. 180. 202—04. 207; J. G. Frazer, The Golden Bough IV [Adonis, Attis, Osiris], Vol. 2, 1914; W. B. Kristensen, Op. cit.; H. Kees, Der Opfertanz des ägyptischen Königs, Lpz. 1912, p. 154 and note 40; 165 ff.; 188 f.; H. Schäfer, Die Mysterien des Osiris in Abydos [Untersuchungen z. Gesch. u. Altertumskunde

747

Ägyptens, ed. K. Sethe, IV, 2] Lpz. 1904; H. Gressmann, Tod und Auferstehung des Osiris nach Festbräuchen und Umzügen [Der Alte Orient XXIII, 3] Lpz. 1923. About the marriage of the God in the shape of the king see Moret, Royauté, p. 48 ff.; Kees, Aegypten in Bertholet, Rel. geschichtl. Lesebuch, 2 ed., 1928, p. 40. In Myth and Ritual, ed. S. H. Hooke, 1933, Blackman gives a detailed account of the Osiris festivals in Egypt from the 12. Khoiakh till the 1st of the next month (Tybi) when it is New Year's day with a *sed* festival, the regeneration of Osiris as Horus, and the enthronement of the king, as well as the creation rites which take place in connection herewith; further the autumn feast in the 9th month in which the king ritually reaps a sheaf "for his father": and the elaborate coronation drama according to a text from the time of Sesostris I 1970 B. C. and rites into which enters hieros gamos.

Among the *Hittites* there was a feast at the accession of the king, see Götze, Kleinasien [W. Otto, Handb. d. Altertumswiss. III, 1,3] p. 83 f., and also a series of great feasts in which the king was active, see ibd. p. 85 f.; 154 f. In Additional Note II we have discussed the significance of the death and resurrection of the god. Not until the large Hittite material has been made accessible can we arrive at an understanding of how this feature fits in with others as part of the royal feasts.

In the *Babylonian* and *Assyrian* world the enthronement of the king does not seem to play such an independent and prominent part in the annual ordinance of the feast as in Egypt, but the regeneration of the king forms part of the great annual feast, the New Year's feast, the *akitu* or *zagmuk* festival in which the regeneration of the God takes place. This feast is known in its main features although the order is uncertain on some points. It was celebrated on the 1—12. Nisan, on exceptional occasions it has been held in the autumn, in Tishrit, in Uruk at both these times (Hommel, Geogr. u. Gesch. d. alt. Orient, 2 ed., p. 221, note 2; Meissner, Bab. u. Ass. II, p. 396; Pallis, The Bab. Akîtu Festival, p. 31). On the 2. Nisan before sunrise the high priest, purified by river water, enters Marduk's chapel in Esagila and sends up a prayer and gives praise to the God. Then the temple doors are thrown open, other priests enter and officiate, inter alia by reciting a prayer to Marduk and his wife, entreating protection from all the enemies of Babel and the temple. The 3. Nisan is passed with a similar service and the making of two wooden figures, with clothes, gold, and precious stones, by a wood-carver, a goldsmith, a stone-cutter, and a weaver. On the 4. Nisan the chief priest again enters Marduk's chapel long before day and does homage to him as king, lord, and creator who gives the king his sceptre; homage is also paid to Marduk's wife, Ṣarpanitu, as the intercessor who protects the king and Babel. In the temple court the chief priest pronounces a blessing on the temple. The doors are thrown open, and the priests come in to officiate at the service. In the evening the chief priest recites before Marduk *enuma elish*, the mythical epic about the creation of the world through the struggle of the gods. The 5. Nisan begins in a similar way to the other days. After the doors of the temple have been opened and the priests have come in, a purification of the temple is carried out by special priests, while the chief priest remains in the court. The purification is effected by sprinkling with water from the river, anointment with cedar oil, the kindling of incense and the sounding of copper cymbals. A special purification takes place in Nebo's chapel. Here a priestly cook cuts the head off a ram whereupon the purification priest passes the body of the animal over the walls of the chapel; the two priests now cast the head and the body into the river and go away to the plain where they remain while Nebo is in Babel. After the further preparation of the chapel Nebo comes from Borsippa, also some other gods (5. or 6. Nisan). When the purification ceremony is over sacrifices are offered to Marduk. Now the priest takes the king into the temple and the latter alone approaches Marduk's chapel. The chief priest comes out of the chapel, takes the diadem, sceptre, and other insignia from the king and lays them before Marduk. The chief priest, who is here acting on behalf of the God, comes out again, boxes and pulls the king's ears; the king kneels down and offers a prayer of penitence. This evidently means that the kingdom is taken from the king, he is like the most lowly of his subjects, without honour and power, without resources. Then the chief priest says on behalf of the God that his prayer is heard, if he will look after Babel and the temple his power shall be increased, his kingdom be exalted, the God will bless him and put down his enemies. Then the priest, i. e. the God, returns the royal insignia to him. In the evening a white bull is burnt with special ceremonies. In these rites we have the regeneration of the king, as repeated annually. We hear nothing of a special enthronement feast in honour of the king as in Egypt, but of course it may have taken place in the palace.

Through his regeneration the king is enabled to take the lead in the great drama that follows. Unfortunately the order of the ritual for the following days is not fixed. On the 6. Nisan amongst other ceremonies an act of atonement is carried out with the above-mentioned figures. On the 8. Nisan the gods who have arrived assemble in the chamber of fate under the presidency of the king of the gods. On the 10. Nisan the king seizes Bel's hands and leads the gods in a procession down the holy way and in a ship down the canal to the festal house outside the city. On the 11. Nisan they return to the chamber of fate in the temple, and on the 12. Nisan the gods return to their home cities. During these days great things have happened. Marduk, the principal god of Babel has died, his death is accompanied by a universal lament, his murderer is punished, and the God is resuscitated. Great contests are fought, probably in the akitu house, identical with the fights with the dragons described in the mythical epic of creation. In all these the resuscitated Marduk is victorious, and he creates the cosmos. As the chief God he takes the lead in the chamber of fate in establishing the destinies, i. e. the creation of the new year with its happiness and fertility for Babel under the leadership of the king. Fruitfulness is also re-created by the holy marriage between the God and his wife; in this as in other sections of the holy ceremonies it may be taken for granted that it was the king who played the part of the God. On the Babylonian feast see H. Zimmern, Zum babylonischen Neujahrsfest I—II, in Berichte u. Verh. d. Sächs. Ges. d. Wiss., Lpz., Phil.-Hist. Kl., 58, 1903 and 70, 1918. The same author, Das bab. Neujahrsfest [Der alte Orient XXV, 3] Lpz. 1926; Thureau-Dangin, Rituels accadiens, Paris 1921, pp. 127—154; Dombart in Journ. Soc. of Orient. Research, VIII, 1924; Meissner, Bab. u. Ass. II, p. 95 ff.; S. Langdon, The Babylonian Epic of Creation, Oxford 1923; S. A. Pallis, The Babylonian Akitu Festival [Vid. Selsk. Hist.-Fil. Medd. XII, 1] Copenhagen, 1926, where the whole material is collected and discussed in detail. For separate items see B. Landsberger, Der kultische Kalender der Bab. u. Ass., 1915, p. 12 f. et al. — It will be seen that in the Egyptian and in the Babylonian festival there is an intimate connection between the regeneration of the God and of the king. The principal object of the feast is to experience the death of the God, and then to re-create his life and his production of the whole world with its order of things. In the death and regeneration of the God resides the decisive difference between Israel and the strangers; the Israelites were unable to appropriate entirely anything directly connected with this. In that respect there is a certain similarity between Yahweh and Apollo. This ancient pastoral God also appropriated agriculture in so far as he received and sanctified the first crops. But the rites representing the death of the God remained foreign to him. Only the Greeks made no protest against such rites for other gods, just like the Baal cult, being incorporated and practised at the same time as the cult of Apollo. Just as the myth of creation, Enuma elish, was recited at Babylon in honour of Marduk who re-created the world at the feast, it seems natural to suppose that the Israelites, when celebrating Yahweh's assumption of power as the creator of the world, recited a myth of creation. The story of the creation given in Gen. 1 conveys the impression of a didactic exposition rather than a cult-myth. Of course it was based on a real myth, but it is highly probable that a myth of creation recited in the temple of Jerusalem had the character of a glorifying account of the work done by Yahweh in primeval ages. The myth of the deluge, ending with the promise of the regular alternation of the seasons (Gen. 8,22), would fit in well with the autumn festival, all the more so since Noah who is saved from the chaos, reintroduced then, is the first vine grower (Gen. 9,20). According to Lukian, De dea Syria § 13, the cessation of the flood was celebrated in the temple of Hierapolis by libations of water. The libations which took place at the Feast of Tabernacles in Israel may, while they sanctified the water of the new year, also have been meant to recall the mythical renewal of the law of water as described in the story of the flood. In a Ras Shamra text, III AB, there occurs a myth about Al'iyan Ba'l's battle with the sea and the flood, i. e. the waters of chaos, which shows that an old Canaanite cult underlies the legend of the flood.

Just as the legend of the deliverance from Egypt was closely connected with the Passover, thus the stories about the making of the covenant on Sinai were no doubt represented, with a renewal of the covenant, at one of the festivals.

ADDITIONAL NOTE IV.

RECENT DISCUSSIONS OF THE DEUTERONOMIC PROBLEM.

The idea which came up already in antiquity that the law-book of Josiah is to be found in Deuteronomy has been generally accepted in critical research since de Wette set forth the grounds for it in detail in 1805 and 1806. Since then it has been universally assumed that Deuteronomy came into existence in the 7th century. Already de Wette was uncertain, however, about its extent. It was generall/ believed that Deuteronomy was based on earlier sources, thus Graf, Die gesch. Bücher, p. 24 f.; Dillmann's Comm. Num.-Josh., p. 604 ff.; Driver, Introduction et al. Wellhausen specially stresses the fact that it is a legislation, the first "public" one, on a prophetic foundation; thus, in general, the theologies of the O. T.; see also Bertholet's comm., introduction p. XIII. The diversified and partly disconnected character of the work led to attempts to find out its literary genesis. At first the paraenetic framework, chapters 5-11.28-30, was regarded as a later addition, thus Wellhausen and others. Staerk, Das Deuteronomium and Steuernagel, Der Rahmen des Deut., both 1894, sought especially by observing the alternative use of the singular and the plural in address to find the original writings underlying the Deuteronomy found under Josiah but later enlarged; see Steuernagel's comm. Interest was concentrated on finding the original Deuteronomy, by which was meant the law-book discovered under Josiah. A guide was sought in what agreed with the centralisation 2 Kings 22 f., thus Bertholet in his comm., introduction p. XIX. This critical principle has been most consistently applied by Puukko, Das Deuteronomium, 1910 [Beitr. z. W. v. alt. Test., Heft 15]. J. Hempel, Die Schichten des Deuteronomiums, 1914, tries to find out how the work came into existence by investigating the coherence of the subject matter and its literary characteristics and arrives at the result that an ancient temple ordinance has been elaborated with a view to centralisation and furnished with social rules and later with a polemic against Manasseh's cults. This book was found under Josiah. Later on various editions saw the light, with introductions which were worked together, and further additions were made. König, in his comm. 1917, also thinks he can show that there was an early Deut. which was found in 621 but was later enlarged, but he disregards the possibility of collecting in units what goes beyond the earliest Deuteronomy (Introduction p. 33 f.). In another way M. Löhr, Das Deuteronomium [Schriften der Königsberger gel. Ges., Geistesw. Kl., 1925] has tried to find a "Buch der Lehre".

Hölscher, Komposition und Ursprung des Deuteronomiums, Zeits. f. d. alttestl. Wiss., 40, 1922, pp. 161—255, discards the usual principle of combining investigations of Deuteronomy with the historical account in 2 Kings 22-23. He maintains that this is a purely literary task which must especially, inter alia, use linguistic criteria. It is his view that Deut. has come into existence by "Ergänzungen", and he strongly stresses the purely abstract character of the demand for centralisation. Altogether he gives a very apt characterisation of that remoteness from reality which is peculiar to many of the commands of Deuteronomy. He thinks that it came into existence in the priesthood of Jerusalem before Nehemiah, among those who were against him. In this connection he investigates the books of the Kings in Forschungen zur Rel. u. Lit. des Alt. u. Neu. Test., N. F., 19, 1923 [Eucharisterion, Commem. Publ. in honour of Gunkel], pp. 158—213. He thinks he can separate a number of Deuteronomic elements from 2 Kings 22-23 and show that the original story, which is due to the Elohist, does not mention centralisation but only a reform of the cult at Jerusalem. In "Hesekiel" [Beihefte zur Zeits. f. d. alttestl. Wiss., 39] 1924, he tries to show in this connection that Ezekiel 40—48 was not written by the prophet, but dates from the 5th cent., being later than Deut. (especially p. 26 ff.). — Oestreicher adopts another method in Das deuteron. Grundgesetz, 1923 [Beitr. z. Förderung christl. Theol., ed. Schlatter & Lütgert]. He, too, solves the connection between Josiah's activity and Deut. He has a keen eye for the political factors and strongly stresses the circumstance that the Assyrian rule involved an Assyrian cult at Jerusalem, an idea which, however, he carries to the extreme, maintaining that the temple was an Assyrian sanctuary and the law of Yahweh forbidden (p. 18 f. 30). The reform of Josiah was a restoration of the Yahweh cult directed against the Assyrians, initiated in 627 or 626 (the year of Assurbanipal's death) and slowly carried through. The law was not found till some time during the reform, as described in Chronicles. The assault on the high places was merely a temporary desecration, and their priests were "interned" in Jerusalem, 2 Kings 23,8 f., so as to prevent the enemy from permanently establishing his cult in the country (p. 47 ff.); but there is no question of centralisation. On the other hand, Deut. also does not demand centralisation, for Deut. 12,14 speaks of "every place that Yahweh chooseth in any of your tribes" (p. 105 ff.), thus it says the same as Ex. 20,24, and D. is an ancient law. This view of Deut. 12,14 is justified by a reference to a linguistic parallel Deut. 23,17 and by the impossibility of the command that the feasts should be celebrated in Jerusalem alone. Oe. carries the political point of view farther than is justified by the evidence, and his conception of Deut. 12,14 is such a sophistical reinterpretation that it cannot well be considered. But he shows his sense of the fact that there are other compelling forces than the letter of the law. His view is reiterated by himself in Zeits. f. d. alttl. Wiss., 1925, pp. 246— 249, and by Staerk, Das Problem des Deuteronomiums [Beitr. z. Förderung christl. Theol.] 1924. Horst in Zeits. d. deutsch. morgenl. Ges., 1923, pp. 220—238, attempts to distinguish between two sources in 2 Kings 22 f., one of which does not know D. Another division of the sources is attempted by Aa. Bentzen, Die josianische Reform, where the question is treated in its entirety with special reference to the activity of the priests. He thinks D. originated among the priests outside Jerusalem, and tries to show how it fits into the religious movements in the time before Josiah. A detailed account and criticism of the various treatments is given by Gressmann in Zeitsch. f. d. alttl. Wiss., 1924, pp. 313—337; a criticism of Oestreicher's interpretations is set forth by König, ibd., pp. 337— 346. Adam C. Welch, in The Code of Deuteronomy 1924 and in an article in the aforementioned periodical, 1925, pp. 250—255 would maintain that Deut. 12,1-7 is the only passage in Deut. which requires centralisation and this is a later addition, though from before the exile. As for the rest Deut. is an ancient law for "the place Yahweh chooseth" throughout the country. B. D. Eerdmans [in Old Testament Essays, London 1929, pp. 77—84] assigns the earliest parts of Deut. to the 7th century, the conclusion including "the sermons" to the time after Ezra. A survey of the various views and the arguments in favour of them by Bewer, Paton, and Dahl will be found in Journ. of Biblical Literature, Vol. 47, 1929, pp. 305—79. — It is difficult to date the ancient material found in Deut. because it has come into existence through practice; and a purely literary separation of this material from the later author's doctrinary demands is impossible because he was not content to make his contributions in the shape of mere additions. Even statements with definite historical associations are difficult to date, thus e. g. 23,2-9, see Mowinckel in Acta Orientalia I, 1923, pp. 81—104. The difficulty of dating the final form of Deuteronomy is due to the fact that the ideas of exilic and post-exilic times had all been in preparation under the monarchy. But even if Deuteronomy were completed in the 7th century, it is not until after the exile that it acquires importance.

INDICES

I. GENERAL INDEX.

Aaron, 103, 123, 166, 170, 186 ff., 190 ff., 206, 284 f., 291, 364, 368, 393 ff., 468, 614, 643 ff., 649, 658 f., 662 ff., 681, 694 f., 731 ff.; A. and Moses leading characters in the drama of the Passover, 402 ff., 408.

Abel, 665.

Abiathar ben Ahimelech, 152, 153 f., 157, 159, 177, 185 f., 223 f., 232, 680, 681.

Abiezer, 203.

Abigail, 489, 529.

Abihu, 186, 188, 357, 659, 663 f., 695.

Abimelech, 39 f., 46, 203, 211, 256, 381, 418 f.

Abimelech of Gerar, 82, 149, 623.

Abinadab, 231, 269.

Abiram, 102, 283 f., 286, 662, 694 f.; A., son of Hiel, 348.

Abishai, 55, 526, 529.

Abner, 44, 58, 76, 379.

Abraham, 82, 149, 207, 211, 213 f., 227, 312, 339, 355, 480, 498, 666 ff.; A., Isaac and Jacob, 403, 501, 517, 534, 643, 668.

Absalom, 60, 63, 80, 325, 378, 488, 513, 528.

abstemiousness, 455 ff.; a. in war, 10 ff.; a. of the nazirite, 36, 328; vows of a., 328 f.; a. of the Rechabites, 522.

Achan, son of Carmi, 30, 215, 272, 331.

Achish, 52, 57.

Adonibezek, 24.

Adonijah, 71, 77, 338, 488.

Adoniram, 69.

Adonis, 738; A. gardens, 259, 740.

Aegaean influence in Canaan, 202, 511.

Agag, 48 f.

'Aglibol, 507, 509.

agriculture, feasts of a., see: feasts.

Ahab, King, 16, 68 f., 70, 71, 75, 109, 112, 126, 129 f., 141, 474, 479, 516, 518 ff., 569, 570 f., 575 ff.

Ahab, prophet, 146.

Ahaz, 143, 164, 165, 242 f., 319, 350 f., 553 ff., 570, 577, 687 f., 693, 721.

Ahaziah, 119, 519, 569.

Ahijah ben Ahitub, 152, 159, 680.

Ahijah, prophet, 119, 127, 575.

Ahimaas ben Zadok, 153.

Ahimelech ben Ahitub, 152 f., 680.

Ahio, 269.

Ahiram, Phoenician, 677, 715.

Ahitophel, 73, 479, 488.

Ahitub, 152, 680.

Ai, 207, 619, 682.

akitu feast, 747 ff.

Alexander Jannæos, 255.

Al'iyan Ba'l, 651, 652, 717, 738 f., 750.

II. INDEX OF HEBREW WORDS.

ERRATA

p. 52, l. 24: Akish, read: Achish.

p. 78, l. 6: Jehojada, read: Jehoiada.

p. 126, l. 4: Ashera, read: Asherah.

p. 146, l. 23; 352, l. 3 from below: Cyrus, read: Kyros.

p. 177, l. 27: Amasiah, read: Amaziah.

p. 342, l. 6: Assur, read: Ashur.

p. 343, l. 6: Siloa, read: Siloah.